The World Today Series®

Africa 2001

CHARLES H. CUTTER

STRYKER-POST PUBLICATIONS

HARPERS FERRY, WV

36th edition

2001

Next Edition, August 2002

Charles H. Cutter . . .

received his Ph.D. in Political Science from UCLA after taking his BA and MA degrees, also in Political Science, from the University of California, Berkeley. His post-doctoral work was done at Yale University in Art History. He has taught at UCLA, Yale (Moore College), Bristol University, England, and is presently Associate Professor of Humanities and Political Science at San Diego State University where he has taught courses ranging from Traditional African Political Systems to Political Change in Modern Africa and an introduction to African civilizations. Professor Cutter has been the recipient of Fulbright-Hays Foreign Language Fellowships to study Bamana and to conduct research in West Africa, as well as a fellowship from the American Council of Learned Societies to study African Art at Yale. He has published on both African art and political history and curated an exhibition of African Art for the San Diego Museum of Art.

First appearing as *Africa 1966*,
this annually revised book is published by

Stryker–Post Publications
P.O. Drawer 1200
Harpers Ferry, WV 25425
Telephones: 1–800–995–1400 (U.S.A. and Canada).
Other: 1–304–535–2593
Fax: 1–304–535–6513
www.Strykerpost.com
VISA–MASTERCARD

International Standard Book Number: 1–887985–31–X

International Standard Serial Number: 0084–2281

Library of Congress Catalog Number 67–11537

Cover design by MidAtlantic Books & Journals

Chief Bibliographer: Edward Jones

Typography by MidAtlantic Books & Journals
Glen Burnie, MD 21061

Printed in the United States of America by United Book Press, Inc.
Baltimore, MD 21207

Photographs used to illustrate *The World Today Series* come from many sources, a great number from friends who travel worldwide. If you have taken any which you believe would enhance the visual impact and attractiveness of our books, do let us hear from you.

Dedicated to

PHILIP FITZHUGH STRYKER

1929-2000

Dreamer, Founder, Friend

CONTENTS

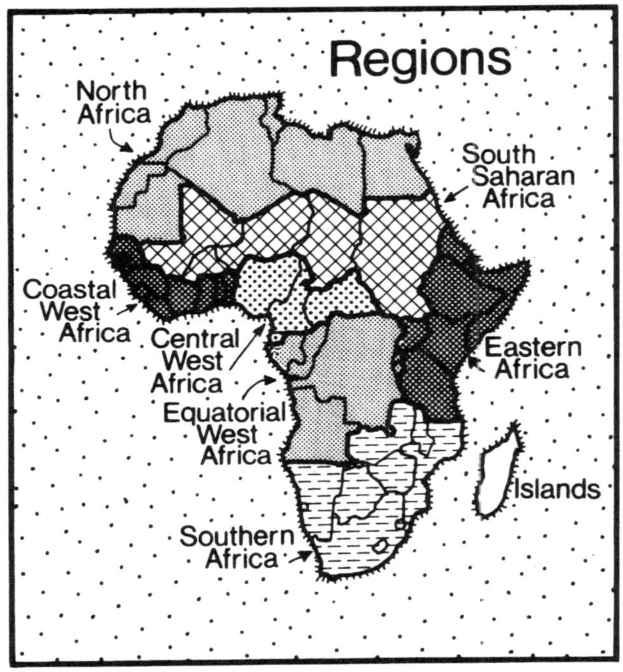
Regions
North Africa
South Saharan Africa
Coastal West Africa
Central West Africa
Eastern Africa
Equatorial West Africa
Islands
Southern Africa

A young Sudanese farmer

Africa Today

Introduction

With the change of administration in Washington, Africa seems at a point of transition. The Clinton administration departed the scene leaving an African legacy more symbolic than concrete. It raised the visibility of Africa, but could do little to quell the fires of conflict that drained blood, hope, and resources from so many African countries. The genocide in Rwanda and a variety of regional wars—in the Horn, in Central and West Africa—all occurred during the Clinton watch.

Expectations for the new Bush administration were low, the candidate himself saying at one point that Africa didn't "fit into national strategic interests." What a contrast, then, to have Secretary of State Colin Powell make his third overseas trip an African odyssey, visiting four countries and making clear his personal, as well as the administration's, commitment to Africa.

Secretary Powell's African journey articulated two important themes: AIDS and good governance. In South Africa he pointedly challenged President Mbeki's dubious stance on the HIV/AIDS connection, going out of his way to assert "HIV causes AIDS." For those paleolithic autocrats, Robert Mugabe and Daniel arap Moi, he offered a diplomatic kick in the shins. For President Mugabe, whose storm troopers brought terror to any opponent of his regime, the secretary's message was stinging: It was, he said, "for the citizens of Zimbabwe to choose their leader in a free and fair election, and they should be given one so that they can make their choice as to how they will be governed in the future." In Kenya he told President Moi, who has been in office 23 years, to abide by Kenya's constitution, which prohibits him from seeking an additional term of office.

It's refreshing to think we might actually have a no-nonsense truth-sayer in Foggy Bottom, the appropriately named home of the U.S. State Department.

President Clinton's most important African legacy is the African Growth and Opportunity Act (AGOA). Signed into law in May 2000, AGOA offers duty-free access for most goods produced in 35 sub-Saharan nations. Early results are encouraging, with U.S. imports from the beneficiary countries up 24% in the first quarter of 2001. Imports from Madagascar and Senegal were up 138% and 544% respectively. Apparel imports, one of the most controversial areas, were up more than 30%. Here, it remains to be seen who benefits the most, as Asian manufacturers rush to establish garment factories in a variety of African countries to take advantage of the new provisions.

Foreign direct investment (FDI) in Africa has slowed as a consequence of continuing conflict, despite rather lucrative 30% profits. Overall, it remains concentrated in the petroleum and mineral sectors. Regional conclaves of the Corporate Council on Africa in places like New Orleans and San Francisco emphasize the point by the featuring the presence of ambassadors from oil-producing states. Some $2.52 billion in FDI has flowed into Africa during the past decade, but nearly 60% of that total—$1.5 billion—went to oil giants Angola and Nigeria ($626 million and $876 million respectively.)

With America's energy problems and an Oil Boys Club operative in Washington, one can expect the oil-producing states to remain privileged locales for American policy makers. Symptomatically, Military Professional Resources Inc. (MPRI) of Alexandria, Virginia, which provides contract military services and expertise to countries having U.S. State and Defense Department approval, is now working to professionalize Nigeria's armed forces. A contract to develop a coast guard for Equatorial Guinea—the "Kuwait of Africa"—has recently been approved, and one involving Angola's army is reportedly pending.

The past year has brought, State balance, more to be optimistic about than not. AIDS increasingly seems to be taken seriously by policy makers. Secretary of State Powell has called it a "national security" issue and made it a key element of his Africa policy. The Bush administration has chucked in a pump-priming $200 million to a UN AIDS fund, and Representative Henry Hyde, has introduced legislation that would grant over a half billion dollars to a variety of AIDS programs in sub-Saharan African and other developing countries. With their image blackened by charges of insensitivity and profiteering, international drug companies have agreed to sell AIDS-related drugs at reduced prices and, in some cases, have even offered to give them away. AIDS vaccine trials on human subjects have been approved, suggesting another avenue of hope.

There even appears to be some hope on the military front. In the Horn of Africa, the guns have fallen silent in the border clash between Eritrea and Ethiopia. A shaky ceasefire and disengagement of troops have begun in the Democratic Republic of the Congo, though the process seems to be heading Burundi towards even greater instability. At midyear Hutu militants are reported to be pouring out of the DRC and Tanzania to harass the Buyoya regime with lethal intent.

In West Africa the signals are equally mixed. Things seemed to have quieted dramatically in Sierra Leone as a direct consequence of a British troop presence. The RUF rebels seem to take the presence of troops from a major power more seriously than the usual rent-a-soldier contingents cobbled together by the UN. Liberia, on the other hand, seems headed towards intensified civil conflict and perhaps all out war with its neighbor, Guinea.

The British engagement in Sierra Leone stands in sharp contrast to French behavior in the Central African Republic, where an attempted coup took place in late May. Where once France had maintained two military bases that made the CAR a virtual tutelary state, this time they opted for non-intervention. President Patassé's government was saved by the speedy intervention of Libyan troops—and a few hundred of Jean-Pierre Bemba's *MLC* fighters who crossed the river to enter Bangui from their northern Congolese bases. It will be important to see if Col. Qadhafi's intervention will remain specific to the mutual defense obligations of COMESSA—the Community of the Sahel and Saharan States—or if he is stationing Libya to be the gendarme of Africa.

And finally, it must be noted that April saw the seventh anniversary of Rwanda's genocide. The guilt and shame of an international community that failed to intervene to prevent this holocaust can only be redoubled by its slowness to apprehend and try those who were the masterminds of horror. Belgium alone has broken new ground by trying four suspects in the

IMPORTANT NOTE:
In the chapters dealing with West Africa, these acronyms are frequently used:

ECOWAS: Economic Community of West African States
ECOMOG: Economic Community Monitoring Group

The homemade guitar—Zambia

Rwanda slaughter in a civilian court before a Belgian jury. It was the first time a jury of citizens had been asked to sit in judgment of war crimes committed in another country, and it marked a step forward in implementing it the notion of "crimes against humanity."

The International Criminal Tribunal for Rwanda (ICTR), seated in Arusha, Tanzania, is a different story. The slowness of its processes has proved shamefully embarrassing. Founded in 1994 to prosecute the architects of the Tutsi slaughter, the ICTR has convicted only eight people. The sloppiness of its procedures has been equally disturbing. In one instance, an investigator in its employ was found to be a genocide suspect himself, working under an assumed name. In another, a defendant, working from his cell, maintained an anti-Tutsi website with a laptop computer he was permitted to use. These are not the events that occasion a belief that justice is being served.

One needs only momentarily reflect on the speed with which the perpetrators of the Nazi holocaust were brought to justice, tried, and dispatched to see that, once again, Africa receives only diminished attention from an international community preoccupied with other things: Kosovo, yes; Rwanda, no. Nuremberg, yes; Arusha, no.

Is it any wonder that bitterness thrives where justice is absent?

C.H.C.

San Diego, CA
June 2001

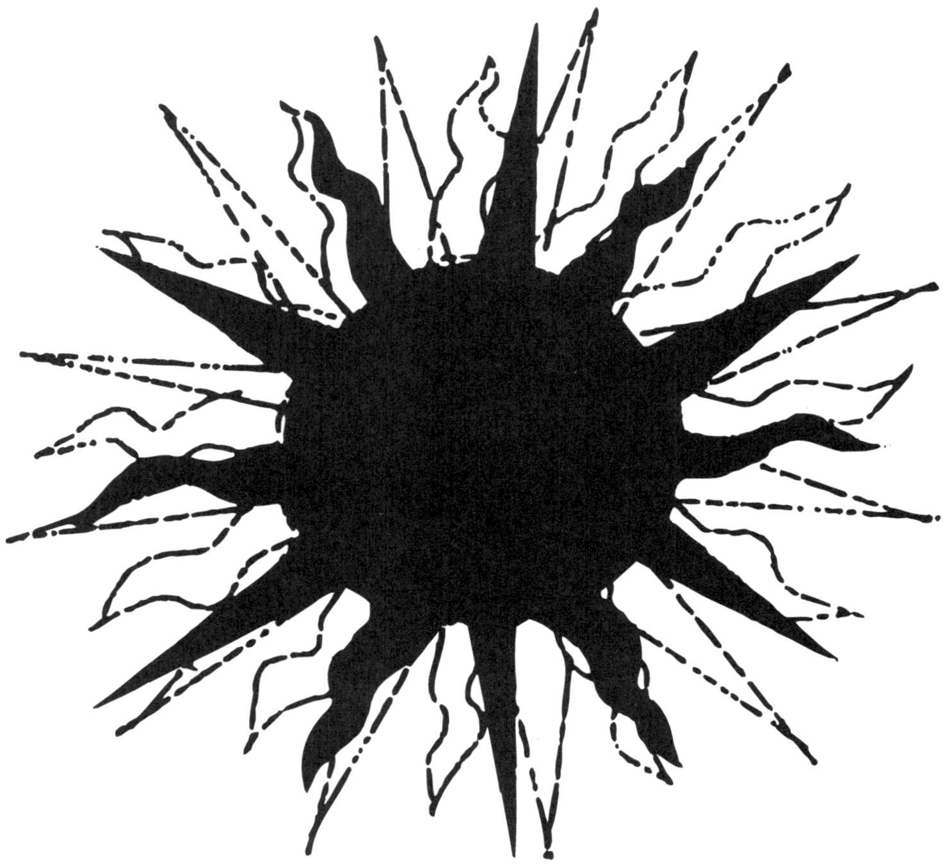

Understanding the Tropical African Environment and Ways of Life

by Louis J. Mihalyi

Africa is a very large continent, some 2 million square miles greater than North and Central America combined, with an estimated population of 550 million in 1997. The landmass shows a very considerable diversity of the physical and cultural environments which, in a simplified approach, may be divided into two broad regions: North Africa, including the Sahara, and tropical Africa, including the Republic of South Africa.

In the North African region, aside from the mountains of the Atlas, Ahaggar and Tibesti ranges, the terrain is characterized by a low topography in the Sahara, often appearing as an "endless" desert landscape. Part of the Sahara is covered with sand while in other areas it has large expanses of exposed gravel and rock. Due to the prevalent trade winds from the northeast, the finer sand and surface soil is generally carried westward and south–westward; this accounts partly for the advance of the desert into the zone of the *Sahel*, greatly affecting life and livelihood in that region.

The climate of North Africa ranges from semi–aridity to aridity with only a narrow strip of Mediterranean climate north and northwest of the Atlas ranges. The environment imposes considerable limits on cultural activities. Below the Mediterranean coastal zone all agriculture requires irrigation; the arable area is limited due to the presence of a single river—the Nile—with a sufficient volume of water year round, although parts of the northern Sahara do contain significant amounts of water in deep–lying bodies which occasionally surface as oases in the otherwise bone–dry landscape.

Dependence on irrigation is aggravated by the ever present danger of soil salinization due to high evaporation and the use of improper irrigation techniques. In addition, the slowly moving waters provide favorable conditions for the spread of *bilharzia;* this disease is transmitted by the miroscopic larvae from fresh water snails which penetrate the body while a person may be either bathing or simply wading in a river or stream. Its effect is to sap human energy permanently, since proper treatment seldom reaches the poor and the isolated who are its principal victims. In the delta of the Nile, this disease affects at least 60% of the rural population with no medicine or vaccine available.

In the Sahara proper, the livelihood aside from the few oases is limited to the practice of nomadic pastoralism by tribes like the Tuareg, formerly a feared group preying on the caravans crossing the desert. The major income earned for the countries is limited to few resources: oil and natural gas in Algeria and Libya, phosphates in Morocco, and tourism—especially in Egypt, in addition to tolls derived from the Suez Canal.

Historically, North Africa was closely associated with the Mediterranean region and the Middle East—not with tropical Africa, due to the barrier of the vast Sahara. This alignment is reinforced by two major unifying cultural factors of the region: the religion of Islam and the Arabic language. Since Greek and Roman times, people from North Africa worked and moved around the Mediterranean basin; presently well over a million Algerians are located in France. These trends are projected to be continued in the future.

The tropical African region, as defined earlier, includes about 8.5 million square miles, with a population of about 390 million in 1985. Topographically, the simplest division would indicate two major parts: "low" Africa in the west, including the Congo basin, then northward from Lake Albert along the watershed of the White Nile to the Red Sea, and "high" Africa containing the rest of the continent and the island of Madagascar, with an average elevation of 3,000 feet or above. On the average, temperatures decrease 3.3°F. per 1,000 feet of elevation. In both areas, volcanic peaks and ranges rise to great heights like the Cameroon mountains, the Mitumba mountains along the west side of the great African lakes, Mt. Elgon in Uganda and Mt. Kilimanjaro in Tanzania.

The Great Rift Valley, an immense fault more than 3,000 miles long, runs from the Dead Sea through the Red Sea and Ethiopia to the mouth of the Zambesi River. It has actually two branches in East Africa, with the western branch occupied partly by the immense lakes of several thousand feet deep. Lake Victoria, the largest of them, is not part of the Rift system, but it received great attention in the early exploration of East Africa by Europeans searching for the source of the Nile.

The low, humid coast of West Africa, the extensive swamps of the Niger delta, the marshy areas along the river, and the "inland delta" of the Niger, are ideal environments for the spread of many diseases like malaria, yellow fever and river blindness. As the early European expeditions often attempted to use the rivers as "highways" to the interior, numerous attempts were made to penetrate West Africa along the Niger. Losing most, if not all their explorers, the European powers gave up the idea of establishing settlers in West Africa. Conversely, the cooler highlands of East and South Africa were favorable to European settlement; partly through government support the lands were seized from native holdings with little, if any compensation. All over tropical Africa the cities were founded by European invaders. Cities on the coast were generally established for easy access, trade or partly military considerations; those founded inland were along a railroad or in a mining area for the most part.

The climate of tropical Africa across the region has basically two traits in common: warm temperatures and a marked seasonality of rainfall, aside from the areas covered by tropical rainforests. Outside the areas with high elevations where the temperatures are lower, the indigenous people are able to survive without constructing substantial, permanent dwellings or producing heavy clothing. The year-round warm temperatures also make it possible to pursue agricultural activities accordingly, *provided there is sufficient rainfall for the crops.* The diverse physical setting supports a great variety of natural vegetation and provides the opportunity for gathering native plants for food during much of the year.

The rainfall pattern in tropical Africa deserves special attention—it is the underlying cause of many of the problems affecting daily life and livelihood. Every day is warm or hot with little exception; but not every night is rainy, even in the most humid regions. The striking features of the rains are the great seasonal differences, their intensity and poor reliability.

The savanna region, an extensive area of grassy woodland, is the largest climatic area in tropical Africa, with a very distinct wet and dry season. The rainfall controls the responses of plants and animals and influences greatly human activities. Where the yearly rainfall is below 25 inches or so, the rains can be very erratic in both arrival and total amount. The areas of Africa affected by famine, the extent of which increased greatly in 1984–1985, are heavily concentrated in the low rainfall regions, like the Sahel zone south of the Sahara, where crop and animal losses can be devastating in any particular year.

Even when the rains come on schedule, they may cause severe problems. Tropical rains often arrive as very heavy showers or thunderstorms. Up to 4 inches of rain *per hour* may fall, causing swift run–off and erosion. Temperatures in the rainforest region are not excessive, practically never over 90°F. Water cannot evaporate rapidly due to the saturation of the air with its vapor; that is the reason for the great discomfort in humid tropical or subtropical climates. In tropical Africa a minimum of 60 inches of rainfall annually is necessary for thick forests; in the high latitudes of the temperate zone, the forests of the "taiga" exist with a precipitation of only 15 inches.

The ecology of the African savanna is remarkable. This area was in the past unexcelled for immense numbers of game which made Africa famous, and due to the favorable habitat, may well have been the location of emergence for *homo sapiens,* suggested by the large number of pre–human remains found in East and South Africa. However, the long dry season promotes the spread of fires, and for centuries the savannas have been burned by accident or design; the existing vegetation is characterized as a "fire climax."

A problem of immense proportions has emerged in the late 1980's in the East African savanna. Game poachers are killing the rhinos and elephants for their horn and tusks, respectively, at unbelievable rates. The 17,000 elephants of Kenya in 1970 now number fewer than 5,000. Uganda, seized by lawlessness, is a poachers paradise. Of all the Black African nations, only Tanzania has a reasonable anti–poaching program, but it is being swiftly undermined by desperately impoverished Zambian poachers. These game thieves have become so bold they assault game wardens sent to protect animals.

In 1989 there was a world pact to end all trade in ivory. Nevertheless, the activities of the poachers continued. In spite of their activity, present estimates of the African elephant population are 573,000–598,000. Zimbabwe, South Africa, Namibia, Botswana and Malawi have asked that the restrictions be relaxed, but there is wide resistance to the move. The argument they use is increased human population needs. The argument used by their opponents is that (1) the population should naturally be controlled and (2) there are a number of other substances which can be suitably substituted for ivory. This item will remain very controversial.

Another continuing problem is that of the chimpanzees. Monkey flesh is regarded as a delicacy in most parts of Africa. The slain animals are singed to remove the hair and then roasted. This is regarded as virtual cannibalism in other parts of the world, where the similarity of the chimpanzee to humans is recognized. Perhaps the worst part is the sale of their young children as pets. Young chimps are cute and adorable. When they pass maturity, they are not. Raucous, generally quarrelsome and wanting to live in their own society, they become very combative and frustrated.

Many "pet" chimpanzees wind up chained to a tree, spending the rest of their lives in misery. They bite (yes, people) and are tremendously strong. It takes four strong men to hold an adult down in laboratories where they are used for testing. (Their genes are about 99% comparable to those of humans.) The old *Tarzan* movies, with their amusing "Cheetah" were not realistic. Ten times as much film as was used in them was thrown in the wastebasket—the female, the more docile of the species, simply would not behave. As adults, they defecate and fling the results with dreadful accuracy. If one goes to Africa and is offered a cuddly youngster, forget it.

The savanna landscapes located in the proximity of the cities and large settlements show a considerable decline due to extensive deforestation. Aside from the small middle and upper class residential areas, the vast majority of Africans use wood or charcoal for cooking. The method used for converting the wood to charcoal is especially wasteful; only about 8% of the total wood piled into the "clamp," i.e. kiln, will actually end up as charcoal.

The environment of the savanna presents a number of hazards to humans and animals. The foremost among them is the presence of the tsetse fly, which excludes the raising of good quality domestic animals in the affected regions. Game animals are immune to the disease *trypanoso-*

miasis carried by the insect, but domestic animals are generally killed by the "nagana," and humans fall victim to the "sleeping sickness."

Getting rid of the fly permanently requires both the killing of the game which is resistant to the "nagana," but still is host to the disease and the cutting of the brush and other vegetation for the conversion of the area to permanent, intensive farming to prevent natural revegetation and return of the game. Presently, perhaps 1/3 to 1/4 of the entire savanna area may be infected by the tsetse.

Of the biological dangers affecting the crops are the presence of a large variety of ants and insects, the occasional flight of hordes of locusts and many grain–eating birds. Due to poverty and the low level of technology, the African farmers have no defense against these enemies. In addition, poor storage techniques result in a yearly crop loss estimated to be from 15% to 30%.

In the semi–arid grasslands of tropical Africa the pastures are reasonably good for animal husbandry and the tsetse fly is seldom a problem. But the prolonged dry season causes great hardships, especially in terms of the water supply. Overall, the wildlife, cattle and other livestock walk long distances for grass and water under the hot sun and show only a small weight gain during the year. In addition, ticks spread a variety of diseases, some of them fatal. However, perhaps the main handicap to proper animal raising lies in the traditions and customs of the pastoral people, especially those of East Africa. The monetary value of cattle is not as important as the *social* one; the prime consideration is to increase numbers for *status*, prestige or dowry. Little concern is given to the carrying capacity of the range; this overgrazing is one important factor in the spread of the desert in the Sahel region.

In tropical Africa good soils are the exception. The fast growth of the rainforest is based not so much on the soils but the rapid recycling of the nutrients from the plants' fast decomposition. The year round warm temperatures provide a perfect setting for the rapid decay of organic material and, with the warm waters carrying dissolved chemicals, essential elements for growth penetrate the soil deeply. The minerals carried downward can be reached by the long roots of the large, long– lived plants; but when these are replaced by short–cycle, 3–5 month crops, plant growth is stunted. This factor, among others, led to the practices of shifting, slash–and– burn cultivation with the ashes from the burned vegetation providing reasonable fertility for a period of 2–4 years.

In the savanna region, coarse sand, rock and clay particles remain after the soluble materials have been carried away by wa-

A child leads a victim of river blindness. A vaccine is now being provided without charge by a U.S. firm which will eradicate infection by this disease as of 2002.

WORLD BANK photo

ters rapidly leaching the soil; this gives rise to a hard, unyielding surface, often forming laterite—reddish in color and generally hard enough to be used for road surfacing. Applying mechanized farming techniques to any part of tropical Africa requires a careful approach and study of the existing conditions to avoid failures such as occurred in Tanzania after World War II.

Often called the "peanut scheme," the British government attempted to raise peanuts on a large scale (for edible oil). The area selected had an erratic rainfall of 6 to 25 inches each year, and the dry soil was extremely hard. The machinery used was mainly war–worn bulldozers and caterpillar tractors from U.S. surplus in the Philippines; they broke down rapidly. The project folded in a few years with a loss of millions of dollars. However, in some parts of tropical Africa, such as on the highlands of Kenya, in Zambia and Zimbabwe, properly established modern farming techniques have proved to be successful.

African cultivation is of two types: (1) permanent, or (2) shifting—slash and burn. The first appears in areas generally limited to good soils, near cities and in parts of the coastal strip. Aside from crops, a variety of fruit trees are also planted.

Far more widespread is the second approach; shifting cultivation developed hundreds of years ago when land was free and plentiful—and there was a relatively low population density. Farming is simple; the major tools are the axe and the hoe. The trees and brush are cut, then burned, and the seeds are sown in the ashes. Animal power is very seldom used, so these farmers, in general, are at the stage which existed in Europe about the time of the Roman conquests. Upgrading such farming techniques is a very difficult task; great leaps forward into mechanized farming have generally resulted in a disaster.

One percent of sub–Saharan African farming is mechanized, draft animals are used in another 10%, but human labor accounts for 89%. Although the men occasionally help out with the heaviest tasks, the burden falls almost exclusively on women to produce food. Yields are modest, being the product of a hoe and hour upon hour of grueling labor. Surpluses are seldom produced and there are large losses due to insufficient storage facilities. However, Africans are very talented farmers, using local plants for food or medicine, and are able to survive even in spite of crop failures.

Partly to overcome the numerous biological hazards, the average family may cultivate several plots at scattered locations. However, in spite of these efforts, food is often in short supply before the harvest of the major staple crop; the children are the first to suffer.

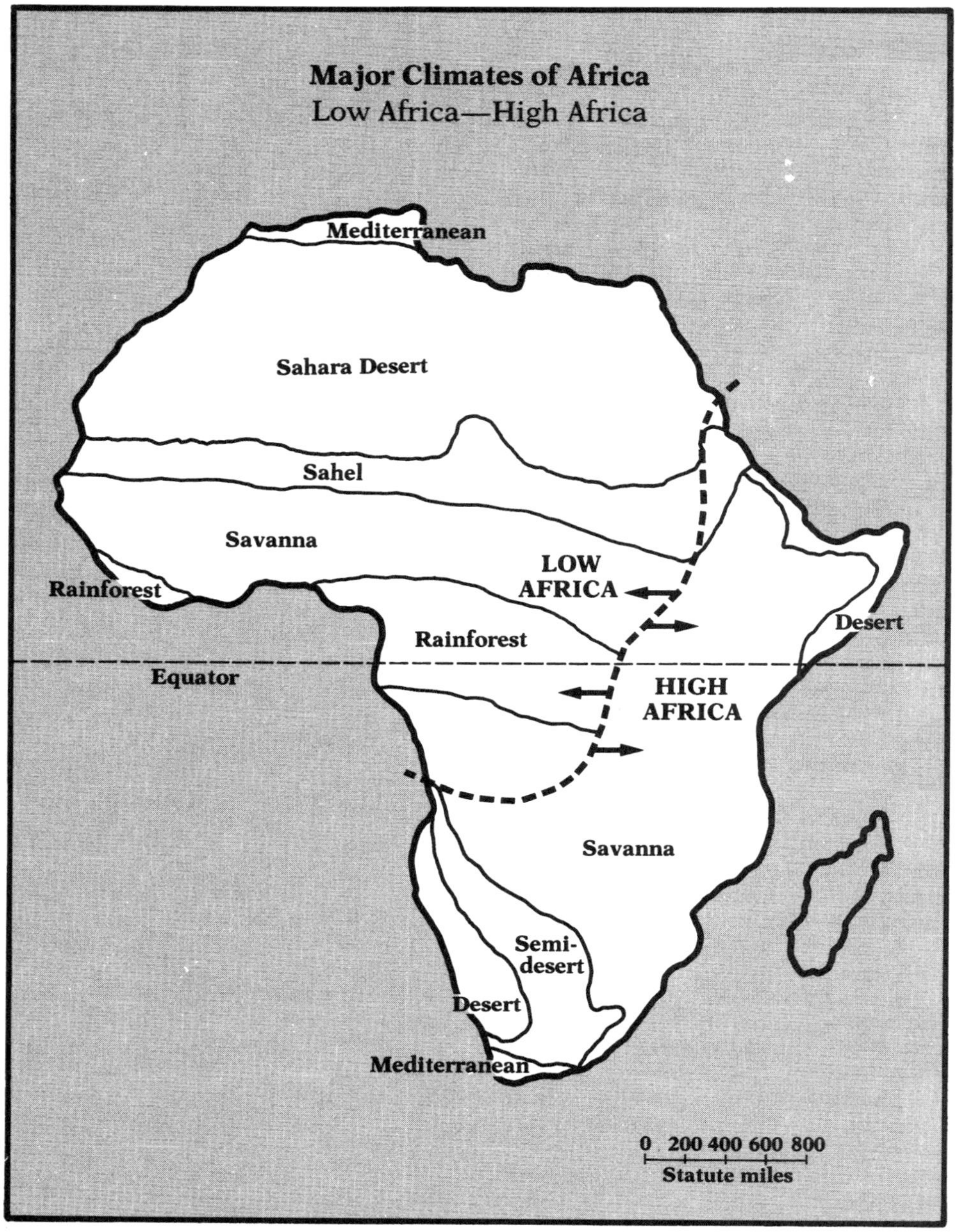

The diet of the African population is usually inadequate. Carbohydrates represent most of the food supply while meat consumption—of very poor quality—is at most about 6% of that in the average American's diet. Malnutrition is widespread, especially among the children, and heavily affects women during pregnancy. The majority of families is limited to one daily meal—in the evening. Even in the cities, the drinking water is polluted by a variety of organisms, but little is done to tackle the problem.

Ideally, western, and in particular American, mechanized agriculturural techniques should be supplied to Africa, particularly legumes (peas, beans, particularly soybean growing should be taught) to raise the bulk, adequacy and protein of the African diet. But this is impossible because of present conditions. National, state, tribal and local leaders usually demand a "piece of the action." Under the circumstances, no capitalist from the more industrially advanced world could be attracted to participate in such an effort. Thus, the people are relegated to their routine, starch–laden diets.

The Republic of South Africa possesses the capacity to change things, and is making efforts in this direction. Western economic measures directed against that nation in the name of racial righteousness, hampered it in its efforts, as well as deprived thousands of black South Africans of something even faintly resembling a decent standard of living.

Because of widespread poverty and the absence of electricity in all but the urban areas, refrigeration equipment is extremely limited. Leftover food spoils rapidly.

Spraying to kill small snails that cause Bilharzia WORLD BANK photo

Where food preservation is practiced, like in the case of fisheries along the lakes and streams, it is a common sight to see fish cut up and laid out to dry in the open—covered with flies and dust. The same is true with animal carcasses after slaughtering, especially in the rural areas. In Lake Victoria man introduced the Nile Perch—a fish that can grow six feet long and weigh several hundred pounds. It ate almost all of the native, much smaller Tilapia fish which was preserved by drying in the sun. Oily and too large for sun–drying, the Nile Perch has to be smoked to preserve it. Thus, forests in the region are suffering from excessive wood loss. Further, the Tilapia ate algae and the snails that transmit *bilharzia*—both are spreading. Ironically, Tilapia are now being farm–raised in ponds here in the U.S. and are proving to be a real seller in supermarket fish counters.

The recent spread of "modernization" led to the availability of Coca–Cola and other soft drinks popular among the younger generation, but with "empty" calories in terms of proper nutrition. Africans in general consume a considerable amount of beer, originally produced from some staple foods—millet, maize or bananas—although bottled, manufactured beer is gaining increased popularity and prestige. "Kat" is a widely–used opiate (excitant) in Ethiopia, and "dagga" (bhang) is smoked by adults on occasion.

The tropical African environment, especially that of the savanna region, harbors a large variety of diseases affecting the human population. Aside from *bilharzia,* which is estimated to affect at least 80 million Africans, amoebic and bacillary dysentery are very widespread and are a major factor in high childhood mortality. Malaria is spreading again, especially in the more humid areas—mosquitos having increased resistance to sprays. *Filariasis,* a disease due to parasites, often causing swelling in the limbs, is commonly found in mosquito–prone areas. Hookworm affects many children who generally go barefoot. *Yaws* and *leishmaniasis* (carried by the parasite which forms ulcers on the skin) are frequently encountered in the region of the equator. *Onchocerciasis* ("river blindness"), spread by black fly eggs, is prevalent along streams in West Africa.

Fortunately this will become a problem of the past. An American pharmaceutical company has developed a serum which, if made widely available, will eliminate the disease. The company has agreed to furnish the medicine at no cost.

To the list must be added Guinea Worm Disease which exists in a belt of the Savanna–Sahel stretching clear across Africa. It is spread by contaminated water. The ovum of the worm is consumed by drinking and locates itself within the human body, most usually in the legs. It grows to a length up to three inches and immediately seeks exit from its victim, a process that is excruciatingly painful, taking several weeks. Seeking relief from the pain of a worm half in and half out of the body, infected persons soak in nearby ponds and streams. The worm exits and starts the cycle again by producing more eggs. This causes substantial loss of work and productivity.

Overall, much of the population and especially the children suffer from widespread incidence of multiple vitamin deficiency. *Kwashiokor,* an almost always fatal disease among youngsters, is caused by a protein–deficient diet and . . . starvation. Ironically, improved vaccination availability against measles and other childhood diseases in the last decade have led to lowered infant and child mortality, resulting in even more mouths to feed with an inadequate food supply.

Because of inadequate medical reporting, it is impossible to estimate the number of cases of AIDS in Africa. Frequently the disease is not identified, or the victim does not seek medical treatment. No relief in the form of a vaccine is now in sight. In the coming years until the turn of the century, it has the potential to infect more than 50 million people on the continent. It knows no class distinctions and is claiming the lives of sorely needed technicians and professionals.

Medical services and facilities, aside from the urban areas, are very simple and utterly inadequate over tropical Africa. Even when the people are "cured," re–infection occurs very frequently, and some diseases—like *bilharzia*—have *no* dependable cure unless the person receives prolonged treatment in Europe. Sanitary and hygienic facilities across the continent are all but absent, and even the hospitals have great problems with proper staffing. Many African doctors trained at considerable expense leave the continent to advance their fortunes; those who remain practice mainly in the urban areas. Communication with patients is very difficult due to the *over 700 indigenous languages* with few competant interpreters.

The social fabric of tropical African life is characterized by a large number of tribes, at least 700, living within closely defined kinship obligations of the "extended family" system. This does not include the "de–tribalized" Africans who left their homelands particularly during and after the World War II period, to live, often in squalor, in urban areas to which they were attracted by industrial or mining employment. The tribal organization provides for relative security of the individual within the tribal area, but makes cooperation difficult on the national level. The dependence on relatives is the main reason for the widespread practice of nepotism (favoritism shown to a relative), with the problems caused by inefficiency and inexperience greatly aggravated by corruption. Other problems in tropical Africa are related to the conquest by European powers and are part of the colonial legacy.

From the start of European domination, education for Africans was left generally in the hands of the missionary societies until well after World War I. The student body had a large majority of boys, with subject matters concentrated on reading, writing and religious instruction—in addition to some training in trades such as carpentry and bricklaying so that the Africans would be "useful workers."

"Higher" education always used the language of the colonial power, which then became the official language of the country once it achieved independence. Few Africans received advanced training, and then almost always overseas in the respective "mother" country. Their education was primarily in the liberal arts and humanities. As a result, at the time they became independent, illiteracy in tropical African countries ranged from 80% to 90% of the total population with only a handful of graduates in engineering and sciences. For these reasons, the newly independent countries have had to rely on foreigners to handle many of the technological and administrative tasks until these can be replaced by sometimes hastily–trained Africans. This has had a detrimental effect on efficiency, and that is the characteristic situation across much of tropical Africa at the present time. On the other hand, where the government maintained the existing foreign personnel and production methods such as in the mines and agriculture, operations were hardly disrupted at all.

The political situation in tropical Africa has had many facets since the arrival of independence. Divergent vested interests of more than 700 tribes and clans, in addition to the selfish motives of the existing elite, have severely limited development. Populations with a high rate of illiteracy cannot possibly decide on the relative merits of any candidate running for election even if there *are* elections. Social, political and economic policies are simply beyond their understanding.

Dictatorial policies and monetary dishonesty of several African leaders have resulted in almost perpetual turmoil and financial crises. Relief efforts to avert starvation in areas such as Ethiopia and Sudan should be via recognized international agencies. Another example of needless economic hardship has been found in Liberia, where three crops of paddy rice can be harvested each year with proper cultivation. Yet this staple food was imported for lack of local supplies. To this has been added the spectre of widespread hunger and malnutrition associated with revolution accompanied by virtual anarchy in that nation for more than two years.

Although foreign investment is desirable, sometimes it results in exploitation. Because of low living standards, cheap labor is available to assemble parts made elsewhere into products at wages as low as $5.00 a week. It is highly unlikely that tropical Africa will enter the stage of the Industrial Revolution within the 21st century without there first occurring basic changes. Subsistence agriculture, disease, and power shortages constitute the only future that one can see for the black–ruled nations of sub–Sahara Africa, unless capital and technological skills can be attracted for improvement.

Processing cotton in northern Cameroon

AFRICA 1905

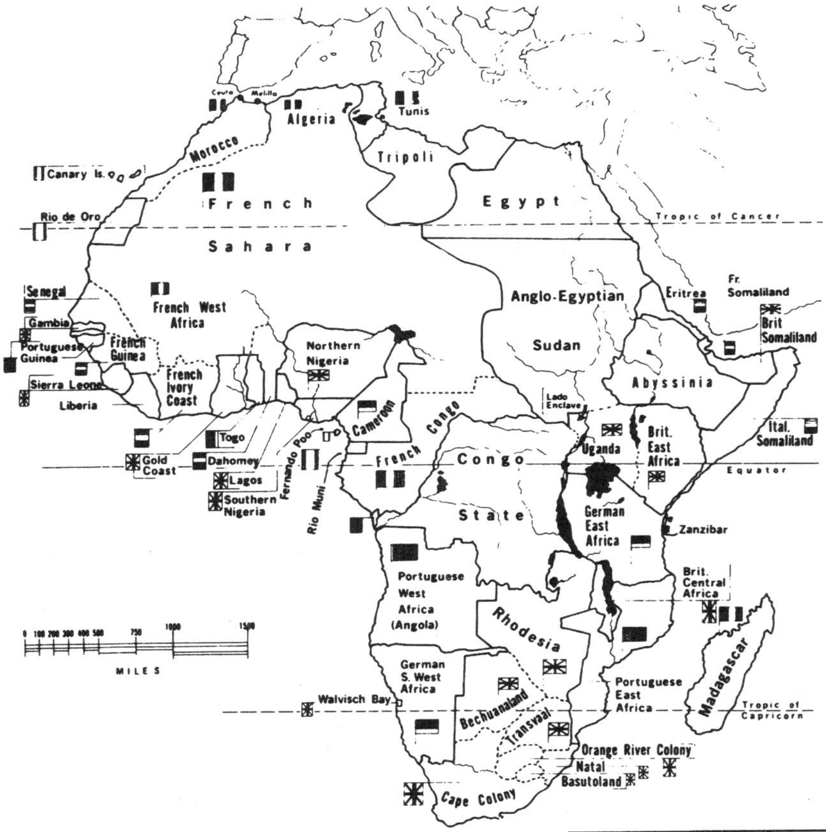

AFRICA TODAY

HISTORICAL BACKGROUND

Sunrise over the Niger River

WORLD BANK photo

PREHISTORIC AFRICA

Advances in archeology, population genetics and linguistics continue to flesh out our understanding of human evolution. Two things are most striking: we are all one human family and our ancestral home is Africa.

The greatest advances have come in biological sciences and the human genome has come to be a new archive for historians and prehistorians. Interpretation of these archival materials remains unsettled. One element of the human cell has its own DNA which escapes he reshuffling of genes in each generation. Inherited just through the mother's line, this material, called mitochondrial DNA, has allowed population geneticists to trace Homo sapien origins. Using this material Dr. Douglas Wallace and his colleagues at Emory University in Atlanta, Georgia, have identified the Vasikela Kung of the northwestern Kalahari desert as the population that lies nearest to the root of modern humans' origins.

Using the same DNA materials, Dr. Elizabeth Watson of Massey University in New Zealand indicates the Turkana people of Kenya show the greatest genetic diversity of any known human group. For Dr. Watson highest diversity is usually indicative of a species' place of origin. Regardless of the specific place of origin what is clear that Homo sapiens, modern humans, evolved in sub-Saharan Africa and, in a later split, migrated out of Africa some 50,000 years ago to populate the rest of the world. And this wasn't the first migration of hominids out of Africa.

Archeologists, like population geneticists, continue to add to our store of knowledge of human development. Only this year scientists digging in the former Russian republic of Georgia have discovered a 1.7 million-year-old hominid skull that shows clear linkages with African fossils. Tools found with the Georgian skulls resembled tools found in the Olduvai Gorge of Tanzania and dated at about 1.8 million years.

Migration routes of early hominids are also beginning to be discovered, allowing scientists to trace this incredible journey. A cave site in Zambia has revealed pigment and paint-grinding equipment that dates back 400,000 years, suggesting the ancestors of *Homo sapiens* were decorating themselves much earlier than ever thought. A recently discovered site along the Red Sea coast of Eritrea appears to be 125,000 years old and documents the utilization of marine resources—clams, crabs and oysters.

These are some of the more tantalizing discoveries that will form the basis of a fuller understanding of human birth and development in Africa. Existing archeological remains testify to the richness of African civilization.

EARLY CIVILIZATIONS OF THE NILE VALLEY AND MEDITERRANEAN SEA

The Nile Valley was settled and agricultural skills developed by 5,000 B.C. This population was able to form one of the first centrally organized societies of the western world by about 3,000 B.C., the beginning of the Egyptians. Under the control of the succession of kings (Pharaohs), the social organization of the people permitted rapid evolution and development of writing, architecture, religion and the beginning of scientific thought.

The Egyptians' early religious efforts were varied; they conceived of a god represented by a variety of animal forms. Under the rule of the dynasties, these individual symbols were gradually discarded in favor of the obelisk (a tall, usually pointed four–sided structure with ornate carvings and frescoes which was used as a symbol of *Re.* It is probable that *Re* was associated with local gods which the people were accustomed to worship, but this concept of God led to the development of the first–known beliefs in life after death. The development of writing, first in hieroglyphics (illustrations portraying a variety of thoughts and concepts) and later in abstract symbols (an early "alphabet") in turn enabled the development of a highly stylized literature. A calendar of 365 days

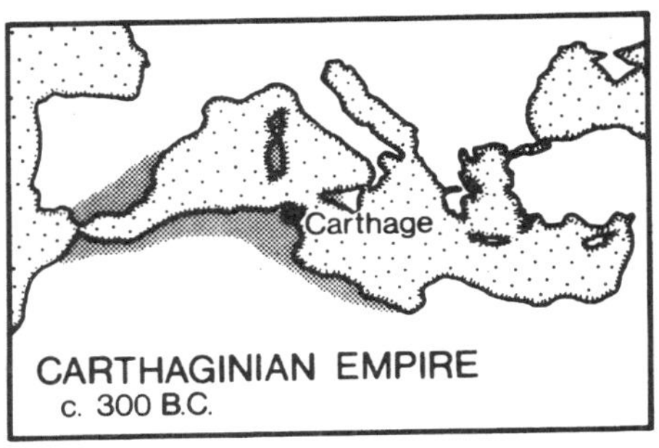

was adopted. The religious concept of life after death led in turn to invention of enbalming methods to preserve the human body after death. This further resulted in the combination of early geometry with architecture, which permitted the construction of obelisks and elaborate and immense pyramids, the burial tombs of the pharaohs.

The Egyptians under the pharaohs reached their period of greatest power in the 2nd millenium before the Christian era, and gradually declined in strength and organization until they were invaded by a succession of other Mediterranean powers—the Assyrians in the 7th century B.C., the Persians and finally the Greeks under Alexander in the 4th century, B.C.

Phoenician traders on the northern coastline of the African continent combined over many centuries with the small number of other people of Middle East origin, emerging into a unified society known as Carthage in the 9th century B.C. in what is now Tunisia and part of Algeria. These aggressive people fought with the inhabitants of Sicily and Sardinia for about four hundred years, eventurally winning control of the two islands after many changes in the fortunes of war in the 2nd century B.C. Carthaginian control was brief—the powerful Roman Empire was able to completely conquer Carthage by 122 B.C.

EARLY CHRISTIAN ERA MOVEMENTS

There was a second but smaller immigration of people to Africa from some other land of the equatorial Indian Ocean and Far East–Indonesian area which probably occurred during the first millenium of the Christian era. These people, known as the Hovas, settled in the highlands of the island of Madagascar and to a much lesser extent in east central Africa, now Kenya and Uganda. There is no way to estimate the numbers of people arriving, nor is there any indication as to the method by which they reached the continent other than that the movement was by sea rather than overland. They remained cohesive on the island of Madagascar, but blended with mainland peoples, becoming part of the local Bantu population.

The Bantu and Sudanic groups expanded at a relatively rapid rate during the first millennium of the Christian era. There was an initial expansion of Bantu peoples into the eastern regions of Africa, into what is now Tanzania, Zambia and Zimbabwe.

The imposing stone constructions at Great Zimbabwe, located in the south-

The Zimbabwe Ruins

western part of the nation now bearing that name, suggest a wealthy and privileged élite in control of a powerful state. The site was the capital of a Bantu kingdom that stretched from eastern Zimbabwe over parts of Botswana, Mozambique, and South Africa. The first known permanent settlement was established around the 11th century and building continued into the early 15th centry. The large quantities of stone used to build on the site suggest control over considerable labor. The state's prosperity was based on trade in gold with Swahili speakers on the eastern African coasts.

Zimbabwe is the Anglicized version of the Shona word *Dzimbahwe,* meaning stone houses—later understood as graves, or dwellings, of chiefs. The significance must run far deeper. Built in a gentle valley, it is believed that this was a sacred place where a person could communicate with his ancestors. Stone huts attached to portions of the ruins indicate that it later became a home for the living. Zimbabwe was abandoned in the early 19th century when fierce Zulu warriors destroyed the Shone confederation. The rituals which took place here are forever shrouded by the mists of time.

In succeeding centuries, the Bantu people emerged into rather powerful societies in what is now Uganda and the Congo River basin. A king of a Bantu state in Uganda who was deposed in 1966 claimed to be the 37th monarch in an uninterrupted rule of a single family. Since there was a lack of the written word during these early centuries, our knowledge of this history is dependent on oral sources. In many societies specialists, like the *griots* of West Africa, memorized the history and traditions of their peoples and passed them on to their sons. Spoken and sung, very much like the epics of Homer, these histories provided inspiration and identity for families and communities. Today, they remain an important source for historians attempting to reconstruct an African past.

The Bantu expansion southward continued at a relatively slow rate. As it pushed more deeply into the south it encountered Khoisan speaking pastoralists. When European sailing ships, mainly Dutch and English, began to make regular voyages around the Cape in the sixteenth century, they too encountered Khoisan pastoralists, eager to sell their surplus animals in exchange for iron, copper, tobacco, and beads.

THE KINGDOM OF ETHIOPIA

By tradition, the Ethiopian kingdom dated back to a visit by the Queen of Sheba (a city in Yemen also known as Saba or Sabah) at the court of Solomon. Menelik I, son of Solomon and the Queen, founded the Ethiopian monarchy. There are other indications that the Ethiopians had pro-

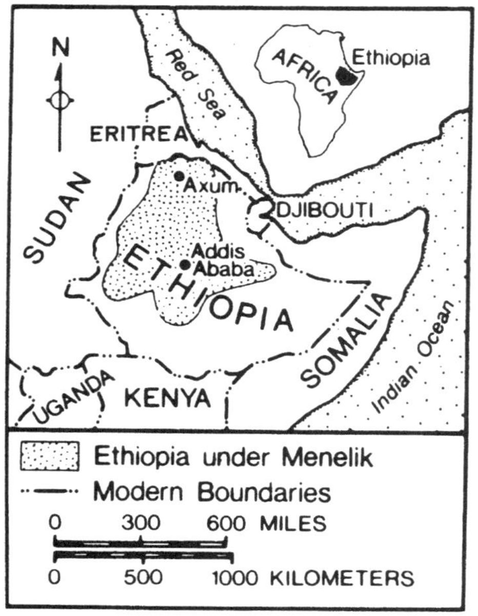

gressed at a relatively early date in African history. Herodotus, a Greek writer of the 5th century B.C. described Ethiopia; Homer refers to the Ethiopians as a "blameless race" in his writing of about 800 B.C. There are numerous references to Ethiopia in the Bible.

Not much is known of the history of Ethiopia at the beginning of the Christian era. The capital was moved from the ancient city of Axum to Addis Ababa and the distinctive Amharic language of the Ethiopians slowly evolved. The Christian Church in Ethiopia was established as a branch of the Coptic Christian Church headed by the Patriarch of Alexandria in Egypt. Contact with other Christians was later severed by the Islamic–Arab conquest of North Africa in the mid–10th century.

THE SPREAD OF ISLAM

The teachings of Mohammed, a religious prophet of the neighboring Arabian peninsula, were the basis for the religion known as *Islam,* sometimes incorrectly referred to as *Mohammedanism.* The writings of Mohammed, together with his teachings, are gathered together in a book known as the Koran. He envisioned his prophecy to be supplemental, or in addition to the other revelations, including those of Judaism and Christianity, of a single God. Preaching a belief in *Allah,* a single, all–powerful God, Mohammed was supposed to be the last prophet of God. He thought that there is a Last Judgment, a duty to donate to the poor, and, most important, there is an obligation to engage in a daily system of prayer.

A line of Islamic rulers established themselves in Damascus in Syria, and from that base other Muslim leaders conquered most of North Africa within a century, even going further to seize most of Spain.

Islam spread southward from the 8th century AD, converting most of the semiarid regions south of the sands of the Sahara. Because of this contact with Islamic Arabs whose faith was based on a written text and who employed writing in their commercial transactions, we have much more extensive materials on which to build a history of this area. Al Umari, Ibn Khaldun and especially Ibn Battuta who visited the Mansa of Mali in the 14th century, have all left important materials to supplement local oral traditions.

ARABS IN EAST AFRICA

From the 8th to the 10th centuries A.D. the Arabs penetrated the shoreline of East Africa in increasing numbers, establishing trading posts at Mogadishu (Somali Republic) and Mombasa (Kenya) and in what is now Mozambique. Ivory and African slaves were the basis of a brisk trade, as well as gold, shipped primarily to India. This continued in one form or another until control of the area was seized by European colonial powers in the last part of the 19th century.

THE EARLY EMPIRES OF WEST AFRICA

A segment of people living in the area south of the Sahara gathered together in the first "empire" of West Africa in the 4th century A.D., eventually controlling a large area which is now part of Burkina Faso, southern Mali and eastern Senegal. The basis of this early group of people was a lively trade in gold and slaves with the nomadic people to the north. *Ghana,* as this empire is historically known, should not be confused with the modern state bearing that name. Its existence continued until it was conquered by the Islamic Berbers from the north in 1076, who converted the local people to their faith.

West Africa's history after Islam arrived in the sub–Sahara dry regions is one of conflict between various tribes and kingdoms, all located within the same general area. The Songhai Empire in western Niger, which had controlled the region since the 7th century, adopted Islam, as did the Mandingo Empire which arose in Mali. Initially, most of West Africa from about 1000 to 1200 A.D. was divided between the Songhai and Mandingo rulers, with the exception of areas closer to the coast in what are now parts of Guinea, Côte d'Ivoire, Ghana and Burkina Faso.

Trade with the Arabs to the north and east was lively for several centuries, with caravans linking Timbuktu, Gao (Mali), Kano (Nigeria) and the Lake Chad region with the Middle East by way of the Sudan and Egypt. The more affluent Islamic people journeyed on traditional pilgrimages to Mecca from this area of West Africa. Other trading was conducted with the Arab–Berber people of the North where Morocco, Algeria, Tunisia and Libya are now located.

The Mandingo rulers gradually acquired more territory at the expense of the neighboring ethnic groups after 1200 A.D. A brief domination by the Sosso people of Guinea, led by Sumanguru Kanté, was ended when the kingdoms of the savannah were rallied to overthrow Sosso's oppression in the early 13th century. The leader of this liberation struggle, Sundiata Keita, became the first of the Mansas or Emperors of Mali. Timbuktu, located in a remote part of what is now Mali, became a center of culture and progress fabled throughout West Africa, and was visited by many Arab merchants and travelers.

The Mandingo Empire disintegrated in the 15th century when Timbuktu was invaded and sacked by desert Tuaregs. A generation later, in 1468, the Songhai rulers were able in turn to expel the Tuaregs. The Songhai reached their greatest power in the following six decades, at a time when the first Portuguese explorers began to penetrate the area.

Several initially non–Muslim kingdoms arose along the southern coast of West Africa at about the same time the Islamic empires of the upper Niger River were powerful. The Fulani, also known as Peulh, established several states from what is now Senegal to Nigeria, occupying an area between the Muslim empires and the coastal lands, and gradually were converted to Islam. Closer to the coastline, the Mossi created two distinct states within what is now southern Burkina Faso and Ghana, also adopting Islam.

The Ashanti became established in what is now central Ghana, as did the Soso in Guinea, the Yorubas in Dahomey and southwestern Nigeria and the Ibos in southeastern Nigeria.

EUROPEAN DISCOVERY AND EXPLORATION

The first exploration of the African coastline started early in the 15th century when Portuguese navigators reached Senegal, Guinea and the islands lying adjacent to the West African coast. By 1492 Fernão Poo reached the island off the coast of Cameroon which bore his name, translated into Spanish—Fernando Poo. Fifteen years later, Bartolomeu Dias, usually referred to in English as Bartholomew Diaz, was blown by a storm in a southerly direction to the bottom of the continent. Turning eastward, he became the first European to navigate around the Cape of Good Hope.

In 1497, shortly after Columbus' second voyage to America, Vasco da Gama sailed around the African cape in search of a way to India, using the primitive navigation information supplied by Diaz. He stopped at Mozambique, Mombasa and Malinda on the east coast of Africa, and was able to obtain the information necessary to proceed onward to India from the Arabs who were already established along the African coast.

With the arrival of increasing numbers of Portuguese vessels, quarrels with the Arab traders intensified. Francisco de Almeida was sent with a squadron to control Arab interference with Portuguese shipping; he took Mombasa in 1505 and ultimately demolished the Arab fleet in 1509, establishing Portuguese supremacy in the eastern coastal area of the continent.

In spite of this rather rapid navigational discovery, there was to be almost no penetration inland by the Europeans for more than three hundred years. With the exception of a Dutch settlement at the Cape of Good Hope, the sub–Sahara inland African regions remained the same dark, forbidding land that was first seen by the Portuguese. Following the precedent of the Arabs of East Africa, the Europeans started a lively West African trade in human cargo—slaves to perform the tasks of labor needed to colonize other parts of the world.

It was an easy task, with little exception, to acquire slaves along the so–called Gold and Ivory coasts of West Africa. Anchoring their slave ships in natural harbors, the Europeans negotiated with the chiefs of the more powerful ethnic groups that lived inland. When a suitable price (in terms of value, almost nothing) was agreed upon, the men and sometimes the women of a weaker neighboring tribe would be brought to the coast in bondage after a brief skirmish. They were delivered as promised to the slave traders. It was in this manner that black Africans, tempted by their desires for the wealth offered by the white slave traders, sold the bodies of other black Africans into slavery.

The Africans had no reluctance in this trade—they were doing no more than disposing of people that were a real or imagined threat to them, their families and their tribe.

Packed shoulder to shoulder in quarters on the slave ships that were so cramped no one could stand, the cargo of humans, regarded as animals, was transported across the sea, usually to the Western Hemisphere. Those unable to survive were dumped overboard at suitable intervals following their death. The remaining survivors were sold at a handsome profit compared to the sum paid for them along the African coastline—a profit possible even if more than one–half of the ship's cargo died during the trip to the "new world." The fact that an individual slave had survived this journey was testimony to his hardiness and stamina as compared to his less fortunate brethren who had perished.

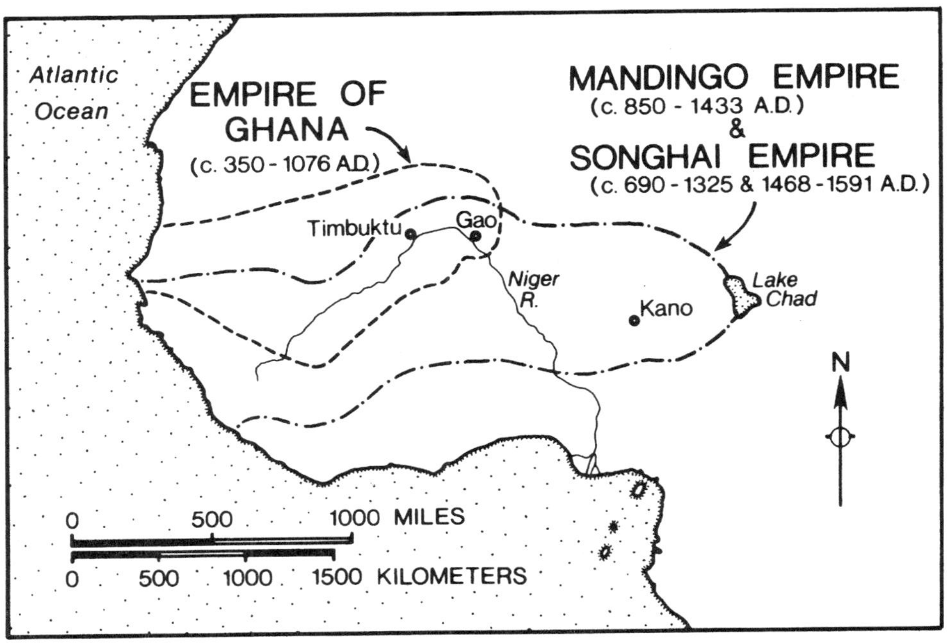

Arriving at a particular destination in the Western Hemisphere where he was sold, the slave was to begin a new and incredibly difficult life in a totally strange surrounding where he would be judged by his physical ability to perform long, long hours of hard manual labor.

EARLY ETHIOPIAN–EUROPEAN CONTACT

In the late dark ages of Europe, a letter from a supposed Christian king of Africa received widespread acclaim as possibly being from an unknown people dating from Biblical times. Inspired by this, a Roman Catholic Pope dispatched several Dominican brothers in the 14th century to locate this Christian kingdom. The results of these efforts are not clear, but an Ethiopian emissary did reach Venice in 1402, arriving later at Lisbon and Rome. In turn, European kings and the Pope sent emissaries to Ethiopia, hoping to enlist help in the continuing "crusades" against the Islamic people of the Middle East and North Africa. This diplomatic effort continued unevenly for four centuries, and there was no other significant contact between this region of Africa and Europe during the passage of those years.

Increased penetration of Ethiopia by Europeans occurred in the 19th century. Although Ethiopia was not formally colonized by any European power, it became subject to a variety of "spheres of influence" of the British, French and Italians in the latter part of the century. The succession to the Ethiopian throne was irregular—every time a king died there was usually a two or three way contest for the throne. The somewhat weak character of the nation was further complicated by periodic skirmishes and quarrels over territory with the neighboring Sudanese who were led by religious–political figures with the title *Mahdi.* The Somalis to the east, who were Islamic, also claimed Ethiopian territory, sometimes with the assistance of the French or the Italians. The borders of the kingdom changed countless times during this period.

The modern history of the country begins with the reign of Emperor Menelik II, the first monarch to choose that name since the reign of the son of Solomon and Sheba. It was under the second Menelik that Ethiopia began to have regular contact with the outside world.

Although he was at first forced to acknowledge an Italian protectorate over Ethiopia, by 1896 he had consolidated his power sufficiently to send a military force which decisively defeated the Italians.

Lidj Yassu, the grandson of Menelik II succeeded to the throne in 1913, but was deposed in 1916. Zauditu, Menelik's daughter, was installed as Empress. Her cousin, Ras Tafari Makonnen ascended the throne in 1930, taking the name *Haile Selassie,* which means "the power of the Trinity" in Amharic.

THE ARABS AND OTTOMAN TURKS IN NORTH AFRICA

The Arab–Berber rulers of North Africa who came to power with the spread of Islam were known first as the Almavorid and subsequently the Almohad dynasty. Initially these Muslim kingdoms were characterized by a centralized power, but in the 13th to the 16th centuries there was gradual division into countless numbers of local rulers. Just as Christianity had split into numberless sects, so also had Islam been divided. Although the internal unity of the Arabs diminished, they were usually able to unite against non–Arabs on the infrequent occasions when outsiders threatened their territory.

The Muslim rulers of the Turkish Ottoman Empire gained control of most of Egypt and Libya at the beginning of the 16th century; their power in this area was not absolute since both regions quickly became no more than tribute–paying vassal states of the Empire. The Ottoman rulers were almost continuously occupied in wars with Europe and had insufficient resources to bring North Africa directly within the Empire as was done in Syria and Iraq. It was not long before most of North Africa was within the Ottoman sphere.

With the exception of Egypt, the remainder of North Africa continued under the loose control of the Ottoman Empire until World War I. Egypt remained under the Ottomans until the invasion by Napoleon in 1798. The Turks sent Mohammed Ali from an Ottoman military family (probably of Albanian origin) as commander of forces opposing the French; together with the British under Lord Nelson, they were finally able to expel the invaders in the summer of 1799.

Mohammed Ali quickly established his personal rule in Egypt as an Ottoman *Pasha.* Although he and his successors were able to avoid absolute domination by the Ottoman rulers, in reality Egypt continued to be a tributary vassal of the Empire for about 75 years until the British influence became paramount.

Khedive Ismail, grandson of Mohammed Ali, ruled as king but under the authority of the Sultan and Caliphs of the Empire; he had received a European education for several years. The Suez Canal was under construction principally in order to provide the British with a shorter route to their possessions in India and the Far East, although the construction effort was in the name of a cooperative effort of most of the European nations and Egypt. In anticipation of the revenues expected from the canal which opened in 1869, Ismail borrowed large sums of money at extremely high interest rates from European banks. When he was unable to repay the loans on schedule, the British used this as a pretext to assert their authority in Egypt, initially with Egyptian cooperation, in order to bring areas bordering the Red Sea waterway and in the Sudan under control.

By 1876 Khedive Ismail had been forced to sell all Egyptian shares in the Suez Canal, and Egypt was placed under the supervision of British and French financial controllers. This is considered the start of the colonial period in Egypt; although the Khedives continued to be the nominal power, they were little more than the instrumentality through which the British ruled.

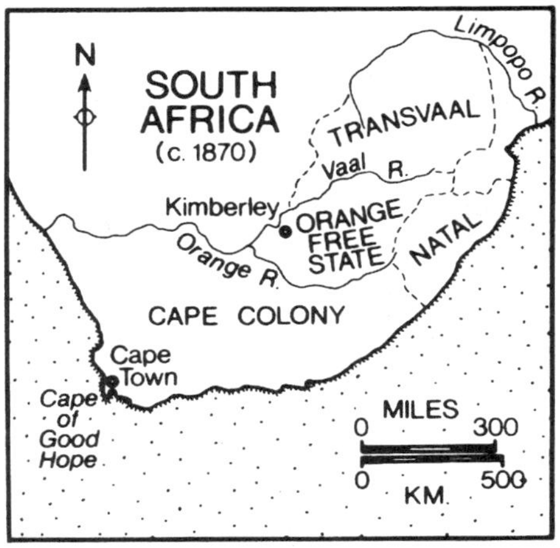

EUROPEAN SETTLERS IN SOUTH AFRICA

The Dutch at the Cape of Good Hope

Holland, seeking a food and fuel station for its ships sailing to the Dutch East Indies, established a small station on the Cape in 1652. A fort was constructed to guard against the Hottentots and Bushmen found in small numbers in the area. This outpost developed rapidly, with the outlying farms worked by slaves brought from the East.

There was a slow expansion of this Dutch community into the interior, though such was not actively pursued by the Dutch East India Company. A substantial number of Huguenot religious refugees from France arrived in 1688, adopting the Dutch social patterns. Further settlement of the interior by the Dutch *Burghers* continued for the next hundred years, since there was little opposition to their desire for additional farmland. It was not until the Dutch had penetrated 200 miles to the northeast that they first encountered the Bantu people who were then in a process of migration from the southeast lake region of Africa. Bitter frontier warfare between the two groups of migratory people continued for the next seventy–five years, with large numbers of casualties on both sides.

The British took possession of Cape Town in 1795 in the name of the Prince of Orange, who then reigned in Holland and in England when his nation was overrun by the French. The British handed the area over to the Batavian Republic, a puppet state of France, in 1803 (all of this was a product of shifting alliances in Europe involving Napoleon's activities). But in 1806 the British returned; the Cape Colony was officially ceded to it in 1814 and it became a Crown Colony. A substantial migration of British settlers arrived in the succeeding 30 years, which by 1834 caused widespread unrest among the Dutch farmers of the Eastern Cape, who resented British rule.

Led by men of courage like Andries Pretorius, for whom Pretoria is named, the *Voortrekkers,* or pioneers, journeyed in covered wagons to the northeast, overcoming severe hardships and fighting the fierce Bantu tribesmen. In 1839 they founded a new republic called Natal, but were later pushed even further into the interior by the arrival of British military forces. Crossing the Drakensburg (Dragon Mountains), they went into the Orange Free State and Transvaal. In each area, a *Boer* republic was proclaimed. Thus, toward the end of the 19th century, there were two *Boer* republics and two British colonies in what is now the Republic of South Africa. Discovery of a huge 84 carat diamond on the banks of the Orange River by an African shepherd boy in 1869 set off the South African diamond rush. Fortune hunters from all over the world flocked to South Africa. In 1886 the world's largest goldfields were discovered on the Witwatersrand, adding to the influx of non-Boers. With these discoveries South Africa was transformed. From an economic backwater it became a major supplier of precious minerals to the world economy.

The Imperial Family of Ethiopia, 1930

THE COLONIAL PERIOD

Nigeria dances for Queen Elizabeth and Prince Philip, 1956

THE PORTUGUESE

Coastal West Africa: Portuguese Guinea

Although the Portuguese explored the coastline of Guinea as early as 1446, the area remained a slave trading coastal region for about the next 450 years. Portuguese control of the area occurred only because it was permitted by the other, more aggressive colonial powers. This was somewhat poor territory and literally what was left after the French and British had colonized West Africa.

The final boundaries were delineated in 1905, after both Britain and France had appropriated parts of Portuguese Guinea. Penetration into the interior was negligible until about 1912; in recent years the Portuguese had only sporadic control of the region, which was still theoretically a part of European Portugal. It was declared independent on September 10, 1974.

Equatorial West Africa: Angola, Cabinda, São Tomé, Príncipe

Angola was first explored in 1482 by Diego Cao of Portugal, who found this region of Africa controlled by the Bacongo people, led by a mighty King of the Congo. A scattering of Portuguese immigrants arrived during the following decades, but they were restricted to the coastal areas by the native Africans as a result of a series of bloody clashes. The King was overthrown, but later reestablished by the Portuguese in 1570.

During the 17th and 18th centuries, Angola was the prime source for slaves deported to Brazil to work the huge coffee plantations in that Portuguese Latin American colony. Also, an infamous penal colony was established in Angola.

During the late 19th and early 20th centuries, a multitude of treaties between Portugal and the British, French, Belgians and Germans gradually fixed the boundaries of Angola and Cabinda. The colony was given a form of internal autonomy in 1914, but this was strictly under White minority rule.

There were periodic uprisings in the 20th century, and in general, Portugal had almost exclusively favored the Portuguese immigrants and their descendants. In a flurry of civil war, accompanied by Cuban assistance for a Soviet–backed group, Angola, after formally being granted independence, became a Marxist state (see Angola).

Economic development under the Portuguese consisted of agriculture in the form of coffee and cotton production and mineral extraction based on diamonds in northeast Angola.

Cabinda is a part of Angola; it is a small enclave north of the Congo River. São Tomé is a tropical island devoted to cocoa production; it is inhabited by a uniform group of people of mixed, but predominantly African ancestry. There also was a small commercial element of Portuguese immigrants, most of whom left following the wars after independence. Príncipe is a small and poor island barely supporting the handful of descendants of freed slaves. These islands became independent on July 5, 1975 as *The Democratic Republic of Sãio Tomé and Príncipe.*

Southern Africa: Mozambique (Moçambique)

The Portuguese presence along the coast of Mozambique dates back to the voyage of Vasco da Gama in 1498. He found a number of trading posts that had been established by the Arabs, who offered little resistance to Portuguese construction of settlements and forts during the next century. These stations were intended more as an aid to Portuguese efforts in India and the Far East and were little more than stopping places for commercial vessels bound to and coming from those areas.

Shortly after Africa was partitioned at the Berlin Conference of 1885, both the French and Germans recognized Portuguese supremacy in Mozambique and elsewhere; Britain, preoccupied with its own colonial ambitions, ignored the Portuguese. Five years later, after expanding into neighboring Nyasaland (now Malawi), the British reached an agreement recognizing Portuguese claims. At the same time, the Mozambique Company was chartered to manage and invest in the colony, backed by substantial amounts of British capital. A massive uprising of Africans at the close of the 19th century hampered economic development in Mozambique. An early attempt was made in 1907 to establish a legislative council with membership restricted to White settlers in the colony.

As a result of the German defeat in World War II, the Portuguese added a small piece of German East Africa to Mozambique. The colonial period was relatively eventless between the two world wars. Railroad lines were extended initially from Beira to Nyasaland (Malawi), Southern Rhodesia (Zimbabwe), Northern Rhodesia (Zambia) and as far as the southeastern province of Katanga (Shaba) in the Belgian Congo, now DR Congo.

Portugal resisted attempts on the part of the native African majority to obtain independence during the postwar period. Following a liberal–army revolution in Portugal itself, this colony was granted independence in mid–1975 (see Mozambique).

THE BRITISH

Coastal West Africa: (The) Gambia

The claimant to the throne of Portugal granted English merchants, in exchange for an undisclosed sum of money, the exclusive right to trade with the people along the Gambia River.

Queen Elizabeth I confirmed this sale by granting letters patent to English busi-

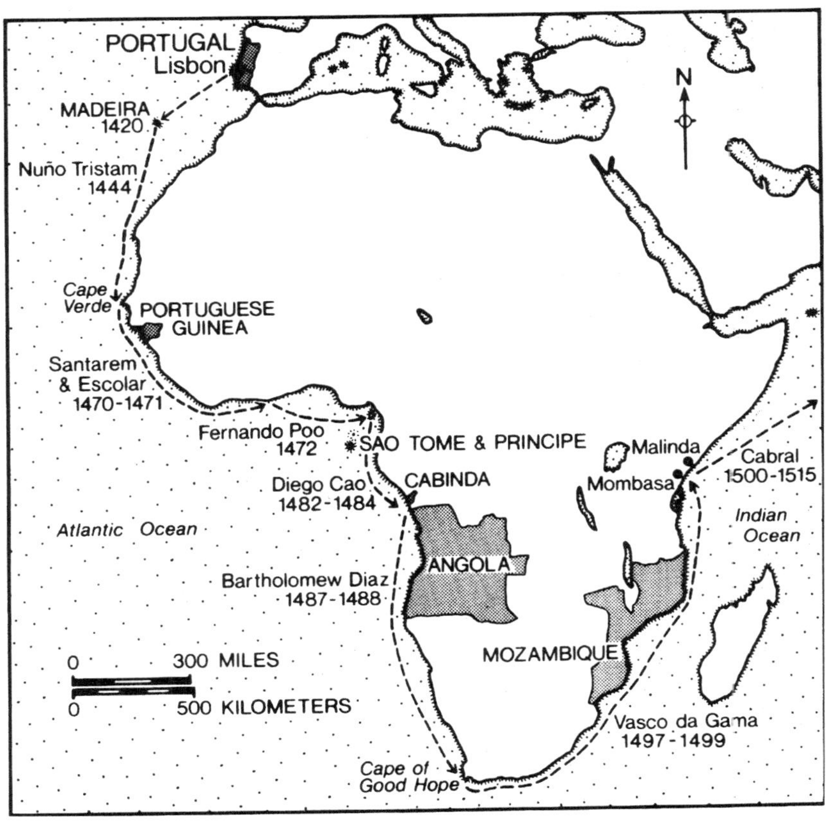

nessmen, and in 1618 James I granted a charter to the Royal Adventurers of England, giving the company trade franchises in Gambia and in the Gold Coast.

At the same time the British merchants were developing trade in the river area, French interests were expanding in Senegal, and the Gambia River was the best route to the interior of Senegal. Hence, an intense rivalry arose between the two nations in this area of colonial Africa. Their disputes were partially resolved by the Treaty of Versailles in 1783 which granted Gambia to the British, but reserved for the French a small enclave across the water from Bathurst.

There had been little exploration or penetration up the river to the interior until after 1860 when British explorers went inland and negotiated treaties with the local chief to obtain additional territory. The city of Bathurst remained a separate entity for the next two decades, sometimes administered from Sierra Leone, otherwise governed as a separate colony.

The present boundaries of The Gambia were delineated by a British–French agreement in 1889. Although the exportation of slaves had been prohibited, it was not until 1906 that the local practice of slavery within Gambia was abolished by British decree.

From the turn of the century until after World War II, there were few significant historical events in Gambia. Periodic efforts of the French to acquire control of the area were unsuccessful. With the exception of Bathurst, no Europeans lived in Gambia.

During World War II, Gambia not only served as an important naval base for military convoys, but contributed soldiers who fought valiantly in the Burma campaign of General Stilwell against the Japanese. The postwar period saw the birth of nationalist sentiment in Gambia. The Governor–General granted increasing powers of self government to the Africans of the country and established an advisory council.

In the late 1950's, Gambian leadership gathered into four political parties: the *Progressive Peoples Party;* the *United Party;* the *Democratic Congress Alliance;* and the *Gambian Congress Party.* The leaders of these groups actually had few differences, except with regard to possible association or federation with Senegal.

In general elections held in 1962, the *Progressive Peoples Party* gained 18 of the 32 popularly elected seats of Parliament. Prior to that time, Pierre Sarr N'jie, leader of the *United Party,* had been Chief Minister. David K. Jawara was selected Premier when his *Progressive Peoples Party* received support from the single delegate of the *Gambia Congress Party.*

Through subsequent defections, the *United Party* of N'jie lost five members to the organization of Jawara. An assembly of tribal leaders were selected by the Governor–General with the advice of the Prime Minister, but they had no vote. Thus, the National Assembly's membership totaled 38.

Internal self–government was granted to The Gambia in 1963, followed by explorations of the possibility of union with Senegal. A U.N. recommendation for unity between the two was turned down.

Coastal West Africa: Sierra Leone

The people of the European mercantile powers, particularly in England, had felt increasing antipathy toward the principle of slavery by the end of the 18th century after the American Revolution. A Society for the Abolition of Slavery was formed under the leadership of Granville Sharp, which planned to establish a colony in Sierra Leone for the slaves that were to be set free. In 1788, the Temne King, Naimbana and his subordinate chiefs, sold a portion of the coastal area of Sierra Leone to the Society, which was then settled initially by a group of 300 Africans freed as a reward for their service in the British armed forces in the battles of the American Revolution, joined by some former Jamaican slaves. The diminutive settlement was administered by the Sierra Leone Company and was immediately burdened by the task of fending off attacks from neighboring groups and French warships.

There was little growth—the burden of defense, development and settlement proved to be severe for the Company, and in 1808 Sierra Leone was taken over by the British as a Crown Colony. The English Parliament had abolished slave trade in 1807. Freetown, the name of the Company settlement, became a base for a squadron of ships which sailed the shores of West Africa searching for and intercepting the privateer slave ships. The first slave ship found was quickly condemned in 1808; its human cargo, so recently abducted from other African areas, was released at Freetown. As further slave ships were captured in the succeeding years, thousands of Africans of great diversity in origin were released, most of whom elected to remain in Sierra Leone, settling largely in the areas closest to the coast.

The period of the 19th century was one of gradual development by the British in Sierra Leone, with the establishment of a flourishing trade, schools, a college and Christian church missions. The former slaves, called *Creoles,* isolated from their native peoples and traditions, adopted many English customs which prevail today among their descendants, now numbering more than 125,000. In 1896 a British protectorate was established over the territory, which by then had definite boundaries with the adjacent French territories as a result of treaties signed in 1861.

The roads to democracy and independence were ones of peaceful development of responsibility and unity among the Creoles and the inland groups, with the first elections for local office being held in 1924. Sir Milton Margai, a Creole leader, was appointed to successive offices in 1954 and the following years, becoming the first Prime Minister in 1960.

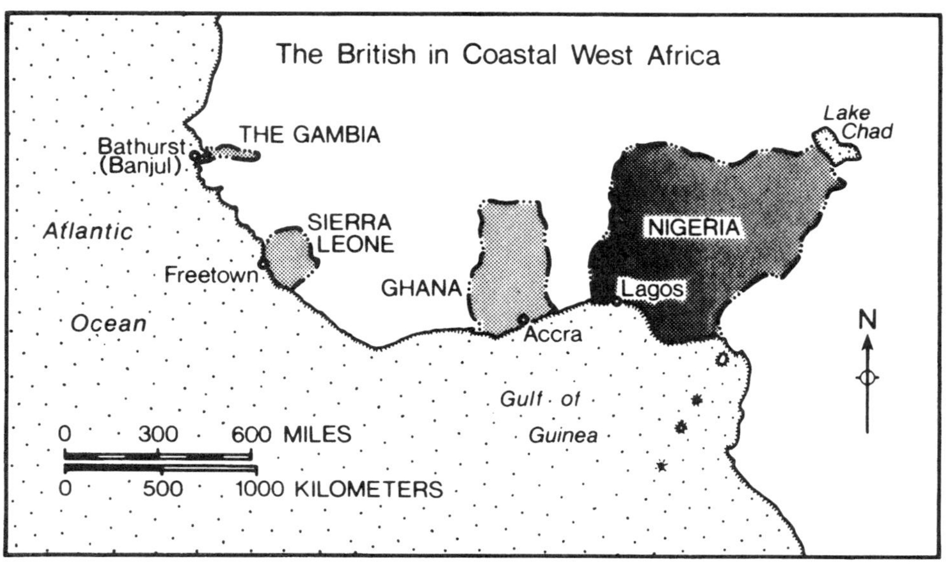

Coastal West Africa: Ghana (Gold Coast)

The Portuguese intially landed in Ghana as early as 1470; they were followed in 1553 by an English arrival on the shores of what was then known as the Gold Coast. Seeking gold, ivory and spices, the Portuguese built a castle which now stands in ruins on the coast. English, Danish, Dutch, German and Portuguese commercial interests controlled ports on the Gulf of Guinea during the next 250 years. By 1750, only the English, Dutch and Danes remained.

Great Britain assumed control of English commercial settlements in 1821, negotiating treaties with the local chiefs in the southern areas in 1844. Shortly thereafter, the Danes and Dutch ceded their interests to the British.

It was necessary for the English forces to fight a long series of battles against the Asante of the interior; there were four major campaigns in which the British subdued them: 1824–27, 1873–74, 1893–94 and 1895–96. It was only in 1901 that colonial authority spread through the entire country. After seizing Togoland (Togo) from the Germans during World War I, the British administered it from Accra. With the exception of the commercial activity in the south coastal area, there was little economic development during the colonial period.

Following World War II, there was a sharp rise of nationalism among the Africans of higher education in Gold Coast, as the colony was called. The *United Gold Coast Convention,* led by J.B. Danquah, exerted continuous pressure for autonomy and independence.

Political developments quickly came to revolve around one person: Kwame Nkrumah. After receiving college educations in the United States and Great Britain, obtaining several degrees in advanced courses of study, he returned to the Gold Coast from England in 1947. As Secretary of the *UGCC,* he assisted in promoting riots and strikes in early 1948. Both he and Danquah were exiled to a remote northern village by the British Governor. The British accused Nkrumah of being a communist.

Under continuing pressure, the British in 1949 promulgated a new constitution and released the exiled leaders. Nkrumah, restless under the leadership of Danquah, formed his own political party, the *Convention Peoples Party (CPP).* Further civil disobedience under Nkrumah's leadership resulted in his arrest, conviction and sentence to a two–year jail term. Constitutional reforms in 1951 provided for election of a greater number of Africans to a legislative council and Nkrumah was freed from prison to head the new government.

A new constitution of 1954 established a cabinet composed entirely of African representatives. The subsequent elections again resulted in a majority for the *CPP.* Two years later, Nkrumah, as Prime Minister, demanded independence. The British, not convinced that this was the will of the people, held new elections in 1956, which perpetuated the majority of the *CPP* (71 out of 104 seats). Independence was declared in 1957.

Central West Africa: Nigeria

The Portuguese were also the first explorers to land at Nigeria in 1472. For the next 300 years, traders from all nations

Kwame Nkrumah

called briefly in Nigeria, but there was no settlement. The principal purpose of their visits was to obtain human cargo to work in the colonies of the Western Hemisphere. The hundreds of Nigerian tribes periodically attacked each other, and the victor carried off the defeated to be sold into slavery for never more than $10.00 each. Transported across the ocean, they brought prices of up to $300.00. Close to 70% died in the slave ships. Slavery was not outlawed internally in Nigeria until 1901. There was a slow penetration of the British into the interior of Nigeria following the Napoleonic wars. The colony of Lagos was founded in 1862. Twenty–three years later, the Niger River Delta was established as a British Protectorate and British influence in Nigeria was formally recognized at the conference of European powers at Berlin in 1885. The British continued to expand in Nigeria through the Royal Niger Company, but in 1900 the territory came under the control of the British Colonial Office.

The people of northern Nigeria were believers in Islam; the Hausa and Fulani, as they are known, were feudally governed by a variety of rulers known as Emirs (also spelled Amirs).

Even after penetrating into areas of Nigeria, the British had difficulty in controlling the people; there were widespread disturbances and revolts in southern Nigeria in 1904 and an uprising in the Sokoto region of northern Nigeria in 1906.

It was not until 1914 that northern Nigeria was fully brought under control, at which time the Colony and Protectorate of Nigeria was formally established. Shortly after World War I, African legislators were included in the Council governing Lagos and southern Nigeria. The British enlarged tin mines on the Jos Plateau and improved the roads, schools and port facilities of Nigeria during the succeeding decades. Following World War II, the Colonial Office adopted successive constitutions which expanded African participation in Nigerian administration on a representative, federal basis. Three political parties evolved on a regional basis: the *Nigerian Peoples Congress* (North), the *National Convention of Nigerian Citizens* (Southeast) and the *Nigerian National Democratic Party* (Southwest). The latter two of these parties pressed energetically for full independence, but the *Nigerian Peoples Congress* advocated a lesser nationalistic outlook because it feared domination by a combination of the other two parties.

Discussions were held in London in 1957, at which time there were demands by 15 ethnic groups that they become individual and independent nations within the territory of Nigeria. The British resisted these demands and established a central parliamentary government with many powers reserved to the individual provinces; independence was granted in 1960.

Central West Africa: Cameroons

The British had early colonial ambitions in Cameroon and dispatched an emissary to negotiate treaties with the local chieftain in 1884. He arrived on the coast five days too late—the German representative had already concluded agreements with the coastal people, and Cameroon was to remain a German colony until 1916.

An extensive campaign was waged by the British and French against the German forces in Cameroon during the first world war. The fighting ended with the surrender of the Germans in 1916 (in Cameroon) and under the Treaty of Versailles Britain was awarded the smaller West Cameroon territory and France obtained East Cameroon. The fact that there were two colonies where there had been one gave rise to the plural name *Cameroons* for the area, creating confusion which persists even after they were again joined together in 1961.

The British held a mandate over its part from the League of Nations and subsequently under a trusteeship from the United Nations. Because of the language difference between the colonial powers of the two countries, there was wide divergence of opinion among the people of West Cameroon as to the political future

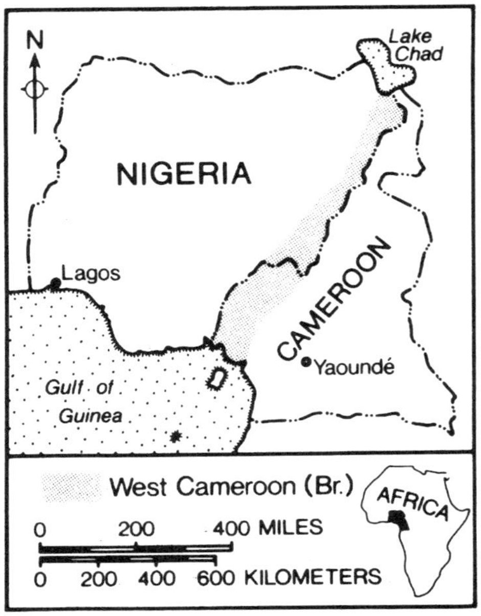

of the territory in the late 1950's. The British conducted a plebiscite under UN supervision in 1961 to determine whether the people of West Cameroon desired to become a part of the English–speaking Nigeria to the northwest, or to join the French–speaking East Cameroon in a federation.

Rather than conduct the plebiscite on the basis of all votes cast in the entire territory, it was decided to count the votes of the northern and southern portions separately. The people of the North voted to become part of Nigeria, which was effected, and the people in the South voted for the federation with the former French Cameroon. The voting procedure was strongly opposed by East Cameroon, considerable opinion existing to the effect that the vote should have been counted as a whole. Had this been done, no part of West Cameroon would have become a part of Nigeria.

———— • ————

The difference in language brought to West Africa by the British and the French has been the basis of post–independence problems. Almost uniformly, the official and commercial language of each area is that of its former colonial ruler. English–speaking Gambia should logically be a part of Senegal where French is spoken; Ghana is an English language nation surrounded by French–speaking nations, and many Ghanians, in the ethnic sense of the word, live in neighboring former French areas.

There also remains an economic pattern which is based on former colonial status; almost every nation of West Africa is economically tied to either France or Britain. Fluctuations and devaluations in currency, trade restrictions and the political problems associated with the European Common Market have all served to prevent a genuinely free flow of commerce among the present–day African nations.

South Africa

Since the period of partial British control of what is now the Republic of South Africa was brief and hotly contested by the *Afrikaaners* of Dutch ancestry, the history of the colonial period appears in the section on South Africa. There were, however, three territories in the area over which exclusive British control was continuous: Botswana (called Bechuanaland), pronounced Beh–*kwa*–na–land), Lesotho (called Basutoland, pronounced Ba–*soo*–toe–land) and Swaziland (pronounced *Swah*–zee–land). During the colonial period, which ended in 1967–1968, all three were economically dependent upon what is now the Republic of South Africa even though they were colonies of Great Britain.

Southern Africa: Botswana (formerly Bechuanaland)

The Tswana, as the majority of the people of Botswana are called, remained split into hundreds of tribes and communities until Khama I, Chief of the powerful Bamangwato tribe, consolidated them into a loosely constituted group in the last half of the 19th century.

As the *Boers* of South Africa were pushed northward from the Cape by the British, they attempted to penetrate into what is now Botswana, and battles erupted between the two peoples. Khama I, a Christianized native, appealed to the British for assistance, and the country was proclaimed to be under British protection.

Khama I reigned over the loosely united country until his death at the age of 93 in 1923, and was succeeded by his son, Sekgoma, who died three years later in 1926.

The British did little more than maintain peace in Bechuanaland during the period of the protectorate, although in later years they provided an annual grant to assist the colony's economy. In 1920 they set up two advisory councils—one for the native African people and one for the European settlers and their descendants who had come in small number to the area. Later, in 1934, they established a constitution which granted authority to the local chieftains and native courts.

The native rule of the Bamangwato passed to Seretse Khama, then the four–year–old son of Sekgoma, under the regency of Tshekedi Khama, brother of the dead ruler. The British had difficulty in controlling Tshekedi—at one time he was deposed as regent for a short time after having had a Britisher flogged.

Seretse Khama left for England in 1945 to pursue higher education; while studying law he met a young English woman, Ruth Williams, and married her. This interracial marriage of 1949 infuriated the white population of South Africa, and the embarrassed British Government removed Seretse Khama from office and forced him to remain in England until 1956.

After obtaining a renunciation of his chieftainship, the British permitted him to return to Bechuanaland in 1956 as "Mr. Khama." Many of the lesser chiefs opposed his return, as did his uncle, Tshekedi. The British established a Legislative Council in 1958 composed of 35 members equally divided between the races to advise and consent to the acts of the British High Commissioner, who was also executive authority in Swaziland, Basutoland and Ambassador of Great Britain to South Africa. Tshekedi was removed as Regent–Chief in 1959; the avowed purpose of establishing the Council was to prepare Bechuanaland for independence.

Political parties emerged rapidly after the first Council meetings—K.T. Motsete formed the *Bechuanaland People's Party* in 1960, demanding immediate independence and removal of political power from the White settlers. The British tacitly permitted Seretse Khama to enter politics because of his popularity, which had grown since his return from exile. He formed the *Bechuanaland Democratic Party,* with membership from both races, and advocated a policy of non–racism in government, a move toward internal self–government by 1965 and independence as soon thereafter as possible.

The British reviewed the status of Bechuanaland in 1963 and established a new constitution in consultation with the representatives of the political parties. The first elections in 1965 under the new system were won by Khama's *Democratic Party* and he was named Prime Minister. Further negotiations led to an agreement for full independence which became effective on September 20, 1966; Bechuanaland took the name *Botswana*—land of the Tswana.

Southern Africa: Lesotho (formerly Basutoland)

The people of what is now Lesotho, although composed almost of what are now referred to as South Sotho people, were organized in a multitude of sub–groups and tribes in the early 19th century. Raids from neighboring Zulus and Matabeles had depleted their number, and the remainder were gathered together in a loosely united kingdom by Moshoeshoe I, a chieftain from the northern region of Lesotho. The land was mountainous, hilly and generally regarded as unsuited for farming by *Boer* descendants of the original settlers of South Africa who had been driven from the Cape region into the interior of South Africa by British pressures.

But pressures for more land led to a twelve year war between the Whites of the Orange Free State and the Sothos between 1856 and 1868 which weakened the latter; they lost a substantial portion of their territory, still referred to as the "Conquered Territory." Facing total defeat, the Sothos appealed to the British for protection in 1868. The land area of the protectorate was poorly defined; the British resisted further *Boer* expansion, but had difficulty establishing control in what was considered a remote (from the Cape) land.

Basutoland, as it was then called, was annexed to the British Cape Colony in 1871, an act which was resented by the Basutos at the time because the English were just as eager for expansion in southern Africa as were the *Boers.* The unstable union was plagued by disturbances within Basutoland; the British, faced with a state of near–anarchy among the people, placed the colony directly under the control of Her Majesty's Government in 1884.

The British High Commissioners spent most of their time in Basutoland settling tribal differences and determining who was Paramount Chief—since the reign of Moshoeshoe I the land had been governed by about twenty–two lesser chiefs, who were in turn superior to approximately 2,000 minor chieftains. Little was done to improve and modernize the lives of the people living in the remote wilderness of the highlands.

The Basutoland Council was informally constituted in 1903 to provide direction in internal matters, and it was recognized officially by the British in 1910 as a legislative body to be consulted on internal affairs of the colony. The Council requested further reform in 1955 in order that its decisions might be conclusive on all internal questions. After a period of negotiation a revised constitution was adopted in 1959, to take effect the following year, which granted the wishes of the Legislative Council.

Pressures for total independence slowly gathered momentum, and Britain decided on a course of action in early 1965. Elections were held in April of that year to determine the popular will with respect to leadership of the colony. The *Basutoland National Party* of then–moderate Chief Leabua Jonathan gained 31 of the 60 parliamentary seats. The opposition party, the *Panafricanist Congress Party,* led by Ntsu Mokhele, a leftist, received 25 seats, and the right–wing *Maramatlou Freedom Party,* which supported the aspirations for power of Moshoeshoe II, hereditary Paramount Chieftain, won 4 seats. One delegate from the *Maramatlou* party defected to the *National Party* shortly after the election.

Although Chief Leabua Jonathan, who conducted his campaign from a helicopter provided by the Republic of South Africa, had received a minority of 44% of the popular vote, he negotiated for independence with the British in London.

Seretse Khama and his wife shortly before Botswana's independence

An independence agreement was reached on June 18, 1966 whereby Basutoland was to become independent and was to be called *Lesotho,* indicating the lowlands of the Sotho—the area they traditionally occupied.

Southern Africa: Swaziland

The Swazis came to their present territory during one of the many Bantu migrations. In the 18th century, Zulu raids into their country forced the tribal chieftain of Mawati to seek British assistance through the Agent General in Natal, who mediated a peaceful relationship between the two groups. For a time, the Transvaal Republic (now a province of South Africa) protected and administered Swaziland. After the *Boer War* (see the Republic of South Africa), control of the territory passed to the British.

In 1907, administration of Swaziland was charged to the British High Commissioner for South Africa. A proclamation was issued in 1944 by the Commissioner which recognized the Paramount Chief and Council as native authority for internal matters.

The British agreed in 1967 that Swaziland was to be independent after September 6, 1968. Internal self–government was established in April 1967 and elections were held shortly thereafter. The *Imbokodvo National Movement* (also known as *The Grindstone Movement),* led by Prince Makhosini Dlamini, won all 24 seats in the National Assembly. King Sobhuza II ascended the throne at the time of independence. Dr. Ambrose Zwane, leader of the opposition *Ngwane National Liberation Council,* pressed charges that the elections were rigged before the Organization of African United and in the UN. Both organizations listened, but did nothing.

Southern Africa: Rhodesia, Zambia, Malawi

A steady, but small procession of traders and missionaries of many European nations established themselves in Mozambique after the Portuguese in the 16th century. Actually, there was no colonial effort until almost four hundred years later. Diamonds and gold had been discovered in the former *Boer* states of South Africa, Transvaal and Orange Free State, both of which were coveted by the British. Transvaal had been successful in maintaining its independence. In an effort to surround the people of Dutch ancestry, the British commissioned the British South Africa Company in 1889, giving it all rights to an area north of Transvaal without limit.

Under the leadership of Cecil Rhodes, Salisbury was founded in 1890 in what

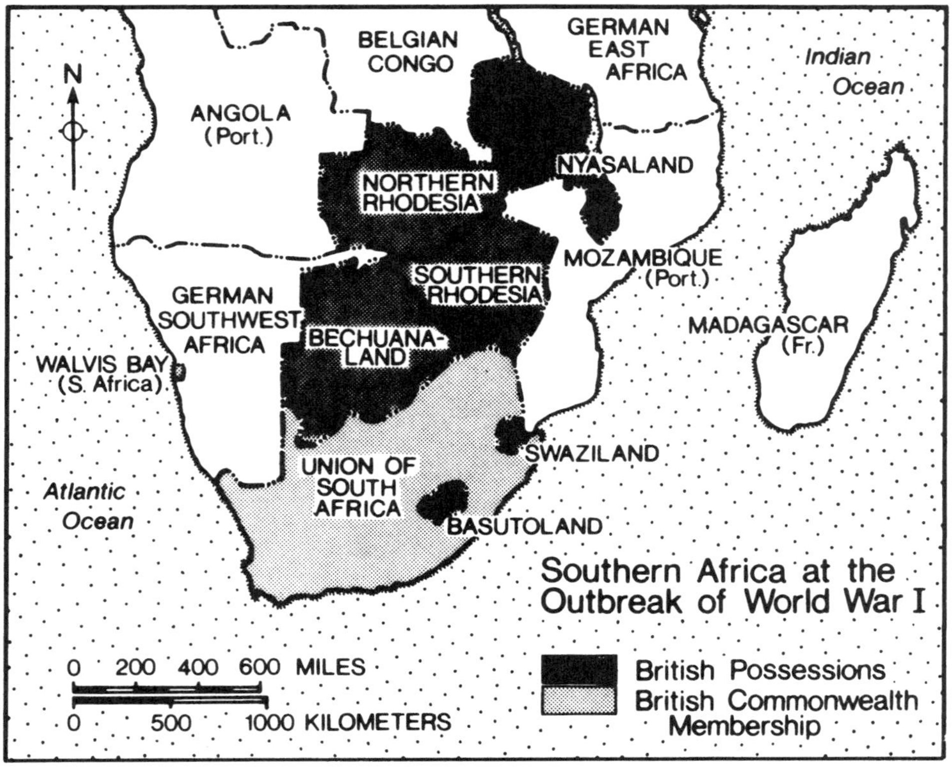

Southern Africa at the Outbreak of World War I

was then known as Mashonaland, inhabited by Matabele (Bantu) people. Leander Jameson, a close friend of Rhodes, was appointed administrator of the thinly–settled area which included what is now Zambia and the name *Rhodesia* was adopted in 1895.

Since the most valuable of the natural resources of this part of Africa were then believed to be only in South Africa, the settlement of Rhodesia was slow. For decades, Salisbury was a rural town with wooden sidewalks and was the only urban settlement in what was a vast agricultural area. In the early 20th century, Zambia was recognized as a distinct state called *Northern Rhodesia;* both areas were granted full internal autonomy in 1923, when Rhodesia was declared to be a Crown Colony instead of the property of the British South Africa Company.

The White Rhodesians were few in number, but steadily grew into an industrious, conservative society. The African people, with the exception of a few missionary efforts, were largely ignored, and restricted to the poorer lands in the ensuing decades. Salisbury emerged as a cosmopolitan and large city by the end of World War II, which was the beginning of a period of migration of more thousands of White Europeans—principally British—to Rhodesia.

The African people of Rhodesia became increasingly restless after 1960 as many colonies of Africa were granted independence under African leadership, but the resulting limited political effort was unsuccessful because of the power of the White minority which was firmly established. Southern Rhodesia was joined with Northern Rhodesia (Zambia) and Nyasaland (Malawi) into the Federation of Rhodesia and Nyasaland in 1953, but this crumbled because of the overwhelming opposition of the African majorities in what are now Zambia and Malawi. Although there were earlier visits by traders and missionaries, the first significant penetration of Malawi was by the intrepid Scotch missionary, Dr. David Livingstone, on September 15, 1859. For almost 15 years he devoted his life to exploration of southeastern Africa and teaching Christianity to the native people. Formal annexation of the area occurred in 1883 when a representative of the British government accredited to the kings and chief of central Africa appeared and negotiated treaties with them. In reality, this was no more than an effort to exclude Portugal and Germany from the area. The British energetically and successfully ended slave trade of Arab raiders.

During the colonial period, particularly after the discovery of gold and diamonds in South Africa and copper in Rhodesia (Northern), the men usually spent several years working in the mines of those territories, bringing their limited wages back home to Nyasaland, as the area was then called. Because of this, and the prevalence of the Christian faith among the people, there was no rapid surge of nationalism. This changed in 1953 when Nyasaland was joined into the Federation of Rhodesia and Nyasaland—the Nyasas greatly feared the White supremacy movements that were strong in the other two members of the Federation. In an effort to suppress opposition, the British tried to arrest the chief of the Angoni tribe who advocated a passive resistance to the Federation. The attempted arrest was unsuccessful, but was the source of an even higher level of mistrust of the British and other White people by the Nyasas. There was a gradual transition to internal autonomy from 1961 to 1963 based upon elections in which the *Malawi Congress Party* of Dr. Hastings Kamuzu Banda won an overwhelming victory. The despised Federation was dissolved in 1963 and independence was granted the following year.

East Africa: Kenya, Uganda and Tanzania (Tanganyika and Zanzibar)

The first British efforts in East Africa occurred in 1823 when Admiral William Owen entered the coastal area, supposedly in an attempt to end the Arab slave trade that had been going on for centuries along the coast. In theory, the Sultan of Muscat on the Arabian coast was the ruler of the region, and his authority was exercised by a viceroy (Sayyid) on the island of Zanzibar. The British, using a combination of threats and treaties, gradually established their control about the turn of the century.

German exploration and annexation of Tanganyika and part of southern Uganda from 1878 to 1885, in turn, aroused the interest of the British in Kenya and Uganda. The Sultan of Zanzibar granted the British East Africa Company a 50–year lease of what is now Kenya in 1887; this in turn was changed to the East Africa Protectorate, governed by a Commissioner, by the British government in 1895.

The last quarter of the 19th century in the eastern region of Africa was turbulent. There were efforts by both the British and Germans to enter Uganda, which was divided into four semi–autonomous kingdoms—Buganda, Busoga, Butoro and Bunyoro, of which Buganda was the most powerful. King Mwanga of Buganda, who reigned from 1884 until he was captured and exiled in 1899, tried to play the British off against the Germans by alternating his allegiance. In addition to this swirl of activity on behalf of Germany and Great Britain, there were roving remnants of Arab slave traders and religious conflicts involving and between Catholic and Protestant missionaries and believers, as well as those of Islamic faith.

The borders of this region were adjusted countless times, and not generally along the lines of actual colonial power. By a process of bargaining and trading, accompanied by line–drawing, particularly in Berlin in 1885, the eventual boundaries of the German, British and Por-

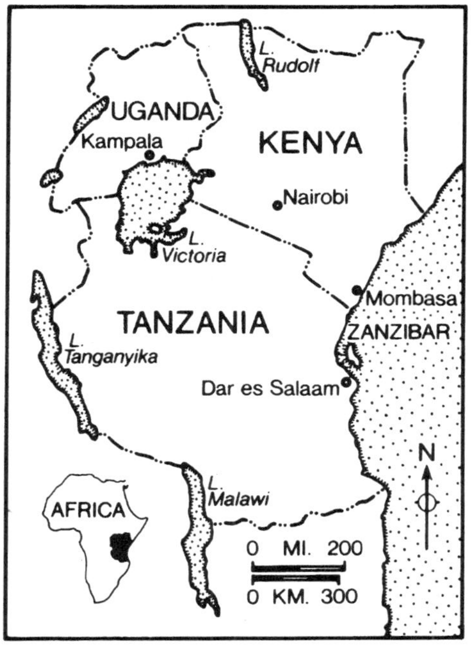

tuguese territories, as well as those of King Leopold of Belgium were fixed. The almost straight line that now separates Kenya and Tanzania cuts almost through the center of the territory inhabited historically by the Masai people.

The British encouraged immigration of White settlers to Kenya after the turn of the century, and they established immense plantations in the most select parts of the colony. The tribespeople of Kenya, particularly large numbers of the Kikuyu (referred to as "kooks" by the British) were relegated to the poorer, tsetse–fly infested farmlands. White immigrants entered Uganda only in very small numbers.

At the start of World War I, 300,000 British, South African and colonial Indian troops invaded German East Africa, renamed Tanganyika following the establishment of British control after the war. A force of slightly more than 200 German officers, commanding native troops numbering between 2,500 and 4,000 fended off the massive force for four years under the brilliant leadership of General Paul Von Lettow–Vorbeck.

After the war, the British sent the German settlers from Tanganyika, confiscating their lands; a small number were permitted to return within a few years. Kenya was completely dominated by the White farmers and a substantial number of Indians who were descendants of workers brought in to complete a railroad between Nairobi and Mombasa which had opened in 1895. Uganda was governed through the local kings, and the cultivation of cotton and coffee quickly rose to be the source of the leading exports, permitting Uganda to become the richest British colony in Africa.

Government in Kenya was through a variety of commissioners sent from Britain; it was at a relatively late date that local councils were permitted, and initially even these consisted of people appointed by the commissioners. The White farmers of Kenya requested a regional council for Kenya, Uganda and Tanganyika as early as 1926, but were turned down since it was felt that this was merely an effort of theirs to preserve and extend their power which excluded the African majority from sharing in government.

Following World War II, the ability of the British to rule effectively in Kenya and Uganda sharply decreased. The population of Kenya was stratified into three groups: the rich, landowning White (a small minority), the Indian and Arab merchant class, and (at the bottom) the huge majority of Africans. The African population had doubled in 25 years, creating tremendous pressure for expansion into the lands exclusively held by White farmers. The White population, instead of recognizing the needs of the Africans, instituted progressively more strict and severe laws directed against the majority.

The restive Africans formed a terrorist organization, the *Mau Mau,* to achieve their goals. Dreadful brutality became commonplace. Not only did the *Mau Mau* seek the lives of the Whites, they mercilessly slaughtered those of their own people who were servile to and worked for the Whites. White retaliation was equally brutal. Jomo Kenyatta, the political leader of the majority of African people, educated in Europe, was arrested, tried and convicted for participating in the *Mau Mau* conspiracy. He was sentenced to seven years in jail. In 1957 Kenya erupted in a total state of civil anarchy. *Mau Mau* terrorism had spread into almost every area of the country. Africans suspected of participating in this secret society were shot on the spot by Whites. Even long–trusted house servants had by this time joined the secret organization.

It became increasingly apparent that in order to bring stability to Kenya, the British would have to accede to the demands of the *Mau Mau.* Most of the British farmers departed, and in 1960 an agreement was reached in London which gave the Africans a majority in the Legislative Council.

Dissension and political quarrels among the Africans in Kenya retarded the goal of full independence. Kenyatta, released from jail, headed the *Kenya–African National Union (KANU),* which represented the larger tribes of the country. The *Kenya African Democratic Union* drew its support from the many smaller tribes. After prolonged discussion in London, a complicated constitution was adopted providing for a loose, federal system of government.

Jomo Kenyatta

The election conducted in May 1963 resulted in an overwhelming victory for *KANU.* Under pressure from the majority, the constitution was amended to strengthen the authority of the central government. The British recognized the independence of Kenya in December 1963.

Uganda was not without disturbance during the postwar period, although not as bloody as that in Kenya. In 1953, with the intent of establishing a central government, the British Commissioner informed the Kabaka (King) of Buganda that there were to be reforms in administration which would undermine his authority. Edward Mutesa II, the Kabaka, adamantly refused to accept these regulations and he forthwith was dismissed as King and put on a plane for London. The Buganda people regarded this as nothing short of an outrage. The British had to constitute a form of martial law to control the people throughout Uganda, and the economy suffered a steep decline.

The British attempted to solve this state of affairs by proposing that the *Lukiko,* the Ugandan tribal assembly, be permitted to vote on whether a new king should be chosen; the Assembly would not listen to the proposal. Kabaka Edward Mutesa was subsequently returned and the British set up a ministerial system of government, increasing African membership in the Legislative Council. The United Kingdom of Uganda was granted full independence in October 1962.

The movement toward independence was relatively tranquil in Tanzania (Tanganyika). The British had received a mandate from the League of Nations to administer the former German colony. This continued under a U.N. trusteeship. A gradual development of internal self–government was undertaken by the British, starting with a Legislative Council appointed by the government in 1926.

Subsequent elections were held in 1958 and again in 1960, the latter of which was won by the *Tanganyikan African National Union* of Julius Nyerere, who was President of Tanzania until 1985. He retired in that year, but is still a figure of power in the country. Full independence was granted in December 1961.

Northeast Africa: Egypt and the Sudan

During the first half of the 19th century, interest in European technology and education grew rapidly in Egypt, ruled by the Khedives (kings) nominally subject to the control of the Turkish Ottoman Empire's sultan. The basis for the construction of the Suez Canal lay in this interest, coupled with British and French desires for a shorter route to India and the Far East.

After negotiation with Khedive Ismail, European powers, working through their financial institutions, began construction of the canal, which was completed and opened amid great fanfare in 1869 with a multitude of European royalty present; they later heard the first performance of the opera *Aida,* by Giuseppe Verdi, erroneously said to have been written for the occasion. Egypt had been enriched by the demand for cotton created by the United States Civil War, but had also heavily borrowed at high interest rates to help finance the construction of the canal. From 1870 to 1883, the British succeeded in conquering most of the Sudan, penetrating as far as Uganda, supposedly in partnership with Egypt. The prime interest initially in this area was to end the oppressive slave trade that was firmly entrenched.

There was a financial crisis which compelled the Khedive to sell all of the Egyptian shares in the Suez Canal to Great Britain in 1876, giving the British a majority interest in the canal. Further financial deficits and inability to repay European loans were the basis of increasing British control of Egypt. The Khedives rapidly became figurehead kings, totally subject to British control, which led to an early rise of Egyptian nationalist desires. An army revolt, coupled with a popular nationalist uprising was the excuse used to invade Egypt, and absolute British control of the region resulted.

Although the Khedives were retained as the nominal rulers, their power quickly became almost nonexistent in the face of growing pressures of the nationalist leaders. Eventually, a scheme of rule was devised under the so–called *Organic Law* which included a legislative council and cabinet with advisory powers. The Khedive was controlled by a "Resident and Consul–General" of the British; all high Egyptian ministers had a British "advisor."

In the Sudan, Mohammed Ahmed, a leader known as *Mahdi,* quickly achieved wide popularity following 1880—in addition to his political military support, he was regarded by his followers, the *dervishes,* as a modern–day prophet of Islam. By 1884, he had all but completely demolished British and Egyptian forces within the territory. An expedition sent by the British offered the *Mahdi* some concessions which were flatly rejected; the Mahdi immediately laid siege to Khartoum where General Charles Gordon and his forces were located.

After several months, the Mahdi entered the city and the British were slaughtered; General Gordon was impaled by a dervish spear. A relief force sent to help arrived in Khartoum three days later, but was greeted only by smoking rubble and the silent stench of death. Fearful of also being wiped out by the fanatical Sudanese, the rescue force beat a hasty retreat. The control of the Sudan remained with the Mahdi and his successor for ten years. The British, faced with the growing French expansion on the western side of the Nile River in the Sudan, sent a large force under General Sir Horatio Hubert Kitchener to reconquer the territory in 1896–1898. The Mahdi had died and the dervishes were disorganized; in the ensuing battle almost 10,000 Sudanese lost their lives and were only able to claim that of 50 British and Egyptians in return. One of the young lieutenants in the British force was none other than Winston Churchill, destined to lead Britain through World War II.

Kitchener was later entitled Lord Kitchener of Khartoum in recognition of his leadership. Entering Khartoum, he emptied the revered tomb of the original Mahdi and dumped the corpse into the river,

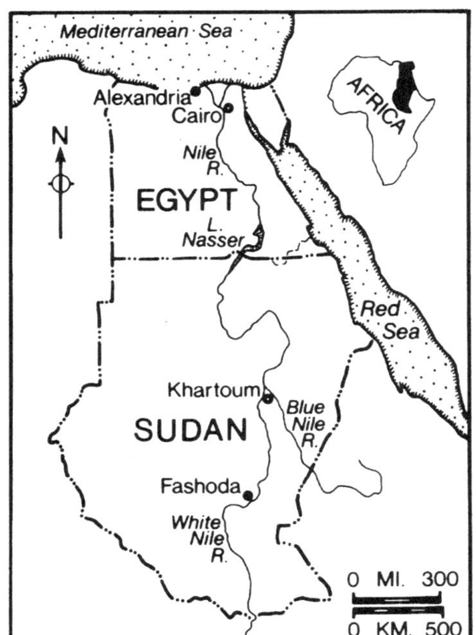

and then quickly captured and killed the *Khalifa,* successor of the Mahdi.

Kitchener marched rapidly southward, meeting the French at Fashoda (now Kodak) in an effort to reassert British power. The result was the Fashoda Crisis (discussed under *The French in Africa)* that was finally ended by agreement on areas of control which roughly defined the boundaries between what is now the Sudan, Central African Republic and Chad.

Great Britain and Egypt set up a joint administration of the Sudan; although they were nominally equal partners, the British were in fact the dominant power.

After World War I, the British had to institute increasingly harsh measures to maintain their control in Egypt and the so–called Anglo–Egyptian Sudan. At the start of World War I, the Ottomans in Turkey demonstrated sympathy for the German cause, and as a result, the British declared war against them. Although the Ottoman control in Egypt was little more than imaginary, the British used the war as a pretext to proclaim a protectorate status over Egypt, which aroused a great deal of local opposition. The *Nationalist,* or *Wafd Party,* quickly became dominant, opposing both the British and the Khedives.

A multitude of administrations under a semi–democratic constitution ruled following World War I. Ahmed Fuad, the Khedive, repeatedly dissolved nationalist governments and announced new elections, in all of which the nationalists scored tremendous victories and returned to power. The nationalist movement was not genuinely popular, however; its primary support came from the wealthy, land–owning *pashas* who had become established during the Ottoman era. The Protectorate status was withdrawn in 1922 and Egypt achieved internal autonomy as a result of *Wafd* efforts.

There were some efforts at economic development during the period between the two World Wars based upon the opening of dams along the Nile to partially control the age–old flood and drought cycle of the river. Constitutional reforms gave increasing power to the Egyptian *pashas.* The worldwide depression of the 1930's further lessened British control, and upon the death of King Fuad I in 1936, his handsome 16–year–old son, Farouk, came to power. Colorful and pleasure seeking, he was at first very popular. With the consent of the British and other European powers, Egypt became nominally independent in 1936 and was admitted to the League of Nations a year later. British military control was limited to the Suez Canal area.

The King dissolved the *Wafd* government in 1938, and the election that followed was a complete victory for the new pro–King party. Initially arming itself for World War II, Egypt maintained a passive

King Farouk at 16 in 1936

King Farouk at 32 in 1952

neutrality during the conflict, although it was the scene of battles between the Allied and Axis powers.

Following World War II, the Egyptians sought to end the last vestiges of British domination. Weakened by the war, England was in no position to offer opposition to this demand. The picture was further complicated by the presence of the newly–born Jewish state of Israel, carved out of a portion of Palestine, opposed by the Arabs, which led to a brief Egyptian–Israeli battle in 1948, won by the Israelis.

The *Wafd Party* again returned to power in 1950 after several changes of government reflecting the desires of the nationalists and unrest among the army leadership. Egypt demanded withdrawal of British troops from the Canal Zone and from the Sudan. Great Britain immediately retaliated with a plan for Sudanese independence; this appeared realistic in view of the traditional hatred for and distrust of Egyptians by the Sudanese. Events moved swiftly—the U.N. requested that Egypt lift its embargo forbidding use of the Suez Canal by ships bound for or coming from Israel. Egypt replied by abrogating its treaties with the British of 1899 and 1936 and the British navy attacked Port Said and landed forces in the area. Riots erupted in Cairo and there were two rapid changes of government. King Farouk, having grown fat and dissipated at the age of 32, was overthrown and exiled by the military in July 1952; a new era began in Egypt which is now generally thought of as the beginning of true independence in the modern age.

Prior to the defeat of Farouk, the British offered the Sudan a plan of internal self–government which was condemned by Egypt. The colonial government was able to work out a compromise arrangement with the military *junta* that succeeded Farouk, which provided that the Sudanese should decide whether they were to be independent or part of a federation with Egypt. In 1953 an overwhelming number of the Sudanese voted for independence, which was granted in 1956.

THE FRENCH IN AFRICA

North Africa: Algeria, Morocco and Tunisia

With the exception of Morocco, all of Arabic–speaking North Africa was at the turn of the 18th century in theory a part of the vast Ottoman Empire; the area consisted of a number of small principalities ruled by Turkish military men who had titles of *Bey* or *Dey*, depending upon the location. Commerce consisted of trade with regions to the south, and piracy of European shipping in the Mediterranean Sea.

The booty seized from the vessels consisted not only of cargo, but the crew as well, which was sold into slavery. After other nations had sent expeditionary forces against the Arab raiders, France sent a force into Algiers in 1830, deposing the Dey and seizing a few of the coastal towns. Another Dey was selected by the local people, who promptly marshaled attacks upon the French. Eventually the occupying forces had to recognize the new Dey, Abd el–Kader. He engaged in sporadic warfare for fifteen years against the French, who relinquished to him their claim to interior lands initially, but later drove him into Morocco where other French forces invaded and captured him in 1847.

Although the French presence in the area now known as Algeria was initially military, efforts were made to settle colonists from France in the 1860's and 1870's when most of what is now Algeria was gradually brought under colonial control. In Tunisia, the French had economic competition from England and Italy. In return for control of Cyprus, the British acknowledged France's authority in Tunisia. Because of an outbreak of violence, a naval force seized Bizerte in 1881 and forced the *Bey* of Tunis to accept the status of a French protectorate over the area. The British, Italians, and Turks all protested, but France had the support of Germany in the move, given in exchange for French support of German colonial ambitions elsewhere in Africa.

Morocco initially escaped domination by a colonial nation, although the major powers had forced a treaty in 1880 which protected the rights of foreigners within the country. After a 13–year–old boy succeeded as Sultan in 1894, the internal conditions deteriorated, reducing Morocco to virtual anarchy by the turn of the century. In exchange for concessions in Libya, Italy relinquished any claim it might have had in Morocco and the British later also acknowledged French supremacy in 1904. A nominal French–Spanish control was established in 1906 after a visit to Morocco by German Kaiser Wilhelm II as evidence of a German interest; negotiations led to an acknowledgment of French domination of the country in 1909. This was given by Germany in exchange for some economic guarantees and a section of the French Congo, which became part of Germany's colony of Kameroun (now Cameroon).

As was true with most colonial efforts, the French purpose in North Africa was primarily to enrich France. Although legally recognized as being in control of the area by 1910, actual control was much less than complete. During the entire colonial period from the 19th century until about 1960, the Arabs were almost in constant rebellion. Riff tribesmen of the Moroccan mountains and the Berber and Tuareg horsemen of southern Algeria never did accept French control. Arab unrest also came from the Muslim *Senussi* sect in neighboring Libya that spilled over into Tunisia which was populated by Italians as well as French immigrants.

Further complicating the peaceful colonization of North Africa, the immigrants to the area from France were principally military personnel and their families—they quickly developed a militant and conservative attitude as evidenced by their armed opposition to French efforts in the 1870's to placate the restless Arabs. Substantial numbers of Arabs went to France during the colonial period, but both in Africa and in France the two ethnic groups—French and Arab—resisted integration with vigor.

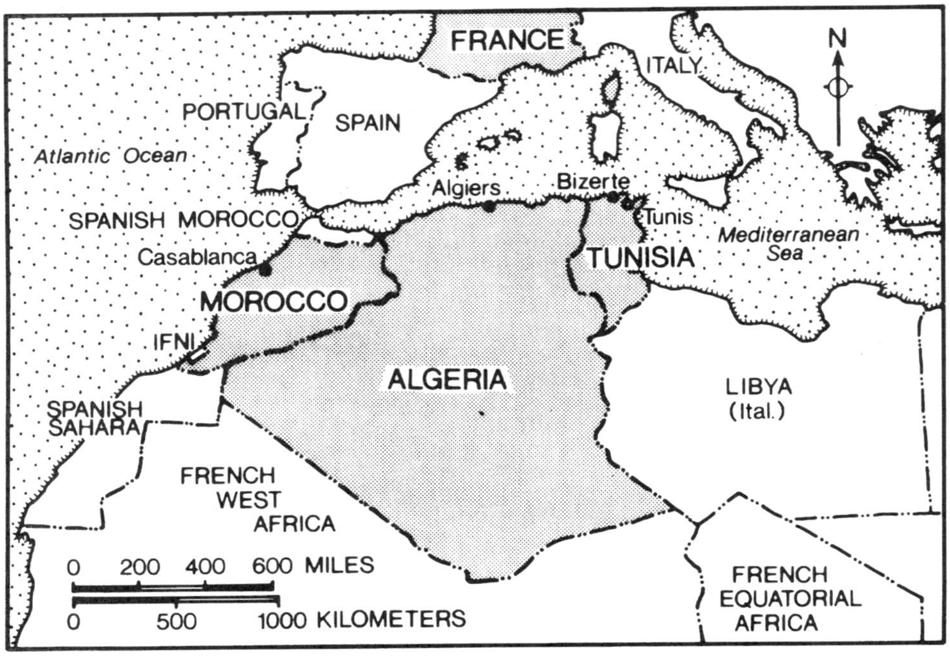

The French colonists assumed the dominant position in North Africa, both economically and in terms of status derived from education. Lower schools were provided for those of French ancestry, but with little exception, no comparable effort was made on behalf of the Arabs. The local rulers were allowed to retain nominal powers, since it was actually easier to rule through them rather than try to depose them.

The earliest signs of Arab nationalism in the region occurred in Morocco in the 1930's, partially because of the world economic depression which had a severe effect on the economy of all North Africa which was based almost entirely on the agricultural production on farms of European immigrants and their descendants. This effort was the basis of continuing anti–French sentiment among the Arabs to which was added growing worldwide liberal–nationalistic ideals that were temporarily interrupted by World War II before making any progress.

Upon installation of a pro–German government under Marshal Henri–Phillipe Petain in France following the German invasion of that country in World War II, Algeria, Morocco and Tunisia were brought under the nominal authority of the *Vichy (Vee–shee)* government which he headed, named after a town in central France from which part of France was administered by his regime in 1940–1944. Although only a relatively insignificant number of French troops loyal to the Axis powers were stationed in the area, the Allies felt that it was necessary to establish Free French control in the area prior to invading Italy.

A combined American–British force invaded Morocco and Algeria on November 8, 1942, and three days later a cease–fire arranged with Admiral Jean François Darlan, the *Vichy* commander, led to Allied control of French North Africa within a short time, with Admiral Darlan achieving the post of Chief of State with Allied approval. Following his assassination shortly afterward, the Anglo–American command tried to install the aging General Henri Giraud as commander of French forces outside France in spite of the more energetic anti–Axis, anti–*Vichy* activities of the Free French led by the younger General Charles de Gaulle. His forces had conducted assaults in and from Brazzaville, French Congo. A brief German offensive in North Africa was repulsed by the Allies in May 1943.

The French were restored to continued colonial control of North Africa following World War II. Their rule was no more effective than the unstable and numerous French governments of mainland France. In Algeria, the conservative colonists *(colons)* of French ancestry completely dominated all phases of government, although Algeria was legally supposed to be an integral part of France. The Communist Party had been outlawed in Morocco, a colony, but this could not be done in Algeria since the communists were not outlawed within France. The *National Liberation Front* quickly rose in power and spearheaded a revolt which started in late 1954 and lasted for seven years. This group was a leftist–socialist–communist Arab party, united in opposition to French colonial rule.

A last ditch effort of the *Secret Army Organization (OAS),* composed for the most part of French–descended Europeans, failed to stem the overwhelming tide of revolution in spite of cruel and terroristic anti–Arab measures in 1961. A cease–fire was finally negotiated in March 1962 and President Charles de Gaulle, who had promised the French to end the bloody conflict, recognized Algerian independence on July 3 of that year.

At the close of World War II, the *Istiqlal Independence Party* was formed in Moroc-

Habib Bourguiba celebrates Tunisian independence

co; it promptly issued a demand for independence which was refused. The party quickly gathered momentum with the tacit consent of the Alouite monarch, Sultan Mohammed V.

The willingness of this ruler to permit existence of the independence movement created great dissatisfaction among the French administrators. The French deposed him in 1953, sending him into exile, first on Corsica and then to Madagascar. Assisted by the Berber *Glaoui* (Sheikh) of Marakesh, the French placed Mohammed VI on the throne—a colorless, subservient member of the ruling family who was generally disliked by Moroccans.

Growing resentment led to severe rioting; terrorists struck swiftly, retreating to the safety of the hills and mountains to regather their forces, in the same manner as the formerly rebellious Riff tribesmen. The United States indicated great dissatisfaction with French policy, and in 1955, because of internal and external pressures, the French returned Mohammed V to the throne. Under the overwhelming influence of a strong and popular king and the independence party, Morocco ended its colonial status in 1956.

In Tunisia there was also a postwar surge of nationalism. A large middle class of well–educated people had emerged and backed this movement, led by an Arab lawyer educated in France, Habib Bourguiba. His *New Constitution Party* succeeded the older *Constitution Party.* Bourguiba's life during the French colonial period alternated between periods of exile and/or imprisonment and periods of nationalistic leadership. Exiled in 1934, he returned in 1936, was rearrested in 1938 and later was freed by the Germans in 1942. He again was arrested when the French returned, but escaped and went into exile. When he returned in 1952, he was arrested, and in 1954 was banished into exile.

By this time Tunisia was in a full state of insurrection requiring the presence of 70,000 French troops to attempt to control the colony. France granted internal autonomy to Tunisia in 1955 which also provided amnesty for all freedom fighters. Bourguiba was permitted to return, and full independence was achieved on July 20, 1956.

The South Sahara: Mauritania, Mali, Upper Volta (Burkina Faso), Niger, Chad.

Colonization of the southern Sahara region of Africa was a much slower process than in other areas of the continent because the almost uniformly arid land held little importance to the French, other than strategic. The only reasons for colonization were in order to connect other more valuable colonies together and to exclude other foreign colonial effort in the region.

At a meeting known as the Berlin Conference, arranged by Otto von Bismarck of Germany and the French foreign minister in 1884–1885, the major world and colonial powers officially decreed that African slavery was to be abolished and that there was to be free navigation of the major rivers of the continent. It was further decreed that colonial power in the area was to be based on presence and actual control. Unofficially, and more important, the representatives took a map of the continent and drew lines indicating areas of interest of the respective powers.

The maps of the continent at that time were uncertain—boundaries differed sometimes more than a thousand miles, depending on the map and the nationality of the cartographer. In their effort to connect the West African and Equatorial African colonies, the French, in 1896–98 sent an expedition under Jean Baptiste Marchand that pushed rapidly northeastward as far as Fashoda (later named Kodak) on the Nile River. At the same time, having defeated the Sudanese, supposedly on behalf of Egypt, British Lord Horatio Herbert Kitchener was leading his forces southward along the Nile from Omdurman, and a second British expedition was pushing north on the river from Uganda. Further complicating the picture was the imminent arrival of an Ethiopian army on the right bank of the Nile at Fashoda, accompanied by another group of French forces.

The result was the Fashoda Crisis in which the British and French were eyeball–to–eyeball on the brink of total war. However, France was preoccupied with a complicated political scandal involving top military figures in Paris (the Dreyfuss Affair) which had political and religious overtones. The French blinked first, ending the crisis with an agreement on the lines of French and British authority in the area, which approximately fixed the present eastern borders of Chad and the Central African Republic with the Sudan.

Although the major powers of the world recognized French authority in this barren land by the end of the 19th century, the nomadic people who lived in the south Sahara region refused fully to submit to foreign rule for several years afterwards. In the final analysis, France was compelled to rule this part of Africa through local tribal leaders who possessed a large measure of autonomy. This permitted nominal French control without large–scale military forces which would have been necessary for direct rule.

The region was administered as a whole; it was part of French West Africa. Mali, Niger, Chad and southern Algeria were also known as French Sudan, the French spelling of which was Soudan.

The lives of the people were hardly disturbed by colonial rule. There was virtually no immigration of Europeans such as occurred in North Africa; the only French presence was essentially military. Occasional revolts occurred which were contained, rather than defeated by the French.

Although there was some sporadic German penetration in World War II during the North African campaigns of 1942–43 in the Mali, Niger and Chad regions, the

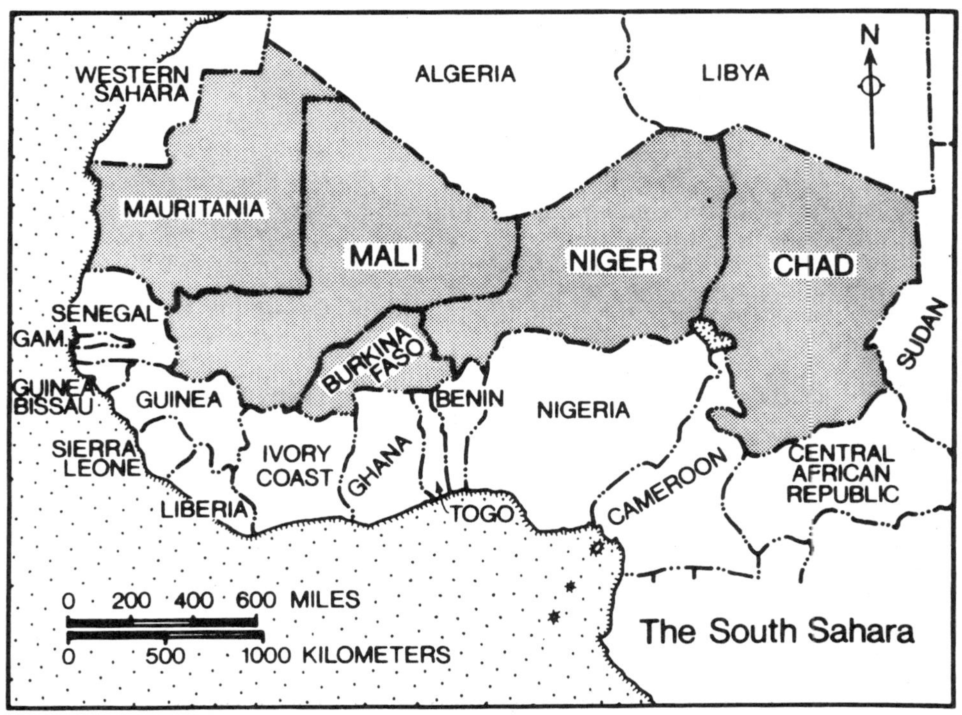

local people were not involved in the battles. Free French forces under General Jean LeClerc fought several engagements with the Germans in the northern Chad area. With little exception, there was no political movement toward independence from France following World War II in the south Sahara. Niger shared in the development of the *Democratic African Rally Party,* but in this respect was dominated by the members from the Ivory Coast under Félix Houphouet–Boigny. As a result of unrest of the Muslim Mossi people in what was then called Upper Coast, the area now constituting Upper Volta (Burkina Faso) was separated after World War II from Ivory Coast, taking the French name *Haute Volta.*

Following the election of Charles de Gaulle as President of France, the *French Community* was established in 1958—a plan whereby France's colonies in Africa were granted internal autonomy. This was an effort to satisfy independence movements in areas of French Africa outside the south Sahara. It proved to be unsatisfactory in many respects, not the least of which was continued opposition to French authority over foreign relations by a multitude of African nationalists within the *Community.* Because of this, France granted independence to the remaining south Sahara and West African colonies, numbering thirteen, in 1960. Thus, without any substantial internal effort to promote independence, the south Sahara region was freed of French authority (which in reality had never been firmly established).

Coastal West and Equatorial Africa: Senegal, Guinea, Ivory Coast, Togo, Dahomey, East Cameroon, Central African Republic, Gabon, Congo.

France initially had no colonial ambitions along coastal Africa—scattered missionary stations were established in the 17th and 18th centuries and slave trade was also prevalent at the time. Following the abolition of slave trade in 1815, France maintained very small "factories" (trading posts) along the various parts of the coast.

Colonial interest quickened during the mid–19th century when the major European powers feared that one or another of them would obtain some valuable territory available to all nations, with a potential discovery of valuable metal ores and gems. In reality, with the exception of widely scattered and exaggerated tales brought to Europe by occasional explorers, almost nothing was known of the interior coastal lands of West and Equatorial Africa.

Senegal was the first area of increased French activity—General Louis Faidherbe headed an armed force in 1854 that was immediately resisted by the natives and their Tukuler ruler, Hajk Omar, but it was gradually able to subdue most of the area. The most commercially important region of Senegal—the Gambia River Basin—had been seized by the British decades prior to the arrival of the French.

At about the same time a military mission was sent to Guinea, but because of the fierce resistance of the people of the region, penetration into the interior was slow. The Mandingo chieftain, Samory Toure, intially signed a treaty which permitted him to claim additional territory to the northwest. This peace was short–lived; further French military efforts were necessary in 1885–6, and a dire threat to the French was mounted when Toure united with the Tukuler people previously driven from Senegal into Mali.

The French offensive was on two fronts—north and east in Guinea and north and west in Ivory Coast, which finally resulted in the defeat of Toure in 1898. He was exiled to Gabon after his capture, where he died two years later. Penetration from southern Ivory Coast had also been slow. Although treaties were signed with the coastal chieftains of the Grand–Bassam and Assime regions, the Agnis and Baoules, two groups closely related to the warlike Ashanti people of Ghana to the west, offered fierce resistance to drives into the interior. Further north, the Mandingo people of Samory Toure and the Tukuler Africans prevented progress; Ivory Coast was not fully conquered by the French until about 1915.

As a result of a treaty signed with the French in 1851 by Ghezo, ruler of Abomey (Dahomey) a small commercial effort was initiated in that country. Coutonou was ceded as a trading post in 1868. The colonization of Dahomey was not uncontested—the Portuguese and British attempted to encourage inter–tribal rivalries in order to unseat the French from the coastal area, but without success.

Dahomey, with the exception of its narrow coastal strip, was left virtually untouched until 1890 when Benhazin, the last powerful king of Abomey, refused to sign additional treaties with France. Military occupation of Coutonou was ordered, swiftly followed by a violent uprising which continued with periodic interruptions until 1894, when Benhazin surrendered. The interior of Dahomey was slowly subdued during the following decades.

Togo was not gained by the French until World War I. The larger part of this former German colony was occupied by French troops in 1916; this control was converted into a mandate by the League of Nations, which divided the colony between France (East) and Britain (West). The British area was joined with the Gold Coast (Ghana). The East Cameroon region was also acquired from Germany in a similar fashion in 1916, also resulting in a League of Nations mandate.

Count Pierre Savorgnan De Brazza of France entered the northern side of the Congo River region of coastal Africa at about the same time that the British–American explorer Henry Stanley was claiming the southern side of the river region on behalf of King Leopold of Belgium in the first part of the 1880's. Both followed the same procedure of entering into so–called "treaties" with the various sub–chiefs of the once–mighty Kingdom of the Congo, a Bantu empire which once had extended from Gabon to Angola including an area several hundred miles inland from the coast. After exploring most of Congo (Brazzaville), De Brazza went into Gabon and established a small coastal outpost.

The area which now is the Central African Republic was not penetrated by the French until about 1889, when an outpost was established at Bangui, the present

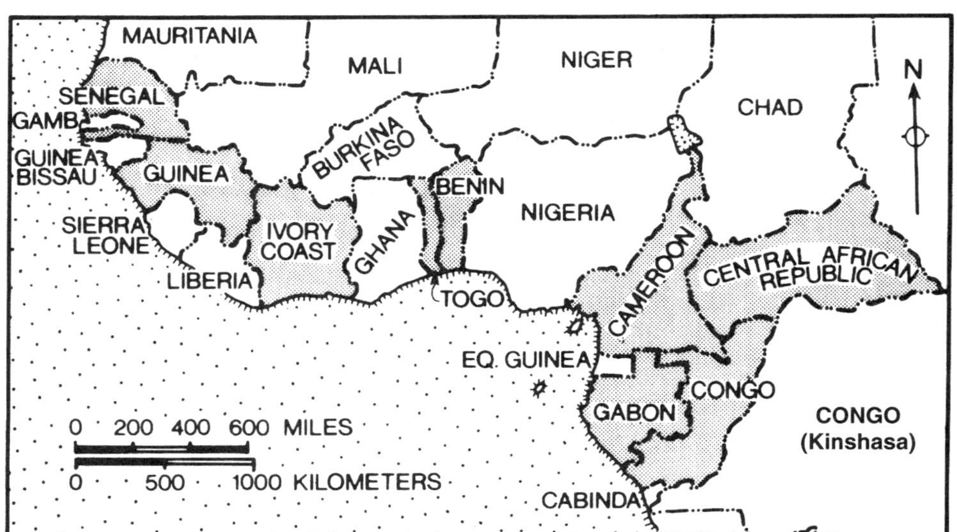

Marketplace vendor, Mali

capital. The French named this territory *Ubangi–Shari* after its two principal rivers. It was not until after the turn of the century that effective French control was imposed on Congo, Gabon and the Central African Republic, all of which were combined in 1910 to form French Equatorial Africa, a distinctive administrative area. Upon receiving a mandate from the League of Nations over East Cameroon, a section of the former German colony (Kameroun) was made a part of French Equatorial Africa.

Mauritania, Senegal, Guinea, Ivory Coast, Dahomey, Mali, Upper Volta and Niger had been joined together as French West Africa in 1904; the entire territory was administered from Dakar, Senegal. The part of former German Togoland acquired after World War I was joined into this vast colony.

A variety of local councils were permitted by the French, giving the Africans a limited voice in their local affairs during the colonial period. European–style education was introduced, but never achieved widespread enrollment due to a shortage of trained teachers willing to live in Africa. Small numbers who did obtain secondary education usually went to France if they desired higher level studies.

Roads and railroads were constructed to the extent necessary to commercially develop this area of the continent, such as in Ivory Coast to permit export of agricultural products and in Gabon to support wood production.

After obtaining the necessary medical education, Dr. Albert Schweitzer, a world–renowned German philosopher and musician, received permission to establish a Protestant Christian medical mission and hospital at Lamborene in the interior of Gabon. He labored among the people, relieving the illness and misery of Africans regarded as little more than savages by the rest of the world—but whom he considered priceless human beings—from 1913 until his death in 1965. He adapted medical methods to harmonize with the customs of the Africans. The mission continues its work under the leadership of his daughter, who engages in fund–raising to support its activities.

Other than medical facilities provided principally for Europeans living in West and Equatorial Africa, almost none were established for the benefit of the African people during the colonial years, but there was some improvement in the post–World War II period. Boundaries were stabilized over a number of years by agreements with the British, Belgians and Liberians; the map of colonial Africa underwent no substantial change in West Africa after 1920.

The World Depression of 1929 and the following years had great impact in the coastal colonies of French West and Equatorial Africa, where agricultural products usually were the sole exports. The sharp drop in prices paid for foodstuffs meant a corresponding decrease of income, and accompanying lower living standards which had not really been much more than marginal.

When France fell to the overwhelming might of the German Nazi military machine, a puppet, pro–German administration was established in France—the *Vichy* government (1940), named for its location in central France. It quickly dispatched administrators and personnel to take control of French Africa; they were generally disliked by the French living in the colonies. Their policies tended in many cases to be openly racist and repressive. French General Charles de Gaulle led a force aided by British vessels which attempted to seize Dakar, Senegal in 1940, but it was repulsed. A month later, he was able to capture Douala, Cameroon; Brazzaville was also occupied and a powerful transmitter was erected in order to make daily Free French broadcasts which were received in distant areas.

Following World War II, colonial rule continued, but there was a rapid upsurge of nationalism among native Africans. France itself had been economically devastated by the war and only slowly recovered with great amounts of foreign assistance provided by the United States. Political extremism, both rightist and leftist (communist) was rampant, making orderly French government all but impossible. Félix Houphouet–Boigny, a nationalist leader in Ivory Coast, organized the *Democratic African Rally (RDA)* with associated parties in most of France's West African colonies; the allied party succeeded in electing almost all of the area's deputies to the Assembly in Paris between 1947 and 1950. The relatively small number of African delegates allowed by the constitution allied themselves with the communist deputies during this period in an effort to gain support for their nationalist viewpoint, but that allegiance was discontinued in 1950.

France was severely drained by the communist rebellion within its Indochinese colonies, including Vietnam, during the postwar period which ended in a military disaster for the French in 1954. Immediately, a second total rebellion was mounted by the Algerian *National Liberation Front* which resulted in devastating warfare within that colony for seven more years, with accompanying additional strain upon the French economy. Principally for those reasons, the French were in no position effectively to oppose nationalist demands of their African colonies.

The Overseas Reform Act *(Loi Cadre)* of 1956 gave the African colonies internal autonomy, leaving matters of defense and foreign policy to France in an effort to quiet the demands for total independence. After Charles de Gaulle assumed almost absolute powers in France in 1958, he announced the creation of the *French Community,* the first step towards granting total independence to the colonies. Guinea, led by Sékou Touré, rejected the plan and that colony gained immediate independence.

Senegal and Mali were joined into the Federation of Mali in 1959 and France made some other minor changes, but granted full independence to all its remaining colonies in West and Equatorial Africa in 1960.

East Africa: Madagascar, French Somaliland

The immense island of Madagascar was known to navigators since the 15th century, but there was no attempt at colonization. The Hindu Merina (Hova) people of Indonesian and Malaysian descent lived in the central highlands; persons of Arab and African heritage inhabited the coastal areas. There was only a brief period when the island was under single control during the 16th century, established by Sakalava (Arab) rulers.

The Merina kingdom became dominant in the 18th century under King Andrianampoinamerina (1787–1810); he and his successors alternately encouraged the French and British in their tentative efforts at colonization so that neither would gain the upper hand. Between 1775 and 1824, the island was a stronghold of marauding pirates, including John Avery, Captain Mission and William Kidd. The pirates even formed a republic called *Libertalia,* which was of brief duration.

Other nations of the world later established commercial relations with the Malagasy people; a treaty of peace, friendship and commerce between the United States and Madagascar was signed in 1881. During this period, British influence in the interior became strong. In 1869, Merina Queen Ranavolona I and her Court were converted to the English Protestant faith. French interests continued to dominate the coastline.

At the Berlin Conference of 1885, as a result of concession by the French to the British in other parts of Africa, Great Britain supported the establishment of a French Protectorate over Madagascar. This status led to the end of the Merina Kingdom. General Joseph Simon Galliene, the first French Governor, with the aid of French troops, unified the entire island.

The people—particularly the Merinas—had little use for French rule. In 1916 they rose unsuccessfully in bloody rebellion. The differences between the pro–French coastal inhabitants and those of the interior was expressed in this movement for independence which was limited to the people of the highlands. After the fall of France in World War II, Madagascar, first administered by the *Vichy* (pro–Nazi) government of France, was occupied in 1942 by the British to prevent possible Japanese seizure of the strategic island. The Free French gained control in 1943. By 1947, an independence movement had become overwhelming and there was a national uprising suppressed only after months of bitter fighting which resulted in the death of more than 10,000 people of the island.

Subsequent constitutional reform in France lessened the tensions in Madagascar, and led to the establishment of the Malagasy Republic within the French Community in 1958. The Republic became fully independent in 1960.

The tiny, sun–blistered colony of French Somaliland came into existence when treaties were signed with local chieftains in 1862. This colonization, as well as that of the British and Italians in the area, was to secure the regions south of the Suez Canal, then under construction, in order to prevent any disruption of shipping. The only asset of the territory was a deep, natural harbor facing the Gulf of Aden. At the turn of the century, a railroad from Addis Ababa, Ethiopia to Djibouti was completed and was thereafter the prime source of revenue. This colony achieved independence from France in June 1977 and is now known as the Republic of Djibouti.

THE UNITED STATES OF AMERICA IN AFRICA

See Liberia: History.

KING LEOPOLD AND THE BELGIANS IN AFRICA

The Belgian Congo, Ruanda-Urundi.

The Belgian efforts at colonization in the Congo region of West Africa call to mind the name of one man: Henry Stanley. Following his birth in Wales, he migrated to the United States where he became an author, soldier and adventurer, fighting on both sides in the American Civil War. Seeking new adventure, he turned to Africa and went to locate the Scottish missionary, Dr. David Livingstone, who had disappeared while exploring central Africa. After locating Dr. Livingstone on the shores of Lake Tanganyika in 1871, he explored the lake regions of the continent and then proceeded westward to the Congo River region. It took him three years to traverse the length of the river; he arrived on the Atlantic coast in 1877 and departed for Europe.

Stanley was immediately summoned by King Leopold II of Belgium, who saw in this explorer a means to compete in the scramble for colonial territory in Africa. Stanley accepted the offer of employment and returned to the Congo, entering into treaties on behalf of King Leopold with the native chieftains. The curious thing about this colonization is that it was not on behalf of the Belgian nation—this was Leopold's personal project.

At the Berlin Conference of 1885 when great portions of Africa were divided between the European colonial powers, King Leopold had personally been awarded the area south of the Congo River as far as Portuguese possessions in the Angola region.

Although the area was referred to as "The Congo Free State," the years which followed were harsh. King Leopold desired wealth from the Congo and all policies in the territory were used toward that desire. Forced labor and torture were used to compel production of wealth; it is estimated that up to 8 million Africans lost their lives during the 23 years of Leopold's exploitation. By 1904, knowledge of these repressive conditions had become known in Europe and the United States; in response to pressure from Britain, Germany and the U.S., King Leopold sent a commission to investigate conditions. The report of the commission, issued in late 1905, indicated that the actions of Leopold's administrators were scandalously cruel and improper. Bowing to continued international pressure, the Belgian parliament passed an act in 1908 annexing the Congo State of Belgium.

During the period at the turn of the century, there was friction between the British, French and King Leopold over control of the upper (southern) Nile area in the region near Lake Albert. As a result of a compromise, the Congo Free State received a small portion of territory known as the Lado enclave, which reverted to the Sudan (Anglo–Egyptian Sudan) at the death of Leopold in 1910. There were a variety of treaties between the several colonial powers that gradually and firmly demarcated the borders of the Congo region.

Under Leopold, the copper–rich Katanga (now Shaba) area had been opened up, and economic development based on that region's wealth proceeded forward under Belgian administrators. The general approach was that the native Africans should not be given too many privileges lest they become restless. Due to efficient administration, however, the per capita income rose to be one of the highest in colonial Africa.

Belgian forces moved to occupy the northwestern part of German East Africa at the start of World War I. This region, consisting of what is now Rwanda and Burundi, was then called Ruanda–Urundi and became a mandated territory assigned to Belgium in 1923; it was joined administratively with the Congo, which was given a wide degree of autonomy at the same time. Between the two world wars, Belgium made substantial capital investments in the Congo, including construction of railways connecting Kinshasa (then called Leopoldville) to the mineral wealth of Shaba (then called Katanga).

Nationalist pressures on the part of the native Africans mushroomed after World War II. Belgium, prostrated by the battles and German occupation of the war, was

Leopold II of Belgium

actually in no position to resist this movement. In a completely unexpected change, Belgium announced in January 1960 that it would grant independence to the Congo as of June 30th of the same year. It is highly probable that the Belgians hoped that a quick grant of independence would result in chaos to a degree that would justify continued colonial control. This hope, motivated by the desire for further wealth, was almost realized.

THE SPANISH IN AFRICA

Spanish Sahara, Spanish Guinea, Ifni, Ceuta, Melilla

The colonization and division of Africa between the major powers in the 19th century was during a period when Spain, having formerly been a powerful colonial nation, was in a state of decline. The result was that Spain succeeded in claiming Spanish Sahara (also called Spanish Morocco, Rio de Oro), a barren desert area, and Spanish Guinea, a small section of oppressive jungle on the west coast at the Equator which included the island of Fernando Poo. The enclaves of Ifni, Ceuta and Melilla along the coast of Morocco were holdovers from the time when both Morocco and Spain were controlled by Moorish Arabs. The areas in which Spain was able to lay claim were available largely because of lack of interest in them on the part of other stronger colonial nations.

Although Spain was technically supposed to be in partnership with the French in Morocco during the colonial period, the actual control was by the French. Spain ceded its theoretical protectorate right to Morocco in 1956 when the French granted it independence; a small part of southern Morocco was relinquished in 1958. The enclave of Ifni was returned to Morocco in 1968; Ceuta and Melilla, coastal cities along the coast where Spain and Morocco are closest, remain under Spanish control with the tacit consent of the King of Morocco.

Wind–swept and arid, Spanish Sahara is inhabited by a handful of nomadic Berber–Bedouin tribesmen who had been left to themselves by the Spanish. There had been almost no interest in this area on the part of the rest of the world prior to 1966 when extensive and rich deposits of phosphate were located. After withstanding pressures from the UN, Morocco and Mauritania for a decade, Spain vacated the territory in 1976 (see Western Sahara).

Spanish Guinea, now the mainland portion of Equatorial Guinea, consisted of an undesirable, oppressively hot and humid area acquired at the Berlin Conference in 1885, which was joined administratively to form a single colony with Fernando Poo, an island ceded to Spain by Portugal in 1778. There was no significant nationalist movement reported during the postwar period and no effort was made to prepare the colony for independence.

In the mid 1960's, Spain began to bring increasing pressure on the British to cede the Gibralter peninsula on the ground that it, lying at the entrance to the Mediterranean Sea, belonged to Spain by virtue of natural geography. In order to reinforce its arguments, Spain granted Spanish Guinea independence in 1968, giving little prior indication of its intention to do so.

THE GERMANS IN AFRICA

West Africa: Togo, Cameroon

Although there was some German missionary and trading activity on the coasts of Togo and Cameroon from 1845 onward, these areas also were open to religious and commercial efforts of the remaining European nations. In the rush to acquire colonies during the 1880's, Gustav Nachtigal negotiated treaties with the Ewe chiefs of the region at Togoville, located on the banks of Lake Togo. The most powerful of these was King Mlapa III.

During the thirty years that followed the announcement of a German protectorate in Togo, there was slow penetration into the interior. The borders with the surrounding colonies were adjusted several times by treaty. The rule of the German administrators was harsh and exploitive; there was no effort to provide any benefit to the people of the region, since the only interest was commercial. Large numbers of Togolese were jailed and forced to labor for the Germans. There was little regret when the British and French arrived early in World War I.

The territory was jointly administered for five years, but was then split into two areas with the British in a smaller, western portion and the remainder controlled by the French. The British area became part of what is now Ghana, formerly known as Gold Coast.

The Portuguese navigator, Fernao Poo (Fernando Po in Spanish) had explored the coast of Cameroon in 1472; the prolific shrimp in the River Wouri inspired the sailors to christen the river *Rio dos Cameroes,* meaning "River of Shrimp" in Portuguese. There was a variety of commercial activity during the 19th century pre–colonial period, a time when no single European nation dominated Cameroon. The British decided in 1884 to annex Cameroon and sent an emissary to sign treaties with the local inhabitants. He arrived five days too late—spurred by the rush for colonies, a German Consul had already visited Douala, the seaport, and obtained the signatures of the chieftains on treaties annexing Cameroon to Germany; the area was named Kameroun, a Germanization of the original Portuguese name.

The colonial rule of the Germans was similar to that in Togo—exploitive and often cruel. There was some penetration into the interior but control was not established in the northern regions by the Germans. Throughout the colony it became difficult to locate the tribal chieftains, who went into hiding to avoid possible punishment or being held hostage by the colonial administrators. In exchange for support of French claims in Morocco, Germany was granted about 100,000 square miles of Congo (Brazzaville).

Cameroon was the scene of an extensive campaign early in World War I. British and French forces wrested control from Germany, and by the terms of the Treaty of Versailles, Cameroon was split between the two powers. The land previously acquired from Congo (Brazzaville) was rejoined with that territory.

South Africa: South–West Africa

The Germans first entered the region of South–West Africa in the 1840's in a strictly missionary effort, similar to British efforts in South Africa among the native Africans. This outpost, called the Bethany Mission, slowly expanded during the following decades, and numbers of Germans went into the interior from Walfish (Walvis, Walvisch) Bay. The German missionaries twice asked for the British to assume protection of the Bay area, and in 1877 this request was granted.

There was substantial German migration into South–West Africa during the last quarter of the 19th century. After quarreling with the British for several months, the Germans proclaimed a protectorate over the area in 1884; administration initially was by the German Colo-

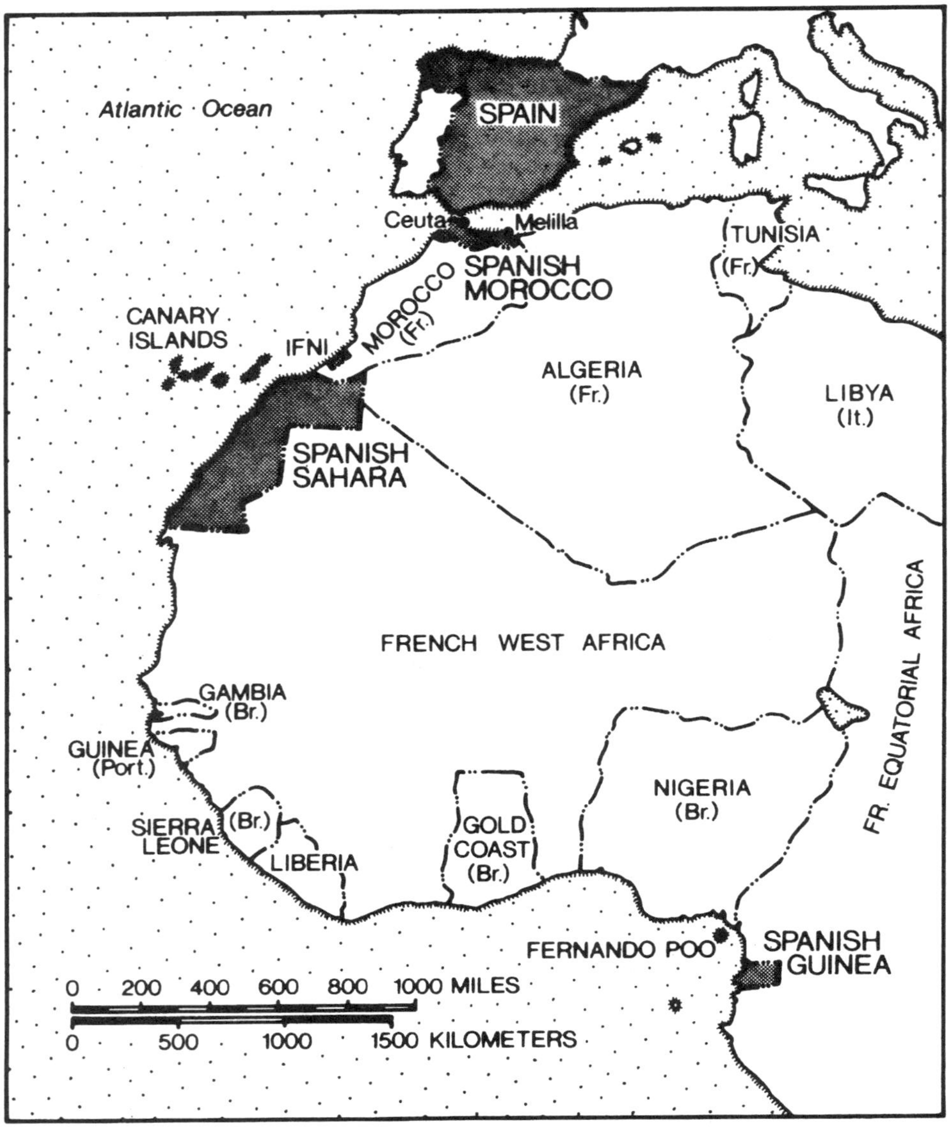

nial Company, but in 1892 South–West Africa came under the control of the German government.

The migrants to the area were principally farmers and herdsmen who occupied the scarce and choice lands suitable for cultivation and grazing. Discovery of mineral wealth led to further measures designed to exploit the wealth of the land for the benefit of the Germans. The Bantu Hereros, also known as Damaras, rose in bloody revolt from 1904 to 1908, requiring 20,000 German troops to finally defeat them. Several thousand of these people fled to neighboring Botswana (then Bechuanaland) during the revolt.

Within a year of the start of World War I, a combined British and South African *Boer* army was able to defeat the German force of about 3,500 stationed in South–West Africa. The territory was assigned to the British–*Boer* Union of South Africa as a mandate by the Allied Council and later by the League of Nations.

East Africa: Tanzania (German East Africa)

Initial exploration of the East African coast area occurred in 1860–1865 when Karl von der Decken entered the region, but it was not until 1884, when Karl Peters signed a series of treaties with native kings that the colonial effort actually started. The agreements provided for a sale of land to the Germans for a very small fraction of its probable value. The German status in the area was recognized at the Berlin Conference of 1885, and the German East Africa Company was created to administer the colony.

In the early colonial period, the Germans also acquired lands in adjacent Uganda and coastal Kenya by signing treaties in the former, and coercing the Arab viceroy in Zanzibar to surrender lands in the latter. These were given up by treaties to the British in exchange for a somewhat worthless island in the North Sea and other minor concessions; treaties were also entered into with King Leopold of Belgium and the Portuguese which fixed the border of German East Africa. Penetration into the interior was slow and difficult. The native Africans resisted the German movement; there was a violent uprising of the Muslim Arabs along the coast (1888–90), a revolt of the Wahehe (Wahaya) people (1891–93) and a combined Muslim–Angoni rebellion (1903–1905). The Angonis, a Bantu group related to the warlike Zulus of South Africa, were all but exterminated during this conflict, known as the Maji–Maji Rebellion, in which the Germans ruthlessly destroyed crops and villages, rendering a large area completely desolate.

In 1914, 300,000 British, South African *Boer* and Indian troops invaded German East Africa. A force of slightly more than 200 German officers, commanding native troops numbering between 2,500 and 4,000 fended off the massive attack for four years under the spirited and brilliant leadership of General Paul Von Lettow–Vorbeck.

With great effort, the allies slowly pushed Lettow–Vorbeck from German East Africa into Mozambique and Rhodesia. The Germans refused to stop fighting, and the battles ceased only when their commander was informed that the Armistice of November 11, 1918 had been signed, ending World War I, and providing for the evacuation of Germans from German East Africa.

The British received a mandate from the League of Nations to administer the former German colony, which was renamed Tanganyika. Substantial numbers of German immigrants who had established large, prosperous farms and plantations, were deported to Germany; a few were later permitted to return to the British colony.

Kaiser Wilhelm II of Germany

A small, northwestern part of German East Africa which had been occupied by Belgian troops at the start of the war was mandated to Belgium in 1923; initially called Ruanda–Urundi, following independence it became the two nations of Rwanda and Burundi.

THE SOUTH AFRICAN "MANDATE"

Namibia (German South–West Africa, South–West Africa)

The Union of South Africa received a mandate from the League of Nations in 1919 over what had been German South–West Africa. After The UN came into existence, it exerted pressures to grant the people of *Namibia* their independence. Finally, on March 21, 1990, that goal was achieved (see Namibia, p. 112).

THE ITALIANS IN AFRICA

The Eastern Horn; Somalia, Ethiopia

In comparison to other European nations, Italian colonial efforts were relatively weak and delayed because of the fact that Italy itself was not closely united as a nation. Following agreement among the stronger powers in 1885, the Italians signed treaties during the next four years with the three Muslim sultans in the "horn" region of East Africa. Although Italian Somaliland was acquired as a colony, full control was not established in the area until as late as 1927. The bleak, uniformly hot and dry region was considered to be valueless as a colony and the nomadic Cushites and Somalis who lived in the region, including part of Kenya and Ethiopia, were difficult to control.

British and French Somaliland, both areas somewhat more desirable, separated Somaliland from Eritrea, a semi–arid expanse given to the Italians by a lack of interest on the part of more powerful colonial nations. Benito Mussolini, the fascist dictator, came to power in Italy in 1922. He began to flex colonial muscles, eyeing with envy the vast territories taken without resistance by the rest of Europe in Africa and elsewhere.

From bases in Eritrea, Italian forces invaded ancient Ethiopia in 1936; Emperor Haile Selassie begged for assistance at the League of Nations, but his plea fell on deaf ears. The fate of Ethiopia had been decided earlier in Paris, when the British and French gave the Italians wide authority over Ethiopia in an effort to appease Mussolini. The figurehead King of Italy proclaimed himself Emperor of Ethiopia, a title recognized at once by Austria and Germany and in 1938 by Great Britain and France.

Ethiopia was joined with Somaliland and Eritrea to form Italian East Africa; initially there was some effort at economic development and road building. However, an attempt was made to assassinate the Italian governor at Addis Ababa in 1937. A reign of terror followed, with wide-

Benito Mussolini

spread arrests and summary executions in an attempt to terrorize the population. Further unrest became intense, and by 1940 the Italians were besieged from within by Ethiopian terrorists and from without by British forces. Exactly five years after the first entry of Italian troops, Haile Selassie entered Addis Ababa at the head of a British–Ethiopian force and Italian rule was ended.

During the postwar period, a plan whereby Eritrea was to become a part of Ethiopia was promulgated at the UN; following its acceptance, the two were joined. The UN granted a trusteeship over Somalia to Italy in 1949; this area had been occupied by the British since the early years of World War II. The trusteeship provided for complete independence within ten years, which was achieved in 1960.

North Africa: Libya

Although many Italian immigrants had settled in North Africa, particularly in Libya and Tunisia, there was no effort to colonize the area until the 20th century. The ambition had then been present for decades—when the British and French settled the Fashoda Crisis (see *The French in Africa*), the Italians protested since they did not share in the division of the Sahara region of the African continent. Using a short–term ultimatum to provoke a conflict, Italian forces invaded Libya in 1911 in an attempt to seize control from the Ottoman Turks. After taking a few coastal towns, a protectorate status was proclaimed by the Italians.

The Muslim *Sanusi* sect immediately organized a revolt that continued until about 1931 at various places within Libya. Because the Arab–Berber people were given only the poorest parts of the land in which to live, the people of Libya, through eventually subdued, continued to have a smoldering hatred for the Italians.

Italian rule was ended in the two years following 1940. Extensive campaigns were waged by the Allies throughout the land against the Nazis who had gained control of North Africa when it became apparent that Italy could not act with military authority in the area. The country, historically divided into three provinces of Cyrenaica, Tripolitania and Fezzan, was split between Allied powers at the end of World War II. Fezzan was occupied by the French, and the remaining two provinces were under British administration.

The question of Libya's status was submitted to the United Nations, which adopted a resolution providing for Libyan independence by the end of 1951.

Haile Selassie enters Addis Ababa in 1941

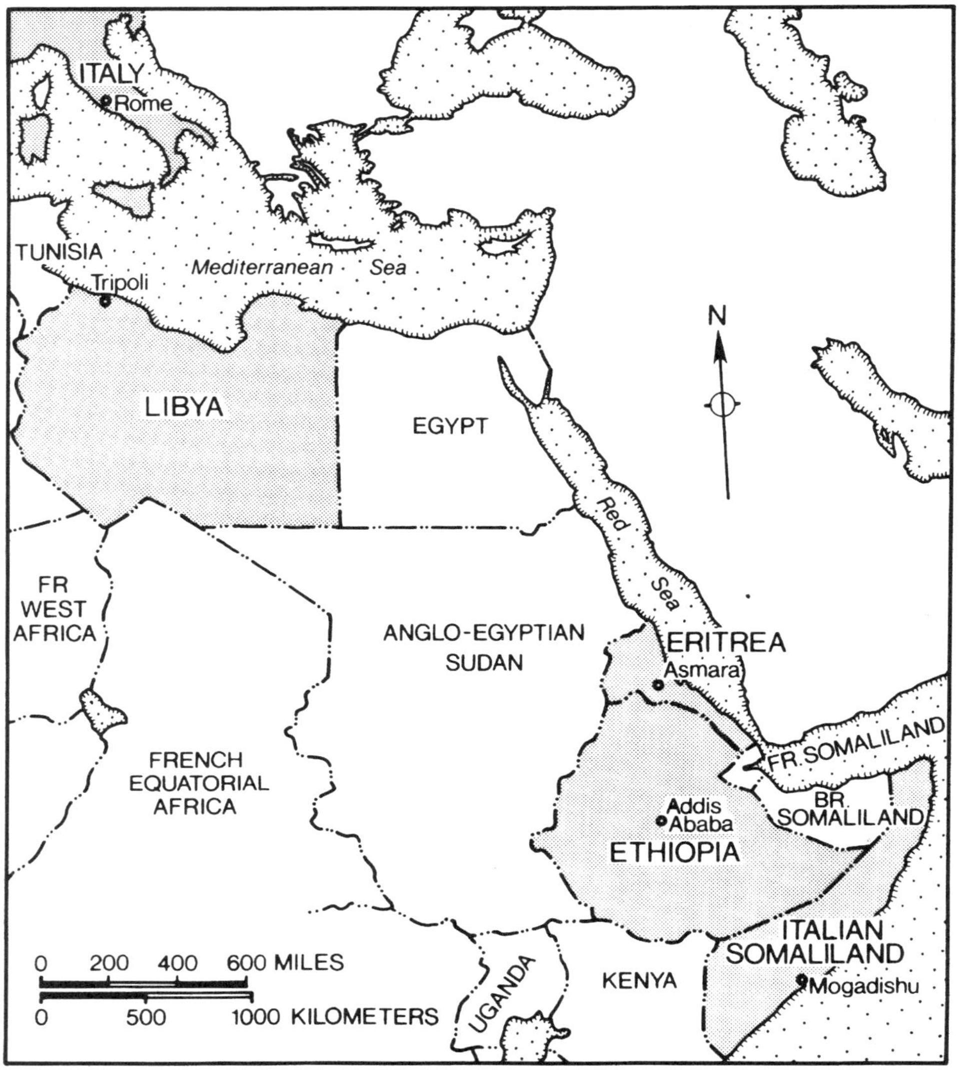

The Italians in Africa

Ethiopia's Emperor Haile Selassie aboard a U.S. warship with President Franklin D. Roosevelt, then on his way home from the 1945 conference in the Crimea.

COASTAL WEST AFRICA

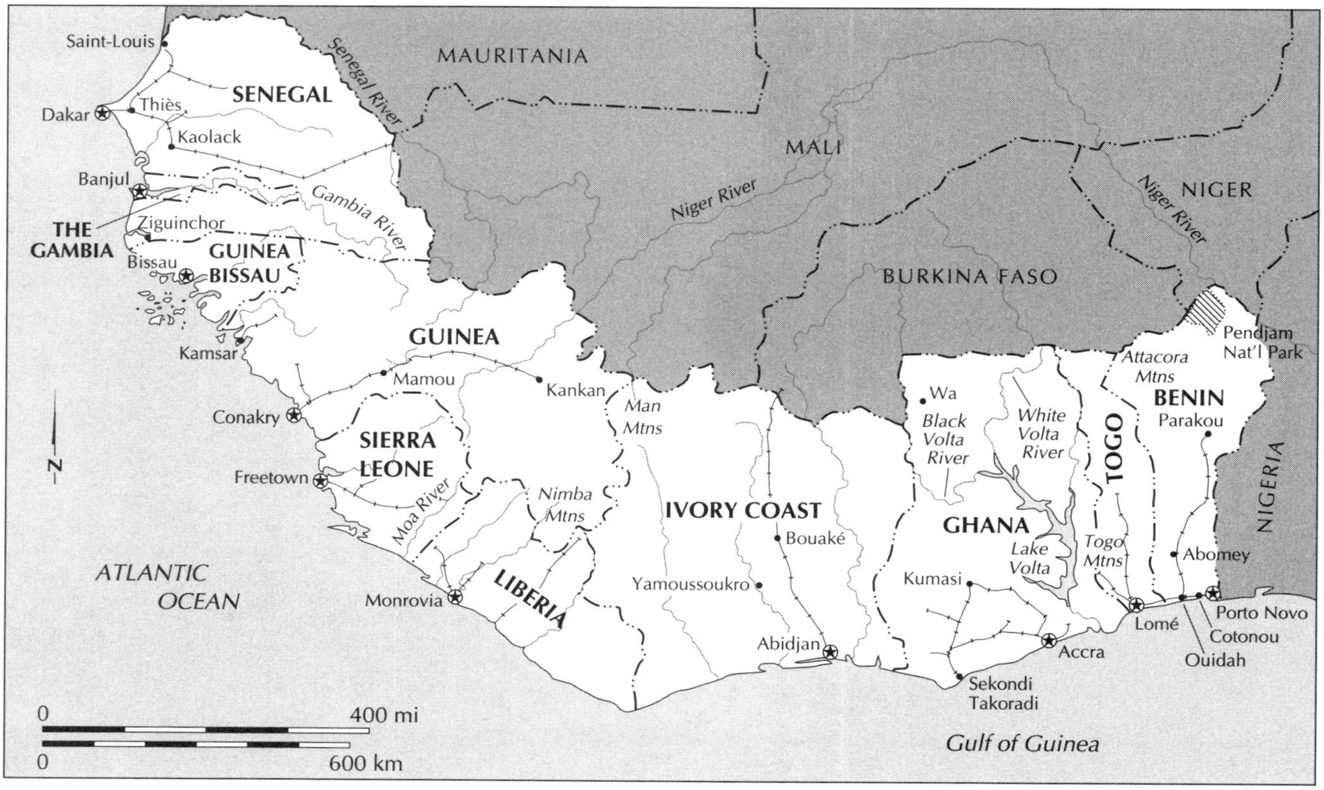

The Republic of Benin (pronounced ben–neen)

Area: 115,773 sq. km. = 44,483 sq. mi. (slightly larger than Tennessee).

Population: 6.3 million (estimated)

Capital City: Porto Novo (pop. 228,000 estimated. The main port is nearby Cotonou, with a population of 550,000. 1996 est.)

Climate: Hot and humid in the South tempered by sea breezes; tropical in the North, with wet seasons in the South (mid–March to mid–July and mid–September to mid–November. Northern Benin historically had a single wet season (June–October) but has been afflicted by drought for the last decade.

Neighboring Countries: Togo (West); Burkina Faso (Northwest); Niger (North); Nigeria (North, East).

Official Language: French.

Other Principal Languages: Fon, Adja, Yoruba, Bariba.

Ethnic groups: There are 42 distinct ethnic groups in Benin. The Fons, Adjas, Yorubas and Baribas are the largest, constituting more than half the population.

Principal Religions: Indigenous beliefs 70%, Muslim 15%, Christian 15%.

Chief Commercial Products: Cotton, crude oil, palm products, cocoa.

GNP per capita: 380 US$

Currency CFA Franc (African Financial Community).

Former Colonial Status: French Protectorate (1892–1960).

Independence Date: August 1, 1960.

Chief of State: Mathieu Kerekou, President (b. 1932, pronounced *Mah*–tyoo *Kair*–uh–koo).

National Flag: A green vertical stripe at the staff with two horizontal stripes of yellow and red filling the remaining area.

Benin lies in a small belt of land stretching from the warm waters of the Atlantic Ocean to a distance of 450 miles inland. The coastline is 78 miles wide, but in the North the width increases to over 200 miles.

The coastal area, with palm trees waving gently in the breezes from the ocean, is a region of picturesque lagoons and inlets. A narrow sandbar lies close to the entire coastline; the lagoons open to the sea in only two places.

A series of clay plateaus extend further inland for a distance of about 50 miles, terminating at the rocky foothills of the stretch of mountains which divides the North from the South. There usually has been abundant rainfall in this region, as well as along the coast, supporting dense vegetation in the areas not under cultivation.

Immediately south of the Attacora Mountains, which rise to a height of 2,300 feet, there is a swampy depression. From these mountains to the north, the land gently descends in a patchy forest with very little undergrowth, to the plains of the Niger River valley. Temperatures north of the mountains have a wider variation than is found in the rest of the country. The dry season from November to May has in recent years been transformed to a year–long drought, creating severe conditions for the people located in the area.

The Pendjam National Park, next to the borders of Burkina Faso and Niger, is a reserve to protect the country's dwindling numbers of wild game. It extends across the boundary into the two neighboring countries. Although hunting is not permitted within its limits, hunters pursue animals in the surrounding areas.

History: The record of shifting tides of migrant people in Benin extends back to the late 16th century. A group of people traveled west from the Mono River and settled near what is now the city of Allada, establishing a kingdom. After a war of succession to the throne in 1610, a young contender named Dacko went to Cana, near the present city of Abomey, and founded the Kingdom of Abomey, becoming its first ruler. This monarchy expanded gradually; Dacko's son conquered the lands belonging to a neighboring king named Dan. Angry with the aggressive invader, Dan is reported to have said "If I don't surrender, you will go so far as to kill me and build over my corpse." Dan was beheaded, buried and a building was erected over his body. The former name of the country, Dahomey, comes from the two words *Dan Home* which literally means "on the belly of Dan." The Abomey Kingdom quickly became paramount over all other tribal rulers in the southern region. Their superior position continued for 350 years until the French abolished the monarchy.

Ghezo, the ruler of Abomey from 1818 to 1858 signed a treaty of friendship and commerce with the French in 1851. His son, Glele, ceded the commercial city of Cotonou to the French 17 years later. For details of the colonial period, see *The French in Africa*.

Shortly before independence in 1960, three major political parties united and brought pressure against a fourth to disband. The combined organization, the *Dahomey Unity Party,* captured all 60 seats in the unicameral National Assembly. There followed a period of behind–the–scene activity by the three prominent leaders, Hubert Maga, Souran Migan Apithy and Justin F. Ahomadegbe.

A rapid succession of governments followed:

1963: Military *coup* led by Col. Christophe Soglo ousted the government; President Maga went into exile in Paris.

1964: Elections were held, Apithy became President, Ahomadegbe became Vice–President.

1965: The leadership resigned under pressure; Soglo again assumed power and sent both in exile to Paris.

1967: A *coup* by young army officers ousted Soglo and sent *him* to Parisian exile. The top military command, after four days of house arrest, picked Chief of Staff Alphonse Alley as head of state.

A new constitution forbade any ex–president, ex–vice president or other ex–ruler to run for office. The Supreme Court held this action to be illegal, but it was adopted. The Parisian exiles urged a boycott of the elections and the military responded by throwing out the results and naming Dr. Emile Zinsou president. He lasted until the end of 1969.

A military *junta* wielded power as a result of political violence, ruling through a Presidential Council of military members. The last military *coup* occurred on October 26, 1972. The then Major Mathieu Kerekou announced "that authority of the State has disappeared everywhere." Many politicians were arrested and some were put to death. In an effort to widen his support, Kerekou established the *National Council of the Revolution* in late 1973; a year later he announced the transformation of Benin into a Marxist, one–party state.

Foreign interests were nationalized. Although ties were established with the U.S.S.R., China, Cuba and North Korea, little assistance was forthcoming from those nations, except endless quantities of advice. These moves alienated western goodwill and resulted in lowered financial assistance.

In 1975 General Kerekou declared the country's name would be changed from Dahomey ("imposed upon us by colonialists") to the People's Republic of Benin (in 1989, to simply Benin). *The Benin People's Revolutionary Party* was the only legal political group, and the 196-member Revolutionary Assembly was its rubber stamp. First elected to a three-year term as president in early 1980, Kerekou was reelected to an extended five-year term in mid-1984 and again in 1989. After 1984, the country veered sharply toward a Marxist style government.

Kerekou's Marxist regime was of course a disaster economically, and with the collapse of communist regimes in Eastern Europe, the people of Benin were increasingly encouraged to speak out against a regime that was economically inept and politically oppressive. Popular protests over Kerekou's disastrous economic policies and repression that included a ban on traditional animist religion led to a National Conference to discuss Benin's problems. In December 1990, a new constitution, adopted by referendum, officially ended seventeen years of militaro–Marxist rule.

A transitional parliament organized multiparty, democratic elections in 1991. Kerekou stood for election, but was defeated by Nicéphore Soglo, a French educated economist with respected experience at the World Bank in Washington. In democratic Benin multiparty exuberance flourished, but the consequence was that

Water dwellers, Ganvie, Benin. The more elaborate house at left is that of the Chief of the Fons.
AP/Wide World Photo

President Mathieu Kerekou

legislative majorities were difficult to obtain. Governance in such a situation is always a fragile affair, as President Soglo found out.

Soglo was not able to lessen Benin's economic woes. Kerekou kept a low profile after leaving office, but Soglo was flamboyant, usually dressed in expensive and colorful clothing. He traveled widely abroad, and installed too many members of his family in the government. The people, forgetting the miseries of the former military dictatorship, returned Kerekou to office in elections held in March 1996. He was greatly helped by two main opposition groups and received 52.5% of the vote to Soglo's 47.51.

President Kerekou has thus far continued the economic and political reforms begun under Soglo. Since these involved privatization or closure of inefficient state enterprises and a streamlining of Benin's civil service, there has been a white-collar resistance to reform. Strikes by public employees are continuing events in Benin and contribute to a climate of unrest. Unions protested the 2000 budget because it failed to appropriate funds for civil service raises contracted in 1994. The government has offered to pay the 1994 raise only if the unions agree to a merit pay scheme, a project vigorously contested by the unions.

Legislative elections in spring 1999 produced another slender majority in parliament—understandable when you realize that there have been at one time or another over 100 political parties in the country. In these elections 2,905 candidates from 35 parties or alliances of parties established electoral lists for Benin's election by proportional representation. When all the ballots had been counted by Benin's autonomous electoral commission, former President Soglo's *Benin Renaissance Party* headed the list of about 10 opposition groups with 27 seats. In total the opposition won 43 out of 82 seats in the National Assembly.

Voter participation was high and there were few complaints about the honesty of an election where voters deposited their ballots in transparent boxes supplied by Denmark. In its third multiparty legislative elections, Benin once again demonstrated a political maturity that makes it a model for African democracy. President Kerekou has had to adjust to working with an opposition parliament and both the executive and legislature must work within the constraints of limited revenues and ongoing unrest produced by Benin's movement to a more liberal economy.

Benin's reputation as a "laboratory of democracy" was severely tested by presidential elections in early 2001. After two relatively successful changes of power in 1991 and 1996, the elections of 2001 proved controversial. In the primary, President Kérékou faced three challengers, including ex-President Soglo. Kérékou received 47% of the vote while Soglo received about 29%. The third-place finisher, Adrieu Houngbédji, President of the National Assembly, garnered 13% while Bruno Amoussou came in a distant fourth with a mere 4% of the ballots.

Without a clear majority, a run-off election was needed, but former President Soglo refused to run, citing a variety of irregularities that added up to massive fraud. The election was, he said, a "masquerade." The electoral commission went to the third-place finisher, Houngbedji, and was similarly rejected.

There being no alternative, Bruno Amoussou's name was placed on the ballot. A member of the Kérékou cabinet who had already asked his supporters to vote for the president in the run-offs, Amoussou did no campaigning and conceded the election before the ballots had been counted. Benin's electoral battle had been won for lack of combatants. President Kérékou was reelected with 84% of the vote, cast by only 53% of eligible voters.

Culture: While Porto Novo is the official capital of the nation, most government offices and embassies are found twenty miles to the west at the port city of Cotonou (*Coo*–toe–new). This is Benin's chief commercial center and has magnificent beaches. It has in the past been a weekend resort for many foreigners, with excellent seafood.

Unfortunately, Cotonou has become afflicted with some of the worst air pollution in West Africa, largely the product of gasoline engine exhaust. It's visibility is zero frequently, and the main culprit seems to be elderly used cars, but motor bikes also produce noxious exhaust. Drivers tend to believe that a vehicle uses less fuel when it's filled with oil, so there's a lot of burning oil to add to the pollution. There's no sign of things getting better: some 31,000 vehicles were added to the streets between 1989 and 1994.

Adding to Cotonou's urban din and pollution are thousands of taxi motor bikes operated by young Beninois with no other job possibilities. Wearing bright yellow shirts, "zemidjans" [literally "take me quickly" in the local language] ferry passengers from place to place during the day. The more entrepreneurial owners rent their bikes for a more macabre evening service: transporting the bodies of the dead. For those families unable to afford standard mortuary charges, the motor bike hearse is an affordable alternative. The cadaver is placed on the bike, lashed to the driver and held by a family member as it is whisked to the family home for appropriate ceremonies.

The palace site of the Kings of Dahomey at Abomey has been on UNESCO's World Heritage list since 1985. The entire palatial site is vast, extending over approximately 108 acres. Each successive Dahomean king added to the site, making it visual symbol of his obligation "to make Dahomey ever greater."

The palaces of King Guézo and his son King Glèlè, with important relief sculptures which document the history and culture of the Dahomean kingdom, have undergone extensive restoration and conservation since 1992. They now house the Abomey Historical Museum, which contains three hundred years of royal history. Thrones, scepters, appliqué umbrellas and hammocks, state swords, royal vestments and commemorative altars called *asin* all form part of the museum's treasures.

Arguably the greatest expression of the kingdom's identity and ideology are the royal bas-reliefs of Abomey, lovingly restored with the aid of the Getty Conservation Institute and others. A book and video of the same name, *History Told on Walls: Bas-Reliefs of Abomey,* tell the story of these preservation efforts.

Economy: Benin's economy is dependent on cotton exports. Ninety per cent of export income comes from cotton, but world commodity prices have fallen significantly in recent years. Benin's largest state-owned company, the National Company for Agricultural Production (SONAPRA), responsible for marketing the country's cotton, was expected to earn around $12 million in 1998, but only earned $5 million. Cotton production declined 25% in 1998, dropping to 300,000 tons from an earlier high of 400,000 tons.

Many of the cotton industry's problems were attributable to the decision to privatize some parts of SONAPRA and allow cotton prices to be determined by the market. After privatization private businessmen, who were less than scrupulous in what they sold, supplied 80% of insecticides. Farmers complained that where they put fertilizer, grass grew and cotton plants died; insects seemed to thrive on the new insecticides. Put them in a bottle of insecticide, said one farmer, and they flap their wings and fly away. Caterpillars and insects invaded cotton fields and severely damaged the crop.

SONAPRA itself had financial problems. Badly mismanaged, it often failed to secure payments it was owed and found itself without funds to pay farmers or truck drivers who transported the cotton to market. Once the decision was made to let the market determine cotton prices, banks were averse to lending SONAPRA funds, so uncertain were they about the ability of the agency to repay its obligations. Benin farmers were equally skeptical. In June 1999 they refused to grow more cotton until the last season's payments, which totaled more than $10 million, had been settled by SONAPRA.

Given the importance of the cotton industry, it comes as no surprise that politics enters almost always to the disadvantage of the farmer. One recent Minister of Rural Development encouraged the establishment of five new cotton-processing factories. Benin now has the capacity to process more than 650,000 metric tons of raw cotton, while producing only 350,000 tons. In 1996 and 1997, SONAPRA increased the price of cotton paid to producers. Both increases were seen as "political prices" to thank producers after President Kerekou's election in March 1996. Such prices were unsustainable and unrealistic given worldwide price declines. (Mali set its price at 150 CFA francs and Burkina Faso at 160 CFA francs.)

Benin's port of Cotonou serves as a regional transit hub important for supplying landlocked Niger and Burkina Faso. Cargo handling at the port has been liberalized, and the Benin Port Authority (SOBEMAP) now competes with the Danish company Maersk. Given this newly competitive environment, the Autonomous Port of Cotonou (PAC) has registered an increase in both traffic and capacity, enabling it to earn revenue of almost 2 billion CFA francs in 1997.

Corruption appears to be a national sport in Benin, and it is estimated that the state loses 25 percent of its receipts annually through fraud and corruption. World Bank officials estimate that only about 30 percent of international credits put at the government's disposal are actually utilized due to corruption and poor administrative practices. For the man on the Benin street everything can be bought, from driver's licenses to diplomas. To get one what wants in Benin, one only needs to know how "to place a pebble on the dossier"—the local euphemism for corruption.

In 1996 when General Mathieu Kerekou returned to power, he set up an ambitiously titled "public morality unit," vowing to stamp out corruption in the public sector. In July 1999 a presidential commission reported that more than $105 million had been misappropriated within Benin's civil service over the last three years. The biggest financial discrepancies were found in the books of two major state-owned companies: SONAPRA and the National Petroleum Product Marketing Society (SONACOP).

Despite the fanfare, Beninois have remained skeptical about bringing the suspects to trial. None of Kerekou's earlier anti-corruption commissions have yielded any results. Trials for crimes related to fraud remain rare. Few investigations, in fact, are ever completed. In the past 10 years, at least 100 such cases annually came before the council of ministers, but barely 10 per year ever resulted in convictions. Under any circumstances, judicial pursuit could only be the slowest given a lack of personnel and funding for Benin's judicial system. The Cotonou public prosecutor's office had only three judges in 1960; 40 years later, in 2000, there are still only three.

Future: Controversies over the 2001 presidential elections will contribute to rising tensions in Benin. These abound, especially those created by the government's attempts to liberalize the economy. There is already a palpable sense of disillusionment with a democracy in which economic benefits remain the privilege of a group of influential businessmen who have lent their support to President Kérékou.

Palace at Ahomey
Photo of Francesca Piqué, courtesy Qetly Conservation Institute

The Republic of Côte d'Ivoire

The government established the French form of *Ivory Coast* as the country's official designation, pronounced *Coat deev–whar.*

St. Paul Cathedral, Abidjan AP Wide World Photo

Area: 323,750 sq. km. = 125,000 sq. mi. (somewhat larger than New Mexico).
Population: 15.8 million (estimated)
Capital City: Yamoussoukro, the birthplace of former President Félix Houphouët-Boigny, is the political and administrative capital with a population of 120,000. Most government departments remain in the former capital of Abidjan (pop. 3.5 million), which is the major center for economic activities.
Climate: Tropically hot and humid in the South, with two wet seasons (March–July and October–November). Warm and less humid in the North with a single wet season (May–October).
Neighboring Countries: Liberia, Guinea (West); Mali, Burkina Faso (Upper Volta–North); Ghana (East).
Official Language: French.
Other Principal Languages: Anyin, Attié, Bale, Bété, Dan, Guéré, Guro, Jul, and Senoufo.
Ethnic Groups: More than sixty ethnic groups. Prominently, Baoulé (15 percent), Sénoufo (10 percent), Bété (6 percent), Lagoon peoples (5 percent), Agni (Anyi—3 percent), and a Mandé cluster of groups, including Juula, Bambara, and Malinké (17 percent). Non-Ivoirian Africans, Lebanese, Asians, and Europeans composed nearly 27 percent of population.
Principal Religions: Muslim 60%, Christian 22%, and indigenous 18% (some of these are also numbered among the Christians and Muslims).
Chief Commercial Products: Cocoa 36%, coffee, tropical woods, petroleum, cotton, bananas, pineapples, palm oil, cotton, and fish.
GNP per capita: 700 US$
Currency: CFA Franc (African Financial Community).
Former Colonial Status: French Colony (1839–1960).
Independence Date: August 7, 1960.
Chief of State: Laurant Gbagbo, after disputed elections, October 2000.
National Flag: Three vertical stripes of orange, white and green.

The Republic of Côte d'Ivoire occupies an area in the center of the south coast of the west African bulge. The coast, warmed by the waters of the Gulf of Guinea, is 340 miles long; from the border of Ghana for a distance of 185 miles to the west, it is flat and sandy, with many inland lagoons. The remainder of the coast towards Liberia has numerous sharp rocks and is higher. The surf along the entire shore line is quite heavy, steadily pounding the sand and boulders. Dense forests and jungles spread their green foliage further inland, covering almost 40% of the country. Tall niagou, samba and mahogany trees struggle against each other for precious sunlight, crowding smaller trees and undergrowth.

Approximately midway to the north, the trees gradually become thinner and are succeeded by low scrub trees, grasses and brush vegetation. This in turn gives way in the extreme northern area to a semi–arid (recently *arid)* climate, which has in the past supported grasslands, occasionally interrupted by taller growth. With the African drought of the past decade, this northern region has become increasingly desolate.

The country is almost entirely level—only the Man Mountains in the area closest to Mali and Guinea relieve the monotony of the plains.

The southern and central portions of the country have traditionally received ample rainfall and have a high humidity. Temperatures are warm in the North, with less (or hardly any) rainfall.

History: Artifacts discovered in Côte d'Ivoire suggest that a Neolithic civilization flourished there in prehistoric ages. Not much is known of the history of this country prior to the 14th century.

At the time of the arrival of the first Europeans, there were three strong kingdoms, the Krinjabo and Bettie in the North and the Boundoukou in the East. There were, besides the three major kingdoms, more than 50 other small tribal groups which had little contact with each other.

The severity of the surf and the forbidding appearance of the land discouraged early European exploration. For greater detail on early history and the colonial period, see Historical Background and *The French in Africa.* When full independence was gained by Côte d'Ivoire on August 7, 1960, Félix Houphouet–Boigny *(Fay–*lix *Who*–fway *Bwa*–nyee) became its first president. He was well–prepared for the tasks which faced him.

One of the Baoulé people, with ancestors including a line of chiefs, he attended the prestigious École William Ponty in Dakar, Senegal. The school brought together the very best students from each of the French West African colonies for advanced education that would prepare them for positions in the colonial civil service or French commercial enterprises. Houphouët-Boigny was trained as a *médecin africain.* Perhaps even more important for future political developments, Ponty created an educated elite which would ultimately bring the various colonies of the French West Africa to independence. The friendships they made at Ponty were crucial for that development.

Houphouët-Boigny traveled the colony extensively as a rural doctor and in 1940 inherited large-coffee producing tracts of land from his father, a wealthy planter and chief. Using modern techniques, he was able to expand their output, becoming a wealthy man in a relatively short time. By the 1940s he was acknowledged as leader of disgruntled African planters and founded the African Agricultural Union in 1945. The group fought colonial policies that favored French planters and worked to end forced labor of Africans on white-owned plantations.

He formed the *Parti démocratique de la Côte d'Ivoire* (*PDCI*) in 1945, mobilized African planters, and was elected a deputy to the French National Assembly in 1945 and again in 1946. In the Assembly, Houphouët initially affiliated with the French Communist Party. After long and persistent harassment by colonial officials, he broke with the Communists in 1950 and began to cooperate with the French. In West Africa his *PDCI* was part of the *Rassemblement démocratique africain*, a Federation-wide party.

In 1958, when General de Gaulle offered the possibility of immediate independence to France's colonies, Houphouët instead campaigned vigorously for self-government within the Franco-African Community. He was an equally vigorous opponent of any large federation of independent states, refusing to see Côte d'Ivoire's wealth used to subsidize French West Africa's poorer states.

Félix Houphouët-Boigny became prime minister of the Côte d'Ivoire in 1959 and in 1960 was elected the first president of the independent state. He was the architect of Côte d'Ivoire's rise from colonial backwater to relatively wealthy republic.

His political base remained with the African planting class, and economic development reflected their interests. Commercial export of coffee and cocoa was encouraged and facilitated by development of roads. The port of San Pedro in the southwest was built to facilitate exports of the two crops. To work the plantations, migrant workers from Côte d'Ivoire's over-populated and underdeveloped north were encouraged to travel south. Similarly, migrant labor from Mali, and what is now Burkina Faso, was encouraged to travel to the plantations. Land ownership and even citizenship were made possible for the newcomers.

For thirty years the *PDCI* remained the country's sole political party, and Houphouët-Boigny governed by crafting an alliance between Akan-speaking southerners and largely Muslim northerners. When young northerners complained of unemployment and uneven regional development in the 1970s, a flurry of projects were started in the north, but by the early 1990s northern resentments and frustrations could no longer be so easily bought off.

As elsewhere in Africa, waves of sentiment for multiparty democracy were felt in Côte d'Ivoire in the late 1980s. In response to popular demand, and a bit of pressure from the World Bank, free formation of political parties was permitted for the first time during the 1990 elections. One of the most critical voices was that of Laurent Gbagbo, a member of the minority Bété community and former history professor who founded the *Front Populaire Ivoirien* (*FPI*) in 1990 and ran for president against Houphouët. Gbagbo's *FPI* gave expression to the frustrations felt by those who had long suffered under a government dominated by Akans.

President Laurent Gbagbo

Côte d'Ivoire's founding father died in December 1993 and was succeeded by his protege—another Akan-speaker—Henri Konan Bédié. Less confident and politically skilled than Houphouët, Bédié seemed not to understand the basic pragmatism by which Houphouët had ruled, winning over opponents through co-optation and cooperation, consensus and compromise.

Northern resentments could no longer be contained. Northerners felt they were not receiving a fair return for political support given over the years. They received fewer political appointments, and economic development of the region was stinted. They were too frequently hassled when trying to obtain national identity cards and complained of being treated not like citizens, but as foreigners. Their answer was to split from the *PDCI*.

The *Democratic Rally of Republicans* (*RDR*), based mainly in the north, was founded in September 1994 only a few months after Houphouët-Boigny's death. Its leader was Houphouët's prime minister and rival with Konan Bédié as his successor, Alassane Ouattara.

Faced with an increasingly desperate economic situation and deprived of the *PDCI*'s traditional northern support, Konan Bédié resorted to the baser instincts of his countrymen. "Foreigners" were stigmatized; a populist Ivorian nationalism was generated. It was not the first time the regime had diverted attention from its problems by arguing the colony's wealth was exploited by foreigners. Dahomeans had been the object of attack in 1958, but now it was the turn of Burkinabé and Malian migrant laborers. It was easy, by extension, to include Bédié's lapsed allies—northern Muslims.

First articulated by Bédié in an August 1995 speech to the *PDCI* faithful, the concept of Ivorian identity—Ivoirité in French—became central to political discourse in the country and was used to justify what developed into violent xenophobia.

A program of *Ivoirization* was instituted in 1996, a direct reversal of the open borders policy of the country when plantation labor was needed. Now, to officially be a citizen, one had to prove his or her parents and grandparents were born in Côte d'Ivoire. Strict nationality rules for presidential candidates were introduced into the Ivorian electoral code.

Alassane Dramane Ouattara, once a prime minister under Houphouët-Boigny, was effectively prevented from running in 1995 because of them. He later accepted appointment as IMF deputy director. When, in April 1998, he announced that he would not seek reappointment and would be available to serve his country, the controversy re-emerged with a vengeance. One *PDCI* leader accused him of being a foreigner. "We must close ranks," he told a party audience, "and not let ourselves be distracted by provocations of messiahs coming from other lands." The party newspaper, *Le Democrate*, charged Ouattara was from Burkina Faso and reprinted documents which, it said, substantiated its claim. The state-owned *Fraternité-Matin* editorialized ominously: "A man whose Burkinabé nationality is irrefutably established wants to lead our country. And we continue to believe nothing can happen to us."

The virulence of attacks on Ouattara suggested the nervousness and even paranoia of the political class. He is both a northerner and Muslim, the "other" for the Akan-speaking Christian core of *PDCI* support. Like his predecessor Houphouët-Boigny, President Bédié is a Christian politician in a country increasingly turning to Islam.

Raw statistics describe a situation ripe for xenophobic reaction: Côte d'Ivoire has an estimated three million people officially described as "residents of foreign nationality." Another two million are residents of foreign origin—migrant workers and their descendents, largely Muslim. In short, some 30% of the population could be demagogically defined as "foreign."

Bédié's campaign to promote Ivorian nationalism produced increasing hostility directed at foreigners and ethnic minorities. Smoldering resentment against "foreigners," particularly in the South, erupted in ethnic pogroms in several communities. Burkinabé farmers were attacked in Tabou, a rich cocoa-growing area on the Gulf of Guinea. Two people were killed and nearly 20,000 fled to Burkina Faso. Malian fishermen, like the Burkinabé farmers, long-settled in the region, were similarly set upon in coastal Ayamé. Their homes destroyed, they escaped to Abidjan, from whence they were convoyed 600 miles north to Mali. Most had never seen the country before.

Anti-ethnic riots and continuing political demonstrations took place against a background of deteriorating economic conditions. Particularly affected was the cocoa industry. The European Union agreed to allow chocolate manufacturers to use less cocoa butter in their confections, and the International Cocoa Organization, which represents the world's largest growers, said the proposal would lead to a $1.5 billion loss of export revenue. The Ivory Coast's exports minister warned that widespread use of substitute fats could reduce Western European cocoa demand by between 130,000 and 200,000 tons and reduce prices by 20%.

The government was already having trouble paying its bills and even the salaries of its workers. A corruption scandal in one ministry, merely the tip of the corruption iceberg, resulted in a cutoff of funds from the IMF and other lenders.

Economic problems fueled political tension throughout 1999 as the country approached its presidential election. The government responded to its critics with a repression that indicated an intolerance of dissent. Opposition leaders were imprisoned and street demonstrations prohibited. The campaign against Ouattara became more and more personal. When one judge ruled that Ouattara qualified as a presidential candidate, the justice ministry forced that judge to resign and replaced him with a jurist who ruled that Ouattara's identity papers were forged. In early December the government issued a warrant for Ouattara's arrest.

The country's cumulative crises were resolved on Christmas Eve, when General Robert Gueï, a former army chief of staff, assumed leadership of disgruntled soldiers demanding back wages and overthrew the Bédié government. France, with significant commercial interests at stake, 20,000 citizens actually resident in the country, and 550 soldiers stationed there, did not act to restore the *ancien régime*. The country at large seemed to greet the coup with an enormous sense of relief.

Military intervention did not, however, cool the political temperature. Quite the contrary. Since the Christmas Eve coup Côte d'Ivoire has been plagued by violence and instability. General Gueï moved with military dispatch, despite two military mutinies and attempted assassinations. A new constitution was written, submitted to voters and massively approved in July 2000, but it carried into the Second Republic the fertile seeds of division cultivated in the first: Presidential candidates were required to have two Ivorian parents. Bédié's *"Ivoirité,"* aimed specifically at his most feared opponent and ultimately anti-Northern, anti-Muslim and divisive, was given formal constitutional recognition.

Presidential elections were organized for October and nineteen people submitted the requisite candidacy papers. Fourteen were declared ineligible by a Supreme Court appointed by General Gueï and headed by his former legal adviser. Muslims, including most prominently Alassane Ouattara, were pointedly excluded. At best, the remaining five candidates, Robert Gueï among them, represented no more than 15% of Côte d'Ivoire's diverse population.

The campaign came down to a battle between General Gueï and Laurent Gbagbo, the former history professor who, as the leader of the *Front Populaire Ivoirien (FPI)*, had opposed the governing *PDCI* since 1990. Security forces engaged in bloody assaults against northerners, judged by dress and religion to be opponents of General Gueï. The worst such incident occured at the Abidjan suburb of Yopougon. There gendarmes slaughtered 57 individuals and dumped them in a mass grave.

When the electoral commission proclaimed Gueï the winner in October elections, people took to the streets in massive demonstrations. The general fled and Laurant Gbagbo proclaimed himself winner and president.

Once installed as president, Laurant Gbagbo refused all suggestions that the election be rerun despite its dubious legitimacy. In December 2000 legislative elections were organized and now a Gbagbo court, echoing Konan Bédié's, excluded Alassane Ouattara from even running for the National Assembly. Demonstrations followed and many thought the country was on the verge of civil war. The *RDR* boycotted the election with such success that in some nothern areas absolutely no one turned up at the polling stations. Only 33% of registered voters summoned courage or interest enough to vote.

The *FPI* obtained 96 seats in the 225-seat Assembly—not enough to govern alone—with the former governing *Ivory Coast Democratic Party* (*PDCI*) garnering 94 seats. With 22 independents subject to government cooptation, the *FPI* has more than a fair chance of getting its legislative way.

Muncipal elections in March 2001 were dominated by Ouattara's *RDR*, now participating on a nation-wide basis, and the party of Houphouët-Boigny and Konan Bédié, the *PDCI*. Laurant Gbagbo's *FPI*, with a comfortable position in the National Assembly, put little effort into the muncipal elections. With these elections the RDP proved to all who might doubt that it was indeed a national party and could be successful in a fair election.

The Gbagbo government speaks of national reconciliation, but its credibility and legitimacy remain shakey. In March 2001 the Ivorian Movement for the Defense of Human Rights (MIDH) released a report illustrated with grisly photographic evidence of victims tortured to death and accused the government of fomenting the violence. MIDH accused President Gbagbo and two senior ministers of inciting sweeping violence, including torture and deaths, in December. The group's spokesman noted that this "barbarism was not accidental but a response to the need to institutionalize terror before annihilating any form of opposition."

Culture: Abidjan, the former capital city, is located on lagoons inland from the coast. The city now has a population of 3.5 million—the equivalent of the population of the entire country at independence in 1960. This is the consequence of a 3.8% birth rate, one of the highest in the world.

Hot and humid, Abidjan brings to mind Paris with its friendly sidewalk cafes. It boasts architecture as modern as any city in the world and its skyline is as impressive as New York City's. Less impressive is the quality of its air, often dense with the smoke of cooking fires.

The Ivoirian population uses charcoal for heating and cooking and this has led to a massive destruction of the country's forests. In 1990 FAO estimated that 9 million cubic meters of wood was burnt to produce 1.24 million cubic meters of charcoal. The government has announced a plan to re-plant trees on a minimum of 42,275 hectares of forests between 1998 and 2000. The use of natural gas, particularly in urban areas, will be pushed.

Music in Côte d'Ivoire's has been an important medium of social expression, and during the repressive year's of Bédié's rule, a covert means of articulating social discontent. Broadcast on the radio, the most accessible means of communication in the country, it became a means of forming and mobilizing public opinion. The Christmas Coup even had a reggae beat.

General Robert Guei

Shortly after they seized the state radio headquarters, and when there was considerable concern that France might intervene to restore Bédié, rebellious soldiers turned to the music of one of the country's foremost reggae singers, Alpha Blondy. Put on the air and repeatedly replayed was his "French Army, get out of here!"

Alpha Blondy is part of a whole generation of musicians who matured under Bédié's authoritarianism and musically expressed their disgust with the regime's corruption and policies of ethnic exclusion. Although Bédié and his government were almost never named in the songs, every listener understood when Tiken Jah Fakoly's lyrics called upon listeners to fight "the powers that divide." Alpha Blondy's 1999 song *Dictature* accused Bédié of "ruling by dividing, dividing by trickery."

During Bédié's rule references to "dictator," "thief," or "national divisions" were sensitive enough to have a record pulled from the airwaves, but as the former president was being hustled to safety in neighboring Togo, mutinous soldiers were themselves singing *"Longue vie a Alpha Blondy."* Of these musicians of protest, one soldier was quoted as saying, "They're people who tell the truth."

Economy: Côte d'Ivoire's economy is heavily dependent on agriculture. Cocoa and coffee are its principal exports. It is the world's largest cocoa producer, with production levels at one million tons a year. Coffee exports rise to 175,000 tons annually. There are some 620,000 cocoa and coffee farmers out of a population of 16 million and another three million people depend directly on the commodities for their livelihoods. The state marketing body, the Agricultural Products Price Stabilization Board (*CAISTAB*), controlled both cocoa and coffee sales, but as part of liberalization undertaken by the government, *CAISTAB* was privatized in May 1999.

Liberalization was intended to make prices to producers more responsive to market forces and ultimately more profitable to farmers. Unfortunately, liberalization took place just as world prices were dropping and a decade-long planting binge had helped to increase cocoa production. Prices slumped and plunged further when the EU voted to allow "chocolate" to be sold with up to five percent vegetable fat substituting for cocoa butter. Farmers protested vehemently, blaming the new *CAISTAB* for low prices.

Signing an enhanced structural adjustment facility (ESAF) with the IMF in February 1998 led to a rescheduling of a portion of the country's accumulated debt. From $16 billion, the nation's public sector debt was reduced to $12 billion. Approximately 38% of Côte d'Ivoire's 1999 budget was committed to debt servicing, but when the military government took power there was so little money available they had to cancel debt payments. "We have temporarily suspended payments of foreign commitments," said Gueï in January 2000. "Only after a thousand gymnastics moves were we even able to pay (December) salaries."

In March 2001 the World Bank declared Ivory Coast to be in non-payment status, making it ineligible for new loans and fresh disbursements from already approved assistance programs. A team of World Bank and IMF economists visited the country in April to assess the country's financial condition. It owes billions and experienced two percent negative growth in 2000. Given more than a year of ethnic, religious and civil turbulence, foreign investors have gone elsewhere. Foreign investment is down 40% and the country teeters towards bankruptcy.

The Future: Political life will remain tense; stability will remain fragile. The xenophobic passions whipped up by former President Bédié have proved useful to the Gbagbo regime. President Gbagbo's principal preoccupation is remaining in power. He is dependent on a restive army whose own appetite for power has been whetted. Keeping unruly soldiers contained to their barracks with regular salary payments may prove difficult in the country's dire financial circumstances.

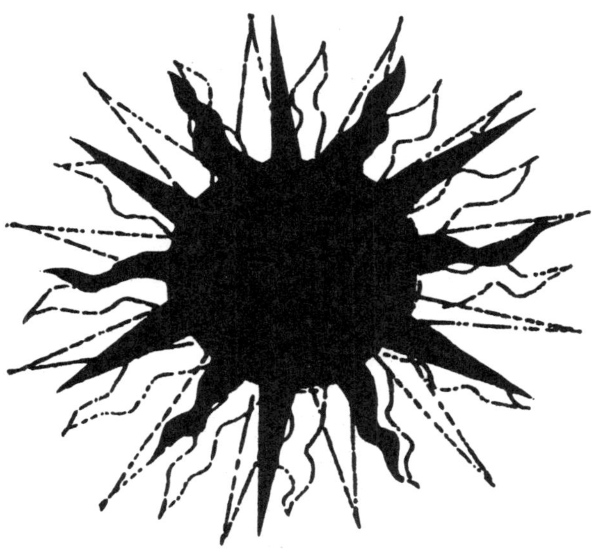

The Republic of The Gambia

Mothers lined up for food Photo by Ken Brown

Area: 10,463 sq. km. = 4,005 sq. mi. (Connecticut is 1/5 larger).
Population: 1,336,320 (July 1999 est.)
Capital City: Banjul (Pop. 240,000. 1996 est.)
Climate: Subtropically warm with a wet summer (May–October) and a dry and somewhat cooler season (November–April).
Neighboring Countries: The Gambia is enclosed on three sides by Senegal.
Official Language: English.
Other Principal Languages: Fulfulde, Jola, Mandinka, Soninke, and Wolof.
Ethnic Groups: African 99% (Mandinka 42%, Fula 18%, Wolof 16%, Jola 10%, Serahuli 9%, other 4%), non-African 1%.
Principal Religions: Muslim 90%, Christian 9%, indigenous beliefs 1%.
Chief Commercial Products: Peanuts and peanut products, fish, cotton lint, and palm kernels.
GNP per capita: 340 US$
Currency: 1 Dalasi (D) = 100 Butut
Former Colonial Status: British Colony (1816–1965).
Independence Date: February 18, 1965.
Chief of State: Capt. Yahya Jammeh, President (1994).
National Flag: Three horizontal stripes of red, blue, and green; thin white lines separate the stripes. Symbolically, the blue stripe (Gambia River) is between the red and green stripes (sun shining on the river as it flows through the fertile land).

The Gambia has the smallest area of any independent nation on the African mainland. Slicing thinly into the northwest coast of Africa and facing the tropical waters of the Atlantic Ocean, this country lies within an area smaller than Jamaica. It was named *The* Gambia by the government to avoid confusion with Zambia.

The Gambia is a finger–like projection into the territory of southern Senegal by which, except for the seacoast, it is surrounded. The wide Gambia is one of the larger and more navigable rivers of northwest Africa—it is possible for ocean–going vessels to travel 150 miles inland and for smaller ships to traverse its entire length. The estuary contains one of the finest natural harbors in Africa.

The entire territory is low–lying, never exceeding a height of 120 feet. On each side of the broad river, thick swamps contain mangrove trees which reach heights of up to 100 feet. Further inland from the river is a region of swamps and river flats. These are often flooded, sometimes by salt water during the wet season. This swampy belt is succeeded by round hills and rolling plateaus with thick growths of grass and periodic clumps of trees. There is ample rainfall for cultivation in this long and narrow nation, seldom more than 20 miles in width.

History: Between the 10th and 15th centuries there was a migration of Hamitic–Sudanic people from the Nile River Valley westward. They arrived in The Gambia and Senegal, settled and intermingled with the West African Negro people already living there. The various waves of migration evolved into distinct tribal patterns, many of which are evident today. The first Europeans to visit The Gambia, about the same time Columbus reached the West Indies, were from Portugal. By 1500 the lower river area had become a regular port of call for traders seeking slaves and gold. For details of early and colonial history, see *The British in Africa* and *The French in Africa*.

Conferences between the British colonial rulers and The Gambia in 1964 led to full independence on February 18, 1965; David K. Jawara was installed as the first Prime Minister. The Gambia elected to become a republic within the British Commonwealth in 1970 at which time Prime Minister Jawara became President.

Elections held in April 1977 (the first in ten years) resulted in a continuation of control by the *People's Progressive Party* led by President Jawara, who was elected to a five–year term. In mid–1981, while he was in London attending the wedding of Prince Charles, a force of leftists attempted to overthrow the government. Elections held in May 1982 resulted in a legislature with 27 *PPP* members, 3 from the *NCP* and 5 independents.

Elections in 1987 were contested by two other parties competing with the *PPP*, the *NCP* and the *Gambian People's Party*. In spite of this, President Jawara was reelected by a comfortable 59% of the vote, although this was lower than the 72.4% in the prior election.

Trials of three charged with attempting a *coup* in April–June 1988 resulted in stiff sentences. President Jawara charged that Libya's Gadhafi was the source of the move to recruit dissidents and foment revolution. President Jawara initially announced in late 1991 that he would not stand for reelection, but in early 1992 he changed his mind, and moved the elections from March to February. The outcome was not unexpected—he won 59% of the vote; his party elected 25 of the 36 members in the legislature.

Unrest had been bubbling just below the surface for a decade, and finally erupted decisively in mid–1994 when Lt. Yahya Jammeh staged a *coup*. The basic problem was army personnel who had not been paid while rampant government corruption was obvious. Jammeh established a five–man ruling council. A referendum was held approving the new constitution. Jammeh resigned his commission and was elected president in September 1996. Parliamentary elections in January 1997 were contested by Jammeh's party, the *Alliance for Patriotic Reorientation and Construction* (*APRC*), the *United Democratic Party* (*UDP*) led by Ousainou Darboe, the *People's Democratic Organization for Independence and Socialism* (*PDOIS*), the *National Reconciliation Party* (*NRP*) and five independents. Only the *APRC*, organized to contest every seat, won more than a two-thirds majority—33 seats. The *UDP* won seven, the *NRP* two and the *PDOIS* one. The elections were controversial and most observers thought them neither fair nor free.

Given its origins in a military coup and fraudulent elections, it is little surprising that the regime is authoritarian and oppressive. President Jammeh dominates the country and controls the instruments of force and fear. He holds the ministry of defense portfolio through which he commands the army. The National Intelligence Agency reports directly to him. Oppositional activity is closely watched and the main opposition group, the *United Democratic Party* (*UDP*) is frequently denied permission to hold public rallies. Members of the *UDP* have been arrested and regularly accuse the police of torture. Members of parliament are prohibited from criticizing the president and denied the right of discussing any matter impending in the courts.

The media is equally subject to abuse and control. At a July 2000 meeting with his party's youth group, President Jammeh threatened to "extend my broom to Radio Gambia because they edit my speeches." Those dismissed, he added, would be "completely destroyed." Reporters, long-suspected by the government of harboring sympathies for the opposition, were warned to stay away from "gatherings of people prone to or engaged in trouble-making"—i.e. political meetings.

The President's warnings to journalists were well reported, for good reason. At one point in the meeting he told Radio Gambia staff members present "you must broadcast all that I have said. Whoever cuts anything out, tomorrow you will forget your job!"

"The broom" swept in January 2001 when a senior broadcaster at Radio Gambia was fired for reporting that President Jammeh had hinted intentions to introduce Sharia, or Islamic law, in the country during a Ramadan message to Muslim elders in Banjul. Wary of such a controversial subject, government officials denied the statement and claimed the Gambian leader had been misquoted.

Jammeh and other members of the regime keep the rhetorical heat on high when dealing with opponents. In a speech commemorating the 1994 coup, the President said that those who would destabilize The Gambia would be denied court proceedings and "never see any face on earth" again. He had earlier in the year promised to "chop up" his opponents, bury those who opposed his policies "like dogs," and warned that those who insulted him would "never see the sun." Political opposition in The Gambia is circumspect.

The regime has seemed to become more authoritarian and brutish as any opportunity for its popular assessment comes near. Municipal elections scheduled for November 2000 were postponed. When the Chairman of the Independent Electoral Commission successfully petitioned the Supreme Court to compel the government to hold them, he was sacked. Needless to say, they have not yet been held.

In April, the regime unleashed its security against students protesting the torture and murder of a nine-year old student leader the month before. At least 12 people were shot dead. It was the bloodiest confrontation yet between the regime and its critics. Succumbing to international pressure, the government set up a commission of enquiry, but then rejected its findings.

The *APRC* has traditionally used its youth wings, trained by Libyans, as its storm troopers, breaking up opposition rallies, bullying and beating hapless candidates and opposition supporters. At a *UDP* meeting in June 2000, things got out of hand and one *APRC* supporter was killed. The *UDP* leader, Ousainou Darboe, and some 20 of his followers were promptly arrested and charged with murder. Though most have been acquitted, the trial of Darboe continues.

The government says the next presidential election will be in October 2001, with the National Assembly elections in January 2002. Deeply unpopular and desirous of maintaining power at any cost, a regime devoid of any notion of responsibility can only be expected to endure through repressive thuggishness.

Culture: The Gambia's population is 90 per cent Muslim and female circumcision is widespread. An estimated 80 per cent of Gambian women have had their clitoris surgically removed. A variety of women's groups have been organized to ban female genital mutilation (FGM), but they receive no support from President Jammeh. In typical rhetorical form, Jammeh declared that those who campaigned against female genital mutilation could continue their work, but "there's no guarantee that after they deliver their speeches they will return to their homes." In January 1999 Jammeh called those working to eliminate FGM "enemies of Islam" who sought to undermine the religion and African culture.

In neighboring Senegal the attitude has swung against FGM and last year it outlawed the practice. Even those accessory to the operation can now be prosecuted in Senegal. One consequence of this new law is that a cross-border trade in female circumcision has grown up. Parents send their infant daughters "on holiday" with relatives in The Gambia where the operation is performed.

It should be noted that the Gambian vice president, Mrs. Isatou Njie Saidy, who is also minister of health and women's affairs, is among the staunch campaigners against FGM.

Economy: The Gambia's economy is agriculturally based and largely dependent on groundnut export earnings. The groundnut sector has been in turmoil since February 1999 when the government closed down the main groundnut company. With insufficient funds to pay farmers fully, the government has seen them sell their produce across the border in Senegal where they receive lower prices, but immediate payment.

A once-promising tourism industry is on the verge of collapse. Tourists, harassed by unemployed locals known as "bumsters" and solicited for drugs or sex, have turned their backs on The Gambia. The country has developed such a reputation as transit point for the drug trade that fresh vegetable growers have seen their produce rot on the tarmac because flights from the Gambia are not accepted.

The Gambia produces no diamonds, but has become a major exporter of the gems. According to a UN report, the importation of "Gambian diamonds" into Belgium averaged over $100 million per annum between 1996 and 1999. UN experts referred to The Gambia as "mini-Antwerp," so notorious had it become as the diamond-peddling center of the subregion. Those most knowledgeable of the diamond trade say that 90% of "Gambian" diamonds are from Sierra Leone.

The Gambia's total debt increased from $390 million in 1992 to $566 million in 1999. Of that total, reported the Secretary of Finance and Economic Affairs, external debt amounted to $425 million dollars, but was expected to increase to $439.5 by the end of 2001. Eager to avoid criticism about its lending policies, the IMF opened its coffers in late 2000 and granted The Gambia $91 million in debt relief. Debt service payments will be reduced by about 43% over 2001-05 and 25% over 2006-15.

The Future: The fate of any military coup leader, no matter how legitimized by a dress of "democratic" elections, is dicey. He himself provides the model of his own fate. Jammeh has already survived several attempted coups from within the armed forces, and it is unlikely future attempts will cease. In any fair election Jammeh would be defeated handily, but this is not a regime that intends to leave its fate to the ballot box.

Capt. Yahya Jammeh

The Republic of Ghana

A farmer clears his land for planting

Area: 238,537 sq. km = 92,100 sq. mi. (Oregon is slightly larger).
Population: 18,887,626 (July 1999 est.)
Capital City: Accra (metropolitan area pop. 3 million estimated; pronounced Ah–Krah).
Climate: Hot and humid in the southwest; warm and less humid in the north. Ghana has a wet season (May–September) and a dry season (October–April).
Neighboring Countries: Ivory Coast (West); Burkina Faso (Upper Volta—West, North); Togo (East).
Official Language: English.
Other Principal Languages: Akan, Moshi-Dagomba, Ewe, and Ga.
Ethnic Groups: Akan 44%, Moshi-Dagomba 16%, Ewe 13%, Ga 8%, European and other 0.2%
Principal Religions: Indigenous beliefs 38%, Muslim 30%, Christian 24%, other 8%.
Chief Commercial Products: Gold 39%, cocoa 35%, timber 9.4%, tuna, bauxite, aluminum, manganese ore, and diamonds.
GNP per capita: 390 US$
Currency: 1 New Cedi (C) = 100 Pesewas
Former Colonial Status: British Colony (1821–1957).
Independence Date: March 6, 1957.
Chief of State: John Agyekum Kufuor, President.
National Flag: Three horizontal stripes of red, yellow and green with a five-pointed black star in the center of the yellow stripe.

Ghana is situated in the center of the Gold–Ivory Coast of Africa and has a 334–mile–long shore washed by the warm waters of the Gulf of Guinea. The coastline is an irregular pattern interrupted by streams and lagoons covered with strand and mangrove growth. The plant cover is not continuous, but gathers in tufted and erect green patches of grass and low vegetation. In the eastern inland coastal area, the terrain consists of a stretch of scrub and grassland, interrupted by clumps of bushes and small trees. Inland from the western coast there is an area of jungle, which receives ample rainfall, supporting dense growths of trees towering to heights of 200 feet.

The dense vegetation gives way 175 miles north from the sea to a somewhat smooth grassland area with less rainfall. The trees of this region are widely spaced among grasses which attain heights of 12 feet. The *harmattan*, a dry wind from the Sahara, penetrates from November to April. The humidity drops during this dry season and both the grasses and trees turn yellow; the trees lose their foliage within a few weeks. Temperatures in this region are high since there is no cooling breeze from the sea. In the extreme North, rainfall rapidly diminishes and becomes nonexistent. Northern Ghana has all but become totally arid during the last decade and faces invasion by the expanding Sahara Desert. There are no true mountains in Ghana—the highest elevation is 2,900 feet in the part closest to the eastern boundary.

History: The folklore of the people of Ghana refers to migrations from the North, and it is probable that these legends relate to the travels of Sudanese people from the Niger River in the 10th–15th centuries A.D. The name Ghana is derived from a powerful kingdom believed to have been centered some 200 miles north of Bamako (now the capital of Mali) as shown on p. 12. For earlier history, see also p. 18.

After independence, President Kwame Nkrumah (*Kwah*–mi N–*kroo*–mah) rapidly transformed the government into a dictatorship patterned after various communist nations. His *Convention People's Party* became the instrument of all political thought, and the government was supposed to be the servant of the party. Nkrumah acquired the power to jail people for ten years without trial; the press was rigidly censored. But in spite of these measures, he initially was an immensely popular figure.

Establishing close ties with Russian and Chinese communists, Nkrumah accused the Western nations of "neo–colonialism" with tedious regularity. He bolstered his ego with titles such as the "lion," "giant" and "prophet" of Africa. He was inconsistent, argumentative and stubborn; although there was an appearance of prosperity in Ghana under Nkrumah, this was only on the surface. He borrowed huge sums of money from abroad and spent them on lavish projects, such as the then modern Accra Stadium adjacent to Black Star Square, home of an able soccer team which has won international awards. Agricultural improvement and industrial development were largely ignored. The economic situation became increasingly difficult, but Nkrumah did give the Ghanaians pride, however imaginary it might have been. When he was deposed, it became apparent that he left Ghana in an economic shambles.

A group of army officers seized power while Nkrumah was visiting China and

North Vietnam in early 1966. A *Liberation Council* was formed, Nkrumah sympathizers were arrested and almost 1,200 political prisoners were released from jails. Communist technical and political personnel were quickly expelled. Nkrumah went to Guinea, where his personal friend, Sékou Touré, bestowed on him the honor of titular head of state.

There followed a succession of governments, military and civilian, none of them able to solve the problems of soaring inflation, dishonesty in government, unemployment and all the ills accompanying a nation deep in debt. Twelve years later, with the military in power, elections were scheduled, but many people knew that the outcome was prearranged; extra ballots had been printed to assure victory for the chosen candidates. At this point, Flight Lt. Jerry Rawlings, with a group of young officers, took over the government. This group of idealistic men went forward with the elections which were held in September 1979. The winner was a highly respected former foreign service officer, Dr. Hilla Limann, who declared his intention to bind up the nation's economic wounds and set Ghana on a solid economic course.

The Limann government lasted only until New Year's Eve, 1981, when Lt. Rawlings again appeared on the scene and deposed the elected chief executive. The new military leaders pledged to reverse that trend and to provide stable democracy. Rawlings, head of a 7–man Council, suspended the constitution, abolished all of Ghana's six political parties, accused the Limann government of failing to provide for the needs of the people, and called upon the citizens to become actively involved in "the decision–making process" (whatever that meant).

The new government, on the surface, appeared to have turned radical—Rawlings was an unabashed admirer of Libya's Colonel Gadhafi. Plans were afoot to install "popular committees" which would, in theory, manage *all* aspects of the lives of Ghanaians. "People's Defense Committees" briefly mushroomed in city neighborhoods, in rural villages and industry. They were supposed to serve as watchdogs against corruption and black market dealings.

Economic hardships added fuel to the fires of dissent which present a continuing threat to the regime. It was this that led to an about–face by Rawlings and his regime in 1987–88. About 45,000 civil servants were fired, foreign investment policy was reversed and a less revolutionary style was adopted.

Encouraged by these and other moves to put Ghana's economy in order, the International Monetary Fund and the World Bank, as well as several western nations, extended credits to the country that had been withheld. Foreigners were invited to use modern techniques in the gold mines, producing favorable results.

Bowing to international pressures, Lt. Rawlings allowed a multiple party system to develop in the early 1990's preparatory to elections scheduled for November 1992. He resigned from the air force (as required by new election laws) and ran as a civilian. Rawlings won with 60% of the vote, but there was substantial tampering in the contest without which he probably would have won anyway.

Ghana's distinguished diplomat, Kofi Annan, was chosen UN Secretary General in late 1996. Elections in December 1996 were won by President Rawlings and his *National Democratic Council* (*NDC*). He won handily, taking 57.4 % of the vote, while his nearest rival, John Kufuor heading the *Great Alliance* (consisting of the *New Patriotic Party* and the *People's Convention Party*) won a respectable 39.6%.

In legislative elections the *NDC* won 132 seats, an absolute majority in Ghana's 200-member parliament. The *NPP* won 60 seats, and its electoral partner, the impotent remnant of Nkrumah's once-dominant *People's Convention Party*, won a paltry 5 seats. Despite huge majorities in parliament and loads of international goodwill, Rawlings and the NDC were unable to revitalize the Ghanaian economy.

By the time the elections of 2000 rolled around the economy was in full decline, worsened by the reluctance of the Rawlings government to take hard decisions in an election year. Prices of Ghana's major exports, gold and cocoa, had declined and petroleum prices had soared. Interest rates were nearly 50% and inflation soared to 60%. Unemployment hovered at 50% while the value of Ghana's currency, the cedi, had collapsed.

In 1981, before Rawlings took power, the cedi was worth 2.75 to the dollar; in 2000 it took 6,800 to buy a single dollar. Per capita income in 1981 was $410; in 2000, it had dropped to $360. Growth was predicted to be a miserable 1%. People were suffering, and the party that had governed for so long was similarly made to suffer at the polls.

Constitutionally prohibited from seeking a third term, Rawlings had handpicked his vice-president, John Evans Atta Mills, to be his successor. The *New Patriotic Party* nominated John Kufuor, an Oxford-trained lawyer, businessman and long a conservative opponent of the regime. A Roman Catholic from the country's influential Ashanti tribe, Kufuor campaigned on a platform of "positive change."

President John Agyekum Kufuor

Though marred by violence, the vote count was generally fair. The opposition *New Patriotic Party* won 100 of the 200 parliamentary seats. Its presidential candidate, Kufuor, nearly won a first ballot victory, taking a lead of 48.44% to John Atta Mills' 44.8%. In the run-off, all five minor candidates threw their support to Kufuor, who won with an impressive 57%. When Vice-President Mills telephoned his concession speech, Ghanaians sighed in collective relief: Ghana had successfully achieved a democratic transfer of power.

Culture: Traditional kingdoms continue to flourish in Ghana, and their rulers exercise influence nationally and outside the borders of Ghana. In spring 1999, Ghanaians mourned the loss of the greatest of its traditional kings, the Asantahene, paramount chief of the Asante Federation, Otumfuo Opoku Ware II. "A great tree has been uprooted," said his memorialists. The Asantahene died at age 79, having occupied the Golden Stool of the Asante for 30 years. He was buried in the full splendor of traditional ceremonies that affirmed the importance of an enduring African culture.

The regency was assured by the Queen Mother, an all–important figure among matrilineal Asante, and after a suitable mourning period, the new Asantahene was named. Nana Kwaku Duah, a London–trained accountant and business executive, aged 48, asserted the long continuity of his office in his official name. As Asantahene he will be known as Osei Tutu II, after the first Asante king. Thousands watched as the new king was carried through the streets of Kumasi, surrounded by bodyguards wielding staffs made of gold. His coronation, an enstoolment among the Asante, took place on the Golden Stool. The stool is believed to have descended from Heaven in a cloud of white dust and to have landed on the lap of Osei Tutu I. Asantes believe it incarnates the soul of the Asante nation.

Ghana's bereavement doubled with the death of the Okyenhene, paramount chief of the Akim Abuakwa traditional area. The Okyenhene was also president of the National House of Chiefs.

The Market Women of Ghana are not mere salespeople—they are a respected institution. Noisy, sometimes quarrelsome, but brilliantly arrayed, they vend their wares in the town and city markets, often occupying the same space for years. They highly resent price "freezes" adopted in recent years, being firm believers in the traditional bargaining method of selling their wares.

Hon. Kofi Annan

Improvement in education has occurred since the Nkrumah years; college and youth organizations are among the most vocal critics of Rawlings' government. About 1 million students attend primary and secondary schools and more than 40,000 are studying in high schools, training colleges and academic universities, including the University of Ghana. The literacy rate is admirably high—over 60%—in dramatic contrast to 30% one short generation ago.

Economy: At the time of independence, Ghana was the world's leading cocoa exporter. Its economic prospects were excellent. When Kwame Nkrumah and his *Convention Peoples Party* came to power, they sought economic development through rapid industrialization, directed and funded through the state. Investment funds were largely derived from accumulated surpluses of the Cocoa Marketing Board. The state enterprises created at this time rarely proved profitable. State budgets went into deficit which could not be covered by cocoa surpluses since the price had precipitously fallen on world markets. A huge accumulated debt was Nkrumah's legacy to his political heirs.

Desperation drove the Rawlings government to work out an Economic Recovery Program with the guidance of the IMF and the World Bank in 1983. Fiscal discipline was restored, better tax collection implemented, and by 1986 the budget showed a surplus. A second phase of the recovery program began in 1986 with structural adjustments. Cuts were made in a bloated civil service. A new investment code created to encourage foreign investment and privatization of state enterprises was actively pursued.

When multiparty democracy was returned in 1992, however, Ghana fell off the straight-and-narrow path it had been following under a military regime. As an inducement to civil service voters to support his party, Rawlings granted large public employee pay raises. He won the election, but five years worth of surpluses disappeared, inflation was fueled, and domestic debt increased.

When President Kufuor took office, the country was saddled with a debt burden totaling $7.5 billion. It represented 224 percent of exports, 709 percent of budget revenue and 124 percent of GDP. (For the World Bank, anything over 220 percent of exports qualifies a country as "severely indebted.") Debt had spiraled upwards during the final months of the Rawlings administration because it refused to take politically hazardous but economically necessary action just before an election.

Costly fuel and electricity subsidies, for example, were maintained. Ghanaians could drive around on gasoline which cost less than a dollar per gallon while the government's Tema Oil Refinery, which processes all imported crude oil, was accumulating nearly $350 million in debts. In February 2001, shortly after it had been inaugurated, the new government announced a 60% hike in gasoline prices in an effort to keep its debt-ridden national refinery from collapse.

Ghana needs to import 45,000 gallons of crude oil a day, and in November 2000 the Rawlings government signed an agreement to import 50,000 barrels of crude a day from Equatorial Guinea under extended favorable credit terms. So cash-poor was Ghana that only a few months later President Kufuor led a team to Nigeria to negotiate oil purchases on a 90-day repayment basis.

There are similar problems in the electrical energy area. Recent droughts have highlighted the inability of the Volta River Authority (VRA), operators of the Akosombo Hydroelectric Dam, to supply steady and reliable energy to Ghanaian industries. Recognizing the vulnerability of hydroelectric power, Ghana has joined with Togo, Benin, and Nigeria in a regional partnership to construct the West African Gas Pipeline (WAGP). The proposed 600-mile pipeline would bring natural gas from Chevron's Escravos terminal in Nigeria to Benin, Togo, and Ghana where it would be used to generate electricity.

The Volta River Authority's major power consumer, the Volta Aluminum Company Limited (VALCO) located at Tema, has indicated that it would switch to electricity generated from gas as soon as the West African Gas Pipeline (WAGP) project is operational. There is some fear that if VALCO switches to electricity from cheap gas the Akosombo dam project may collapse. The fragility of one of Ghana's largest undertakings symbolized the perilous state of the economy inherited by President Kufuor.

Kufuor and the *NPP* campaigned on the virtues of free enterprise. In his maiden speech as President, Kufuor spoke of "mismanagement, mass unemployment, low wages, high cost of living, a rapidly depreciating currency, a colossal national debt, [and] high dependency on foreign aid." The economy was a shambles, he said, because his predecessor didn't believe in the private sector as the engine of growth and didn't manage the public sector efficiently. In contrast, his government would be "the most business friendly Ghana has had to date".

President Kufuor's first budget has targeted a Gross Domestic Product growth rate of 4%. It also pledged to contain the inflation rate at 25%. Wasteful subsidies would be phased out, and efforts would be made to accelerate diversification of an economy acutely vulnerable to market swings in the price of gold and cocoa. The tasks are daunting.

The Future: Ghana voted for change, but change, particularly in the economic realm, will be slow and painful. Entrenched interests and ways of thinking will resist. But President Kufuor's call to open the economy may well unleash entrepreneurial energies long suppressed and restore Ghana to its role as an economic model.

The Central Library, Accra AP/Wide World Photo

The Republic of Guinea

(pronounced *Gih*–nee)

Guinean family outside traditional thatch hut. Note the ventilation opening to allow hot air to escape.

Area: 245,857 sq.km. = 95,000 sq. mi. (about the size of Oregon).
Population: 7,538,953 (July 1999 est.)
Capital City: Conakry (Pop. 1,558,000, estimated).
Climate: In the extreme Southeast and Southwest there are small hot and humid areas of jungle with two rainy seasons (May–July and September–November). The climate gradually changes the terrain to a warm, semiarid region in the North with a single rainy season (April–October).
Neighboring Countries: Guinea Bissau (West); Senegal, Mali (North); Ivory Coast (East); Liberia, Sierra Leone (Southeast).
Official Language: French.
Other Principal Languages: Baga, Dan, Fuuta Jalon, Kissi, Malinke, Maninka, Mano, and Susu.
Ethnic groups: Peuhl 40%, Malinke 30%, Soussou 20%, smaller tribes 10%.
Principal Religions: Muslim 85%, Christian 8%, indigenous beliefs 7%.
Chief Commercial Products: Bauxite, alumina, diamonds, gold, coffee, fish, and agricultural products.
GNP per capita: 540 US$
Currency: Guinea Franc.
Former Colonial Status: French Colony (1894–1958).
Independence Date: October 2, 1958.
Chief of State: Col. Lansana Conté, President.
National Flag: Vertical stripes of red, yellow and green.

Facing to the southwest on the Atlantic Ocean in the western extension of Africa, Guinea has an irregular, but level coastline. Immediately inland there is a gently rolling area, covered with dense vegetation in the more southern coastal area. Grassy plains, interspersed with trees, are found in the north coastal region.

Further inland the landscape slowly rises in a series of flat plains and table mountains. The Fouta Djallon mountains rise to heights of 6,000 feet in central Guinea and are the source of three large West African rivers: the Niger, the Gambia and the Senegal.

Further to the northeast, the land slowly descends to a flat grassland which has greater variation in temperatures than the more humid coastal area. These grasslands attain a rich, green color towards the end of March and the vegetation grows rapidly in the ensuing rainy season which lasts until November.

In southeast Guinea the terrain becomes somewhat higher, containing dense forests with a pattern of rain quite similar to that of the plains land. As the dry season commences in the latter part of November, the leaves of the trees turn into a panorama of brilliant colors, not because of cold weather, but because of the lack of moisture. This is the equivalent of "winter" in Guinea, and it is not until April that the landscape is again green.

History: Guinea was dominated in early times from the 10th to the 15th centuries by kingdoms overlapping from neighboring countries. The vast empires of Ghana, Mali and Songhai successively occupied the country during the period. Earlier migrations of people to Guinea remained during the period of these kingdoms. The nomadic Fulani (also known as Peulhs), the agricultural Mandingos, Malinkes and Soussous had become established in times unknown and today inhabit this area of West Africa. For details of early and colonial history, see Historical Background and *The French in Africa.*

Under pressure for independence from its African colonies, France enacted the *Loi Cadre* in 1958, extending to the colonies the choice of full independence or autonomy within the *French Community*. Guinea quickly elected to become fully independent—the only French colony to make that choice—and it was proclaimed a nation on October 2, 1958.

Following independence, Guinea was actually a total dictatorship under the iron rule of its first president, Ahmed Sékou Touré. There were trappings of democratic government, i.e. elections for the president every seven years and for seats in the National Assembly every five years. However, the *Democratic Party of Guinea* was the sole political force in the country. Sékou Touré was its Secretary—General. Membership in the party was said to be as many as 2 million, organized into thousands of local committees. Therefore, elections were a mere formality.

Sékou Touré's one–man rule ended very swiftly in a Cleveland hospital when he died on March 26, 1984 during an operation to correct a blood vessel defect. His closest confidante, Prime Minister Louis Lansana Beavogui immediately took control of the government. A 40 day period of mourning for the late "hero" was proclaimed. The party's 14–member political bureau was scheduled to meet in order to select the successor of Touré.

Early in the morning of April 3, 1984, junior military officers, disgusted with prior civilian rule, took over the country, proclaiming that Touré's rule was no more than a "bloody and ruthless dictatorship." This undoubtedly had something to do with the fact that Touré regularly "purged" the military to insure his own seat of power. A Military Committee was established which assured all foreign nations that Guinea would live up to its commitments; it immediately began to release some political prisoners from Conakry's notorious

Camp Boiro, a barracks where many atrocities were said to have taken place. At least 10,000 political prisoners had been seized during Sékou Touré's regime, of whom some 2,500 simply "disappeared."

The *Democratic Party of Guinea* and the constitution were suspended. Political prisoners surviving Touré's holocaust, numbering 250, were given radio time to relate their experiences to the people. The new regime was initially led by Col. Lansana Conté, President, and Col. Diarra Traoré, Prime Minister; rivalry led to the latter's demotion in December 1984.

Dissatisfied, Traoré and others attempted a *coup* in July 1985 while President Conté was in Lomé (Togo) at a conference. The President returned to Guinea after giving a speech at the conference and had no difficulty in restoring control. Some 30 people involved in the attempt were summarily executed, including Traoré. The whole affair had tribal overtones.

Since the death of Touré, Guinea has embarked on a new course. A $2.3 million loan was negotiated with France and the International Monetary Fund soon granted a line of credit to begin the refurbishing of a potentially wealthy African nation. The Soviet bloc belatedly came forward with promises (not money) of future assistance. Programs were undertaken to cut the government bureaucracy (87,000) drastically and to sell several government–owned enterprises to the private sector.

Human rights conditions did not immediately improve in Guinea. The results of military trials in 1986–7 of about 200 officials of Touré's regime resulted in 60 death sentences, 21 of them *in absentia*. Some of the accused were presumed to be already dead. The purpose was to instill fear, particularly in urban areas, where the government popularity had plunged because of severe economic conditions.

The president elaborated in 1989 on a prior plan for a new constitution which may possibly provide for a political government; parties were legalized in 1992 and there are now about 40 of them, squabbling endlessly over things of little import. The "legislature" is the National Assembly, dominated by the *Party of Unity and Progress* (*PUP*) of President Conté (71 of 114 seats) since 1995 elections.

President Conté took office in 1994 after multiparty elections were deemed by the opposition as an "electoral masquerade" and "a comedy." He barely survived a military mutiny in 1996 when army units rebelled demanding higher pay. They burned down the presidential palace, looted shops and led the president off to an army base. Fifty people were killed in the incident. President Conté was forced to sign a five-point accord with the mutineers before being returned to power. Amnesty, apparently, was not of the agreement. Long-delayed trials began in early 1998 and exposed confessions extracted by torture and ethnic bias against soldiers not of the president's Soussou group.

The Soussou make up only 15% of the population, but dominate the machinery of repression—the ministries of the interior, police, and security; they dominate the *PUP*, and even the finance minister, Kassory Fofana, is a Soussou. Risen to power by a coup, terrified by another, President Conté often exhibits a bunker mentality, viewing other ethnic groups with the greatest of suspicion and withdrawing to the safety of his own.

Presidential elections held in December 1998 demonstrated the sharpness of ethnic division in Guinea. Conté faced four opponents, three of whom concluded an electoral alliance aimed at stopping president Conté from winning on the first ballot. Linked together within the *Coordination of Democratic Opposition* (*COD*) were the Malinké Alpha Condé, the Peul Mamadou Ba, and Jean–Marie Dore of one of the smaller ethnic groups. If the alliance could force the president into a second ballot, all agreed to support his opponent. It was to no avail in a situation where the election is controlled by the regime in power. In dubious balloting, Conté was officially given a first–round victory of 56.12% by the Ministry of the Interior. Ba won a quarter of the vote and Alpha Condé slightly less than 17%.

Two days after the announcement of his victory, President Conté had his rival Alpha Condé arrested, despite his status as a member of parliament, and charged with state security offenses. These included allegedly recruiting mercenaries to overthrow the regime of Lansana Conté. Riots broke out in the principal Malinké communities and several people were killed. In Conakry, women protested bare-breasted, a traditional sign of mourning. For their political expression, they were arrested for assaulting public modesty. Fourteen leading members of the Malinké opposition, including members of parliament, were arrested, charged with threatening public order, found guilty and jailed.

Faced with Malinké radicalization, President Conté sought appeasement through appointment. He failed to reappoint his technocratic prime minister, Sidya Touré, creating a prominent opening in political space. Accused of being too soft on the opposition by the president's Soussou inner circle, Touré was replaced by Lamine Sidimé, the Malinké head of Guinea's supreme court. A lawyer and professor, educated and trained in Senegal and France, Sidimé had long tilled the regime's fields, having supervised three of Guinea's elections as chief justice. That one of those elections was the notorious presidential race of 1993 where Lansana Conté was elected with 51.7% of the votes—only after balloting in areas favorable to the opposition had been annulled, did not lend much confidence to the situation.

President Conté conducted a major purge of the army in March 1999, sacking the armed forces chief of staff, Col. Oumar Soumah and 30 other officers in connec-

French President Mitterrand greets Guinean President Conté in Paris, 1987

AP/Wide World photo

The Guinean coastline

tion with the 1996 army mutiny. How quickly they forget. It was the army mutiny of 1984, prompted by repeated purges conducted by Sékou Touré, that had first brought Lansana Conté to power.

A repressive regime creates enemies everywhere. Opponents who have fled the country represent a continuing threat, and in the fall of 2000 the Liberian leader Charles Taylor—a man who never forgets or forgives an enemy—focused his full attention on Guinea, making use of enemies of the regime both internal and external.

As things seemed to calm in neighboring Sierra Leone, RUF fighters there, dependent on Taylor, launched border raids on several northern Guinean towns. As usual with RUF engagements, death, plunder and devastation ensued, but their surprising military sophistication was attributed to training offered by Guinean officers, some of the mutineers of 1996 who had fled Guinea.

A second front in Taylor's campaign to destabilize the country was opened in the south when a previously unknown group began making cell-phone calls to radio stations claiming responsibility for a series of incidents. A spokesman announced the attacks were by the *Allied Democratic Forces of Guinea* (*RDFG*), described as a group of "dissident Guineans."

The two countries stand at the brink of war. President Taylor has demanded that Guinea expel Liberian dissidents—*ULIMO-K* members—harbored and trained there. President Conté has accused Guinea's huge refugee population of ingratitude and of facilitating rebel infiltration. His countrymen responded by breaking up refugee camps and savaging their inhabitants. Local militias were organized throughout the country for better surveillance of non-Guineans, and the Guinean army lobbed a few heavy artillery shells into northern Liberia. Liberia described the action as "tantamount to full-scale war."

In April 2001, President Conté significantly raised the ante for potential internal violence. On the occasion of the 17th anniversary of the army's seizure of power, Conté told assembled soldiers: "If you meet people with weapons who do not belong to the military, you must simply annihilate them. That is what I am saying, and it is an order that you must execute, if you are good citizens. There must not be a second army. You must fight them."

It was in this atmosphere of rising violence that the long-delayed trial of Alpha Condé finally concluded. In September 2000 an emergency session of a State Security Court convicted him of sedition and sentenced him to five years in prison. Seven of the 47 people accused along with Condé were also given prison sentences ranging from 18 months to three years. The others were released or acquitted. Condé himself remained in virtual isolation, denied audience with his lawyers and family members.

The deplorable nature of Guinean justice made Condé a focal point of regime criticism internally and externally. President Wade of Senegal offered asylum and encouraged his release, but a regime fearful, threatened, and paranoid showed neither flexibility nor mercy. Guinea's justice minister has indicated he is convinced that members of Condé's *RPG* party along with elements of the national army and administration have collaborated with Guinea's neighbors to destabilize the country. He threatens to dissolve the *RPG*. Under heavy pressure from France and Senegal, President Conté released Alpha Condé in May 2001.

Guinea should have held parliamentary elections in November 2000. But the multifaceted crisis facing the country has led the government to postpone them indefinitely.

Culture: More than 80% of the people of Guinea live a rural life on small farms that provide their basic needs. Artistic and literary expressions, formerly limited by the single political party and its leader, are re–emerging. About 10,000 people who fled the nation during the Touré years have returned and are being resettled with international assistance. There are more than 16 distinct ethnic groups within the country, the great majority of which profess Islam as religion. When splinter groups of Islam began to appear, the government banned them and established the *National Islamic League*, the only group authorized in Guinea. In spite of the efforts of the former ruling party, basic values have been retained. Female circumcision is still practiced in Guinea and opponents have struggled for 14 years against the practice. In November 1999 there was a symbolic breakthrough in the campaign against well-ingrained cultural practices. Several hundred women who performed the operation handed in their ceremonial knives in the eastern town of Korosa. The campaign to abolish the practice continues, led by women, many of whom were once practitioners.

Economy: Guinea is a land rich in natural resources—bauxite, iron, gold, and diamonds—and the water to produce the energy needed to process and convert those raw materials. The Senegal, Gambia, and Niger rivers all flow from Guinea's mountains. Its land could produce a rich bounty of agricultural goods, but despite its mighty potential, Guinea's economy languishes. Ports, roads, and schools—the central aspects of the economy's infrastructure—are deficient. Only a third of the population is literate, and life expectancy does not exceed 45 years.

Guinea's non-development has its origins in the Marxist economic thinking of the Touré years. State-led development has proved an abject failure. With about one-third of the world's bauxite reserves—the principal ore used in making aluminum—government planners, fixated on modernization through industrialization, transformed Guinea from an exporter of agricultural products into a major bauxite exporter. That meant that Guinea ultimately had to import food to feed its citizens.

Other state enterprises created bloated bureaucracies whose salaries devoured any profits from bauxite. With little money to invest productively, there was neither growth nor development. Controlled prices acted as a disincentive to producers who turned to the informal economy. Smuggling flourished and the government lost tax revenues as the clandestine economy grew. By the 1980s the informal sector met an estimated 80% of urban consumer needs and the entirety of those needs outside the capital.

As its revenues declined, a consequence of the informal sector's growth and generally lower prices for raw materials, the government was less able to provide health and social services and the country's infrastructure deteriorated.

Even Touré realized the root of Guinea's problems, and turned to the West for help in his waning years. Failing to become a full economic partner in the Soviet bloc, Guinea turned once again to France and the West for development capital and expertise. In 1996 President Conté restructured his government to emphasize economic reform. Structural adjustment programs initiated by the IMF have been followed successfully, and 1997 marked an economic stability in Guinea not seen since 1989.

Though the vast bulk of its population is engaged in subsistence agriculture, Guinea's economy is dominated by its mining sector. Mining generates about 20% of GDP, while bauxite, alumina, gold and diamonds produce about 80% of export revenues. For the year 2000 the government estimated that exports from Guinea's mining sector reached $700 million.

Bauxite, a basic element in making aluminum via alumina, is the biggest element of the mining sector, accounting itself for nearly 85% of foreign exchange earnings. Guinea's *Companie des Bauxites de Guinée* (CBG) is the world's largest exporter of bauxite. CBG is a joint venture between the government and Halco, whose shareholders include Alcan of Canada, Alcoa and Reynolds of the US, plus French, Australian and German concerns. In June 1999, the government, while retaining its equity share, invited Alcoa to take over the management of the project. CBG produces an annual 13 million tons of bauxite, making Guinea the world's second largest producer after Australia.

Guinea's number two bauxite company, the *Société des Bauxites de Kindia* (SBK), was established primarily to supply bauxite to the Nikolaeyev alumina refinery in Ukraine. It produces about 1.3 million tons of bauxite a year. In April 2001, it was announced that Russian Aluminium (RusAl), the world's No. 2 aluminum producer, would take over management responsibilities of SBK. RusAl will spend US$40 million over the next three years upgrading and expanding SBK's mining activities.

Madina, the commercial center of Conakry

Significantly, Guinea has to import aluminum! At this point neither the infrastructure nor the investment capital is available to build a bauxite refinery. Guinea has vast potential in hydroelectric power needed for industrial development, but historically it has failed to develop it.

Gold and diamond mining are both growing. Gold output in 1999 output was about 14,000kg, with two commercial operations—*Société Minière de Dinguiraye* (SMD) and *Société Ashanti Goldfields de Guinée* (SAG)—contributing 9,285 kg. The remainder was produced by small-scale artisanal mining. Commercial diamond production in 1999, with a high proportion of gem-quality stones, was 21,908 carats. Artisanal mines raised the 1999 output to 30,281 ct.

Malaysia has become an important investor in the Guinean economy, especially in the telecommunications sector. Telekom Malaysia has invested $US45 million for a 60% stake in Sotelgui, a joint venture with the Guinean government. Sotelgui has a ten-year contract to develop Guinea's telecommunications system and has grown from 19,000 subscribers in 1996 to 40,000 in 1999. By 2010 it hopes to have 500,000 subscribers.

The Malaysian agricultural conglomerate Padiberas Nasional (Bernas) is involved in similar joint ventures with the government, including rice farming and breeding chickens for eggs and broiler chicken. The Malaysian Prime Minister, Mahathir Mohamad, has also indicated that Malaysia is interested in setting up oil palm and rubber estates in Guinea.

Guinea, surrounded by political instability in Liberia, Sierra Leone and Guinea-Bissau, has more refugees than any other country in West Africa—some 750,000, representing a significant drain on its resources. Recent cross border attacks on refugee camps from both Sierra Leone and Liberia have scattered many of the inhabitants and closed off delivery of humanitarian aid.

The Future: Guinea has all the hallmarks of another victim of Charles Taylor's regional ambitions. The campaign to destabilize the country is well under way, and it is unlikely Guinea has the institutional capacity to halt its slide into disorder. The United States has sent a team of ten U.S. Army Special Forces troops to Guinea to offer a month of basic military training to sixty Guinean soldiers, and ECOWAS has committed some 1600 soldiers to monitor Guinea's borders. Neither seems more than gesture and symbol. Guinea will need more than that will against impending anarchy.

The Republic of Guinea–Bissau

A quiet area near Bissau

Area: 36,260 sq. km. = 14,000 sq. mi. (the size of Connecticut and Massachusetts; includes the Bijago Archipelago).
Population: 1,234,555 (July 1999 est.)
Capital City: Bissau (Pop. 170,000, estimated (pronounced Bee–*sow*).
Climate: Very warm and humid with a wet season from May to October and a drier period from November to June.
Neighboring Countries: Senegal (North); Guinea (Southeast).
Official Languages: Portuguese
Other Principal Languages: Balanta, Crioulo (the lingua franca in much of Guinea-Bissau), Fulfulde, Mandinka, Mandyak, Papel.
Ethnic groups: Balanta 30%, Fula 20%, Manjaca 14%, Mandinga 13%, Papel 7%, European and mulatto less than 1%.
Principal Religions: Indigenous beliefs 50%, Muslim 45%, and Christian 5%.
Chief Commercial Products: Cashews 95%, fish, peanuts, palm kernels, and sawn lumber.
GNP per capita: 160 US$
Currency: CFA franc (as of 1 May 1997)
Former Colonial Status: Portuguese Colony (1885–1974). During this period, the area was considered by the Portuguese to be an integral part of European Portugal.
Independence Date: September 10, 1974 (The date on which Portugal recognized independence; unilateral declaration of independence was on September 24, 1973).
Chief of State: Kumba Ialá, President. (Pronounced Ya-*la*).
National Flag: Three stripes—red, vertical nearest the staff upon which there is a centered, black star and two horizontal stripes of yellow (top) and green (bottom).

Bordering on the waters of the Atlantic, most of Guinea–Bissau is a swampy coastal lowland with about sixty small islands lying close to the shoreline. On its eastern and southern borders it is protected by the Foutah Djallon mountains of Guinea. The level land, coupled with more than adequate rainfall, contributes large quantities of produce with less labor than is found in most areas of Africa.

History: The Balante people are probably the oldest inhabitants of Guinea–Bissau, joined only during the last millenium by the Mandingo and pastoral Fulani (Peulh) people. For details of earlier history, see Historical Background, *The Portuguese in Africa.*

Nationalist guerrilla warfare was unevenly conducted from the dense interior jungles beginning in 1961; as a result of this rebellion, Portugal had to maintain up to 26,000 troops, half of whom were African, stationed within the territory to oppose some 7,000 rebels. The colonial forces controlled only the coastal areas, and the interior was dominated by the rebels, who established basic schools and government services. Occasional Portuguese raids into the interior were made, but little more than temporary control resulted. The time of day or night was often the determining factor in deciding which force controlled what territory.

Initially there were two resistance movements, but one, the *African Indepen-*

dence Party of Guinea and Cape Verde (PAIGC) initially led by Amilcar Cabral emerged as the sole effort. By the early 1970's the rebels held one–half of the country and threatened another one–fourth. They were able to bombard Bissau periodically. Their support came from Soviet and Chinese arms and Cuban trainers all located in neighboring Guinea. Portugal retaliated by transporting Guinean rebels from Bissau to Conakry in late 1970 to raid *PAIGC* headquarters there, as well as other installations.

Fighting between the mulatto Cape Verde troops and the Black African soldiers marred the struggle for independence; the army of Guinea had to intervene to stop the strife. Cabral was assassinated in early 1973 and was succeeded as head of *PAIGC* by his brother, Luis. The revolution was successful because of a governmental change in Portugal; liberal military officers there realized it was futile to hold on to the rebellious colony. Independence was recognized on Sept. 10, 1974 and the Portuguese were gone within a month.

Cabral rose to the office of President by common consent and was "reelected" in March 1977. Economic conditions took a sharp turn for the worse; this led to Cabral's ouster in 1980 in a bloodless *coup* led by General João Bernardo Vieira. President Pereira of Cape Verde was accused of being a part of the whole problem. Although the quest for independence united the two territories, what little unity they had dissolved in the early 1980s. Although a return to constitutional rule was supposed to occur in 1984, the government still had all the trappings of a communist–style regime—a Central Committee, Politburo and single party.

General Veira was elected to a term of five years as President in 1984 and again in 1989. Communist rhetoric all but vanished, but until 1992 there remained only one political party, when opposition was permitted in response to international and local pressures. Elections scheduled for 1992 were repeatedly postponed, attracting considerable criticism, and were finally held in July 1994. The president and his party were elected in a multi–party contest (but not without accusations of election fraud). International observers termed the contest a fair one.

After 24 years in power the *PAIGC* had grown complacent, divided, and directionless. In June 1997 the sixth party congress was paralyzed by conflicts between two major party factions—one led by its President "Nino" Vieira, and another led by a former Prime Minister, Manuel Saturnino da Costa, the party's national secretary. President Vieira's removal of da Costa as Prime Minister and replacement with Carlos Correia had set him at odds with major *PAIGC* factions. Fateful for the president, those factions came to control parliament and would ultimately be responsible for his own removal.

Latent hostilities within the political class broke into open conflict with President Vieira's sacking of the Army Chief of Staff, Ansumané Mané, in June 1998. Mané was charged with insufficient control of cross-border arms trafficking. The army rose in revolt to support its popular leader and soon controlled most of the capital city. President Vieira called upon Senegal and Guinea for assistance against the rebels, but foreign troops were not enough to crush a popular rebellion.

The army and its civilian supporters controlled the countryside and a good portion of the capital, now largely destroyed and abandoned by most of its inhabitants. A bloody impasse resulted. In November President Vieira and General Mané signed an agreement in Abuja (Nigeria) which called for an extension of the cease fire, the withdrawal of foreign troops, and the deployment of an intervention force to separate the warring parties. Elections were to be organized by the end of 1999.

In December, President Vieira designated Francisco Fadul, General Mané's political advisor, as prime minister heading a government of national unity. The governments of Togo, Benin, Niger, Mali, and The Gambia all agreed to provide troops for an ECOMOG peace-keeping force, while Guinea and Senegal, somewhat reluctantly, agreed to pull out their contingents.

In early May 1999, with Guinean and Senegalese troops withdrawn from the country and only a token ECOWAS force on hand to supervise the Abuja and later Lome agreements, the army once again rebelled. President Vieira was driven from the burning executive palace to seek ultimate sanctuary in Portuguese exile.

Parliament has demanded that Vieira stand trial for corruption. Some understanding of popular resentment against the former regime may be found in the country's division of rich and poor. Seventy per cent of the population lives below the poverty line of $26 per person per month. Guinea-Bissau's richest 20% receive 56.2% of total income. The leader of Guinea-Bissau's Catholics has weighed in, saying the people "rightly or wrongly" attributed their misery to Vieira's corruption.

Parliament drafted a new constitution and set multiparty elections for both parliament and president. The new constitution, approved in July 1999, seems to settle long term tensions about Cape Verdean leadership and domination of the revolutionary struggle in Guinea-Bissau. One constitutional provision stipulates that high-level state positions may be held only by citizens with both parents of national origin.

Elections were held in November and January and the leading contenders for the presidency, Malam Bacai Sanhá and Kumba Ialá, both emerged out of the *PAIGC*. As leader of one of the anti-Vieira factions in parliament and its speaker, Sanhá had been made interim President when Vieira fled to Portugal. A former philosophy teacher, Ialá was a *PAIGC* defector, having gone into opposition and courageously run against Vieira in the 1994 elections.

Ialá's *Party for Social Renewal* (PRS) and the *Guinea-Bissau Resistance* party (*RGB*) led by Helder Vaz were the principal opposition to the *PAIGC*. In the race for 102 parliamentary seats, the *PRS* won 38 and the *RGB* claimed 28. The *PAIGC* came in third place with 24 seats, while five other parties shared the remaining 12 positions.

With 12 presidential candidates in the field, Ialá and Sanhá were thrown into a January runoff. The result was a decisive victory for Kumba Ialá who won 72% of the ballots. With the defeat of Malam Bacai Sanhá, a quarter century of *PAIGC* domination came to an end. The party refused to join in a grand coalition, choosing instead to become the principal opposition.

In February 2000, the *PRS* and the *RGB* formed a coalition government, and President Ialá set about the enormous task of recreating Guinea-Bissau. Political coalition did not produce stability, however, for the delicate issue left unresolved was the relationship of army and junta to the new civilian government.

In October, President Ialá appointed the constitutionally required State Council to advise him on key decisions, like declarations of war or a state of emergency. The Council, which includes members of all political parties represented in parliament and a variety of civic organizations, was

Former President João Bernardo Vieira

intended primarily to perform the functions carried out by the junta in the transitional government. Long-simmering tensions between state and army culminated in November when General Mané canceled army promotions made by the president, declared himself army chief of staff, and once again plunged the country into turmoil.

The PAIGC and other opposition parties welcomed Mané's declaration, but the rebellion was short-lived. The general was tracked down and killed in a shootout with loyalist troops. When the general's widow was presented with her husband's body in a coffin—not part of Muslim burial practice—rumors circulated that he had been beaten to death. Thousands accompanied his remains to their final resting place shouting "Allahu Akbar" and calling for justice in Guinea-Bissau.

A hero of Guinea-Bissau's liberation war against Portugal, Ansumané Mané was a member of the country's Muslim community—some 30% of the population. Reflecting continuing social tensions in the country, public reaction in some quarters seems to have made the general a martyr. One photographer was quoted as saying that selling the general's photograph had now become a lucrative business.

Rid of the one man who had done so much to keep him from governing in peace, President Ialá did little to ease political tensions by ordering the arrest of opposition politicians who had supported General Mané. Those detained were held for almost a week at a police station until a judge ordered their release for lack of evidence. Internal dialogue was not enhanced.

Against a background of continuing strikes by public employees for back wages and protest over detentions of and reprisals against opposition leaders, the fragile governing coalition in parliament fell apart. The *RGB* withdrew in January 2001 and condemned the government of Prime Minister Caetano Ntchama for failing the quell political and social unrest. Members of the president's own party made similar calls for new leadership as a means of extricating the country from its political paralysis.

In March, the president appointed Foreign Minister Faustino Imbali to the job, but there appears little likelihood the appointment will resolve the country's institutional crisis. The two largest opposition parties—the *African Party for the Independence of Guinea and Cape Verde (PAIGC)* and the *Guinea-Bissau Resistance/Bafata Movement (RGB)*—said Imbali was simply not up to the job of dealing with the country's concurrent crises.

Life in Guinea Bissau remains uncertain and insecure. Fuel, energy and water shortages plague the capital. Unemployment remains high. During the most recent civil conflict some 20,000 mines were laid, with 11,000 in the capital Bissau and its environs. With the death of General Mané, the government may be able to effect greater control over the arms trade with Casamance rebels in Senegal, but the border remains insecure. National police are insufficiently equipped to deal with an upsurge of banditry in the countryside. In short, the government has much to do.

Culture: The Balantes live in a subsistence agricultural manner in the coastal lowlands; the Mandingos (Mandyakos) and Fulani people of the interior place greater emphasis on the ownership of livestock. Contact between the Portuguese and the Africans was minimal during the colonial period; almost no educational facilities were provided for the black people. A tiny handful of Africans lived as *assimilados,* speaking Portuguese and adopting European customs.

The Cape Verdians (of mixed blood) long dominated the business scene in Bissau and always assumed a higher position on the social scale than their darker-skinned brethren. This was the cause of smoldering resentment, among others.

Economy: An economy already in crisis was devastated by the civil war. An estimated 2,000 citizens were killed and 500,000 were internally displaced. Roads and bridges were left a shamble. Disease and epidemics threaten as medical facilities were destroyed and personnel fled. Chronic food shortages have been worsened by 11 months of fighting.

Under normal circumstances Guinea-Bissau's economy is heavily dependent on exports of cashews and timber and the sale of fishing licenses. The government remains the country's largest employer. In December 1999 Prime Minister Fadul announced the state payroll had risen from 15,000 to 40,000 since the country's recent conflict. A good portion of that increase came as a consequence of the government's decision to fully integrate more than 10,000 military and paramilitary "volunteers" into the army. Finding the money to pay the wages of state employees remains a continuing source of anxiety for the government.

One of the world's poorest countries, Guinea-Bissau is burdened with a huge external debt, amounting to more than $920 million. Annual debt servicing drained away $34 million from state coffers. Significant debt relief became possible when Guinea-Bissau became eligible for the Highly Indebted Poor Countries (HIPC) program. In December 2000, a World Bank and IMF debt-relief package totaling $790 million was granted, alleviating some 85% of the country's total debt.

Agriculture provides jobs for 82% of the population and generates about 50% of GDP and 93% of exports. Subsistence farming and animal husbandry presently dominate the sector. The main food crop is rice, which is grown on nearly 20% of all cultivated land.

Guinea-Bissau's internal trade is dominated by barter and exchange among producers. A kilo of cashews, for example, can be exchanged for a kilo of rice. In 1986 cashew nuts overtook groundnuts as the main export crop. Guinea-Bissau is currently ranked as the world's sixth-largest producer of cashews. Other cash crops include palm kernels, coconuts, tobacco, and sugar.

Other areas for potential development are fishing, mining and timber. Coastal fishing resources are extremely rich. Guinea-Bissau currently sells the right to fish in its 200-mile Exclusive Economic Zone, and industrial fishing trawlers take their catch home for processing. Phosphate deposits have been discovered near Farim by Champion Resources of Canada, but production will not begin before 2002.

The Future: Difficult at best.

The Republic of Liberia

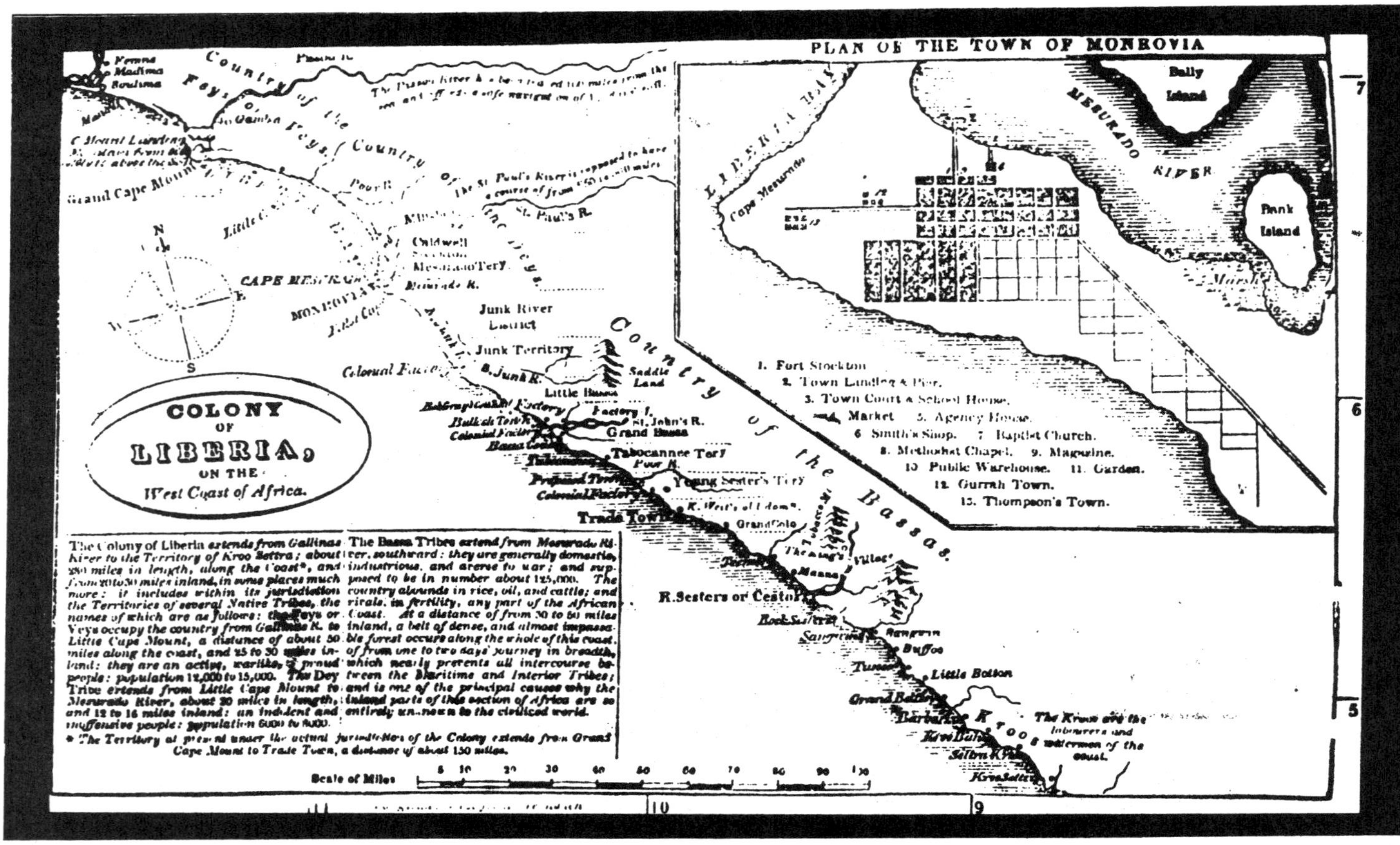

Map of the colony of Liberia, ca. 1827

Area: 111,370 sq. km = 43,000 sq. mi. (Pennsylvania is slightly larger).

Population: 2,923,725 (July 1999 est.)

Capital City: Monrovia (Pop. 400,000, swelled by about 125,000 refugees in 1992–93).

Climate: Warm and humid, with a wet season (April–November) and a drier season (December–May).

Neighboring Countries: Sierra Leone (West); Guinea (North); Côte d'Ivoire (Northeast, East).

Official Language: English.

Other Principal Languages: Over thirty, including Bassa, Dan, Gola, Grebo, Kisi, Kpelle, Krahn, Loma, Mano, Manya, Vai.

Ethnic groups: Kpelle, Bassa, Gio, Kru, Grebo, Mano, Krahn, Gola, Gbandi, Loma, Kissi, Vai, and Bella, Americo-Liberians 2.5% (descendants of immigrants from the US who had been slaves).

Principal Religions: Traditional 70%, Muslim 20%, and Christian 10%.

Chief Commercial Products: Diamonds, iron ore, rubber, timber, and coffee.

GNP per capita: Not available.

Currency: Liberian Dollar.

Former Colonial Status: Liberia has traditionally been an area of United States development.

Independence Date: July 26, 1847.

Chief of State: Charles G. Taylor, President (since August 3, 1997).

National Flag: Eleven horizontal stripes of red and white, with a single white star on a blue rectangle in the upper left–hand corner.

Liberia is located on the southern part of the west coast of Africa, facing the warm equatorial waters of the Gulf of Guinea. It is within the tropical region of Africa and as such, has a warm, humid climate. Its jungle areas are thickly carpeted with roots, dead leaves and debris, which are quickly made a part of the earth by the rapid rate of decay. From the floor of the jungle, shrubs and small trees entangled with vines, rise from 40 to more than 100 feet. Interspersed with this thick growth are the so–called *crown* trees which bear foliage only at immense heights, having trunks up to twelve feet in width. The coastal area of Liberia, receiving the most rainfall, is dotted with lagoons, tidal creeks and marshes. Further inland the terrain rises slowly to a level of 1000 feet in a series of plateaus obscured by the dense undergrowth. Low mountains rise occasionally throughout the country, seldom reaching a height of more than 3,000 feet, with the exception of the Nimba and Wale mountains, which are 4,500 feet high.

Six rivers flow from the interior southwest to the Gulf of Guinea; they are not navigable for more than a few miles inland and are bounded by level land suitable for cultivation.

During the 8–month rainy season, hardly a day passes without an inch or more of rainfall, including sharp thunderstorms intermingled with a steady, tedious downpour.

History: In all the world, Liberia's birth as a nation was unique. The Kru, Mandingo and Gola ethnic groups had lived for countless centuries in Liberia prior to the arrival of the white man. Easily reached by the ships of slave traders plying the south Atlantic, local chiefs greedily sold conquered peoples to them. The market for field labor on the plantations of the southern colonies of America and in the West Indies was immense. Often, the traders took only the men for heavy work, leaving the women and children to fend for themselves.

The origins of Liberia took vague shape as early as 1691 when the Virginia legislature passed a law requiring slave owners who granted freedom to any to arrange for their passage out of the colony within half a year. Where they went was not spelled out, but a feeling was growing that danger lurked if both slaves and freed blacks mingled. But Blacks who were born free could remain.

More than a century passed before Virginia lawmakers once again considered the problems caused by slavery. An idea was put forth to establish a penal colony for any Blacks (in the judgment of their masters) fomenting rebellion. The 1789 slave revolt in Haiti had sent a chill through plantation owners. Thomas Jefferson had openly expressed the view that there should be a plan for colonizing blacks; he advocated a separation of the races, and that appeared to be the only reasonable way to accomplish this.

Finally the Virginia legislature, in the forefront of the movement, requested President James Monroe to obtain land outside the United States, preferably in Africa for this purpose. Voices were being raised against the slave trade (but not always *slavery),* and the idea of a colonization project developed. The African slave trade had been outlawed by the U.S. Constitution as of 1808.

Just before Christmas in 1816, with the support of clergymen from many denominations and with the backing of such influential friends as U.S. Speaker of the House Henry Clay, he helped to organize the *American Society for Colonizing the Free People of Color in the United States.* This group targeted two classes—originally, blacks *born* free, and subsequently *freedmen* (those who had been slaves). The plan was designed strictly for those who wanted to be resettled, and the Society had no intention to interefere with the institution of slavery. The intended communities would be established in Africa in the pattern of American society.

However noble these efforts might have appeared at the time, an underlying reason for the action might be found in Clay's own words in which he counseled that such colonization would "draw . . . off" free blacks.

Northerners emphasized the missionary nature of the plan and the uplifting from bondage of an exploited and oppressed people. Southerners, on the other hand, stressed the possibility that free blacks might incite a slave rebellion; remote Africa offered an ideal place to send such potential troublemakers.

Finally a sum was allotted by Congress to transport Africans rescued from illegal slave ships and resettle them on their home continent, but that sum was *not* for the purchase of land. The American Colonization Society (as it had come to be known) pressured the government for a portion of the money to be used for land purchase.

In 1820 a small expedition of 86 landed on a small island off the west coast of Africa, just south of Britain's earlier–established colony of Sierra Leone. The two government–appointed agents died within a few weeks from yellow fever or malaria which had no known cure at the time. Others in the party also died and the remaining settlers sought British protection in the nearby colony.

The following year another expedition suffered the same fate, but in 1822 a third group of colonists arrived about 240 miles south of Sierra Leone. The land had finally been purchased by the U.S. from local chieftains for about $300, but it was left to the Society to raise money for the maintenance of the colony.

By 1830 the tiny colonization effort had grown to a thousand people. This new "land of liberty" was named Liberia, and the colony continued to expand; trade increased because the settlers preferred American food which had to be brought in by ship.

The people united in 1839 to form the Commonwealth of Liberia under a governor appointed by the American Colonization Society, and in 1847 the Free and In-

Sketch of first settlement

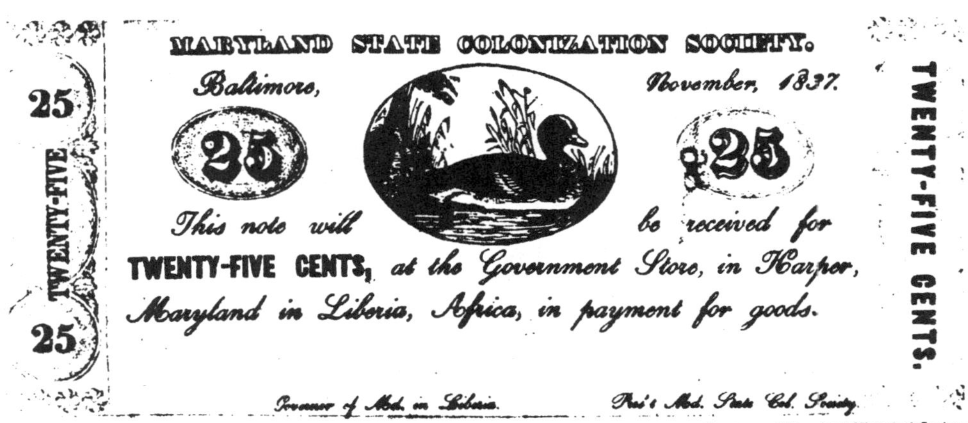

Courtesy of Maryland Historical Society

Sample of currency made available by Maryland

dependent Republic of Liberia was proclaimed. The new nation was recognized within a short time by the European powers, but not by the United States until 1862.

The life of the descendants of the freed slaves was harsh. This was a hostile land—a difficult place in which to survive, though the tribes of the interior were not aggressive people. It was not until the 1930's that there was any real penetration of the interior by the Americo–Liberians via routes hacked through the dense jungle.

Shortly after World War I there were rumors that the Americo–Liberians were engaging in slavery, using people from the tribes of the interior. A commission was established in 1929 to investigate the charges. The findings indicated that there was widespread shipment of so–called "contract labor" to neighboring colonies. There was evidence of involvement of government officials in this activity; the report also indicated that a custom of pawning people for terms of years to pay off debts existed.

Under pressure of other nations as a result of the report, the government resigned and some officials were prosecuted. The U.S. withheld recognition of the succeeding regime until it was clear that these practices had ended.

William V.S. Tubman was elected to a four–year term of office as president in 1944 and again in 1948. The constitution was amended in 1952 to permit him to serve another term of office. In later years, this formal and conservative executive accepted a "draft" election to office at the call of the *True Whig Party.*

Both President Tubman and Vice–President William R. Tolbert were reelected to four year terms of office in 1967 and 1971, but Tubman died suddenly in mid–1971. Tolbert was inaugurated the 10th president of Liberia in 1972 in ceremonies attended by a multitude of world dignitaries. He was reelected in 1975 and at the same time a constitutional amendment

M/Sgt. Samuel K. Doe

Assassinated President Tolbert in a "swearing–in suit"

was adopted providing for an eight–year term of office which he strongly supported; the president may no longer run for a second term. Tolbert was the first Liberian president to speak an interior tribal dialect.

The True Whig Party, named for a political party in the U.S. which was dominant in days before the Civil War, had for over a hundred years been run by the Americo–Liberians who had carefully excluded from "the club" all but their own, except in the 1970's when a few "safe" outsiders were invited to join. In efforts to promote reforms for more press freedom, expand educational opportunities and bring people from the interior into the elitist government, President Tolbert was said to have "let peasants into the kitchen."

Signs of trouble surfaced in 1979. When rice supplies dropped as inefficient and often growers found it more profitable to work as laborers on the large rubber plantations, the government proposed that the price per hundred pounds be raised from $22 to $26 to encourage greater production. Since rice is the staple food of the people, the plan touched off populist riots in Monrovia; there was widespread looting. About 50 people were killed and another 500 injured.

Ninety percent of the businesses in the capital were either partially or totally destroyed, with damage said to be about $50 million. President Tolbert imposed a curfew on the city and the Congress granted him emergency powers. These measures proved to be too late to stem the tide of rebellion. Enemies of the establishment surfaced and on April 12, 1980, a group of non–commissioned officers led by Master Sergeant Samuel K. Doe stormed the Executive Mansion, assassinated President Tolbert (and disemboweled him), seized power and set up a *People's Redemption Council (PRC)*. Doe (who installed himself as Commander–in–Chief and Chairman of the *PRC*) and his fellow non–commissioned officers represented a variety of back–country peoples who had traditionally been excluded from power by Americo–Liberians. (Members of the ethnic groups could achieve NCO status, but most of the upper ranks were dominated by Americo–Liberians.) Doe was a member of the Krahn people, while his two principal partners, Thomas Quiwonkpa and Weh Syen, were Gio and Kru respectively. Ten days later the *PRC* organized the public execution of thirteen high officials of the deposed government. Its birth in blood continued to characterize the Doe regime.

Rivalries soon brought bloody death within the ruling junta. Weh Syen, now a major–general and Vice-Chairman of the *PRC*, and four others were executed for plotting to kill Head of State Doe a year later. A *coup* involving Thomas Quiwonkpa, commander of the Armed Forces of Liberia (AFL) was discovered in November 1983. Granted clemency by Doe, he returned to his home base but ultimately fled the country when it was obvious his life was in danger.

During the same year Charles Taylor (the current president of Liberia) who was serving as Deputy Minister of Commerce in the Doe government, was charged with corruption. Among other things, he had ordered $1 million worth of bulldozers which never arrived. The money was stashed in American bank accounts and when he fled Liberia for his life, Taylor headed straight to the U.S. Arrested, he was represented by ex–Attorney General Ramsey Clark and held awaiting trial in an old Plymouth, Mass., jail. Hacksawing the window bars on the second floor, he escaped and made his way back to Africa. In 1988 Taylor, still a fugitive from American justice, was reportedly supported and trained by Moamer al–Qadhafi at a Libyan terrorist base.

Doe set about transforming himself into a civilian ruler, all the better to become the recipient of foreign aid from those who had any qualms about people who shoot their way into office. A new constitution was approved in July 1984, and in October 1985, general elections were held to implement its provisions. Doe, now head of the *National Democratic Party of Liberia (NDPL)* was elected president. The *NDPL* claimed victory by a slender margin: 50.9%, but the election was seen as utterly fraudulent by most observers. Under President Doe one saw the increased "ethnicizing" of the armed forces. Krahn people were given most of the authority in the military and the most significant posts in government. Ethnic rivalry intensified as a consequence.

The illiterate former master sergeant played the cold war obsessions of the United States symphonically. Successive U.S. administrations poured over $400 million into President Doe's eager hands. Liberia became an important listening post and staging base for CIA operations in central and southern Africa. By 1987 most of the money given Liberia couldn't be accounted for and the U.S. was forced to send in the auditors. Needless to say, it was an impossible mission. Doe simply refused to cooperate.

Shortly after the 1985 presidential elections, Thomas Quiwonkpa, the former army commander, returned to Liberia via Sierra Leone and staged a *coup* against his former companion in arms. It failed. Quiwonkpa was apprehended, killed, and dismembered. According to some reports (and a recurring theme in the Liberian tragedy) part of his body was consumed by his executioners. A nationwide pogrom against members of Quiwonkpa's Gio people and closely related Mano ensued. Execution, flogging, castration, dismemberment and rape became all too common as Liberia sank into bloody civil strife.

Liberia's civil war broke out in earnest in December 1989 when Charles Taylor led an invasion of insurgents from Côte d'Ivoire. They called themselves the *National Patriotic Front of Liberia (NPFL)*. The insurgents received support from Libya, Burkina Faso, Côte d'Ivoire and Liberians living abroad. From Libya they received training and money; Col. Qadhafi supported any group that would undermine American interests, and by now, America was deeply invested in Liberia. The Ivoirian president, Houphouët–Boigny, apparently condoned and the French Ambassador winked. For Houphouët–Boigny the support was personal. A step–daughter had been married to A.B. Tolbert, murdered by the Doe regime like his father, the Liberian president. Burkina Faso was at the time caught up in the excitement of leftist ideology and generously funded by Libya. The Burkinabé president, Blaise Compaoré, also needed to buff his revolutionary credentials. These had been seriously damaged by Compaoré having been implicated in the 1987 murder of his predecessor, Burkina Faso's charismatic young revolutionary, Thomas Sankara.

Mano and Gio youth flocked to Taylor's *NPFL* to avenge the sufferings of their people consequent to the 1985 attempted coup against Master–Sergeant Doe. The general disgust with Doe rallied others and soon Taylor's forces had overrun most of the country. Control of rich diamond–producing areas supported the rebellion. The violence was grim, the brutality bestial. The scale of operations favored a breakup of the Front as local warlords sought to control territory and resources. By August 1990 the situation had become anarchic and other West African states decided to intervene militarily to spare the nation. The military force they created was called ECOMOG, standing for the ECOWAS Monitoring Group. Charles Taylor would long remember the ECOMOG intervention, thinking it cheated him of total victory.

One of Taylor's principal aids, Prince Yormie Johnson, broke up the *National Patriotic Front* when he formed his own rebel force, called the *Independent National Patriotic Front of Liberia (INPFL)*. In September 1990 Johnson's forces captured President Doe when he left the besieged Executive Mansion to meet with the head of ECOMOG. He was cruelly tortured, mutilated and executed. The violence was preserved on videotape.

Other rebel groups formed around local leaders. *The United Liberation Movement of Liberia (ULIMO)* was organized by Alhaji Kromah in March 1991. This would later fragment along ethnic lines into *ULIMO–K* for Kromah's Mandingo faction, and *ULIMO–J* for a faction organized around Roosevelt Johnson and his Krahn supporters. All the while a bewildering series of agreements were brokered and signed, and just as quickly ignored or broken. Nothing and no one seemed able to curb the destructive violence. Nigeria, principal provider of the ECOWAS forces, with immense domestic political problems, decided it could no longer sustain the Liberian effort; its withdrawal effective April 1, 1994 was announced. The U.S. persuaded Nigeria to postpone the move.

By mid-1995 even Monrovia had become a wasteland in which teenage rebels cruised the streets with loaded automatic weapons and medium artillery. When rebel factions began ambushing ECOWAS forces, the Nigerian military ruler, Sani Abacha, had had enough. Faction leaders were summoned to Abuja, disarmament ordered, an election date set, and an interim ruler—Ruth Sando Perry, who had been a senator during the Doe period—appointed.

Multiparty elections were finally held in July 1997 and Charles Taylor emerged victorious. Seventy-five percent of the Liberian electorate placed their desires for peace in the hands of the man so much responsible for the devastating civil war.

Swearing in the Council of State (left to right) Chairman Wilton Sankawulo, Charles Taylor, Alhaji Kromah, George Boley, Oscar Quiah, Chief Tamba Tailor, on September 1, 1995. The thinly–threaded Council by mid–May was falling apart at the seams.

His *National Patriotic Party (NPP)* won an absolute majority in both houses of the legislature.

The extent of the destruction that has taken place in Liberia is staggering. More than 5% of the population has been killed and more than half a million Liberians have fled the country. Almost 50% of those remaining have been displaced from their home villages. Indeed, so great was the dislocation that the traditional electoral system based on geographical representation had to be abandoned, replaced by a country–wide, party based system of proportional representation.

Given the choice of conducting himself as a statesman or a warlord, Charles Taylor has opted for both, with a decided preference for the latter. Liberia has taken on the appearance of a security state. Security agencies are everywhere. The army has not yet been reformed and is still dominated by President Doe's Krahn. Then there are the National Police, responsible in theory for internal security. The Special Security Service (SSS), large and heavily armed, is another name for the presidential guard. The president's son, Charles Taylor, Jr., who is in his twenties and generally goes by the name of "Chuckie," heads up a secret military unit of some 600 fighters. The unit, named SWAP, includes Liberians and Gambians, as well as fighters from Burkina Faso and Guinea.

In September 1998 security forces assaulted the Monrovia headquarters of Roosevelt Johnson. Hundreds of SSS members, police, and other armed men employed automatic weapons, rocket–propelled grenades and mortars. Much of the 17–hour battle took place at night. Firing was indiscriminate, and an estimated 300 people, mostly Krahn, died. Johnson and a few followers attempted to gain refuge in the American Embassy and were pursued to its gates. Police opened fire on Johnson and seven others in the Embassy entryway, killing two and wounding others, including two U.S. Marines. Johnson was given asylum and later spirited out of the country. The U.S. State Department described the shoot–out as "below the rule of law."

One of Taylor's most influential opponents, Samuel Dokie, his wife, and his sister were found murdered, along with three other family members, in November 1998. The car in which they had been riding had been stopped at a police checkpoint and they were detained. The next day five SSS officers forcibly removed the Dokie party from police custody. That was the last they were seen before their bodies were discovered, mutilated and burned. Five SSS officers were charged in January 1999, but when the trial began in February, the prosecutor dropped charges against three of the five and a jury unanimously found the other two not guilty.

Power in Liberia tends to be personal and arbitrary, even occasionally just bizarre. In May 1999 President Taylor sacked almost his entire cabinet because they failed to attend a church service as he had ordered. "God is responsible for our survival," he said. "Anybody who does not love God will not serve on my Cabinet." It was just one of a string of surprising actions. The month before he decreed a month off for nearly the entire civil service, telling government workers to plant crops.

Power in Liberia is also coercive and frequently brutal. Most of the main faction leaders of the civil war live in exile, fearful for their lives had they remained in the country. Public complaints of harassment and abuse by state security forces are common in Liberia. Singled out as a particularly notorious perpetrator of flagrant human rights abuses is the special unit headed by the president's son, Chuckie Taylor.

Liberia's New Penal Law provides that a person is guilty of sedition if he "advocates rebellion, incites or promotes insurrection against state authorities by word of mouth." Sedition charges are little more than a means of silencing criticism. The Taylor regime is, shall we say, hypersensitive to criticism. In general, criticism seems to be viewed as dissidence and dissidence as treason.

The regime's intolerance of independent, critical thought is particularly manifest in its relations with the media. In March armed policemen surrounded the premises of two private radio stations in Monrovia, banned their operations, and seized their equipment "for being agents of people bent on creating security problems in Liberia" according to the Information Minister.

When independent newspapers staged a news blackout to protest the closure, the government ordered a tax audit. It also announced that state institutions would no longer advertise in the newspapers. Chillingly, the government statement indicated that "All newspapers that refuse to carry government stories and attend government functions are 'dissident' papers."

The international community has spent much of the past year seeking ways to curtail President Taylor's regional destabilization. A panel of experts created by the UN Security Council found "unequivocal and overwhelming evidence" of Liberian support for the RUF in Sierra Leone at all levels: "training, weapons and related *matérial*, logistical support, a staging ground for attacks and a safe haven for retreat and recuperation."

The effort is paid for by Sierra Leone di-

Rural gas station

WORLD BANK Photo

amonds mined by the rebels. The experts noted that at Kono, Sierra Leone, a Liberian said to be a representative of President Taylor supervised diamond operations. The rough stones were transferred to Liberia by Foday Sankoh's lieutenants, Sam Bokarie and Issa Sesay. The magnitude of this trade is seen in the statistics. Liberia's official diamond exports in 1998 were 8,000 carats, valued at $800,000. In the same year Belgium recorded imports from Liberia totally 2.56 million carats, valued at $217 million.

The December 2000 *Report of the Panel of Experts* documented several arms shipments to the RUF rebels. One shipment made in March 1999 involved 715 boxes of weapons and cartridges and 408 boxes of cartridge powder. It also included anti-tank weapons, surface-to-air missiles, and rocket propelled grenades and their launchers. The weapons came from a Ukrainian state-owned company, and end-user certificates indicated they were for the sole use of the Burkina Faso Ministry of Defense. The cargo was duly offloaded in Ouagadougou, the Burkina Faso capital, then trucked to Bobo Dioulasso. From there, said the panel, the bulk of them were trans-shipped "within a matter of days" to Liberia.

In March 2001 the UN Security Council voted unanimously to impose sanctions on all direct and indirect diamond exports. In addition, President Taylor and other officials are subject to travel restrictions. The council reiterated its 1995 arms embargo on Liberia.

Implementation of sanctions was delayed for 60 days at the request of the Economic Community of West African States (ECOWAS) to give President Taylor a chance to demonstrate behavioral change. By mid-April neighboring Guinea, in a state of virtual war with Liberia, requested the sanctions be expanded "to all commerce in wood and rubber, which are Liberia's main exports." When the May deadline came, President Taylor's attempts to avoid sanctions were found insufficient, and the sanctions commenced. They did not include the really meaningful sanctions on timber and rubber exports.

While international pressures built up against him, President Taylor actively crushed internal opposition. Four journalists were arrested and accused of spying in February 2001 after revealing the government had spent $50,000 to repair helicopters while civil servants had gone months without pay.

In March, when university students protested their continued detention and organized a rally to express solidarity and raise funds for them, Liberian security forces invaded the university. Members of the Special Operations Division indiscriminately flogged and beat students and faculty. Several homes near the university campus were broken into, looted and destroyed by marauding security men searching for students involved in the rally.

Liberian dissidents, members of *ULIMO-K*, continue to attack the northern border areas from bases in Guinea. The two countries remain on the brink of full-scale war.

Culture: There has been a basic divergence of cultural traditions in Liberia. The descendants of freed slaves living in the coastal regions were for the most part urban, Christian people. English is the language of choice and they prefer American styles in dress. They particularly valued formal attire, including, until lately, tuxedos and top hats notwithstanding the close, tropical climate.

The people of the interior were relegated to a rural life based on subsistence agriculture. Clothed in the manner of West Africans, with flowing styles and brilliant colors, all had a high rate of literacy. But schools have been wrecked and plundered during the strife of the last years and few remain.

Economy: Liberia's seven-year civil war pretty much destroyed its economy. GDP dropped 25 to 50% of its prewar levels, and per capita income sank to less than $200. By most UN indicators, Liberia vies with Sierra Leone as one of the two poorest countries in the world. At least 70% of the population is unemployed, and an equal percentage is illiterate.

Prior to 1990 the economy was primarily based on iron ore, rubber, timber, diamond and gold exports. With substantial investments in rich iron ore deposits, Liberia had become the world's fifth largest exporter, but war completely disrupted the industry.

Before the war the rubber industry generated over US$100 million annually in export earnings. Some 50,000 people earned their living through the industry. The Firestone rubber plantation, roughly 188 square miles containing 8 million rubber trees and 670 miles of roads, was the largest rubber plantation in the world. It has yet to recover fully from war damages. Many of its trees were overtapped by looters and will have to be cut down and replanted. It takes seven years for a rubber tree to mature and be ready for tapping.

In 2000 Liberia recorded exports of $61.6 million, led by rubber and timber. The figures represent a 23% increase over 1999 and probably illustrate feverish logging activity in Liberia's forests. Like much of Liberia's economic activity, the timber industry is dominated by Charles Taylor. Global Witness, an investigative human rights group based in the United Kingdom, examined the importance of timber for President Taylor and concluded it was more financially valuable to him and his security forces than was the diamond trade. A significant portion of timber-derived revenue, Global Witness concluded, was used by Taylor to train, arm and supply the RUF.

Taylor awarded a huge logging concession—more than 3.5 million acres—to the Oriental Timber Company (OTC) headed by one of his intimates, Gus van Kouwenhoven. OTC also has been given a virtual monopoly over the country's transport. It controls the port of Buchanan to which logging trucks deliver their cargo and then can pick up arms shipments. Roads built and maintained for timber extraction are thus conveniently used for weapons movement within Liberia and ultimate shipment to RUF fighters.

Logging is reportedly done at an unsustainable rate and threatens to devastate the Liberian rainforest within the decade. France and China, two destinations for Liberian timber, both voted against imposing an embargo on these "logs of war."

OTC is simply another indication of Liberia's continuing warlord economy. Charles Taylor funded his insurrection by seizing control of the diamond, gold and timber areas in the north and selling their resources. Diamond and other natural resource sales funded his weapons purchases, helped organized the administration of the state within a state he created, and contributed to his personal fortune.

President Taylor has built an elegant mansion with an Olympian-size swimming pool and basketball court for himself. His entourage tools around Monrovia in flashy and very expensive vehicles. Elsewhere in Monrovia there is no running water, and the electricity supply is more nonexistent than sporadic.

Future: At this point there are more negative than positive indicators. Charles Taylor's election eased the fighting in Liberia. Civil conflict had killed more than 200,000 people and displaced at least half the prewar population of 2.5 million, but despite what some saw as a end to the disturbances, it is clear that President Taylor has powerful enemies still capable of disrupting and destabilizing the county.

Taylor's continuing support of rebels in Sierra Leone is seen as a source of regional instability. "As long as Taylor is in power in Liberia, the Sierra Leone crisis will never end," charged the ECOMOG commander, General Timothy Shelpidi.

Bullying and brutality by state security forces have produced an appalling human rights record, and it is precisely that record, coupled with insecurity in the country and region, that will discourage potential investors from risking their money and international lenders from offering anything beyond the barest minimum. Without that investment and assistance, any Liberian renaissance is a long way off.

The Republic of Senegal

Independence Plaza, central Dakar

Courtesy: Embassy of Senegal

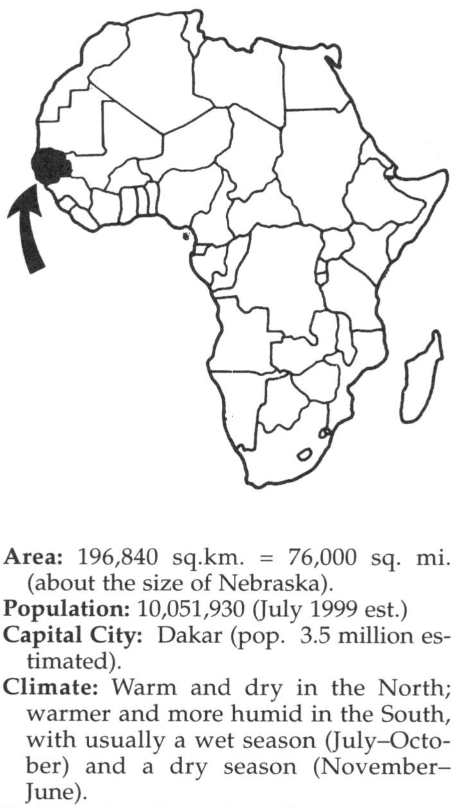

Area: 196,840 sq.km. = 76,000 sq. mi. (about the size of Nebraska).

Population: 10,051,930 (July 1999 est.)

Capital City: Dakar (pop. 3.5 million estimated).

Climate: Warm and dry in the North; warmer and more humid in the South, with usually a wet season (July–October) and a dry season (November–June).

Neighboring Countries: The Gambia is a finger–like projection extending eastward from the Atlantic coast to the interior; Mauritania (North); Mali (East); Guinea–Bissau, Guinea (South).

Official Language: French.

Other Principal Languages: Over 30. Prominently: Bambara, Pulaar (Peul), Diola (Jola), Malinke, Serere, Soninke, and Wolof, spoken by about 75% of the population.

Ethnic groups: Wolof 43.3%, Pular 23.8%, Serer 14.7%, Diola 3.7%, Mandinka 3%, Soninke 1.1%, European and Lebanese 1%, other 9.4%.

Principal Religions: Muslim 92%, indigenous beliefs 6%, Christian 2% (mostly Roman Catholic).

Chief Commercial Products: Fish, ground nuts (peanuts), petroleum products, phosphates, and cotton.

GNP per capita: 530 US$

Currency: CFA Franc, no longer tied to the French Franc.

Former Colonial Status: French Colony, a part of French West Africa (1895–1960). French commercial interests were active in Senegal prior to the formation of French West Africa.

Independence Date: June 20, 1960.

Chief of State: Abdoulaye Wade, President, since March 2000.

National Flag: Three vertical stripes of green, yellow and red, with a green star on the middle yellow stripe.

The Republic of Senegal, the westernmost portion of Africa, lies in a transitional zone between the steaming jungles of the Gold–Ivory Coast to the south and the endless, dry Sahara to the north. Its unique position has made it a true "crossroads" of the world—between Europe and Latin America, the United States and the Near and Far East, and finally, between South Africa and the European and American continents.

This is a flat, rolling plains country with characteristic grasslands and low tree vegetation. In the Southwest there is a small area of jungle and the coastline is often marsh or swampland. There are no high mountains in Senegal, but there are four large rivers flowing in parallel courses from east to west. These rivers are navigable to a substantial distance inland from the Atlantic, particularly during the wet season.

The hot breath of strong winds from the Sahara ushers in the traditional dry season each November. This wind of dry months, call the *harmattan* by the people, occasionally rises to almost torrential velocity, producing severe dust and sandstorms. In the last decade, all too frequently the wind is year–around, creating severe drought problems and intrusion of the Sahara at the rate of about four miles per year.

History: From the characteristics of the people who today live in Senegal, it is apparent that many centuries ago there was a migration of Hamitic–Sudanic groups from the Sudan area of the Nile River, but it is impossible to pinpoint the period of these migrations. These groups were well–established in approximately twenty distinct parts of the country at the time of the first European explorations. For details of early and colonial history see Historical Background and *The French in Africa.*

For a brief period in 1959 Senegal and the former French Soudan were joined to form the Mali Federation, which was ultimately dissolved when Senegal withdrew and proclaimed itself a republic. France had, prior to this move, granted full independence to the federation.

The constitution of Senegal first provided for a President with a seven–year term of office and a Prime Minister chosen by the legislature. The first president was Leopold Sedar Senghor, a well–known educator and literary figure, apart from his political stature, who had been a respected statesman not only in Senegal, but throughout the former French West Africa. The largest political party, the *Progressive Senegalese Union,* now the *Socialist Party,* was led by him. Political rivalry between the president and Prime Minister Mamadou Dia, led to an attempt by Dia to seize control of the government in 1962. This was quelled without bloodshed, but caused Dia's imprisonment and the adoption of a new constitution replacing the former parliamentary system with a presidential government for a period of time.

The *Socialist Party (PS)* won all 100 seats in the National Assembly in elections held in January 1973; all were selected from a single–party list. President Senghor was reelected to a five–year term.

Constitutional amendments provided for additional political parties and indefinite eligibility of the president to be reelected. Further provision was made for succession to the presidency by the prime minister after that office was reestablished. The additional political parties had little success; President Senghor was overwhelmingly reelected in 1978 to another five–year term.

In perhaps the most orderly transfer of power seen in post–independent present–day Africa, the aging president resigned his office on December 31, 1980, and turned it over to his able prime minister, Abdou Diouf, who completed his predecessor's term of office.

Senegal's first president, Hon. Leopold Sedar Senghor

In February 1983 President Diouf rolled up an impressive victory in democratic elections; both he and the *PS* received more than 80% of the vote. Seven other parties competed in the contest. The candidates for president included Mamadou Dia.

Democracy prevails in Senegal, but within limitations. Opposition to the administrations of Diouf centered around Abdoulaye Wade's *Senegalese Democratic Party (PDS),* the principal non–government in 1983 and 1988 elections. The result of these contests was heavily weighted in favor of Diouf's supporters. After brief bitter opposition following the 1988 elections, Wade and three other opposition leaders joined in a coalition government with the socialists; this lasted until late 1992 when they resigned, complaining that they had been influential on only minor and trivial decisions.

The real reason for the resignations was a desire to freely compete in early 1993 elections. Because the opposition was divided into five parties, including one devoted to the cause of the rebellious Casamance people, Diouf won handily. The same situation prevailed in March 1996 when the president was elected to yet another term.

May 1998 legislative elections confirmed the dominance of the *PS,* which won 93 out of 140 parliamentary seats. Its closest rival, Abdoulaye Wade's *PDS,* won only 23 seats. New electoral procedures had been voted for the election and these gave a big advantage to the better organized and financed *PS.* Seventy deputies were elected by proportional representation; 50 others were elected in simple majority districts. By this mixed procedure, President Diouf's *PS* won a marginal 50.2% of the vote, but won 66% of parliamentary seats. The election was also important for being Senegal's first organized by an independent electoral commission.

The new upper house of Senegal's parliament, the Senate, was chosen in early January 1999 by an electoral college composed of deputies and regional, rural and municipal councilors. Forty–five members of the sixty–seat house were chosen in this fashion and the *PS,* which controls local governments throughout the country, won every position. Twelve additional seats were appointed by President Diouf and three members were elected by Senegalese living abroad.

Amid mounting tensions, Senegal held the first round of its presidential elections in February 2000. Eight candidates were on the ballot, but only four had any reasonable expectations of electoral success. The two principal candidates were familiar opponents. President Diouf was the standard bearer of the PS and the long-time opposition leader, Abdoulaye Wade represented the *Parti Démocratique Sénégalais* (*PDS*).

After forty years in power, the *PS* had become increasingly dysfunctional as a

political family. Two *PS* defectors, both one-time party heavyweights, entered strong candidacies, made stronger by their ability to criticize Diouf and the PS from inside knowledge. Djibo Leity KÂ, representing the *Union for Democratic Renewal* (*URD*), had served in various ministerial positions under Diouf and was part of the *PS* leadership until he lost favor in 1998. Moustapha Niasse, a former foreign minister, enjoyed an international reputation and access to considerable campaign financing.

Niasse had announced his candidacy in June 1999 and was promptly expelled from the *PS.* Without denying his own past, Niasse was devastatingly critical of the present regime. Senegal was, he said, only a façade democracy. Hinting at the regime's corruption, he spoke of putting an end to "illicit enrichment practices, the Mafia stranglehold of the economy, the threats on the democratic system."

At 73 years of age, Abdoulaye Wade was the grand old man of Senegalese opposition, but the darling of the young. His campaign stops drew enthusiastic crowds. Change was in the air and "*Sopi,*" the Wolof word for change, was the chant of the crowds. If elected, he promised, he would organize a referendum to dissolve the national assembly and change the constitution—change the system.

Change, indeed, was what the Senegalese voters wanted. With a host of international observers watching, the usual mechanisms of electoral manipulation were put aside. Dramatically, President Diouf failed to obtain a majority in the first round of voting. In the runoff, Wade won 58.5 percent of the vote. Diouf graciously admitted defeat and announced his retirement from politics.

Change, indeed, was what the Senegalese voters wanted. With a host of international observers watching, the usual mechanisms of electoral manipulation were put aside. Dramatically, President Diouf failed to obtain a majority in the first round of voting. In the runoff, Wade won 58.5% of the vote. Diouf graciously admitted defeat and announced his retirement from politics.

The winds of change have blown hard in Senegal during the past year. President Wade moved quickly to draft a new, more democratic constitution. Among a number of important changes, presidential terms were reduced to five years from seven. The Senate, an ineffective retirement home for faded PS politicians, was abolished and the National Assembly reduced from 140 members to 120. The president granted the right to dissolve the Assembly (dominated by the PS) after two years of existence. The right to form opposition parties was entrenched; the Prime Minister's duties were specified and enhanced and the judiciary given more independence. For the first time women were given equal property rights with men.

In early January 2001 Senegalese voters in massive number returned to the polls and voted for more *sopi.* Ninety-four percent approved the new constitution. Elections to choose the members of the new National Assembly were held at the end of April and a coalition of 40 pro-Wade parties calling itself "*Sopi*" swept the field. In a complicated voting procedure which combined single member districts with national lists chosen by proportional voting, *Sopi* won 90 of 120 seats.

The Caliph of Murid

The Caliph of Tijanis

The landslide victory gave President Wade a free hand to effect the changes his constituents demanded. Some feared Senegal had moved from one single-party system to another.

Casamance

The *Movement of Democratic Forces of Casamance* (*MFDC*) has been intermittently fighting some 16 years for the region's independence. Located south of The Gambia, the province has long thought of itself as exploited, virtually colonized by northerners. Unlike most north/south conflicts in Africa, the struggle in Casamance does not pit an Islamic north against an animist south because most of the region's people are Muslims, including a slight majority of the dominant ethnic group, the Diola. Instead, the conflict is economic.

Casamance produces peanuts, like the rest of Senegal, but also has rich fishing grounds off its coast and has over the years become a tourist Mecca for Europeans. It produces cotton for northern factories, and its forests provide charcoal for Dakar. Coastal waters hold the promise of petroleum yet to be found. Despite the region's wealth, however, Casamançais have seen few benefits. They question where the money has gone and deplore the degradation of the region's resources.

Industrialized fishing fleets are depleting coastal waters, and forests are shrinking rapidly. They note that traditional rice cultivation, based on natural inundation, was destroyed by the importation of cheap foreign rice. At the same time they point out huge investments in the north to create a rice industry based on much more expensive damming and irrigation. Insufficient development of roads has hampered the marketing of local fruits and vegetables; Casamançais oranges and mangos rot on the ground. Currently, one of the most productive crops is "*yamba,*" the local name of cannabis. Driven by a huge demand in Dakar, *yamba* has become one of the principal sources for rebel financing.

Over the years the struggle has resulted in thousands of deaths. The French, with military bases in Senegal, quietly assisted the Senegalese army in putting down the rebellion until 1997 when they began to urge negotiation between the parties. The secessionist leader, Abbé Daimacoune Senghor, was urged to negotiate on the basis of greater autonomy, rather than insisting on full independence. By the beginning of 1998 Abbé Senghor himself was calling for peace, but the rebel field commanders, whose troops sometimes conducted themselves as much as bandits as anything else, have been harder to convince.

The rebels have for years been able to replenish their arms supply through weapons smuggled from Guinea-Bissau, where much of the army is made up of

A small industry: military arm patches
WORLD BANK photo

ethnic groups closely akin to the *MFDC* fighters. Mines, too, were secured and laid with lethal consequences for the Senegalese army. Thus one can understand the willingness of the army to intervene to support President Vieira when the Guinea-Bissau army rose in rebellion against him in June 1998. It provided an opportunity to destroy *MFDC* support and training bases protected in Guinea-Bissau. If successful, the intervention would prevent the installation of a new government thought to favor the *MFDC.* Vieira had already drawn closer to Senegal, encouraged by France, which had permitted Bissau's entry into the franc zone. The two countries had signed agreements on sharing future offshore oil discoveries, and Bissau had destroyed its stock of surplus weapons to reduce arms smuggling across the border.

The era of cooperation came to an end with General Mané's attempted coup and the unsuccessful intervention of both Senegal and Guinea to support President Vieira. The civilian government of President Kumba Ialá, who replaced Vieira, had difficulty controlling its armed forces. The army closed an eye to the cross border activities of *MFDC;* its commander, General Mané, was alleged to have helped smuggle arms to the Casamance separatists. They paid with income from the cannabis trade.

With General Mané's death in November 2000, the political situation changed dramatically, but tensions between the two countries remained. Guinea Bissau's government accused some members of the *MFDC* of trying to kill president Ialá and of fighting beside General Mané in the Novmber 2000 show-down in which he was killed. The army subsequently launched an offensive to push the *MFDC* guerrillas back into Senegal.

By March 2001 even President Jammeh of The Gambia, where *MFDC* had also found refuge, recognized the changed circumstances in the region. After a three-day visit to Senegal, Jammeh said his government would never allow forces to attack Senegal from The Gambia. That, of course, remains to be seen, but it does suggest the pressures on the rebel commanders to negotiate seriously.

Culture: The gleaming beauty of Dakar, the busy seaport and capital of Senegal, is almost unique among the cities of Africa. The city has grown by leaps and bounds and is peopled by modern, urban dwellers of many cultures. There are, of course, inevitable slum areas, which have grown dramatically in recent years when the eastern part of Senegal has been gripped by drought.

With two million inhabitants Dakar can boast a cyber café on nearly every corner in the center city, but its transportation system is paralyzed by rush hour gridlock that rivals Lagos. Urban transport is one of President Wade's first and most demanding problems. Dakar's buses are known for air pollution. The city's drivers are noted for bad manners and frayed tempers. Rubbish collection, too, tests the patience of those living in the capital.

Wielding great influence in this largely Islamic nation are "the brotherhoods." The clout of these conservative societies is through their religious hold on the people. Their opinions strongly influence the political, commercial and social life of the country.

The most numerous of these is the *Tijanis* (Tea–*jan*–is), although the *Murid* (*Moo*–reed) owns the largest peanut plantations and is considered the most influential. The *Hadria* (*Hod*–ria) is the third. Each has its own spiritual leader, or *Caliph General* (pronounced *Hah*–leaf). The power of this high office is passed down through the family.

In November 1998 the last living Senegalese veteran of World War I died, a few hours before the 80th anniversary of the armistice that ended the war. Abdoulaye N'Daye, aged 104, was the last of thousands of black Africans who had been recruited to defend France during the Great War. He was to have received France's highest award, the Legion of Honor, at ceremonies commemorating the conclusion of hostilities in 1918.

Economy: Senegal's economy has been totally dependent upon the production of peanuts for the past three decades; production now exceeds well over one million metric tons a year, made possible by improved methods of cultivation and development of plantations to replace smaller farms. France supported peanut prices until 1967. Production has been uneven since then because of adverse weather conditions. Other problems have included what the government has termed "peasant malaise." This actually was a boycott consisting of a refusal to (1) grow peanuts and (2) to market them through the national monopoly. Higher prices and immediate payment led to widespread smuggling of the crop into The Gambia. (The direction reversed periodically when prices were higher in Senegal than in The Gambia.)

The state–run monopoly pays only half of the export price to the farmer; the remainder is supposed to be held against the threat of low yields in future years. In reality, it is used for government support and ordinary expenses, and a small part simply disappears into the teeming bureaucracy of Dakar.

The dependence on peanuts has been markedly reduced since the early 1980s. A drought parched the land for more than a decade, forcing the abandonment of marginal land and decreased peanut crops. The price of this primary export took a tumble (but has risen since the late 1980s). One of the largest obstacles to higher Senegalese prosperity is U.S. protection of its own peanut farmers (paid for by U.S. consumers). A switch to other crops has been steadily underway, but with limited success. In spite of being agriculturally–based, the per capita annual income of Senegal is relatively high for West Africa.

Periodic loans from the International Monetary Fund have enabled Senegal economically to survive. The conditions for these loans have been difficult: austerity and more austerity. This has included disposing of several government monopolies and reduced salaries for government workers, as well as the "final" solution: elimination of government jobs.

Nutrient-rich cold waters off the Senegalese coast have made an extremely rich fishing area, but since the arrival of foreign trawlers, particularly from the EU, fish stocks have crashed. Several hundred trawlers from Spain, the Netherlands, Portugal and other EU nations have badly overfished the area. Senegal's agreement with the EU is up in 2001. Faced with Morocco's refusal to renew its agreement, the EU is bringing pressure on Senegal to increase fishing quotas by an unconscionable 61%. EU trawlers already have an annual catch of 100,000 tons. Biologists warn that fish stocks are at a critical point.

One bright economic note is the interest a number of independent oil companies have shown in Senegal's off-shore prospects. ROC (Australia) has invested heavily in three blocks known as the Casamance blocks. The concession covers over 8,000 sq. km. and lies north of two oil discoveries made by Houston-based Vanco oil company.

Almost a million Europeans are annually attracted to Senegal's beautiful beaches and warm sun during northern winter months.

The Future: Given the expectations raised by the election, the burdens on President Wade are enormous. The economy is sluggish at best. The Casamance insurgency remains vexatious and unresolved. Relations with Guinea-Bissau, where the Casamance rebels often retreat, remain tense.

MARDI 9 FEVRIER 1999
28e année - N° 8607
ISSN 0856-0793
150 Fcfa
FRANCE 8FF CÔTE D'IVOIRE 250 Fcfa GABON 350 Fcfa • CAMEROUN 300 Fcfa GUINEE, TOGO, BURKINA FASO, MALI 250 Fcfa

le soleil

Mamadou Diop présidera le Sénat

A quelques jours de la date probable, en tout cas annoncée, de la première réunion du Sénat, lundi prochain, les supputations vont bon train quant à la liste complémentaire des 12 sénateurs que le président de la République doit désigner et à la personnalité qui dirigera la nouvelle institution. De nombreux noms circulent sur la composition de la liste présidentielle non encore rendue publique si elle est déjà élaborée.

A ce niveau, il n'y a encore aucune certitude. Tout au plus tient-on pour hautement probable l'inclusion dans la liste complémentaire de personnalités du Parti libéral sénégalais (PLS, formation dirigée par Ousmane Ngom) et, sans doute également, du PDS/R de Serigne Diop. Cette ouverture à des formations non-socialistes permettrait de décolorer quelque peu une chambre sinon totalement verte. Les observateurs ont noté que lors d'un débat à ce propos au bureau politique du P.S., le Premier secrétaire, Ousmane Tanor Dieng, soutenu, dit-on, par le seul Abdourahim Agne, avait défendu la nécessité d'octroyer des sièges, par la liste supplémentaire, à des personnalités non socialistes. L'osmose entre le Premier secrétaire et le président du parti autorise à conclure que l'esprit d'ouverture du Premier secrétaire correspond à l'option faite au sommet.

La décision est également prise, apparemment, en ce qui concerne le poste de président de la deuxième chambre du parlement, qui semble maintenant acquis à Mamadou Diop, l'actuel maire de la ville de Dakar. Des recoupements effectués de diverses sources et des démarches entreprises par le maire lui-même confirment que le poste lui reviendra. Mamadou Diop, qu'il ne nous a pas été possible de joindre hier soir, se concerte depuis deux jours avec des membres de sa famille, des camarades du parti à Dakar, des dignitaires de la communauté lébou et certains de ses collaborateurs au sein du conseil municipal.

L'attribution de la présidence du Sénat à Mamadou Diop sera lue comme un carrière politique personnelle particulièrement riche pour l'ancien ministre et responsable politique.

Mamadou Diop n'hésitera certainement pas à passer d'une municipalité, fût-elle la plus grande et puissante, avec son budget de 13 milliards de francs, à la position de troisième personnage de l'Etat. D'autant qu'il déménagera de l'Hôtel de ville au siège flambant neuf du nouveau Sénat, qui a commencé d'être édifié sur le terrain de la place Soweto à l'angle du boulevard Mandela face à l'Assemblée nationale.

Mais il ne peut y avoir de cumul de mandat à ce niveau et le maire actuel de Dakar chercherait, apprend-on, à obtenir soit une période transitoire durant laquelle il pourrait cumuler, soit à placer un de ses adjoints directs à l'Hôtel de ville, son souci étant de jouer un rôle dans la mairie après Mamadou Diop. Ces intentions qui lui sont prêtées n'ont cependant pas vraiment de chances de se concrétiser. Du moins peut-on raisonnablement arriver à cette conclusion, le cumul étant difficilement défendable, et de toute façon impossible, le choix d'un maire pour Dakar étant d'autre

Le président Abdou Diouf, accueilli hier matin à son arrivée au Palais des congrès du Méridien-Président par le président du conseil de l'UE, Joschka Fischer, le président du conseil des ministres ACP, George Saitoti et le commissaire européen, Joao de Deus Pinheiro.

UE-ACP

Les exigences d'une nouvelle coopération

Le président Abdou Diouf a officiellement ouvert hier, le premier round des négociations sur les accords de la future Convention qui prendra le relais de celle de Lomé IV, dès février 2000.

Devant un parterre de représentants de 87 pays ACP (Afrique-Caraibes-Pacifique) et de l'Union Européenne (UE), il a plaidé pour une coopération mutuellement avantageuse aux deux partenaires. Ce partenariat, souhaité par les deux parties, va certainement s'établir dans un contexte marqué par de nouvelles exigences. Le chef de l'Etat s'est en effet appesanti sur les défis que doivent relever les pays ACP en terme de politiques macro-économiques de qualité. Tandis que le président du Conseil de l'UE, Joschka Fischer, a demandé aux Etats ACP de s'inscrire dans une dynamique de promotion des valeurs démocratiques, dans un environnement de paix et de sécurité.

PAGES 4 - 5

G 15
Abdou Diouf en Jamaïque

CAHIER ECONOMIE
Riz : la filière tourne mieux
Production record, entente sur le prix du paddy

A leading newspaper in Dakar

The Republic of Sierra Leone (pronounced See–*air*–uh Lee–*own*)

Panoramic View of Freetown Photo by Doug Brooks

Area: 72,326 sq. km. = 27,900 sq. mi. (slightly larger than West Virginia)
Population: 5,296,651 (July 1999 est.)
Capital City: Freetown (Pop. 530,000, estimated).
Climate: Equatorial, very warm and humid.
Neighboring Countries: Guinea (North and Northwest); Liberia (Southeast).
Official Language: English.
Official Language: English (regular use limited to literate minority).
Other Principal Languages: Mende (principal vernacular in the south), Temne (principal vernacular in the north), Krio (English-based Creole, a lingua franca and a first language for 10% of the population but understood by 95%. The dominant language of the younger generation).
Ethnic groups: 20 native African tribes 90% (Temne 30%, Mende 30%, other 30%), Creole 10% (descendants of freed Jamaican slaves who were settled in the Freetown area in the late-eighteenth century, refugees from Liberia's recent civil war), small numbers of Europeans, Lebanese, Pakistanis, and Indians.
Principal Religions: Muslim 60%, indigenous beliefs 30%, Christian 10%.
Chief Commercial Products: Diamonds, rutile, cocoa, coffee, and fish.
GNP per capita: 140 US$.
Currency: Leone.
Former Colonial Status: British Colony (1808–1961)
Independence Date: April 19, 1961.
Chief of State: Ahmad Tejan Kabbah, President. Returned to Freetown on March 10, 1998.
National Flag: Three equal horizontal stripes of green, white and blue.

Sierra Leone lies on the legendary Gold Coast of the immense portion of Africa that extends westward into the Atlantic above the equator. Its climate is almost identical with that of the Congo River basin to the southeast—hot, rainy and oppressively humid. The Freetown area along the seacoast receives 150 inches of rain each year, and the relative humidity seldom drops below 80%. The coastal belt, averaging sixty miles in width, is a region of dense mangrove swamps quite similar to the Florida Everglades.

Stretches of wooded hill country rise from the coastal belt to gently rolling plateaus in the North. Mountains tower to heights of 6,000 feet in the southeast area near the Moa River. Although there is a nominally dry season from November to April, heavy rains, especially in July, August and September, contribute to the dense, jungle growth characteristic of portions of Sierra Leone. This compact green vegetation contains the many species of the rain forest, but few of the hoofed animals of the African plains.

History: Sierra Leone was thinly populated by the Mende and Temne people, who date back to unknown times when the Portuguese explorer Pedro de Cintra visited the coastal area in 1460. Impressed by the beauty of the mountains of the southeast, he name the territory *Sierra Leone*—"Lion Mountains." For details of earlier and colonial history, see Historical Background and *The British in Africa.*

Following achievement of independence in 1961, the constitutional parliamentary government was controlled by the *Sierra Leone People's Party (SLPP),* led initially by Sir Milton Margai, and, after his death in 1964, by his brother, Sir Albert Margai. Elections held in 1967 were hotly contested by a rival party, the *All People's Congress,* led by Siaka Stevens. The Mende and Temne people of the interior supported the *SLPP* and the coastal Creoles favored the *APC.* A pre–election attempt of Margai to outlaw the *APC* failed. Early returns indicated that the *APC* had captured 32 seats in the parliament to 28 for the *SLPP.* Governor General Sir Henry Josiah Lightfoot Boston (a Creole) quickly gave the oath of office to Siaka Stevens, making him Prime Minister. The military arrested both Stevens and Boston ten minutes later.

The National Reformation Council, established by the officers, continued in power until April 1968. Both Margai and Stevens were imprisoned and later exiled—Margai died in 1980 near Washington, D.C.

A group of non–commissioned officers ousted the *National Reformation Council* in 1968 and brought Siaka Stevens from exile in Guinea to be Prime Minister. He ruled during the following years with increasing repression, subduing rioting of Margai supporters in the interior with army troops. A state of emergency was proclaimed in late 1970 because of continued agitation against Stevens.

Sierra Leone became a republic in 1971, with Siaka Stevens as President for a five-year term. In 1978 Stevens proposed a constitutional referendum to create a single-party state. Not surprisingly, 97.1% voted "Yes." In one northern province not one brave soul voted "No." Stevens was sworn in for a 7-year term under the new constitution, the sole party being his *APC.* He rejoiced in the voters' rejection of "... the worn-out, multiparty (system) ... inherited from our colonial master, Britain."

Much of Sierra Leone's current civil strife began during Siaka Stevens' repressive single-party rule. As his term of office was drawing to an end in 1985, the elderly Stevens designated Army Chief Maj. General Joseph Momah his successor. Momah sought to continue the single-party, authoritarian rule of Stevens and the *All-People's Congress* (*APC*).

President Momoh made some effort to bring order to the chaos which gripped the economy. Subsidies of rice and fuel were gradually reduced. Diamond smuggling continued in spite of efforts to suppress it. The company buying and exporting diamonds closed its doors in 1988 because of instability associated with smuggling.

Austerity measures insisted on by the IMF lowered the standard of living. Government corruption became pathological. When workers were forced to appear personally to pick up their pay in cash, it turned out that 75% of those listed as employees didn't exist. A rebel insurgency led by Foday Sankoh, aided by Charles Taylor's *National Patriotic Front of Liberia,* broke out in the early 1990s. Increasingly Momah had no control over corruption, government, or insurgency. His poor prosecution of the war against Sankoh's *Revolutionary United Front* (*RUF*) and failure to support his troops in that effort, led junior officers, under Captain Valentine Strasser, to take power in late April 1992.

Under the inexperienced Strasser, then 26 years old, the situation continued to disintegrate. Senior officers lost control over their troops and being a soldier became regarded as a license to murder and steal. His administration collapsed and he was replaced by an army colleague, Brigadier Julius Bio, on January 16, 1996.

Faced with economic and political chaos, Bio agreed to hold elections to restore civilian rule. The agreement to hold elections in March 1996 was implemented and, despite harassment and intimidation, voters went to the polls and chose members of the legislature and a new president.

As testimony to Sierra Leone's fragmented political culture, 13 parties competed and six managed to elect members to the House of Representatives. The largest number, 27, came from the *Sierra Leone's People's Party* (*SLPP*), followed by 17 seats for the *United National People's Party* (*UNPP*).

The *SLPP*'s Ahmad Tejan Kabbah and the *UNPP*'s John Karefa-Smart topped the field of ten presidential contenders, and in the runoff election Kabbah was declared the victor with 59.5% of the vote. A former UN official, he slowly built confidence in his leadership to the extent that in late 1996 the RUF agreed to discontinue its rebellion and surrender all arms. What appeared a promising beginning came to an end in May 1997 when the army revolted over unpaid wages, threatened cutbacks in their rice rations, and possible reductions in force were announced by Kabbah. (He had little trust in the army that had failed so miserably against the *RUF.* Indeed, it was actually thought to be working with the rebels: soldiers by day, bandits by night.)

A corporal, Tamba Gborie, organized the coup and led his followers to Central Prison where they freed Major Johnny Paul Koroma, awaiting trial for conspiring to overthrow Kabbah in September 1996. Koroma was recruited to head an *Armed Forces Revolutionary Council* (*AFRC*) that would govern Sierra Leone. President Kabbah fled his capital, and Sierra Leone descended into anarchy.

Soldiers looted indiscriminately and within days were joined by fighters of the rebel front hungry for a share of the spoils. Their common experience was poverty and they expressed their sense of injustice in robbery and mayhem. The coup was universally rejected, by both the population of Sierra Leone and the international community.

Captain Valentine Strasser

ECOWAS foreign ministers met in Conakry in late June to see if they could negotiate a return to civilian rule, but diplomacy with the *AFRC* failed. The army and its allies seemed more interested in plunder than peace. The West African states decided to intervene militarily.

Warfare would be waged for nearly ten months, involving three major components. ECOWAS forces, army mutineers and their guerrilla rebel allies, and groups of traditional hunter societies called Kamajors, loyal to the deposed Kabbah. It is likely the Kamajors had been armed and trained by private security companies employed by owners of Sierra Leone's diamond mines, but true or not, they became a major element in the ensuing struggles.

In February 1998 ECOWAS forces (dominated by Nigerian troops) drove the military junta from Freetown. President Kabbah was triumphantly returned in March to his war-ravaged capital. Mutineers and rebels had pretty much stolen anything of value. Schools and Fourah Bay University were stripped; students' chairs were used as kindling. They even sacked foreign embassies before withdrawing to the countryside where their depredations continued with murderous intensity. Opponents of the AFRC, local supporters of President Kabbah, members of the Kamajor hunting groups were singled out for particularly venomous reprisals.

The tenuous control Kabbah's ECOWAS-supported government had over the country was dramatized when the rebels renewed their offensive against the government in late 1998. In early January they launched a brutal attack on Kabbah's capital. The cruelty one had come to associate with the rebels seemed to reach new heights. Random killing, mutilation, and rape were horrifically widespread. The entire populations of residential compounds were executed for refusing to obey instructions to dance and make music on the streets. Death became a game where executioners, high on alcohol, cocaine, or other drugs, teasingly chose whom to kill, whom to spare.

After nine days of intense fighting, the rebels, who had come close to capturing the city, withdrew. A fifth of all the capital's buildings were destroyed as the country descended into some hellish lower depths seeking a modern Dante to describe its suffering and loss.

The international community, with heavy American involvement, brought pressure on both parties to work out a power-sharing solution. Negotiations went on throughout spring and early summer 1999. An accord between government and rebels was signed in July in Lome, Togo, and its content could not give heart to humanitarians. Violence, fear, and intimidation received their reward.

The Lome Accord named the *RUF* leader, Foday Sankoh, Chairman of the Commission for the Management of Strategic Minerals, National Reconstruction, and Development, with the rank of vice-president. In effect, Sankoh was put in charge of Sierra Leone's diamond production. President Kabbah was not allowed to dismiss him from this post. Sankoh was also given the right to name four members of the cabinet in key slots. Major Johnny Koroma, head of the *Armed Forces Revolutionary Council* (*AFRC*) that overthrew President Kabbah, was named Chairman of the Commission for the Consolidation of Peace.

Provisions were also signed for the demobilization of combatants. Rebels would be disarmed and reintegrated into civil society; some were integrated into the army. For those who elaborated, directed, and implemented a brutal policy of rape, mayhem, murder, and maiming, amnesty would be granted.

Reality on the ground was, unexpectedly, different. UN peacekeepers received little cooperation from *RUF* leaders. Few rebels turned in their arms, and peacekeepers were not permitted to enter areas controlled by the *RUF*. Rebel diamond production continued and was easily filtered out through The Gambia, Burkina Faso or Liberia.

In May 2000 when the Nigerian-led ECOWAS peacekeeping force announced its departure, the rebels attacked, held several hundred UN peacekeepers captive, and advanced on Freetown. British intervention saved the capital and the Kabbah government.

Three things have changed the Sierra Leone situation. First, the May British intervention effectively prevented the *RUF* from taking Freetown, and thus the country. Second, Foday Sankoh, the *RUF* leader, was captured and imprisoned in May. Third, the international pressure on Charles Taylor, the Liberian president, to end his support of the rebels has been consistently ratcheted upwards.

The direct British intervention was critical in creating a modicum of optimism in Sierra Leone. "We have," one British official was quoted as saying, " a responsibility for a dying African colony." British "advisers" occupy critical positions in both the Sierra Leone police and finance ministry. To all intents and purposes, they run the defense ministry. A contingent of 400 British soldiers is retraining the armed forces.

The rebels, now led by General Issa Sessey, signed a ceasefire in November 2000 and have found new areas to ravage and plunder as part of Charles Taylor's efforts to destabilize neighboring Guinea. The UN has the largest number of troops in any peacekeeping mission in Sierra Leone—more than 10,000—and has been permitted by the *RUF* to share areas under its control. The *RUF* still refuses to disarm or surrender its control over the diamond producing areas, which leaves the Kabbah government's budget dependent on foreign aid.

President Kabbah's term of office expired in March 2001, but both presidential and parliamentary elections have been postponed six months. There is little prospect of meaningful elections in the near term. As long as rebels control most of the countryside, donors will remain unwilling to provide funds to establish new electoral rolls necessary for the conduct of any election.

In the meantime, a demonstrably ineffective and increasingly unpopular government remains in nominal charge, propped up by British and multilateral forces and sustained by foreign financial assistance. With government and parliament likely to extend their tenure for six-month periods during the foreseeable future, Sierra Leoneans are increasingly calling for an Interim Government chosen by a national conference of civil society groups and political organizations.

Culture: The Mende of the North and the Temne of the South constitute 60% of the population, largely rural people dwelling in the interior regions. There are 18 smaller groups each with its own language and cultural traditions in the inland area. Krio, the "pidgin English" of the coastal Creoles, is widely spoken among all of the ethnic groups of the nation, a language perpetuated by many folk tales and proverbs.

President Ahmad Tejan Kabbah

Economy: The Kabbah government has little control over the country's territory and no control over its economy. Roads have been devastated by warfare, and it's often easier for farmers to smuggle their commercial produce, coffee and cocoa primarily, across borders. A recent lull in overt conflict has permitted the government to begin a program to repair feeder roads in and around Freetown. The aim is to boost trade by easing the flow of traffic in and out of the capital. Housing remains in critically short supply in the capital.

Sierra Leone's greatest riches, diamonds, lie in areas controlled by the rebels. The bulk of diamond production is smuggled to Liberia. Official figures show the value of Sierra Leone's uncut diamonds dropped from $66 million in 1998 to $31 million in 1999. Simultaneously, the value of diamond exports from Liberia, with virtually no diamond deposits at all, rose from $268 million in 1998 to $298 million in 1999. This nearly perfect match of decline and increase is less coincidence than connivance—of Liberian authorities.

The *RUF* economy is founded on diamonds which fund their arms purchases. De Beers estimates that $70 million worth of rough diamonds were produced in rebel-held areas of Sierra Leone in 1999. Additional income is derived from the sale of looted property. Arms are sourced in Ukraine or other eastern European states and supplied to the rebels through Liberian or Burkinabé connivance.

To stop the flow of what are called "blood" or "conflict" diamonds, the government has introduced a certification system. Mining licenses have increased from 400 to 700; dealers' licenses have risen from 105 to 144. The government generated about $10 million from these licenses in 2000—up from $1.5 million in 1999.

Warfare has similarly deprived the government of revenues from Sierra Leone's second most valuable export, rutile, a titanium dioxide. The first legal shipload in three years left the country in June 1999, but many of the mining sites for both rutile and bauxite are still in rebel hands.

Given the government's lack of control over the economy, at least 60% of its budget is being funded by grants and loans from international financial institutions. There has been some recent tantalizing evidence of off-shore oil deposits, and the government has announced that deep water offshore drilling of oil and gas will begin in January 2005.

The Future: Much will depend on the effectiveness of UN sanctions against Charles Taylor and Liberia. Taylor, the *RUF's* patron, has profited handsomely from regional disorder, and only when those profits are strangled will arms to the rebels be cut off.

The Republic of Togo

A balanced converstion in Lomé

AP/Wide World Photo

Area: 56,950 sq. km. = 21,988 sq. mi. (Half of Mississippi, vertically).
Population: 5,081,413 (July 1999 est.).
Capital City: Lome (pop. 810,000 est. in 1996.)
Climate: Warm, humid and tropical.
Neighboring Countries: Ghana (West); Burkina Faso (Upper Volta, North); Benin (East).
Official Language: French (the language of commerce).
Other Principal Languages: Ewe and Mina (the two major African languages in the south), Kabye (sometimes spelled Kabiye) and Dagomba (the two major African languages in the north), and Gourmanché, also spoken in the north.
Ethnic groups: Over thirty, among the most prominent the Ewe, Mina, and Kabre. 99%; European and Syrian-Lebanese less than 1%.
Principal Religions: Indigenous beliefs 70%, Christian 20%, and Muslim 10%.
Chief Commercial Products: Cotton, phosphates, and coffee, and cocoa.
GNP per capita: 330 US$
Currency: CFA Franc (no longer tied to the French franc).
Former Colonial Status: German Colony (1885–1916), French Colony (1916–1960).
Independence Date: April 27, 1960.
Chief of State: General Gnassingbé Eyadema, President, b. 1930. (Pronounced Nah–sing–*bay* Aye–ah–*day*–mah).
National Flag: Green, yellow, green, yellow equal horizontal stripes. A red square at the staff top half with a superimposed white five–pointed star.

Lying almost in the center of the Gold and Ivory coasts, Togo is a long, narrow country stretching 360 miles from the blue Atlantic into the interior. This small nation is only thirty–one miles wide at the coast and 100 miles in width at its broadest point. As is common to this region of Africa, the climate of Togo is predominantly hot and humid on the coast with a drier and slightly cooler region in the North. Picturesque Lake Togo, with quiet, fresh water, is located in the central coast region, a center of modern recreational facilities. The central section is traversed by the Togo Mountains and is succeeded in the North by a level territory of farms.

History: Not much is known of the pre–colonial history of this region of Africa. That which is known is based on tradition passed on verbally through many generations of people living in Togo at the time of the first European explorations. From the ethnic background of the people, it is certain that the majority of the population, of West African Negro origin, had lived there for countless centuries. A smaller group, of Sudanic ancestry, settled in northern Togo during the period of their migration westward from the Sudan–Nile region in the 10th–13th centuries. For details of early and colonial history, see Historical Background and *The Germans in Africa* and *The French in Africa.*

Pre–independence elections installed Nicholas Grunitzky of the *Togo Progressive Party* as president. The *Togo Unity Party* subsequently gained in popularity and membership under the leadership of Sylvanus Olympio. This well–educated man spoke many foreign languages as well as the native Ewe dialect. Olympio was not a native of Togo, having been brought to Africa from Brazil by his father when he was a small child. Ostensibly a moderate, after becoming president in 1960, he disqualified the *Togo Progressive Party* from participating in 1961 elections; the *Togo Unity Party* won 90% of the vote and all 51 seats in the assembly. Grunitzky, who was Olympio's brother–in–law, went to Benin in semi–exile.

Shortly after a state visit to the United States, Olympio was assassinated in early 1963 outside the U.S. Embassy in Lomé where he had been seeking refuge. Grunitzky returned later and was named Prime Minister by Sgt. Etienne Eyadema who was in the group that killed Olympio. A new constitution was adopted and four political parties participated in elections held in 1963 which were officially won by Grunitzky's *Togo Progressive Party;* he became president.

The followers of Olympio attempted a *coup* in 1966, but Eyadema, by then a Lt.

Colonel, assisted in resisting the move successfully.

Dissatisfied with a general lack of progress which he attributed to the time–consuming bickering of politicians, Etienne Eyadema seized power in 1967, abolishing all parties. He later formed the *Togo Popular Rally* and ran in 1972 as the sole candidate for president, receiving about 90% of the vote in a "yes" or "no" contest.

Assassination and torture have been used routinely by Eyadema and the military in Togo for almost three decades. Educated Togolese regard the president as crude and low–class. In 1991 it briefly appeared that Eyadema's strangle–hold on Togo might be broken when the presidency was stripped of almost all power. However, Eyadema's support by the military remained steadfast. His chosen prime minister, Kokou Koffigoh quickly became subservient to his wishes, and presidential powers were gradually restored.

The potential rival in the 1993 elections, Gilchrist Olympio, son of Sylvanus, was almost killed in an assassination attempt. He chose treatment in France, fearing he would not survive in Togo. A 1993 election was a sham—as many dead people as live ones voted. Legislative elections in 1994 resulted in no party winning a majority. For a time, Eyadema's *RPT* and the *Togolese Union for Democracy* (*UTD*) of Prime Minister Edem Kodjo, formed a majority coalition. Following by-elections in August 1996, President-General Eyameda's *RTP* won a majority in the Legislative Assembly. It no longer had need of an alliance with the *UTD*. Edem Kodjo was dismissed as Prime Minister and Kwasi Klutse, a technician, was appointed in his place. President-General Eyadema resumed control of most aspects of government.

The mid–summer presidential elections of 1998 were prepared with care. A new constitutional court was created to hear any election disputes, filled with Eyadema supporters. A new communications authority was established to oversee the media. It too was controlled by Eyadema appointees. A new Electoral Code was passed, giving responsibility for organizing and supervising the elections to the Ministry of the Interior. The preparation of new electoral rolls was advanced, catching the opposition unawares and, of course, they were uninvolved in the preparation. And finally, in March 1998 the elections, originally scheduled for August, were advanced to June. Surprise, the President–General knows, is a tactical element.

To the surprise of none, the election proved that dinosaurs live, sustained by a DNA of fraud. Eyadema was re–elected, according the Interior Minister, General Seyi Memene, by a modest 52.13% of the votes cast, just enough to avoid a runoff election. Just prior to the Minister's announcement, the head of the Electoral commission resigned, saying she had been threatened physically and had received telephone calls threatening her life. Four other members of the commission also resigned. Eyadema's principal rival, Gilchrist Olympio, was allotted a generous 34.1% of the ballots by the interior ministry. Opposition protests were met with tear gas grenades. Olympio said his own calculations showed he won 59% of the vote and vowed to use all peaceful, legitimate, and constitutional means to have the results annulled, all of which, of course, would be of no avail. The President–General, who had already served 31 years as head of state, became Africa's longest serving leader and second only to Fidel Castro in longevity of rule.

Spring 1999 legislative elections did not rise much above the level of electoral farce either. The opposition boycotted and candidates of Eyadema's *RPT* won 79 of 81 parliamentary seats. The interior ministry claimed that over 66% of registered voters participated; the opposition claimed the figure didn't pass 10%. The European Union, which suspended economic cooperation with Togo in 1993, called for an "internal dialogue" between the opposition and the regime, but the positions of each seemed so entrenched that dialogue seemed a distant possibility.

President Eyadema

In May 1999 Amnesty International described Togo as a "state of terror," characterized by executions and extrajudicial executions perpetrated by authorities throughout the political crisis from 1993 to 1998. Hundreds had been killed in the days leading up to the 1998 elections alone. Evidence gathered from Togolese and Beninois fishermen indicated that manacled opponents had been thrown into the sea from Togolese air force planes.

The Togolese army, on which President-General Eyadema's repression relies, consists of 14,000 men, more than one for every 300 citizens. The army, like the other forces of order, is largely recruited in the North, President–General Eyadema's region of origin. Four new brigadier–generals were appointed in early 1998, and all of them were, like Eyadema, northerners. Of the nine Togolese generals, five, including the president, are of the same ethnicity. Togo's air force is completely dependent on French military cooperation.

President-General Eyadema's brutal repression and cavalier attitudes toward democratic processes left Togo in a permanent political and economic crisis. Only in 1999 were there signs that the President-General was willing to compromise with his opponents, and then, only after years of economic sanctions had taken their toll. "National reconciliation" discussions took place in July under the authority of four "facilitators" designated by Germany, France, the European Union (EU) and La Francophonie, the French equivalent of the Commonwealth. President Jacques Chirac of France visited West Africa and, dropping in to see the President-General, provided the carrot complement to EU economic sanctions. Only national reconciliation, he said, would enable the EU to resume aid, which was suspended in 1993.

Chirac himself announced that Eyadema would step down at the end of his presidential term in 2003, respecting the constitution by not presenting himself for a third term. The President-General announced he would dissolve the contested National Assembly and call new parliamentary elections in March 2000. He also agreed to the creation of an independent electoral commission.

At this point Togo looked as though it were on track to end its long term political crisis, but one did not fully appreciate the intransigence of Eyadema's foes, so long kept at arms length. Gilchrist Olympio, Eyadema's main political opponent living in exile in Ghana, refused to participate in the Lomé reconciliation talks for security reasons. Internal opponents of the regime found numerous details to quibble and complain over. In exasperation, the four "facilitators" sent their recommendations directly to the National Assembly, which approved a new election code in March.

The new code envisaged the creation of a permanent independent national electoral commission to oversee future voting. The commission would include an equal number of government and opposition members and represented a remarkable break with present practice: elections conducted by the interior and security ministries of the President-General. The new code opened the way for Eyadema to honor his pledge to dissolve parliament and redo last year's legislative election, but those elections promised for March were not to be.

The opposition, objecting to an amendment made to the code legislation by parliament, once again had withdrawn from political engagement. By early spring, it appeared to remain sulking, and it looked as though the President-General had bested the opposition once again. There were clear signs that EU sanctions imposed on Togo since 1993 might be lifted "in order to alleviate the undue suffering of the Togolese people."

That possibility was quashed when the latest human rights scandal broke. On the eve of President Chirac's visit, the Benin League for the Defense of Human Rights confirmed Amnesty International's charges that hundreds had been summarily executed and their bodies dumped into the sea in the run-up to 1998's presidential elections. The League reported finding more than 100 bodies in coastal villages. Some were headless, handcuffed, or riddled with bullets. They were, said the League, "pushed from low-flying planes and helicopters coming during the night from Togo."

From the Togolese government there was much bluster and bravado about legal action against Amnesty International. Later it emerged that the government had hired witnesses to perjure themselves at hearings and journalists to write articles questioning the facts and motivations of those who presented them.

By June 2000 a joint commission between the United Nations and the OAU was set up to investigate the allegations of state-sponsored massacres, no doubt much to the embarrassment of President Eyadema who had begun serving a term as OAU chairman. Shortly before the commission of inquiry was to release its report in February 2001, the government's disinformation machine was cranked up. Amnesty International was accused of accepting a bribe of $500,000 from Gilchrist Olympio to prepare its "highly negative human rights reports" about Togo.

When the inquiry team released the results of its investigation, it made clear its belief that individuals linked to Togolese security forces, working in co-operation with the Togolese police and allied militias, had indeed carried out summary executions of the government's political opponents. It was not the first embarrassment with which the President-General had had to deal.

The Fowler Report to the UN Security Council of March 2000 had identified Eyadema as one of those facilitating the continuing arms supply of Jonas Savimbi's UNITA forces in Angola. A follow-up experts report issued in December accused Togolese authorities of accepting "blood diamonds'" from Savimbi in exchange for illegal arms and fuel shipments.

International opprobrium and a changing political situation in West Africa had their impact on the Inter-Togolese dialogue being facilitated by European mediators. The facilitators left Togo at the end of January 2001, admitting their efforts to get both opposition and government to agree on a date for new elections had "ended in failure." To break the deadlock, the group gave "the Togolese political stakeholders three days within which to get their acts together or have themselves to blame."

Barely 24 hours after the departure of the facilitators, the government shocked all involved by presenting its "sincere apologies to the mediators for any embarrassment the government's earlier position may have caused them." It requested the National Independent Electoral Commission to hold an emergency meeting on January 29 to set up an electoral timetable. The Commission, composed of 10 members each from the government and opposition groups, met and set the next parliamentary elections for October 14, 2001.

It is likely that even the radical opposition will agree this time. Ghana's recent election of John Kufuor as president has changed the regional landscape politically: Togolese dissidents will no longer find safe harbor in Ghana. Kufuor, committed to an open economy and interested in developing regional trade, made his first official trip abroad to Togo in January 2001. In response to reporters' questions, he announced that "During my term, I will never allow people to attack Togo from Ghanaian territory."

Culture: The people of the populous southern coast area are better educated and economically better off than those of the sparsely settled North—a pattern common to many countries in this area of Africa. The Ewe people have dominated the cultural life in Togo and extend beyond its borders well into Ghana to the west. There are few communities that lack educational facilities within the Ewe country. Although a few of this group continue the animist customs of their past, most are Christians, widely employed and leading modern, urban lives. In spite of this, the literacy rate of Togo ranges from an estimated 67% for men to 37% for women.

The lives of the people further inland are based upon small family holdings of farmland, and they have little daily contact with the larger cities of the South. The brilliantly–colored costumes of these people, with their lengths of shining beads and elaborate headdresses, are distinctive.

Economy: The Togolese economy is mainly dependent on agriculture, which accounts for 40 percent of the GDP, 75 percent of jobs, and more than 50 percent of export earnings. Combined exports of commercial crops like cotton, cocoa, and coffee, account for nearly 30 percent of export earnings.

Togo's cotton exports rose from 49,200 tons in 1995 to 66,900 tons in 1998. Overall production during 1998-99 was approximately 200,000 tons, but world market prices have declined sharply. According to the Togolese Cotton Society (SOTOCO), more than 230,000 Togolese earn their living from cotton.

The mining sector accounts for more than one-third of export earnings, of which phosphates contribute a quarter. Togo is the world's fifth largest exporter of calcium phosphate and possesses large reserves, estimated at over 150m tons. The country currently produces 2.7 million tons per year, but its income has suffered as world prices have declined. The state-owned *Office Togolais de Phosphates* (*OTP*), which has a monopoly on phosphate sales, is currently being privatized.

Despite expanding the tax base, lowering inflation, and cutting public spending, the economy stagnates and Togo suffers economic malaise. The causes are several, but the political situation is the principal factor. Dependent on foreign investment for economic development, Togo has been largely cut off from international aid since death and violence marred its transition to democracy in 1991.

The World Trade Organization has described Togo's economy was among the most open in West Africa, but state incentives to lure international investors to Togo have proved unattractive. For private investors, political repression represents economic risk. For state donors, a democratic ethos—democratic procedures and civil rights—has become a requirement for economic assistance.

The European Union (EU) has withheld the greater part of aid for Togo since the disputed elections of 1993. EU sanctions are believed to have lost Togo over $600 million in terms of economic aid. It is also believed to have lost more than 60 per cent of its external trade with the Union.

The absence of aid and investment explains Togo's low growth rates. From 1987 to 1997 the economy averaged only 2.7 percent growth. In 1998 this fell to 0.6, illustrating another structural weakness of the economy: insufficient power generation.

Togo generates only 30 per cent of its own electricity needs. For the rest it depends on electricity supplied by Ghana's Akosombo Dam. In 1998 water levels at the dam fell precipitously. Electricity rationing was introduced, and the entire economy suffered a setback. To rectify its power insufficiencies, Togo is participating in a pipeline project to distribute Nigerian natural gas to Benin, Togo, and Ghana for the generation of electricity.

The Future: Togo will remain politically stifled until Eyadema goes, and army control is ended. Most adults have lived their entire life under Eyadema and know nothing about genuine democracy. With agreement on October elections, Togo's long-lasting political crisis may be nearing an end. Transparent democratic elections will in turn open the spigot for vitally needed economic aid to help end Togo's even longer economic crisis.

CENTRAL WEST AFRICA

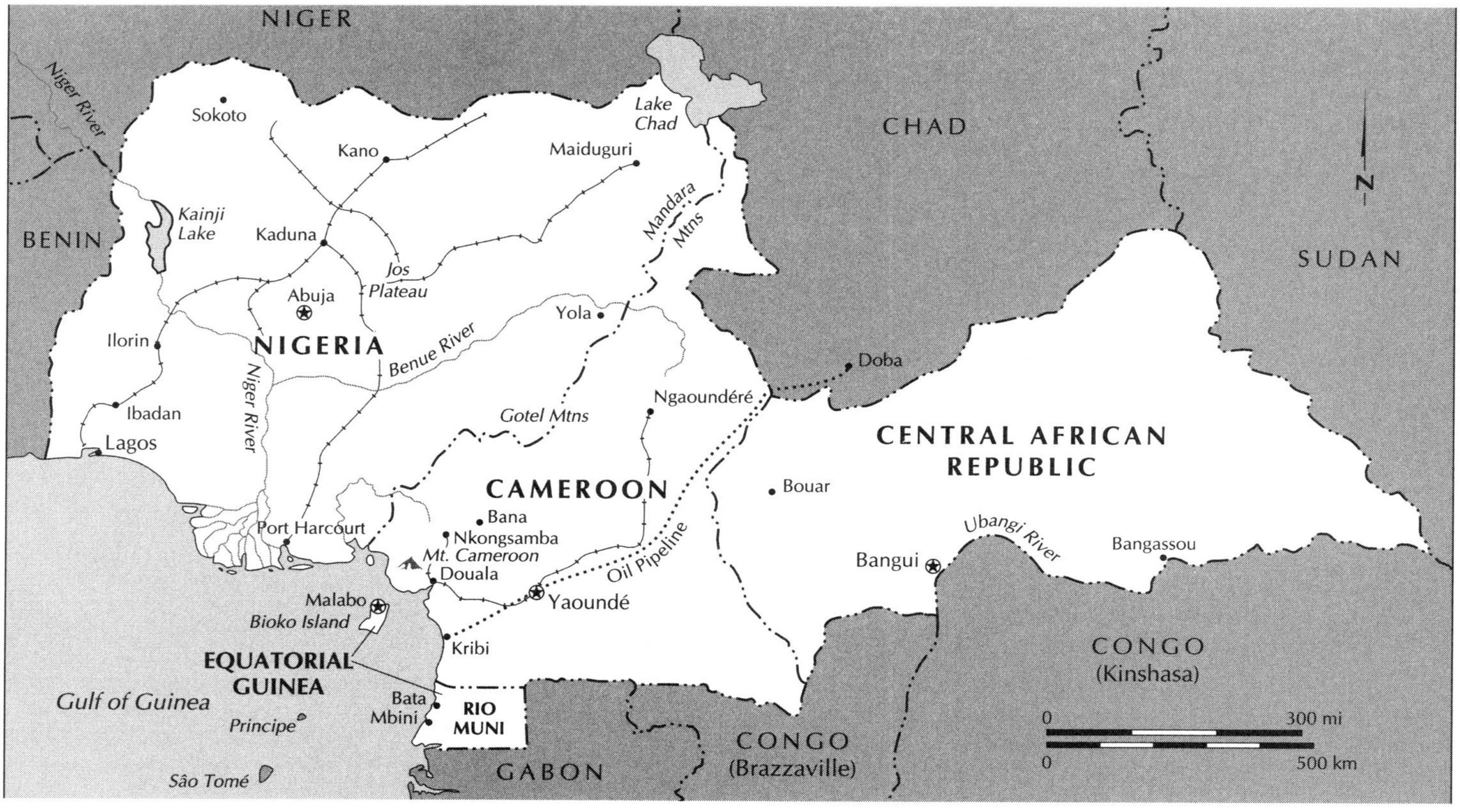

The Republic of Cameroon

Area: 475,400 sq. km = 183,552 sq. mi. (Size of California and 1/4 of Oregon).

Population: 15,456,092 (July 1999 est.).

Capital City: Yaoundé (pop. 900,000, estimated; pronounced Yah-oon-*deh*).

Climate: Hot and humid in the South, progressively becoming drier to the inland north; arid in the Lake Chad area.

Neighboring Countries: Nigeria (Northwest); Chad (Northeast); Central African Republic (East); Congo, Gabon, Equatorial Guinea (South).

Official Languages: French (East Cameroon) and English (West Cameroon).

Other Principal Languages: There 24 major African language groups, involving more than 275 separate languages. Prominent are Akoose, Bafia, Bafut, Bakoko, Bakundu, Bamileke, Bamun, Basaa, Beti, Bulu, Duala, Eton, Fang, Fe'fe', Fufulde, Gbaya, Kanuri, Kenyang, Kom, Lamnso', Limbum, Mafa, Makaa, Masana, Mbo, Medumba, Mungaka, Musugu, Ngiemboon, Ngembe, Tupuri,Yemba. Cameroon Pidgin, an English-based Creole language is spoken primarily in the Southwest and Northern provinces and has become a widespread lingua franca in Cameroon, spoken as a second language by more than half the population.

Ethnic groups: Cameroon Highlanders (Bamilike, Bamoun) 31%, Equatorial Bantu (Beti) 19%, Kirdi 11%, Fulani 10%, Northwestern Bantu 8%, Eastern Nigritic 7%, other African 13%, non-African less than 1%.

Principal Religions: Christianity (about 53%), traditional beliefs (about 25%), Islam (about 22%).

Chief Commercial Products: Crude oil and petroleum products, lumber, cocoa beans, aluminum, coffee, and cotton.

GNP per capita: 610 US$

Currency: CFA Franc

Former Colonial Status: German Colony (1884–1916), British Colony in West Cameroon (1916–1961); French Colony is East Cameroon (1916–1960).

Independence Date: January 1, 1960 (East Cameroon); October 1, 1961 (West Cameroon independence and federation with East Cameroon).

Chief of State: Paul Biya, President (1982).

National Flag: Three vertical stripes of green, red and yellow with a yellow star in the red stripe.

This land of contrasts, containing almost every species of flora and fauna of tropical Africa and numerous varieties of wild game, stretches north from the Atlantic in a "hinge" position between West and Central Africa. From the Polynesian– like beaches, washed by the waters of the Bight of Biafra, there rise towering mountains which proceed directly north into West Cameroon. Mount Cameroon, the tallest peak in western Africa, towering almost 14,000 feet high, is presently an active volcano located close to the seacoast. Reportedly christened *Chariot of the Gods* by Hannon, a Carthaginian chief of the 6th century B.C., this volcano, with a base of about 700 square miles, erupted as recently as 1959. The southern part of Cameroon, extending eastward in a horizontal line, is characterized by a low coastal basin with equatorial jungles. In the more north–central part of the country there is a series of grassy plateaus whose heights reach 4,500 feet, but in the extreme northern Lake Chad region, the dry climate supports only seasonal grazing and nomadic herding, culminating in a marshland. This area has been gripped for the last decade in the drought of the *Sahel,* with disastrous results, causing inhabitants to flee southward in order to live.

History: Cameroon has been inhabited since early times, containing relics of prehistoric societies in the North. Commerce with the Mediterranean region was active, with trade routes across the Sahara Desert used to transport ivory, panther skins, ostrich feathers, bronze and salt to Egypt and other early civilizations. Originally populated by pygmies, who are now found only in small numbers along the southern border, Cameroon was successively dominated by other native groups. The Bantus arrived in substantial numbers in the 15th century, settling in the central plateau region. In 1472, a Portuguese explorer, Fernão do Poo (Fernando Po in Spanish) arrived on the coast of what is now Cameroon. For details of early and colonial history, see Historical Background, *The British in Africa, The Germans in Africa* and *The French in Africa.*

France granted independence to East Cameroon on January 1, 1960; the British relinquished West Cameroon on October 1, 1961, and there was a reunification of the two Cameroons. A Federation Constitution was adopted and a single–party system emerged, based upon the *Cameroon National Unity Party (UNC).* President Ahmadou Ahidjo (from East Cameroon) and Vice President John Foncha (from West Cameroon) received 97.5% of the vote in 1970 elections. Constitutional reforms in 1972 eliminated the state government of the two regions, but guaranteed the continuation of the French language in the East and English in the West.

Ahmadou Ahidjo, possessing a high school education, was a master politician in his ability to pull about 200 tribes together under a single government. Legislative elections were held in 1978 and presidential elections in 1980 at which time President Ahidjo was elected to a fifth five–year term. All candidates were from the *Cameroon National Union (UNC).*

Coming as a complete surprise, President Ahidjo resigned on November 6, 1982, handing over power to the Prime Minister, Paul Biya, who completed Ahidjo's term of office. The former president was said to be exhausted. In January 1984 elections, President Biya, a Christian from the south, was elected in his own right to a five–year term of office by a margin of 99.98% Although it was technically possible for persons to run against him, in reality, legal obstacles made this impossible and practicality made it unwise.

In an effort to consolidate his power and eliminate potential competition, President Biya saw to it that the constitution was amended to eliminate the office of Prime Minister. The name of the nation was changed from the "United Republic of Cameroon" to simply the "Republic of Cameroon."

In early April 1984 there was an attempted *coup.* Fierce fighting erupted in Yaoundé—mutinous members of the Republican Guard, which was supposed to *protect* the president, composed mostly of Islamic northerners, waged a pitched battle with regular army units. Biya, after the rebellion was snuffed out, announced that it was on behalf of Ahidjo, who still was in Paris. The official number of deaths was "about 70," but the actual number was probably close to 1,500. Within weeks, 35 were tried and summarily executed. Almost 1,000 others who had been detained were released.

In order to demonstrate his "New Deal" policies, President Biya changed the name of the sole legal party in 1985 to the *Cameroon Democratic Rally (RDPC).* This was done at a convention in Bamenda, the capital of the English–speaking portion of Cameroon; in 1986 party balloting (secret) resulted in the ouster of several officials who had served under Ahidjo—a consolidation of power by the president.

President Paul Biya

President Biya advanced elections scheduled for early 1989 to April 24, 1988. The *RDPC* approved 324 candidates to contest 180 seats; the result was a National Assembly with younger members. The president was reelected with a 98.75% majority. Having received the mandate he sought, Biya announced wide–ranging programs to pare the size of the bureaucracy and cut government expenditures. The result was a positive response to requests for foreign aid.

Summary arrests of journalists and widespread unrest followed the approval of a multi–party system in 1990. Regrettably, the opposition was divided into 48 parties, none very strong. But this was translated into reality in legislative elections in March 1992; the *RDCP* received 88 of the 180 seats. Principal opponents were the *National Union for Democracy and Progress (UNDP)* which elected 68 members and the *Union of Peoples of Cameroon (UPC)* which won 18. There were boycotts of the balloting by 16 of the opposition parties, including that of popular English–speaker John Fru Ndi's *Social Democratic Front.*

Presidential balloting was advanced from the spring of 1993 to October 1992 in order to catch the divided opposition unprepared, and was marred by massive fraud and irregularities. The state–owned television gave 2½ hours of time to Biya, but only 16 minutes to the opposition.

The ruling *RDPC* won May 1997 legislative elections, taking 109 of 180 seats. The opposition *Social Democratic Front* captured 43 seats. Thirteen seats went to the *National Union for Democracy and Progress*, five to the *Democratic Union for the Liberation of Cameroon Youth*, and the *Democratic Movement for the Defense of the Republic.* As expected, widespread intimidation and fraud were reported.

October Presidential elections were virtually meaningless. President Biya refused to allow an independent electoral commission to organize them and the main opposition parties refused participation. Most citizens treated it as a non-event, but the government reported that 60% of registered voters participated and gave 80% of their votes to Biya.

Political power in Cameroon is concentrated in the office of president. The president appoints the cabinet, which serves at his pleasure. He names judges, generals and governors, district administrators and the heads of state corporations. Parliament, dominated by President Biya's *Cameroon People's Democratic Movement* (*RDPC*), consistently defers to the legislative program submitted by the government. That control has been used to increase presidential powers. Constitutional amendments in 1996 increased the presidential term to seven years and created an upper house of parliament and regional councils. Thus far, only the extension of the presidential term has been implemented. Presidential power is maintained through active repression of the political opposition, especially in election years. When Titus Edzoa, Cameroon's health minister, long–time aide and personal physician to the president, declared himself a candidate for the presidency, charges of financial misconduct were immediately filed. Edzoa was found guilty and safely dispatched to jail, from which there is no campaigning.

The government closely controls the electoral process, which is administered through the Ministry of Territorial Administration. Members of oppositional ethnic groups and those living in areas dominated by the opposition are effectively prevented from registering to vote. The government operates almost all broadcast media (a small private Catholic station rebroadcasts programs from Vatican Radio), and coverage of opposition activity is underwhelming. Print media, of small circulation and limited to urban distribution, are tightly circumscribed by criminal libel laws. Political cartoonists seem to be a particular object of presidential wrath. In late December 1998, copies of *L'Expression de Mamy Wata*, a Douala–based satirical weekly, were seized because they had cartoons insinuating the president beat his wife.

Tensions continue in the Anglophone areas of Cameroon, which feel increasingly marginalized by Cameroon's Francophone majority. Separatist demonstrations were staged late December 1999 and early January 2000 in English-speaking parts of the country, and security forces detained 23 members of the *Southern Cameroon National Council* (*SCNC*). Prime Minister Mafany Musonge visited the English-speaking southwest provinces, reiterating his attachment to Cameroon's territorial unity. In the delicate ethnic and regional balancing necessary in the Cameroonian government, prime ministers are traditionally English-speakers. Musonge is a native of the English-speaking Southwest Province. Holding an engineering degree from Stanford University, he was president of Cameroon's largest agro-industrial enterprise, the Cameroon Development Corporation, when President Biya first appointed him prime minister in 1996.

Cameroon faces border tension with several neighbors. With Nigeria, there is tension over the Bakassi peninsula, a 400-square mile swamp-infested area of southwest Cameroon thought to hold significant oil reserves. Both countries have submitted their claims to the International Court of Justice (ICJ), but these hearings were complicated when Equatorial Guinea entered its own claims. Submissions from all sides will continue through mid-2001.

In the parched northern region, Cameroon's plans for irrigated agriculture have brought it into conflict with both Nigeria and Chad. Nigeria has threatened to bring the country back to the ICJ over disputes involving development projects on the Benue River. Chad has threatened similar action over irrigation and rice production projects on the Logone River. Even the border with the Central African Republic has seen several incidents of incursion.

Culture: For two years in a row in the late 1990s Cameroon topped Transparency International's list of countries perceived as being corrupt. Stung by its classification as the world's most corrupt state and with its consequent investor mistrust and diplomatic chastening, President Biya's government lumbered into an anti-corruption campaign.

In November 1999, *On corruption in Cameroon* was published in Yaounde. Compiled by the Cameroonian branch of the Democracy and Economic and Social Development Study and Research Group (Gerddes), the book urged Cameroonians to combat the culture of corruption, which it said was destroying the fabric of society. The authors found that "for any service an agent provides he expects the user to provide him, in return, with a bonus, the nature of which depends upon the circumstances."

So commonplace are corrupt acts that Cameroonians, like the proverbial Eskimo describing snow, have elaborated a rich vocabulary to describe them. *Magouiller* means "to scheme," *pistonner le dossier* "to pull strings;" *bien parler* is to "do what you have to," while *engraisser la patte* is to "grease someone's palm."

The government's anti-corruption campaign has had some success. A few high ranking officials have been arrested, and the sense of impunity which surrounded corrupt officials has diminished a bit. President Biya has pointedly excluded people jailed for embezzlement of public funds, corruption, nepotism, and favor trading from the magnanimity of presidential pardon.

Transparency International took note. In September 2000 Cameroon moved from 90th and worst on its corruption index to a mere 84th. Progress, as T. S. Eliot might have noted, is measured in coffee spoons.

Economy: Cameroon's economy was traditionally based on agriculture until the discovery of oil, but oil production peaked in 1985 at 158,000 barrels a day. In 1999 production was at the level of 100,000 barrels a day. Diminished production has been caused less by exhaustion of reserves than by bureaucratic and financial impediments created by the government. Recently a new investment code has been elaborated to attract investors.

The most significant oil development in Cameroon is the planned oil export pipeline from neighboring Chad. Peak production from Chad's Doba fields is projected to be around 225,000 to 250,000 bb/d. Crude oil from some 315 wells would be transported through a 650-mile pipeline to an offshore marine terminal near Kribi, Cameroon.

The World Bank, despite stiff opposition from environmentalists, is supplying 3% of the financing for the pipeline project. ExxonMobil, Petronas—the Malaysian National Oil Company—and Chevron will undertake construction of the project. The pipeline is the largest single investment project in sub-Saharan Africa.

An aggressive construction schedule has been drawn up, involving rapid mobilization and commencement of critical infrastructure work by the end of 2001. The project is expected to create between 3,000 and 4,000 jobs, while roads will have to be resurfaced and bridges built. Some 400,000 tons of equipment will have to be landed at Douala. Known for its high costs and slow services, the port is being restructured and rehabilitated to accommodate pipeline activities.

Aside from oil, the country's main cash crops are cocoa, coffee, cotton, and timber. Cameroon is the world's fifth largest cocoa producer, and cocoa provides about 40% of its exports. But declining world

The old way of cultivation, Cameroon

market prices have resulted in reduced production. Farmers are expected to produce around 90,000 tons of cocoa in the 2000-2001 season, down by 10,000 tons from the previous year. In several areas parts of cocoa plantations have been destroyed to pave way for food crops such as tomato, vegetables and plantain.

In response to depressed coffee prices members of the Association of Coffee Producing Countries (ACPC), including Cameroon, agreed to withhold 20% of coffee exports from world markets starting in September 2000.

About 40% of Cameroon's land is forested, but the forests are disappearing rapidly because of irresponsible logging activity. Logging concessions are awarded by a bidding system. The winner is traditionally not the highest bidder, but the company prepared to offer the highest financial inducements to officials. So flagrant is corruption in the industry that the Commonwealth secretary-general has warned of the "debilitating effects of corruption in the forest sector."

Cameroon is now the largest producer of logs in Africa. It currently exports three million cubic meters of wood, but in January 1999 the government announced it would stop issuing export permits for raw timber. Forest preservation was less the goal than the encouragement of the local saw-milling industry. The government hopes to increase exports of processed sawn wood and veneers.

Cameroon qualified for $2 billion in debt relief under the Highly Indebted Poor Countries program in late 2000. The relief cuts the country's debt by 27% and will free up about 100 million dollars of annual debt service obligations over the next three years. The savings are to be invested in poverty reduction programs. The debt reduction reflects a new donor confidence with Cameroon's ability to deal with its finances. Increased oil income has helped, but growth is steady—in the 4% to 5% range, inflation minimal, and privatization programs on track. Much of the credit is due to finance minister Edouard Mfoumou. Unlike his predecessor, Mfoumou has had the political clout to win presidential backing for actual implementation of the policies promised to foreign donors. It may help that he is a presidential cousin and widely seen as a potential successor to President Biya.

The Future: The opposition is fragmented and was incapable of even choosing a single candidate to oppose President Biya in the last election, so one can't expect much from it. Economic growth is insufficient to mask the repressive nature of the political system. There is, however, a new optimism in Cameroon that may facilitate necessary change. A gold medal in soccer at the Sydney Olympics, coupled with World Bank approval of the pipeline financing and debt reduction, have transformed a mood of pervasive gloom.

The Central African Republic

Area: 626,780 sq. km. = 242,000 sq. mi. (the size of Texas and New Mexico).
Population: 3.5 million (estimated).
Capital City: Bangui (Pop 640,000, estimated; pronounced Ban–*ghe*).
Climate: Temperate, with a rainy season (June to October) and a dry season (November to May).
Neighboring Countries: The two Congos (South); Cameroon (West); Chad (Northwest); Sudan (Northeast and East).
Official Language: French.
Other Principal Languages: Sangho (lingua franca and national language), Arabic, Hunsa, Swahili.
Ethnic groups: Baya 34%, Banda 27%, Sara 10%, Mandjia 21%, Mboum 4%, M'Baka 4%, Europeans 6,500 (including 3,600 French).
Principal Religions: Indigenous beliefs 24%, Protestant 25%, Roman Catholic 25%, Muslim 15%, and other 11%. Note: animistic beliefs and practices strongly influence the Christian majority.
Chief Commercial Products: Diamonds, timber, cotton, coffee, tobacco.
GNP per capita: 300 US$
Currency: CFA Franc (no longer tied to the French franc).
Former Colonial Status: French Colony (1894–1960).
Independence Date: August 11, 1960.
Chief of State: Ange-Felix Patassé, President.
National Flag: Four horizontal stripes (from top to bottom) of blue, white, green and yellow, divided by a red stripe down the middle, with a yellow star on the left hand side of the blue stripe.

Located in almost the exact center of Africa, the Central African Republic is a vast, rolling plateau rising 2,000 to 2,500 feet above sea level. Lying more than 300 miles from the sea, this sun–drenched land of agricultural and forest products found its original wealth in ivory from its once large herds of massive elephants. Prolific groups of wild animals roam the land today, making it one of the most zoologically interesting areas of Africa.

There is a small area of jungle in the southwest which is rapidly succeeded by the rolling plateaus of the plains, rising gently to the mountains of the northeast. Heavy rainstorms occur almost daily during the wet season from June to October, seldom permitting the ground to become dry. The shift of the sun to the south in November is the start of the dry season when the leaves of the trees turn to brilliant hues because of lack of moisture. In the following weeks the leaves fall, and the grass, having grown to the height of more than five feet, changes its lush green color to a tinder–dry yellow. Fire becomes a great danger as the drought continues. This grassy highland, shared with other countries by the Central African Republic, extends more than three thousand miles westward to the coast of Guinea on the Atlantic Ocean.

The Ubangi River flows along a good portion of the southern border, then plunges south to join the waters of the mighty Congo.

History: Little is known of the early history of this remote area of Africa. The Central African Republic shared the numerous migrations of different ethnic groups, most of which are of Bantu origin. For details of earlier and colonial history, see Historical Background and *The French in Africa.*

The country gained independence on August 11, 1960, taking the name Central African Republic. The constitution initially provided for a unicameral National Assembly with 50 members elected for a five–year term by universal suffrage. David Dacko's *African Social Evolution Party* immediately won a majority in the assembly, and banned all other parties. He became the first president and was reelected in 1964 by a majority of 99.4%. Dacko established close relations with the communist Chinese; the influx of Chinese technical and diplomatic personnel aroused the resentment of the military, which ousted Dacko in 1966. General Jean–Bedel Bokassa assumed power and abolished the constitution, dissolved the legislature and transferred administrative duties to his appointed cabinet.

There were constant Cabinet changes during Bokassa's rule and several attempts on his life. In early 1976, one resulted in death sentences for alleged conspirators, including the President's son–in–law.

Bokassa proclaimed himself president for life in 1972 through the country's sole political party, the *Movement for Social Evolution of Black Africa*, but that was not nearly enough for the short Field Marshal. In late 1976 a new constitution brought into being the Central African *Empire*. In late 1977 in sweltering Bangui, a crowd of over 3,000 guests witnessed Jean–Bedel Bokassa place a 2,000–diamond encrusted crown on his head and proclaim himself Emperor Bokassa I. The spectacle was said to have cost well over $22 million in this land–locked country where the average per capita annual income was $120. The Emperor was outraged by some of the tongue–in–cheek news stories of his coronation. An admirer of Napoleon, Bokassa tried to give the colorful pageant as much pomp as had the one in 1804. But, muggy Bangui is no Paris.

Student riots broke out in early 1979 following an order by the Emperor that they should wear school uniforms. The demonstrations quickly spread and assumed an anti–imperial tone. They were brutally suppressed by the Emperor's forces. Agitation continued, however, until April when the Emperor had several hundred students arrested and over one hundred killed in a Bangui prison. The commission of African jurists investigating reported that Bokassa had taken an active part in the slayings; the atrocities created outrage in world public opinion. Opposition to Bokassa continued to harden in the country and abroad.

While the Emperor was visiting Libya, he was overthrown by his cousin and advisor, David Dacko (from whom Bokassa had seized power in 1966). With the support of French armed forces, Dacko reestablished the Republic; Bokassa was given asylum in Côte d'Ivoire. But the CAR continued to be plagued by corrupt, inept government swollen by useless insiders and relatives of the elite. Elections held in 1981 were clouded by accurate charges of fraud. When Army Chief of Staff General André Kolingba demanded President Dacko's resignation four months later, he quickly received it.

Former Emperor Bokassa I

Food shortages, student unrest and general unrest marked the ensuing years. In a referendum in late 1986 a new constitution was approved which provided for only a single political party; President Kolingba, having changed from his uniform to a tuxedo, was sworn in for a six–year term. He duped former Emperor Bokassa into leaving his luxurious chateau in France and returning to the CAR, promising a hero's welcome for the witless monarch. (Although France desired his departure, it denied having anything to do with his exit.)

Bokassa was tried for multiple murders and embezzlement, but cannibalism charges were dropped. His defense was that he didn't know what his underlings had been doing. Found guilty, he was sentenced to death in 1987. This was later lowered to life imprisonment which was reduced in separate acts (all by Kolingba) to 20 years, 10 years and he was released in early September 1993. He was immediately welcomed as a guest in the presidential palace. In full regalia, he compared himself to Jesus Christ in a speech. It reasonably may be assumed that each instance of leniency was fully supported by a suitable bribe with the money he had appropriated during his years in power. He died in late 1996 of natural causes.

In response to pressures for multi-party democracy that increased in the early 1990s, resulted in Kolingba summoning a "Grand National Debate." Fourteen parties opposed to Kolingba's *Central African Democratic Rally (RDC)* boycotted the session. He then advanced the date of elections from 1993 to October 1992 in order to catch the opposition off balance; this strategy failed in the face of unrest, and Kolingba ruled by decree. When the two–stage contest was held in late 1993, Kolingba was eliminated in the first round by an "anti" vote.

Ange–Felix Patassé won in the second round in an apparently fair contest. Since that time he has been sustained in office against mutinous army troops by resident French forces on four different occasions. The grievances were almost always the same: the inability of an inefficient government to pay its own troops. The latest came in late 1996 and continued for nearly two months. The longer it lasted, the more mutineers escalated their demands, finally demanding the ouster of President Patassé himself. The demand highlighted the regional conflicts that beset the coun-

General Kolingba

President Patassé

try. The mutineers were southerners, loyal to ex-President Kolingba. Patassé is a northerner. Finally, Mali's highly respected former military ruler, Amadou Toumani Touré, was invited to mediate. The Bangui Accords he brokered involved amnesties for mutineers, a government of national unity, and the deployment of African peace-keepers to replace French troops. The Accords were signed in January 1997.

The *Inter-African Surveillance Mission for the Bangui Accords (MISAB),* comprised of troops from Burkina Faso, Gabon, Mali, Senegal, Chad and Togo, was barely in place before it faced another outbreak of hostilities in June. Chadian troops conducted what was described as a "muscular offensive" against the mutineers, and French helicopters flew over the capital to guarantee security of the main roads, blocking mutineers and their supporters in their barracks. Having been soundly whacked, the mutineers signed yet another cease-fire in early July and the Bangui Accords have held since then. In September the French began the process of withdrawing their troops from the country. They would be withdrawn by mid-April 1998 and replaced by UN peace-keepers.

The United Nations approved sending a peace-keeping mission to the Central African Republic for an initial period of three months in March. The mission, with a military component of 1,350 personnel, replaced departing French troops. The United Nations approved sending a peacekeeping mission to the Central African Republic for an initial period of three months in March. The mission, with a military component of 1,350 personnel, replaced departing French troops. *MISAB* soldiers exchanged their headgear and were integrated into the new force, called the UN Mission in the Central African Republic *(MINURCA).*

In March gala festivities observed by the presidents of the two Congos, Sudan, Gabon, Chad, and Mali celebrated the signing of a national reconciliation pact. The pact, unanimously agreed to by some 400 delegates to a National Reconciliation Conference, set forth procedures for integrating former mutineers into the army as well as rules for what was called "good governance" under a non–military prime minister.

There remained a lot of reconciling to be done. André Kolingba, the president's long–time foe, condemned the "climate of hate, division, tension and terrorism, created by the present regime" in late March—after he had signed the grand pact of reconciliation!

Legislative elections in November and December did little to build a climate of trust. More than 800 candidates from at least 26 opposition parties entered the contest for 109 parliamentary seats. In the first round, President Patassé's *MLPC* had a slight lead, winning 26 seats to the opposition's 17. For the second round, fourteen opposition parties signed an electoral pact to support the best–placed candidate against those of the *MLPC.* The results were, shall we say, inconclusive. The *MLPC* and its allies held 51 seats; the opposition, were it to be united, held 53. Seven independents were elected, making them the focal point of everyone's attention and blandishment. Seeing the potential for continued volatility, Secretary General Kofi Annan recommended that *MINURCA's* mandate be extended through the end of 1999.

"Discussions" with the independents went on. First the opposition announced it had secured the support of two, enough for a majority in parliament. More "discussions" and, suddenly, there were defections to President Patassé's coalition. The defector was "bought," said the spokesman for the opposition coalition. "We have a majority," said the president as he proceeded to appoint a prime minister. Recognizing who has the best "talking points" other parliamentarians swing to the president. Political parties sue their disloyal members, but the courts decide a member is elected to represent his constituency, not his party. When parliament finally begins its session, the opposition boycotts the meetings.

This was the political climate that preceded the September 1999 presidential elections. The opposition could not agree on a single candidate to confront President Patassé, so ten names appeared on the presidential ballot. The most prominent candidates were former presidents David Dacko and André Kolingba. The opposition found much to complain about and rejected the results even before the election was held. Hopes that Patassé would be forced into a runoff election were dashed. Some 56% of registered voters went to the polls and the president won by a razor slim majority: 51.6%. General Kolingba received 19.3% of the votes and David Dacko came in third with 11.1%. Observers declared the election free and fair. Any irregularities, they said, were not of a kind to affect the overall result.

Desperately poor, the Central African Republic has teetered on the brink of implosion since the election. Unable to pay civil servants their salaries, students their stipends or retirees their pensions, the government has faced an on-going series of protests and demonstrations. A near-permanent strike of government workers began in November 2000 when demonstrators set up barricades and burned tires in the capital before being dispersed by security forces. They demanded nearly 30 months of wage arrears.

The opposition seized on the issue to escalate tensions by demanding President Patassé's resignation, and the government has resorted to a variety of less than liberal measures to defend itself. Demonstrators and even members of parliament have been arrested and jailed for encouraging violence. The publisher of a local news letter was speedily dispatched to jail after publishing a poll which indicated that 173 of 200 respondents wanted the president to resign.

More effective in quelling passions has been the periodic distribution of monies begged and borrowed from a variety of sources. A call by the Public Sector Employees Union to turn the Bangui into a ghost city on January 19, 2001, went largely unanswered as most civil servants rushed instead to their banks to receive three months back pay offered by the government.

In April 2001 the president dismissed his prime minister and cabinet, charging most with incompetence. It is unlikely that new faces will bring new responses to old problems, however. CAR represents a worst-case scenario for the abjectly poor state: economic crisis exacerbates political tensions and facilitates social disintegration.

Crime in the capital and banditry in the countryside are increasing. Armed banditry has reached insurrectional proportions, threatening the state's authority in the provinces. Armed with Kalashnikovs and 12-gauge shotguns, the bandits, known locally as Zaraguinas, operate in gangs of ten to 20. They rape, rob, and murder at will, disrupting trade between nearby Chad and the Cameroonian port of Douala, the CAR's main outlet to the sea. The Central African army has traditionally been viewed as ineffective against the brigands, but a newer version of the military has begun to strut its stuff.

For the first time since the 1996-97 mutinies, the CAR army paraded on the streets of Bangui in April 2001. Restructured with financial and technical assistance from France and the international community, the army now has over 4,000 men.

The CAR has remained, as best it can, neutral in the conflict which has engulfed the neighboring Democratic Republic of the Congo (DRC). Neutrality has, however, few rewards. The CAR has had to receive refugees from the conflict and occasional incursions by one fighting force or another. Fuel supplies have been cut off by fighting on the Ubangui River, and in one instance Laurent Kabila held back a fuel shipment at Kinshasa by claiming it was going to MLC rebels. The fuel shortages only contributed to increasing local tensions.

Culture: Within this vast, thinly populated nation, nine out of ten people live in rural isolation, cultivating traditional subsistence crops on small farms, raising livestock as well as engaging in hunting and fishing. HIV/AIDS is well-established in the Central African Republic. The government officially estimates some 300,000 people out of the 3.5 million population are affected. At a July 1999 seminar the Minister of Health observed that every citizen had already lost at least one family member because of AIDS.

Researchers have noted a disturbing phenomenon in the CAR's AIDS epidemic—the presence of elevated HIV/AIDS rates among the best educated sectors of the population. AIDS was the principal cause of death among teachers, for example, between 1996 and 1998. "It's a profession," said one researcher, "where one is more exposed to easy sexual relations."

One expert called the official figures of a 10–15% infection rate "too timid." Based on a recent sample of 2,059 persons, he estimated the infection rate closer to 24%.

Economy: Like the political scene, the CAR's economic situation remains precarious. President Patassé has inherited an economy in shambles. Mismanagement under Bokassa and continuing civil strife since the army mutinies have led to a general economic deterioration and deepening poverty for most citizens.

Following implementation of the broad program of nationalization which followed the coronation of Emperor Bokassa in December 1976, GDP per capita declined. Between 1985 and 1995 the country registered annual declines of 2.4%. Recent economic restructuring is bringing more positive results. GNP grew by 5.6% in 1999. According to one UN report, more than 60% of the population still lives on less than a dollar a day.

Agriculture and forestry are the mainstay of economy, accounting for 51% of GNP in 1996 and employing 66% of the workforce. Subsistence farming dominates, with farmers growing cassavas, yams, bananas, sorghum, millet, and rice. Cotton and coffee are cash crops, grown for export, but prices for both commodities have declined on world markets. Coffee exports were $8 million in 1998, down from $17million in 1997.

Second only to cotton as a cash crop, coffee is grown in several regions of the country and covers over 138,000 acres, mostly in the south-west. Ninety percent of coffee growing is done on small plantations, often less than an acre in size, with relatively low yields. Some 300,000 to 400,000 families gain their livelihood from coffee production. In 1999 the country exported 200,000 bags of robusta beans, significantly up from the 115,000 exported in 1997, but slightly down from 1998's production of 214, 000 bags.

Central African Republic has significant forestry potential, with over 60 commercially viable trees. Typically it exports around 21 species, but further development of the sector is hampered by high transportation costs and delivery problems. Landlocked, the state is dependent on the political stability of its neighbors for getting its production to sea. Civil conflict in the Republic of Congo closed the Brazzaville-Pointe Noire rail line used to export much of the timber production. Cameroon has plans to build a rail link from the port of Kribi into the Central African Republic, but their implementation is presently remote. Output of logs increased in 1997 to 429,208 cubic meters, from 290,902 in 1996. Forestry contributes about a quarter of CAR's export revenues.

Diamonds have traditionally contributed half of foreign earnings, but production is affected by political instability. Central African Republic is ranked among the top ten diamond producers of the world. An estimated 50,000 small-scale miners recover about 500,000 carats each year, over half of which are of gem quality. In 1997 diamond exports of $67 million accounted for only 39% of the nation's export earnings, down from 48% in 1996. Diamond exports earned only $59 million in 1998, but accounted for 42% of total export income. Smuggling remains a significant problem, reducing government revenues from diamond sales.

As a result of fighting in the DRC, fuel has often been in desperately short supply. Tanker barges have been unable to reach Bangui by river, and fuel has had to be transported by road through Cameroon. This has added transport costs to already high fuel prices and forced the government to stint on salaries in order to import oil.

An attempted coup in late May was bloodily repressed with the aid of Libyan troops and several hundred of Jean-Pierre Bemba's *MLC* fighters, who crossed the Ubangui river from their northern Congolese bases. Their participation gave credence to reports that Bemba was receiving financial support from Col. Qadhafi.

General André Kolingba, once again, seemed to be the man behind the coup. With little evident self-mockery, he denied that it was a coup attempt. It was, he said an effort to bring "peace and security to the country." The fighting further damaged the capital, already devastated by three previous coups, and mop-up operations focused on General Kolingba's minority Yakoma tribesmen.

President Patassé remains ensconced in his presidential palace surrounded by a protective force of Libyan troops. General Kolingba, stripped of his medals and demoted to private, is in flight. The government has offered a bounty of $38,000 for the general, dead or alive.

Future: Precarious at best.

The Republic of Equatorial Guinea

A catch off Rio Muni

Area: 28,051 sq. km = 10,830 sq. mi. (slightly larger than Vermont).
Population: 465,746 (July 1999 est.)
Capital City: Malabo (on Bioko Island, pop. 50,000, projected).
Climate: Tropically hot and humid.
Neighboring Countries: Cameroon (North); Gabon (East and South). The island portion of the country lies some twenty miles off the west coast of Cameroon.
Official Languages: Spanish and French.
Other Principal Languages: Fang, Bubi, Ibo, and Pidgin English.
Ethnic groups: Bioko (primarily Bubi, some Fernandinos), Rio Muni (primarily Fang), Europeans less than 1,000, mostly Spanish.
Principal Religions: Most people are nominally Roman Catholic; traditional tribal beliefs are intermingled with their Christian faith.
Chief Commercial Products: Petroleum, timber, and cocoa.
GNP per capita: 1,500 US$
Currency: CFA Franc
Former Colonial Status: Spanish Colony (island, 1778–1968, mainland 1885–1968).
Independence Date: October 12, 1968.
Chief of State: Col. Teodoro Obiang Nguema Mbasogo, President, Supreme Military Council (Pronounced Tay–oh–*dor*–oh *Oh*–be–ang N–*gway*–mah M–bah–*so*–go).
National Flag: Three horizontal stripes of green, white and red, with a blunt aquamarine triangle next to the staff.

Note: Between 1974 and the present, geographic place names have been changed from Spanish to African and then to *other* African designations and back to Spanish. The island, first known as Fernando Poo, was renamed by the late president in his own honor. It then was designated *Bioko* after an early king of the region. The mainland, formerly Rio Muni, became Mbini but is now again generally called Rio Muni.

On the protected shoreline of mainland Equatorial Guinea, hot and humid Rio Muni, the narrow white sandy beach quickly gives way to thick growth of interior jungle, where immense ebony, mahogany and oak trees crowd each other to bask in the sun. It is uniformly hot and oppressive. Few roads penetrate into the interior, but the land is thick with streams which are the home of giant frogs (as long as three feet and weighing up to six pounds!) which perch motionless on the spray–drenched rocks, their tongues darting out to catch unwary insects. Here in the steaming jungle back in the mid–1960s was found a baby gorilla which, through a genetic quirk, had a pink face and white fur.

The scenic Island of Bioko is large and was productive until the 1970s, being the source of one of the best qualities of cocoa in the world. Production was on large plantations; contract help from Nigeria was imported, but almost all fled when brutality entered the nation under the hand of the demented former ruler, Macías Nguema. Ships from many nations called at the port, and the international airport was the base from which relief supplies were flown into strife–torn Nigeria in the early 1970s.

History: Almost nothing is known of the pre-colonial period of this remote part of Africa; the Fang and other Bantu people settled thinly in Rio Muni and the Bubis settled on Bioko. For details of early and colonial history, see Historical Background and *The Spanish in Africa*.

Spain granted independence to Equatorial Guinea in 1968; the territory had been internally self–governing since 1964. Elections held in 1968 under UN supervision resulted in a plurality of votes for Francisco Macías Nguema; in the run–off ballot he won a majority and was installed in office.

Disputes between the remaining Spanish people and the government of Macías in 1969 led to a demand that all Spaniards and troops be withdrawn from the country. This was not done immediately and violence erupted that threatened thousands of lives.

Almost immediately following independence Macías Nguema arranged for the arrest and execution of political figures on the ground that they were plotting his overthrow. He rapidly installed members of his family in key government posts—but he even kept a close eye on *them*. Conditions steadily worsened until by early 1969 the country was in a state of anarchy and there was widespread starvation.

Life became increasingly grim in this two–part nation. In 1972 Macías Nguema's hand–picked National Assembly named him "president for life."

His mental condition worsened by leaps and bounds; in 1974 he had a high wall built around the palace in Malabo. A report sent to the UN states that by 1974 two–thirds of the members of the 1968 National Assembly had just *disappeared*. Stories increased about imprisonment, torture and execution of anyone who so much as lifted an eyebrow against the government, and rumors of forced labor were proven to be correct. All boys between 7 and 14 were forced to receive military training or their families would suffer the consequences—generally meaning death.

Macías Nguema used the youth organization *Youth Marching with Macías* to accomplish his more grisly missions. After

more than 25,000 Nigerian laborers fled the country to save their lives, arriving home penniless because their labor contracts had not been paid for, Macías Nguema expelled all the rest—there had been about 45,000 Nigerians working on the cacao plantations; he then ordered the arrest of 25,000 people on the mainland, Rio Muni, to be used as slave labor to replace them.

His madness increased. After an attempt to overthrow him in 1976, he decided to abandon Malabo on the island and set up shop in his home village of Mongomo, near the easternmost mainland border of Equatorial Guinea. In closing down government operations, he saw to it that some $60 million left in the national treasury was moved to a wooden hut in the village. Day–to–day government affairs were placed in the hands of his nephew and deputy defense minister, Lt. Col. Teodoro Obiang Nguema Mbasogo.

The nation fell into a state of abandonment; journalists were barred for many years. The national currency, formerly the Ekoule, disappeared from circulation; primitive bartering was the only salvation of the people. Most of the fishermen's boats had been destroyed so that no more citizens could escape the terrorized nation. Civil servants went unpaid and the gates of the finance ministry were shut with a huge padlock. There was no electricity; the capital's generator had blown up in the summer of 1978 and there was no money to repair it. Malabo dwindled from a city of 60,000 to 20,000. Shops were shuttered since there was nothing to sell—no fish, no meat, clothing, medical supplies. It literally became a ghost town where the people went out of their homes only when absolutely necessary because of thieves. The provincial capital of Rio Muni, Bata, was even worse. It is estimated that a third of the population fled and about 40,000 were used as forced labor; the same amount were executed.

In the summer of 1979 Macías Nguema was suddenly overthrown by his nephew, Teodoro. He was captured hiding in the bush at Mongomo; he and six close associates were executed by firing squad within weeks.

"Elections" were held in 1983 and again in mid–1988 for candidates hand-picked by the president. The basic problem continues to be ethnic. The Fang of Rio Muni are less cultured and educated than are the Bubi of Bioko. The latter are effectively excluded from government; there was no legislature until 1994. It now consists of members produced by massive election fraud.

The *Democratic Party of Equatorial Guinea (PDGE)* of the Nguema clan was the only political party after independence until 1993. Elections in that year were no more than a farce; opposition candidates had been murdered or jailed for years, leading to a boycott of the contest by any meaningful opponents. Conditions were so bad that voters fled into the jungle rather than register to vote at the point of a gun. After the U.S. denounced the elections, the security chief of Equatorial Guinea (Capt. Manuel Nguema Mba) accused the U.S. ambassador of taking medicine from the opposition, administered by a witch doctor, in order "to make the vote come out badly."

Although multiparty elections were introduced in 1993, nothing approaching democracy exists in Equatorial Guinea. President Obiang was elected to a seven-year term in 1996 in a contest dominated by fraud and intimidation. The government and 14 opposition groups signed a national pact in April 1997 agreeing to the basic conditions for future legislative elections. One month later, however, the government announced a plot to overthrow the president had been uncovered. The alleged leader was Severo Moto, leader of the *Partido del Progreso de Guinea Ecuatorial (PPGE)*—one of the most influential of the opposition groups. This set off another wave of political repression. Relations with Spain deteriorated. Obiang was infuriated when Spain granted Moto asylum. In pique, Obiang made French the official language of this former Spanish colony. In May Severo Moto, along with eleven others, was tried *in absentia* for treason, found guilty and sentenced to 101 years imprisonment. The *PPGE* was banned in June, indicating just how quickly the opposition can be dispatched in Equatorial Guinea.

A new separatist group emerged in January 1998, attacking three police posts and killing several people. It identified itself as the *Movement for Self-determination for the Island of Bioko (MAIB)* and demanded independence for the island's indigenous population of Bubi peoples, marginalized and excluded from the country's political and economic life by the mainland Fang. Mass arrests followed. Fifteen Bubi were condemned to death by a military court. The sentence was reduced in September, by presidential grace, to life imprisonment after an outpouring of international protest.

Legislative elections in March 1999 could be called farcical were it not for the thuggish brutality of the Obiang Nguema regime. Opposition candidates were threatened, arbitrarily arrested and prevented from campaigning. For the election itself, additional polling places were set up in schools, barracks and state–owned enterprises, close to the governing party's adherents. Alliances between parties were prohibited. Electoral lists were unilaterally established by the government and the *PDGE*. On election day those lists went frequently unposted at precincts, while armed soldiers or other security agents stood inside the polling area. Voters were often forced to cast their ballots publicly. The European Union and most other bodies who had been requested to send observers refused to sanction any of this by their presence. Spanish journalists who wanted to travel to Malabo to observe the elections were denied visas. Little wonder Freedom House lists Equatorial Guinea as one of the 13 worst dictatorships in the world, right up there with North Korea and Iraq.

Unsurprisingly the *PDGE* won seventy-five of eighty parliamentary seats. In some constituencies, like President Nguema's hometown, the party captured 100% of the vote. Only two opposition parties managed to get their candidates elected. The socialist *Popular Union* won four seats; the *Convergence for Social Democracy* obtained a single seat. The eleven parties of legal opposition that failed to elect a representative to parliament faced extinction. The electoral law of February 1998 provides for the dissolution of any party not having elected a candidate to office in the last three elections. Since the election, both the *Popular Union* and the *Convergence* have continued to criticize its procedures and refused to take their seats in parliament.

The government held municipal elections in May 2000, and unsurprisingly the *PDGE* swept all 30 city councils, winning 230 out of 244 seats. The three main opposition parties had stigmatized the elections as a "parody" and refused participation. Symptomatic of the tightly controlled political environment in Equatorial Guinea is one simple fact: the Minister of the Interior, in charge of police and security, is simultaneously chairman of the National Electoral Commission!

The government strictly controls freedom of speech and press. Press laws authorize government censorship of all publications. All electronic media are censured. The ruling party controls the country's main publications, radio and television. It owns and operates Radio Malabo, the most widely heard station. Only in 1998 did the government allow the country's first private domestic radio station, but that is reportedly owned by the Minister of Forestry, Environment, and Fisheries, Teodoro Obiang Nguema, the president's son.

At this point political opposition in Equatorial Guinea is both futile and heroic. Threats, kidnapping, torture and murder have all be employed by the government to control its opponents. In March 2001, eight opposition parties headquartered in Madrid set up a coalition with the aim of bringing international attention to the dismal record of the regime. Given Equatorial Guinea's developing oil-wealth, however, President Obiang has received welcome and entrée where once, one would have hoped, ethical sensitivities would have barred the door.

President Obiang Nguema Mbasogo

Culture: The oil economy means the people of Rio Muni no longer live in rural solitude. Four–wheel-drive vehicles tooling along the faded elegance of Spanish colonial boulevards suggest the ruling elite has begun to enjoy the economic fruits of political power. The dispossessed must suffer through daily water and power cutoffs and drinking water regularly polluted by drainage water, mainly because of broken pipes.

The use of marijuana is widespread and traditional. Referred to as the "sacred weed of the people" and once used only in traditional ceremonies, marijuana has found its way into every level of Equatorial Guinean society. The plants are grown locally between cassava plants or banana trees, and on the streets of Malabo a poor man's joint can be had for 100 CFA francs (about 20 US cents.). The drug provides, for the poor, escape from worsening poverty amid the riches of an oil boom. "We can neither go to school nor to work and people think we are thieves," said a young unemployed woman. Another of Malabo's poor said he and his companions "take refuge in marijuana. At least it helps us to take a less aggressive view of life." Perhaps. A senior police officer was less sanguine. Most young smokers, he thought, "turn into dangerous delinquents. Under the influence of the sacred weed, they do not hesitate to use machetes, knives, and guns to carry out armed robberies." The process has already been seen in places like Liberia and Sierra Leone.

Economy: The export of cocoa and coffee had been the traditional backbone of the nation's economy, but under Macías Nguema the plantations were nationalized and destroyed. In the 1960s nearly 98,000 acres were devoted to cocoa production, mostly on Bioko Island; by the 1980s, only 7,400 acres remained in production. Annual yields fell from 38,000 metric tons to a low of 4,500 tons. Coffee production similarly collapsed. About 8,500 metric tons, most of it grown by African farmers on small plots in Rio Muni, were produced in 1968. By the late 1980s production had fallen to 1,000 tons.

There are few incentives for farmers to continue cocoa cultivation. The Equatorial Guinea Institute for Agricultural Promotion (*INPAGE*), which buys and sells farm produce on behalf of the state, offers farmers significantly less for their produce than farmers earn in nearby Cameroon. In September 2000, over a hundred farmers besieged *INPAGE*'s offices to demand payment for cocoa rendered but not yet recompensed. Little wonder, then, that plantations are increasingly abandoned by workers migrating to seek jobs in the burgeoning oil sector.

Equatorial Guinea's reversal of economic fortune began in the 1990s with the discovery of oil in the Gulf of Guinea. By 1998, Mobil Oil was pumping 90,000 barrels a day; reserves at its Zafiro field, northwest of Bioko Island, were estimated at 300 million barrels. Dallas-based Triton Energy operates a second field, La Ceiba, with estimated reserves of 500 million barrels. In 1999 and 2000, daily production from the two fields averaged 102,000 barrels a day. The Energy Ministry forecasts that output will rise to 200,000 barrels per day by the end of 2001. At that rate Equatorial Guinea will overtake Gabon, sub-Saharan Africa's third biggest producer.

For a number of years Equatorial Guinea survived on foreign aid which accounted for 25% of GDP, one of the highest rates of aid-dependence in the world. Since the discovery of oil in 1995, Equatorial Guinea has attracted well over a billion dollars in foreign direct investment. It is money that knows few ethical hesitations before a regime that is more authoritarian than democratic. The huge multinationals present in the country have shown little interest in pressing for political liberalization or fairer distribution of new wealth. Endemic corruption has brought little improvement in the economic fortunes of the average citizen.

Two American independent energy companies are partnering with the government to develop the country's largest project—a $450 million methanol plant outside the capital. The plant would stop the wasteful and ecologically damaging flaring of natural gas associated with oil production. Production is estimated to produce revenues equivalent to another 25,000 barrels per day of oil. Construction was initiated in 1999 and production scheduled to begin by mid-2001.

Financing for the plant was facilitated by the quasi-governmental U.S. Overseas Private Investment Corporation (OPIC). In June 2000, the corporation's Board of Directors approved a $173 million guaranty for the construction, ownership and operation of the plant. It was the agency's largest-ever loan to sub-Saharan project. Gilding the lily, the Board also approved another $200 million in political risk insurance for the project. In September, OPIC hosted President Obiang at its Washington headquarters.

Washington's new enthusiasm for the country could also be seen in the Clinton State Department's approval of a license to an America private military company to bolster government security capacities. Military Professional Resources Inc., or MPRI, of Alexandria, Va., will help the government develop a coast guard to protect its off-shore oil fields. How soothing is the balm of petroleum: in 1993 the American ambassador received a death threat for trying to save opponents of the Obiang regime.

People have begun to refer to the country as "Africa's Kuwait." The economy grew by more than 40% in 1996 and by about 50% in 1997. In 1999 growth registered 28.4%. The country is earning $200 million annually, with a population of nearly 465,000. The run-down capital has been spruced up. Roads and bridges, seriously dilapidated, have been repaired and rebuilt. An impressive convention center was completed just in time to host the May 1999 summit of the Central Africa Economic and Monetary Community (*CEMAC*). Afterwards it houses the National Assembly.

Developments in the petroleum sector have far overshadowed the other important resource for the country's ruling clan: timber. Initially small scale, logging operations exploded around 1994 when huge transnational companies from Malaysia, China and North Korea moved in. By the mid-1990s there were more than 20 logging companies exploiting the rain forest. Timber operations accounted for at least 70% of government revenue, and much of the work was done on concessions reportedly owned by President Obiang.

There are approximately 3.2 million acres of forestland in mainland Equatorial Guinea. By 1997, an estimated 800,000 cubic meters of valuable hard woods were being logged, and timber revenues represented about 5.9% of GDP. At the port at Bata, only 238 miles from the timber concessions, ships never seemed to stop loading. Exports slowed during the Asian economic slowdown, but by 2000, timber exports were estimated to be around 811,000 cubic meters.

In June 2000, the World Wildlife Fund (WWF) and the Washington-based World Resources Institute (WRI) released a long suppressed report on worldwide logging operations which condemned the expansion of destructive logging practices by largely Asian firms, mainly from Malaysia, Indonesia, Korea, and Hong Kong. The authors were so disturbed by what they saw in Latin America, the Pacific and Africa that they recommended a complete moratorium on logging in eleven countries, one of which was Equatorial Guinea.

Unfortunately the oil revenues have mostly allowed the Obiang regime to enrich and further entrench itself. As it had controlled jobs in the bureaucracy, awarding them to its faithful supporters, the clan Nguema controls access to the new, high–paying jobs of the oil industry. The best jobs are reserved for the *PDGE* faithful. The national budget is also a means of reward and punishment. Malabo, the nation's capital and largest city of more than 50,000 inhabitants, is controlled by the opposition. Its budgetary allocation for 1999 is a little over $4,000. The city's mayor criticized the government and aptly pointed out that municipal authorities were unable to carry out their responsibilities, especially since taxes due the city are collected, and retained, by the interior ministry. President Nguema responded to this with brutal honesty: "We don't bother ourselves with opposition city halls and we didn't come here to pick up Malabo's garbage."

The Future: Equatorial Guinea's oil bounty is not without its problems. Boundaries of the oil fields could become contentious with neighboring Nigeria and São Tomé. Nigeria has already allotted exploration rights to the French oil giant Elf Aquitaine in areas claimed by Equatorial Guinea. The Obiang clan intends to stay in power as long as possible and the best the opposition can hope for from the new oil wealth is that the presence of hundreds of foreigners might restrain regime repression.

The Federal Republic of Nigeria

Tire advertisement does not help this traffic jam in Lagos AP/Wide World Photo

Area: 924,630 sq. km. = 357,000 sq. mi. (the size of the traditional southern states east of the Mississippi River, omitting Florida).
Population: 113,828,587 (July 1999 est.)
Capital City: Abuja (Pop. 850,000, estimated).
Climate: Hot and humid in the coastal belt and southern interior; hot and less humid in the central plains regions; semi–arid to arid and hot in the extreme north.
Neighboring Countries: Benin (West); Niger, Chad (North); Cameroon (East).
Official Language: English.
Other Principal Languages: There over 450 languages spoken. Prominent are Edo, Fulani, Hausa, Ibibio, Igbo, Ijo, Kanuri, Nupe, Tiv, and Yoruba.
Ethnic groups: Prominent are the Hausa, Fulani, Yoruba, Ibo, Ijaw, Kanuri, Ibibio, and Tiv.
Principal Religions: Muslim 50%, Christian 40%, indigenous beliefs 10%.
Chief Commercial Products: Petroleum and petroleum products 95%, cocoa, rubber.
GNP per capita: 300 US$
Currency: 1 Naira (N) = 100 kobo
Former Colonial Status: British Colony (1914–1960).
Independence Date: October 1, 1960.
Chief of State: Olusegun Obasanjo, elected February 27, 1999.
National Flag: Three vertical stripes of green, white and green.

Nigeria, the fourteenth largest country on the African continent with the largest population of any African nation, lies facing the Gulf of Guinea on the southern coast of West Africa. From the warm waters of the ocean the land has a flat appearance; there is a belt of dense swamp and towering mangrove trees 10 to 15 miles wide. This marshy coastal area resembles the bayous of Louisiana, particularly in the delta of the Niger River.

Further inland, there is a region 50 to 100 miles wide where the vegetation is thick green jungle rising from more stable ground. The trees of this warm and humid area reach heights of 200 feet where vines entwine all growth. This jungle area and the coast receive up to 150 inches of rainfall per year.

The land rises slowly in a series of foothills to the Jos Plateau, reaching altitudes up to 1,000 feet. Tall grasses grow rapidly between widely spaced trees. The dry season, from October to April, evaporates moisture from the ground, hardening the earth so that when the spring rains come, the soil erodes into the rivers.

There is a semi–arid to arid region in the extreme north, close of Lake Chad and Niger. This is the transition zone lying between the Sahara Desert and the green forests and jungles of the South, receiving 25 inches or less of rain per year. In the last decade, the "or less" has been the rule. This area is threatened by the expansion southward of the great desert.

During the dry season, particularly in December and January, the *harmattan,* the hot wind blowing from the desert, penetrates to the Gulf of Guinea, lowering the humidity and raising dust storms in the interior.

History: The early history of Nigeria is traced through the people by their poetry and legends. The Yoruba tribes were established between the 11th and 14th centuries in the southern coastal region. The Hausa kingdoms were gradually established after the 12th century in the North; the people, of Sudanic–Hamitic descent, were converted to Islam in the 14th century. The Fulani (Peulh) nomadic cattle herdsmen became rulers in the Hausa regions of the North in the late 19th century. The Ibo occupied the southeast region for many centuries before the arrival of the first Europeans, organizing themselves into family units. For details of early and colonial history, see Historical Background and *The British in Africa.*

Following its independence granted in October 1960, Nigeria became a part of the British Commonwealth, but altered its status to that of a Republic within the Commonwealth in 1962. President Nnamdi Azikwe replaced Queen Elizabeth II as titular chief of state with this change.

Regional differences were inevitable; Nigeria was at that time divided into three regions: the largest, the North, inhabited predominantly by Islamic believers, and two smaller states in the South. Of these latter, the Eastern Region was dominated by the progressive, Christian Ibo people and the Western Region was controlled by the religiously mixed, but predominantly Christian Yorubas. Each of the three groups was split into innumerable factions, tribes and groups, and none of them constituted a unified factor in Nigerian politics. At the top of government was the Federal Prime Minister, Sir Abubakar Tafewa Balewa.

There were four short years of apparent harmony, but this was true only on the surface. Elections in 1965 provided a scenario in which corruption and ethnic strife has continued at higher and lower levels since that year. With the exception of a few brief periods, the leadership of Nigeria was determined by *coup* and assassination. Widespread lawlessness accompanied the confusion.

The basis for this virtual anarchy was the more numerous Islamic Northerners dominating either of the two main southern groups, and the inability of the latter two to cooperate with each other. Conditions worsened in 1965–66, leading to an attempted *coup* by Ibo army officers. Ibos had settled throughout Nigeria, with occupations such as technicians, clerks and civil servants. There ensued an effort by the Hausas and other groups of the North to eradicate as many Ibos as possible. Conferences to settle the conflict were fruitless.

Colonel Odumegwu Ojukwu, an Ibo, assumed control of the Eastern Region and proclaimed independence of the area, naming it *Biafra.* Strife immediately intensified, continuing until early 1970. The innocent suffered the most. The bellies of Biafran children became swollen and their black hair turned orange by the dreaded *Kwashiokior*—the Ghanaian word for protein starvation. Collected into orphanages, they became too tired to eat, sat down—and died. Burial, when possible, was usually in mass graves. The conflict abruptly ended when Ojukwu fled and the Ibos surrendered.

Based upon the 1967 performance of the Northerners, widespread genocide and starvation was generally expected, but thankfully averted. A military government emerged in firm control. Recovery from the civil war was rapid, but uneven. During the latter 1960s and the years succeeding, a mass migration to the cities occurred in Nigeria, severely straining the ability of the government to provide essential services.

Starting in the 1970s, petroleum production burgeoned (exported principally to the U.S.) and contributed an additional basis for dispute. One in five barrels simply evaporated and the money from its sale went directly into the pockets of one or more Nigerians in a position to steal, either in or out of government.

Adopting a new constitution in 1979, Nigeria made an attempt at democratic government until 1983. The constitution, however, only presented a theater for a replay of ethnic differences. Oil revenues, which peaked in 1980, provided prosperity that drew attention away from them. More than 1 million Africans from neighboring nations (principally Ghana) were allowed in to work in positions related to oil production. This changed in the 1990s when they were summarily expelled in order that Nigerians could claim the same jobs.

With its candidate reelected in 1983, the northern *National Party* pressed for installation of its stalwarts in office. It was not long before they were in office, shipping money to foreign accounts while the good days lasted. But they didn't. By 1983 income from oil had dropped in half. The military, disgusted with rampant corruption, seized control. Mismanagement and corruption were everywhere. It instituted military tribunals for officials suspected of corruption and placed strict controls on currency to lower all forms of thievery. Public executions of violent criminals became commonplace.

The construction of the new federal capital city at Abuja was a classic example of Nigerian corruption. By the mid–1980s half–completed government buildings and luxury hotels were everywhere, replete with poor quality, design, workmanship and materials. Transfer of governmental bureaus from overcrowded Lagos to Abuja is still underway, although the official goal for completion of this was 1992. The new buildings are not stable because of the moist heat typical of the area.

When in 1985 oil prices plummeted to less than $10 per barrel, chaos in the Nigerian economy resulted. The military regime imposed yet another round of austerity measures, including pay cuts for the military which were most unpopular.

External and internal pressures led to planning for a return of multi–party civilian government by the beginning of the 1990s. The military chief of state was charged with having a secret goal: maintenance of military control over Nigeria. This was untrue; he sought to prevent the total collapse of his country. Legislative elections were held in 1992, but the victors were put on "hold" awaiting further developments. The promised legislature simply evaporated. The military dictated that there be only *two* parties in order to coerce the population into making political sense. One, the *Social Democratic Party* was to be "a little" to the left; the other, the *National Republican Convention,* was to be "a little" to the right.

After three postponements, elections were finally held in mid–1993. Moshood K.O. Abiola, a billionaire Yoruba Muslim of the *Social Democratic Party,* promised instant

President Shehu Shagari (from 1979 through 1983)

paradise for all if elected (prosperity within six months!) Both he and his *Republican* opponent were close friends of the military leader, Ibrahim Babangida. Only about 30% of the disbelieving Nigerians voted, but they apparently chose Abiola, who was an astute politician, a conniving thief or an *Uncle Tom* (or a combination of all three) depending on who is relied upon.

Babangida and the military, correctly sensing Nigeria was heading for disaster, arranged the filing of a series of pre–arranged lawsuits alleging the election was riddled with irregularities (there weren't that many by Nigerian standards). While the cases were pending in court, the military nullified the election "to save our judiciary . . ." (!)

Promising elections in August 1993, Babangida instead stepped down. An insignificant tribal chief was briefly president until the real power behind the military stepped forward in November to personally attend to the leadership of Nigeria: General Sani (Sanni) Abacha.

Political parties were outlawed, their candidates were silenced and labor strikes were promptly abolished; state, local and federal government offices were seized. The usual internal and external protest was loud, and the response was that civilian government "had not been abandoned."

A promise that is perennial in Nigeria was heard. There must be a constitutional convention to bring about reconciliation. To mute criticism at home and abroad, General Abacha decreed that the 1979 Nigerian constitution be restored. His cabinet contains several former supporters of Abiola, who has termed the military takeover an act of God. The military rules a fragmented Nigeria which just barely avoided disintegration and anarchy. The composition of the members of and date of a constitutional convention remained unannounced as of mid–1994, although an inconclusive meeting of prominent persons was held in February. The U.S. and other western nations grumbled about the latest military takeover. The U.S., opposition to military rule and insistence on a return to the civilian president, has been almost totally absent, compared to Haiti.

Northern Nigeria's ancient Muslim city of Kano at the edge of the Sahara AP/Wide World Photo

The reason: Nigeria has oil and Haiti doesn't. It is most predictably (but inefficiently) extracted and exported to the U.S. under Nigerian military rule.

Moshood Abiola addressed popular anti–military rallies in 1994 and was arrested on charges of treason in mid–year. Legal proceedings against him (which the British described as being "irregular" but are more properly termed a serial farce) are not yet complete, yet he is confined to jail and is reported to be ill. The latest wrinkle came when the trial judge walked out of the courtroom because he felt "threatened," most certainly true.

A pro–democracy oil workers strike was broken in late 1994; the workers demanded the installation of Abiola as president. But economic necessity forced the workers to return to their labors. The government responded by publishing decrees granting itself "absolute power."

The military government worked through and with local, traditional rulers to maintain control of Nigeria, particularly in the oil producing regions. Nigerian playwright Ken Saro–Wiwa and eight other activists from the Ogoni people of Rivers State decided in 1994 to make a play for the wealth of the oil–rich region. They claimed the environment of the Ogoni people was being ruined. Four traditional Ogoni leaders were gunned down; the government charged that Saro–Wiwa and his cohorts arranged the deaths. There was a trial in secret by a court selected by Abacha, which resulted in death sentences for all nine. In spite of international howls of protest as well as those in the liberal press of the United States, the death sentences were carried out (very clumsily).

The life of a military dictator is not an easy one. Another coup was discovered in December 1997, this time involving Abacha's second in command, General Oladipo Diya, the highest ranking Yoruba in the military government. Great efforts were made to prove the authenticity of the plot. Video tapes of Diya and others confessing were played for select audiences. Prominent among those selected for government briefing were traditional rulers, whose backing President Abacha seemed particularly eager to secure.

It was clear that General Abacha was planning on running for the Nigerian presidency later in 1998. Relative success in Liberia and Sierra Leone, though terribly expensive, had given a temporary boost to his reputation as a regional leader. As of late April, all five legally permitted parties had asked Abacha to be their candidate. In effect this meant that the presidential election was now a referendum: Abacha or not? Elections for state assemblies in December went off smoothly, but the turnout was low. National Assembly elections in April were boycotted by the opposition and showed similar lackluster participation. The army could maintain security, but it couldn't excite people about the electoral theater it provided.

The Abacha era came to an abrupt end in early June when the dictator suddenly died. He was succeeded as head of state by General Abdusalam Abubakar, Chief of the Defense staff, appointed to the position by his fellow generals on the Provisional Ruling Council. General Abubakar's transition to civilian rule was remarkable in its swiftness and general efficiency. Political detainees were released, including General Obasanjo who had been detained since 1995 as a suspect in an anti-Abacha coup. Chief Abiola, in detention since 1994, suddenly collapsed on July 7. All efforts to save his life failed.

Moshood K.O. Abiola

His passing from the scene eliminated a major problem for General Abubakar and facilitated the relatively smooth transition to civilian rule in late May 1999.

General Abacha's self–serving transition structure was swept away and its five political parties disbanded. An independent electoral commission was instituted and elections for the civilian government were organized and successfully carried off. Northern power brokers, the Kaduna mafia, agreed to a shift in power that would bring a Southerner to the presidential office for the first time. In the presidential election, two Yoruba opposed each other. Olu Falae, a former finance minister, was the standard bearer of two allied parties, the progressive *Alliance for Democracy* and the more conservative *All People's Party*. Olusegun Obasanjo, the only military man to actually hand back the reins of government to civilians, represented the centrist *People's Democratic Party (PDP)*. Obasanjo, who clearly had the backing of northern politicians and the army won 62.8% of the vote to Falae's 37.2%. The *PDP* also won a clear majority in both houses of parliament.

General Abubakar also moved on the economic front, but here the results seemed less positive. A plan to privatize some of Nigeria's unproductive and expensive state corporations was finally announced in early May. The plans called for privatization of electricity, telecommunications, oil refining and other companies. Given the lateness of the proposal and the importance of the issue, little action was expected. Nigeria has more than 1,500 state–owned companies, and they cost the country more than $2 billion annually. State corporations provide huge patronage possibilities and were the basis of much of the power wielded by the old élites. There are more than 4,000 directors, members of boards and executives of the largest corporations appointed by the president. Privatization will be a major stumbling block for the civilian regime.

Halfway through his term of office, President Obasanjo has experienced two years of crisis-to-crisis management. The return to democracy has placed extraordinary demands on the government. Freed from 15 years of iron-fisted military repression, Nigerians of all levels erupted in what appeared at times a volcanic expression of grievance, complaint and demand, devolving, at times, into ethnic or sectarian conflict.

In many ways the new Nigeria has begun to resemble old Nigeria. Regional conflicts persist. Fuel and electricity shortages continue. Government resources are turned to projects of dubious economic value. Law and order are uncertain and the security of person and property at risk. A culture of corruption is so embedded that it is likely to be an enduring feature of Nigerian life.

At the heart of current controversies is the nature and definition, if not the existence, of the Nigerian state: What should be the balance of resources and power between the central government and individual states? Resolving these political questions in deplorable economic circumstances will not be easy. For the remaining two years of President Obasanjo's term of office, the tensions and conflicts of Nigerian life are likely to be exaggerated as all eyes begin to look toward presidential and gubernatorial elections in 2003.

President Obasanjo is confronted with regional tensions in both north and south. In the south, crisis is sited in the Niger Delta area, source of Nigeria's wealth, but an area in which the processes of extracting that wealth have created an ecological hell. Since 1986, between two and three million barrels of oil of been spilled on the land and creeks of the Delta region, killing the soil and polluting the waters, depriving local inhabitants of their traditional means of livelihood. Every day eight million cubic feet of natural gas are flared, adding deadly illumination to the processes of extractive destruction

Despite its generation of fabulous wealth, the Niger Delta area remains one of Nigeria's poorest and least developed regions. For residents there is a near total absence of schools, drinking water, electricity, and medical care. A crescendo of regional complaint has been raised, demanding a greater share of petroleum profits. The most intractable of demands came from young members of the Ijaw community, probably the fourth largest group in Nigeria.

On December 11, 1998, some 5,000 members of the Ijaw Youth Council (IJC) from the Delta region had met in Kaiama, Bayelsa State. The 11-point resolution they passed, which became known as the Kaiama Declaration, gave vent to their frustrations with the leadership of an older generation that had achieved so little in terms of communal and environmental improvement. "We are tired," the resolution said, "of gas flaring, oil spillages, [and] blowouts..." In many ways it amounted to a declaration of secession from a Federal Nigeria. The IJC declared that it ceased to recognize all decrees "enacted without our participation and consent."

The Declaration went on to claim ownership of all natural resources found in Ijaw territory and demanded that the oil companies stop exploration and exploitation activities. Oil workers were given an ultimatum to vacate Ijaw land or face the consequences. The deadline for cessation of activities and withdrawal of personnel was set for 30 December. Then, the Declaration said, "Ijaw youths in all communities in all Ijaw clans in the Niger Delta will take steps to implement these resolutions..."

Continuing violence in the area brought army intervention with bloody consequences. At Odi, a community of perhaps 15,000 people, the army razed the entire town, with the exception of the bank, the Anglican church, and a health clinic. At nearby Choba, the army was accused of mass rape. President Obasanjo's visit did little to ease the situation. Ijaw youth activists virtually closed down the entire Texaco operation in the region.

To ease tensions, the government agreed to implement a constitutional provision which allocates 13% of oil revenue to each oil-producing region. But the legislation creating a Niger Delta Development Commission (NDDC), caught in a dispute between legislature and executive, was long delayed. Once created,

President Olusegun Obasanjo

Natural gas storage sphere, Escravos Project Photo courtesty Chevron

however, the NDDC has been starved of funding to begin its activities, adding to the general distrust in which federal authorities are held.

Nor was trust and credibility enhanced when the Obasanjo government sought to adjust the percentage due the Delta downwards. This numerical sleight of hand came when the government said the constitutional 13% applied only to revenues derived from on-shore drilling; revenues derived from off-shore drilling were the exclusive right of the federal government. The issue has been sent to the Nigerian Supreme Court for resolution.

Perhaps the Obasanjo government faced its greatest crisis after the governor of an obscure northern state decided to implement Sharia law for the state's Muslim population. Sectarian and communal riots broke out in Kaduna, one of the largest cities in the north, and for three solid days in March 2000 the city was one vast killing zone. Estimates put the number killed at more than a thousand. Street after street was burned down, and the Red Cross estimated some 80,000 people had been driven to reception centers.

When retaliatory riots broke out in the southeast, Nigerians had an uneasy sense of *déja vu*. The events looked ominously like those that preceded the Biafran civil war. Once again, the stability of the country was at risk. Its very definition as a country was open to question.

Massive military intervention quelled the rioting in Kaduna, but eleven northern states have adopted Sharia law which, in some interpretations, violates the constitution. Increasingly one hears calls for a Sovereign National Conference to thrash out the many grievances held by Nigerians and to create a new constitution defining anew the rights of states and their relationship with each other in a federal arrangement.

In late April 2001 the government, certainly not wanting a potentially uncontrollable body claiming sovereignty, began its own process of constitutional consultation. Some 92 proposed amendments are being submitted to public hearing and debate in six regional centers. After this a six-month national debate is scheduled to follow, during which a variety of educational meetings would be held to review, analyze and debate the proposed amendments.

Culture: In almost no other nation of Africa is there so much diversity as is found in Nigeria. Colorful clothing, worn by the women, consists of a blouse, a wrap-around skirt, which sometimes covers the blouse, and an elaborate headdress to match. The men wear trousers and a shirt, covered by a long, flowing robe.

The Fulani and Hausa of the North are organized under local monarchs called Emirs, but the family is the social unit among the Ibos. Throughout Nigeria the songs and dances, performed in great varieties, provide entertainment and are part of religious rituals. The complex rhythm of drums predominates in the accompaniments.

English is the language of instruction in all high schools and universities. There are more than four million pupils in primary schools, a substantial number in courses through junior college and many are enrolled in the technical colleges and 12 universities. In spite of sometimes ineffective efforts in education, the literacy rate is high—in many cases the result of self–education. The Nigerians have enjoyed sports and for many years were the first Black African nation to participate in the Olympic Games. There are widespread organizations of Boy and Girl Scouts.

Lagos on the coast, Kano in the North and Ibadan in the West are the three largest cities, containing up–to–date architecture, and modern conveniences. Television and radio programming is varied and of high quality. A campaign to reduce the number of accidents on the highways has fizzled; driving in Nigeria was traditionally spirited at minimum and more often simply wild, harrowing and dangerous.

Economy: Nigeria is Africa's most populous country. As such it is an enormous market for goods and services. Its economy was radically transformed by the advent of oil production. From an agricultural economy, deriving 65% of foreign exchange earnings from food exports, Nigeria moved to become a major oil-exporting nation. The petroleum industry, centered on the delta region of the Niger River, dominates Nigeria's economy. It accounts for nearly 95% of foreign exchange earnings and around two-thirds of federal government revenues.

Nigeria contains an estimated 22.5 billion barrels of oil reserves and, with extensive off-shore exploration, hopes to increase its reserves to 40 billion barrels by 2010. Work towards this goal has been stymied by the inability of the state owned Nigerian National Petroleum Company to come up with the capital to fulfill its joint venture contracts with private oil firms. That Nigeria lacks investment capital while pumping 2 million barrels of oil a day suggests the pervasive nature of Nigerian corruption and its deadly impact on economic growth. Royal Dutch/Shell is the biggest company in the oil patch, accounting for nearly half of Nigeria's total oil production.

Oil production has been interrupted by local protest and ethnic violence in the delta region. Sabotage, occupation of oil facilities, hostage taking and kidnapping have all been employed by local activists. In 1999 delta protests forced production cuts of 300,000 barrels a day—accounting for a total revenue loss of $1.5 billion.

One of the great ironies of Nigeria is the importance of oil and the persistence of fuel shortages. The average driver spends hours, often overnight, waiting to buy gasoline. Part of the problem is refinery capacity: starved of money to upgrade facilities by a corrupt military regime, the country's four refineries gradually deteriorated.

The major problem is the enormous price subsidy given gasoline in Nigeria. A liter of gasoline—which for Americans paying nearly $2 a gallon, equals 2.64 gallons—costs a piddling 18 cents. Corruption diverts much production to more profitable venues, creating constant shortages. To rectify this, the government has proposed to deregulate the gasoline market, but labor unions, fearing the price rise this would entail for members, have threatened to make the country ungovernable if the proposal is implemented.

Nigeria is moving to diversify and decrease its dependence on oil. Natural gas, closely associated with oil, will replace it as the backbone of Nigeria's economy in the next century. The move to gas production comes from the government's desire to curb flaring, the simple burning off of gas associated with oil drilling and pumping. Seventy percent of all associated gas is currently flared, making Nigeria one of the world's worst heat polluters. Quite justifiably environmentalists have heaped abuse on the oil industry for such practices. The government has targeted an elimination of flaring by 2010.

Nigerian gas reserves are put at about 160 trillion cubic feet, and already a number of projects have been started for their exploitation. The Chevron project at Escravos, opened in 1997, processes 165 million cubic feet a day of natural gas for domestic and international markets. Agreements have been signed for construction of a 400-mile pipeline to bring gas to energy-starved Benin, Togo, and Ghana. The pipeline promises to make natural gas the basis of industrial development throughout coastal West Africa.

One of the single most expensive engineering projects in the history of Africa, the Nigerian Liquified Natural Gas (NLNG) plant at Bonny Island, opened in October 1999. NLNG was developed by an international consortium which included the Nigerian National Petroleum Corporation—the biggest shareholder at 49%—Shell, Elf Aquitaine, and Agip. The plant is expected to process 252.4 billion cubic feet of gas annually.

Gas production in Nigeria faces the same problems of order and stability as the oil industry. Only 30% of Nigeria's gas reserves are offshore. Another 30% are in swamplands and the rest are on dry land where production is vulnerable to the escalating violence which characterizes the region.

Nigeria's total external debt was estimated to be nearly $33.5 billion at the end of 2000 when international creditors gave the Obasanjo government a democracy dividend: rescheduling of $23.4 billion of that debt. The deal is expected to save Nigeria an estimated $1.4 billion.

An even greater priority for the government is its privatization program. Action has been sluggish because it's hard to give up statist thinking and even harder to give up potential sources of political patronage. Movement on privatization—selling off an abundance of state corporations—is essential for a variety of reasons, the least important of which is money gained through the sales. In a post-military Nigeria, the control exercised by the federal government will need to be decentralized. The state can no longer afford to subsidize inefficient corporations when regions and local communities demand a share of scarce resources for their own development; privatization will help redress the balance between center and periphery. If handled properly privatization can also make a greater contribution to job creation and poverty elimination than continued donor support.

Nigeria remains an important hub in the international illicit drug trade which seems to expand wherever Nigerians go. When ECOMOG forces were sent to Liberia, Monrovia's port became an important drug distribution point, and when a Nigerian peacekeeping force went to Sierra Leone, the first thing that happened was that the Freetown airport became a drug trafficking platform. Nigerian drug trafficking rings are a worldwide phenomenon. One was identified working the Philippines in 1995 and in the same year, Cambodian law enforcement authorities claimed that most drug traffickers in that country were from Nigeria or Ghana. Traffickers have a preference for repatriation of their profits and the consequence of this has been the growth of elaborate money-laundering schemes. Outright fraudulent schemes, usually involving the alleged transfer of funds, also tumble creatively from the minds of Nigerian criminals. So extensive are these schemes that he American Secret Service maintains a separate Nigerian fraud squad in metropolitan Washington.

The Future: The tragic consequences of years of corrupt and venal rule by military dictators will lay heavily on the efforts of the Obasanjo government. A cult of lawlessness permeates all levels of Nigerian society. One senses a need for moral as well as economic and political regeneration to bring Nigeria out of the depths into which it had been cast by Sani Abacha and his cronies. The inequities of the present, products of past abuse, require readjustment. Inevitably a new constitution will have to be elaborated in which the centralizing tendencies of successive military regimes are reversed and resources and decision making are returned to lower levels of government.

Abuja—National Mosque (upper left), National Ecumenical Center (upper right), International Conference Center (center)

Photo by Tony Azogu

EQUATORIAL WEST AFRICA

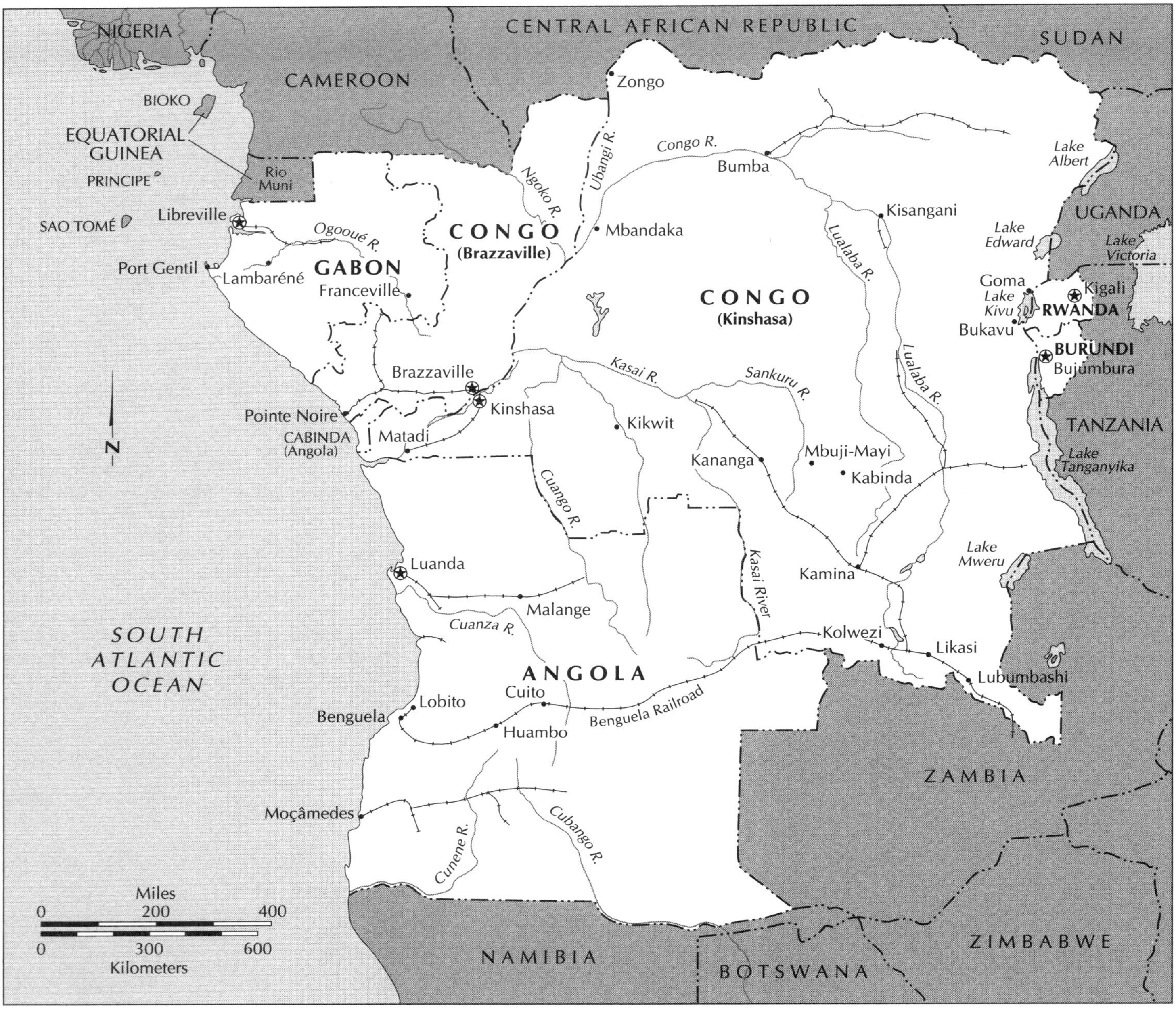

The Republic of Angola

Area: 1,245,790 sq. km. = 481,000 sq. mi. (about four times the size of New Mexico).

Population: 11.2 million (estimated).

Capital City: Luanda (Pop. 4 million, est.).

Climate: Moist and warm in the North, dryer and hot in the large, central plateau area; arid, semi–desert in the South.

Neighboring Countries: Congo–Kinshasa (North); Namibia (South); Zambia (Southeast).

Official Language: Portuguese.

Other Principal Languages: Over forty African languages, including Tchokwe, Kikongo, Kwanyama, Mbundu, Nyaneka, and Umbundu.

Ethnic groups: Ovimbundu 37%, Kimbundu 25%, Bakongo 13%, mestico (mixed European and Native African) 2%, European 1%, and other 22%.

Principal Religions: Indigenous beliefs 47%, Roman Catholic 38%, Protestant 15% (1998 est.).

Chief Commercial Products: Crude oil 90%, diamonds, refined petroleum products, gas, coffee, sisal, fish and fish products, timber, cotton.

GNP per capita: 340 US$

National Flag: Two horizontal stripes of equal width, red and black, upon which is centered a 5–pointed yellow star, halfway surrounded by a wheel and crossed by a machete.

Currency: Kwanza.

Former Colonial Status: Portuguese Colony until November 11, 1975; actual control passed in early 1975.

Independence Date: November 11, 1975.

Chief of State: José Eduardo dos Santos, President.

For most of its sprawling area, Angola is a high, grassy plateauland ranging from 3,000 to 4,000 feet above sea level, dotted by occasional trees and brush hardy enough to withstand the scorching heat of the day. The coastal belt, home to about 20% of the population, is from 15 to 60 miles wide, stretching from the tropical mouth of the mighty Congo River, down to the palm–lined central beaches, and then on to the reddish sands of the Namib Desert in the extreme south.

Lofty mountains drive eastward, splitting the country in half until the terrain gradually levels out, dipping first northeast into the hot, steaming jungles of Zaïre's river basin and then southeast to isolated, semi–arid land. The mountains are the source of rivers which fan out in all directions.

The Cuanza River, Angola's largest, twists north for 600 miles in a wavering half–circle and then drains into the Atlantic below cosmopolitan Luanda. The Cunene's cold waters gush south down the mountains, slow as they pass through the plains, become sluggish in the silent desert, then lazily turn westward and are caught by the huge Cunene Dam, which regulates its flow as it forms the 175–mile border with Namibia to the ocean. Another river, in the northeast, offers unique drama.

Meandering aimlessly across the sun–parched grasslands, the Lucala unexpectedly reaches a wide, curved rock shelf where the placid waters suddenly plunge into a 350–foot gorge, sending up a heavy spray–mist which transforms the immediate area into a lush oasis, rich with dark mosses and tropical foliage—the Duque de Bragança Falls—a truly spectacular sight. Again docile, the river moves across the flat land and joins the waters of the larger Cuanza.

Cutting across otherwise unspoiled country teeming with wildlife is the Benguela Railroad. Its tracks have clattered to the tune of millions of tons of rich copper ore shipped from the vast mines in Zaïre and Zambia to coastal Benguela and then to Lobito, Angola's principal port. Due to guerrilla activities, the line has not been in regular use since 1975 except in the coastal region.

History: The Bushmen were probably the first inhabitants of Angola during the late Stone Age; they were driven southward by a Bantu migration which was to occupy most of Africa below the Sahara Desert. This region constituted the southernmost part of the once–mighty Kingdom of the Congo—a loose confederation of Bantu tribes dominated by the Bakongo prior to the arrival of European explorers. For details of early and colonial history, see Historical Background and *The Portuguese in Africa.*

Portuguese troops fighting in Angola, 1971

Portugal's colonial policies generated increasing resistance and resentment by the 1950s. Assimilation had produced a small group of educated Angolans, mostly *mestiços*, who recognized there was no equality of treatment for an African, even if assimilated. In the countryside, the settlement of white farmers and use of forced labor embittered the rural peasantry.

Anti-colonial, nationalist sentiment first coalesced in Luanda, the capital, with the formation of the *Popular Movement for the Liberation of Angola* (*MPLA*) in 1956. The heart of the movement was a multiracial core of leftist urban intellectuals. Its ethnic core resided in the Mbundu people of Luanda and the surrounding area. As of 1962, the group was headed by Agostinho Neto, an assimilated Mbundu physician.

The *MPLA*'s greatest rival in the early years was the *National Front for the Liberation of Angola* (*FNLA*). Led by Holden Roberto, *FNLA* began as a spokesman for ethnic interests of Angola's northern Bakongo peoples, but by 1958 it expanded its goals to independence for all Angola. A national liberation army was created, and young Angolans were sent to North Africa to train with Algerian forces engaged in their own nationalist struggle. A *Revolutionary Government of Angola in Exile* (*GRAE*), headquartered in Leopoldville, was also created and claimed sole representation of the interests of the Angolan people.

A falling out between Holden Roberto and his foreign minister in the *GRAE*, Jonas Savimbi, led to the creation of *National Union for the Total Independence of Angola* (*UNITA*) in 1964. The group's membership was rooted in Angola's largest ethnic group, the Ovimbundu, peasant farmers who dominated the fertile central highlands. In 1965 Savimbi (who earned a doctorate in political science from the University of Lausanne, Switzerland) and several of his followers went to China where they received military training and became disciples of Maoism. Like its rivals, *UNITA* claimed to be the sole representative of the Angolan people.

Angola's march toward independence centered on these three military-political groups. They had one common enemy, Portugal, but differing nationalist visions. Each was specifically rooted in the geographical and ethnic reality of Angola and drew on different sources of external support that intensified rivalries both personal and ideological. At a time of intense ideological competition internationally, each of the groups ultimately became an extension of Cold War rivalries between East and West.

With its Marxist-Leninist orientation, the *MPLA* attracted the support of the international left. Its military cadres received training in Eastern Europe and Cuba. Recently independent African states with similar left-leaning inclinations provided sympathetic support. Soviet arms transited through Tanzania and Zambia to supply its forces.

The nationalist struggles in its African colonies drained Portugal's will and resources. Some 11,000 Portuguese soldiers had been killed by 1974, and on April 25 of that year disgruntled military officers overthrew the Portuguese government and began the process leading to independence. Angola's transition to independence was difficult. A transitional government involving all three nationalist groups was created, but Portuguese settlers resisted and rioted. Rivalries between the three nationalist groups intensified. External aid and intervention increased.

The United States supported the pro-Western *FNLA* when it seemed the strongest of the groups, but it later shifted its support to *UNITA*. The Soviet Union responded with increased arms deliveries to the *MPLA*, and Cuba sent military instructors and combat troops. OAU negotiators brought Neto, Roberto, and Savimbi together in June 1975 to produce a draft constitution for independent Angola, but soon afterwards the transitional government collapsed. The *FNLA* and *UNITA* withdrew, and, recognizing their military weakness individually against the *MPLA* army, united and declared war against the *MPLA*. Group rivalry turned into civil war.

In support of the *FNLA-UNITA* alliance, South Africa, which had already worked with Portugal fighting nationalist guerrillas in Angola and *SWAPO* guerillas fighting for the independence of South West Africa from their Angolan bases, sent in an invasion force to protect hydroelectric facilities on the Cunene River in August 1975. A larger South African-led force invaded Angola in October. Six provincial capitals were occupied, and the invaders came within 62 miles of Luanda.

International reaction had major consequences for Angola's nationalist groups. The *MPLA* received a massive increase in Soviet military aid, while Cuba poured thousands of troops into the country; the military balance tipped in its favor. South African support of the *FNLA* and *UNITA* tainted both groups. Portugal granted independence amid the chaos of civil war on November 11, 1975, marking the end of four hundred years of Portuguese colonial rule.

The *MPLA*, in control of the capital, proclaimed the People's Republic of Angola. A rival "Democratic People's Republic of Angola" was proclaimed by the *FNLA-UNITA* alliance, but it was clear the *MPLA*, backed by some 10,000 to 12,000 Cuban troops, had emerged on top. International recognition followed, and the *MPLA* moved to create a Marxist-Leninist single-party state. Agostinho Neto served as both *MPLA* secretary-general and president of Angola. With Cuban assistance the *FNLA* was defeated militarily, leaving only one rival to dispute its legitimacy, Jonas Savimbi's *UNITA*.

President Neto flew to Moscow in September 1979 for political discussions and medical treatment. Following an operation, he died on September 10 and was succeeded by his foreign minister, José Eduardo dos Santos. Angola faced continuing instability from internal and external elements. *UNITA* continued armed resistance to the *MPLA* government. The presence of *SWAPO* guerilla bases brought frequent South African incursions, and this resulted in clashes between Cuban and South African troops.

The linked external problems were resolved in a grand diplomatic solution of 1988. South Africa agreed to the independence of South West Africa, while Cuba and South Africa jointly agreed to withdraw their troops from Angola. There remained only the irksome presence of Jonas Savimbi and *UNITA*.

Negotiations between the two nationalist rivals resulted in a ceasefire that commenced on June 1, 1991. The lull in military conflict prepared the way for political conflict. Angola's single party constitution was amended to permit multiparty elections, and these were scheduled for September 1992. President dos Santos won a plurality of votes on the first ballot, but *UNITA* refused to accept the results, claiming widespread fraud. Within a few days *UNITA* had resumed the civil war. *UNITA* supporters were chased from Luanda, and the second round of elections were never held.

Full-scale fighting continued until a peace accord was signed in Lusaka in November 1994. In the military area the Lusaka Protocol called for demilitarization of *UNITA* and the creation of a national army integrating *UNITA* elements into the Angola Armed Forces. In the political area, it called for a government of national unity and the extension of state administration to areas formerly under *UNITA* control. Neither side seemed genuinely committed to the peace accord. Indeed, the government has never been committed to less than the total destruction of *UNITA* and the elimination of its leader, Jonas Savimbi.

Localized fighting continued throughout 1995 and 1996 despite the Lusaka Protocol. The year 1995 was marked by a major UN effort to bring peace to Angola. *UNIVEM III*, a multinational "peace–keeping" force was deployed to the country late in the year. Underfunded and understaffed, the force could hardly observe activity throughout the country, but it did begin to implement the Lusaka provisions.

By April 1998 it looked as though virtually all the Lusaka provisions had been implemented. *UNITA* had turned over almost all of the territory under its control to government administration; its soldiers, for the most part, were disarmed, and its propaganda radio shut down. For its part, the Angolan government recognized *UNITA* as an unarmed political party with the right to organize and campaign throughout the country. Savimbi was officially recognized as the main opposition leader with rights to hold regular consultations with President dos Santos, access to government media and the right to visit Angolan embassies abroad. For his personal safety, Savimbi was permitted a bodyguard of 400 men, to be ultimately reduced to 150. *UNITA*'s participation in a *Government of National Reconciliation (GURN)* was made real with the inclusion of 70 deputies in parliament and the grant of seven ministerial portfolios in the unity government. Four deputy–ministerial posts were also allocated the former rebels, as well as six ambassadorships and several senior positions in the administration.

Dr. Jonas Savimbi of *UNITA*

The Lusaka Protocol's seeming successful implementation was entirely superficial. The process had been intermittent and at each stage suggested the reality of *MPLA* intentions towards its bitter rival. In September 1997 the ruling party suspended *UNITA*'s ministers, vice–ministers, and parliamentarians, threatening *GURN*'s existence. Under international pressure, the suspension was lifted by the end of the year. The government also mounted an effort to destroy *UNITA* as a political party by successfully inducing a number of *UNITA* figures participating in *GURN* to break with Savimbi and form a new party. *UNITA–Renovado*, as it was called, deposed Savimbi as president and achieved government recognition as the authentic "interlocutor for national reconciliation." The government also sought to peddle it as such to the international community.

In the countryside, far from the probing eyes of reporters of UN monitoring teams, the Angola National Police (ANP) pursued another systematic approach to *UNITA*'s destruction. Party leadership and grassroots structures in those areas returned to the government's administration were targeted. *UNITA* administrators, party officials and even persons merely accused of collaborating with *UNITA* were simply murdered, hardly suggesting a government interested in reconciliation.

In April 1998 as part of the Lusaka agreement, *UNITA* closed down its radio station, Voice of the Resistance of the Black Cockerel–Vorgon. The station had broadcast anti–government commentary for 19 years. The government now fills its airwaves with what Western diplomats refer to as "fabricated news reports of *UNITA* atrocities." London's *Economist* reported that the propaganda campaign had become so virulent that both the UN and the Americans had issued statements denouncing the use of "false information" and "provocative rhetoric." The intent was clear: to create an atmosphere of fear and justify a renewal of hostilities against its foe.

Mobutu's Fall and Its Consequences

Angola aggressively aided and exploited the collapse of the Mobutu regime in Zaïre as part of its campaign to destroy

UNITA. It intervened militarily in the two Congos with the strategic goal of destroying support and supply for Savimbi. Mobutu, who had long aided *UNITA*, was an obvious target. Angolan troops were sent to assist Kabila. President Lissouba of Congo (Brazzaville) too had aided *UNITA*, so when devastating civil war erupted there between Lissouba and his foe, ex-president Sassou–Nguesso, Angolan planes bombed the capital and helped dispatch Lissouba to unhappy exile. Troops were also sent into Congo–Brazzaville to ferret out *UNITA* bases from which attacks on Cabinda had been made. Leaving nothing undone, the heaviest of diplomatic sticks was waved at Zambia, where *UNITA* bases were alleged to exist near the western border. In 1999 the pressures on Zambia were increased as Angola named names and accused Zambia's vice–president and a former defense minister, among others, of smuggling arms to *UNITA*.

If the *MPLA* government was willing to use its armies against sovereign states, it was clear they would once again be used against *UNITA*. At the *MPLA* party Congress in December 1998 President dos Santos made that clear, bluntly saying that "the only way to achieve peace in Angola is through the political and military neutralization of *UNITA* and its president." The campaign, it appeared, would be directed by dos Santos himself. He has restructured his cabinet, dismissed the prime minister and assumed his powers, as well as those of the supreme command of the armed forces. Other cabinet appointees are committed dos Santos men, fully expected to do his bidding. All appear to be hardliners on the war against *UNITA*. A close advisor, General Kundi Payama, was appointed defense minister. One of his nephews, Fernando de Piedade, has been promoted to the position of Minister of the Interior, a position from which he oversees state security.

Dos Santos moved to consolidate his personal power in the party as well as the state. Former *MPLA* Secretary–General Lopo de Nascimento, a critic since 1993, was removed from the party's central committee. Potential rivals like former prime ministers França van Dunem and Marcolino Moco also lost their places on the central committee. All were replaced with dos Santos loyalists.

By spring 1999 both the government and *UNITA* had restocked their armaments and engaged in feints and tests of each other's capabilities. With no peace to observe, the UN withdrew, its $2.2-billion mission having expired in utter failure. The National Police aggressively implemented conscription, and reporters, even if female, who investigated stories of draft resistance were subject to violence and incarceration.

Having spent a half a billion dollars on new armament, the Angolan army kept *UNITA* forces on the run once the war began. *UNITA*'s central highland cities were captured and its forces fragmented and dispersed. The government obtained permission from its close ally, Namibia, to pursue fleeing rebels into Namibian territory. Retaliatory strikes by *UNITA* troops brought death to Namibians, created an outpouring of refugees into Namibia, and, when foreign tourists were killed, dimmed the prospects of Namibian tourism. It was good permission to pursue the rebels had been granted after President Nujoma's election.

President José Eduardo dos Santos

By 2001 the government had achieved considerable success against *UNITA*. It had eliminated its capacity to conduct conventional warfare, but was incapable of destroying the group. *UNITA* forces melted into the landscape and resorted to traditional guerilla tactics. Occasional raids to replenish supplies asserted the group's continuing power and presence, but check points on roads in areas supposedly controlled by the group were almost never established. By being nowhere, *UNITA* projected an image of being everywhere. Travel outside government-held cities remains hazardous. Beyond five to thirty kilometers roads are mined and subject to attack.

Having failed to destroy its enemy militarily, the *MPLA* government found itself faced with growing demands for some negotiated settlement from civil society. Over the years Angola's civil society had grown larger, stronger, and bold enough to condemn the government's war that had destroyed the country but not the enemy. Increasingly vociferous church groups and humanitarian organizations lead the way. Independent journalists and opposition parties contribute choral support to the pro-peace movement, and Jonas Savimbi, in a dramatic Voice of America interview and a letter to Angola's Catholic bishops, aligned himself with the movement by calling for a negotiated solution.

Externally, both Washington and London seemed to draw back from a hard line effort to isolate Savimbi. *UNITA* reconnected with conservatives in Washington who had given support during the Cold War, and at least one meeting between a deputy assistant secretary for Africa in the defense department and a *UNITA* representative was reported. A similar meeting between a representative of the British government and *UNITA*'s former representative in London was reportedly held in Paris. At the UN, it was reported that Secretary-General Annan's advisor on Angola, Ibrahim Gambari, had begun to involve the oil companies in a search for peace based on a national dialogue.

The *MPLA* also appeared to have a pro-dialogue faction emerging within its ranks. Two former party secretaries-general, Lopo do Nascimento and Marcolino Moco, have criticized the *MPLA* leadership for rejecting calls for a negotiated solution to the war. Most remarkable was an August 2000 interview given a Portuguese publication by General João de Matos, the army chief of staff. De Matos expressed doubts about the possibility of a military solution to the war, suggesting it would only cease when democracy was installed in the country.

After eight years of loyal service to the *MPLA* state, General de Matos was removed as army head in January 2001. Both sides said it was a routine rotation, but the timing looked suspicious. Military destruction remains the preferred option for the government, which continues to buy arms that will only prolong Angola's agony. In March 2001, Spanish customs authorities in the Canary Islands found 636 tons of war material on the *Anastasia*, a ship of Georgian registry, traveling from a Ukrainian port bearing a shipment of Russian arms destined for an Angolan state-owned company, Simportex. There were 20,000 boxes of ammunition, mortar grenades, ground-to-air missiles and night-vision equipment—all listed on the ship's manifest as "automobile parts."

The government, of course, does not give any indication of how much money it is spending for arms, or for much else for that matter. In December the cabinet did issue a statement saying its spending priority in 2001 would be national defense. When the $5.5 billion budget was presented to parliament in February, opposition lawmakers were infuriated by the absence of clear figures, but they sought answers to their questions in vain.

There hasn't been an election in Angola since 1992, and the government is talking about holding one in the second half of 2002. This is rather unlikely, but if it did occur, it might help the regime's public image, one that even hired PR flaks have had trouble with recently. French judges have been investigating a series of scandals collectively called "Angolagate." The most serious charges involve illegal shipments of a half billion dollars worth of arms to Angola by a cast of characters worthy of a good spy novel, including Jean-Christophe Mitterrand, son of the

View of Luanda from its harbor AP/Wide World Photo

former French president, François Mitterrand.

President dos Santos was so exercised about the revelations, which he thought part of a planned defamation of his country, that he berated the new French Ambassador when his credentials were presented. Those involved, he averred, were of great help to Angola; their actions were seen as gestures of confidence and friendship between the French state and Angola. That was the reason, he pointedly remarked, for the spectacular increase of cooperation between the two countries, especially in the petroleum sector.

He concluded his remarks with a proverb-like reminder to the French representative: "Friendship is like a plant that withers if it is not watered and fertilized regularly. At this time, I think that it's up to your government, by means of concrete gestures, to do more for the friendship and cooperation between our two peoples." Being little sympathetic to the niceties and nuances of such things as the rule of law, transparency, or separation of powers, he perhaps hoped that the French president could call off the judicial hounds and tell them they'd gone too far.

Cabinda

The former president of Portugal, Mario Soares, probably provided as much discomfort for President dos Santos as French investigative judges when he commented on the continuing struggle for self-determination in Cabinda. The nearly 30-year liberation struggle was, said Soares, "no internal Angolan affair." "Anyone who supports self-determination," he added, "cannot deny the right of a population to discuss the issue, and when this reaches the pitch it has in Cabinda, it moves out of the realm of domestic politics."

The April 2001 speech was occasioned by kidnappings of Portuguese workers by various elements of the *Frente de Libertação do Enclava de Cabinda* (*FLEC*)—the *Liberation Front for the Cabinda Enclave*. Abducted to focus international attention on *FLEC*'s demands for self-determination, some of the captured workers had been held for nearly a year when Soares spoke.

With an area of just a bit more than 2,800 sq. miles, the Cabinda enclave is completely separated from Angola by a narrow stretch of land on either side of the Congo River. It exists as a consequence of colonial power politics. Leopold II, the brash and entrepreneurial Belgian King, wanted access to the sea for the Congo Free State, his personal fief in the heart of Africa. The Portuguese government, possessed of little capacity to protest, was pressured into making the concession.

The enclave contains around 250,000 Cabindans, most of whom would probably prefer independence if given a chance. It produces nearly 70% of Angola's oil from its off-shore wells. Like the people of the Niger Delta, Cabindans feel exploited, abused, and short-changed. Cabinda reportedly receives 10% of the taxes paid by the oil companies—Chevron is the dominant player on the Cabinda fields—but *FLEC* has long argued this is insufficient. It's not an argument that finds much sympathy in Luanda.

Cabindan separatism stems from several sources. Ethnically and linguistically, Cabindans are more closely akin to the peoples of southwestern Congo. Historically, the enclave was administered separately by the Portuguese until 1956, and this provided a clear sense of distinctness from Angola. "In our souls, we don't feel we are Angolans, we are Cabindans," said one FLEC leader.

There is also a sense of historical exclusion. Cabindan interests were not represented in discussions between mainstream nationalist groups and Portugal that resulted in independence. The feeling then, and now, was that the enclave was simply arbitrarily annexed to Angola at independence. Even the more recent Lusaka agreement was restricted to the *MPLA* government and *UNITA* and ignored *FLEC*'s troublesome demands.

As with its efforts to destroy *UNITA*, the dos Santos regime has failed to eliminate the various *FLEC* factions. One reason for Angola's military advance into the two Congos was to eliminate the support and refuge both *UNITA* and *FLEC* groups found there.

There is a sense that pressure is building on the government to negotiate with *FLEC*, as the comments of former president Soares suggest, but the question remains: which *FLEC*? Ever since its founding in 1963, the group has been fractious. *FLEC* has broken into at least three factions, two of which, *FLEC-Renovata* and *FLEC-Armed Forces of Cabinda*, engaged in the recent kidnappings that once again brought international attention to their long quest for independence.

Culture: Until 1974 there were two cultures in Angola—the approximately 300,000 Europeans, mostly Portuguese, who were the businessmen and farmers, and that of the original inhabitants of the land. The latter lived a marginal existence in the cities and in the hinterland, working as laborers in the factories and fields of Angola. A small group of these lived as *assimilados*—they adopted European customs, the Portuguese language and passed an educational test. They now are the leadership of the *MPLA*.

Between the *MPLA* and *UNITA* leadership lies the chasm of culture and history and race. *UNITA* emerged as a factor in the liberation struggle from the perception that the *Movement for the Liberation of Angola* was dominated by mixed–race intellectuals from the coastal cities. Historically the Luandan élites had looked down on countryside folk as inept and inferior. Jonas Savimbi sought to exploit and mobilize those differences. *UNITA* is based on the highland Ovimbundu people. It has always claimed to represent "real Africans," "sons of the soil," "living in the bush" against a better–educated, wealthy, cosmopolitan urban élite. As almost living proof of the cultural division, President dos Santos has left Luanda to visit the rest of the country only once in seven years, during a brief campaign swing. Savimbi's populist nationalism, with potential appeal to the dispossessed masses living in the squalor of squatter shacks on the outskirts of Luanda, is deeply threatening to the status and perks of that urban élite.

The capital, Luanda, a modern city once bustling with life and commerce, is now depressing—its people are discouraged by the lack of food, unemployment, the lack of city services and shortages of just about everything. Huambo, Angola's second largest city, is devastated; it formerly was a thriving agricultural center whose markets once rang with the voices of vendors. Stalls were heaped high with fruits and vegetables. All this is gone.

It is almost impossible to describe the devastation produced by more than 30 years of continuous conflict. A culture of violence is both physical and mental; some of its aspects can be described in statistics while others remain hidden, perhaps for years to come. While the *MPLA* élites enjoy the good life, the mass of the population suffers. On the 1998 Human Development Index, Angola was ranked 156th out of 174 countries, putting it in the depths of human misery. Some 82.5% of its population lives in absolute poverty and life expectancy is a mere 47 years. Fifty–eight percent of the population is illiterate. Forty percent of Angolan children die before they reach the age of five, one of the highest infant morality rates in the world. Angola has the greatest concentration of land mines in the world—some 15 million; and it has been estimated that anywhere from 70,000 to 200,000 people have lost limbs to them. One and a half million Angolans have been uprooted and displaced by war, refugees in their own country.

Hundreds of thousands of them have relocated to the outskirts of the capital where they live in shantytowns of utmost squalor and misery. Luanda now has four million inhabitants. Only about 20,000 of them have running water or modern toilets. The government could easily afford to build a sewage treatment plant and pipe drinking water to the city. Rivers are nearby and the war is distant. In the absence of such services, millions of Luanda's poor pay up to 10,000 times more for drinking water than the elite, who merely open a tap.

With the bulk of government resources devoted to defeating its armed opponents or corruptly siphoned off to private coffers, Angola's health system, which might provide some alleviation of peoples' misery, has totally collapsed over the years. In an unusually frank report, *Medecins Sans Frontières (MSF)* reported that Angolan authorities displayed "a striking lack of interest in the health of their population." The report, issued in November 2000, deemed government spending on the health system "inconsequential" and its provision of drugs and medical supplies "completely insufficient."

MSF calculated that the government covered only 1.2% of needs of one hospital it served and noted that although the government was a major oil producer, there was "not a drop of diesel for the hospital generators, the only source of power in most large hospitals." This was not, the group asserted, a consequence of war as the government claimed, but the consequence of "deliberate choices."

The choice was clear: let humanitarian agencies fund health; let the government fund war. The consequence was equally clear: the Angolan population benefited not a jot from the wealth of its land.

The Catholic University of Angola, Luanda

Economy: Just what is the reality of Angola's great wealth? The country is presently the second most productive oil state in sub-Saharan Africa. New offshore discoveries seem to be announced daily. Angola currently produces 750,000 barrels of oil per day, a total expected to rise to over a million within the next decade. This accounts for some 80% of the state's revenues.

As of 1998 more than sixty per cent of daily production was exported to the United States, generating substantial hard currency reserves. The government also produces about $850 million in diamonds every year. Yet in a recent year-end message, President dos Santos indicated that GDP, which had been growing since 1994, saw a decline in 1998 and was expected to decline further in 1999.

The 1999 budget was in deficit and Angola is a major debtor, having accumulated an estimated $12.5 billion in debts. Inflation was a galloping 1,650% in 1996, slowed to a mere canter of 91% in 1998, and is estimated at 250% for 1999. Domestic savings are impossible in these circumstances.

War of course is only excuse and justification. Equally contributory is an Olympian corruption that provides a comfortable life for President dos Santos, his family and supporters. They have enriched themselves through their government connections while the average Angolan earns $340 a year. The books of the national oil company, Sonangol, are virtual state secrets in an authoritarian state where transparency has no value. A Swiss judge elicited from the former President of Elf-Gabon the revelation that oil companies had paid hidden commissions—"bonues" in petrospeak—of more than a billion dollars to secure Angolan exploration permits in 1998.

Angola's wealth is tightly restricted to a narrow elite. The President's eldest daughter, Isabel, is widely reported to have extensive holdings in both oil and mining operations. Many of the Angolan generals own or have shares in the numerous security firms that are essential to business, especially the diamond business, in Angola.

The Catoca diamond mine in northeast Angola, for example, currently produces about $8 million worth of diamonds a month. Catoca pays $500,000 a month to a private security firm reportedly controlled by the Army Chief of Staff, General João de Matos. About 300 armed guards, most former soldiers of the Angolan army, man a defensive perimeter around the mine.

If oil allows the government to wage war, diamonds do the same for *UNITA*. Global Witness, an investigative human rights group based in the United Kingdom, has recently estimated that from 1992 to 1998 Unita earned at least $3.7 billion from diamond mines under its control. To feed its soldiers—the diamond income goes to buy arms—*UNITA* subjects citizens living in areas it controls to crop seizures. They are also subject to forced labor and mandatory military service.

Canada has launched an international campaign to embargo UNITA-supplied diamonds through the UN. It is part of the international community's effort to remove Jonas Savimbi as a destabilizing actor.

The Future: Even if Jonas Savimbi were removed, a venal, corrupt and violent regime would remain. The real test of each side in this seemingly interminable conflict will be its response to growing popular pressures for peace. Negotiating peace is no longer a matter of two parties only. The growth of an articulate civil society requires the participation of new and more varied voices. Future peace negotiations will also, this time, need to be global, including not only the *MPLA* government and its *UNITA* antagonist, but also representatives of the interests of Cabinda.

The Republic of Burundi

Aerial view of Bujumbura and the northernmost extent of Lake Tanganyika

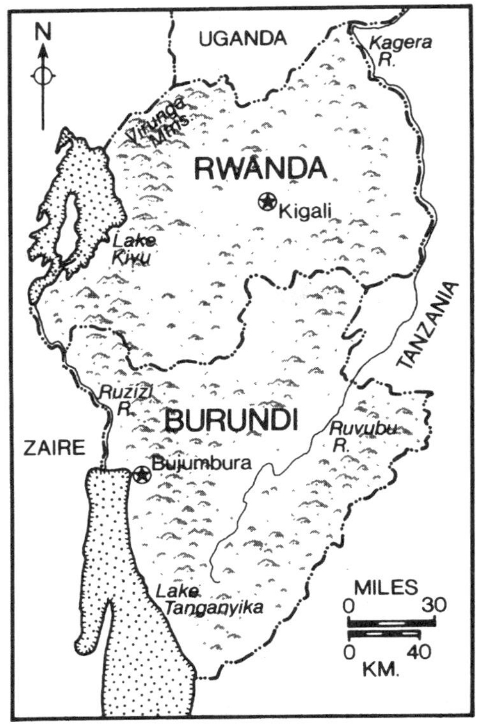

Area: 28,490 sq. km. = 11,000 sq. mi. (slightly larger than Maryland).
Population: 5,735,937 (July 1999 est.)
Capital City: Bujumbura (Pop. 186,000, estimated).
Climate: Temperate, with an alternating wet season (October–April) and dry season (May–December).
Neighboring Countries: Rwanda (North); Tanzania (East): Congo-Kinshasa (West).
Official Languages: French, KiRundi.
Other Principal Language: KiSwahili.
Ethnic groups: Hutu 85%, Tutsi 14%, Twa (Pygmy) 1%, Europeans 3,000, and South Asians 2,000.
Principal Religions: Christian 67% (Roman Catholic 62%, Protestant 5%), indigenous beliefs 32%, and Muslim 1%.
Chief Commercial Products: Coffee, tea, cotton and hides.
GNP per capita: 140 US$
Currency: Burundi Franc.
Former Colonial Status: Part of German East Africa (1899–1917); occupied by Belgian troops (1916), Belgian trust territory under League of Nations and United Nations (1923–1962).
Independence Date: July 1, 1962.
Chief of State: Pierre Buyoya (a Tutsi), President (since July 1996).
National Flag: Divided by a white diagonal cross into red panels (top and bottom) and green panels (hoist side and outer side) with a white disk superimposed at the center bearing three red six-pointed stars outlined in green arranged in a triangular design (one star above, two stars below).

A cool, pleasant land of mountains and plateaus, the Republic of Burundi was known as Urundi before its independence; it was the southern portion of Ruanda–Urundi. Burundi is situated in the highlands of central Africa, and though only two degrees below the Equator, the climate is tempered by altitude. Fabled Lake Tanganyika, the longest fresh water lake in the world, separates Burundi and Zaïre. This amazing body of water is more than 2,500 feet above sea level on the surface, yet its floor reaches a depth of about 2,000 feet below sea level. The lake abounds in fish, hippopotami, crocodiles and other native species.

Countless eons ago a great strip of land between parallel faults in the earth sank to great depths, forming the basin of the Red Sea and continuing into the land mass of east and central Africa. This unique land feature is known as the Great Rift Valley, an area of grassy, upland plains. The wet season has characteristic daily downpours with intermittent clear, sunny weather. Almost no rain falls during the five–month dry season.

History: The old Kingdom of Burundi dates back to the 15th century; tradition indicates that the Twa (Pygmies) were the first inhabitants, a few of whom are found in the remotest parts of Burundi today. They were succeeded by the Hutu, a peaceful Bantu agricultural group, who in turn were subdued by the extremely tall Tutsi, who reduced the Hutu to serfdom. For details of early and colonial history, see Historical Background, *The Germans in Africa* and *The Belgians in Africa*.

Following independence in 1962, it appeared that Burundi would emerge as a stable nation. It seemed that the Tutsi and Hutu people had been able to work together in government with representation from both groups.

The Kingdom of Burundi was established as a constitutional monarchy with Mwami (King) Mwambutsa IV as ruler. The legislature, or National Assembly, was dominated by the *Burundi National Party of Unity and Progress (UPRONA)*. This was a coalition of Tutsi and Hutu leaders, but was dominated by the upper class Tutsi nobles known as the *Ganwa*. The coalition underwent a severe setback in 1965 when a group of Hutu leaders attempted a *coup*. Prime Minister Biha was seriously wounded by gunfire, Mwambutsa departed for Switzerland, 76 Hutu leaders were executed and the de-

President Pierre Buyoya

fense minister, Michel Micombero, was given absolute power.

Mwambutsa made a half–hearted effort to return to his kingdom, but was ousted by his son, Ntare in 1966. When the youthful King was out of the country, Micombero proclaimed himself president of the *Republic* of Burundi. He had the support of the *Bahima* clan of the Tutsi, who traditionally were jealous of *Ganwa* power.

Restless Hutus living in exile in Tanzania plotted a revolution with the aid of that country in mid–1972. Emboldened by drugs and assurances of invincibility from local folk priests, they mounted a swift campaign. The plot involved Ntare, but after being put under house arrest, he was later killed "while escaping."

About 2,000 Tutsis were mercilessly slaughtered; they responded with a blood bath that took the lives of more than 200,000 Hutus within six weeks. Worst of all, this vengeance was directed against educated Hutus needed to perform a multitude of important tasks. A second wave of Hutus poured over the Tanzanian border in May 1973, creating further strife. Unconfirmed reports give totals up to and exceeding a half million people who were casualties of the inter–tribal strife.

The first constitution was adopted in 1974 and contained some unusual features. The head of the sole party, *UPRONA*, was both President and Premier. Micombero's tenure was extended for seven years. Then came the inevitable. Rivalries between army groups within the Tutsi tribe flared, and Col. Jean–Baptiste Bagaza led a bloodless *coup* in 1976. *UPRONA* was dissolved; a military council was formed which selected Bagaza to lead the country.

In 1980, Bagaza commenced anti–Catholic Church measures which led by 1987 to the expulsion of more than 450 foreign priests. He viewed the Church as a instrument of potential Hutu rebellion. He was ousted in 1987 by a military–backed fellow clansman, Pierre Buyoya. The new leader welcomed back the expelled Catholics in spite of suspicions of right–wing Tutsis. Leftist Hutus based in Rwanda (where they were the majority) convinced other Hutus that the Tutsis were plotting their annihilation. Attempting to strike preemptively, the Hutus slaughtered about 500 Tutsis. This was but another outbreak of the communal violence between Hutu and Tutsi that has kept the country in a state of perpetual tension. Elections were organized in 1991 and a Hutu, Melchior Ndadaye, won Burundi's first democratic presidential poll. He was assassinated in a coup attempt in October 1993 and since then Burundi has been gripped by a cycle of terror and counter-terror referred to as *la crise*—the crisis. The conflict has claimed the lives of 200,000 people.

Parliament elected a moderate Hutu, Cyprien Ntaryamira, as Ndadaye's successor in early 1994. Just a few months later President Ntaryamira was killed in the same plane crash that killed Rwanda's president and set off the genocide of that year. Amid general agreement that the security situation did not permit another round of elections, parliament eventually appointed another moderate Hutu, Sylvestre Ntibantunganya to the presidency.

Communal tensions were not eased. Tutsi politicians claimed the government was biased against Tutsi. Rogue elements of the army, controlled by Tutsis, and extremist Hutu militias engaged in nearly daily atrocities against civilians. In November 1995, at the urging of the UN secretary-general, Burundi and its neighbors agreed to a regional peace initiative. Former Tanzanian President, Julius Nyerere, was designated as mediator between the various factions.

Mediation only seemed to intensify hostilities. Fearful and frustrated, the army intervened in July 1996. President Ntibantunganya went into hiding and Major Pierre Buyoya seized power, for a second time. Burundi's neighbors united to impose economic sanctions on the country in an effort to force a restoration of democracy. As with many such efforts, the goal was not achieved but the consequences were disastrous. The economy further deteriorated, malnutrition rates soared, and the atrocities continued, for sanctions could not stop the flow of arms into Burundi.

Given the continuing security threat, the government decided to create a group of resettlement centers that would gather rural and isolated communities, mostly Hutu, into more controllable and protected camps. This involved relocating more than 800,000 people—about 12% of the population—into 58 camps whose conditions were appalling by the most generous of appraisals. In one there were only 25 latrines for 5,000 inhabitants. The Hutu opposition called them "concentration camps," and the international community condemned them. By early 2000 the government began to dismantle some, but not before the project had set off another wave of refugees fleeing to camps in Tanzania.

Getting peace discussions going was more of a problem, but Major Buyoya has thread his way through mine fields of conflicting demands from Hutu and Tutsi, regional politicians and international organizations. In June 1998 a Transitional Constitutional Act (TCA) designed to pave the way for the Tutsi–led government to share power with the mainly Hutu opposition was signed into law. The party of Hutu militants, the *National Council for the Defense of Democracy (CNDD)*, condemned it from exile in Brussels as nothing more than a ploy by Buyoya to legitimize his power. Tutsi militants were equally skeptical.

The TCA transformed the structure of Burundi's government. Under new provisions, parliament was enlarged by 57 new seats to make government more representative. The government appointed 27 members from Burundi's civil society; small parties not heretofore represented appointed 9 of the new members, and the Hutu opposition party, *Front pour la démocratie au Burundi* (*Frodebu*), designated the remaining 21 seats. The post of prime minister was eliminated and two vice-presidencies were created, one of whom was a Hutu, a member of *Frodebu*. The new cabinet of 22 members also included ten members of *Frodebu*.

With these power-sharing reforms as background, seventeen delegations gathered in Arusha, Tanzania, to begin peace discussions. The most militant of the Hutu rebel groups, *the Forces for the Defense of Democracy* (*CNDD-FDD*) and the hard-line *Paliphatu* were excluded from the talks. Progress, which was sluggish at best, was brought to a halt by the death of the mediator, Julius Nyerere, in October 1999.

Africa's most distinguish ex-president, Nelson Mandela, was prevailed upon to take on the role of mediator and assumed his duties in February. Mandela brought a sure star-power to the talks. His presence brought the klieg lights of publicity to previously obscure discussions. His moral stature allowed him to publicly chastise all parties. His international prestige and contacts allowed him to proffer the carrot of aid to reconstruct a devastated country.

With both ethnic communities deeply divided, the participants at the Arusha meeting proved a fractious lot that tested Mandela severely. By August 2000, a Peace Agreement was signed, though key issues, including the leadership of the transitional period and agreement for a cease-fire had not been reached. Several

Rural Tutsi tribesmen in a ritual ceremony

parties signed with reservations, and two key armed opposition groups, the *CNDD-FDD* and the *Forces nationales de liberation* (*FNL*), did not attend and were not part of the agreement. Indeed, following the signature of the Arusha Accord, both groups increased military activity against President Buyoya's government.

Mandela entrusted cease-fire negotiations to the South African Deputy President, Jacob Zuma. A series of meetings in Nairobi and Libreville failed to reach agreement on a ceasefire by April 2001. The Arusha Accord was ratified by the Burundian National Assembly in early December. Shortly afterwards an international donors' conference in Paris agreed to provide $440 million for reconstruction programs.

The deadlock on transitional leadership was not ended until March 2001, but agreement here reflected no unanimity. Eight of the ten pro-Tutsi parties proposed former Interior Minister Epitace Bayaganakandi as candidate for president, while six of the seven pro-Hutu parties presented Domitien Ndayizeye, secretary general of the largest pro-Hutu party *Frodebu*, for the post of vice president. Tutsi groups opposed to President Buyoya succeeded in excluding the president from this selection of transitional leadership. But it is unlikely the president, who regards himself as the only man capable of holding the country together, would be so easily excluded.

In April 2001, while President Buyoya was meeting in Libreville with his armed Hutu opponents, a small group of very junior officers took over the Bujumbura radio station and announced he had been deposed. They drew no support from other elements of the army and ultimately surrendered to loyalist forces, but the incident underscored the political reality of Burundi: nothing is settled, nothing is certain.

Culture: In terms of its rich African heritage, the customs of the people of Burundi are unique and beautiful. The Tutsi are unbelievably tall, reaching heights of seven feet, and possess a high degree of unity based on social order, with the *Ganwa* traditionally at the top and the *Bahima* somewhat lower. A great variety of dance accompaniments with highly stylized rhythms have been among the most intricate to be found on the continent. Rural Tutsi dancing is breathtakingly graceful—the unison movements of the men are accented by headdresses ornamented frequently with monkey hair. Due to the massive ethnic warfare of 1993–4, these customs are now difficult to find.

European night life had invaded Bujumbura before the strife, with several nightclubs featuring the latest western clothing styles and music—very popular among urban residents. A substantial number of people are now of both Hutu and Tutsi ancestry as a result of intermarriage between the two groups. Radio, widely available for years, both government and clandestine, was used with vigor to incite people to violence.

Economy: Agriculture is the mainstay of Burundi's economy. Most cultivated land is devoted to subsistence crops—mainly cassava, bananas, and sweet potatoes. Cattle rearing is also an important source of food, as was fishing on Lake Tanganyika until it was banned by the government as a security measure to prevent rebel infiltration.

The main cash crop is coffee, more than 90 per cent of which is higher quality arabica. The Gourmet Coffee Project, sponsored by the International Coffee Organization, is active in Burundi, seeking new and attractive specialty coffees. Coffee exports account for at least 75% of Burundi's foreign exchange revenues. A total of 514,000 bags were exported in the 1999 season, up from less than 300,000 bags in 1997.

Other cash crops include tea, which produces about 15% of foreign exchange revenues, cotton (increasingly important), palm oil and tobacco.

The instability experienced since 1993 and sanctions imposed against the government of President Buyoya by his neighbors have damaged the economy enormously. GDP fell every year between 1993-96; only in 1997 did the economy return to growth and then only 1.5 per cent. The national cattle herd dropped by 20% because sanctions prevented the import of veterinary medicines to fight livestock diseases. Food shortages developed as large areas of the country remained uncultivated. Fuel imports shrank to 10% of normal requirements because of sanctions. This led to a collapse of the transport sector and made it impossible to collect crops. Coffee and tea exports declined and smuggling was given a significant boost. Today the informal economy (or, more commonly, black market) is larger than Burundi's formal economy.

The Future: President Buyoya has made it clear that that his government will not hand over power to the transitional institutions until a cease-fire is reached with dissident Hutu rebels. Even then, one can't be sure if he will be ready to give up power.

The Republic of Rwanda (pronounced Roo–*wahn*–dah)

Typical rural Rwandan dwelling near Kigali, with a woman working her garden plot AP/Wide World photo

Area: 28,900 sq. km. = 11,158 sq. mi. (slightly larger than Maryland).
Population: 8,154,933 (July 1999 est.)
Capital City: Kigali (pop. 236,000, est.)
Climate: Temperate, with dry seasons (January–February, June–September) and wet seasons (March–May, October–December).
Neighboring Countries: Congo-Kinshasa (West); Uganda (Northeast); Tanzania (East); Burundi (South).
Official Languages: English, French, and KiNyarwanda.
Other Principal Languages: KiSwahili
Ethnic groups: Hutu 80%, Tutsi 19%, Twa (Pygmy) 1%.
Principal Religions: Roman Catholic 65%, Protestant 9%, Muslim 1%, indigenous beliefs and other 25%.
Chief Commercial Products: Coffee 55%, tea 21%, hides, and tin ore (1997).
GNP per capita: 230 US$
Currency: Rwanda Franc.
Former Colonial Status: Part of German East Africa (1899–1916); occupied by Belgian troops (1916); Belgian trust territory under the League of Nations and the United Nations (1923–1962).
Independence Date: July 1, 1962.
Chief of State: Paul Kagame, President.
National Flag: Blue and green with a rising sun in the middle.

Rwanda, often called the "African Switzerland," is a land lying in the eastern lake region of Africa, composed for the most part of a gently rolling plateau land. Sharp volcanic peaks rise to towering heights in the West on the border of Lake Kivu, generally considered one of the most beautiful of the unspoiled great lakes in Africa. Another mountain range lies to the northwest, topped by Mt. Karisimbi at a height of 13,520 feet.

Rwanda has a mild and temperate climate—the temperature seldom rises above 80°F. during the daytime and the nights are always cool, with frost in the highlands and the mountains.

Many centuries ago, the Virunga volcanoes, some of which are still active, dammed up a section of the Great Western Rift Valley, creating Lake Kivu, with fjord–like bays and inlets. This lake, now the site of resort towns, with swimming, boating and fishing, drains into Lake Tanganyika to the south through the waters of the Ruzizi River. The volcanic activity thus diverted water which flowed upward to the Nile River, forcing it to flow westward to the Atlantic through the immense Congo River, since Lake Tanganyika drains westward to the Congo through the Lukuga Creek.

History: As is true in Burundi to the south, the original inhabitants of Rwanda were dimunitive pygmies who seldom reached a height of more than five feet. The Twa were succeeded in turn by the Hutu, sometimes called Buhutu, an industrious people of hunters and farmers having Bantu ancestry. About four centuries ago, a warrior tribe, the Tutsi, sometimes called the Watusi, invaded Rwanda from the north. The Hutu were unable to defend themselves against the Tutsi, who were seldom less than six feet tall! The Hutu were reduced to serfdom, each choosing a Tutsi lord protector who gave them the use (but not ownership) of cattle, the most important status symbol and source of wealth among the Tutsi. For early and colonial history, see Historical Background, *The Germans in Africa* and *King Leopold and the Belgians in Africa*.

At the close of the colonial period, the restless Hutu, weary of their serfdom, rose in revolt in 1959 and the years following. They sought equality for all groups in Rwanda, acting through the *National Party of Hutu Emancipation.* Civil war broke out after the death of a Hutu leader and the Mwami, or Tutsi king, and his advisors departed from the country hastily—this was a period when the Tutsi justifiably feared for their lives.

Under Belgian supervision, communal elections were ordered in 1960, resulting in a landslide victory for the more numerous Hutus. Gregoire Kayibanda was selected to head the first government. After a republic was proclaimed in 1961, Kayibanda was appointed Prime Minister. General elections under the supervision of the UN were held in 1961; independence was recommended for Rwanda, which was granted in 1962.

Led by Kayibanda, the *Parmehutu Party* of the Hutus had controlled the government since independence, electing all 47 members of the single–chamber assembly. Alternate members of the party were usually provided as candidates for each seat.

The period 1967–1969 was marked by tension with nearby Zaïre arising out of the continuing struggles within that country. Kayibanda and the *Parmehutu Party* were routinely returned to office in 1969.

Renewed strife between the Hutus and the Tutsi minority occurred in March 1973. Kayibanda was criticized for being too lenient with the Tutsi, who were slaughtering thousands of Hutus in neighboring Burundi. Kayibanda had hoped to change the constitution to permit his return to office for a fourth term in 1973.

Suspecting his Defense Minister Juvenal Habyarimana—the lone northerner in the Cabinet—of disloyalty, Kayibanda ordered him arrested. The attempt triggered a takeover by the army and General Habyarimana was named the new president. A death sentence against Kayibanda was later commuted to life imprisonment. After the 1973 *coup* the government pushed economic reforms vigorously, with limited success because of the ever–swelling population.

The constitution of 1973 effectively limited the presidency to a Hutu, but in the presence of pressure for multi–party government, it was amended in the early 1990s and the restriction was ended. Multi–party elections were scheduled, but postponed because of political unrest and a festering rebellion in the North by Tutsi who fled Rwanda when the Hutus took over the reigns of government. As the contest drew nearer in early 1994, the revolt continued, and Habyarimana was faced with growing pressure from within his own party and the military, both of which thought he was being "too soft" generally in dealing with Tutsis. This feeling had been heightened when Habyarimana

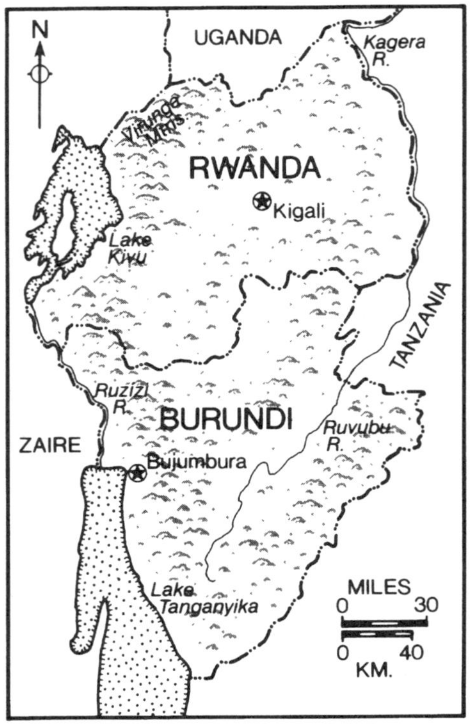

agreed in 1992 to an interim government in which power was shared with the rebel Tutsis.

Fighting that erupted in late 1993 in neighboring Burundi largely between the two ethnic groups, proved to be a major factor in igniting warfare in Rwanda in April 1994. Tutsis from Burundi poured into Rwanda by the tens of thousands. Clandestine and government radio stations in both nations fueled the flames of sheer hatred ("You [Tutsis] are cockroaches! . . . We will kill you!"). The Rwanda fighting started in early April 1994 when a plane carrying President Habyarimana (and the Hutu president of Burundi) was shot down while landing at Kigali airport. The enraged presidential guard embarked on the merciless, barbaric killing of any Tutsi found, believing that persons from that group had downed the aircraft. It is most probable that disgruntled Hutu military personnel were the perpetrators. Habyarimana had been quietly arranging the eradication of his Hutu opponents for several weeks.

In March 1999 the Paris–based International Federation of Human Rights (IFHR) and the U.S.–based Human Rights Watch released a nine hundred page report on the killings in Rwanda. Entitled *Leave None to Tell the Story*, the report surveyed the unfolding of Rwanda's tragic genocide. It has become increasingly clear that upon Habyarimana's death, members of his inner circle moved to take control of the state and turn it into an instrument of genocide to maintain themselves in power. The holocaust unleashed was horrifying in its dimensions. Conducted largely through the Interahamwe militia of the Habyarimana party, the slaughter took upwards of 800,000 people over a 13–week period. Seventy–five percent of the country's Tutsi population was killed, most of them in the first five weeks. At the slaughter's peak five people per minute were being killed.

Sadly, the IFHR report argues that the genocide was preventable. Western powers and the UN all had advance warnings, and failed to take action. One CIA analyst predicted in January 1994 that as many as half a million could die. General Dallaire, the Canadian commander of the UN peacekeeping mission in Rwanda, warned his bosses of what was to come and repeatedly requested more troops and a mandate to act. He was turned down, and the bulk of the UN force was evacuated after the execution of ten Belgian peacekeepers on the opening day of the genocide.

Once the slaughter began, the Western countries acted timidly and ineffectively, allowing the regime to consolidate its position and continue the genocide. The report is devastating in its condemnation of Western governments. "The Americans were interested in saving money, the Belgians were interested in saving face, and the French were interested in saving their ally, the genocidal government," said the report's chief author. "All of that took priority over saving lives."

The *Rwanda Patriotic Front* (*RPF*) army, made up of diaspora Tutsi who had lived and worked in Uganda, where they had been an important part of Yoweri Museveni's efforts to topple the government there, invaded Rwanda and took the capital of Kigali in July. Former members of the Rwandan army and militias fled to Zaïre with thousands of Hutu who now feared for their lives. Hutu militants took over the refugee camps and turned them into training grounds for another round of ethnic confrontation. The Tutsi search for

Former President Bizimungu

President Paul Kagame

Rebels with the Rwanda Patriotic Front patrol Kigali, June 1994 AP/Wide World Photo

security in this situation dominated every action of the *RPF* coalition government established by General Paul Kagame.

When President Mobutu proved incapable or unwilling to control Hutu extremists resident in Zaïre, the *RPF* intervened and supported a successful rebellion against Mobutu. Laurent Kabila was installed in his place in 1997, and a year later when Kabila himself had failed in his commitments to Rwandan security, a second intervention was undertaken, this time in support of Congolese Tutsi, called Banyamulenge, and other groups disenchanted with Kabila. The rebel coalition now controls most of the eastern third of the Democratic Republic of the Congo. Rwandan military activity has not been without criticism, including smuggling, corruption, and human rights abuses.

Internally, the Rwandan government struggles to maintain security and rehabilitate the economy. In certain areas where security remains low, officials have said they will build special protected villages to accommodate 650,000 Rwandans displaced by war and genocide. The high-density villages will be surrounded by security fences, making them easier to patrol and defend. In a more positive sign of normalcy returning to Rwanda, nationwide local elections were held in April 1999. Voter turnout was high and Vice President Kagame called it "the beginning of a new era."

The delicate façade of an intercommunal government ended when President Bizimungu, an ethnic Hutu, bowed to what seemed mounting pressure and resigned his office in March 2000. He was not the first Hutu forced from office in the previous year. Parliament had found two Hutu cabinet ministers guilty of corruption. The parliamentary Speaker, Joseph Sebarenzi, fled the country in January, and the Hutu Prime Minister, Pierre Rwigema, resigned after being accused of corruption.

In April parliament elected Vice President and Minister of Defense Paul Kagame Rwanda's first Tutsi president. The election only made manifest Rwanda's political reality: Kagame had controlled the government for the past 6 years anyway.

In his inaugural address, Kagame called upon diaspora Rwandans to return home to rebuild the country. He also rejected the notion that Rwandan troops in the Congo meant the country liked to fight or wanted to become a superpower in the region. The issue, he stressed, was the nation's security concerns. Hutu militiamen and former Rwandan soldiers who had carried out the genocide were granted shelter in the Congo. They were allowed to carry out military training there and were given arms with which to kill Rwandan citizens and destroy what had been reconstructed.

One problem President Kagame will have to deal with are tensions with neighboring Uganda in the Congo. Each government is backing different factions of the Congolese rebel movement and their forces have actually engaged in shoot-outs around Kisangani.

Rwandan policy throughout 2000 was consistent. Military action focused on *Interahamwe* elements armed and employed by the Kabila government. Joint action with rebel *RCD-Goma* units in Katanga resulted in a crushing defeat of government alliance forces defending Pweto in early December. Congo's army chief of staff, Joseph Kabila, had to beat a humiliating retreat, abandoning his helicopter to escape the rout by ferry boat.

Pweto marked a high water mark for Rwandan arms and suggested the difficulty of its position before the international community. Hundreds of *Interahamwe* escaped across the border into Zambia, but the army held back from pursuing and destroying them, fearful of international reaction. President Kagame's reception in Washington was noticeably cooler than that afforded Congo's new leader, Joseph Kabila. Both had accepted invitations to a congressional prayer breakfast in February 2001, and it was the first opportunity President Kagame had had to meet members of the new administration.

The Clinton administration, perhaps driven by the guilt of inaction during Rwanda's genocide in 1994, had been lavish in praise and generous in support of the *RPF* government. Emergency military aid amounting to $75 million had been dispatched soon after the *RPF* had installed itself in Kigali. The Bush administration, in contrast, seemed more concerned about Rwandan militarism and the need it had to advance so far into the Congo. Less praise and more pressure to commit to the Lusaka peace process seemed to be the new administration's position. As America's acting representative to the UN said in February: "We do not believe that Rwanda can secure its long-term security interests via a policy of military opposition to the government of Congo."

The Rwandan army and its allies have increasingly been criticized for human rights abuses in their campaign against the *génocidaires*. Certainly there was a tendency, immediately after the genocide, to view all Hutus as guilty, and massive human rights violations have occurred in the occupied regions of Eastern Congo. In response to such criticism, President Kagame agreed in April 2001 to allow the United Nations International Criminal Tribunal to try Rwandan army officers accused of human rights crimes.

The Rwandan army and its *RDC-Goma* allies have also begun their pull back from the battle zones. But President Kagame has made it quite clear that withdrawal of his troops from the Congo "has to come after a solution is found to the genocide suspects who are still in the Congo, who wish to continue in a genocidal policy," as he said at Harvard's John F. Kennedy School of Government in February.

Part of the solution lies outside the Congo, in those countries that continue to shelter some of the principal *génocidaires*. Kigali considers the arrest and trial of the worst perpetrators to be of critical importance in promoting stability and creating the conditions necessary to ensure the genocide never again occurs. "If we do arrest the top guys," said one senior official, "we know the rest will give up. If we do not, the threat of another genocide will remain."

The government's priority of priorities is thus the arrest and trial of those Hutu strategists who conspired to create and implement the plan to wipe Tutsi's from the face of the Earth. To cite but one example, Felicien Kabuga, described as "a mastermind behind the genocide," remains at large. He was Rwanda's richest man, possessed of tea estates, transport companies and a variety of shops and factories. Part of the *akazu*—the Hutu elite that controlled wealth and power in Rwanda under President Habyarimana—Kabuga used his wealth to create Radio Mille Collines, the most vile of the anti-Tutsi propaganda machines. He also used his wealth to import vast numbers of machetes to arm the *génocidaires*.

Kabuga remains at large, reportedly living in Kenya, where money can blind the eye to the most heinous of crimes. Thousands of unrepentant Hutu extremists still shelter in the Congo, armed and paid by the Kabila regime. As long as they remain a threat, and they will remain so until arrested and brought to trial, there is little likelihood Rwanda will withdraw its forces from the DRC.

Domestically, President Kagame's principal goal is national reconciliation, without which there can be no peace, development, stability or progress. A National Unity and Reconciliation Commission has been created, and it has begun a number of programs to alter the way people think of themselves and their country. National identity cards, which bore the owner's ethnic identification and were made mandatory by the Hutu regime, have been abolished. "Solidarity camps" re-educate both Hutu fighters returning from the Congo to seek re-integration into the Rwandan army and young Hutus, who were arrested and imprisoned as child participants in the genocide of 1994.

The re-education of those child participants is designed to facilitate two national objectives: justice and reconciliation. More than 120,000 prisoners now await trail for crimes arising from the 1994 genocide, and the conditions of their incarceration are appalling. The Red Cross had to ask that some prisoners' feet be amputated. They had simply rotted after standing in water in spaces too crowded even to move. Averaging some 600 trials a year, it would take the judicial system 200 years to complete its caseload. To break the logjam, the government has recently passed two pieces of legislation. One defines four categories of criminality, and the other creates a system of grassroots justice—traditional village courts called *gacaca*.

Under the new judicial legislation, only category one criminals—masterminds of the genocide—would be tried in the regular court system. All others would be brought before *gacaca* courts—ten villagers elected to hear and pass judgment. Suspects would have to confront relatives, their own and those of their victims, a process that might provide catharsis and reconciliation. It is hoped those who had participated in the genocidal events of 1994 as children and have passed through a solidarity camp will bear witness against those who ordered and directed their murderous activities.

Truth-telling is at the heart of the child-participant's re-education, and truth, perhaps more than justice, is the goal of the *gacaca* system. Rwanda's minister of justice has described the system succinctly: "We've already seen in group trials that when people are brought together in a commune they do tell the truth. We take them to where the crime was committed, everyone comes, including witnesses, and they are charged there. The suspect fears to lie because everyone knows what happened."

The *gacaca* system has its flaws—resources for the suspect's defense are limited and ethnicity or class status may play inappropriate roles in determining guilt or innocence. But it has its roots in traditional processes of reconciliation and may represent the best solution for a practical problem. Victims lament being deprived of what they see as justice, but Rwanda's attorney-general pinpointed the ethical reality: "There is no justice for crimes of mass violence," he said. "Where participation in atrocities is so widespread, the justice can only be symbolic. It would be impossible to provide the survivors with real justice. What punishment could ever satisfy them?"

President Kagame runs a pretty tight ship, so to speak. Rwanda isn't much of a liberal democracy, but the government has begun a process of decentralizing and democratizing local political institutions. A second set of elections was held in March for local councils and had a relatively strong participation rate, though there is some indication people thought they would be fined if they did not vote. Political parties were not allowed to campaign for candidates who stood as individuals, not party representatives. Forming a political party in the present circumstances is risky business. Former President Bizimungu was clapped into house arrest in May after announcing the creation of a new party.

Parliamentary and presidential elections are slated for 2001 or 2004, after approval of a new constitution by popular referendum.

Culture: More than 90% of the people of Rwanda are agricultural, rural folk, densely crowded (708 per square mile) on the large, grassy plateaus. Although most are Christian, particularly among the Hutus, almost half retain traditional beliefs. Relations between the Rwanda government and the Catholic Church remain strained. Two priests have already been sentenced to death for participation in the genocide, and there are reports that Catholic churches and institutions have been special targets in the DRC.

Catholic orders in Europe are accused of harboring priests and nuns on the run from genocide-related criminal charges. In March 2000 a Belgian court ruled that two accused nuns sheltered in Belgium by their order should be tried there and when the trial concluded, an all-white jury found the two guilty. They were sentenced to lengthy prison terms.

HIV/AIDS has become Rwanda's new genocide. The virus was already working its way into Rwandan society by 1990, but the genocide contributed to its explosive growth. The mass rape of Tutsi women was an integral part of the planned genocide. Radio propaganda taunted Hutus with a mythology of Tutsi women: they were taller, more beautiful, arrogant and threateningly dangerous because of their sexual wiles. They had to be tasted and humiliated before being killed.

More than 50% of the rape survivors are now HIV-positive. So great is the stigma attached to rape that few survivors have been willing to admit it. Few have had the courage to identify those who had brutalized them, justifiably fearing retribution from friends and relatives of the accused. With thousands of men imprisoned and accused of the crime of genocide, the Ministry of Justice gave little attention to the crime of rape. As a result Rwandan women received neither attention nor justice until recently.

The shift of thinking came in 1999 with the trial of the former mayor of Taba, Jean

Paul Akayesu, before the International Tribunal on Rwandan Genocide in Arusha. In 1994 Akayesu had kept 300 women prisoner in the Cultural Center of Taba for several weeks. They were raped repeatedly before being killed.

In an historic judgment the Arusha court ruled that rape and sexual violence "also constitute genocide in the same way as any other act, as long as they were committed with intent to destroy a particular group targeted as such." The court concluded that rape of Tutsi women was systematic, was perpetrated against all Tutsi women, and had constituted an integral part of the Rwandan genocide. Akayesu was condemned to death.

Rwandan courts handed down their first rape sentences in April 2000. Maximum sentence for the crime is twenty years. None of the HIV-infected will live that long.

Some 350,000 Rwandans, including over 200,000 children, died of HIV/AIDS-related diseases in 1999. An additional 60,000 children were orphaned by HIV/AIDS. Some 70% of patients in Kigali's main hospital are suffering from illnesses related to HIV.

Rwanda's silent death is spread by another consequence of 1994's genocide. So many men were killed during Rwanda's genocide that female survivors are prepared to share husbands in order to have a family. The practice of sharing men, known as "*kwinjira*," is widespread in rural areas. Health officials say that it represents the greatest challenge to their efforts to combat the spread of AIDS.

Economy: Often described as the land of a thousand hills, Rwanda is a country whose economy is largely based on subsistence agriculture. It has, for the past five years, been engaged in a process of economic and political reconstruction. Roads, bridges, and whole sectors of the economy were destroyed by civil war in 1994. Thanks to the relative peace established, GDP has grown—10.3% in 1997 and 10% in 1998—and the economy is now about 88% of its prewar level.

Farmers contribute 75% of the GDP and Rwanda's most important exports are coffee and tea, which bring about 80 to 90% of export revenues. In 1999 coffee production rose 20 percent to 17,000 tons, but it is still a long way from peak production of 45,000 tons a decade ago. The government has identified tea production as strategically important to the country's economic development. Over the past 30 years it has grown consistently, contributing 30,000 jobs to the economy. In 1998 tea exports brought in $19 million in foreign exchange. The government plans to privatize 10 state-owned tea factories as part of its general privatization program.

Local production of foodstuffs is insufficient for consumption needs, so most foodstuffs are imported from neighboring countries. Rwanda imports between 8000 and 10,000 liters of milk each day from Uganda. There are plans to redevelop the dairy industry by importing some 3,000 cows from Germany, but few have yet been purchased.

The 2000 budget was $545 million. Seventy million dollars—3.2% of GDP—is allocated for defense spending because, as the finance minister said, "Rwanda is still under threat." Russian combat helicopters have reportedly been purchased in the past year, along with a number of used Ukrainian tanks.

To improve social services and deal with the AIDS crisis, the budget reduces nonpriority services by 30 percent. Nonessential ministries are being closed down, government houses sold and the number of Rwandan diplomatic missions abroad will cut in half. Still, about a third of the budget will come from foreign donations.

The government's biggest problem, apart from security, remains the integration of more than two million refugees returning home. Some have been living as such since 1959. So many returnees did not speak French the government was compelled to make English an official language. There are political as well as economic tensions between those who returned and those who stayed and survived the genocide.

In addition to criticism of its human rights abuses in the Congo, the Rwandan government faces intensive scrutiny over its exploitation of the DRC's natural resources. The UN panel of experts examining the issue was withering in its criticism of the Rwandan Patriotic Army and its allies, who were, it said, financing the war through a variety of commercial activities. With Uganda and Burundi, Rwanda had, said the panel, engaged in "mass-scale looting," extracting diamonds, gold, timber, elephant tusks and other resources. Presidents Museveni and Kagame were identified as "the main sponsors of the three-year rebel war" and had "indirectly given criminal cartels a unique opportunity" to exploit Congo's mineral wealth.

The report was so unbalanced that it was easily criticized. "The reason we went to Congo," said President Kagame, "is to make sure that what happened in 1994 does not happen again. We are not there looking for precious stones . . . We cannot exchange lives for gold."

Future: The challenge facing President Kagame is to create a unified Rwanda. It is not a task that can be achieved overnight. Nor does the gulf between the rhetoric of a united nation espoused by the *RPF* and the recent elimination of Hutu participation in government suggest the task will be an easy one. Increasing criticism of President Kagame and his government suggests the benefit of doubt accorded Rwanda as victim may have run its course.

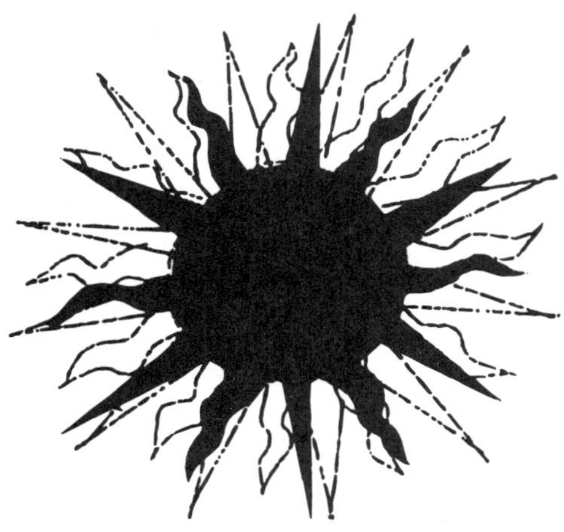

The Democratic Republic of the Congo

A poster of former President (of Zaïre) Mobutu Sese Seko burns

AP/Wide World Photo

Note: This country has been known as Belgian Congo, Congo (Leopoldville), the Democratic Republic of the Congo, Zaïre, and most recently, Democratic Republic of the Congo.

Area: 2,343,950 sq. km = 905,000 sq. mi. (one–third the size of the U.S.).

Population: 50,481,305 (July 1999 est.)

Capital City: Kinshasa (pop. 6.55 million)

Climate: Warm and humid tropical weather in the western and central areas, temperate in the eastern highlands.

Neighboring Countries: Congo (North, West); Central African Republic, Sudan (North); Uganda, Rwanda, Burundi and Tanzania (East); Zambia and Angola (South).

Official Language: French.

Other Principal Languages: Over 200 African languages are spoken. Most prominent are the Alur, Bembe, Chokwe, Fuliiru, Hunde, Kituba (a creole based on the KiKongo dialect spoken in Manianga area of the lower Congo River), Kinyarwanda, KiKongo, Lega, Lingala (a lingua franca trade language), Luba, Lugbara, Mangbetu, Mongo, Nandi, Ndo, Ngbaka, Phende, Sanga, Shi, Songe, Swahili, Tetela, and Zande.

Ethnic groups: Over 200 African ethnic groups of which the majority are Bantu; the four largest peoples—Mongo, Luba, Kongo and the Mangbetu-Azande make up about 45% of the population.

Principal Religions: Roman Catholic 50%, Protestant 20%, Kimbanguist 10%, Muslim 10%, other sects and traditional beliefs 10%.

Chief Commercial Products: Diamonds, copper, coffee, cobalt, and crude oil.

GNP per capita: 110 US$

Currency: Congolese franc (CF)

Former Colonial Status: Personal possession of King Leopold II of Belgium (1885–1907); Belgian Colony (1907–1960).

Independence Date: June 30, 1960.

Chief of State: Joseph Kabila, President (since January 2001).

National Flag: A plain blue field upon which is centered a large gold star, with a line of five small stars at the pole.

The deep green region of the Congo has intrigued explorers, adventurers and writers for centuries, becoming one of the popular stereotypes of Africa in the western mind. Dark jungles and rain forests abounding in game, and almost as unknown today as at the time of Stanley's explorations, adjoin huge mining developments and vast plantations, some of which have been broken down into smaller farms. The very size of the Congo is

one of its most distinctive features. Even more interesting, this huge nation has only a 25–mile–long coastline which allows it to "breathe" on the South Atlantic Ocean.

There are three distinctive features of this land mass: the immense river basin of the Congo and its tributaries, tropically hot and humid; the rich mining areas are located in the eastern sector and the upland plains in the northeast and southeast with tall, rippling grasses and snow–capped mountains rising to almost 17,000 feet in the East near the Equator. The eastern lake region, which includes Lake Kivu and the western shores of Lakes Tanganyika, Mweru, Albert and Edward, is unsurpassed in scenic beauty and abounds in wildlife.

Tributaries of the great Congo River flow from these lakes into the Lualaba River, which in turn becomes the Congo after it reaches 4° south latitude. From this point, the Congo surges in a wide, island–dotted course through the jungles, joined by its other tributaries. Three hundred miles inland from the Atlantic, at Malebo Pool (near bustling Kisangani), the river widens into a lake, continuing on to the sea with a width of up to ten miles. The river is navigable for the most part and widely used in commerce, interrupted only by cataracts at Malebo Falls (formerly Stanley Falls) and below Kinshasa. Railway by–passes have been constructed at these cataracts to maintain the continuity of commerce.

History: Before the arrival of European explorers, the mighty Kingdom of the Congo, with an age–old way of life, included not only the present–day Democratic Republic of the Congo, but what is now Angola and west equatorial Africa. Until the middle of the 19th century, this area was virtually unknown to the western world. Earlier, Portuguese penetration was not significant, though it did result indirectly in the consecration of the first Black bishop by the Roman Catholic Church in 1520. For details of early and colonial history, see Historical Background and *King Leopold and the Belgians in Africa.*

There was little effort made prior to independence to prepare the people of the Congo for self–rule, although the Belgians did establish primary and secondary schools which would have eventually served as a basis for higher education; much of this effort was through Catholic missionaries. In the middle 1950s, two leaders became prominent when political activity was first permitted. Joseph Kasavubu led *ABAKO*, an organization composed of Bakongo people. Patrice Lumumba, a Batetela from the interior, headed the *MNC*, which had almost no tribal identity and was composed of memberships of a number of smaller ethnic groups.

Belgium proposed in 1956 that the Congo become independent in 30 years, but Kasavubu demanded freedom in "much less than 30 years." For the first time, elections were scheduled in 1957 in which Africans were to participate; they were limited to lesser municipal offices. When French Congo, across the river, was offered independence by French President Charles de Gaulle in 1958, there was renewed pressure brought on Belgium to grant independence to its colony. An impending threat of independence, coupled with tumbling world copper prices, led to a withdrawal of foreign capital from the country in the late 1950s, making a shambles of the economy and creating widespread unemployment.

In this turbulent atmosphere, Belgium summoned the African leaders to Brussels in early 1960 and announced that independence would become effective on June 30th. The Congolese politicians hurried home to gain support; the people were tantalized by a multitude of promises of good things to come with independence (under the "right" leadership, of course). A multitude of new parties sprang up, almost overnight. The intense political and tribal activity served as a forewarning to thousands of Europeans, who began to leave the Congo in droves.

President Kasavubu (center) and Premier Lumumba confer with Belgian army chief, 1960

Although pre–independence elections were relatively calm, the result was an impossible splintering of representation. Lumumba's *MNC* won the greatest number of seats—33 out of 137 in the House and 24 in the 84–seat Senate. After ten days of bargaining behind closed doors, Lumumba announced a coalition with a 37–member cabinet containing officials from no less than 16 parties. Amid pomp and ceremony, independence was declared on the chosen date with Kasavubu as president and Lumumba as premier.

The situation in the new nation quickly deteriorated into lawlessness, rebellion, anarchy, revolt and secession. It started when the *Force Publique*, consisting of 1,000 White officers and 24,000 African soldiers, disintegrated into open mutiny. Hundreds of whites were mercilessly slaughtered and thousands of others were beaten and tortured; within a week there was a renewed mass exodus of white people.

The turmoil which had almost immediately engulfed the new nation brought a new and ambitious actor to the scene. Moise Tshombe, premier of the copper–rich southeastern province *Katanga*, announced that the area would be a separate nation; a neighboring province, South Kasai, also seceded from the Congo. With President Kasavubu and Premier Lumumba literally at each other's political throats, Belgium flew in paratroopers to put down the civil war. In the meantime, a UN peace–keeping force was sent in to help maintain some semblance of stability.

Two months after Katanga had announced its severance from the Congo, President Kasavubu decided to eliminate his rival, Lumumba, once and for all—he had the army seize power and hand Lumumba over to the self–proclaimed President of Katanga, Moise Tshombe. Kasavubu's plan worked—Lumumba was promptly killed. A year later, the country was still caught up in civil war, and UN Secretary General Dag Hammerskjold was killed in a plane crash on his way to try to talk peace with the tough Tshombe.

The fierce fighting continued into August 1962 when the UN submitted a plan for peaceful settlement of the civil war. Tshombe was riding high and would have no part of it; Katangan troops even fired upon UN forces in late 1962 to show their scorn for the world organization's interference in their independence movement. But it was a losing battle against too many outside forces, and Tshombe gave in to the central government in early 1963. Under these conditions, UN troops withdrew in mid year.

Another rebellion of rival factions began to take shape. In a move made out of desperation—and urgently needing a strong individual to take charge—Presi-

Premier Moise Tshombe greeted by spear-carrying warriors in Kivu Province, August 1964

dent Kasavubu appointed Tshombe to become premier. The defeated leader used foreign mercenaries and Belgian paratroopers to put down the rebellion.

He got no word of thanks from President Kasavubu, who, frightened and envious of Tshombe's growing popularity, fired him as premier, whereupon Colonel Joseph Désiré Mobutu took center stage and ousted the president in late 1965.

Mobutu's power over the Congo lasted until 1997—32 years. It can be divided into three periods:
1965–1970—Consolidation of power, dependence on foreign aid.
1970–1981—Seizure of foreign interests; emulation of Mao Zedong; drop in productivity.
1982–1997—General deterioration; Mobutu became useless to the U.S. and western nations as the Cold War faded, and a ruthless, thieving recluse in his own country.

Consolidation of Power

Mobutu was able to maintain the loyalty of the army as he nationalized the huge Belgian copper mines. Tshombe was ordered to leave the country; his plane was hijacked when leaving and he was then held under house arrest in Algeria until his death of an alleged heart attack two years later.

By juggling bureaucrats and the cabinet constantly and by sewing seeds of suspicion to pit one tribe against another Mobutu all but eliminated opposition. Pressured by the U.S. and other foreign powers to hold elections, he created the *Movement for the Revolution (MPR)* in order to prepare for them to be held in 1970. He and the party were victorious since there was no effective opposition.

Being president went to Mobutu's head. Instead of taking what Congo had and building upon it, he blindly tore it apart. All names had to be African, not Christian; when the Catholic Church opposed this move, he sent the resident Cardinal back to Rome. Mobutu became "Mobutu Sese Seko Kuru Ngebendu Wa Za Banga," donning a leopard skin cap as the symbol of his status and power. Congo (Kinshasa) was renamed *Zaïre,* supposedly an African word meaning "Big River," but actually a corruption of a Portuguese word.

Seizure of Foreign Property

The constitution was revised in 1974 to contain "Mobutuism" which embodied his thoughts and teachings. It was forced upon the Catholic schools. All plantations and farms owned by foreigners were seized, to be compensation for over a period of ten years (this did not happen). All ore had to be refined within Zaïre, which didn't have adequate facilities to perform the task.

Elections in 1977 resulted in another victory for Mobutu and his party; however, the legislature was no more than a debating place—Mobutu was actually ruling by decree. Yet, he continued to receive foreign assistance from the U.S. and other nations on the theory that Zaïre was a bastion against communism.

Faced with increasing criticism at home, Mobutu closed newspapers and became increasingly reluctant to appear in public as his popularity waned. But he, his family and friends were reaping huge fortunes—it was estimated that 40% of all revenues found their way into their pockets.

General Deterioration and Anarchy

Mobutu, realizing that his personal security and future were clouded, summoned Israeli military personnel to train a Presidential Guard in 1982. They performed well, and the elite guard slowly became the only force in Zaïre. The armed forces were expected to make their way by theft and corruption. Government workers were unpaid, and were expected to survive the same way. Most failed to even appear at work except to collect a bribe.

The currency ($Zaïre) became a bad joke. The military would appear on currency printing day to grab as much as possible and spend it immediately before it was devalued—it quickly became utterly worthless.

Descent into Anarchy; Reclusiveness of Mobutu

During 1982 Mobutu began his withdrawal that in later years became extreme—he trusted almost no one except his presidential guard. He had a palace (actually a fortress) erected, costing a tremendous sum, at Gbadolite in northwest Zaïre. His income was increasingly derived from diamonds and forcing farmers to grow cotton and staple crops which could only be sold through government markets at woefully low prices. The copper mines of Sha-

In Kinshasa, an enthusiasm for education but a destruction of schools.
Photo by Marie-Françoise Plissart

ba had been flooded and idle for years. With his fortune, he paid his presidential guard and ignored the rest of the world and his countrymen. In 1996, probably after a period of denial associated with his reclusiveness, Mobutu traveled to Switzerland for extensive treatment of prostate cancer.

Militias abounded, existing by thievery. The loyalty and morale of the army descended to virtually zero. Foreign aid was limited to humanitarian needs, but even this went awry. The army appropriated it upon arrival and sold it to black marketeers. Thus, while people were dying for lack of medical care, doctors were unable to treat them because they had no medicines or supplies.

Without knowledge of usual sources, another ominous event was taking place in 1996: Tutsi troops from Rwanda and eastern Zaïre were being equipped and trained to seek out and destroy the remains of the Rwandan Hutu army living in eastern Zaïre. This effort quickly included rebellious Banyamalenga Tutsis native to Zaïre, who were willing to fight to end the wretched conditions within their own country. These forces in training were supported by Uganda, Tanzania and Angola.

Laurent Kabila

Plucked from obscurity to provide a non-Tutsi face to the insurgency was the semi-retired roly-poly professional revolutionary Laurent Kabila. A Luba from Katanga, he had been long engaged in the anti-Mobutu struggle, but always in secondary roles.

He eventually emerged as the head of a Marxist political organization, the *People's Revolutionary Party*, and established an enclave in eastern Zaire's Kivu province. There, along the shores of Lake Tanganyika, he lived and governed outside the rules of Mobutu's rigid state as a typical African warlord.

When Che Guevara, the charismatic Cuban revolutionary who was looking for further fertile fields to ply his trade, arrived in eastern Zaire he ran across Kabila and provided a withering critique of his revolutionary potential. Despite being "the best of the Congolese leaders," Kabila was seen as "too addicted to drink and women." Reluctant to engage in any actual fighting, Kabila seemed to take his best shots across the bar.

After the early revolutionary days Kabila appears to have settled into the life of a warlord businessman, making a decent living through smuggling and selling Zairian gold. He apparently made enough money to keep two large homes in Dar es Salaam and another in Uganda. He was, as they say, available when the call to leadership came.

Once the insurgency began, some 2 million Hutus living as refugees in Zaïre were terrified and started to flee back to Rwanda They did this in spite of loud protests by the Hutu army that they would be killed if they returned. Possibly 1.2 million of them made it back to Rwanda, where they live in squalor as refugees. There were slaughters and burials in mass graves of untold hundreds of thousands.

This was not a military battle. The Zaïrian army fled in terror before the onslaught; they had little loyalty except to themselves. The only thing that impeded Kabila's forces was the fact there are no roads or bridges, just rutted, frequently flooded and muddy areas that allow trucks to pass irregularly. Because of these conditions, it took until May 1997 for them to reach Kinshasa.

Laurent Kabila took the oath of office on May 31, 1997. He promised democracy, but said elections could not be held for two years because of the need to bring order to the Democratic Republic of the Congo, Mobutu's *Zaïre*. He spent most of 1997–98 consolidating his power.

In August 1998, when it had become apparent that Kabila had become little more than a mini–Mobutu, discontent grew more vociferous. The security demands of Rwanda and Uganda were still unmet, Hutu rebels still posed threats from bases in the Congo, and enemies of the Museveni regime scampered back and forth across the border, doing damage to Ugandan citizens. Inside the Congo Banyamulenge Tutsi had little sense they would be incorporated into any national dialogue, and it became evident that Kabila was moving to place relatives and members of his own ethnic group in the most important positions of power. Nepotism was accompanied by its sister vice, corruption.

When Kabila moved to sack his Rwandan military advisors and send them packing—the very people responsible for elevating him to presidential status—the crisis of confidence came to a head. The second rebellion arose in the East no sooner than the plane bearing the exiled advisors landed. A brilliant tactical flight to the West brought rebel forces close to the doors of Kinshasa and for a moment it looked as though the regime were doomed. A fearful Kabila called upon his fellow authoritarians in Angola and Zimbabwe. Both presidents dos Santos and Mugabe responded with interventionist forces. The western threat was ended and military action focused on the Eastern Front.

The Second Rebellion developed into Africa's first continental war. Besides Angola and Zimbabwe, Namibia, Chad, Sudan and Libya came to the support of the Kabila government. Rwanda and Uganda supported local Congolese rebel factions. By mid–1999 it looked very much as though the Democratic Republic of the Congo had been, *de facto*, partitioned. The rebel coalition controlled the eastern third of the country. Laurent Kabila remained in office by virtue of foreign arms. It was difficult to talk of the central government exercising control over its territory.

"To those who hold out longest, good things come" might very well be Laurent Kabila's personal motto. Having enjoyed initial military success, the rebel forces opposing him soon fell to bickering among themselves.

The *RCD* split in two. After months of infighting, the rebels removed their original leader, Ernest Wamba-dia-Wamba, replacing him with Emile Ilunga. Rwanda and Uganda, themselves divided on the best way to fight the war, supported different rebel factions. Uganda supported Wamba, who moved to Kisangani where he was better protected by Ugandan troops; Rwanda backed Ilunga, whose *RCD* faction remained headquartered in Goma. Yet a third rebel faction emerged under the leadership of Jean-Pierre Bemba, the leader of the *Congolese Liberation Movement* (*MLC*). Backed by Uganda, Bemba took charge of the rebellion's northern front. Rwanda and Uganda themselves engaged in heated fighting around Kisangani on at least two occasions.

The Lusaka Agreement

War and peace have continued intermittently bringing hope and despair to everyday Congolese. Peace prospects seemed hopeful in the summer of 1999 as warring states gathered in conference. In July six participating governments signed an accord in Zambia's capital, Lusaka, setting the conditions for ending war in the Democratic Republic of the Congo. The conditions were defined and a timetable was set, a sign of the terminal optimism of conference participants.

Within 24 hours of the signing, hostilities were to cease. Within a week a Joint Military Commission (JMC), consisting of two representatives of each belligerent party, under a neutral chairman designated by the OAU, would be appointed. It was to oversee implementation of the accord until the deployment of a UN peacekeeping force.

The international force would take the necessary action to ensure compliance, collect weapons from civilians and supervise the withdrawal of all foreign troops. The agreement also envisioned tracking down and disarming armed groups, screening for mass killers and war criminals, and ultimately the handing over of suspected *genocidaires* to the International Criminal Tribunal for Rwanda (ICTR) in Arusha, Tanzania.

Signatories agreed to repatriate members of the "armed groups" to their countries of origin, with an additional commitment of amnesty granted to those not found guilty of genocide. The "armed groups" were identified as the Rwandan ex-FAR and Interahamwe, the Ugandan *Allied Democratic Forces* (*ADF*), *Lord's Re-*

Mobutu Sese Seko

sistance Army (*LRA*) and *West Nile Bank Front* (*WNBF*), the *Uganda National Rescue Front II* (*UNRF II*), the Former Ugandan National Army (FUNA), the Burundian *Forces de Défense pour la Démocratie* (*FDD*) and Angola's *UNITA*.

Forty-five days after the signature of the Lusaka agreement, the DRC government, the *Rassemblement Congolais pour la Démocratie* (*RCD*), the *Mouvement de Libération Congolais* (*MLC*), unarmed opposition groups and Congolese civil society were to begin open political negotiations leading to the creation of a new political dispensation for the Congo.

On paper the plan looked excellent, but political reality and diplomatic brilliance are hardly the same. Nearly a year and several cease-fires later, the international peace force was not yet in place.

In February 2000 the Security Council approved a Congo peacekeeping force. It called for a monitoring force of some 500, backed by about 1000 soldiers; 4,000 additional personnel would function as a support staff. Its assignment is to oversee the implementation of last year's Lusaka agreement to end the Congo civil war. One wondered about the capacity of the 500 to monitor a cease-fire only reluctantly and intermittently followed in a country the size of Western Europe. President Kabila signed the Lusaka ceasefire agreement to avoid losing the war. Quibble, protest, rejection and delay provided time to rebuild his forces, but additional Chinese arms and Northern Korean training were of little avail. The year 2000 was punctuated by regular violations of the cease-fire and dramatic successes of the rebel alliance.

Kabila's Military Failures

In August 2000, President Laurent Kabila announced that his government would no longer observe the Lusaka accord because Congo was occupied by Uganda and Rwanda. On the 9th of August a force sent up the Ubangui River to attack Jean-Pierre Bemba's *MLC* rebels was ambushed. A river ferry mounted with cannon and antiaircraft guns was destroyed, along with some 800 Congolese and Zimbabwean troops according to the rebels. The government denied it lost the gunboat, but with Orwellian attention to the uses of the press release, it announced that it had successfully concluded its offensive. On the 11th government troops were ordered to halt their offensive.

In October the Congolese army (FAC) and its allies attacked Rwandan and rebel forces on the southern Katangan Front, hoping to open a corridor for Burundian Hutu rebels—members of the *Forces de la Défense de la Démocratie* (*FDD*)—to infiltrate Burundi. Burundi has always been considered the weakest link in the anti-Kabila alliance. If it could be destabilized, the government would have to withdraw its troops from the Congo.

The government coalition was initially successful, but its lines were overextended. Roads were in such miserable shape the Zimbabwean heavy artillery could not be resupplied. When the Rwandan Patriotic Army (RPA) and its allies counter-attacked, Kabila's troops fell back precipitously. The government's military failure was completed in early December when Rwandan troops and their *RCD-Goma* allies captured the strategic southeastern city of Pweto, a critical gateway to the riches of Katanga province, Kabila's homeland.

At least 200 of Pweto's defenders—Rwandan Hutu *Interahamwe,* Burundian Hutu rebels, and members of FAC—were killed. Those not killed, up to 10,000 including a full battalion of Zimbabwean soldiers, fled across the border into Zambia.

Material losses to Kabila's allies were equally staggering at Pweto. Zimbabwe lost a MIG jet-fighter, shot down by a Rwandan surface-to-air missile, and a huge store of equipment—armored vehicles, ballistic missiles, rocket launchers, 122 mm and 130 mm guns, about 1,000 brand new individual arms—fell to the rebels. With the capture of Pweto and the scattering of its defenders, the road to Congo's second-biggest city, Lubumbashi, lay open.

The Belgian-based International Crisis Group has called the battle of Pweto "a turning point in Rwandan strategy." The rout of Kabila's forces prompted a debate within the Rwandan government. Some thought the victory should be exploited to destroy the *Interahamwe* in Katanga completely, and some even argued for tracking them down in Zambia. The diplomatically attuned successfully argued that the backlash against such a move would simply be too costly. Indeed, Pweto may be the high-water mark of Rwandan arms in the Congo, for other events were soon to tip the balance towards more peaceful solutions.

Laurent Kabila Assassinated

Many in Kinshasa had the feeling the Kabila regime had entered its final stages by September. By then, Angola, one of its strongest backers, had become fed up with the pudgy president. Angolan emissaries were reported to have met with both President Museveni of Uganda and Jean-Pierre Bemba, head of the Uganda-backed *MLC,* which controlled the northern third of the Congo. President Kabila's regular search for plots, conspiracies and opposition culminated in turning on his initial supporters.

One of those was Anselme Masasu, a founding leader of the *AFDL.* Masasu had commanded the army of child soldiers (*kadogos*) from Eastern Congo that swept into Kinshasa in the wake of Kabila's victory. In October he was reported to have made subversive comments at a meeting of some 1,200 *kadogos* and was subsequently arrested and tortured, along with many others of eastern origin. Some 47 were executed in the presence of President Kabila, who allegedly killed several himself. Anselme Masasu and eight of his companions were reportedly sent to Katanga where they were murdered on 27 November.

Masasu's murder resonated strongly among the *kadogo*s, and its rumor was a factor in their massive desertion at the battle of Pweto. Others plotted more direct action to avenge the murder of their commander—the assassination of Laurent Kabila.

Kabila was assassinated on 16 January 2001, forty years, to the day, after the murder of Patrice Lumumba. According to the official version, he was shot by one of his own *kadogo* bodyguards, Rachidi Kasereka, who was, in turn, shot to death by Kabila's aide-de-camp, Col. Eddy Kapend. That Col. Kapend and more than fifty others—including Gen. Nawej Yav, one time commander of Kinshasa's armed forces and other security officials—now rot in prison suspected of involvement in the assassination, suggests the Byzantine nature of the regime and how difficult it might be to ever get the real story.

The real story is probably less important than the consequences of Kabila's death. UN officials have set the tone by regularly referring to it as a "window of opportunity." There is a new found optimism regarding Congo's prospects. Laurent's son, Jospeh Kabila, elevated to the presidency by his father's inner circle and their Angolan and Zimbabwean backers, has broken a diplomatic stalemate by reversing many of his father's decisions that had blocked implementation of the Lusaka agreement.

Moving swiftly to gain international support, Joseph Kabila visited Washington and all the major European capitals, consented to the UN mission in the Congo, accepted the OAU's designated mediator—the former Botswana president, Ketumile Masire—and agreed to begin an inter-Congolese dialogue. Laurent Kabila

Former President Laurent Kabila

lost the war; his son may very well win the peace.

Joseph Kabila

Joseph Kabila had long enjoyed the confidence of his father, alternating military assignments with more confidential missions on his father's behalf. Quiet, direct and frank, Joseph is stylistically very different from his father. He rejected the "Marble Palace," built by Mobutu and favored by his father, and works from the OAU's Kinshasa headquarters, protected by Zimbabwean troops. Educated in Tanzania and Uganda, Kabila reportedly feels more comfortable speaking English than French. When elevated to the presidency he was serving as the army chief of staff. He was 29 years old, Africa's youngest president.

Peace in the Congo depends on three issues: disengagement, disarmament and dialogue. Each poses different problems for Joseph Kabila. Under the Lusaka agreement, disengagement requires belligerents to withdraw some 9.3 miles behind their front lines. By mid-2001, Burundi, Rwanda, Uganda and all the rebel factions had agreed and commenced to do so.

Thus far there has been no action by the armies of the government coalition—Angola, Namibia, Zimbabwe. Their governments have always argued they will start withdrawing their troops from the Congo only after Rwanda, Uganda and Burundi finish theirs. The latter three still have security concerns, and a total withdrawal before those concerns, are settled is unlikely. Angola, too, has security concerns, though with troops already stationed in Congo-Brazzaville, these may be largely met. Zimbabwe has no security concerns and could easily withdraw its troops were it not for their financial entanglements in the DRC economy and Robert Mugabe's fear of having the opposition use withdrawal as the ultimate sign of policy failure in next year's presidential election.

Disengagement will be observed and overseen by international institutions. The Joint Military Commission (JMC), the OAU group overseeing the peace plan, is in place and its new chairman selected: Brig. Gen. Njuki Mwaniki, a senior Kenyan officer. The JMC has already agreed on draft proposals for the withdrawal of all foreign troops in the country. The UN Military Observer Mission in Congo (MONUC), which will observe withdrawals and monitor ceasefire violations, is also getting in place, though it has been reduced in size. Instead of some 5,000, the mission will now be 3,500 strong—500 to observe and the rest to protect UN facilities and stores from theft.

Sir Ketumile Masire, the OAU facilitator, has announced Congo's internal dialogue is scheduled to start on July 15, 2001. A major step towards the inter-Congolese dialogue was taken when Joseph Kabila permitted political parties to organize. Banning parties had been one of Laurent Kabila's first steps once he reached Kinshasa. The purpose of the dialogue is to lead to the creation of a transitional government which will prepare for eventual presidential and legislative election throughout the DRC.

Any genuine inter-Congolese dialogue is dangerous for Joseph Kabila and what remains of the *AFDL* regime. He lacks legitimacy and doesn't command much of a political constituency. He is maintained in office by foreign armies. There are two models of dealing with the transitional government problem before him. In Comoros, Colonel/President Azali announced he would not be a future candidate for president and took charge of the island's transitional process. In Burundi, President Buyoya has used the dialogue process in every way possible to avoid being excluded from leadership of the transitional government. For him negotiations have been a means of clinging to power.

Joseph Kabila's choice will depend on the kinds of pressures exerted on him from internal and external sources. The barons of his father's regime, none of whom wants willingly to lose power and its acquisitive possibilities, will press for controlling the process and maintaining power. Zimbabwe, with all its cozy financial arrangements with Laurent Kabila at risk, has the most to lose by Joseph Kabila's removal from office. To secure its interests, it has moved to diminish Angolan influence in the circles that surround the young president. As tensions between Angola and Zimbabwe grow, Joseph Kabila seems to be trying to firm up relations with South Africa.

Complex as the dialogue issue is, it remains less problematic than disarmament of Congo's "negative forces." Hutu elements, be they ex-Rwandan army (FAR), *Interahamwe*, or Burundian *FDD* forces, remain armed and dangerous. Their object is the overthrow of the present governments in both Burundi and Rwanda and, if past is prologue, the destruction of their "race enemy." Certainly with the Rwandans, many bear, to varying degrees, the guilt of 1994's genocide. Disarming them will be difficult. Reintegrating them into Rwandan society will be even more so.

President Joseph Kabila

There has been some softening of Rwanda's demands for justice against FAR and *Interahamwe* forces. A new form of community trial, *gacaca*, is being developed in Rwanda to reduce the backlog of genocide cases, and these could be used for many of the non-leadership *FAR* and *Interahamwe* people. Joseph Kabila's government seems to be encouraging them to leave, but is doing little if anything to disarm them. A general pattern of easterly Hutu migration has been seen by mid-2001, forcefully dramatized by the killing and eating of two mountain gorillas by starving *Interahamwe* forces trying to enter Rwanda. Barefoot, hungry and only lightly armed, they have been, so far, easily controlled by the Rwandan Patriotic Army.

Culture: The social structure of the Congo is almost unchanged from what it was prior to the arrival of Europeans. Family, clan and tribe are the units of organization. Tribes are usually names for a distant ancestor or a nearby river. Dance is associated with every important event from birth to death, accentuated by the clapping of hands and the accompaniment of varieties of drums, bells, horns and locally–fashioned flutes.

Kinshasa, Congo's capital, remains a testament to the Congolese capacity to suffer and endure. A hugely swollen population escaping the devastation of war, estimated now to be near seven million, survives cut off from the city's traditional sources of food. Half of Kinshasa food supply was lost when rebels captured fertile Equateur province and controlled the river that once carried food to the capital. Virtually every available parcel of ground in the city is planted with foodstuffs to supplement the meager food supply.

The consequences are heart rending. The majority of *Kinois* (the city's inhabitants) must content themselves with a single, frugal, daily meal, usually eaten at night so they can go to sleep with a full stomach. Parents fast for two or three days to provide food for their children, but malnutrition grows and with it, an increase in childhood disease and death. The DRC's child mortality rate is 200 per 1,000 live births, one of the highest in the world. The New York-based International Rescue Committee estimates the total number of lives claimed by the Congo war now approaches three million—most of them from malnutrition and disease.

In the markets of Kinshasa it is easier to find rice from Pakistan or Vietnam than it is to find manioc, the *Kinois'* traditional starch. Those who can afford it pound rice to make a substitute manioc flour to create their traditional *fufu*. Meat of almost any kind—pig, chicken, or beef, for example—is beyond the budget of most *Kinois*. Bush meats, even endangered species, have become an important source of protein for the well-to-do. For the most impoverished, dog meat, at 50 cents a pound, is now the only affordable meat.

Economy: At the time of independence, this was one of the potentially richest nations in the world, with vast deposits of copper, cobalt and diamonds. But government corruption, mismanagement and thievery was a ball and chain around the economic leg of Zaïre through the 1980s.

The immense copper mines of Shaba remain flooded and unworked. Half of the money from diamond mining under forced labor conditions went to pay the army until 1993; after that, troops were expected to "live off the land."

At independence there were about 80,000 miles of good to fair roads in this huge country; most have been swallowed up by jungle growth, leaving few passable by vehicles larger than a jeep. Transportation in the interior is by primitive river barge on the Congo River, the avenue of almost all internal trade.

Until the 1990s the government bought all farm crops at prices set by it; this depressed output by imposing a layer of bureaucrats between the farmers and their markets. Well over 1,000 businesses were taken from their owners and distributed to Mobutu's friends. Not possessing the skills and motivation to run them, the new owners let them simply rot away.

Little changed under Laurent Kabila. He early lost the confidence of businessmen by reneging on contracts originally made to finance the rebellion. Once in power Kabila could more profitably re-negotiate those contracts and so he did. Efforts to centralize gold and diamond purchases to secure government interests and revenues have been less than successful. The interventionist forces, on both sides, engaged in massive exploitation of Congo's resources to finance their military endeavors and enrich their political and military elites.

President Kabila made it worthwhile for his allies by granting privileged access to Congo's mineral riches. He appointed Zimbabwean businessman Billy Rautenbach to head up Gecamines, the Congo's largest mining company. In addition, Rautenbach was granted lucrative cobalt and copper mining concessions to be operated by his Ridgepointe Overseas Developments company. The appointment was remarkable for the amount of foreign control over Congolese mining assets it gave and came after interventions with Congo authorities on Rautenbach's behalf by Zimbabwe's then Minister of Justice, Emmerson Mnangagwa, a confidant of Robert Mugabe.

By the end of 1999 the deal had already gone sour. When Gecamines experienced tremendous financial, operating and industrial relations difficulties and could not generate the revenues desired by Kabila, Rautenbach was replaced by a Belgian executive. Production at Gecamines has fallen drastically since the late 1980s, and today it is estimated to be producing at a mere 10% of its capacity. It requires $150 million just to revive production. To reach its maximum output will require an investment of $1 billion.

When rebels threatened the critical diamond-mining center of Mbuji-Mayi, a thousand Angolan troops were dispatched to its defense. Congo is the world's third-largest exporter of diamonds, and in the past 10 years diamonds have replaced copper as Congo's major source of foreign exchange. Diamond exports—mostly of industrial-quality diamonds—account for about 70% of the DRC's total export revenues. The diamond mining company, MIBA, like Gecamines a traditional government cash cow, has fallen on hard times, however. In 2000 the company produced around 4,600,000 carats, which was 75% lower than in 1999. The Congolese government owns 80% of MIBA shares.

Other diamond resources were employed by Laurent Kabila to pay off his supporters. In January 2000 the Zimbabwe Defense Forces and the Armed Forces of the Democratic Republic of the Congo announced a joint venture to operate the Senga diamond mines. None was left unrewarded by President Kabila: he also granted the Namibian army a diamond mining concession.

Congo's deputy-minister of mines, Ambroise Mbaka, estimates that massive exploitation of the country's diamonds by various elements of the rebel alliance deprives the DRC of an estimated $50 million a month. To regain control over its vast mineral wealth, Joseph Kabila's government agreed to implement a certification system already working in Angola and Sierra Leone. Officials in Antwerp, the world's largest diamond trading center, claim the system stops the flow of rebel-sold gems.

To liberalize the diamond sector, Joseph Kabila's government cancelled a license his father granted the Israeli International Diamond Industries (IDI) to buy and export DRC diamonds exclusively. IDI had agreed to pay Laurent Kabila's cash-strapped government $20 million for a flow of diamonds worth up to $600 million a year. Israeli security services were also alleged to be part of the payment. A UN report called the deal a "nightmare" for Congo's government and a "disaster" for Congo's diamond trade.

The Future: For the first time in years a modicum of optimism seems possible. Tentative, and at times hesitant, implementation of the Lusaka disengagement provisions will test participants, but of all the critical areas, this will show the most progress.

Joseph Kabila's democratic credentials are as yet uncertain. More than 200 political prisoners are still locked away, and there has been little effort to dismantle his father's wide-ranging security apparatus. He has little or no control over a deeply divided political establishment, and his control over the army may not be much greater.

Congo's economic problems are enormous. The economy is a shambles, and Kabila needs an estimated $8 million a month just to supply fuel to his unhappy country. A $125 million contract signed with Thebe Petroleum of South Africa in April to supply motor fuels suggests a shift away from reliance on Angola.

There is little infrastructure to link the regions to Kinshasa, so any plans for a centralized state will simply repeat the failures of the past. Political reconstruction might best look at a variety of federal arrangements. Economic reconstruction of the Congo will require billions. The country will be dependent on outsiders for decades to come.

The Republic of Congo

Area: 349,650 sq. km = 135,000 sq. mi. (twice the size of Missouri).
Population: 2,716,814 (July 1999 est.)
Capital City: Brazzaville (Pop. 850,000, estimated).
Climate: Tropically hot and humid.
Neighboring Countries: Gabon (West); Cameroon (Northwest); Central African Republic (North); Democratic Republic of the Congo (East, South).
Official Language: French.
Other Principal Languages: Lingala and Munoukutuba (a Kikongo-based creole); both are lingua franca trade languages. Many local languages and dialects (of which Kikongo has the most users).
Ethnic groups: Kongo 48%, Sangha 20%, M'Bochi 12%, Teke 17%, Europeans NA%; note—Europeans estimated at 8,500, mostly French, before the 1997 civil war; may be half of that in 1998, following the widespread destruction of foreign businesses in 1997.
Principal Religions: Christian 50%, animist 48%, Muslim 2%.
Chief Commercial Products: Oil, wood products and timber, potash, palm oil, cocoa, bananas, peanuts.
GNP per capita: 690 US$
Currency: CFA Franc (no longer tied to the French franc).
Former Colonial Status: French Congo (1883–1910); one of the four territories of French Equatorial Africa (1910–1960).
Independence Date: August 15, 1960.
Chief of State: Denis Sassou-Nguesso, President (since January 1998).
National Flag: Diagonal green, yellow, and red stripes; the yellow is narrower dividing the two fields.

This lush, green land of ancient tradition lies immediately to the north of the great Congo River. Formerly a part of French Equatorial Africa, the country has the same general geographical features as Congo (Kinshasa) to the south.

As early as the fifteenth and sixteenth centuries, this land was part of the great native Kingdom of the Congo. Its present day boundaries, as is so often the case in Africa, are based upon arbitrary determinations of the 19th century European powers rather than on cultural and physical reality.

A low–lying, treeless plain extends forty miles from the coast to the interior, succeeded by a mountainous region parallel to the coastline known as the Mayombe Escarpment. This is a region of sharply rising mountain ridges covered with jungle and dense growth. Continuing further, the Niari River Valley, an important agricultural area, extends to the east, and to the north lies The Pool, a region of treeless hills and a succession of grassy plains, covering some 50,000 square miles. Part of the Congo River Basin lies in the extreme northeast, a region of dense jungle and all but impassable plains. The climate is uniform and equatorial—hot and humid all year.

History: As in the neighboring country of Congo (Kinshasa), legend common to this region conveys the story of the mighty Kingdom of the Congo, said to have been founded by Wene, also known as Nimi Loukemi, the first king, who reigned more than 400 years ago. For details of early and colonial history, see Historical Background and *The French in Africa.*

Following independence, Fulbert Youlou, who had been instrumental in charting the course toward independence, was installed as president in 1960. A single–chamber assembly of 55 members was established under the constitution, which had the power to remove the president.

Corruption, incompetence, massive labor unrest, and lack of French support led to Youlou's ouster in 1963. His successor, Alphonse Massamba-Débat, shifted policies leftward, creating the *National Revolutionary Movement* (*MNR*) as the country's single party.

Continuing regional tension and administrative weaknesses led the military to replace Massamba-Débat with Major Marien Ngouabi in 1968. Ngouabi maintained the socialist line. He insisted that Marxism was a "universal science," though with different application in each country. He renamed he country the People's Republic of the Congo on Dec. 31, 1969 and announced its sole political party would be the *Congolese Labor Party* (*PCT*), replacing the MRN.

Ngouabi was a northerner, and his regime shifted control of the country away from traditional power centers in the south. This created opposition among workers and students in the highly politicized environment of Brazzaville and other southern cities. He was assassinated in March 1977; a military tribunal was hastily convened which quickly accused and convicted Massambat-Débat of being behind the killing. He was executed and an 11-man military committee took control.

Ngouabi's military successor lasted two years and was ousted in 1979; Colonel Denis Sassou-Nguesso took over as "caretaker" president—and was confirmed in that office in later March. More politically attuned than his predecessors, Sassou-Nguesso maintained a delicate political balance among the leading political groups—the army, the trade unions, and intellectual Marxist civilians. The regime's political language even became more moderate, and his governments included former critics. He was popular enough to capture the 1989 elections, winning a third five-year term.

The fall of the Berlin Wall had its repercussions on Congolese Marxism. Required membership of government officials in the *PCT* was dropped in 1990 and a new constitution establishing a multiparty system was drafted. Dropped was the word "People's" from the country's official name. Adopted by referendum in March 1992, the constitution provided for a new set of multiparty elections. Ultimately 14 political parties participated.

The elections were held in two rounds; the first eliminated Sassou-Nguesso and in the second round Pascal Lissouba, of the *Pan African Union for Social Democracy* (*UPADS*) was chosen president by a majority of 61%. Former president Sassou-Nguesso was granted amnesty for any acts committed during his years in office. Neither graceful defeat nor political retreat seemed to rest easily on his personality.

Legislative elections were inconclusive and a coalition government lasted only until late 1992. New elections, highly disputed, were held. President Lissouba's party controlled 65 out of 125 seats in the National Assembly. A period of shaky parliamentary government ensued.

Political opponents organized private militias to oppose the government and President Lissouba deemed it best to create his personal militia, avoiding any reliance on the national army. Each of the militias had its own distinctive, colorful, and threatening name. Bernard Kolelas, the charismatic mayor of Brazzaville, had the "Ninjas." Sassou-Nguesso's were "Cobras," and President Lissouba's, trained by Israeli's, were "Zulus." After Lissouba appointed Kolelas Prime Minister in 1997 and moved to eliminate Sassou-Nguesso's militia, bloody and destructive conflict broke out in Brazzaville.

Having begun negotiations with an American oil company, Lissouba lost the support of the French who refused to aid him against the forces of ex-president Sassou-Nguesso. Lissouba later charged that Sassou-Nguesso was supported by money coming from the French oil giant Elf, which is pretty likely. More certain was the support offered Sassou-Nguesso by Angolan forces. In the battle of the warlords Brazzaville was bombed and targeted by mortars, laid waste by internecine strife. Lissouba lost and fled into bitter exile. Elf returned to its damaged skyscraper office building and offered to contribute significantly to the rebuilding of Brazzaville. Angolan forces seemed to be a permanent presence in the Congo.

Denis Sassou-Nguesso's bloody conquest of Brazzaville did not end Congo's civil conflict. In December 1998 Ninja rebels in the south cut the railroad line from Pointe Noire to Brazzaville, cutting off its food supplies which then had to be airlifted into the capital. Ninjas infiltrated the capital's southern districts, which were promptly bombarded by Sassou-Nguesso's artillery and Angolan assault helicopters. The President, whose return to power with the aid of foreign interventionists had already brought death and desolation to the capital, continued to butcher his own citizens to maintain that power.

The civil war continued in the south throughout most of 1999. Pointe Noire, Congo's economic capital, was virtually cut off from the rest of the country. Water and electricity supplies were disrupted by rebel activity. Some 800,000 people in the south were dislocated, many fleeing to the forest to escape the depredations of both rebels, the government, and its allies. Supported by Angolan troops and helicopter gun ships, remnants of the Hutu Interahamwe, and a few Chadian and DR Congo fighters, government troops turned the tide of battle against the rebels by mid-year.

By the end of 1999, offers of amnesty and integration into government security forces in exchange for disarmament had secured cease-fire agreements with major militia commanders. Since then over 13,000 weapons have been collected and over 6,000 militiamen have demobilized, a small portion of the 25,000 militiamen eligible for the government offer, but a definite sign of progress. Congo's security situation has improved significantly.

Politically, a "national dialogue," carefully managed by President Sassou-Nguesso, has been taking place. Its first phase was a series of localized debates in the regions and municipalities. The second was a "national convention," which met between March and April 2001. It involved 550 delegates representing the Congolese government, the internal and external opposition, plus other political groups and civic organizations.

The process has been mediated by Sassou-Nguesso's son-in-law, President Omar Bongo of Gabon, and delegates were focused on producing a draft constitution and preparing follow-up elections. There was little, if any, opportunity to address the causes which led to the Congolese conflict in the first place.

Although billed as "all-inclusive," the national convention carefully excluded former President Pascal Lissouba and his last prime minister, Bernard Kolelas. The two men have been sentenced to death in absentia by Congolese judicial authorities and were, for that reason, not authorized to take part in the deliberations.

The national convention did approve a draft constitution for the new Congolese republic. It is tailored to the style and personality of Denis Sassou-Nguesso, featuring a strong presidential regime. The president of the republic, elected for a seven-year term—with one renewable mandate—would wield exclusive executive power. The president would appoint the prime minister and could not be impeached by parliament. Some participants strongly criticized what were seen as excessive presidential powers. One even went so far as to suggest the constitution created "a sort of republican monarchy."

President Sassou–Nguesso

If all goes as planned, the constitution will be submitted to a national referendum by the end of 2001. Presidential and parliamentary elections would be organized following its approval.

Angolan forces remain in Congo and provide strong backing for Sassou-Nguesso. When Laurent Kabila was assassinated, Angolan tanks in Brazzaville crossed the river to Kinshasa to maintain security there. At the start of the "national dialogue" Angolan troops were dispatched to the country's third largest city, Dolisie, a center of opposition to President Sassou-Nguesso in recent civil disturbances.

Culture: Tribal patterns dominate the social life of the Republic of Congo. Although discrimination is legally prohibited, tens of thousands of indigenous Pygmy people, living largely in the northern forest regions, enjoy less than equal treatment at the hands of their Bantu neighbors. Many have Bantu patrons to whom they are obligated in perpetuity. At the death of their patron, the eldest son inherits them.

AIDS has begun to make its appearance in Congo, not unsurprisingly, traveling in the wake of civil disturbance and disruption. According to armed forces health officials, AIDS is the number one cause of death in the Congolese armed forces. According to the director of the First Military Zone's health service, Colonel Prosper Kinzonzi, AIDS accounted for more than 60 percent of army deaths during the period 1989-1993. This was the equivalent of three companies of men during the period. The colonel attributed this mortal toll to prostitution and the sexual violence committed by soldiers while participating in the conflicts that have devastated Congo. Fourteen percent of Congolese servicemen have tested HIV-positive.

Unlike some of its neighbors, Congo has a relatively strong tradition of urbanization. One sixth of the population has traditionally lived in the two principal cities, Brazzaville and Pointe Noire. As a consequence, the country has one of the highest literacy rates on Black Africa, estimated at nearly 77%, though female literacy is generally lower—about 70%. Also related to this urban tradition is the relatively high percentage of Christians—mostly Roman Catholic—in the population and the early development of labor unions.

Economy: The object of armed struggle in Congo is the state's oil revenue, about 80% of state income and 94% of all its export earnings. The value of oil production has risen dramatically since 1994. Then it generated $820 million and in 1999 earned $1.5 billion. Mostly conducted offshore, the oil sector was virtually untouched by the events of the civil war. The rest of the economy was severely damaged by those events.

Some 20,000 people are estimated to have been killed in the various phases of the war, and 800,000 people were displaced. Half of the agricultural output was destroyed, particularly in the south, where the richest agricultural land is located. A good proportion of the country's cattle was also destroyed. Congo's highly urbanized population, especially in Brazzaville, the capital, has felt the impact deeply. Since 1997, the percentage of the urban population below the poverty line has increased from 30% to 70%. Life expectancy has fallen from 53 to 48 years.

The December 1999 ceasefire and the relative peace that followed have returned a sense of hope to the Congolese. Critical to the welfare of Brazzaville's population has been the reopening of the rail connection to Pointe Noire, Congo's chief port and economic capital. Fuel and foodstuffs can now reach the city directly. Previously it was often dependent on shipments through neighboring Kinshasa. So desperately short was fuel that the government had to fly in supplies at a huge premium.

Cessation of conflict has allowed the government to resume operations at the state-owned oil refinery in Pointe-Noire. Halted for nearly four years because of delayed repairs, the plant is now refining 75 tons of crude an hour. It has a capacity of one million tons a year, but never produced more than 600,000. The port of Pointe Noire is also being dredged to enable large ships to dock. Since 1987, when it was last thoroughly dredged, the port had silted up and lost some six feet of depth.

The reopening the Congo River, the railroad, and the port dredging all significantly benefit the timber industry—after oil, Congo's most important source of income. Many fine hardwoods such as *okoumé* and *limba* are in much demand in foreign markets. Officially, Congo annually produces 600,000 cubic meters of timber, the bulk of it from northern forests. When river and rail transport were disrupted, lumber had to be exported through Cameroon. That transshipment is no longer necessary.

Wasteful and destructive over-cutting by the lumber companies is a major concern. To reduce exportation of raw logs and increase employment opportunities, the government would like to require companies to process all timber locally.

Congo's fishing potential is largely underdeveloped, but the government has recently banned shark fishing off its Atlantic coast to prevent depletion of stocks. The calamitous over-fishing was caused by massive demand in Asia for shark fins. Shark fishing in the area took off in 1998 and was dominated by Ghanaian and Senegalese fishermen.

Congo's small mining sector is dominated by developments in magnesium. Used in automotive parts, high purity magnesium alloys allow manufacturers to decrease the body weight of their cars and improve fuel efficiency. Demand is expected to increase as manufacturers are faced with higher emission standards. Major automotive firms expect the magnesium content of each vehicle to increase from 5 pounds to as much as 300 pounds over the next 15 years.

A Canadian magnesium mining company, Magnesium Alloys Corporation (MAC), plans to begin annual production of 60,000 tons of magnesium metal and high purity magnesium alloys by 2005. The facility is located on the Kouilou River, 50-kilometres to the north of Pointe Noire. MAC has signed a memorandum of understanding with Siemens of Germany to develop a hydroelectric plant to supply power to the facility.

Given the terrible damage inflicted by years of civil war, private investment is hesitant about placing its money in the Congo. The country's biggest problem is finding the resources to repair infrastructure and productive capacity—estimated at nearly $2 billion. Government deficits over the yeas have created a huge total debt of $5.4 billion, which is approximately 245% of Congo's annual GDP. Some 46% of the projected 2001 budget will be absorbed by debt servicing, and the government is actively working with the IMF and other lenders to reduce this enormous burden.

The Future: Regional and personality differences will continue to keep Congo tense. Exclusion of leaders like Lissouba and Kolelas casts doubt on the government's sincerity to conduct a genuinely "national dialogue." It is unlikely Denis Sassou-Nguessou could win a free and fair election if it were held. so electoral shenanigans should be expected.

Militarization of Congolese society with its pervasive violence poses an ongoing threat to future stability. Certainly there are still a lot of arms that haven't been turned in by militia members. It is also unlikely the government will be able to integrate all former militia members into its security services. It is equally unlikely these youth, unskilled except in the ways of violence, will take easily to employment in "civic improvement" activities like rebuilding police stations destroyed in the war. For them, hammer and hoe are less attractive than the Kalashnikov.

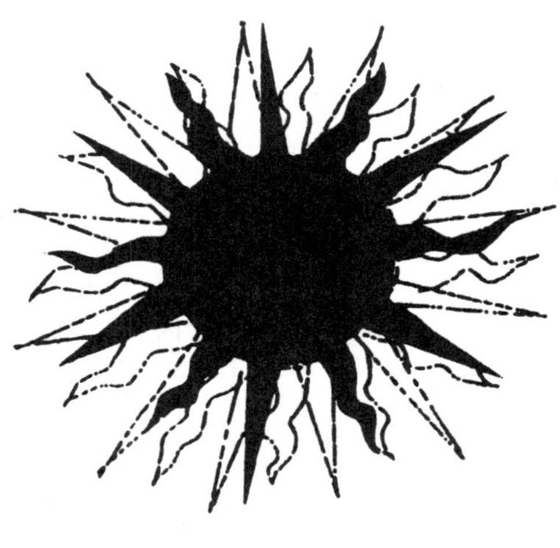

The Republic of Gabon (pronounced Gah–bonh)

Gabonese mechanics replace an outboard motor on the Ogooue River
WORLD BANK photo

Area: 264,180 sq. km. = 102,000 sq. mi. (about the size of Colorado).
Population: 1,225,853 (July 1999 est.)
Capital City: Libreville (pop. 400,000)
Climate: Hot and humid. Although there is almost no rain from June to September, the humidity remains quite high. Rainfall in the remaining months totals more than 100 inches per year.
Neighboring Countries: Equatorial Guinea (Northwest); Cameroon (North); Congo (East, South).
Official Language: French.
Other Principal Languages: Around 40. Prominently: Mbere, Myene, Fang (a widely used *lingua franca*), Njebi, Punu, Sira, and Teke.
Principal Religions: Christian 55%–75%, Muslim less than 1%, and animist.
Ethnic groups: Prominently: Fang, Eshira, Bapounou, Bateke; about 6,000 French.
Chief Commercial Products: Crude oil 81%, timber 12%, manganese 5%, and uranium (1996).
GNP per capita: 3,950 US$
Currency: CFA Franc (no longer tied to the French franc).
Former Colonial Status: French Colony (1903–1960).
Independence Date: August 17, 1960.
Chief of State: Omar Bongo, President.
National Flag: A tri–color, with horizontal stripes of green, golden yellow and royal blue.

Lying astride the Equator on the west coast of Africa, Gabon is a land of hot and humid jungle with a heavy rainfall. The coastal lowlands from 20 to 120 miles in depth receive up to 150 inches of rain per year. A series of plateaus rise further inland, spreading from the northeast to the southeast of the country with altitudes from 1,000 to 2,000 feet. They are densely packed with lush green vegetation. The remainder of the land is covered by gentle, round mountains extending to heights of 5,200 feet.

History: For countless generations, the Bantu tribes, divided into many distinct groups, lived undisturbed by explorers and adventurers. For details of earlier and colonial history, see Historical Background and *The French in Africa.*

At the time of independence there were two major political parties—*The Gabon Democratic Bloc* and the *Social Democratic Union of Gabon.* The parties, led respectively by Leon Mbá and J.H. Aubame, were evenly divided in the first election; neither captured a majority of the 40–seat Assembly, but Mbá's party, joined by four independent representatives, selected him as the first Prime Minister. Through a series of measures, Mbá was able to get rid of the opposition party and then he dissolved the Assembly in 1964 to hold elections under rules excluding his opponents. The army revolted, but French troops intervened the next day and reinstated Mbá's government. It later won an overwhelming majority in the Assembly; since 1964 *The Gabon Democratic Party* became the sole party, winning all seats in each election. When Mbá died in 1967, he was succeeded by Vice President Albert Bongo.

Bongo announced in 1973 that he was renouncing Roman Catholicism and adopting Islam, changing his name from Albert–Bernard to *El–Hadj* Omar. He ran a tight ship and was "reelected" to three seven–year terms.

In spite of pressures, a multi–party system was rejected by the president in 1990, but he quickly reversed his position. He was re–elected in a contest in December 1993 by a 51% majority. His principal opponent was Paul Mba Abessole of the *National Rally of Woodcutters (RNB),* but there were ten more candidates who effectively diluted opposition voting. Unrest for two months followed the election, which although officially proclaimed to be untainted, was most probably riddled with irregularities. The radio station of the woodcutters in Libreville was seized by presidential forces in early 1993 after Abessole had proclaimed himself president of a "parallel" government.

Disputed elections are almost always the sign of leadership desperate to retain power and privilege. Gabon held disputed elections in December 1998. President Bongo was again opposed by the Mayor of Libreville, Paul Mba Abessole, leading the *Rassemblement national des bûcherons* (*RNB*) and Pierre Mamboundou of the *Haut conseil de la résistance* (*HCR*). The Ministry of the Interior announced final

results: Bongo 66.55% and elected on the first ballot; Mamboundou won 16.54% and Abessole collected 13.41%.

Observers noted that the interior ministry had managed to add another 30,000 voters to the electoral lists, which it prepared, in the 48 hours immediately preceding the election. Voters in precincts known to favor the opposition discovered their polling place had been transferred to another site, usually at some distance. And the regime even managed to hire its own election observers—long time friends of President Bongo in French legal circles. They dutifully reported that all was well.

Washington, Paris and Geneva investigations have revealed the nature and extent of President Bongo's personal enrichment from Gabon's oil production. A US Senate investigation named him as one of a "rogues gallery" of foreign leaders who have funneled millions through American banks.

In Switzerland an investigative judge, probing the activities of French oil giant Elf-Aquitaine, developed testimony on the practice of offering "bonuses" to leaders of oil producing states to secure exploration permits. André Tarullo, the former head of Elf-Gabon, spoke of commissions of 60 cents to a dollar per barrel of oil. Money—at least $100 million—went into at least three accounts held in Tarullo's name, but actually belonging to Bongo.

The investigations by two French judges into Elf-Aquitaine's business practices continue, with the Bongo name surfacing with regularity. *Le Monde* has reported that at least twice the president had made personal appeals to French President Chirac to halt the investigations.

In March 2001, Bongo's lawyers were in a Parisian court charging a French author, Francois-Xavier Verschave, and his publisher with insulting the head of state. In his controversial *Noir Silence* (*Black Silence*), Verschave examined the relationship between France and its former colonies and described President Bongo as heading a "predatory elected dictatorship."

In October 2000, the Gabonese parliament offered protection to the president by amending the constitution to give former heads of state immunity from legal prosecution. By the terms of this amendment, no president who has ceased to exercise his functions may be "challenged, pursued, sought, arrested, detained or judged" for any action arising out of the performance of his presidential duties.

Culture: The majority of Gabon's people live in cities and larger towns. Most of the interior is densely forested and minimally populated. Libreville, the capital city, contains over a third of the population of the entire state.

Situated on a strategically located peninsula Libreville has experienced rapid growth. With a population of nearly 450,000, the city is dependent on imported food and is ranked as the fourth most expensive city in the world to live in, more costly than London, Paris or Gene-

President Omar Bongo

va. The poor of Libreville, seeking food and firewood in the surrounding area, contribute to enormous environmental pressures building up on the peninsula.

Over 60% of the population is literate. Two institutions of higher learning, Omar Bongo University (OBU) in Libreville and the Masuku University of Science and Technology at Franceville in the east, together enroll some 11,000 students in somewhat difficult circumstances. Built in the prosperous 1970s, OBU was designed to accommodate 3,000 students, but currently enrolls 9,000. There are no current subscriptions for scientific journals, the most recent of which go back to the 1980s, and there are reportedly only twenty or so computers available.

Economy: Gabon is the richest of the sub-Saharan states because of oil, timber and mineral extraction. Gabon is sub-Saharan Africa's third largest oil producer, and crude oil exports are the backbone of the economy. Oil contributes over 40% of GDP and represents 80% of total export revenues. Sixty percent of government revenue comes from the oil sector, and budgets are seriously affected by price fluctuations in the world market.

With recent price increases, the government has experienced a budgetary windfall. Long term, however, oil production will begin slowing as fields age and are exhausted. No major discoveries have been made in recent years, and oil production has not grown since the mid-1990s. At the moment, much hope rests on ultra-deepwater drilling. In March 2001 TotalFinaElf began ultra-deep drilling 8,071ft below the water surface; the well is expected to reach a depth of 13,288 ft.

Gabon's forestry sector is the country's second largest industry. Timber products represent around 15% of total exports and contribute over 5% of GDP. Thick forests cover 76% of the country, and exports of timber have risen in recent years. In 1957, less than 10% of Gabon's forests were allocated as logging concessions, today more than half have been designated for logging.

Okoumé, a moderately soft wood suitable for plywood, accounts for three-quarters of total wood production. Most Gabonese timber is exported as logs, with little domestic processing that would add value. Only 20% of okoumé production, for example, is locally turned into plywood and veneers. About half of Gabon's timber production is exported to Asian countries, and China has replaced France as the principal market for Gabonese wood.

Gabon is a significant producer of manganese. Uranium mining has ceased, but there is some small scale but promising gold production.

Bad investment strategies and mismanagement have produced a sizable debt for Gabon. As of 1999 it was estimated to be $4.6 billion. Large arrears in debt payments have been whittled down with the revenue windfall from higher oil prices. Debt servicing takes 48.6% of the 2001 budget, down from 67.4% in 2000.

The Future: Eager to encourage oil exploration, the government will liberalize investment codes and offer other inducements to attract a wider range of participation. A lot of eggs are being placed in one basket.

Gabonese boxers

SOUTHERN AFRICA

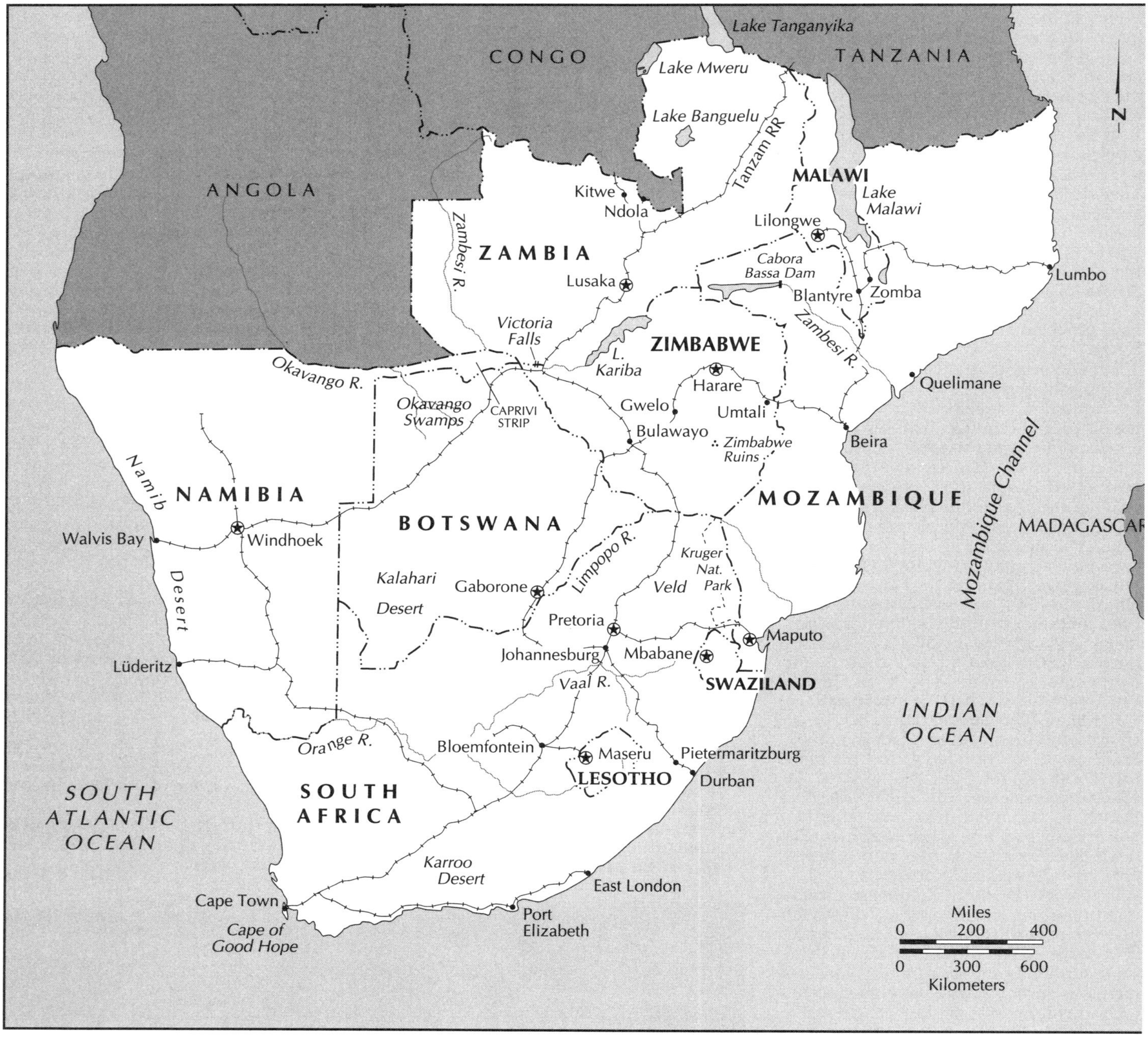

THE MIDWEEK SUN

WEDNESDAY
APRIL 1 1998
ABC CONSUMER PRESS MEMBER OF THE AUDIT BUREAU OF CIRCULATION
BOTSWANA'S LEADING MIDWEEK PUBLICATION
95t Incl. Sales Tax ZIMBABWE $3.00 Incl. Sales Tax RSA R1.35 Incl. Vat.
REGISTERED AT THE G.P.O. AS A NEWSPAPER

Clinton praises Botswana

by Sun Reporter

ABOUT 3 000 people flocked to State House on Sunday to get a glance of the United States President Bill Clinton when he arrived on a two-day visit.

The US President arrived some hours later than the initial planned time, and the awaiting crowd stood impatiently in the hot sun until the American delegation arrived.

Clinton and his wife, Hillary, were driven from Sir Seretse Khama International Airport in a black limousine, which had bulletproof windows and tyres, as well as shooting holes and an air conditioning system. There were also other special vehicles transporting other officials.

Shortly after meeting with Sir Ketumile Masire and Vice President Festus Mogae, Clinton addressed the crowd who had gathered on the lawn at State House.

"We have seen the promise of a new Africa whose roots are deep here in your soil, for you have been an inspiration to all who cherish freedom," the US President said.

"America is proud to be Botswana's partner and friend."

When making reference to Masire's retirement today, Clinton said "I am deeply honoured to be among those here as you leave your distinguished tenure....

"On behalf of all Americans, I salute you and your achievements. I would say you have earned the right to go back to your cattle ranch."

He announced America's intention to establish Radio Democracy for Africa, a voice of America service aimed directly at encouraging progress toward freedom and democracy, respect for human rights and an independent and objective media.

The 15-minute long remarks were commended by some of the people in attendance, who described them to be of substance.

"The relationship between the two countries is already there, and what the speech did is just to silver it," said the Bank of Botswana governor Baledzi Gaolatlhe. "The trip is good for Botswana as people around the world will get to know what Botswana is."

Minister of Commerce and Industry George Kgoroba was impressed

▷ To Page 2

LEFT: President Clinton of the US, has commended the government of Botswana and Sir Ketumile Masire for upholding the principles of democracy. (Pic: Oaltse Sejakgomo)

President Mogae!

by Sun Reporter

THE Vice President and Minister of Finance and Development Planning, Festus Mogae, will be sworn in by the Chief Justice Julian Nganunu, as the third head of state since Botswana gained her independence in 1966.

The swearing in ceremony is billed for 9am today, Wednesday April 1, in front of the parliamentary buildings after which Mogae is expected to announce his Cabinet. Thousands of Batswana, and members of the diplomatic community are expected to attend the ceremony.

On Monday, the staff of the National Assembly, assisted by the BDF, were busy preparing for the ceremony.

The Constitution allows the new President 14 days in which to announce his Cabinet including naming his vice president. The vice president's name has first to be brought before the parliamentary caucus for approval.

So far it is still not known who will be in Mogae's Cabinet. He is, however, expected to make an announcement either today or Thursday.

Delegates at the BDP National Council, held at Denman Rural Training Centre in Sebele on Saturday, pledged their loyalty to Mogae. One of the speakers from the floor was applauded after saying that it will only be seen whether the party is united when Mogae appoints his Cabinet. He said unity will only be evident when there are no dissenting voices and, if all BDP parliamentarians cast their vote in favour of the BDP candidate.

Meanwhile, the outgoing president of both Botswana and the ruling Botswana Democratic Party (BDP), Sir Ketumile Masire, assured his party colleagues that he will remain a loyal, disciplined member of the party.

Masire said this when he gave his valedictory address at the BDP National Council.

He told the democrats that as of April 1, after duly being sworn in, Vice President Mogae will become His Excellency

▷ To Page 2

Using a cellular phone given to him by Mascom last Friday, the new president Festus Mogae is probably calling on those he thinks might make good ministers. He will be sworn in today. (Pic: Oaltse Sejakgomo)

The Republic of Botswana

Area: 569,800 sq. km = 220,000 sq. mi. (slightly larger than France).
Population: 1.5 million (July 1999 est.).
Capital City: Gaborone (pop. 180,000 est. 1997).
Climate: Subtropical, with temperatures as high as 100°F. in the summer (November–April) and as low as 20°F. in winter (May–October). Rainfall varies from 25 inches per year in the North to 9 inches or less in the southern Kalahari Desert.
Neighboring Countries: Namibia (West and North); Zambia ((North); Zimbabwe (Northeast); South Africa (South).
Official Languages: English, seTswana.
Other Principal Languages: Afrikaans, Herero, Kalanga, Kgalagadi, Kung and other Bushman languages, Mbukushu, Subia, Tswana, Yeye.
Ethnic groups: Batswana 95%, Kalanga, Basarwa, and Kgalagadi 4%, white 1%
Principal Religions: Indigenous beliefs 50%, Christian 50%.
Chief Commercial Products: Diamonds 76%, copper, nickel 4%, and meat.
GNP per capita: 3,600 US$
Currency: 1 Pula = 100 Thebe
Former Colonial Status: British Protectorate (1885–1966).
Independence Date: September 30, 1966.
Chief of State: Festus Mogae, President (since April 1998).
National Flag: Five horizontal stripes of blue, white, black, white and blue.

Botswana is a large, landlocked country which lies in the transition zone between the dry deserts of South Africa and the jungles of Angola. In the South, a vast area is covered by the shifting red sands of the Kalahari Desert, occasionally interrupted by limestone rock formations and clumps of grass and scrub brush at the few places where water is close to the land surface.

The change from desert to grassland is so gradual that it is hard to see where the first ceases and the latter begins. The growth becomes increasingly thicker and there are frequent patches of trees. Annual rainfall slowly increases until it reaches a level required to support farmland where the food and cattle of the nation are produced in non–drought years.

Vegetation becomes dense in the North and the land turns into the dismal marshland in the Okavango Swamp, fed by the Okavango River flowing from the low mountains of Angola. There is no exit to the ocean for these waters.

The country's elevation, averaging 3,300 feet, modifies its subtropical climate.

History: The original inhabitants of Botswana were tribes of primitive Bushmen who lived for untold centuries in isolation from the world. The Bantu tribes of central and east Africa migrated into the area in the 16th century; during the following centuries, intermarriage and population growth of the Bantus reduced the number of pure Bushmen to a handful.

The Tswana remained split into hundreds of tribes and clans until they gathered together under Khama III, Chief of the powerful Bamangwato tribe; this was a loose federation which emerged in the last half of the 19th century. For details of pre–independence history, see Historical Background, *The British in Africa* and *The Republic of South Africa.*

After gaining independence on September 30, 1966, the pre–independence government continued in office. Elections since then have resulted in substantial majorities in the 36–seat Legislative Assembly for the *Botswana Democratic Party.* There are three other small political parties which actively compete in the free elections, but their following is not significant.

The chiefs of the eight largest tribes are permanent members of the House of Chiefs, and are joined by seven other sub–chiefs. the Legislative Assembly consists of 36 representatives, 4 of whom are appointed by the government, but it cannot act upon matters concerning internal tribal affairs without first submitting a draft to the House of Chiefs.

Elections in October 1979 resulted in a resounding victory for President Sir Seretse Khama (who had been reelected chief executive since independence), with almost 60% of the voters turning out at the polls. He was to have served for another five years, but the President died in June 1980; Vice President Quett K.J. Masire was installed to fill out his term and was reelected in September 1984. Khama's eldest son, Ian Seretse Khama, was installed in May 1979 as Chief of the Bamangwato Tribe; he served as Commander of the Botswana Defense Force numbering about 1,500 men until 1998.

For eighteen years President Masire maintained the multiparty traditions of democratic Botswana and exercised a conservative fiscal restraint on the use of the country's riches, producing 16 years of budget surpluses and large foreign reserves. After his initial election as President in 1984, he led his *BDP* to successive electoral victories in 1989 and 1994. Only in the last election did the party lose some ground to the opposition *Botswana National Front*, strongly supported by unemployed youth and urban voters. In November 1997, Masire announced his retirement, effective in six months, and on April 1, 1998, he was succeeded by his Vice-President and Finance Minister, Festus Mogae.

Almost simultaneously, Lieutenant-General Khama resigned as chief of the Botswana Defense Force. Having consulted with traditional Bamangwato leaders, he was given temporary release from his chieftaincy to pursue a career in politics. Moving swiftly to fill the vacant Vice Presidency, Mogae nominated General Khama to the position. With the popular Khama on his side, Mogae effectively closed off internal opposition to his leadership of the *Botswana Democratic Party* (*BDP*).

President Masire's chosen successor, Mogae, an Oxford University graduate, was seen as a straight-talking, pragmatic, no-nonsense leader, capable of uniting and energizing a fractured and complacent *BDP*. In the fall 1999 parliamentary elections, Mogae's political wisdom in appointing Khama became manifest. The dashing young general campaigned vig-

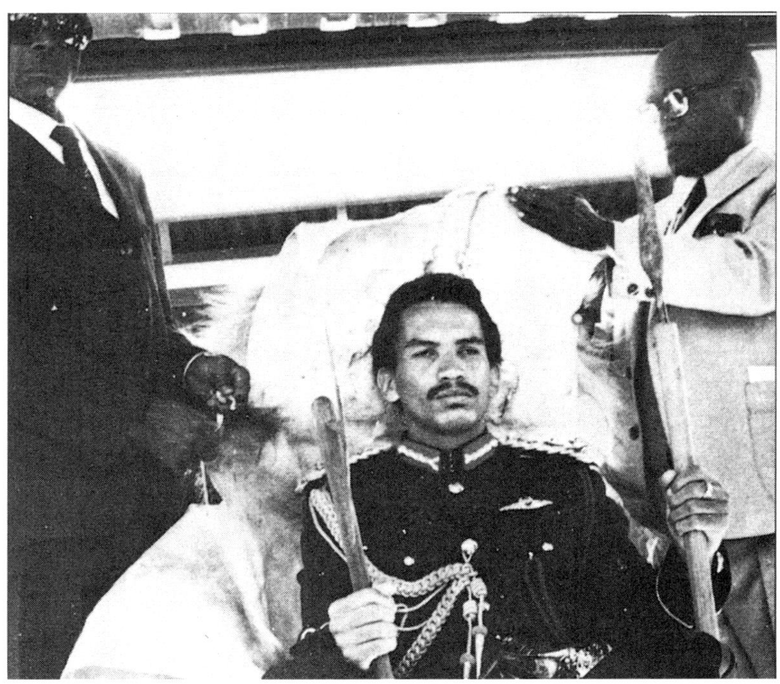

Brigadier Ian Seretse Khama having draped over his shoulders the traditional lion skin on his installation of Chief of the Bamangwato

orously, often flying about the country in military helicopters to galvanize a complacent party and electorate.

The *Botswana Democratic Party* (*BDP*), which has governed Botswana since independence, was also aided by a serious split in the opposition. In 1998, *Botswana National Front* (*BNF*) dissidents withdrew and formed the *Botswana Congress Party* (*BCP*). Separated, the two parties, along with the smaller *Botswana Alliance Movement* (*BAM*), contested the October 1999 parliamentary elections. Divided, the opposition was decimated. The victorious *BDP* swept 33 of 40 seats, even winning four of eight urban seats traditionally occupied by the opposition.

Vice President Khama returned to his official duties in September 2000 after an eight-month sabbatical. Having helped to unify the *BDP*, he appears in the best position to be the ageing President Mogae's successor in the next Presidential elections. Both the *BNF* and the *BCP* are also undergoing a generational change of leadership, but there is little indication that more youthful leaders will be better able to unify the opposition.

Culture: Botswana has the highest HIV/AIDs infection rate in Africa. Nearly 36% of sexually active adults are infected. These grim figures emerge even after an extensive government education campaign. Billboards, posters and bumper stickers in cities and villages throughout the country warn of the dangers of unprotected sex, with messages like "Don't let casual sex kill Botswana's future" and "Be wise, condomise."

President Mogae mentions the HIV/AIDS crisis in every speech, and during her reign as Miss Universe, Botswana's Mpule Kwelagobe campaigned against AIDS at home and abroad. Still, for a significant number of Batswana youths AIDS remains a joke—"America's Idea of Discouraging Sex."

Christian clergymen have actively opposed the distribution of condoms, arguing it would lead to promiscuous extramarital sex, while the infection rate only increases. The life expectancy rate has dropped and could fall to as low as 29 years if the spread of the virus is not slowed or reversed. Half of all natural deaths in Botswana are currently linked to the disease, while one in eight infants is infected with the virus at birth.

The economic implications for business and the national economy are staggering. Economists estimate Botswana's GDP growth rate will drop by 1.5%; within 25 years the country's economy will be 31% smaller than it would have been without the pandemic. In March 2001, President Mogae delivered a chilling warning to his countrymen: Botswana faced extinction if it failed to slow the spread of the deadly virus within the next five years.

Botswana's HIV/AIDS educators face a difficult uphill battle where elders and parents are reluctant to talk about sexual matters with young people and where religious figures stint their support. Increasingly they are turning to drama, song and poetry as a means of reaching those bored by politicians' speeches, bleak billboard campaigns and scary statistics.

Gospel singer Jerry Moremi argues that since pastors haven't been effective in preaching the anti-HIV gospel, it's time to try music. The traditional artist Duncan Senyatso dedicates his "African Rain Song" to the struggle against HIV/AIDS. Rain, he says, is symbolic of cleanliness, and in drought-plagued Botswana it symbolizes hope for the future.

Economy: Since independence Botswana's economy has shown impressive growth, averaging of 10% per year from 1976 through 1991. More recently it has showed signs of slowing down, a disappointing 3% in 1994 and a healthy, but more modest 7% in 1995. The effects of the Asian market collapse were reflected in an estimated 5% in 1998/1999. By most estimates, economic growth in 1999/2000 is likely to exceed 7%.

Botswana's economy is diamonds. The country is the world's largest producer of diamonds by value, with sales in 2001 expected to exceed $2 billion. They account for 80% of its export earnings, 30% of its gross domestic product and 55% of government revenues. All of this is generated by Debswana, a company equally owned by the government and De Beers of South Africa. Company production now exceeds 25 million carats annually. This follows the $410 million expansion of its Opara mine—the biggest capital project ever seen in Botswana. Opara output was doubled to 12 million carats a year.

International concern with "conflict" or "blood" diamonds fueling conflict in Angola and Sierra Leone, and suggestions of a consumer boycott of diamonds, have sent a tremor of concern through Debswana officials. Similarly, the economic downturn in the United States, which accounts for over 50% of diamond retail jewelry sales, has made the industry nervous.

Despite the economic dominance of diamonds, the bulk of Botswana's workforce is employed in agriculture. Meat production (including beef for export) is a major component of the sector, while cotton and peanuts are grown as cash crops. Sorghum, maize, millet, beans, vegetables, and melons are grown by the country's subsistence farmers, most of whom live below the poverty line.

The driving imperative of Botswana's government is diversification of the economy. Mining jobs account for only 3.6% of the country's workforce, and attempts to diversify into manufacturing have barely dented an unemployment rate estimated at 21%. Young, jobless voters have been the principal support of opposition parties, and the government has been unable to generate sufficient new jobs to absorb the 27,000 school leavers who enter the employment market each year.

One of the government's major diversification projects is to turn Botswana into a "Switzerland of Africa" by establishing an international financial center. With one of the best educated work forces in southern Africa, a liberal investment regime, and stable economic fundamentals, the government hopes to attract investors in banking, insurance, fund management, and other financial services to Gaborone.

Perhaps the biggest single challenge facing the country now, along with the rest of southern Africa, is the HIV/AIDS pandemic. In March 2001 Debswana announced it would pay 90% of the cost of antiretroviral treatment for its employees and their spouses.

Tensions with neighboring Namibia, which increased defense expenditures, have somewhat diminished. Their border dispute over an island in the Okavango River was settled in Botswana's favor by the International Court of Justice in December 1999. Unresolved are tensions created by Namibian desires to pump water from the Okavango to its parched capital, Windhoek. The river goes nowhere, but in good years it floods the vast Okavango delta in Northern Botswana, attracting millions of birds and animals which are the country's principal tourist attraction. Namibia's plans would threaten the delta, which accounts for 75% of Botswana's earnings from tourism, contributes 6% to its gross national product, and employs thousands.

The Future: President Mogae has brought unity to his own party and triumphed in the latest parliamentary elections. With a solid majority in parliament, foreign reserves of $5.6 billion—the envy of any state—he now confronts the hard task of dealing with the consequences of Botswana's superficially successful economic development: inequalities, unemployment and dominance of the economy by a privileged few.

The Kingdom of Lesotho (pronounced (Leh–*su*–tu)

A home in the style of a Basotho hat, Maseru AP/World Wide Photo

Area: 30,303 sq. km. = 11,700 sq. mi. (somewhat larger than Maryland).
Population: 2,128,950 (July 1999 est.)
Capital City: Maseru (pop. 386,000 est.)
Climate: Temperate. The western lowlands, about one–quarter of the country, have temperatures ranging from a high of 90°F. in the summer to 20°F. in the winter. The remaining area of highlands has a wider range of temperatures, with readings below zero on the snow–capped peaks of the Drakensburg Mountains.
Neighboring Countries: Lesotho is completely surrounded by the Republic of South Africa.
Official Languages: Sesotho, English.
Other Principal Languages: Zulu, Xhosa.
Ethnic groups: Sotho 99.7%, Europeans 1,600, Asians 800.
Principal Religions: Christian 80%; the rest indigenous beliefs.
Chief Commercial Products: Manufactures 65% (clothing, footwear, road vehicles), wool and mohair 7%, food and live animals 7%.
GNP per capita: 570 US$
Currency: 1 Loti = 100 Lisenti. At par with South African Rand.
Currency: Maloti, at par with the South African Rand.
Former Colonial Status: British Protectorate (1868–1966).
Chief of State: King Letsie III.
Head of Government: Prime Minister Pakalitha Mosisili.
Independence Date: October 4, 1966.
National Flag: Divided diagonally from the lower hoist side corner; the upper half is white, bearing the brown silhouette of a large shield with crossed spear and club; the lower half is a diagonal blue band with a green triangle in the corner.

Lying deep within the lofty peaks of the Drakensburg Mountains, Lesotho is the only nation of the world which is completely surrounded by another country. One–fourth of the land is relatively low—from five to six thousand feet above sea level. The warm sun of Africa raises the temperatures in this agricultural region during the summer. The rest of the nation is made up of scenic highlands from 6,000 to 9,000 feet, with some peaks rising as high as 11,000 feet above sea level.

The snow–capped Drakensburg Mountains form a natural boundary between Lesotho and Natal Province of the Republic of South Africa; they also provide water for the neighboring country. The mountain snows melt, and, augmented by gentle and usually uniform rainfall, the water flows into the small streams which unite to form the Orange and Tugela rivers, which flow into an otherwise somewhat dry South Africa.

The mountain scenery of Lesotho is comparable to the pastoral setting of Malawi and the mountainous parts of Kenya. Remote and unchanged by modern civilization, it is one of the truly virgin areas remaining in the world.

History: In times immemorial the Bushmen established a thinly populated primitive society high in the mountains of Lesotho. The waves of Bantu migration from east and central Africa of the 17th century reached the country as did the Bafokeng, Maphetia and Baphuthi tribes, which settled among the Bushmen. The two ethnic groups intermarried during succeeding generations and their descendants are a somewhat uniform people known as Basutos, or Basothos. For details of early and colonial history, see Historical Background, *The British in Africa* and *The Republic of South Africa.*

An independence agreement was reached in 1966 whereby the colony, called Basutoland, would become independent under Chief Leabua Jonathan. The royalists and left–wing representatives had walked out of the independence conference, and Jonathan signed the treaty. The Union Jack was finally lowered at Maseru on October 4, 1966, and was replaced during the ceremonies by the unusual flag of Lesotho.

Chief Jonathan visited South Africa and was received by the then Prime Minister Hendrik Verwoerd in late 1966. Recognizing the need of each nation for the other, mutual cooperation and respect was pledged. The meeting only lasted a few hours so Jonathan could return to Lesotho rather than spend the night in South Africa, racially separated by the doctrine of *apartheid.*

Friction between Leabua Jonathan and King Moshoeshoe (pronounced Mo–*shway*–shway), the hereditary monarch, developed rapidly after independence. The King was placed under house arrest and several left–wing leaders who had participated in Maseru riots were jailed in 1966. Elections held in early 1970 were contested between Chief Jonathan's *Basotho National Party* and the leftist *Basotho Congress Party,* led by Ntsu Mokhele. When Jonathan realized he was being defeated, he announced a state of emergency, arrested the opposition and took steps which led to the exile of the King. (After agreeing to stay out of politics, the King returned the following year.)

Jonathan rescinded the emergency orders in 1973; Mokhele had been released from prison in mid–1971 after 17 months in jail. In late 1973, the *BNP* and Jonathan announced plans to make Lesotho a one–party state. Mokhele and his followers attempted a *coup* in early 1974 which failed. Reprisals were taken not only against the leadership (some of whom escaped to South Africa and Botswana) and members of the *BCP*, but villages suspected of harboring *BCP* followers were destroyed.

A four–way struggle commenced in 1982. South Africa, charging that Lesotho was harboring members of the *African National Congress (ANC)*, outlawed in South Africa, which advocated Black rule within that country, raided Maseru and other parts of the country in 1982–1983. Leabua Jonathan hotly denounced the move, charging that it was an effort on behalf of the Lesotho Liberation Army, the military wing of the *BCP*. South Africa countered with a charge that Jonathan was simply trying to divert attention from his own internal troubles. Jonathan denied granting a haven to members of the *ANC*. Further complicating things, Jonathan visited communist China, North Korea, Yugoslavia, Romania and Bulgaria in mid–1983 to establish diplomatic and economic ties. This infuriated both the South Africans and the Catholic clergy, who in prior times gave strong support to the government (Jonathan was Roman Catholic). Elections were not held after 1970 and there was no indication whether or when they would be held until November 1984 at a Congress of the *BNP*. On July 31, 1985, Chief Jonathan announced that balloting would take place on September 17–18. He later stated that since no opposition candidates had registered to run for seats in the National Assembly as of the August 14 deadline there would be no need for an election. The move was denounced as a farce. Jonathan went two steps further. He formed *Youth League of Chief Jonathan's Basotho National Party* and imported about 14 North Korean "advisers." This set the conservative element within the military on edge, since the orientation of the Youth League was clearly radical, if not communist.

South Africa continued to charge that Lesotho was harboring members of the *ANC* in 1983–1986 and periodically closed the borders and conducted raids in Maseru to root out the rebels. Finally, on January 20, 1986 the Lesotho military acted, ousting Chief Jonathan. A Military Council was installed, headed by Major General Metsing Lekhanya. The border was promptly opened as South Africa hailed the move. The Pretoria government denied having anything to do with the *coup*.

The military government announced amnesty for all opposition leaders, including Ntsu Mokhele. The King, however, decreed that all political activity would cease for two years. From 1987 increasing powers were wielded by the King—too many for the comfort of General Lekhanya; the King was sent into exile in the spring of 1990 and was said to be studying toward his Ph.D. in Britain.

In an effort to bestow legitimacy upon itself, the military promoted a royal *coup*,

His Majesty King Letsie III

installing the eldest son of the king, Prince Mohato Sereng Seeisa (King Letsie III) as monarch in late 1990. Military control was tenuous, and under pressure, parliamentary elections were held in 1993 after being postponed. The result gave the *BCP* all 65 seats in the National Assembly, and Ntsu Mokhele, now a centrist rather than a leftist, became Prime Minister. Moshoeshoe II was restored to the throne in January 1995. He died in an auto accident in early 1996 and was succeeded by the crown prince. A factional attempt to oust Mokhele in early 1997 failed, lacking support in the legislature.

Mokhehle responded in July by leaving the *BCP*, taking a majority of 40 members of parliament with him and creating the *Lesotho Congress for Democracy (LCD)*. The new formation then declared itself the government and took over the *BCP*'s black, green and red colors. Court cases ensued, but the LCD ultimately prevailed. In February, King Letsie dissolved the squabbling parliament to prepare for May 1998 elections.

When the election results were announced, the *LCD* had won 79 out of 80 parliamentary seats. Ntsu Mokhele having been sidelined from active politics by age and health, Pakalitha Mosisili was chosen Prime Minister. The opposition, stung by the magnitude of its defeat, could only imagine it the consequence of fraud. Protests were mounted and became virtually round–the–clock affairs. When the King's palace was blockaded by protesters, electoral experts from Botswana, South Africa and Zimbabwe, guarantors of Lesotho's democracy since 1994, were called in to examine the election. The probe was completed in two weeks, but its publication was delayed, which only added fuel to the protesters' indignation. When finally released, the commission's report evinced "serious concerns" about the general election, but its overall conclusion, expressed in tortured prose and double negatives, was that "We are unable to state that the invalidity of the elections has been conclusively established. We cannot postulate that the result does not reflect the will of the Lesotho electorate."

Demonstrators closed down government offices in the capital, Maseru, locked the gates of parliament, and shut down the Lesotho Bank. In the midst of the demonstrations junior army officers mutinied, took their seniors prisoner and forced their resignation. Sensing a coup very much in the air the government requested assistance from the Southern African Development Community (SADC).

South Africa and Botswana agreed to intervene in a joint maneuver to restore order in the kingdom. South Africa sent in an initial force of 600 soldiers on September 22, but was unprepared for stiff resistance from the Lesotho army. Botswana forces, responsible for establishing order in Maseru, were delayed in their arrival, which had disastrous consequences for the city. Young Lesotho nationalists vented their rage at South Africa by looting, burning and destroying businesses known to be owned by South Africans. The flames spread and much of the capital was reduced to ruins. About 60 people died in the events.

Negotiators produced an agreement to create an Interim Political Authority (IPA) which would steer the country to new elections. The IPA was to consist of two members from each of Lesotho's 12 political parties. It would not replace the government, but was designed to work with it—a task which would prove most difficult.

The IPA proposed to increase the members of the National Assembly from 80 to 130, elected by proportional representation. But when the proposal was sent to parliament to enact, the *LCD* used its majority in the National Assembly to amend. Eighty seats, said the Assembly, would remain single member districts with the remaining distributed by proportional representation. The opposition screamed; the Interim Political Authority objected, and finally Lesotho's Senate saved the day by rejecting the proposal.

In December 1999, political leaders agreed to elections by April 2000. But when that time drew near, Prime Minister Mosisili postponed them for a year, claiming there was insufficient time to prepare. By March 2001, Lesotho's upper house of parliament had finally agreed on the composition of the country's National Assembly. There would be a total of 120 members—80 would be elected by the "first past the post" method, and 40 through proportional representation.

The decision seemed to resolve the ongoing conflict between Senate and Assembly and set the stage, finally, for parliamentary elections. In mid-March, Lesotho's Independent Electoral Commission announced that the general election would be held in 2002 after voter registration in August and September.

Culture: The people of Lesotho have a very high rate of literacy—70%—in spite of the fact that they live, for the most part, in rural isolation. Sheep and cattle raising occupy their daily lives among the scenic peaks and plateaus.

Economy: Lesotho is completely surrounded by South Africa and, possessing no significant natural resources, is economically dependent on its larger neighbor. Only 13% of the country is suitable for agriculture.As a consequence, large numbers of Basotho traditionally leave to work in the mines of South Africa. At one time 70% of rural household income came from remittances sent by migrant workers.

The Basotho are a nation of horsemen

With the drop in gold prices and the shrinking of mining jobs, many Basotho men were forced to return to Lesotho and faced extended unemployment. From 1995 to 1999, the number of migrant mine workers employed in South Africa declined from 104,000 to an estimated 65,000. By mid-2000, more than 10,000 additional miners had lost their jobs, adding to an already serious unemployment problem. In 2000, unemployment was estimated at between 40 and 45%.

Remittances by emigrant workers, so critical to the Lesotho economy, have plummeted. They contributed about 67% of the country's gross domestic product (GDP) in 1990, but declined to about 33% in 1996 and are less today.

Lesotho's economy was devastated by the 1998 political calamity. Damages amounted to $70 million. Some 4,000 jobs were lost, and GDP plunged to negative figures. By 1999, however, the economy had clawed its way back to a positive 0.2%.

The Kingdom's principal revenues are now customs receipts from the Southern African Customs Union (SACU) and payments made for waters produced by the Lesotho Highlands Water Project (LHWP). SACU receipts accounted for $17million of budget revenue in 1998/99, out of $40 millon total. In the 1999/2000 budget, SACU revenue was forecast to rise by 14%.

In an elaborate series of dams, tunnels and canals, the LHWP diverts the waters of the Orange River, in the mountains of Lesotho, to drier industrial areas of South Africa. Estimated to cost around $4 billion, the project is one of Africa's biggest civil engineering undertakings. Once completed it will pump 79 cubic meters of water a second northwards to South Africa and generate an estimated $23 million in royalties for the 1999-2000 budget.

The Future: Lesotho will maintain its reputation as Southern Africa's most unstable state. Despite massive poverty and unemployment—issues which demand unity for solution—tensions between the country's main political forces will persist. Prospects for future stability are further diminished by bitter internal struggles within both the *Lesotho Congress for Democracy* and the *Basotho Congress Party*.

The Republic of Malawi

A village chief examines his corn near Lilongwe

Area: 95,053 sq. km. = 36,700 sq. mi. (the size of Indiana).
Population: 10,000,416 (July 1999 est.)
Capital City: Lilongwe (Pop. 340,000, estimated).
Climate: Hot in the low–lying extreme South; cool and temperate in the highlands with heavy rains (November–April); the amount of rainfall is related to the altitude.
Neighboring Countries: Mozambique (South, Southwest, Southeast); Zambia (Northwest); Tanzania (Northeast).
Official Language: English and Chichewa.
Other Principal Languages: Lomwe, Ngoni, NyakYusa-Ngonde, Nyanja, Sena, Tonga, Tumbuka, and Yao.
Ethnic groups: Chewa, Nyanja, Tumbuko, Yao, Lomwe, Sena, Tonga, Ngoni, Ngonde, Asian, and European.
Principal Religions: Protestant 55%, Roman Catholic 20%, Muslim 20%, traditional indigenous beliefs.
Chief Commercial Products: tobacco, tea, sugar, coffee, peanuts, and wood products.
GNP per capita: 200 US$
Currency: 1 Kwacha = 100 tambala
Former Colonial Status: British Colony (1883–1964).
Independence Date: July 6, 1964.
Chief of State: Bakili Muluzi, President (since May 1994).
National Flag: Three equal horizontal bands of black (top), red, and green with a radiant, rising, red sun centered in the black band.

Malawi, formerly known as Nyasaland, is a country of high mountains covered with lush, green foliage, interspersed with large, sparkling lakes and fertile plateaus. Situated on the western edge of the Rift Valley, Lake Nyasa (also known as Lake Malawi) spreads its long, deep waters over three–fourths of the eastern boundary of Malawi. The surface of this body of water is 1,500 feet above sea level; the water extends to a depth of 2,300, thus the floor of Lake Nyasa is over 700 feet below sea level. The lake pours into the River Shire, which flows southward to join the Zambesi River 250 miles away.

The countryside of Malawi has characteristic plateaus in the middle and on the top of steep mountains. For the most part, these are 3,000 to 4,000 feet above sea level, but rise as high as 8,000 feet in the North. Immediately south of Lake Nyasa are the Shire Highlands, gently rolling plateau country which is 3,000 feet high. From this green, almost level land, the mountain peaks of Zomba and Mlanje tower to heights of 7,000 and 10,000 feet, respectively.

The altitude modifies an otherwise equatorial climate for the most part. The summer, from November to April, is pleasantly warm with equatorial rains and sudden thunderstorms. Towards the end of March, the storms reach their peak, after which the rainfall rapidly diminishes. During the winter from May to September, wet mists float down from the highlands, invading the cool and dry reaches of the plateaus. There is almost no rainfall during these months.

For strikingly beautiful scenery, Malawi is almost unexcelled by any other nation on the African continent.

History: Before the waves of Bantu migration arrived many centuries ago, Malawi was probably very scantily settled. The restive Bantu tribes from the north expanded slowly southward from about the 10th century onward, sending successive waves of transients through this country on their journey to the south. Some stayed as permanent settlers, forming into distinct tribes based on common ancestry. There is no written record of these people; legend must be relied upon. For details of early and colonial history, see Historical Background and *The British in Africa.*

During the latter part of the period when Malawi was part of the Federation of Rhodesia and Nyasaland (1953–1962) the British devised a constitution which for the first time provided for legislative members directly elected by native Africans. In 1961 and in elections held thereafter, the *Malawi Congress Party* led by Dr. Hastings Kamuzu Banda claimed all 50 seats in the assembly; three additional members were selected from a list limited to white voters.

After independence was granted in 1964, Dr. Banda served first as Prime Minister and then as President when Nyasaland, renamed Malawi, was proclaimed to be a republic. The only disturbance in the system occurred in 1965 when there was a minor revolt within the party which resulted in the exile of a few persons.

In a series of moves that were vehemently criticized by Nyerere of Tanzania and Kaunda of Zambia, Dr. Banda entered into trade and aid agreements with White–controlled South Africa, establishing diplomatic relations with that country in 1968.

Confiscation of the holdings of a small number of resident Asians was undertaken in 1975–76; they were permitted to live in only three Malawian cities—Blantyre, Zomba and Lilongwe.

Dr. Banda was made "Life President" in 1970. During his time in office he was an intellectual, dynamic and demanding person, a reflection of his early years as the only Black student at the University of Chicago in 1931 when he received a Ph.D. and completed his medical education in 1937. He was critical of what he considered emotional responses of Black African leaders to post–independence problems. Many of them, in turn, derided him as an "Uncle Tom" in dealing with Whites, particularly those controlling the Republic of South Africa.

During the 1980s, elections only involved the *MCP* candidates selected by Banda. Opposition figures died under very suspicious circumstances. His rigid rule was typified in the 1990s by accusations of human rights violations, particularly those involving the *Malawi Young Pioneers* which emerged as a paramilitary organization and personality cult devoted to Banda. Strife in neighboring Mozambique closed rail lines vital to Malawi's exports, forcing the use of South African facilities.

Under external and internal pressures, the life president grudgingly agreed to a referendum which was held in 1993. He was stunned when 67% voted for multi–party democracy. Illness overtook the president in late 1993 when he had to go to Johannesburg for brain surgery. During his absence a presidential council was formed and the life presidency was abolished; the grip of the *MCP* was ended; the youth group was officially disbanded and a new constitution was adopted.

The government started a publicity trial of Banda and his supporters in 1995 for the 1983 murders of opposition leaders. Well into his 90s, he was totally deaf, senile and too ill to attend the sessions. A seven–member court, in a controversial decision, acquitted all defendants in December. In early 1996 Banda addressed the nation on radio and apologized for any and all wrongs that might have occurred during his 30–year tenure. He did not, however, admit any improper personal involvement. Ex-president Banda died in November, remembered for his leadership of the nationalist struggle that gave Malawi independence and the encouragement he gave some liberation movements abroad. He was also remembered by Malawians for thirty years of autocratic rule, quirky, almost Victorian, morality and a lavish life style. During his tenure in office he built two palaces, one of which cost 100 million US dollars, while most Malawians lived in abject poverty. He died a very wealthy man. At his death Malawi's national debt was close to two billion dollars.

Malawi held its first democratic, multiparty elections since independence in 1994. President Banda was defeated when Bakili Muluzi of the *United Democratic Front* (*UDF*) received 47% of the vote over Banda's 34%. Muluzi's *UDF* won an 83 seat plurality in the 177–member National Assembly, but was able to join with independents and disaffected opposition members to create a working majority in parliament. The elections demonstrated a marked regional division within the country. The *UDF* dominated the south, while Banda's *Malawi Congress Party* took the center and the *Alliance for Democracy* (*AFORD*) the north.

The same forces contended in the May 1999 elections. The *MCP* and *AFORD* formed an electoral coalition in their effort to oust President Muluzi. The MCP leader, Gwanda Chakuamba, was designated the alliance's presidential candidate, and *AFORD* leader Chakufwa Chihana was chosen for the vice-presidential slot, much to the annoyance of the *MCP* deputy leader, John Tembo.

President Muluzi was reelected with 52.4% of the vote to Gwanda Chakuamba's 45.2%, and his *United Democratic Front* won 93 seats in the National Assembly—less than a majority in the 192 seat house. The *MCP* won 66 seats and its *Alliance for Democracy* ally picked up 29 seats.

The opposition protested irregularities and took their case to the courts, but found no support there. Efforts to boycott

President Bakili Muluzi

parliament failed to find unanimity within the opposition, and division seemed to become a dominant theme in Malawi's politics.

The *Malawi Congress Party* was split by a sulfurous clash between Gwanda Chakuamba and John Tembo, still smarting from being pushed aside as a vice-presidential candidate in the 1999 elections. When Chakuamba was suspended from parliament in June for truancy and being disrespectful to President Muluzi, he was replaced as party leader by Tembo, who promptly began to pay salaries to his own supporters despite a protesting party treasurer.

The conflict worsened when the High Court ordered Chakuamba's reinstatement to parliament and resumption of his role as leader of the opposition. The party now had two leaders and two factions, each of which proceeded to hold separate party conventions in different cities to elect their own party leader. The ultimate showdown took place in December when Tembo rallied a majority of MCP deputies to support him as leader of the opposition.

The ruling *UDF* fared little better. As it became increasingly obvious President Muluzi was interested in seeking a third term (which would require a constitutional amendment), internal opposition mounted. Critics of the president were ruthlessly dealt with.

A senior cabinet minister, Brown Mpinganjira, was fired and accused of accepting a piddling $731 in bribes. Found innocent in court, Mpingangjira claimed it had been a political trial and that the whole political system was on trial.

Mpingangjira founded what he called a new "pressure group"—the *National Democratic Alliance* (*NDA*)—in January 2001, and by March the *UDF* had become fearful enough to form an intelligence unit to monitor allegiance of party, officials. Rebels were cast out of the party and in at least one case a *UDF* member of parliament was roughed up by fellow party members on suspicion of supporting the *NDA*.

The third term issue has become central to Malawi's internal politics, dividing both the ruling party and opposition. The other issue that continues to dominate political discussion is corruption. President Muluzi is under continuous and mounting pressure to act decisively. In March 2001, Malawi's seven Roman Catholic bishops sharply criticized the regime, noting the frustration of people who "see how people elected to public office quickly get very rich and live in luxury, while masses are in poverty."

Culture: The Malawis are modern, religious, industrious and thrifty people, known for their advanced culture throughout southeastern Africa. As in the past decades, thousands of men go each year to find work in other countries, returning sometimes only after many years of economic exile. The tribal life strongly resembles that of neighboring Zambia. Education is common through the eighth grade, but rare above that level. With the assistance of a loan from South Africa, the capital was moved from Zomba to Lilongwe in 1975.

Economy: Malawi is desperately poor. With little in the way of mineral resources, its economy is agriculture–dependent. Its four major export crops—tobacco, tea, sugar and coffee—account for more than 90% of the country's export revenue. Per capital income is extremely low—less than $200—and inflation has been extremely high. Growth in GDP registered 5.2% in 1997, but slowed in 1998 to around 3%. Landlocked, Malawi faces high transport costs—estimated to be about 40% of total import costs.

Tobacco, which alone accounts for about 60% of export revenue, demonstrates many of the problems of economic development in Malawi. World prices have declined and despite bumper crops in 1997, farmers earned barely enough to repay loans taken out for this year's crop. Malawi's "green gold" is tainted if not tarnished as an export crop given current agitation against smoking in Europe and America. Substitutes need to be found, but farmers, being conservative, are reluctant to move away from something generally profitable. High in profitability is the cultivation of cannabis, known in the southern African region as "Malawi Gold." The UN Development Assistance Framework reported in December 1998 that some 385,000 acres of land were under cannabis cultivation, mainly in the northern and central sections of the country.

Malawi has an external debt of $24 billion. The country has qualified for debt relief under terms of the HIPC program. In January 2001, the IMF and World Bank announced terms that would save the country an average of $50 million per year in debt service payments over the next 20 years.

The Future: Pervasive corruption will brake development, and erratic government conduct will continue to frighten businessmen. Until credible efforts are made to curb corruption, poverty alleviation will continue to be found mostly within cabinet circles and the higher ranks of the police.

The Republic of Mozambique (pronounced Moe–zam–*beek*)

View of central Maputo AP/Wide World Photo

Area: 786,762 sq. km. = 303,769 sq. mi. (twice the size of California).

Population: 19,124,335 (July 1999 est.) Note: the 1997 Mozambican census reported a population of 16,542,800; other estimates range as low as 16.9 million.

Capital City: Maputo (Pop. 800,000, estimated).

Climate: Tropically hot and humid, modified somewhat in the mountain areas close to Lake Nyasa, the uplands bordering Zimbabwe and in coastline, cooled by ocean breezes.

Neighboring Countries: Tanzania (North); Malawi, Zambia (Northwest); Zimbabwe (West); South Africa, Swaziland (Southwest); Madagascar lies 300 to 600 miles off the coast.

Official Language: Portuguese.

Other Principal Languages: Over 30, including Chopi, Chwabo, Lomwe, Makhuwa, Makonde, Marendje, Nyanja, Ronga, Sena, Shona, Tsonga, and Tswa.

Ethnic groups: Indigenous tribal groups 99.66% (Shangaan, Chokwe, Manyika, Sena, Makua, and others), Europeans 0.06% Euro-Africans 0.2%, Indians 0.08%.

Principal Religions: Indigenous beliefs 50%, Christian 30%, and Muslim 20%

Chief Commercial Products: Shrimp 40%, cashews, cotton, sugar, copra, and citrus.

GNP per capita: 210 US$

Currency: 1 Metical (Mt) = 100 centavos

Former Colonial Status: Portugal claimed that Mozambique was an integral part of Portugal until September 7, 1974; a provisional government was decreed to wield power until formal inde pendence.

Independence Date: June 25, 1975.

Chief of State: Joaquim Chissano, President.

National Flag: Three equal horizontal bands of green (top), black, and yellow with a red isosceles triangle based on the hoist side; the black band is edged in white; centered in the triangle is a yellow five-pointed star bearing a crossed rifle and hoe in black superimposed on an open white book.

The flat terrain of the coastline of Mozambique, filled with dense, tropical jungle in areas which are not cleared, gives way gradually to a series of plateaus and highlands which gently rise toward high mountains in the part closest to the western borders. Towering green peaks are located in the Lake Nyasa area, and the temperature is moderated by the altitude. Most of the intense agricultural production takes place in the coastal lowlands and surrounding plateaus.

History: Prior to the arrival of European explorers, Arab traders had established active trading posts along the coast of Mozambique, dealing in the notorious slave trade, principally, and in commerce involving agriculture to a much lesser degree. For details of earlier periods and colonial history, see Historical Background and *The Portuguese in Africa.*

Nationalist resistance to Portugal's particularly benighted colonialism was organized in 1962 by left-wing Mozambique exiles living in neighboring Tanzania. Under the leadership of Eduardo Mondlane they formed the *Mozambique Liberation Front* (*Frente de Libertação de Moçambique—Frelimo*) and began a guerrilla war against the Portuguese in 1964. Mondlane was assassinated in 1969, but the war effort was continued and expanded by his successor, Samora Machel.

Portugal poured some 70,000 troops into the colony to suppress the insurrection, but by the early 1970s it could do little more than defend the cities. *Frelimo* controlled most of the countryside and drained Portuguese manpower, resources and will. Disgruntled army officers overthrew the Portuguese government in April 1974, and the new government granted Mozambique its independence a year later. *Frelimo* created a single-party state organized on Marxist-Leninist principles with Machel as president.

The Portuguese colonial legacy was appallingly meager. After more than 400 years of Portuguese presence, more than 90% of Mozambique's population was illiterate. For the entire country there were only 80 doctors and 100 high school teachers. The new government's imposition of socialist organization and planning, including large-scale nationalization, led to a massive exodus of Portuguese colonists.

Over 100,000 left and they took with them the bulk of the country's administrative and managerial skills. What they could not take with them, they destroyed. Some drove tractors into the sea; others ripped plumbing out of buildings. Factories were destroyed; government files and business records were burned.

Some 4,000 commercial farms were abandoned, resulting in disastrous declines in export-crop production. The *Frelimo* government sought to make these abandoned farms once again productive by collectivization. State farms were created; agricultural cooperatives and communal villages were organized. Major

portions of export earnings were devoted to the purchase of farm equipment, but there weren't enough skilled mechanics to maintain them nor enough income to buy spare parts. Costly farm machinery lay idle as Soviet theories of mechanized agriculture proved inadequate to African reality.

Created, for the most part, by Lusophone urban elites, the *Frelimo* government, like its colonial predecessor, based itself on the cities, especially the capital—renamed Maputo. It increasingly grew out of touch with the countryside which had once been its base against the country's Portuguese rulers. The government appointed village "presidents" loyal to *Frelimo* and discarded traditional chiefs. Government-set prices for food crops were kept low to placate *Frelimo*'s urban constituency, but offered peasant farmers no incentive to produce. Not unexpectedly, they returned to subsistence farming.

By 1983 even the most starry-eyed Marxists had to admit that socialism as practiced, particularly in agriculture, was a miserable failure. Eighty percent of state resources had gone to state farms, but they represented only 10% of the country's agricultural sector and had proved costly failures. Given a shortage of trained manpower, basic record keeping and production reports were virtually impossible. One major state farm operated 42,000 acres with one book-keeper and a novice economist. State farms and enterprises sent false reports to the government because they had no facts to report, and when the government made it a crime to submit false reports, it got none at all. Communal villages, often organized by force as part of the government's policy of urbanizing rural areas to provide a better distribution of services, were unpopular and ineffective.

Overt opposition to *Frelimo*'s policies had coalesced with the aid of the white government of neighboring Rhodesia in 1976. Fearful of Mozambican aid to the rebel forces of Robert Mugabe fighting to dislodge it, the Rhodesian government organized Mozambican dissidents into an opposition army which called itself the *Mozambican National Resistance* (*Resistência Nacional Moçambicana—Renamo*). When Mugabe's forces triumphed in Rhodesia, support of *Renamo* fell to the apartheid government of South Africa, equally terrified of black radicalism on its borders that lent support to its own black opposition, the *African National Congress* (*ANC*).

Rural, conservative, traditional and speaking indigenous languages, based on the illiterate populations of central and northern Mozambique—everything, in short, that *Frelimo* was not—*Renamo* was implacably opposed to the Leviathan state *Frelimo* sought to create. For some sixteen years it would engage the *Frelimo* government in bloody civil war, the objects of its wrath any and everything that symbolized the *Frelimo* state. Roads and rails, utility lines, schools, clinics and stores, farms and factories were all destroyed. The economy was brought to a standstill. Well over 100,000 were killed; more than a million were displaced.

Faced with civil war and a collapsed economy, *Frelimo*'s Fourth Party Congress, held in 1983, began to shift the state away from inept centralized planning and forced social organization. President Machel, who once thundered to his audience that "Our country will be the grave of capitalism and exploitation," began to solicit western investors.

By 1984, the government sought to cut off its *Renamo* opponent by severing its ties with South Africa. A mutual agreement was reached at the border town of Nkomati: Mozambique would end sanctuary and support for *ANC* forces, and in exchange South Africa would end its military support for *Renamo*. Despite the Nkomati Accord, the South African army continued to aid and supply *Renamo* forces, and they, in turn, continued their depredations in Mozambique.

In October 1986 President Machel was killed when his plane, Russian built and piloted, crashed under mysterious circumstances shortly before landing in Maputo; suspicions of South African involvement have yet to be allayed. *Frelimo*'s central committee met and elected Mozambique's foreign minister, Joachim Chissano, party chairman. As such, he automatically became president.

President Chissano, regarded as a moderate and the man who had convinced Samora Machel to make overtures to western capital, expanded Machel's tentative opening to the West. As elsewhere in Africa, the end of the Cold War brought reassessment and reorientation to Mozambique's Marxists. With Chissano as party leader, *Frelimo*'s Fifth Congress dramatically ended the party's official Marxist-Leninist orientation in 1989. Chissano learned the language of Western democracy and economic liberalism. Multiparty elections became possible, and dutiful acquiescence to IMF economic reform policies was offered.

In October 1992, President Chissano and Afonso Dhlakama, who emerged as *Renamo*'s chief, signed a peace accord. Deep mutual suspicion, sixteen years of devastating civil war and diametrically opposed ideological visions separated the two. *Frelimo* has never accepted *Renamo* as a legitimate representative of those rejected and marginalized by its policies. To this day it still refers to *Renamo* as "bandits," but Mozambique has now seen two multiparty presidential and parliamentary elections.

The first electoral competition between the two antagonists came in 1994. Opposition to President Chissano came not only from *Renamo* and Dhlakama, but from ten other presidential candidates. The elections graphically showed the regional cleavage of Mozambique. *Frelimo* was popular in southern, more populated areas and of course swept the capital of Maputo. Chissano won slightly more than half the votes cast for president. Dhlakama ran strongly in the north—a thousand miles from Maputo—and central areas, winning 34% of presidential votes. *Renamo* ran ahead of its leader in parliamentary races, winning 112 of 250 seats in the Assembly of the Republic to *Frelimo's* 129.

Municipal elections in June 1998 were meant to implement *Frelimo*'s decentralization policies. Instead, they displayed the continuing gulf that separated the two opponents and *Frelimo*'s fundamental resistance to surrendering its control of local authorities. *Frelimo* proposed to devolve authority to only 33 larger cities already organized and dominated by executive councils appointed by, and totally integrated into, the structure of the *Frelimo* state.

Renamo, encouraging the power of traditional authorities in the rural areas, demanded official recognition of their role in

A precarious road deep within Mozambique

Cashew Workers Photo by Ferhat Momade

local communities. These too, it argued, should benefit from the devolution of financial and administrative responsibilities. This position was rejected by the government, and *Renamo* declared an election boycott. So successful was the call nationally that 85% of registered voters absented themselves from the polls. In 19 of the 33 constituencies allowed to elect municipal assemblies, *Frelimo* was the only party competing. In the northern cities of Nampula and Beira, abstention rates were 92% and 90%.

At the national level, parliamentary majorities permitted the *Frelimo* government to engage on a remarkable liberalization of a state-dominated economy, becoming, in the process, the darling of donors and international lending agencies. Development money poured into Mozambique. Growth rates were eye-popping.

Mozambique has been in a state of tension since the December 1999 elections. According to official figures, President Chissano won a surprisingly close victory, winning 52.3% of the vote to Afonso Dhlakama's 47.7%. In elections for the 250-seat Assembly of the Republic, all minor parties received less than 5% of the vote and were completely shut out. *Frelimo* took 133 seats, *Renamo* 117. There were serious questions about the results. Indeed, some diplomatic observers suspected Dhlakama actually won. But Mozambique's Supreme Court rejected, by a split vote, the request by *Renamo* and a coalition of smaller parties to invalidate the results.

Renamo, which won the six northern provinces convincingly, moved its headquarters to the central port city of Beira, due to what it called "popular pressure" from its constituents in central and northern parts of the country. Dhlakama himself darkly threatened to set up a parallel administration in the northern provinces. Pressure was brought to bear on the party leader to accept the results, imperfections and all. Mozambique's Christian bishops met Dhlakama in February 2000 to advise him to accept the election results despite what they called "irregularities" in the ballot.

Political tensions were heightened when pamphlets appeared urging northerners to boycott southern markets. Producers of prawns, cashew nuts, timber, cotton, fish and beans were asked to withhold their products from markets south of the Save River. Since economic man has replaced political man in the new Mozambique, there was no sign that anyone paid any attention at all to the boycott call. This did not prevent the government from detaining a number of *Renamo* faithful in the port city of Beira, whom they accused of possessing "inflammatory leaflets which called for a division of the country."

The election crisis peaked in November 2000 when national protests against rigged elections went tragically awry in the northern community of Montepuez. The demonstrators, a "sea of people," according to one policeman, converged on the police station and began to liberate arms and prisoners. One policeman admitted firing into the crowd, but said his bullets failed to hit the demonstrators who were, he thought, protected by magic. Seven policemen were beaten to death after they had fired on the crowd; at least 18 demonstrators were shot to death. Nationally, over 40 people were killed in the demonstrations, most of them by police bullets.

The next day security forces began a dragnet to arrest *Renamo* leaders and sympathizers throughout the northern region. Hundreds were arrested. Most were jailed in deplorable conditions of overcrowding. In Montepuez, 84 prisoners died in a single night from asphyxia. Record keeping was so bad the police did not even know the names of those who had died. Their bodies were buried in a mass grave.

Almost before the bodies had been buried Mozambique received one additional shock: Carlos Cardoso, the country's best and most respected investigative journalist, was assassinated, gangland style. His exposés had revealed growing and pervasive corruption in the *Frelimo* state; his death highlighted the country's growing crime and criminality. Indeed, he had recently started campaigning against what he called the "gangster faction" in *Frelimo*, a group that provoked violence to cover its own misconduct. Just the week before his murder he had condemned both *Frelimo* and *Renamo* hardliners for instigating the election riots.

President Chissano and Afonso Dhlakama agreed to meet personally—something that had not occurred in over two years—to calm the situation and resolve differences. Three meetings from December through April 2001 failed to produce agreement on anything. It became clear that *Frelimo* had no interest in doing anything that would diminish its hold on power. In April the president pointedly refused to allow *Renamo* to nominate individuals for governorships in the six northern provinces carried by *Renamo* in the 1999 elections. Dhlakama walked out of the last meeting, and Mozambique remains in a state of heightened political tension.

Culture: The European minority was located almost exclusively on the coastline and larger interior plantations of Mozambique. Although most left before and after independence, there are about 30,000 Portuguese in Mozambique, principally in Maputo. Other Europeans assist in furnishing technical services not otherwise available. Mozambique needs doctors, teachers, civil servants, and technicians, and in an about–face has been actively seeking white Europeans for such positions.

Economy: The international community is determined to make Mozambique a showpiece of capitalist development. Five years after hostilities ended, it remains a darling of the donor community: 60% of Mozambique's budget is made up of foreign aid. What has the government done to warrant this support? Basically, it's created one of the most open economic regimes in Africa, aggressively pursued foreign investment, and actively dismantled the state-centered economy of its Marxist past. The consequence of this liberalization has been a series of remarkable economic growth figures, suggesting Mozambique has one of the most dynamic economies in southern Africa. All is not steadily progressive, however. Mozambique remains afflicted by periodic flood, famine, and drought, each of which takes its toll on the country's growth and efforts to lift its population from the miseries of poverty. After climatic devastation in 2000, for example, the economy grew only 2.1%. Since population growth is an annual 2.6%, this means that per capita GDP has actually declined. More than 70 % of Mozambique's nearly 20 million people continue to live in absolute poverty, the vast majority in rural areas distant from the economic success story of Maputo, the capital city.

Prawns are Mozambique's biggest ex-

President Chissano

port earner. In 2000, 9,729 tons of prawns were exported, earning $92.4 million. This represented a significant increase from 1999's 8,000 tons, which earned $72 million. The fisheries sector also includes exports of lobsters, and in 2000 Mozambique exported 102 tons of the crustacean, earning $1.1 million.

Over-fishing and illegal fishing are constant threats to the industry, and the government plans to reduce the number of vessels involved in prawn fishing in the coming year. Prawn farming is being developed to supplement exports. One such project, a joint venture between Mozambican and Chinese businessmen, is slated for the port city of Beira. Another is planned at Quelimane, the capital of the central province of Zambesia.

Cotton and cashews are Mozambique's two largest cash crops and the nation's largest foreign currency earners after prawns. Production of both crops fell dramatically during the civil war, and both are subject to the less than tender mercies of fluctuating demand and prices in the world market.

Cotton, mostly grown in northern Mozambique, involves about 200,000 peasant families. Collapsing market prices have severely weakened production enthusiasm on the part of farmers, and the EU is considering economic assistance to help them shift to alternative crops.

Mozambique was once the world's largest producer of cashews, but the stock of trees has been destroyed by war, ravaged by disease and reduced in production as a consequence of aging. An estimated one million trees die or go out of production each year because of age, disease or neglect. On average only 300,000 have been planted annually to replace them.

The cashew industry has also suffered from trade liberalization imposed by the World Bank and the International Monetary Fund (IMF), which forced most processing plants to close. The last plant, largely owned by South Africa's Anglo-American Corporation, closed in mid-2001.

A number of mega-projects suggest the country's economic vitality and potential. One is an aluminum smelter located at Maputo. A joint venture between British, Japanese and South African investors, Mozal represents an investment of $1.34 billion. The first aluminum was poured in July 2000, and Mozambique's first aluminum exports, 1,350 metric tons worth $2 million, were shipped in August. Production will be systematically raised to 250,000 tons per annum. The company expects to reach this goal in 2001, but the Council of Ministers approved an expansion of the smelter's capacity in February 2001—to 500,000 metric tons per annum.

The smelter is a catalyst for Mozambique's development. Success will encourage other large-scale investment. Construction employment was almost 9,000 workers, 70% of them Mozambicans. More than 5,000 people have been trained in basic building skills, and when the plant is fully operational, it will employ a staff of 800, 700 of them local.

Some sense of the scale of the Mozal project lies in its consumption of electricity. When fully operational the smelter will use twice as much electricity as the whole of Mozambique today.

Bitter competition between the South African energy company Sasol and its US counterpart Enron over plans to commercialize Mozambique's natural gas riches has been resolved. Sasol acquired Enron's rights to the Pande gas field and agreed to supply gas to Enron's Maputo Iron and Steel Project on favorable terms.

Unifying the Pande gas field with its own Temane field gives Sasol proven reserves of 2.8 trillion cubic feet—enough gas for 30 years. The company will construct a pipeline to carry the gas to Maputo and South Africa. Ownership of the pipeline will be shared: 50% owned by Sasol with the governments of South Africa and Mozambique each holding a 25% share. Natural gas could easily replace prawns as Mozambique's most valuable export.

Work progresses on Mozambique's largest industrial enterprise, the Maputo Iron and Steel Project (MISP), being built 18 miles west of Maputo. The project will manufacture steel slabs from South Africa magnetite, and it involves an international consortium of Swiss, Japanese, Australian, Italian and American steel companies. MISP will be the largest customer of the natural gas pipeline to be constructed by Sasol.

Years of upheaval and economic mismanagement left Mozambique heavily indebted. By 1999 its external debt was estimated at $7.7 billion, but it had made impressive strides in dealing with its economic weaknesses. As a consequence, the IMF decided in April 1998 that Mozambique qualified for the Fund's Highly Indebted Poor Country (HIPC) initiative. It is estimated that debt relief under this plan will reduce Mozambique's debt service to less than 20 per cent of export revenues.

The Future: All parties seem to have agreed to seek first the economic kingdom in Mozambique. The important thing will be the extent to which economic development makes a difference in the lives of average citizens. Thus far the evidence indicates it hasn't.

Major investments in human capital will be required if growth and development are to be sustained. Current adult literacy rates of 45% and school enrollment of only 25% will remain a challenge to development plans.

Development remains highly unbalanced, with most centering in the southern regions, especially around Maputo. This disequilibrium, adding to northern poverty, will continue to fuel political tensions.

View of the Cabora Bassa Dam AP/Wide World Photo

The Republic of Namibia

Herero women in their finery Courtesy: CALTEX

Area: 823,620 sq. km. = 318,000 sq. mi. (twice the size of California).
Population: 1,648,270 (July 1999 est.)
Capital City: Windhoek (Pop. 115,000, estimated).
Climate: Hot and dry except in the Caprivi Strip, which has more rainfall.
Neighboring Countries: Angola (North); South Africa (South); Botswana (East); Zambia (Northeast).
Official Language: English.
Other Principal Languages: Afrikaans common language of most of the population and about 60% of the white population, German 32%; indigenous languages: Oshivambo, Herero, Damara, Nama and Kavanga.
Ethnic groups: Black 86%, white 6.6%, mixed 7.4% About 50% of the population belong to the Ovambo people and 9% to the Kavangos people; other ethnic groups are: Herero 7%,Damara 7%, Nama 5%, Caprivian 4%, Bushmen 3%, Baster 2%, Tswana 0.5%.
Principal Religions: Christian 80% to 90% (Lutheran 50% at least, other Christian denominations 30%), native religions 10% to 20%.
Chief Commercial Products: Diamonds, copper, gold, zinc, lead, uranium; cattle, processed fish, and karakul skins.
GNP per capita: 1,940 US$
Currency: Namibian Dollar
Former Colonial Status: The Republic of South Africa asserted control of the territory (as South–West Africa), claiming a mandate under the League of Nations continued since the formation of the United Nations. The UN passed a resolution in 1966 declaring South–West Africa to be under direct UN control and designated the area *Namibia* in 1968.
Independence Date: March 21, 1990.
Chief of State: Sam Nujoma, President (pronounced Noo–*yome*–ah).
National Flag: Diagonal stripes of blue, red and green separated by thin white stripes. On the blue stripe, near the pole, is a golden sunburst.

The narrow white beach of Namibia is quickly replaced by a 60–mile–wide stretch of red–colored Namib Desert which runs the entire length of the coastline. The barren Kalahari Desert stretches along the north and eastern borders of the territory, occasionally interrupted by harsh formations of gray rock and thin scrub vegetation. The only rain in this region comes from torrential storms which occasionally gather—their rapid downpour is swallowed up quickly without leaving a trace of moisture.

The central area of Namibia is a vast plateau suited to pastoral raising of sheep and cattle. Here, there is somewhat more rain, which permits a thin forage to cover the soil. This region produces thousands of karakul sheep, the lambs of which are treasured for their shiny black, curly pelts used in fur coats. The mineral wealth of the region lies in the northeast sector adjacent to the Kalahari Desert.

History: In times unknown, the Bushmen commenced living in what is now Namibia, followed by several Bantu tribes. The Ovambos and Damara–Hereros became the most numerous groups. For details of early and pre–World War II colonial history, see Historical Background and *The British in Africa, The Germans in Africa* and *The South African Mandate.*

South Africa controlled this territory under a mandate from the League of Nations after having occupied the area in 1915. When the United Nations came into being, its Charter provided that all previously mandated dependent territories came under its supervision. In most cases, the mandates were transformed into *trusteeships,* but with the requirement that annual reports be presented to the UN concerning the development of the territories and their progress towards eventual independence.

South Africa applied for "permission" to make South–West Africa part of that nation in 1946. The UN rejected the proposal, but offered South Africa a trusteeship. South Africa rejected that offer (undoubtedly on the ground that what was given could be taken away) and made moves to incorporate the land within its national boundaries regardless of UN protests. By 1949, certain laws had been extended to South–West Africa, and its white representatives sat in the South African parliament. The League of Nations mandate was, it insisted, still in force. The UN passed a resolution condemning South Africa for its failure to live up to the terms of the UN Charter, but this meant nothing in substance in the absence of force.

During the 1960s, a political group took shape in South–West Africa. It called itself the *South–West African People's Organization,* or *SWAPO* for short. *SWAPO's* aim was to gain independence for the territory with majority rule. Although its headquarters was actually in Dar es Salaam, Tanzania, the guerrilla fighters it sponsored roamed the land, recruiting volunteers, terrorizing black and white farmers, sabotaging public utilities and ambushing army patrols. South African punishment

came quickly; hundreds of guerrillas were rounded up and jailed, including the group's leader, Herman Toivo ja Toivo; he was sentenced to 20 years imprisonment on dreaded Robben Island, South Africa, after being convicted of "crimes against state security" (1968). The fighting escalated, backed by surrounding black African nations, which, like Angola and Zambia, provided refuge for *SWAPO* forces.

Finally the UN had enough. It decided in 1966 once and for all to terminate the South African "mandate." The UN renamed the territory *Namibia* (derived from the name of the Namib Desert) and established a *Council for Namibia* as a temporary, transitional government, but the Council operated in New York, not in Namibia; this move failed to affect the South African government, except to harden its resistance to what it considered outside interference in its affairs by elements without knowledge of the true state of affairs. In another landmark decision, the UN recognized *SWAPO* as the "representative" of the Namibian *people.*

The years passed without change. *SWAPO* guerrillas and South African troops engaged in bloody skirmishes. After considerable diplomatic pressure from the U.S., Canada, Britain, France and West Germany, South Africa gave in to a plan for peace discussions which would include *SWAPO* representatives. With *SWAPO* approval, Justice Marthinus Steyn (Mar–*tee*–nus Stain) was appointed by South Africa to administer the area during its transition to independence.

The first talks in early 1978 ended in failure when *SWAPO* representatives demanded that half of South Africa's 3,000 troops must be withdrawn before UN–supervised elections could be held.

South Africa made another move to find an "internal" alternative to *SWAPO* government in late 1978. It promoted mid–1979 elections in Namibia which were won handily by the *Democratic Turnhalle Alliance (DTA),* a multi–racial coalition of conservatives with White leadership. *SWAPO* boycotted the contest and did what it could to disrupt the elections.

The *DTA* insisted that the United Nations back down on its recognition of *SWAPO* as the sole "representative" of the Namibian people, but that organization was, in the eyes of the UN, the only "strong entity" which existed.

Negotiations dragged on and on. The situation was further complicated by Angola's Marxist regime, its endorsement and support of *SWAPO* and the presence of about 50,000 Cuban troops, necessary to ensure continued communist control of that country (see Angola). A strong South African force invaded Angola in 1982–1984 to clean out *SWAPO* rebels. Angola accused South Africa of assisting *UNITA* rebels in *that* country (probably true, although denied by South Africa). Clashes between South African forces and Cubans were inevitable.

South Africa declared a "linkage" policy in 1983: South African troops in Angola would not be withdrawn until Cuban troops were first withdrawn. Angola and Cuba responded with a firm declaration that Cuban troops would not depart unless South African forces were first withdrawn.

As the Namibian armed forces grew, *SWAPO* increasingly resorted to terrorist tactics within Namibia which contributed to its lowered popularity. Government forces included the infamous *Koevoet* ("Crowbar") units which in turn engaged more frequently in widespread atrocities, to the disgust of many. Further complicating the total picture were about 1,000 Namibians held by *SWAPO* in crude prisons located in Angola because of accusations they spied for South Africa.

By 1988 the Soviet Union's Gorbachëv decided that the expensive Cuban presence in Angola had to come to an end. At about the same time, former President Botha of South Africa decided that continued participation in Angola's civil war and guardianship of Namibia were counter–productive. An agreement was reached in December 1988 for a far–reaching regional settlement. Free elections would be held for a national assembly which would draft a constitution leading to independence in April 1990.

Indeed, after a brief transition period, elections for the constituent assembly were held with almost 98% of registered voters participating. *SWAPO* took 57% of the vote, just short of the two-thirds majority that would have given it free reign in writing a new constitution. The *Democratic Turnhalle Alliance (DTA)*, in opposition, received 29% of the vote. By February 9, 1990, the Constituent Assembly had drafted and adopted a constitution that created a multiparty system, limited its executive president to two five-year terms and enshrined a bill of rights. Distancing itself from its socialist background, *SWAPO* participants voted to include provisions which granted private ownership of property and affirmed a mixed economy where foreign investment would be encouraged. The collapse of the Soviet Union had diminished the allure of socialist utopias.

The Constituent Assembly converted itself into the National Assembly on February 16, 1990, and unanimously proceeded to elect Sam Nujoma Namibia's first President. Local elections were held in 1992 to chose members of 13 newly created Regional Councils as well as municipal officials. Two members of each Regional Council serve simultaneously as members of the National Council, the upper chamber of Parliament, and here too *SWAPO* claimed a wide majority. Namibia's first presidential election was held in December 1994 and Nujoma swept to triumphant victory, thrashing his *DTA* opponent, Mishake Muyongo, with nearly 70% of votes cast.

Nujoma's political dominance posed problems for *SWAPO* as it contemplated presidential elections in 1999. Like Robert Mugabe in Zimbabwe, Nujoma neither prepared nor designated a possible successor. Despite the constitutional prohibition on more than two terms, Nujoma announced in April 1997 that "I am still young and if the people of Namibia want me to continue making a contribution I will continue to do so." Dutiful and deferential to its leader, the 1997 *SWAPO* party congress recommended the constitution be amended to permit the President to run for a third term.

SWAPO used its parliamentary majority to change the constitution before the 1999 elections, but the move helped pro-

Bustling Windhoek Courtesy: CALTEX

Republikein

SWA/NAMIBIE SE GROOTSTE NUUS- EN ADVERTENSIEMEDIUM

50c

(AVB INGESLUIT)

First National Bank

FINANCE BRANCH

l. 33111/4 — Posbus 3436 — Windhoek Woensdag 21 Maart 1990 Jaargang 13 Nr. 67 By die Poswese as Nuusblad geregistreer

Namibië vry

Windhoek's *Republikein* on March 21, 1990, in Afrikaans: "Namibia Free"

voke a split in the party. Ben Ulenga, a former guerrilla, trade unionist and Namibian high commissioner (ambassador) in London, resigned from *SWAPO* to form the *Congress of Democrats.*

Ulenga had impressive credentials as a candidate. His liberation struggle credentials were impeccable—wounded in combat and 15 years detention on Robben Island. His disillusionment with *SWAPO* began even before independence when thousands of fighters disappeared without explanation in *SWAPO* detention camps. Nujoma's decision to seek a third term confirmed that disillusionment. Ulenga shocked the party with a scathing attack on Nujoma's autocratic rule, corruption and the very idea of a third mandate for the president.

The *Congress of Democrats* was the first credible alternative to *SWAPO* to emerge, particularly in its traditional northern strongholds. Ulenga himself was also an Ovambo from the Omusati region in the north, a center of *SWAPO* strength. The election was hard fought and not without the usual bullying tactics by *SWAPO* and its supporters. Ulenga accused his old party of corruption, arrogant leadership and mismanagement of an economy struggling with a 35 percent jobless rate. "The leadership of *SWAPO* belongs on the retirement benches," the 47-year old Ulenga told his audiences.

The opposition *Democratic Turnhalle Alliance* (*DTA*) was terminally wounded by the call of its long-time leader, Mishake Muyongo, for Caprivi's secession. When Muyongo fled to Botswana, he was expelled from the party and leadership passed to Katuutire Kaura, but there was little hope the party could provide an effective challenge to *SWAPO*. The third contender in the presidential race was Justus Garoeb, leader of the *United Democratic Front* (*UDF*). Garoeb was also chief of the Damara ethnic group, numbering about 100,000 and mainly based in the west and northwest.

The December election proved a smashing success for *SWAPO*, closely identified in voters' minds with a successful independence struggle. Nujoma obtained 76.8% of the vote, while Ulenga garnered 10.5%. The *DTA's* Katuurike Kaura won 9.6% and Chief Garoeb trailed the field with a mere 3%.

In the National Assembly elections SWAPO increased its electoral support, winning 76% of the vote. Seats in the 72-member house are distributed proportionally. *SWAPO* was allocated 55 seats. The *Congress of Democrats* and the *DTA* were each allocated 7 seats, while the *UDF* got two and the small *Monitor Action Group* settled for one.

Nujoma was given an impressive mandate to deal with Nambia's problems, which remain multiple and extensive. There was no indication that his fundamentally authoritarian leadership style would change in any way. Nor was there any indication that a red-hot rhetorical style would be cooled. "Shooting from the lip" takes on a whole new meaning when one listens to his political rhetoric. Responding to an escalating crime rate in the early 1990s, Nujoma urged citizens to shoot any burglars whom they might find on their property. He similarly instructed border guards that it was their duty to shoot anyone seen crossing the border illegally.

The President's autocratic nature has been seen in his single-handed commitment of Namibian armed forces in support of Laurent Kabila in the Congo. The actual number of troops committed, the number dead or even the overall costs of the adventure remain shrouded in mystery. After his re-election, Nujoma allowed Angolan troops to enter Namibian territory, without any reference to parliament, to search out and destroy bases and personnel of Jonas Savimbi's *UNITA*. A number of foreign tourists as well as Namibian citizens died in the ensuing actions along the northern border. Newly placed landmines now provide additional hazards. In January 2000 the Namibian military began to offer escorts to people taking the trans-Caprivi highway, and these continue.

In late 1998 Nujoma faced secessionist agitation in the remote Caprivi. The Caprivi Strip, Namibia's panhandle, had long been a center of opposition to the Ovambo-dominated *SWAPO* and tended to support the rival *Democratic Turnhalle Alliance* (*DTA*). During the struggle for independence, South Africa stationed forces in Caprivi to fight *SWAPO* and received the collaboration of local peoples—a fact which hardly generates sympathy among *SWAPO* decision makers. As an opposition area Caprivi has usually been shorted in the distribution of development funds, for *SWAPO* believes that friends are rewarded, enemies deprived. The main highway through the strip, for example, has only recently been paved.

The troubles ultimately resulted in the flight of several hundred residents to neighboring Botswana, including the *DTA* leader, Mishake Muyongo. Muyongo, once *SWAPO*'s second-in-command for 16 years, was roundly denounced by Nujoma. Caprivi secessionists were "terrorists," he said, and secession was "the highest crime that citizens can be charged with." With Muyongo's flight, the government quickly controlled secessionist agitation.

One of Namibia's greatest needs is water, and the government is constantly seeking new and alternative sources of supply. This has meant maintaining the closest of ties with Angola and, to a lesser extent, Botswana. President Nujoma is deeply committed to plans for a hydroelectric development on the Cunene River at Epupa. Opposed by the Himba peoples, whose lands would be inundated by the project's waters, Epupa has generated international controversy. Environmentalists have analyzed the project's feasibility study and claim it is so riddled with incorrect conclusions, false assumptions and missing data that it cannot be used as a basis for a well-informed decision.

Despite opposition, Nujoma continues to push the project vigorously. Angola, which shares the river border, has alternative site plans for hydroelectric development and potentially far greater capacity to finance the project. Participation in the Congo war at Angola's side and permission for Angola to operate against *UNITA* within Namibian territory are both related to the country's regional water policy.

Tense relations with Botswana, created by Namibia's expressed desires to pump waters of the Okavango River to its parched capital, Windhoek, remain. A long-running dispute with South Africa over property rights along the Orange River has yet to be resolved.

Culture: A small minority—some 115,000 whites—have enjoyed the wealth of Namibia and the vast majority has been living, for the most part, in backward poverty, engaging in herding livestock to support themselves. The racial bloodbath which many nervous whites had predicted as a result of "communist" rule never happened. *SWAPO* certainly never had a communist agenda, though it certainly favored state intervention in the economy.

Race relations in the country are much better today than at probably any other time;

Windhoek is a pleasant city with marked German architectural styles dating back to that country's prior colonial period. These buildings are now side–by–side with tall structures possessing the latest styles in design and appearance. The city is neat and well–kept. On weekdays, the Damara–Herero women wear ordinary clothing, but on formal occasions and Sundays for Christians, they dress in ankle–length ornate dresses reminiscent of the Victorian era, together with large hats, even when the temperatures are high—a throwback to the dress of the German colonial era.

HIV/AIDS has become a critical problem for Namibia. While official figures claim a conservative 150,000 infected persons as of 1998, unofficial estimates provide a closer picture of reality: 320,000 Namibian are infected with the virus. According to UNAIDS, Namibia has the second highest HIV infection rate in sub-Saharan Africa after Botswana. The UN Development Program (UNDP) report for Namibia in 1998 concluded that if Namibia followed the same patterns as in Botswana and Zimbabwe, life expectancy would fall by 10 to 20% by 2015. There are already 67,000 HIV/AIDS orphans in Namibia. By 2006 it is estimated that about 13% of children under 15 would be AIDS orphans.

The budgetary implications of HIV/AIDS are significant. Government policy prohibits discrimination against anyone because he has HIV or AIDS. This has resulted in ever-increasing budgetary allocations to cover medical expenses for civil servants. In the budget submitted to parliament in March 2001, the finance minister indicated the "cost for chronic medication" would be increased by 60%.

In Namibia no closet doors, nor those behind them, seem safe. Namibia's gay and lesbian community has become a special target of governmental condemnation and harassment. The minister of home affairs has urged police to "eliminate gays and lesbians from the face of Namibia." For his part, President Nujoma has called gays and lesbians "unnatural," "ungodly," "un-African," and "idiots who should be condemned."

In March 2001, while addressing students at the University of Namibia, Nujoma asserted that Namibia did not allow homosexuality or lesbianism. Police, he said, "are ordered to arrest you, and deport you and imprison you too." In Namibia words have consequences. Shortly after one of these presidential outbursts, arsonists destroyed the office of *Sister Namibia*, a women's magazine known for championing gay rights.

Economy: Namibia's modern market sector produces most of its wealth; its traditional subsistence agricultural sector supports most of its labor force. Principal exports are diamonds and the Namibian economy depends greatly on Namdeb, its largest mining company. Namdeb, jointly owned by the Namibian government and De Beers of South Africa, accounts for 10% of the country's GDP and 30% of its exports; it is the biggest tax payer and, apart from the government, the country's biggest employer.

Namdeb produced 1.36 million carats of diamonds in 1996. As rich diamond ore deposits from a 150km beach near the mouth of the Orange River have been mined away over the last 70 years, however, lower yield, less labor intensive areas are being worked. The company now uses a huge dredge capable of stripping 2,500 tons of beach sand an hour to mine low-grade diamond ore. The shift from man to machine means a reduction of employees. Other diamond companies are using high-tech equipment to mine seabed diamonds off the Namibian coast.

President Sam Nujoma

Offshore diamond production in Namibia is growing at such a fast pace that marine output has already overtaken onshore production. Of the 1 million carats produced in the country in 1990, less than 100,000 carats came from offshore operations. In 1998 900,000 carats of Namibia's total production of 1,6 million carats came from marine operations. Geologists estimate that the marine deposits contain between one and three billion carats of diamonds, most of which lie in the Namibian territorial waters.

By 2000 offshore diamonds made up 56% of Namibia's total diamond production, and the Namibian Minerals Corp launched a project to comb the ocean floor in search of new underwater deposits. Geological surveys have already identified 163 areas with diamond potential.

In parched Namibia, water is a central concern and a potential limitation on meeting the demands of economic development, urbanization, and population growth. Approximately 80 percent of the country consists of desert, arid and semi-arid land. Yearly rainfall averages roughly 12 inches, but ranges from less than 2 inches along the coast to more than 27 a year in the northwest and Caprivi Strip. The country's water consumption was estimated at 250 million cubic meters per year in 1990; by 2005 it is projected to increase to 400 million.

The government has covetously eyed the waters of the Okavango River as one major possible solution to the country's perennial water crises. Following a devastating drought in 1996 the government proposed a 250-kilometre pipeline connecting the central area (especially the capital city of Windhoek) to the Okavango River. It has already built a series of canals and pipelines to carry groundwater to the capital from the northern community of Grootfontein. (Windhoek is already one of the few capitals in the world to recycle and reuse 80% of its water.) Plans to divert the Okavango waters pose a major problem: the river feeds into one of the most delicate and beautiful ecosystems in the world, the Okavango Delta, Botswana's premiere tourist attraction. Needless to say, Botswana is stiffly resistant.

Some of Namibia's most grandiose projects reflect the desperate need for water of South Africa's driest country. The hydroelectric project at Epupa is presently estimated to cost $540 million. Translated into Namibian dollars, that's $2.5 billion—the equivalent of one-fifth the total 1996 GDP. The actual site is not yet determined, with Angola and Namibia each proposing a different location, but the government's 2000-2001 budget funded a feasibility study, proving its determination to forge ahead on the project, regardless of criticism.

Budgetary profligacy probably means there won't be enough capital for major investments such as these. The principal cause: ever-increasing spending on the state bureaucracy and its creature comforts. Described as a " high priority project" is a lavish new State House to accommodate the president. Like Louis XIV escaping the din and danger of Paris for Versailles, President Nujoma plans to construct a vast new presidential village on a mountainside south of Windhoek.

Inspired by a presidential visit to North Korea, the project includes a residence and office for the president, cabinet chambers, conference and banquet halls, and a guesthouse complex designed to accommodate six heads of state and their entourages. The estimated cost is $25 million, and that's just preliminary.

Other large building projects included in the 2000-2001 development budget were an enlargement of the National Assembly chambers to accommodate joint sessions of the two houses of parliament, a new headquarters for the ministries of home affairs and labor, and a Heroes' Acre and Memorial Museum in Windhoek "to honor the fallen heroes of Namibia."

Namibia has a hugely bloated civil service—some 77,000 workers in a country with a population of around 1.7 million people—which has expanded to accommodate the needs of the *SWAPO* faithful. Efforts to trim this fatty mass were incorporated into the 2001 budget: $3.7 million to fund early retirement schemes.

It will be a while before the effects of retirement inducements will shrink Namibia's bureaucracy. In the meantime the budget remains in deficit. Much of this is attributable to the cost of maintaining some 2,000 to 2,500 troops in the Democratic Republic of the Congo (DRC). Though Namibia is very much a junior partner in the alliance supporting the Kabilas, father and son, it still spent an estimated $13 million in the Congo over a seven-month period in 2000. In November the finance minister had to request a supplemental budget allocation from parliament—over $70 million—of which more than 50% was to go to the defense department to maintain its Congo operations. Since 1998 Namibia's defense budget has doubled.

The opposition regularly deplores Namibia's involvement in the Congo, and during the budget debates, one regretted that the country had joined those African states that "have money for war but seek aid for development." The government defends itself on the somewhat dubious grounds that if the Kabila government fell, the successful rebels would team up with *UNITA* forces to overthrow Angola's government, which would impact negatively on Namibia. The negative impact of expanding the space of Angola's war against *UNITA* into Namibia can already be seen: tourism has experienced its lowest growth in years.

For its services to the DRC, Namibia has been given at least one diamond mine—just a little something to reduce the budgetary deficit. The mine is operated through a front company of the Namibia Defense Force, August 26 Company, which also owns the military equipment manufacturer, Winhoeker Maschinen Fabrik. Directors of August 26 reportedly include the Namibian army chief, two police inspectors general, and the permanent secretaries of the defense and trade ministries.

The Future: In many ways *SWAPO* is still caught up in its identity as a liberation movement. It believes it legitimized itself in the independence struggle and is owed deference on that basis. The perquisites of victory, thus, are natural. Sweeping electoral majorities have produced delusions of grandeur and invincibility. President Nujoma himself has become increasingly less tolerant of foreigners, gays and critics of his style of government, whom he lambastes as "unpatriotic".

The tasks facing the government are enormous. Unemployment is estimated between 30 to 40%. An estimated 25,000 school leavers enter the job market every year with few prospects of finding a job. The indirect costs of HIV/AIDS, added to the direct costs of medical care, will mean a loss of over $1.2 billion to the Namibian economy by 2001. To meet the challenge of these problems, which require the mobilization of all available national energies, *SWAPO* will need to think of itself less a liberation movement than a genuine political party, gathering and synthesizing a variety of societal demands. To hear those demands it will have to create a more genuinely democratic environment.

President Nujoma's basic authoritarian approach does not give such environmental promise, and there is little evidence he is interested in ever giving up the reins of power. Given strong backing for his third-term bid, President Nujoma is now talking of a fourth term. In April 2001, the 73-year old Nujoma announced that if Namibians wanted him to run at the end of his term in 2005, he was at their disposal.

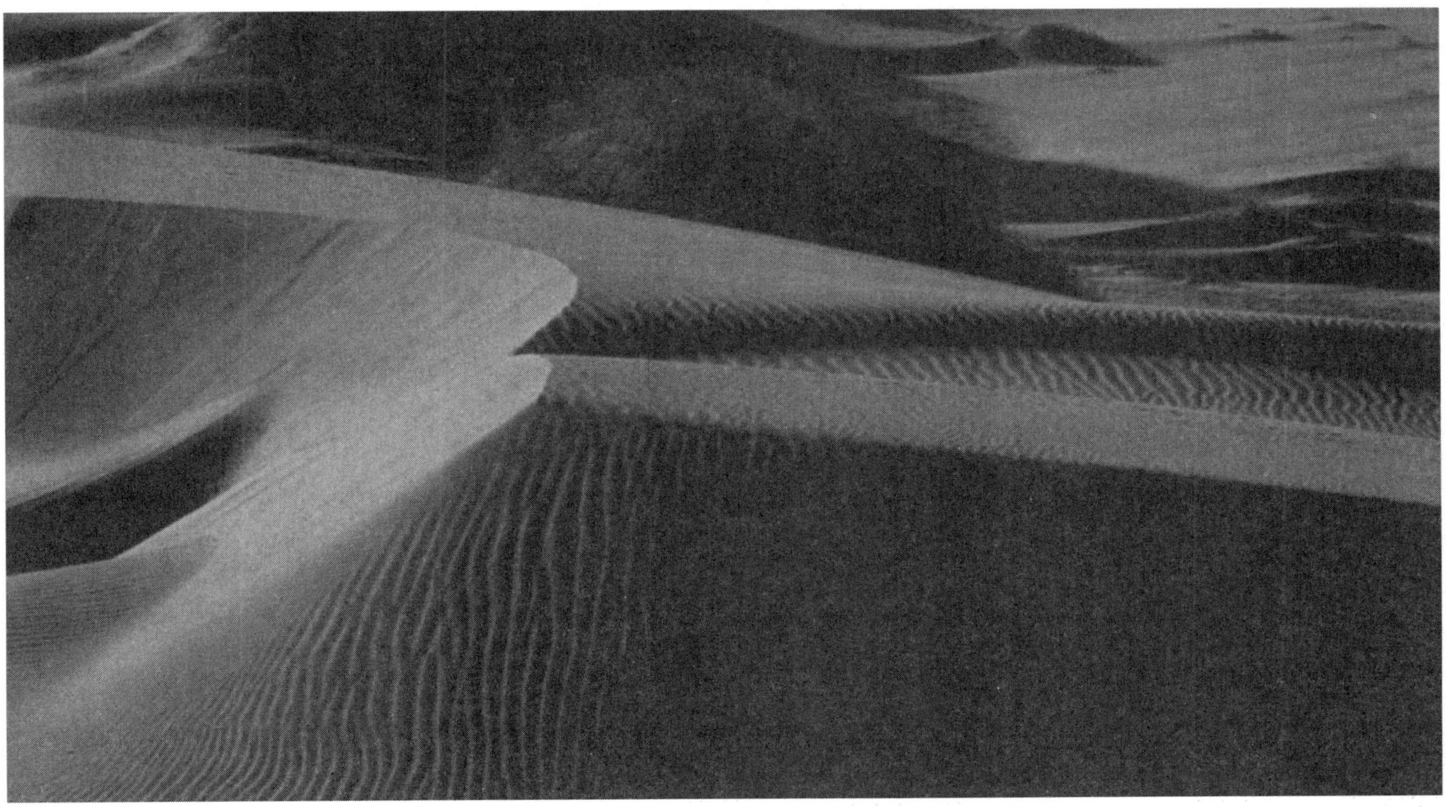

Sunset draws intricate patterns on the Namib Desert

The Republic of South Africa

Modern, sophisticated Johannesburg at night

Area: 1,222,470 sq. km. = 472,000 sq. mi. (three times the size of California).

Population: 43,426,386 (July 1999 est.)

Capital Cities: Pretoria (administrative, pop. 1.1 million); Cape Town, (legislative, pop. 2.2 million); Bloemfontein (judicial, pop. 260,000).

Climate: Temperate and sunny. The eastern coastal belt is hot and humid, the western areas are dry and hot. Only high mountain peaks are covered with snow during winter.

Neighboring Countries: Namibia (Northwest); Botswana, Zimbabwe (North); Mozambique, Swaziland (Northeast); Lesotho is enclosed by South Africa.

Official Languages: 11 official languages, granted "parity of esteem" in the Constitution. They include Afrikaans, English, Ndebele, Pedi, Sotho, Swazi, Tsonga, Tswana, Venda, Xhosa, and Zulu.

Other Principal Languages: Fanagolo, a Zulu-based pidgin, widely used in towns and gold, diamond, coal, and copper mining areas. About 70% of the vocabulary comes from Zulu, 24% from English, 6% from Afrikaans. Also Tamil and Urdu, especially in KwaZulu-Natal.

Ethnic groups: Estimated 76 percent black Africans—Nguni (Zulu, Xhosa, Swazi, Ndebele), Sotho-Tswana, Venda, Tsonga-Shangaan, Khoisan; 13 percent whites—Afrikaners, British, other Europeans; 8.5 percent colored, 2.5 percent Indian.

Principal Religions: Christian 68% (includes most whites and Coloreds, about 60% of blacks and about 40% of Indians), Muslim 2%, Hindu 1.5% (60% of Indians), traditional and animistic 28.5%.

Chief Commercial Products: Gold 20%, other minerals and metals 20%–25%, food 5%, chemicals 3%.

GNP per capita: 2,880 US$

Currency: Rand.

Former Colonial Status: Member of the British Commonwealth as the Union of South Africa (1910–1961). Previously, British authority in a colonial sense was sporadic in the Orange Free State and Transvaal.

Independence Date: 31 May 1910 (from UK).

Chief of State: Thabo Mbeki (pronounced Mm–*beh*–kee), since June 1999.

National Flag: From the pole, a black triangle separated by a thin gold stripe from thick green stripes which join to extend horizontally across the flag; there is a white stripe on either side of it separating the green from a field of red at the top and one of blue at the bottom.

Washed on the west by the South Atlantic and on the east by the Indian Ocean, the Republic of South Africa occupies the southernmost part of the continent. This land of bright, sunny days and cool nights has a consistently uniform climate year around, with a mean annual temperature of slightly less than 60°F.

In the extreme southern Cape area, there is a period of rain between April and September, but the summer (December–May) is warm and dry. The western coast is washed by the cool Benguela Current originating in Antarctica, which produces a climate that supports a large colony of penguins on the shore line. Further inland to the north, after the interruptions of the Cedarburg, Swartberg and Louga Mountains, the land stretches forth in a vast, semi–arid region known as the Karroo Desert. This is not a true desert as encountered in the central Sahara, since the periodic light rainfall supports vegetation which provides food for many species of wildlife. Occasional sharp projections of volcanic rock stand prominently in an otherwise flat land.

The eastern coast along the warm Indian Ocean is hot and humid, supporting almost every type of wild game known to southern Africa. In modern times, this climate has fostered the growth of high intensity agriculture similar to that found in southern California. Multi–colored coral formations are prominantly displayed by the brilliant white sands of the beaches. The northwestern central territory, is a high plains land (veldt), stretching to the north from the scenic peaks of the Drakensburg Mountains. Receiving ample rainfall for the most part, its temperate climate supports rich farmland; the land also contains huge gold and diamond deposits.

The northeastern plains are lower than the high veldt to the south. Kruger National Park, on the eastern border, is visited by tourists from all over the world. Here, all game is preserved, and visitors are not permitted to get out of their autos, which proceed slowly along the road to enable their occupants to see and photograph the many species.

Actually, two–thirds of South Africa is desert, semi–desert, marginal cropland or urban. Altogether, only 12% is ideally suited for intensive cultivation.

History: Before the arrival of Dutch East India Company employees in 1652, South Africa was thinly populated by Bushmen (Hottentots) and a very few pygmies. Bartholomew Diaz had reached the southern cape in 1486, six years before Columbus touched the West Indies. The rough, inhospitable appearance of the cape region attracted only free Dutch burghers, sent to grow grain and make wine to supply ships bound to and from Dutch East India possessions.

Settlement

They were joined by French Huguenot refugee settlers at the close of the century, who were accepted by the Dutch as equals; the two peoples gradually melded into a single society. Expansion of the Dutch–French was slow and generally in a northeastly direction; cattle–raising was their principal undertaking. Because of the need for farm labor, slaves were introduced from West Africa and later from Asia. They were added to modest numbers of Hottentots working under conditions of virtual slavery. Large families were common among the pioneers living in the equivalent of the American West at the time, and children were born of frequent non–marital unions of settlers and slaves, becoming the ancestors of today's Coloured (Cape Coloured, mulatto) population of South Africa.

It was not until the swirl of events in Europe surrounding intense rivalry and competition between the British and French at the turn of the 18th–19th centuries that non–Dutch persons began to enter the Cape Colony. Slave trade was abolished, creating labor shortages. The British initially acted under color of the authority of the exiled Dutch Prince of Orange, but later discarded that fiction and in 1814 came into legal possession of the Cape. This heralded the arrival of substantial numbers of British colonists who had been preceded by numerous missionaries determined to make the lives of natives better, much to the consternation of the *White* natives.

When slavery was abolished in 1834, about 35,000 people were emancipated; there were many protests about the inadequacy of compensation to the former owners.

The Dutch chafed under British authority, and many went northeastward into what were Orange Free State and Natal. At the same time, the area was being occupied by numerous Bantu tribes from points further north. Conflicts with the settlers were inevitable as the rivalry sharpened and as white settlers became more numerous. Their numbers grew substantially during the period of the Great Trek which penetrated north and east of the Orange River in 1835–42. Just as Americans are fascinated by tales of the western frontier during the 19th century, *Boer* South Africans never tire of retelling life during the treks.

The conflicts of this period and the years which followed are said to involve *Kaffirs* (i.e. black people). This is a misnomer the remnants of which exist to this day. *Kaffir* is a word borrowed from Arab slave traders used to refer to East African natives sought by them.

Kaffir today is a racial insult in South Africa, equivalent to the use of *nigger* in the United States. Yet, further compounding the confusion, the British in South Africa founded *Kaffraria* in 1847, a mini–state, later incorporating it into the Cape Colony in 1866. This was but one of many British efforts to legally establish and perpetuate black "homelands" promoting racial segregation in South Africa, an aim usually associated with the *Boer* population.

A busy shopping area in Cape Town

In Kruger National Park

Boer–Anglo Disputes

The *Boers,* Dutch–descended people, were not the only ones on the move. Ostensibly under pressure from missionary zealots to protect black populations, the British fought many skirmishes, battles and wars of words with the *Boers.* Their zeal was not entirely innocent, however, since they were, as in other colonies, seeking means of wealth to add to what became the Commonwealth (which by the last half of the 20th century turned out to be neither common nor wealthy). British problems were compounded by the fact that many of the people who they nominally sought to protect hated them as much as they did the *Boers.* At an early time (1846) the British initiated the ancestor of racial separation *(apartheid)* when they established a Location Commission in Natal.

Over a period of years, various forms of government were tried by the British the success of which was directly related to their ability to leave the *Boers* alone. Self–government was tried in Natal, Transvaal and the Orange Free State. Discovery of immense sources of wealth in diamonds (1867) and gold (1886) proved to be a lure which was virtually irresistable to fortune seekers, not dissimilar to the California and Alaska gold rushes of the United States. The *Boers* actively disliked the new people, calling them *outlanders.*

One of these opportunists, Cecil Rhodes, an energetic Welshman, accumulated a vast fortune by wheeling and dealing. His treaties with black chieftains in particular were heavily weighted in Rhodes' favor. He belatedly tried to salvage what was left of his reputation by establishing the Rhodes Scholarship program which provides the cost of a period of education in England to aspiring students.

Towns sprang up virtually overnight as a result of the wealth. Johannesburg, laid out in 1886, soon had a population of more than 100,000, about half of whom were black. Rhodes evidently satisfied both the *Boers* and the British, since he became Prime Minister of Cape Colony in 1890, nominally functioning under President Paul Kruger from Transvaal. The latter is generally thought of as the founding father of South Africa, affectionately referred to as *Oom* ("Uncle") Paul Kruger.

President Kruger correctly concluded that Rhodes, in order to advance his own interests and, secondarily, to maintain the appearance of British supremacy in South Africa, was financing an anti–*Boer* movement among the *outlanders.* The first tangible act was the aborted Jamison Raid (1895) which led to the ouster of Rhodes as prime minister. In the remaining years of the century, relations between the British and the *Boers* soured. Kruger was elected to a third term as president at the same time the British high commissioner was promoting war between the two societies.

A minor dispute over voting rights of immigrants was a pretext for the Boer War of 1899–1902. By the end of the conflict the British were hopelessly mired down. They had to build concentration camps for *Boer* women and children, several thousand of whom died of disease and neglect. Some 300,000 British troops were required to barely "win" over about 75,000 *Boers,* who then took up guerrilla warfare. The weary British woke up to the fact that the riches of South Africa were being squandered on a meaningless quarrel and offered $113 million and self–government "when possible" to the *Boers* if they would stop fighting. The offer was accepted and the money was used in part to rebuild *Boer* farms which had been ruthlessly destroyed.

The Union of South Africa

Principally in response to the pleas of General Jan Christiaan Smuts *(Boer* commander–in–chief of the Republican forces in the Cape Colony during the final months of the war), the British established the *Union of South Africa* in 1910, thereby granting self–government in Transvaal and Orange Free State. The constitution bound together the two former *Boer* republics with the British Cape Colony and Natal. An administrative capital was established at Pretoria (Transvaal), a legislative capital at Cape Town (Cape Colony) and a judicial seat at Bloemfontein (Orange Free State), an arrangement that prevails to this date. Thus the two groups—the descendants of the Dutch and the British—were encouraged to form a closer bond and still retain the dignity of being important parts of the whole union.

At the same time, a political party was founded by General Louis Botha and James Hertzog, the *South African Party.* It was moderate, encompassing both English and *Afrikaans* speakers stressing the equality of both and pressing for independent status within the British Empire. Within a short time, however, Hertzog and the rural, conservative *Boers* split off to form the *Nationalist Party.*

A basic law was drafted and passed in 1912 which included provisions limiting the areas in which black persons could own or purchase land and further restricting the movement of Asiatics. The latter caused severe unrest among the Indian population, then led by Mohandas K. (Mahatma) Gandhi, which widely demonstrated against its provisions. This law was the beginning of legal separation of the races—*apartheid*—which would be more fully enacted into law after World War II.

World Wars and the Interwar Period

South Africa joined in World War I, fighting the Germans in their possessions in Africa (German S.W. Africa, German East Africa, now Namibia and Tanzania). Hertzog appeared at the Paris peace conference at the close of the conflict to demand independence for South Africa, which was ignored. Because no other logical power was in the region, South Africa was given a League of Nations mandate to control the former German colony of South West Africa. This continued without interruption until 1990 when South Africa became convinced that communism no longer posed a threat in what is now Namibia. Countless international protests over its continued control of the territory and annual United Nations resolutions were ignored (see Namibia). The British did, however, recognize the Union of South Africa as an independent nation within the British Commonwealth in 1931.

Until 1934 government power was exercised by either or both the South *African*

Party (Smuts) and the *Nationalist Party* (Hertzog). When the two united, adopting the name *United South African Nationalist Party,* the conservative members of Hertzog's party re–formed under the old party name with the leadership of Daniel F. Malan. Since the turn of the century, anti–black sentiments had been slowly crystallizing. Initially they were not matters of law, but a product of social organization.

Problems were settled in the church forum and enforced by practices such as shunning those held in disrepute. An informal system of informants existed, particularly in rural areas, and little that went on escaped the notice of church elders. In the pulpits, elaborate Biblical justifications were developed to explain the need for the races to stay apart, thus justifying segregation.

The sentiment for racial segregation was by no means limited to the *Boers.* English–speaking conservatives accepted the notion readily and supported it politically. A very small number of *Boer* liberals did not support segregation, joining with a minority of English–speakers politically. However, liberalism was unfashionable in South Africa among whites, who were largely able to withstand the ravages of the worldwide depression of the 1930s by virtue of the country's vast mineral wealth.

Black persons were allowed to vote, but on a special ballot whereby three white persons represented them in the Union parliament.

South Africa declared war on the Axis Powers of World War II, but its participation was minimal because of its distant location from the fighting. Further, there was a sizable *Boer* element in the parliament which had no use for liberal English–speakers. During the opening years of World War II, this group expressed little regret at a possible defeat of England by Germany. The end of the conflict was the end of the Hertzog–Smuts coalition which had been in power since 1934. As 1948 elections approached, the *National Party,* then led by Daniel F. Malan, campaigned on an openly racist platform, advocating that white South Africans insure their moral and financial future by enacting into law that which already substantially existed by virtue of social customs and economic patterns: *apartheid,* the Dutch Boer word for "separate" (pronounced A–*par*–tate).

Apartheid

Prime Minister Malan and the *National Party* wasted no time in their efforts to deliver the promises made during the 1948 campaign. Within a year citizenship and other important rights were curtailed or eliminated. A person who took up residence in South Africa, no matter what his origin, was able to claim South African

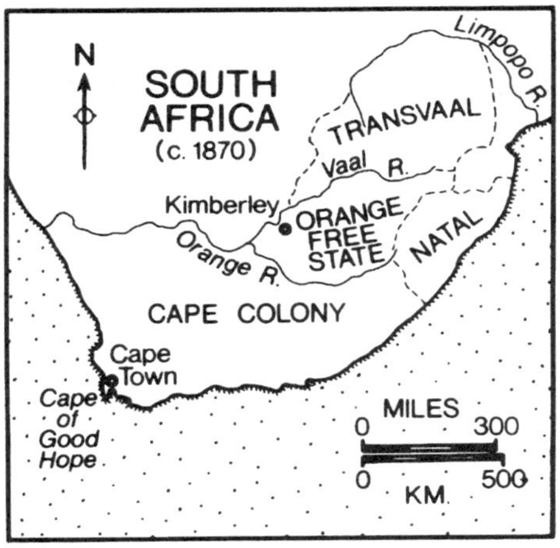

and Commonwealth citizenship almost immediately. A five–year waiting period was enacted and enforced which had the effect of limiting access to the voting booth. Mixed race marriages were banned by law (they had not been widespread before it was passed).

Perhaps the most fundamental law calculated to change the face of South Africa was the *Group Areas Act* of 1950. Combined with the land acts of 1912 and 1936, it strictly limited the area in which a person was allowed to live based on race. Under it, together with enabling regulations, an estimated 3.5 million black people were removed from lands they occupied.

The *Group Areas Act* and associated laws had the effect of denying blacks any possibility of ownership based on occupation of land. Thus, if a given tract was within a "white only" area, all that was necessary to oust a black person was proof that he wasn't white and therefore it was illegal for him to occupy the tract by living on it.

The *Population Registration Act* classified everyone by race at the time of their birth: black, white, Asiatic, Coloured, other. This determination controlled almost every aspect of a person's future—where he lived, worked, went to school, wages, voting (if any), property ownership, etc., and became a foundation for the laws requiring that everyone have a passbook. In many cases, it was illegal for a person to merely *be* in a given area.

The *Internal Security Act* of 1982 granted virtual dictatorial powers to the government and abolished any semblance of civil rights which remained. It provided for the banning of organizations opposed to the state, made it illegal for individuals to belong to them, imposed involuntary censorship on the press, allowed detention without trial of persons suspected of terrorism, and imprisonment of anyone for 10 days without any charges.

To carry out the aims of the *apartheid* laws, the police ("South African Defense Force, SADF") developed a highly intensive system of espionage, informants and control calculated to strike fear into the hearts of all. In particular, the use of informants was widespread, enabling police to arrest would–be criminals before their crime could even be attempted. Prison facilities were designed as tools of the police and to further the ends of justice under *apartheid.* If the degree of proof of the guilt of an individual was dubious or flawed, he or she might well die in prison awaiting trial . . . "slipped on the soap while taking a shower" . . . "fell downstairs" . . . "was assaulted" . . . "died while trying to escape" were all heard with frequency in South Africa if, indeed, anything was heard at all.

Before the days of compulsory censorship, newspapers were guided by the principles of "voluntary" censorship. In its most fundamental regard, this simply meant that anything embarrassing to the state should not be published. If a newspaper violated this imperative too seriously or too often (elusive quantities), paper supplies, bank credit and often telephone service evaporated. Worst of all, no official at whom a finger could be pointed ever did anything illegal. Things just happened.

The *Publication Bill* unashamedly was directed at reporting of black activities in the press. It demanded that the media exercise "due care and responsibility concerning matters which can have the effect of stirring up feelings of hostility between different racial, ethnic, religious or cultural groups" in South Africa. True to the form of the Dutch–descended *Boers* it professed to "avoid the spirit of permissiveness and moral decay sweeping the world and communications media in the country."

The African National Congress

The *African National Congress* was initially formed in response to the enactment

General Jan Christiaan Smuts

of a 1912 *Basic Law* which regulated the areas in which black people were allowed to own land. Passage of the act resulted in the expulsion of some people without adequate compensation from lands they and their ancestors had occupied for generations. The organization had little mass appeal prior to 1948 because of a general lack of political awareness of blacks, and their limited economic condition. The leadership was generally conservative, hoping to deal with the white–dominated government to seek redress of land seizures. Its outlook was not unlike that of the NAACP in the U.S. during the initial years of its existence.

After 1948, with the advent of *apartheid* it became a militant, openly communist organization determined to oust the white minority from power with a commitment to seizing the economic wealth of the nation in the name of black power.

By the early 1960s, South Africa's government was gripped with an obsessive fear of militant black leaders. It outlawed not only the *Communist Party* but also the *ANC,* whose leaders without exception were dedicated communists. In 1962 both organizations went underground and warrants were issued for the party leadership of each. Militant blacks countered with the *Umkhonto we Sizwe* ("Spear of the Nation") in 1961, the militant branch of the *ANC.* Its purpose: guerrilla warfare to replace mass popular demonstrations which had been made illegal.

After a year and a half as a fugitive, Nelson Mandela (45) and Walter Sisulu were tried in 1964 (the Rivonia trial) and found guilty. The sentence: life imprisonment without possibility of parole. The leadership that was not arrested remained underground, taking refuge in neighboring and nearby nations such as Zambia (the location of its headquarters), Mozambique, Tanzania and Botswana. From these exile posts they directed the affairs of the *ANC.* Nelson Mandela was sent to Robben Island prison, noted for its harsh conditions.

During the 25 years after the trial of Mandela and Sisulu, the *ANC* grew steadily as the rigid separation and denial based solely on the basis of race became far more onerous. Ironically, it helped to found the *Inkatha Freedom Party* of the Zulus in 1974, feeling that the anti–apartheid movement ought to have some lawful (i.e. non–communist) presence in South Africa.

ANC Lobbying in the U.S.

The ANC took its cause to the United States, enlisting the aid of the Congressional Black Caucus. Embargoes on trade with South Africa were also demanded, and, most importantly, economic sanctions against South Africa were aggressively pursued.

The sanctions enacted in September 1986 included (1) a ban on all investments and loans in South Africa, (2) a ban in the import of iron, steel and agricultural products as well as uranium, coal and textiles, (3) termination of South African airlines landing rights in the U.S., (4) exclusion of all South African bank deposits in the U.S., (5) a continued ban on the export of U.S. oil, arms or equipment connected with nuclear power, (6) approval of $40 million in aid to disadvantaged South Africans (technically, regardless of race) and finally a "request" that the *ANC* end its ties to the *South African Communist Party,* suspend its terrorist activity, and commit itself to a free and democratic future.

Urban Overcrowding and Resulting Unrest

During the 1960s and onward, there was a continual influx into black townships which were located on the edge of every major and smaller city of South Africa; this was caused by starkly primitive conditions prevailing in rural areas and an influx of immigrants from surrounding African nations. South Africa tried to limit expansion of these urban slums by adopting an identity card (pass book) system intended to protect employed workers around the cities from competition by illegal immigrants.

The pass laws were, among other measures, repealed in 1986.

The government established "homelands" in order to take the pressure off of black townships to reduce its burden to provide decent housing and services. It also sought to neutralize Black political power. Technically, all township residents were required to vote in the homeland from which they or their ancestors had come, or to which they had been assigned. To further encourage migration to the homelands, and in spite of their continuous growth, the government also decreed that no new high school facilities could be built in them.

Soweto

The government had, back in 1953, ordered that instruction in all high schools be 50% in Afrikaans and 50% in English,

Part of Durban as seen from the harbor

but not in the native language of the pupils which was used during the first six years if schooling.

Soweto, outside of the large city of Johannesburg, was one of the early black townships, and thus had a great many four–room houses built by the government which on the surface appeared reasonably presentable. But only about 15% of them had inside running water and toilet facilities. The great majority of the homes had 6 to 8 people crowded in very limited space with no heat.

As early as 1960 (Sharpeville) there had been demonstrated the capability and willingness of black citizens to use firearms against the white police (which had a substantial number of black officers also). The disturbance which is remembered most widely, occurred in Soweto in mid–1976. The cause is traditionally remembered as a directive that all school education be in *Afrikaans*. That is not an accurate statement.

The 1953 agreement on 50–50 use of English and Afrikaans had gradually been ignored in black high schools in favor of English only. This was a sensible move—*Afrikaans* was and is an outdated, parochial language compared to English. The *Boer* members of the parliament, led by the arch–conservative, Dr. Andries Treurnicht, insisted on 50% *Afrikaans* in high school classrooms, and the announcement was made by the then education minister Pieter Botha.

The teachers in Soweto undoubtedly spread the word of this occurrence, using words of polarity, and they were repeated by the students at home. Within hours on June 16th a disturbance that turned into a riot started that lasted until the 24th; before it was over, 174 blacks were killed (compared to 2 whites). There were 1,222 black casualties, contrasting sharply with 6 whites wounded. The disturbance–riot was suppressed with excessive force. Botha retracted the demand for the use of *Afrikaans*.

Another counter–productive program emerged following the Soweto riot: a boycott of schools. The slogan "liberation before education" became a watchword which has proved to be costly. As black majority rule approached in 1994, it became evident that 18 years of school boycotts had left a generation of young illiterates in South Africa.

Apartheid at the beach in Durban

Black Homelands

A "solution" to racial problems for the government was adopted under President Vorster in the form of a Black Homelands Act. This consisted of granting internal self–government to ten areas either traditionally associated with or assigned to a tribal group. When each requested independence, it was to be granted. The first to take the plunge was the Xhosa area in southeast South Africa, *Transkei*, with then about 3 million inhabitants (1976). The next occurred the following year when Bophuthatswana ("homeland of the Tswanas"), a nation in six separated areas with 2.1 million people, was granted self–rule; most of its parts lay to the north, bordering Botswana. Venda, with almost a half million, became independent in 1979 and Ciskei in 1981.

Although the new homeland republics did not receive diplomatic recognition except by South Africa, they maintained offices in major foreign capitals. Neighboring African nations were strongly opposed to what they saw as a plan to keep white South Africa in control of the most productive and desirable land, and to retain economic and political strength.

Of equal concern during the early 1980s was a move to relocate thousands of black South Africans living in rural areas who had acquired their land legally in "white only" areas before the 1912 *Group Areas Act* was adopted. Strong adverse reaction in the foreign press brought a halt to this attempt at forced moving, although the government denied being influenced by such expressions.

The Black Homelands solution addressed only a portion of a social and economic impasse. More than 14 million black people lived in townships adjacent to the largest cities and industrial areas of South Africa; even the government classified them as "detribalized." But to express themselves politically, they were *required* to vote in the homeland to which they had been assigned (which had no role or vote in the government of South Africa) whether or not they had ever been physically present. The system of identity cards was used, in part, to determine who could live outside his or her "homeland."

Viewing the homelands as potential rivals in the quest for black supporters, both the *ANC* and the *UDC* vigorously opposed the homeland concept.

Attempted Reforms

Former President Botha, as early as 1980, saw the need for additional reform and embarked on a wide–ranging series of measures, stating that revolution was not just a remote possibility. He proposed elimination of the *Group Areas Act*, the *Slums Act* and the *Community Development Act;* the names sounded innocent, but the laws were tools of *apartheid*. But the conservative element of the National Party, led by the intractable Andries Treurnicht resisted any reform whatsoever. They persuaded the usually astute president to embark on a "new" approach that would lead to violence and change in South Africa.

The plan was an attempt to placate both international opinion and internal resistance by blacks to white rule. It was supposed to be the answer to the exclusion of blacks from *any* participation in government. Sometime in the mid–1970s a scheme had been devised to constitutionally create

A Three–House National Assembly . . . . . . (With No Blacks).

To appear to be as democratic as possible, a scheme was devised to create a three–house National Assembly with a large body restricted to white membership, two smaller units to represent Coloureds and Indians, and no blacks. The latter were to be given control of the townships in which they were a majority.

In this way, it was felt, black leadership could be used to contain increasing unrest in the townships and, at the same time, satisfy the hunger for self–rule. The *Boer* leadership actually convinced themselves that something was being given to the blacks of South Africa. The *ANC* leadership felt it was no more than just another chapter in the book of *apartheid.*

The National Assembly had a 185–seat white parliament, a 92–seat one for Coloureds and a third for Asians (46 seats). The smaller houses had no powers except with respect to matters of concern to the minority they represented. The larger white parliament could veto any act of the other two. This three–tiered system of parliament, coupled with black "home rule" proved to be white South Africa's most costly and serious mistake; it was instrumental in the downfall of white–controlled government.

The plan itself was unworkable, and quickly gave way to a government by oligarchy: the Presidential Council of about 60 members proposed all laws and the parliament became a rubber stamp. But even worse was Black reaction: instead of seeing a half full glass, they saw only a half empty one. A fundamental decision was made in response to the measure—*make South Africa ungovernable!*

The *ANC* devised a two–pronged agenda to accomplish its aim of seizing control of South Africa (it did not envision doing its will through the ballot box until the early 1990s). First, using violence as a tool against non–Zulu Black South Africans, an effort was made to make all persons, particularly within the townships, either members of *ANC* or sympathizers with the cause it espoused. This was accomplished by making it dangerous *not* to fall within one of the two categories. Second, the *ANC* leadership recognized that *Inkatha,* led by Mangosuthu Gatsha Buthelezi, was a potential rival that had to be eliminated or at least controlled in the struggle for power that was to come. Both of these programs unleashed terrible violence, which immediately increased tremendously; the police were virtually helpless to deal with it because of sheer quantity.

In most cases, well–meaning blacks ran for township office—mayor and council—and with an *ANC* led boycott of elections, they were voted in by a small minority of the electorate. Interestingly, Zulus did not run for these offices, as will be explained. The ones chosen were treated dreadfully—they were regarded as subservient Uncle Toms, cooperating with the despised white–controlled government. They, and anyone cooperating with, talking with, being seen with or simply not opposing them with suitable enthusiasm, became acceptable targets of *ANC* and *MK* violence.

After violence rose to the level hoped for, the *ANC* and those in sympathy with its aims began to use the turmoil as the greatest reason for economic disinvestment and sanction programs directed against South Africa by foreign businesses.

In the decade 1984–1994, a grand total of over 20,000 blacks were killed in South Africa; of these, about 11,000 were murdered after 1990 when Nelson Mandela was released from prison by the white government. Of the total, about 1,500 were killed by the South African Defense Forces of the White government. Those who perished included common criminals who resisted arrest or attempted violence on the police or others and could not be restrained without the loss of life. The significant figure is that 94% of the murders were of *blacks by blacks.*

The commission which developed those figures also concluded that of the black on black homicides, those killed were about 85% *ANC* members or supporters, or lived in *ANC*–controlled areas.

Inkatha Freedom Party and Chief Buthelezi

By the early 1970s the *ANC* had been all but eliminated as an imminent threat by the white–controlled government of South Africa, and the organization was somewhat demoralized. The system of spies and informants which was developed by the South African Defense Forces made it dangerous to belong to the underground organization or to be a communist comrade–in–arms. In order to try to maintain some form of legal pressure against *apartheid,* the *ANC* leadership recognized the need to have a Zulu–based organization to bring pressure on the white government.

The Zulus live primarily in Natal province, surrounding areas and homelands, and have traditionally never been friendly with the Xhosas, who are the core of the *ANC,* together with the Sothos and Tswanas. Thus, although they had no particular affinity for potential rivals, it was a matter of practicality for the *ANC* to enourage and assist in the founding of the *Inkatha Freedom Party* in 1974. Its leader was and is Chief Mangosuthu Gatsha Buthelezi (Man–go–*soo*–too *Gat*–sha Boo–teh–*lay*–zee), a well–spoken moderate leader, known for his ability to communicate with the white leadership, in spite of *Inkatha's* staunch opposition to *apartheid.*

Buthelezi firmly believed that change in South Africa was possible, but also steadfastly believed that if basic changes occurred in such a manner as to impoverish the country, they would be worthless. His attitudes largely reflected the lifestyles of most of the members of *Inkatha,* as well as most Zulu non–members.

The Xhosas and Sothos tended to cluster with their families in shantytowns around the large industrial and mining centers of South Africa, where children were raised in poverty and hardship. The Zulus, on the other hand, were the chief clientele of hostels—shelters for male workers with a minimum of comfort and convenience—where they lived for usually 27 out of 30 days. In the period of respite from work, they went back home (where they had been sending their wages

A group of Zulu women at market

Xhosa farmers in the Eastern Cape

after expenses) to their wives and children. Living in this manner, their needs are minimal, their wages are comparatively high and family tensions and quarrels are usually at a low level since they didn't have time to escalate. Of equal importance, their wives and children weren't exposed to the crime, violence and deprivations of the townships, where living is harsh and often unruly.

When the *National Party* leadership perceived that the *ANC* was attempting to destabilize South Africa with violence, the conservatives and military of the government sought and obtained an informal alliance with *Inkatha* to combat the rise in violence. There is a substantial body of evidence, all unproven, however, that the Zulus were armed and trained by members of the South African Defense Force and the armed forces. As this became evident to the *MK* leadership, efforts against Zulus were redoubled.

Among Zulu customs, the carrying of traditional weapons, referred to also as *cultural weapons*, is important. They are uniquely associated with the passage from boyhood to manhood. Although not universally carried at all times, their presence certainly marks the bearer as a Zulu for all to see, a fact in which not a small amount of pride is held. For reasons that are not clear, an obscure South African judge in 1989 ruled that they were dangerous weapons in the eyes of the law, and therefore could not be carried in public. Making a bad mistake, the government agreed, and told the Zulus they could not carry spears and axes as was their right in the past, even though the Zulus, when resorting to violence (usually considered by them to be defensive) used *modern* weaponry.

Chief Buthelezi and his followers, as well as Zulus in general, were shocked at the decision. Within limits, they had remained loyal to the concept of change as produced by law, not violence. It appeared that in the name of appeasement the government was caving into the whims of the *ANC*, which had been complaining bitterly about the weapons. *Inkatha*, and the Zulus appeared to have become in a sense the sacrificial lamb at the altar of injustice.

Chief Buthelezi, and Goodwill Zwelethini, King of the Zulus, denounced the measure in no uncertain terms, widely supported by Zulus in Natal and elsewhere. Together with conservative white South Africans, the chief began to speak with regularity of a black state seceding from South Africa under his leadership. In the alternative, in the event that agreement could be reached on a non–racial government, a system of strong federalism was favored, creating the equivalent of states' rights. This attracted favorable interest among many white conservatives, who sought to establish a "white homeland" in the event of a black–dominated government in South Africa.

Exit President Botha, Enter President de Klerk

Nelson Mandela wrote to the then President Pieter W. Botha in 1988, urgently stating that the two should confer about matters vital to the future of the nation. Although it was not publicized, the conservative president met with Mandela.

A generally astute leader, President Botha suffered a stroke in January 1989. After a brief recuperation, he announced in March 1989 he would resume his duties as president, but there was immediate opposition from the party leadership, which secured the nomination of Frederik W. de Klerk to run in September elections.

Three weeks before the elections, an angry and frustrated Botha made a television broadcast denouncing de Klerk, the *ANC* and all others perceived by him to be hostile, and resigned as president. His successor showed a generally more conciliatory approach and was able to ignore the white conservatives who were a continuous source of aggravation in South Africa.

Nelson Mandela

Nelson Mandela, born in Umtata (later within the homeland of *Transkei*) in 1918, turned 77 in July 1995. When the *ANC* was banned in 1962 he went underground, as did many others among its leadership. Apprehended, he was charged under the anti–communist and anti–terrorism laws in force in South Africa and was sentenced to life imprisonment without hope of parole. This received almost no attention in the U.S. because he was at the time just another communist revolutionary.

While in prison, he kept abreast of current matters in South Africa, including the turn to violence and terrorism in 1984.

It was not until F.W. de Klerk became president in 1989 and had a chance to solidify his power base that further contact was established with Mandela leading to his release from prison. At about the same time, others, including Walter Sisulu, were released.

President de Klerk correctly concluded that continued detention of Mandela would be counter–productive and his chances of meaningful negotiations would be more possible if they were with the older leaders of the *ANC*. Oliver Tambo had suffered a major stroke and had been largely neutralized by it.

Thus, in February 1990 de Klerk ordered the release of Nelson Mandela, whose name by that time was a legend among the black people of South Africa. There was dancing and widespread celebrating in the townships. He was almost immediately made Deputy President of the *ANC* effectively being transformed overnight from the status of prisoner to head of the organization from which he had been removed almost 27 years past when seized.

Although he made some mistakes following his release, he was quite astute in walking a tightwire, engaging in negotiations with President de Klerk, traveling abroad in search of desperately needed funding, and acknowledging that the anti–*apartheid* rival *Inkatha* movement of South Africa had to be given some sort of recognition. His conduct, however, infuriated the more radical members of the *ANC* who for so many painful years cherished the visions of black power, confrontation, seizure of the state and bloody revolution.

He had not been adequately informed of the fact that communism had been rapidly crumbling in the Soviet Union and Eastern Europe nor could he be expected to foresee the utter collapse of the doctrines he had come to cherish. His initial statements, made in a large stadium in Soweto, shocked white South Africans:

> "We have waited too long for our freedom. We can no longer wait. Now is the time to intensify the struggle on all fronts. To relax our efforts now would be a mistake which generations to come will not be able to forgive."

In the speech, he saluted the *MK*, the *South African Communist Party*, and several members of that organization, including Secretary General Joe Slovo ("one of our finest patriots"), regarded by most whites as little more than a shabby opportunist.

A hammer and sickle flag was displayed (but not on U.S. television) imme-

The misery of *Crossroads* and the new town, *Khayalitsha*

diately below the platform from which he spoke. What was not realized is that those words were for (1) home consumption and (2) more importantly, to assure Mandela of an undisputed claim as leader of the *ANC* as opposed to the militant wing of the organization. His strategy worked, for it was not long before he was proclaimed Commander of the *Umkhonto we Sizwe* (an honorary title). But within a day he was saying: "Whites are fellow South Africans and we want them to feel safe and [to know] that we appreciate the contribution they have made towards the development of the country."

The major mistake he made then and after the speech was to insist upon nationalization of South African industries, in particular, the immense Anglo–American Mining Company, a multi–national consortium with worldwide interests as well as its diamond and gold mines of South Africa. When in 1992 Mandela had concluded that his advocacy of sanctions and disinvestment was the wrong policy, to his remorse, he found that trying to turn away from these policies in order to attract investment to South Africa was far harder than he had imagined. His earlier position had laid the foundation for an atmosphere of suspicion and distrust.

Mandela had been expected by many to be a dedicated, violent revolutionary gripped by the misjudgments of an uniformed old age. To the contrary, he showed great astuteness and flexibility walking the tightwires where there often was no visible wire. It is clear he understood the difference between a revolutionary movement and a political party charged with governing a country. It became clear in all he did that he understood too the necessities of politics in a South Africa about to change. Development of the country and improvement in the lives of its citizens would require, above all, the political stability that would give confidence and assurance to investors on whom that development largely depended.

The pressures under which Mandela survived were tremendous. He had to risk the disfavor of the militant wing of the ANC conditioned by years of a struggle mentality and ideologically shaped by economic thinking which exulted the role of a highly centralized state. The tensions between Mandela's perceived need of moderation as a governing party and the militants' more radical claims were often less lofty, and in the case of his wife Winnie Mandela, even personal. After many months of pondering what to do about her, he finally opted to part ways, separating himself from a figure romanticized by some of the most youthful and radical elements of the party.

With her husband in prison and being far from the "action" in South Africa, Winnie Mandela was bored. Violating her exile in 1986, she worked her way to Soweto, a black township outside of Johannesburg. A luxurious home, complete with swimming pool had been built for her amid the two–room tar paper and tin shanties of the town. There was a minor uproar of protest, so she did not immediately move in.

When she did, she formed "The Winnie Mandela Soccer Team," a gang of young thugs which proceeded to terrorize Soweto and other nearby black townships. Trials of real and imagined offenders took place in her home, where she often "presided." Sentences of beating and death were meted out.

The structure was rebuilt and the terrorism was resumed. A very damaging event occurred in 1988 when a 13–year–old boy was kidnapped from a Soweto Methodist Church shelter by the "team" and taken to the house. He was accused of being a police informer and was beaten severely, reportedly partly by her. Taken to a nearby field by the "team," he was murdered.

Acting through his lawyer from prison, Nelson Mandela ordered her to release three other kidnapped youths and to disband the "team." She was ousted from the *ANC*, losing her informal title "Mother of the Nation." A trial was held sporadically because radical members of the *ANC* kept threatening and actually kidnapped co–defendants and state witnesses, removing them from the country. After listening to her testimony the judge (there is yet no jury trial in South Africa) called her a "calm, composed, deliberate and unblushing liar." She was sentenced to six years in jail; an appeals court sustained the conviction in early June 1993 but, in a political decision which was wise, vacated the prison sentence.

Winnie Mandela is sixteen years younger than her former husband; she had a marriage prior to their union. President Mandela now enjoys the company of his new wife, the widow of Samora Machel of Mozambique.

The trial was held after the release of Nelson Mandela from prison; neither he nor the *ANC* leadership directly rallied to Winnie's defense. She was rebuffed in an effort to rejoin the *ANC* leadership when Walter Sisulu's wife withdrew from the race for president of the Women's Auxiliary and threw her support to an opponent. While her husband was trying to engage in meaningful negotiations with the white government, Winnie appealed to the militant sector of the *ANC*; they remembered her for her famous 1987 state-

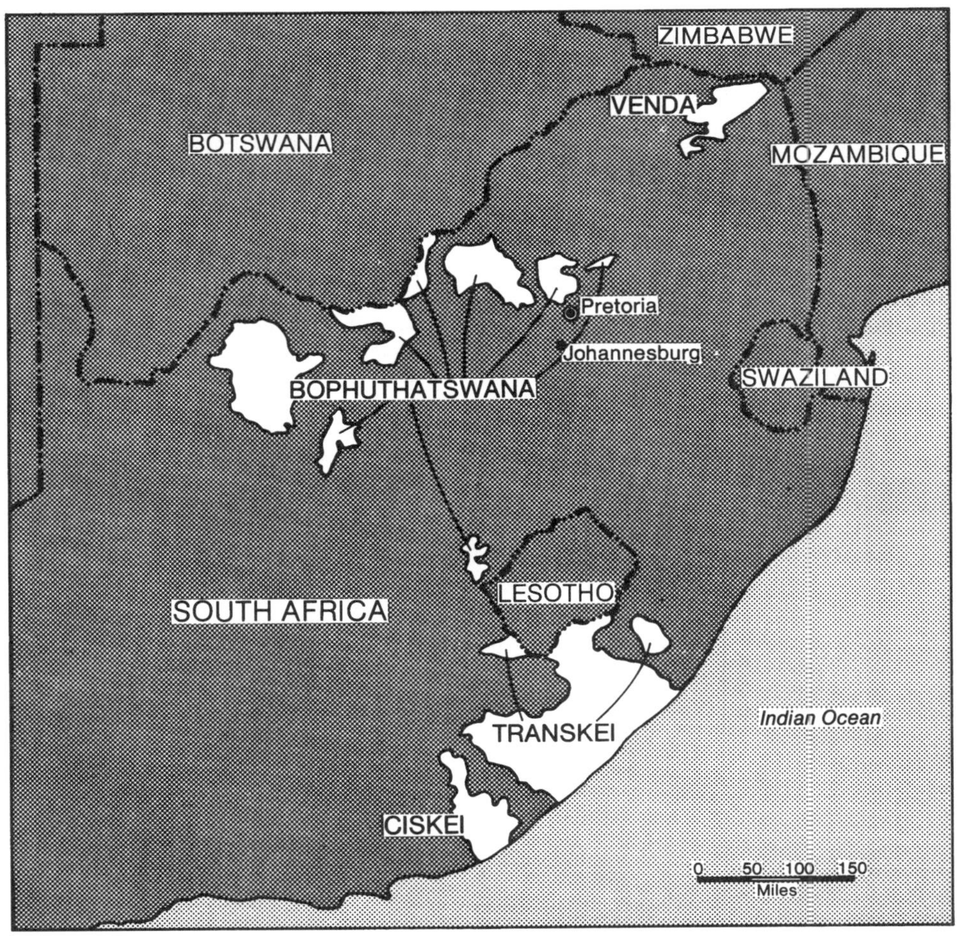

Black "homeland" republics

ment: "With our matchboxes and our necklaces, we shall liberate!"

"Necklacing" occurred when an old tire was jammed down over the shoulders of the victim. Filled with gasoline, it was ignited. As the victim writhed in abject agony, the crowd gathered for the occasion yelled and cheered with glee usually associated with a holiday gathering. Who got this treatment? Anyone disapproved of by *MK* leaders was chosen, including a woman past the age of 80 suspected of being a witch. It was used time after time against blacks believed to be unsympathetic to the aims of the *ANC*, including township mayors, councilmen and police.

Nelson Mandela decided in the spring of 1992 that he had to separate from Winnie because of "tensions" of an unspecified nature. In fact, she was openly carrying on an affair with another man. Acting like a woman scorned, she lashed out at the *ANC* leadership, including her husband.

> "The *NP* [National Party] elite is getting into bed with the *ANC* in order to preserve its silken sheets, and the leadership of the *ANC* is getting into bed with the *NP* to enjoy this new–found luxury."

This and other statements of hers immensely appealed to the younger militants of the *ANC*. And in a wink, she was rehabilitated to her old prestigious stature with the title "Mother of the Nation" restored. Because of name recognition, she polled No. 5 in popularity among *ANC* voters in April 1994 elections.

Under pressure from senior *ANC* officials, Mandela divorced his wife in early 1996. The reason: foreign investment was discouraged by her presence in an apparent present or future position of power.

The Repeal of Apartheid

President de Klerk and the *National Party* wasted no time in 1990–1 to repeal *apartheid* laws in South Africa.

VIOLENCE OF THE 1990s

Repeal of *apartheid* meant that it was legal for black people to be in any area they wish at any time.

Criminal opportunists used the changes in the law to "do their thing" both in Johannesburg and in the black townships with virtual impunity. If accosted by the police, they claimed to be part of *ANC*'s effort to throw off the chains of *apartheid*. The police, fearing an "incident" with attendant publicity, did nothing even under the most suspicious of circumstances.

Compounding the situation was *ANC* insistence that criminals in prison for offenses related to resistance of *apartheid* were entitled to immediate freedom. This led to release of a "political prisoner" who in 1986 had planted a pipe bomb which killed three White women and injured 87 others.

At night there was almost no one on the streets of the formerly bustling city of Johannesburg. Luxury hotels closed, reopening several months later at bargain prices to attract customers. Fences and walls around homes in white suburbs grew higher and higher. Prison bars at the windows, together with elaborate security systems became the order of the day. Purse snatching and petty thievery were common.

In the rural areas and small towns it was no better. White people were brutally assaulted and killed without cause or for robbery. One elderly, retired farmer rigged his house with booby–trapped shotguns actuated by almost invisible nylon fishing line. He explained that his wife was bedridden and helpless and "the police don't come any more."

Morale of the South African Defense Force and local police organizations descended to an all–time low. Turnover in personnel was high, resulting in a training period of only six weeks. Recruits had to be constantly reminded they were a "legal" target for just about any gun–toting person, criminal or otherwise, who bore a grudge against the police in general or simply wanted to escape criminal responsibility for an act.

Constitutional Negotiations

In 1991 the competing elements in South Africa began meeting informally and later in conferences of *CODESA,—* "Congress for a Democratic South Africa." The white leadership met demands of the *ANC* when possible and refused them when impossible. Prior to negotiations, *apartheid* laws had been repealed and political exiles (often common criminals, numbering 50,000) were allowed to return to South Africa with amnesty from charges that they left the country illegally (but not from other charges).

The talks were interrupted periodically by rising tides of violence, but settled down in May 1993 with a renewed sense of purpose. Political sniping from the conservatives had led de Klerk to have a national referendum on the direction desired in the talks by White South Africans. His efforts were supported by 70% of whites, who thus for the first time voted to share power peacefully with the black majority.

The *ANC* had to be careful of what was said because blacks distrusted the idea that whites would genuinely negotiate away their control of South Africa. In statements outside of the conference room, Mandela was careful to level gross insults at de Klerk calculated to reassure his own supporters that he wasn't giving in to white pressures.

Inside the room, there was a consensus: (1) an interim government had to be elected to draw a permanent constitution and to govern, and it (2) would have to see to minority (i.e. white) protection. Black power without limit was quietly discarded by the *ANC* senior leadership (but not its membership). Why?

President Thabo Mbeki

The approach of white negotiators brought home to the *ANC* the idea that revolutionary skills are not productive of administrative ability needed to run a large nation.

A New Constitution

Ink was signed on an interim constitution on November 17, 1993, which was the result of months of painstaking negotiations. The substance of the document was a fundamental victory for the *ANC* and a radical departure from the most widely accepted principles of democratic government. This was necessary, in the opinion of *ANC* leadership, to prevent regionalism and factionalism in the government which would come into being in 1994.

The constitution provided for elections and specified that the 400–member National Assembly members *would not* represent any specific constituency. They were to be chosen from lists prepared by each national party and from their state units, selected from popularity polls. The number of seats for each party is based on the party's percentage of the total (national) vote. A Senate of 90 members consists of 10 members selected by each of the nine states made up from the previous four provinces and 10 black homelands.

This in effect places all power in the hands of the national parties. Most important was the fact that it is an interim constitution—the legislature was charged with the responsibility to draft and enact a new one within five years. At the time it was adopted, there was a reasonable expectation that the *ANC,* particularly in the absence of *Inkatha*–Zulu voting, would win more than two–thirds of the popular vote. If that happened, the party would be in a position to dictate the language of a new constitution.

After its adoption, plans proceeded forward toward elections on April 26, 1994. The *ANC,* in anticipation of the elections, had started a registration drive the previous March (1993). Thorny questions remained to be settled—who was a voter, what were the requirements or lack thereof, where and how would he or she vote?

A Last Minute Accord

Because of increased political violence and apprehension over the imminent elections, President de Klerk declared a state of emergency in KwaZulu–Natal on March 31, 1994, which infuriated Chief Buthelezi and made him even more adamant. According to statements, he demanded the constitution be amended to secure the position of King Goodwill Zwelithini and the historic Zulu kingdom. As part of the state of emergency, 3,000 members of the SADF were dispatched to enforce it, all to no avail. On April 5, 15,000 Zulus armed with spears and clubs marched through the town of Empangeni; the SADF forces considered them too dangerous to disarm.

The election commission said balloting in KwaZulu would have to be postponed. Mandela rejected this, and the possibility of a constitutional violation because of delay was raised. International mediators, including Henry Kissinger from the U.S., failed to budge the parties who continued their intense negotiations. Finally there

Chief Mangosuthu Buthelezi

was a breakthrough on April 19th after two days of talks. The Zulus would, after all, participate in the balloting, abandoning demands for amendment of the constitution. But there were guarantees as to the continued status of the monarchy and the kingdom of KwaZulu–Natal.

The real nature of the settlement was not apparent until almost a month after the elections. More than a million acres of KwaZulu–Natal land was promised to Zwelithini. Buthelezi (jobless after the elections) would become Minister of Home Affairs in the expected new government lead by Mandela. A quiet session of the KwaZulu legislative assembly approved the land deal on April 22, 1994. And thus Zulu participation in the election came to pass. One further matter is important: the Chief and the King were aware of increasing Zulu impatience with the idea that they would not be participating in the first elections in modern South African history.

The Elections

Elaborate and painstaking preparations were made for the first popular balloting including all races in South Africa.

The problem of illiteracy was immense—50%—so it was decided that the pictures of the leaders of each party would be listed above that choice on the ballot. But Clarence Makwetu, leader of the *Pan Africanist Congress,* who resembles Mandela closely, wound up in the number one position on the ballot. People were told to look down the list carefully for the true Mandela. Some white employers told black employees the only way to vote *against* de Klerk was to put an "X" by his picture!

Overcoming well–grounded fears, and waiting in line for hours on end, more than 70% voted. The time for voting was extended for 24 hours because it took longer than expected. Another several days were used to tally the result, which was announced on May 10, 1994.

Other Political Parties and Groups

The *Freedom Front (FF)* was formed in March 1994. The *Freedom Front* is headed by former defense chief General Constand Viljoen whose less than right–wing approach appealed to many conservatives.

White conservatives formerly belonged exclusively to the *Conservative Party (CP),* which is led by the Dr. Ferdi Hartzenberg, successor of Andries Treurnicht. Its principal objective was the creation of an all–white state by the interim constitution, a proposition that was never taken seriously. It refused to register as a political party for the elections.

The *Afrikaner Resistance Movement (ARM)* is a right–wing militant group which also refused to participate in elections. It is led by Eugene TerreBlanche, who was recently sentenced to prison for his anti–state activities.

The *Democratic Party (DP)* is the successor of two liberal parties popular among English speakers which opposed *apartheid.* It is headed by Tony Leon.

The *Pan Africanist Congress (PAC)* and its militant wing, the *Azanian Peoples Army)* is a radical black party led by Clarence Makwetu; it is a fringe party which adopted a slogan "one settler [a white], one bullet."

The results, awaited with great suspense, were predicted before announced. The *ANC* did well in areas where it was expected to as did the *National Party* and the *Inkatha Freedom Party.* The *National Party* did well among Coloured and Asiatic Indian voters. The *Freedom Front* of the right did well in areas dominated by rural whites.

King Goodwill Zwelethini

The ANC in Power

Once in power the *ANC* demonstrated the balancing of ideology and practicality required by the responsibility of governance. Its initial budget envisioned a million new housing units and a million new jobs over a five-year period, without the necessity of new taxes.

The Restitution of Land Rights Act, a very controversial measure, was adopted in late 1994 and established a Land Claims Commission and a Land Claims Court. The act directs "balancing the desirability of remedying past human rights violations against...the need to avoid major social disruption."

South Africa's arms industry, condemned by liberals, was recognized as the moneymaker it was and maintained. As a concession to liberal critics, arms exports would be limited, said the government, to nations using the arms for legitimate purposes and not for human rights violations. Since no known purchase order had ever been submitted with this as a justification for purchase, one was left to wonder how it would be implemented.

To the chagrin of those who preferred a state-controlled economy, foreign investment was encouraged and the government announced plans for a significant privatization of state-owned companies. The two policies were interrelated, for privatization was seen as a means of assuring the international business community that the state was moving towards a more liberal economy.

So great was President Mandela's moral authority that he could successfully say "No" to the more outrageous demands from various sectors of the liberation struggle. When the leader of former guerrilla forces threatened to return to armed struggle over problems arising from the integration of these forces into the South African army, Mandela warned against a "suicidal plot."

Tensions between the *ANC* government and *Inkatha* continued, though the bloody warfare which had characterized the parties' relationship was significantly diminished.

Zulu Rumblings

After the April 1994 elections, control over Zulu King Goodwill Zwelithini's royal purse and security guard passed to the *ANC*–dominated government, weakening the influence of his uncle, Chief Mangosuthu Buthelezi, over the monarchy. A celebration commemorating 19th–century warrior–king Shaka Zulu in September touched off a vitriolic quarrel between the two, particularly because at the same time, the king was seeking to replace Buthelezi with Prince Mcwayizeni Israel Zulu, a member of the executive committee of the *ANC*.

Buthelezi in turn used his support in the Kwazulu–Natal legislature to establish a *House of Traditional Leaders* consisting of all the Zulu kings, princes and chiefs in which Zwelithini would be no more than an equal. *ANC* opposed the move; tensions remained high. Even Nelson Mandela tried to intervene and mediate a settlement between the king and the chief with no results.

Social Discontent

Tensions ran high among South Africa's black population. During the election campaign they were promised far, far more than could be realistically delivered. As the months wore on after the contest, their lives have not changed. Symptoms of this malaise include a high crime rate, near–anarchy, corruption, squatting on land, moving into nearby homes after ousting the occupants, illegal strikes. As in the U.S., some in South Africa have viewed unrest, particularly in the form of protest marches, as an opportunity to loot business areas, particularly retail stores.

All of this was strongly condemned by President Nelson Mandela in his February 1995 speech opening parliament. He criticized what he termed "a culture of entitlement," and accused blacks who "misread freedom to mean license." He condemned those guilty of murder of police officers, taking hostages, riots, looting and other crimes.

The Constitutional Commission completed its work in May 1996. The notable provisions pave the way for expropriation of and transfer of land to black people. It calls for market–based compensation which the government cannot afford. The Senate is changed to a Provincial Council of premiers of the nine provinces and others chosen provincially.

The Supreme Court initially disapproved the new constitution, but accepted it with changes. Adopted in 1996, it has a Bill of Rights that is far more liberal than that of the U.S. It essentially continues the government without change—maintaining a strong central authority, with the powers of provinces and smaller areas being limited.

From Transition to Transformation

The *ANC* party congress in December 1997 chose Thabo Mbeki as party President. President Mandela increasingly relinquished governmental affairs to Mbeki in preparation for the 1999 presidential elections. It put Mbeki in the spotlight. There was little question Mbeki would be the party's presidential nominee, nor any question the *ANC* would win the election.

Thabo Mbeki had long been groomed for leadership. Son of one of the principal *ANC* leaders, Govan Mbeki, Thabo was early marked for leadership by his father and his father's friend and colleague, Nelson Mandela. He left South Africa in 1962 for England where he studied economics at Sussex University; his Master's thesis was on small businesses in Ghana and Nigeria. Like his father Mbeki was a member of the Communist Party and in 1970 he went to Russia for military training. On his return to South Africa in 1990 he pragmatically resigned from the party.

Mbeki's brief biography captures the ambiguity of the man. Steeped in Marxism, he is also trained in Western economics. Nurtured in the idealism of a revolutionary movement and well-versed in its Stalinist organizational style, he is practical and pragmatic. The breadth of his intellectual background would be needed to hold together his coalition partners and to get a handle on a legacy of problems created by apartheid.

Thabo Mbeki's accession to power marked a change in tone and language in the *ANC*'s relationship with South Africa's white minority. The shift was signaled by Nelson Mandela's valedictory speech to the 1997 *ANC* party conference. In this speech, reportedly prepared by Mbeki, President Mandela departed from the soothing rhetoric of multiracialism that had eased the transition to majority rule. Whites had "demonstrated consistently" a desire to cling to the privileges they enjoyed under apartheid. Some were accused of being involved in a "counter-revolutionary conspiracy." It was vintage Marxist rhetoric, stylistically out of character, highly controversial, and an affront to those white South Africans who had long opposed apartheid.

During his first term as president, Mbeki would repeatedly return to the theme. "Racist" would become a potent political charge leveled against white critics of his policies. At times it seemed President

A view of Rhino Peak
K Kohler, Courtesy KwaZulu-Natal Tourism Authority

Mbeki saw criticism as proof that mentalities had not yet been transformed in the new South Africa. "Racist" had the added advantage of undermining black support of any such criticism. Thabo Mbeki's emphasis on race was one indication of how difficult the transition from liberation movement to political party would be for the *ANC*.

The *ANC* has discovered being the party of power is quite different than being in opposition, and this has deeply affected its relationship with its traditional partners, the *Congress of South African Trade Unions* (*COSATU*) and the *South African Communist Party* (*SACP*). Membership in the three groups often overlaps. Leadership of the two partners is frequently co-opted and interlocks with ANC leadership. After the 1999 election, for example, COSATU had to replace four of its principal officers elevated to parliament by virtue of membership on the ANC lists.

COSATU's new president, Willy Madisha, developed his career in the teachers' union and the *SACP*. Its new general secretary, Zwelinzima Vavi, was a National Union of Mineworkers (NUM) organizer as well as a member of the *SACP*.

Both *COSATU* and the *SACP* remain deeply socialist in orientation. They were not part of the process that created a major piece of the government's economic legislation, GEAR (Growth, Employment and Redistribution), and both fear GEAR leans much too much towards a liberal capitalist economy. Both seem to prefer nationalization to privatization. The collision of the three partners seems inevitable, though "unity of the movement," at least in the short term, trumps the obvious divisions among the partners.

Big election issues for the *ANC* were jobs and crime. Unemployment was unofficially estimated at 50%, making it one of the country's most urgent problems. An estimated 4.7 million people were unemployed and looking for work. GEAR had set a goal of 252,000 new jobs for 1997, but this did not adequately take into account the continuing recession in mining. When the price of gold fell to $280, its lowest point in years, the industry had to cut 50,000 mining jobs. Restructuring of the industry to increase efficiency and productivity also contributed to the shrinking of mining jobs.

The close relationship of the *ANC* and *COSATU* is always at the heart of any discussion of job creation and retention. In the run-up to the 1999 elections, the government was already locked in contentious pay negotiations with its public service unions, a formidable political force. The government desperately needs to restructure its civil service; in some provinces nearly 90% of the budget goes to salaries. But to do this it needs the cooperation of the unions, and the unions need to be able to take some tangible benefit back to their members.

There is little talk in South Africa of Export Processing Zones which have done so much to stimulate employment in Mauritius. In these investors are given special incentives—tax holidays, duty free imports and exports—to set up small factories in which local or imported materials undergo some degree of processing before being exported. But in South Africa, with tight control of the labor market exercised by its unions, anything that suggested larger employment, but with lower wages, was anathema.

The 1999 Election

South Africa's second multiparty democratic election took place in early June 1999. Some 42 political parties participated. They ranged from *God's People Party*, dedicated to fighting Satan, to *Keep it Straight and Simple* (you work out the acronym). The *ANC* overwhelmed all comers, nearly winning a two-thirds majority with 266 seats. The *National Party*, burdened with the historical weight of apartheid and deprived of forceful leadership, fell to a fourth-place finish. Not even calling itself the *New National Party* (*NNP*) helped to slow its decline; it won only 28 seats in the legislature.

Its role as official opposition was assumed by the *Democratic Party* a distant second-place finisher with a mere 38 seats. The *Democratic Party* is the home of white liberals and has benefited from *NNP* defections, especially the Western Cape Province. Its leader, Tony Leon, is articulate and fiery as an orator. As leader of the opposition he has provided some of the best and much-needed criticism of the *ANC*. Chief Buthelezi's *IFP* won 34 seats.

The only other party to win more than ten seats in the new parliament was the *United Democratic Movement* with its biracial leadership. Bantu Holomisa, its president, is a former military general and former deputy to Nelson Mandela after the 1994 elections. Popular, but perhaps too honest for his own good, Holomisa was thrown out of the party in 1996 after accusing some of his government colleagues of corruption. Roelf Meyer, an early defector from the withering *NP*, served as Holomisa's deputy leader. After the election Meyer seemed to disappear from politics and it is doubtful the *UDM* will cut much of a figure in upcoming local elections.

South African voters do not vote directly for their representatives and have

Nelson Mandela

AP/Wide World Photo

President de Klerk and Mr. Nelson Mandela (February 1990)

no idea who will represent them because of South Africa's proportional representation system. Parties create national and provincial lists and individuals enter parliament in terms of their ranking on those lists, which represent much internal politicking. Winnie Madikizela-Mandela was number ten on the *ANC* national list, guaranteeing her a position in parliament.

In June 2000 the *Democratic Party* (*DP*), under the leadership of Tony Leon, merged with the *New National Party* (*NNP*) to form the *Democratic Alliance* (*DA*). In many ways it was a merger of fish and fowl. The *DP* was the inheritor of South Africa's white-minority liberal tradition. Formed prior to the 1989 elections, it had assumed the mantle of the *Progressive Federal Party*, which itself had replaced the *Progressive Party* (*PP*). Founded in 1959, the *PP* was long represented by a single MP—Helen Suzman, one of apartheid's most vigorous critics. The *NNP* was, of course, the recently re-baptized *National Party*, which had created and enforced apartheid for 46 years.

In many ways the merger represented a voluntary death for the *NNP*. Loathed by black Africans as the party of apartheid, the *NNP* had little to offer, and its cosmetic name change proved of little value in the last election. It won less than 7% of the votes cast. The question that remained was whether its negative reputation would damage the new *Democratic Alliance*.

According to the constitution, MPs lose their seats in parliament if their party is disbanded. It was therefore agreed that the *NNP* and *DP* would continue to exist in parliament until the 2004 national election. Together the two parties would have a parliamentary delegation of 66 members—small potatoes in face of the *ANC*'s 266.

Mbeki and Transformation

Thabo Mbeki's presidency inaugurated a new phase in South African politics. From the transition years of Nelson Mandela, the system moves to transformation. Nelson Mandela had used his moral authority to convince his fellow Africans to accept the new political system. His moderation and restraint similarly convinced whites to support the new dispensation. A Truth and Reconciliation Commission sought to soothe the emotional pains on both sides of the racial divide. Acceptance and reconciliation seemingly gained, the new government moved to transform the legacy of injustice that characterizes contemporary South Africa. Symptomatic are four laws passed early in the year 2000: the Promotion of Access to Information Bill, the Promotion of Administrative Justice Bill, the Preferential Procurement Policy Framework and the Promotion of Equality and Prevention of Unfair Discrimination Bill.

Together the four bills extend provisions of the South African Constitution, already the most liberal in the world. They are intended to transform the relationship of citizens to their government. Two of the bills give ordinary citizens the right to make the

Winnie Madikizela Mandela

government—at all levels—accountable. The Promotion of Administrative Justice Bill forces government to create mechanisms to explain their decisions, such as cutting welfare grants, to affected members the public. In theory bureaucrats will think before acting, realizing they may have to justify any action they take.

The Promotion of Access to Information Bill is a reaction to the secrecy with which the former white regime shrouded state affairs, but seems to go much further than opening government to the scrutiny of its constituents. The bill affirms a right of access to "any information held by a public or private body," subject only to restrictions that are reasonable and justifiable. Its goal is to foster a culture of transparency and accountability in public and private bodies and permits the government to act in pursuit of these objectives when it is in the public interest. In short, the government is granted potential enormous power to probe "private bodies."

A wide list of exclusions may limit the potential impact of the bill: It will not apply to the Cabinet and its committees, to judicial functions, or to individual members of the national or provincial legislatures. Individual privacy is specifically protected as regards such things as tax records, commercial and confidential information. Defense, security and foreign affairs information is also excluded.

The two remaining bills seek to transform apartheid's legacy of racial hurt and injustice. The Preferential Procurement Policy Framework Bill provides that companies which best reflect the country's racial demographics be given preference when the government solicits bids for contracts or purchases. Probably better known to Americans as "affirmative action" and to South Africans as "positive discrimination," the bill is designed to redress post-apartheid inequalities. Preferences are to be given to people who have been historically disadvantaged on the basis of race, gender or disability.

The Promotion of Equality and Prevention of Unfair Discrimination Bill seeks nothing less than an end of discrimination. It closes the books on apartheid and on 300 years of legalized racism and discrimination. Considered by many as second only to the constitution in asserting and protecting the principals of human rights, the new law bans both behavior and attitudes. Its scope is vast. Discrimination is defined in the broadest possible terms: any act "that has or is likely to have, the direct or indirect effect of unjustly or unfairly causing disadvantage to a person or group of persons on one or more prohibited grounds."

The "prohibited grounds," seventeen in number, include "race, gender, sex, pregnancy, marital status, ethnic or social origin, color, sexual orientation, age, disability, religion, conscience, belief, culture, language and birth or any other recognized ground."

Effective implementation of such laws, each of extraordinary breadth, will depend on budgetary allocations necessary to set up guidelines, procedures and hearing venues—often specially charged courts. The ambiguities of provisions in the four laws suggest that years of legal wrangling can also be expected before full implementation is achieved. In the meantime the government has to deal with issues more pressing.

Crime

South Africa is awash in a tidal wave of crime that threatens to sink the state's capacity to protect its citizens. Car–jacking has become one of the most common crimes. Stolen vehicles are taken to the depressed townships surrounding large cities and are either stripped for parts, reregistered (often with the assistance of corrupt officials) or exported to neighboring countries by crime syndicates. Between January and November 1998 there were 32.7 car–jackings for every 100,000 South Africans, up from 29.1 in 1997. Given a population of 40.5 million, that represents 13,000 car–jackings in an 11–month period. The police and courts remain helpless before the onslaught: only one in ten carjacking cases ends up in court and only one in 50 ends in a conviction. Only in South Africa, one suspects, would someone invent a flame–thrower for car security. It blasts out a jet of fire to engulf the hijacker and your car's finish is untouched!

Frequently the car-jacking results in violence to the car owner. Kwon Yong-koo, the 50–year old president of Daewoo South Africa, was shot dead in his car in what appeared to be an attempted car hijacking. His death sent off alarms in an already–nervous business community. Samsung ordered its expatriates to stay at home after dark, and one Daewoo director darkly warned that "this is the worst thing to happen to South Africa." (Thirteen Korean concerns have South African investments worth about $100 million.) Foreign diplomats as well as foreign businessmen are the targets of South African criminals, which only increases publicity and further embarrasses the state.

In 1996 the Lebanese *chargé d'affaires* was burgled twice in ten days, prompting a speedy repatriation to Lebanon where he thought he would be safer. "Johannesburg is a jungle," he told the press. "The problem in Beirut is political, not criminal." Things were no better in 1999. The son of the Nigerian High Commissioner was abducted and held for a couple of hours, and Burundi's ambassador was forced to hand over his car to gunmen—the second time he had been attacked in a week. Putting a brave face on things, President Mandela told parliament in February that the "statistics show there has been a reduction or stabilization in most serious crimes." Absent from the gallery to hear the president's speech was James Bartleman, Canada's High Commissioner. He was in the hospital with bruises and a broken nose after being mugged in his hotel.

According to Interpol statistics, South Africa's murder rate was the world's third highest in 1997, 56.9 per 100,000 people, behind only Swaziland and Colombia. South African police statistics show there were nearly 140 murders or attempted murders a day in 1998. At least 30 people are shot dead every day, and there are more than four million registered firearms in the country. Millions more are unregistered, creating a culture of violence against which the police are increasingly helpless. The police themselves are an object of assault. There were 216 members of the South African police killed on duty in 1998. Since South Africa became a democracy in 1994, 1,000 police officers have been murdered. It is a scale of anti-police violence unprecedented in the world. In some places, private security firms guard police stations.

Rape attacks are more than double the annual murder rate in South Africa—116 rapes per 100,000, making South Africa the rape capital of the world. A South African journalist shocked her readers with a first-person account of her own rape. "Every half minute in South Africa a woman is raped and on April 1 it was my turn," began Charlene Smith's story. The ugly story that unfolded has forced a crime-hardened country to face the shame of sexual violence and the contempt of women it implies. In Johannesburg, which has the highest incidence of rape in South Africa, results of a survey among 4,000 woman were released in early 1999 that showed one in three women had been raped in the past year. In a related survey conducted among 1,500 school children in Soweto township, a quarter of all boys interviewed said that "jackrolling"—a South African term for recreational gang rape—was fun.

The Mbeki government announced its most visible attack on the crime problem in early 2000. "Operation Crackdown," as it was called, targeted illegal immigrants, particularly Mozambicans. Thousands were arrested, particularly in the Johannesburg area, and, it was claimed, valuable loot and arms were recovered. The population of a transit center near the town which held those awaiting deportation soared from 2,000 to 8,000. For a while a deportation train bearing 2,500 people left for Mozambique every few days.

Human rights activists criticized the operation as a short sighted publicity stunt that only pandered to South African xenophobia. In practical terms, it required saturation policing and could not be sustained. When crime persisted, South Africa's minister of safety and security, Steve Tshwete, ordered an indefinite moratorium on the release of crime statistics, saying the system for collecting was flawed and unreliable. Their biggest problem, of course, was their capacity to embarrass the government.

The moratorium was still in place in mid-2001, and crimes of property and person continued, unabated. Johannesburg and its suburbs were among the hardest hit areas. In May some two dozen businesses in one suburb petitioned their mayor to stop the crime wave crippling their area, or else, they said, "we will close our doors and retrench hundreds." In the suburb of Soweto, all commuter services had to be cancelled because electrical cables controlling the system had been stolen overnight.

One justice department official, speaking, it should be noted, on his own behalf, indicated that some 5% of all cars on the country's roads were "reregistered stolen vehicles." Criminal syndicates were probably responsible, he said, for about 80% of property crimes, and South Africans who bought cheap goods from "truck jackings" without regard to their source only provided incentive for continued predation.

The sense for many that crime, especially violent crime, was out of control was probably best symbolized by the case of Nkosi Johnson, the 12-year old AIDS activist who had movingly addressed the 2000 International AIDS conference in Durban. Dying of AIDS himself, Johnson was robbed at gunpoint in his own Johannesburg home. Armed men broke into the house, threatened to kill his nurse, ordered him to be silent, and stole his television, CD player and other valuables.

Aerial view of bustling Cape Town

Education

Among the most important issues facing the Mbeki government are the distribution of social services, particularly education. The crisis in education has been ongoing, a consequence of apartheid policies on curriculum and funding and of the absence of a clear policy direction from the *ANC* government. President Mbeki has spoken often and with conviction of an African Renaissance. His new African century must produce doctors and engineers and scientists, but the education system remains a shambles. Its desperate state is symbolized by the results of matriculation exams announced in January 2000. Overall, only 48.9% passed, down from equally deplorable results in 1999 when only 49.3% passed.

The worst results came from rural areas where issues of race and gender predominate. The bottom slot was occupied by the Northern Province, which usually comes in last on most lists of social indicators. Only 35.2% passed the exams, which mark students' readiness for advanced education.

Causes are manifold, and certainly the basic material provisioning—classrooms and books—is tragically slighted. Beyond the physical, however, the whole delivery system—an educational bureaucracy, too many of whom are unqualified, unprepared and unmotivated—remains a challenge. A culture of learning has yet to be cultivated, and individual classrooms remain sites of threat and intimidation against both staff and students. Those who can afford it are sending their children to private schools.

When President Mbeki appointed Kader Asmal as education minister, there were high expectations. By many accounts he had been one of Nelson Mandela's most successful cabinet officers while in charge of the water affairs and forestry portfolio. Against daunting odds, Asmal has begun to show results at education. With a 57.9% pass rate, the 2001 matriculation exams showed a 9% improvement over 1999's 48.9% pass rate.

The results continued to reflect the legacy of apartheid and the unequal distribution of educational resources. Lowest pass rates were recorded in the poor provinces with huge black and rural majorities. Well-endowed private schools, on the other hand, scored an average 99% pass rate.

Gender also continued to be a factor. The pass rate among females was significantly lower—55.2% as opposed to 61.3% for males. Although the results project a worrisome under-utilization of women, more worrisome was the reduced number of students taking the maths and sciences exams—only 58%—with a relatively low pass rate of 45.1%. One teachers' union warned of the "dire consequences" for the skills necessary to support a modern economy.

Asmal has announced that mother-tongue education is soon to become compulsory for the first four years of schooling, which may positively effect students' grasp of new materials and ideas.

Northern and Eastern Cape provinces demonstrate the deplorable conditions in which education must function in South Africa's poorest areas. In Northern Province there was a shortage of about 19,000 classrooms; in Eastern Cape, a shortage of 15,538. Of 4,155 schools in Northern Province, 78% had no electricity and 49% no water. Almost three-quarters of the schools in the Eastern Cape were without electricity, and almost a third were without water.

Education is but one example of the government's difficulties in delivering social services. Many of these were to have been handled by provincial governments, but they have been wracked by a variety of problems. In some provincial education departments personnel costs eat up more than 90% of the budget, leaving little left over for spending on school facilities, and the provinces have limited taxing powers of their own. These can be exercised only when they do not prejudice national economic policies and economic activity across provincial boundaries.

Poor financial controls by provincial governments over the funds they are allocated by central authorities also affect their capacity to deliver on education. In Mpumalanga, for example, the province was not even sure of its total debt commitments at the end of the last fiscal year and required a $38 million bail-out from the central government in early 2001. Free State, Eastern Cape and KwaZulu-Natal all had to be rescued in 1997.

Some provincial governments have failed as instruments of service delivery because they have been paralyzed by internal bickering. In most cases the conflict, exacerbated certainly by personality and ambition, is between *ANC* "neo-liberals," on one side, and the party's left-wing alliance partners, frustrated with the slow pace of social and economic transformation. Executives in Free State, Gauteng, and Mpumalanga, for example, have all been replaced by the *ANC* to assure party discipline. At the provincial level the ideological conflicts that pit *South African Communist Party* and *COSATU* loyalists against *ANC* liberals simply mirror the larger problems of the *ANC*'s triple alliance. But the consequence is that the effectiveness of the provincial government as a delivery system is compromised.

Municipal Elections

The government's failure to deliver on its promises was one of the issues seized by the opposition in the municipal elections of December 2000. Local government had been completely overhauled previously. Jurisdictions had been combined, and municipalities were reduced from 543 to 284. For the first time black townships and white suburbs were combined in a single unit. Six "megacities," each with a single powerful mayor, were also created. Some 8,900 seats were contested by 79 political parties fielding 30,477 candidates.

Widely billed as a verdict on President Mbeki's first 18 months in office, the elections were essentially a battle between the *ANC* and the recently created *Democratic Alliance*. Campaigning aggressively, Tony Leon effectively mobilized resentments in the black community over President Mbeki's refusal to admit that HIV causes AIDS and to make life-sustaining drugs available. It did not help the *ANC*'s case that Cape Town, controlled by the *DA*, routinely made anti-retrovirals available to rape victims and HIV-positive expectant mothers.

Discontent with the failure of the *ANC* to deliver on its slogans of "Jobs, jobs, jobs" and "A better life for all" created similar opportunities for the *DA* to make some inroads into black townships. The *DA* also successfully pitched its message to the colored and Indian communities, both of which were feeling increasingly marginalized by *ANC* policies.

When indications of an anti-*ANC* backlash emerged, the party brought in Nelson Mandela who labeled the *Democratic Alliance* a party of "white bosses" and "black stooges." When the final results came in, the *DA* did surprisingly well, picking up 22% of the vote. In the 1999 voting, its constituent parts had won only 16%. The *ANC* won a conclusive 59%, but that was down from the 66% it had won in the 1999 elections. In KwZulu-Natal, the *Inkatha Freedom Party* held its own, but nationally only won 9% of the vote.

The *DA* won overwhelmingly in white areas, but it also won even the poorest colored and Indian areas. In the black townships of Soweto and Thembisa it won 5%, and in Alexandria 7%. The *ANC* had focused its fiercest energies on Cape Town, South Africa's second largest city and a melting pot of white, black and mixed races, but lost to the *Democratic Alliance* which prevailed by a relatively small margin.

After the elections Tony Leon claimed the *Democratic Alliance* had entered a new phase. It was no longer just the official opposition, but now should be thought of as an alternative to the *ANC*. Despite Leon's enthusiasm, however, it's doubtful one can attribute any indications of seismic change to the election. Certainly the *ANC* failed to mobilize its base of support—only 48% of registered voters participated in the election. It's also clear the election sounded a wake-up call for the *ANC* and perhaps even gave ammunition to Thabo Mbeki's enemies within the party.

Truth and Reconciliation Commission

Racial tensions still exist in South Africa, but given the bitterness of past experience, it is remarkable that any harmony at all is possible. One important institution which helped advance the reconciliation process is the Truth and Reconciliation Commission (TRC) established by act of parliament in 1995. Its purpose was to investigate crimes committed during the *apartheid* era, and as commission chairman, President Mandela appointed Archbishop Desmond Tutu, the 1984 Nobel Peace Prize winner. Tutu had been the first black Anglican Dean of Johannesburg and had led the church in South Africa into an active struggle against *apartheid*. Time and time again he courageously told those in power their racist policies defied the will of God and would not succeed. As one of the leading figures in the anti–*apartheid* fight Archbishop Tutu had immense moral authority, all of which would be needed to carry out the Commission's mandate.

One TRC panel met over a two-year period, heard over 20,000 witnesses and compiled a dossier of human rights crimes committed by all sides during the *apartheid* era. A 3,500–page report submitted to President Mandela in October

Flea Market at Pretoria

Summary of *ANC* Activities, 1990–1994

1990–1: *ANC* engaged in fund–raising in U.S. and other overseas locations. There was a readjustment and evaluation of possibilities and alternatives. The result was an encouragement of *ANC* and *MK* aggression against *Inkatha*–Zulus.

1991–2: Fund raising abroad, consolidation at home. Continued aggression directed against Zulus. Preliminary conferences with whites via CODESA, with posturing, walk–outs and ultimatums, some of which were impossible.

1992–3: Continued confrontation, but greater emphasis on cooperation, all without surrender of goals. Constitutional negotiations held with *Inkatha* absent, a pre-empt by virtue of numbers.

1993–4: After 23 months, a negotiated settlement on constitution and elections, to be held if necessary without *Inkatha*–Zulu participation. *ANC* went to the brink of disaster without the Zulus, but retreated at the last moment in 1994 in order to include them in the elections.

April 26–30, 1994: Elections (the voting period was extended).

1998, marked the conclusion of its investigative work. Even before it was released the report engendered criticism from all sides. F.W. de Klerk went to court and prevented publication of material linking him to state–sponsored bombings in the 1980s. The *ANC* too made a last–minute bid to get a court order blocking findings that the party had committed human rights crimes in its fight against *apartheid*. Tutu denounced the attempt and accused the *ANC* of tyranny. "The fact that they are a majority party in government," he said, "does not give them privileges. I did not fight against people who thought they were God to replace them with others."

There was guilt aplenty in the report. Archbishop Tutu, ever emotional, said he was "appalled at the evil we have uncovered." The most serious culprit was the South African State itself. The State, including the government, civil service and security forces was, the report said, "the primary perpetrator of gross violations of human rights in South Africa." The Commission's analysis of why this came about was simple and direct: Racism was at the center of state action designed to protect the power and privilege of a racial minority. As a consequence, white citizens adopted a dehumanizing attitude towards black citizens. They ceased to think of them as citizens and this "created a climate in which gross atrocities committed against them were seen as legitimate." Against its perceived enemies, the State engaged in torture, abduction, arson, sabotage and murder. It even investigated chemical and biological means of rendering blacks infertile. *Apartheid*–era President P.W. Botha was held responsible for human rights violations sanctioned by the State Security Council, an inner cabinet that directed *apartheid's* implementation.

The commission also held the opponents of *apartheid* responsible for their actions. Its report emphasized the legitimacy of the liberation struggle, but held the *ANC* and other liberation movements morally and politically accountable for human rights violations. Thabo Mbeki, for example, had told the TRC that a number of *ANC* members—including 34 in Angola when the party was in exile—were executed by the movement's own security officials. At least one of those was wrongly executed by two *ANC* cadres who themselves were later put to death.

Important political figures did not escape the Commission's condemnation. Winnie Madikizela-Mandela was found accountable for crimes committed by the Mandela United Football Club (MUFC). Killing, torture, assault and arson were all MUFC activities. Madikizela-Mandela herself was aware of this criminal activity, it reported, and chose not to address it.

Mangosuthu Buthelezi was held accountable as leader of the *Inkatha Freedom Party* for all the violence committed by its members. Between 1982 and 1994 *IFP* supporters caused the deaths of about 3,800 people in KwaZulu-Natal province alone, against 1,100 caused by the *ANC*. It was, the Commission thought, a "systematic pattern" of murder and attacks by the *IFP* against its opponents, often in collusion with State security forces.

The TRC report was, as one reporter described it, "an encyclopedia of *apartheid*," but many wondered just how much reconciliation would be achieved by exposing the dark secrets of a dark past. In accepting the report, Nelson Mandela said the "wounds of the period of repression and resistance are too deep to have been healed by the TRC alone." Much of the criticism leveled at the Commission came from a lack of understanding of its purposes. It was never meant to punish people, just to expose their crimes. The hearings allowed some families to bring closure to uncertainty over the fate of loved ones. For others, old wounds are too painful to be assuaged. In choosing between justice and reconciliation, clearly South Africa's leadership had chosen the later. There would be no Nuremberg trial for South Africa, but neither, one suspects, would reconciliation be easy.

Less well known were two additional TRC panels on amnesty and reparations. The Commission was empowered to grant amnesty to those who asked for it and a separate panel was established to hold these hearings. Applicants were required to prove their crime had a political motive

The magnificent forests of northern Transvaal

White horses, San Rock Art, Drakensberg Mountains
G Stewart, Courtesy KwaZulu-Natal Tourism Authority

or was performed acting under direct orders. They were also required to offer full disclosure of their crimes and demonstrate genuine contrition.

The commission received over 7,000 applications for amnesty. By the end of 1999 6,343 had been processed and 5,310 rejected outright. It rejected the killers of Chris Hani—not a political crime the panel said. It also rejected the amnesty application of five policemen involved in the death of Steve Biko, and refused a blanket amnesty to *ANC* leaders, arguing the amnesty was designed for individuals. Thus far only 618 amnesties have been granted. In early 2000 the TRC still had 779 applications, about 12% of the total submitted, to review.

The legislation establishing the TRC entailed the idea that victims of state-sponsored violence should be compensated by the state for their suffering. Since the conclusion of hearings, the third of the Commission's panels has dealt with reparations to the victims. Progress has not been fast, or the rewards great. The TRC itself recommended awards of R17,000 and R23,000 ($2300 to $3200) for a maximum of six years. It estimated that some 22,000 victims would be entitled to such awards. This would cost about R500 million ($70 million) a year for the six-year period.

For its part, the government has allocated much less to the program: only R100 million ($14 m) in the 1998/99 financial year and a further R200 million for 1999/2000. There is, in some quarters, a feeling of resentment with the token payments offered under government allocations. It is as though the victims have been denied both justice and reparations and offered only truth. To many, reparations are a necessary link between truth and reconciliation. The TRC is scheduled to submit its final report to President Mbeki in September 2001

Testing Thabo

President Mbeki and his government have come under increasing scrutiny in the past year as they have confronted a number of issues and problems, many of their own making. Both the president's judgment and action on these have raised questions about his capacity to lead the nation. Part of the problem lies in the president's own style and personality.

The Mbeki style is more restrained than his predecessor's. He is seen as cool, distant and lacking a common touch. His rapport with the masses, that ineffable quality some like to call "charisma," pales beside that of more popular and populist leaders. Indeed, it is widely reported that Nelson Mandela preferred Cyril Ramaphosa, the mine workers' leader and principal negotiator of the transition from apartheid to majority rule, as his successor.

Lacking a fundamental popularity and charisma and surrounded by those who have them can, one assumes, lead to a certain nervousness. Enemies can lurk and conspiracies abound, but the organizational and ideological traditions of the *ANC* stress internal discipline and external solidarity. Historically the movement could enforce discipline by rough revolutionary justice justified as necessary to the achievement of its goals—an elimination of the apartheid system.

Once apartheid was ended and the movement had attained control of the apparatus of the state, divergences over the use, direction, and speed of government action to improve the everyday life of South Africans became evident. Managing those differences, and the personalities and factions that have gathered around them, has tested Thabo Mbeki's judgment leadership.

Some personalities, or perhaps it's a unique category, seem to be untouchable by party discipline. Winnie Mandela went off to Zimbabwe, for example, where she loudly expressed sympathy for war veterans' farm invasions. It was a direct challenge to President Mbeki, who claimed the efficacy of "quiet diplomacy" to critics who demanded he condemn Zimbabwe's state-sanctioned violence against its opponents. The wisdom of that approach became ever more dubious as the situation in Zimbabwe worsened.

The *ANC*'s refusal to condemn comrade Mugabe and his thuggish antics—solidarity with a fellow liberation movement—reached an embarrassing nadir when an *ANC* parliamentary delegation returned from Zimbabwe in September. Headed by *SACP* stalwart Tony Yengeni, the *ANC*'s parliamentary whip, the delegation reported that voting and ballot counting had been "orderly," with the chances of any foul play "negligible." Election results, they thought, " fairly reflected the will of the Zimbabwean people," despite violence that had cost the life of over thirty people, most of them opponents of the regime. That violence, concluded the lawmakers, could not be blamed exclusively on the ruling party.

In contrast, the European Union's observers had blamed the violence solely on the ruling party and said the elections

A Traditional Artisan at Work
Phaoto courtesy KZN Tourism Authority

could not be judged as "free and fair." Even the more cautious Commonwealth observation team declared that political violence, mainly by the ruling party against its opponent, inhibited free choice.

Tony Leon used the issue to criticize Mbeki and the *ANC* in December's municipal elections, and the American Secretary of State, Colin Powell, left little room for ambiguity on the issue when he visited South Africa in May 2001. It was, he said, "for the citizens of Zimbabwe to choose their leader in a free and fair election, and they should be given one so that they can make their choice as to how they will be governed in the future." His South African audience burst into to applause.

Despite lavish public praise, President Mbeki could derive little comfort from the Powell visit. The Secretary not only challenged Mbeki's judgment on Zimbabwe, but seemed to go out of his way to say, while visiting a group of AIDS sufferers, that "HIV causes AIDS." It was a connection Mbeki had long questioned, and his comments on the subject were those that most raised questions about his judgment.

Similar questions were raised over the handling of fraud corruption charges that engulfed the huge arms deal the government had signed with companies in Britain, Germany, Italy, Sweden and France. The contracts, worth more than $5 billion, were controversial from the start. In 1999 the government justified the arms purchases by what are called "offset agreements" which, the defense ministry argued, would result in investment and job-creation. Basically, the government would buy new submarines, helicopters, jet fighters and warships from European companies, and the offset agreement committed the seller country to invest in the purchasing country. The government argued the program would generate $17 billion in foreign investment and 65,000 jobs.

Once corruption charges emerged, the *ANC* seemed to do everything possible to suppress discussion and investigation. Charges of "cover-up" soon overtook the initial corruption charges. By May 2001, officials were investigating at least 24 individuals and 68 statutory bodies, and public hearings, long delayed by a variety of tactics, were about to open. South Africa's Auditor General said 30 full-time officers were probing allegations of conflict of interest and bribery in the purchase of helicopters, fighters, submarines and ships. The highest profile allegations were those against the *ANC*'s parliamentary whip, Tony Yengeni. Comrade Yengeni was accused of taking advantage of very capitalist sweetheart deals on several Mercedes luxury vehicles.

As if the *ANC*'s cup of public embar-

Final Results in the June 1999 Election

Party	Votes	Percent	National Assembly
African National Congress	10,589,180	66.03	266
Democratic Party	1,524,696	9.55	38
Inkatha Freedom Party	1,370,447	8.59	34
New National Party	1,097,573	6.88	28
United Democratic Movement	546,358	3.42	14
All Eleven Others	848,772	5.53	20
Total:	15,977,026	100	400

Port Elizabeth's Pier 14 Shopping Center

Courtesy: Eastern Cape Tourism Board
Photo by Ivor Markman

Part of a huge multiracial crowd attending a Pop Music Festival

rassment were not yet full, security minister Steve Tshwete dropped a political bombshell by naming three of the most popular and easily recognized *ANC* leaders as conspirators in a plot against President Mbeki. Named were Cyril Ramaphosa, a former union leader and secretary-general of the *ANC* who helped negotiate the end of apartheid, and two former provincial premiers: Tokyo Sexwale, an *ANC* member jailed for 13 years under apartheid who later became premier of Gauteng Province, and Mathews Phosa, a former *ANC* guerrilla who became premier of Mpumalanga Province.

All three were now successful businessmen (Ramaphosa is reportedly South Africa's wealthiest black entrepreneur), and all three had their roots in the internal, rather than exiled, wing of the *ANC*. The accusations came from such a dubious source that condemnation was heard from *COSATU* and *SACP* officials and a host of *ANC* figures. Nelson Mandela gave no credibility to the charges at all, saying that "Until there is evidence to substantiate the allegations, I will always regard them in high esteem."

The press was virtually unanimous in treating the charges as a trumped-up attempt by a paranoid Mbeki to involve police and espionage agencies illegitimately in efforts to dispose of potential party rivals. Much of the luster that initially surrounded the president was severely tarnished by the incident.

Culture: South Africa now has one of the highest rates of HIV infection in the world. Unlike Uganda where that rate is dropping, South Africa's keeps rising. The government was slow to recognize the problem. Its response has been confused and unfocused. Its policy is in disarray. The statistics are appalling: one in eight people are already HIV positive. The national health ministry estimates another 1,600 South Africans are infected daily. Five thousand babies are born each month infected with HIV. Patients with AIDS-related infections already occupy 70 per cent of South African hospital beds. It is estimated that between 25% and 30% of all South Africans will be infected by 2010. As parents die, an estimated 700,000 AIDS orphans will be left behind by 2010.

As elsewhere, the infection rate is growing fastest among the young. More than 60 percent of new infections are occurring in people 15 to 25 years old. And worse yet, the pandemic is expected to wipe out large segments of the very people who are needed to fight it—teachers, health professionals and government workers. In the face of catastrophe the government has invested in an educational musical to spread the word. Millions of rand were lost when the government commissioned Durban's internationally renowned playwright Mbongeni Ngema to develop the AIDS-awareness musical, *Sarafina 2*. When the health minister's advisory board criticized the project, she fired them.

The government has also funded dubious pseudo-scientific "cures," one of which, Virodene, had as its active ingredient an industrial dry-cleaning solvent. Virodene's active ingredient, dimethyl formamide (DMF), had previously been blocked for human use in South Africa and elsewhere because of dangerous side effects. In September 1997 the journal *Aids Research and Human Retroviruses* printed a report suggesting that DMF might actually activate HIV.

The government currently calls for more research and refuses to employ vaccines known to reduce the incidence of mother to child transmission of the HIV virus. AZT is rejected as too expensive.

A short course of the drug AZT, now the standard treatment to prevent the transmission of HIV to newborns, costs $120—a price few South Africans can afford. State-run hospitals could provide the AZT treatment for about $60, but the government says it, too, cannot afford the cost. "There are very many competing priorities in South Africa," said Dr. Manto Tshabalala-Msimang, South Africa's health minister. "We are just in the transition period. Everything needs money."

Research in the United States and Uganda employing an alternative drug, nevirapine, found that administering just two doses—one during labor and another three days after birth—is even more effective than the short course of AZT. By contrast, nevirapine costs just $4 a dose. But here too the South African trials of the drug have given the government reason to refuse its use. Five South Africans who got the drug in a clinical trial died of liver complications. Although nevirapine is widely used around the world, liver-related deaths have never been linked to it before.

Despite an abundance of scientific evidence that HIV transmission from mother to infant can be reduced significantly, President Mbeki himself has waded in and muddied the waters further. In his discussions criticism of AZT moved from cost to toxicity, a notion picked up from his reading of the scientific dissidents, those who refuse to admit a relationship between HIV and AIDS. To the chagrin and disillusionment of South African health workers, the President formed an AIDS advisory panel on which the dissidents, self-styled "Galileos" of modern science—those who reject establishment consensus—were given a prominent place.

The government's refusal to allocate funds to reduce mother to infant HIV transmission rates has drawn international condemnation. It also raises disturbing moral, social and political issues. For a government so sensitive to past discrimination, the medical care of pregnant women is biased. Only those who are HIV negative will be treated. For a government that believes in "inclusiveness," the HIV-infected are excluded. For a government that preaches hope, the rejection of preventative treatment is hope denied. As a white South African jurist, Judge Edwin Cameron, himself HIV-positive, has commented, "it simply does not seem that the government can begin to get it right on AIDS." For Judge Cameron the benefits of the government commitment to the use of vaccines to reduce mother to infant HIV transmission would be both psychological and symbolic. Those affected would have

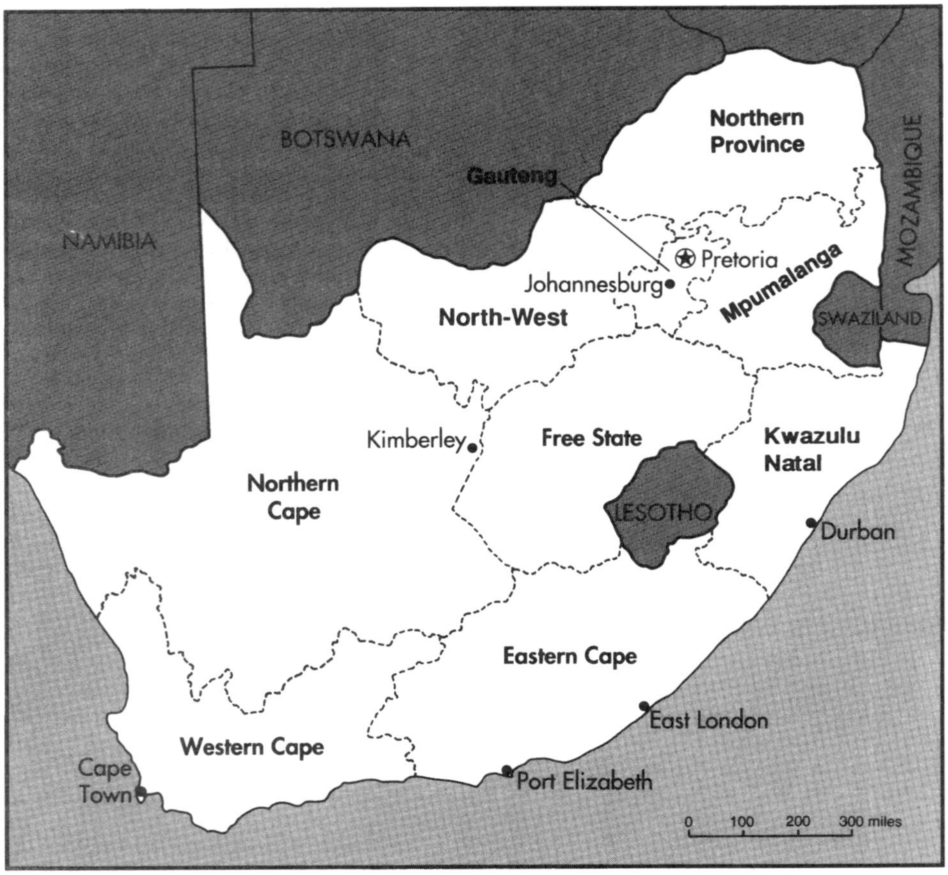

hope restored. Those excluded would once again feel included. To the government's indirection and indecision, Cameron's critique offers a dynamic of hope.

Because the government has so long delayed and vacillated, HIV infection is still highly stigmatized. For many it is still something that happens to "bad people." Those who reveal their illness are shunned, even subjected to violence and death. The stigma remains so great that people often do not wish to know if they are infected. Unknowing, they become one of many carriers whereby the disease is diffused throughout society. In KwaZulu-Natal, the most severely impacted province, only 4,800 people took voluntary HIV tests in 1999. The province has a population of nearly 8.5 million.

South Africa's notorious rape rate is also associated with HIV/AIDS diffusion, but here it is not only the more widely known sexual violence against women, but also the less discussed homosexual rapes that occur in South Africa's prisons. AIDS testing is not mandatory in South African prisons and the HIV status of both the offender and victim is generally unknown. Prisoners are denied treatment for AIDS, regardless of whether they enter prison with it, whether they contract it in prison while tattooing themselves with infected needles or whether they contract it from consensual sex or brutal sexual assault.

The consequences of the government's unwillingness to face up to the realities of the crisis can be seen in other ways, suggesting perhaps misplaced priorities. To prevent discrimination, pre-employment HIV testing is now illegal in South Africa. Banks, however, require loan applicants to hold life insurance policies that cover the value of their loan, and life insurance companies require HIV tests as a prerequisite for coverage. They can legally reject those who test positive.

The currently accepted fashion is to describe President Mbeki's views on HIV/AIDs as "unorthodox." They go well beyond that, suggesting at times the kind of paranoia that has led to acceptance of "conspiracy" accusations in other areas. In October 2000, for example, he told a gathering of *ANC* officials that the CIA was part of a "conspiracy to promote the view that HIV causes AIDS."

According to South Africa's *Mail and Guardian* newspaper, Mbeki told the group the CIA was also working with big U.S. pharmaceutical manufacturers to undermine him. The reason for this, he explained, was the fear that his questioning of the HIV/AIDS link would lead to reduced profits in the sale of anti-retroviral treatments.

The problem with this sort of thinking is that it has delayed action where action is necessary. AIDS in South Africa continues its rapid expansion. By 2002 it is expected that 25% of the population will be infected. Many of those will be the best educated and trained, the ones most necessary to running the country.

Economy: By regional standards, and even continental ones, the South African economy is huge. With a GNP close to $130 billion and a misleading per capita income of nearly $3,000, South Africa dwarfs its neighbors. Its GNP is 20 times greater that Zimbabwe's; its per capita income figures are 36 times those of Mozambique. But the giant is sluggish. Growth is modest and unemployment remains high. Three-fourths of South Africa's unemployed are black Africans, the principal constituency of the *ANC*.

South Africa is rich in natural resources, but the mining sector is in decline. It accounted for 15% GNP in 1985, but only 8% in 1996. Nowhere is that decline better seen than in South Africa's fabled diamonds and gold. Asian demand for polished diamonds—17% of the global market in 1996—has virtually disappeared in the wake of that region's financial problems. The Japanese market alone, second only to the United States, was down 20% in 1997. Nearly 10 million carats of diamonds were produced in 1996, contributing 12% to total export earnings.

Gold contributed 22% of total South African export earnings in 1996, while workers employed in the industry represented 2.3% of the total economically active population. In December 1997, however, the price of gold dropped to its lowest ever setting off a wave of work force reductions. Aging mines and low productivity have left the mines uneconomical and the collapse of world gold prices brought several to the verge of closure. Gold output fell to 493 tons in 1997, a 40-year low. Since 1985, the industry's total work force has shrunk from 515,000 to 298,000. One-third of South Africa's gold mines are losing money, about $10 million a month. The industry would have collapsed entirely if mining companies had not reinvested billions of dollars in new technology and new mines, many of which are outside South Africa. Within the country the National Union of Mineworkers, the most powerful of South Africa's labor unions, has warned that it will undertake nationwide industrial action if gold industry employers fail to keep mining a labor-intensive sector.

Unlike neighboring Angola, South Africa is not endowed with rich oil resources. Coal is the primary fuel produced and consumed in South Africa. It is also the country's second most important foreign exchange earner, after gold, contributing 7% of export earnings. Nearly one-third of total coal production is exported, primarily to the European market. The majority of domestic coal consumption is for the production of electricity, through a significant portion is used by

Ndebele women

the steel industry. Sasol, South Africa's third-largest coal producer, is active in producing oil from coal. With a capacity to produce 150,000 barrels per day Sasol has been the world's largest manufacturer of oil from coal. The technology was originally developed in the 1950s to help reduce South Africa's dependence on imported oil, but the company has been privatized and the government has ended subsidies for this undertaking. Iran is the principal supplier of crude oil to South Africa—300,000 barrels a day—and Middle Eastern imports are likely to remain important for some time to come. South Africa only began production at its first offshore field in May 1997, a relatively small 25,000 barrels a day. Large natural gas reserves discovered off the southern Cape coast are sufficient to produce another 25,000 a day.

South Africa has a diversified industrial sector which accounts for 22% of GNP and employs 27% of the work force, much of which is engaged in processing natural resources. With the major exception of clothing and textiles, most manufacturing draws upon local raw materials. Steel production dominates and is closely associated with automobile manufacture (both Mercedes Benz and Toyota produce vehicles in South Africa), but the metal industry is not a place for labor growth. Technology has greatly reduced the number of workers required for most operations. In 1981 South Africa's metal industries employed 454,000 hourly paid workers. In 1996 the number was only 270,000. Food and tobacco processing remain important, but their share of total output has fallen significantly. South African wine exports increased 35% in 1996, to 11.1 million cases, the highest number ever exported.

One bright spot in food processing is found in macadamia nuts. The South African macadamia nut industry is now the third largest in the world. Production has grown from 500 tons per year in 1996 to about 1,400 tons currently. Production is expected to continue growing at 20 to 30% per year because of new tree plantings. To add value to macadamia production, a factory capable of producing 4 tons per month of chocolate-coated macadamias and macadamia-and-fruit bars has been commissioned. Its target production is 10 tons a month.

South Africa ranks among the world's largest producers of cannabis. An estimated 83,000 hectares yield 176 million kilograms of the drug. First introduced into the region some 500 years ago by Arab traders, cannabis is widely regarded as a traditional crop in many rural areas, particularly the Eastern Cape and KwaZulu-Natal. In some areas it is possible to produce up to three crops per year. In 1998 government eradication efforts were halted mid–year due to a lack of resources required to maintain the helicopters used in spraying operations. The U.S. State Department reports that there are more than 100 drug syndicates operating in South Africa.

Tourism was the only sector which showed a noticeable employment rise in the 1996–97 economic year. An estimated 550,000 people are employed in the industry which contributed 3.6% of GNP in 1996. The industry catered to nearly 5 million visitors in 1996, with the bulk, 3.6 million, coming from Africa. Crime stories continue to have a negative impact on the industry.

The most pressing need for the government is to create an environment of economic stability in order to attract the direct foreign investment through which growth and jobs will be created. In many ways the government has sought to do this. Budgets which display fiscal restraint, an announced willingness to cut back on high public employment, controlled inflation, and steady privatization have all characterized the ANC govern-

Former South African President F.W. de Klerk (left) and African National Congress foreign policy specialist Thabo Mbeki (right) were deputy presidents in President Nelson Mandela's first Cabinet

A spectacular mountain landscape, KwaZulu-Natal
KZN Tourism Authority

ment, and set it at odds with its labor partner, *COSATU*. The government has sold off regional radio stations and a regional airline, but its most important step in disengaging itself from the economy was the partial privatization of Telkom in 1997. Thirty percent of the company was sold to a consortium of Malaysian and American companies for 5.58 billion South African Rands. This represents the largest partial privatization anywhere in sub-Saharan Africa.

The government inherited a huge bureaucracy from its National Party predecessor—affirmative action for Afrikaans speakers—and the wage bill for public service employees currently costs South Africa 40% of its annual revenue. It plans to trim the civil service by some 300,000 jobs by the year 2000. Though most reductions will result from retirements, the thought of thousands of teachers, soldiers, and clerks given their pink slips has raised ominous objections from the unions. They continue to press for increased wages for their members, just compensation, they argue, for the effects of *apartheid* discrimination. Many economists argue that the drive by unions for higher wages will actually result in greater unemployment. A recent World Bank report on South Africa's labor market for example, says a 10% wage increase above the inflation rate leads to a 7% loss of jobs. In part, this can be explained by the changing nature of the desired labor force. In 1981, for example, 15% of the work force consisted of skilled artisans, 17% of those with middle skills and 68% was made up of lower-skilled workers. Today, 17% are skilled, 55% middle-skilled, and only 28% are lower-skilled. The situation will only get worse. As companies respond to greater competition by employing more technology, the need for more highly trained workers will increase and the demand for unskilled labor will diminish. Unfortunately, as job requirements have become more sophisticated, education and job training have not. In the long term education and skills training are the highest priorities.

The AIDS pandemic will have severe consequences for the South African economy. At the most basic level, population growth will be reduced. In 1991—before the scale of the AIDS crisis was fully appreciated—South Africa's Human Sciences Research Council predicted the country's population would rise to between 77–85 million by 2020. Today social scientists estimate South Africa will have a population of no more than 52 million by 2021.

Analysts believe blue-collar industries, such as the mining and transport, will be most affected. The Road Freight Association says that AIDS is killing about three truck drivers a day. It warns that, if this death rate continues, South Africa will have no drivers left by 2003.

The Future: Nelson Mandela's government sought to allay the fears of white South Africans. Thabo Mbeki's will seek to placate the aspirations of black South Africans. The task will not be easy. The *ANC* in power has largely abandoned its Marxist rhetoric and opted for a more open economy as the agent of economic growth. Under Mandela, its great success was in maintaining stability after coming to power in 1994. Under President Mbeki, intensifying ideological differences between the *ANC* and its triple alliance partners, *COSATU* and *SACP*, will threaten that stability. Ultimately, the partners will separate into more natural left and right wings, but that's a long way off. For the short and intermediate term, movement unity trumps all.

The *ANC* enjoys overwhelming power in South Africa. In parliament it commands a near two-thirds majority with which to impose its will in any area. Thabo Mbeki combines the roles of party president and state president. As party leader he can control all provincial and subordinate leadership, as the example of Gauteng illustrates. As state president he has concentrated enormous powers of direction and coordination in his office. In other countries single party dominance of this sort has almost always led to a regime of patrons and clients, disconnected from the needs of those outside the networks of patronage. The real test of Thabo Mbeki's leadership will be the extent to which he avoids the pitfalls of enormous power. Given what appears to be a paranoid personality, one has a right to be uncertain.

The Kingdom of Swaziland

King Mswati III

Area: 17,364 sq. km. = 6,705 sq. mi. (about the size of Hawaii).
Population: 985,335 (July 1999 est.)
Capital Cities: Mbabane (Pop. 40,000, estimated—administrative); Lobamba (Pop. 23,500, estimated—legislative).
Climate: Temperate, with chilly nights during the winter months.
Neighboring Countries: Mozambique (Northeast); Republic of South Africa (North, West, South).
Official Languages: siSwati, English.
Other Principal Languages: Zulu, Afrikaans.
Ethnic Groups: Swazi, a small number of other Bantu groups; European.
Principal Religions: Christian 60%, indigenous beliefs 40%.
Chief Commercial Products: Sugar asbestos, wood and forest products, citrus, cotton, iron ore.
GNP per capita: 1,400 US$
Currency: Emalangeni (at par with the South African Rand).
Former Colonial Status: Under South African protection (1894–1906); British Protectorate (1906–1968).
Chief of State: King Mswati III (b. 1966).
Independence Date: September 6, 1968.
National Flag: Horizontal stripes of dark blue, red and dark blue, divided by thin yellow bands. A shield and spear design is in the center of the red stripe.

High plateaus with groups of forested mountains are found in western Swaziland which gradually descend from a maximum of 4,500 feet to a central region with a 2,800 average height. This gives way to a lowland in the East, and the Lubombo Mountains rise at the easternmost border. The temperate climate is warm enough to permit large quantities of sugar cane to grow, but at the same time it is ideally suited for forest growth of excellent hardwoods. The rolling landscape closely resembles the Appalachian mountain region of the United States.

History: Swaziland was thinly inhabited by a variety of Bantu groups in the 18th century. The Swazis (Emaswati) migrated to the area from what is now Mozambique about 1750. The British–*Boer* competition in the last two decades of the 19th century resulted in Swaziland becoming a British protectorate. For details of early and colonial history, see Historical Background and *The British in Africa.*

The British agreed in 1967 to grant independence to Swaziland on September 6, 1968, which was done in formal ceremonies in Mbabane. Many foreign representatives were present, including high officials from the Republic of South Africa. King Sobhuza's 112 wives were also included among the spectators.

All 24 seats of the National Assembly were held initially by King Sobhuza's *National Movement.* Reigning since 1921 until his death in 1982, he was the oldest ruling monarch on earth. Elections in 1972 reduced the party to 21 seats; Dr. Ambrose Zwane's *National Liberatory Congress Party* won three seats and six additional members were appointed by the King. However, within weeks the King abolished the constitution, dismissed the Assembly and announced he would rule the old–fashioned way—by decree. Later, in 1979, a new bicameral parliament was opened consisting of a 50–member lower house and a 20–member upper house. Ten of each were chosen directly by the King.

King Sobhuza died in August 1982. Intrigue and plotting among the wives and 70 sons of the dead monarch began before he was buried. The numerous persons involved are not now important. The struggles revolved around (1) The Queen Regent, (2) the *Liqoqo* (National Council), (3) the "Authorized Person" (4) The Prime Minister and (5) The House of Assembly and the Senate.

The young Crown Prince, the second–youngest son of the late king, studied in Britain until 1986, when he reached the age of 18; his coronation was held on April 25, 1986. Three days of celebration were attended by numerous heads of state in southern Africa, including President Botha of South Africa. The young king quickly moved to assert his power, reshuffling the cabinet, dismissing the *Liqoqo,* and replacing the Prime Minister.

The Swazi King is one of the world's last absolute monarchs. While the country has a bicameral legislature, the king appoints a number of its members, has the power to dissolve it, and can rule by decree. Political parties have been banned in Swaziland since 1973, and it is the king who appoints the cabinet.

Legislative elections were held in September and October 1998. As a result of the ban on political parties, candidates for parliament emerged through the three-tiered *Tinkundla* system. Tinkundlas, or traditional assemblies, nominate candidates—generally conservative and loyal to the king—in all the chiefdoms of Swaziland. These hopefuls are pared down in primary elections, with the remaining candidates vying in secondaries for 55 seats in the House of Assembly. Candidates run as individuals and of course cannot run on a party platform. The king appoints a further 10 members of the assembly.

From the assembly, the king appoints his government, the cabinet. In 1998 King Mswati II re–appointed his Prime Minister, Sibususo Dlamini. Of the 16 members of the cabinet, only 3 had been elected. All the others had been appointed to the assembly by the King. There is no such thing as electoral accountability in an absolute monarchy.

The Swazi senate has 30 members, none of whom are directly elected. Twenty members are royal appointees. The remaining 10 are selected by the assembly. The whole system is designed to keep the King and his relatives in powerful positions.

The *Swaziland Federation of Trade Unions* (*SFTU*) and the unofficial opposition, the *Swaziland Democratic Alliance,* remain the most vocal opponents of Swaziland's absolute monarchy. With their leadership subject to arrest and intimidation, however, the groups have not yet been able to turn the monarchy to a more open and pluralist political system.

The *SFTU* did pressure authorities into creating a commission to draft a new constitution in 1964 , but royalists and traditionalists make up the bulk of the committee. The commission was to have completed its work in 1998, but the King has postponed its deadline indefinitely. He continues to rule by decree.

In October 2000, one such arbitrary decree by the absolute monarch began to erode the King's support among the rural faithful. He appointed an older brother to a chieftaincy already occupied, and some 100 peasant farmers had to be forcibly evicted when they refused to recognize the new chief imposed on them. "We thought the king was a father to us all" said one, "but it seems that he only looks after his own family."

The evictions plunged the kingdom into an unprecedented political crisis. Unions and student organizations led protests against official excesses. One group of elderly Swazi women took matters into their own hands—some 50 of them tried to flash their naked buttocks at the princely brother. The insult is considered a curse and is one of the most severe forms of disrespect in traditional Swazi culture.

Less dramatically, even the courts ruled against the King. In December Swaziland's Court of Appeals ruled in favor of two original chiefs. Relatives of King Mswati, meanwhile, concerned the mooning had cast a spell on the King and his brother, looked about for an African root to cleanse them and remove the magic of the curse.

Culture: About 80% of Swazis live as peasant farmers on Swazi national land, "king's land," distributed through local chiefs. Deeply conservative, rural Swazi are fully aware that had not foreign ideologies been resisted by kings past, there would be no Swazi nation today. Modern urbanites talking of human rights and democracy are in many ways out of touch with Swazi reality.

The King, by custom the father of all his subjects and the embodiment of the nation, has stated that he would never recognize "anyone who comes to me saying he represents other Swazis." It's a statement that dramatizes the tensions between tradition and modernity that bedevil the Kingdom.

Lacking the age and stature of his father, Mswati seems to have been unable to resist the pressures of royals and traditionalists. Many increasingly wonder if he has the internal resources to provide the leadership Swaziland needs. King Mswati seems no Alexander the Great, capable of cutting the Gordian knot of Swazi politics and liberating his people to move into the 21st century.

A 1999 UNICEF report described the terrifying advance of AIDS among Swazis. More than 300,000 Swazis are already living with HIV/AIDS. Between the years 2000 and 2015 up to 40,000 will die of AIDS each year. Five skilled workers in Swaziland's manufacturing sector die weekly. With surveys showing as many as one third of all young and middle-aged adults in Swaziland infected with the virus and the age expectancy dropping from 38 to 30, King Mswati III at last declared HIV/AIDS a "national disaster."

Enlightenment on the subject is not necessarily to be found among the King's advisors. One described HIV/AIDS sufferers as "bad potatoes" and said they must be removed from society lest "all will go rotten." His solution was an isolation camp for victims of the disease.

Nor has parliament come to grips with sociological reality. In an effort to cut down on the number of babies born with AIDS/HIV and the number of orphans created by the death of infected parents, legislation was proposed to sterilize those infected with the disease. Unexplained by proponents of the law was how it would reduce transmission of the disease or prevent the death of those already infected. Similarly misdirected was the effort to reduce what was considered contributory "sexual promiscuity," by banning miniskirts in schools to prevent sexual relationships between teachers and young girls.

Each time King Mswati decides to take a new bride, gender issues are brought to the fore in Swaziland. One day after accepting a national development document that stressed national progress could not be achieved without full legal and cultural equality for women, the King watched thousands of bare-breasted teenage virgins dance before him in the annual reed dance (*Umhlanga*). From these he selected his newest bride.

Wives of the Swazi king are selected from a prescribed roster of clans. Traditionally, his first wife must come from the Matsebula family. Though traditionally selected, the Swazi queens may very well become agents of change. One wife, Queen LaMbikiza, obtained her law degree, while the other queens spearhead causes devoted to AIDS awareness and the plight of street children. Their engagement with Swaziland's realities has made them role models for younger women.

Mbabane, Swaziland's capital in the Mdimba mountains

Economy: Swaziland's economy has been anemic in the past few years, with a growth rate between two and three percent. Against a population growth rate of 2.7%, there is little hope the average Swazi's standard of living will improve. High unemployment rates (40%) persist, and direct foreign investment is negligible. Private investment in Swaziland has grown minimally, a reasonable indication of investors' confidence in an undemocratic country where opposition political parties are banned, labor unions are harassed, and the government clamps down on any form of political dissent.

The Swazi economy is highly dependent on neighboring South Africa, which surrounds it on three sides. Its currency is pegged to the South African Rand; all its oil is imported from South Africa, as is nearly all its electricity and 85% of its consumer goods. When Johannesburg sneezes, Mbabane gets feverish.

Fifty percent of government revenue currently comes from customs receipts from the Southern African Customs Union (SACU), but these will be lost when the union is dissolved as part of a larger regional trade reform. To compensate for the loss, the government has embarked on an ambitious program to develop transportation and tourism. A new international airport, international conference center, new highways, luxury hotels, an industrial park and an amusement park, were launched in mid-2000 as part of King Mswati's Millennium Projects initiative.

One relative bright spot is Swaziland's principal export, sugar. The country is one of the world's lowest cost producers of sugar. In 1999 it expected to produce 529,000 tons, up from 475,000 tons in 1998. Despite a glut of sugar on world markets, Swazi sugar is protected by a series of conventions with the EU and the US, which guarantee quotas and prices above the world market. Even the 260,000 tons sold within the four-nation Southern African Customs Union (SACU) market receive a higher price than world market standards.

The European Union-African Caribbean Pacific (EU-ACP) Sugar Protocol expires soon, however. Swaziland and other developing countries are lobbying hard for its indefinite extension.

The Future: It's difficult to see much of a future for absolute monarchy, even in such a deeply traditional society as Swaziland. It's equally difficult to see much movement towards change as long as Mswati remains paralyzed by multiple pressures.

Weakened government revenues will add pressure on the regime. Increased social and political tension should be expected.

The Republic of Zambia

Victoria Falls

Area: 745,920 sq. km. = 288,000 sq. mi. (The size of Nebraska, South Dakota, Iowa and Minnesota combined.
Population: 9,663,535 (July 1999 est.)
Capital City: Lusaka (Pop. 1.2 million, estimated).
Climate: Temperate, because of its altitude, although Zambia lies close to the Equator. There is a wet season (October–April) and a dry season (May–September).
Neighboring Countries: Angola (West); Congo-Kinshasa (Northwest); Tanzania (Northeast); Malawi (East); Mozambique (Southeast); Zimbabwe and Botswana (South).
Official Language: English
Other Principal Languages: Over 30, including Bemba, Kaonde, Lamba, Lozi, Lunda, Luvale, Mwanga, Nsenga, Nyanja Nyiha, Tonga, and Tumbuka.
Ethnic groups: African 98.7%, European 1.1%, other 0.2%.
Principal Religions: Christian 50%–75%, Muslim and Hindu 24%–49%, indigenous beliefs 1%.
Chief Commercial Products: Copper, cobalt, zinc, lead, and tobacco.
GNP per capita: 330 US$
Currency: 1 Zambian Kwacha (ZK) = 100 ngwee.
Former Colonial Status: British South Africa Company administration (1895–1923); British Colony (1924–1964).
Independence Date: October 24, 1964.
Chief of State: Frederick Chiluba, President (since November 1991).
National Flag: Green, with an orange eagle in flight over a square block of three vertical stripes, red, black and red, on the right side.

The Republic of Zambia is located in south central Africa, stretching 750 miles west from the mountains of the great Western Rift. This is a high plateau country with an average elevation of 3,500 feet above sea level, which modifies its otherwise equatorial climate. It is only in the low river valleys that any oppressive heat and humidity are encountered.

The gently rolling country alternates between the waving grasses of the plains and forests of widely spaced trees. Great numbers of wildlife are supported by the vegetation which grows rapidly during the rainy season of the year. The country is drained by two major river systems: the tributaries flowing north to the Congo River, and the Zambezi River, which flows southeast through Mozambique to the Indian Ocean. One of the greatest sheets of flowing water in the world is found at incomparable Victoria Falls, near Livingstone in the South. Swampy Lake Banguelu spreads its great width in the north–central part of the country; the deep blue sparkling waters of Lake Mweru and Lake Tanganyika are found in the North.

History: Like many of the adjacent countries, Zambia was probably inhabited in early times by primitive pygmies and other groups. The great wave of Bantu migration over a period of several centuries virtually took over this country, and very few indications remain of earlier civilizations. For details of early and colonial history, see Historical Background and *The British in Africa.*

Northern Rhodesia became fully independent in 1964, taking the name Zambia from the Zambezi River. A republic form of government was established with a single legislative house initially composed of 75 members, but increased to the present 125. Until 1969, ten seats were reserved for White voters. The president is chosen by direct election; Kenneth Kaunda was selected as the first president in 1964.

Initially there were two major parties—the *United National Independence Party* (*UNIP*), led by Kaunda and the *African National Congress* (*ANC*), led by Harry Nkumbula (who died in 1984 in neighboring Zimbabwe). After winning a large majority in 1968, Kaunda abolished the opposition party in the name of "national unity."

Racial, religious and tribal frictions have been frequent in Zambia since independence. Political repression and suppression added to dissatisfaction with Kaunda by many. A dramatic program of nationalization of every major enterprise was started in late 1970. A system of state–owned and managed enterprises and marketing facilities was instituted. Because of poor planning and lack of technical skills, the economy, particularly in the agricultural sector, suffered.

In the early 1970s, Kaunda silenced all organized political opposition by jailing Simon Kapwepwe, a former vice president and boyhood friend who had formed an opposition party. The party was banned and in addition to Kapwepwe, 123 leaders were imprisoned. Although Kapwepwe was released in 1973, Kaunda had made several changes to get rid of opposition permanently.

Zambia was officially made a one–party state, with *UNIP* the sole party. The Assembly was dissolved in 1973 and new elections were set. A "primary" election was first held; before a successful candidate could run in the general election he had to have the approval of the *UNIP* Central Committee; several who won in the primary were eliminated in this way. Twenty candidates were announced as "official candidates" of the party, insuring their election.

Kaunda exhibited qualities of statesmanship during his tenure. Until 1976, he worked long hours to assist in resolving the Rhodesia conflict revolving around minority white control in that nation. He also was initially receptive to the détente efforts of the Republic of South Africa. He responded with enthusiasm to the election of President de Klerk in South Africa in 1989, and met with him shortly before he took office. He strongly urged negotiations without preconditions between the *ANC* and the government of South Africa.

In order to receive desperately needed funds from the International Monetary Fund and the World Bank, austerity programs were instituted in the 1980's which were unpopular and failed to improve economic conditions. Zambia broke with the IMF in May 1987 and decreed that only 10% of its export earnings would be used to repay and service external debt. Of course this led to a freeze on outside assistance at a time when the country was again gripped by drought.

Unopposed, President Kaunda was reelected to a sixth five–year term in late 1988. Voting turnout was substantially lower than in prior elections, indicating increasing dissatisfaction with the government. This was further evidenced by the arrest on suspicion of an alleged *coup* of nine prominent persons.

The year 1990 was filled with political and economic change. A *UNIP* spring conference endorsed the single–party system. But in June, an announced increase in the price of cornmeal from $2.80 to $6.70 provoked riots and an attempted *coup*, the latter of which was unsuccessful. Bowing to intense dissatisfaction, President Kaunda announced multi–party elections would be permitted.

Thus, on October 31, 1991, Zambians voted to decide the fate of one of Africa's most senior statesmen in the first multi–party elections in 23 years.

The campaign during 1991 leading up to the elections of October was hard–fought. Kaunda's references to his opponents were insulting. He was accused of being out of touch with the people and failing to stem the tide of economic events which had produced an annual inflation rate of 400%. Frederick Chiluba, his opponent, a labor leader and head of the *Movement for Multi–Party Democracy (MMD)*, also stressed the need to eliminate almost universal corruption and theft in the government.

Kaunda, a senior African statesman who had been in power for 27 years, was soundly defeated. Chiluba's party gained 125 of the 150 legislative seats. During his first term he did relatively well, reversing the socialist patterns of government and privatizing 140 state–owned, unprofitable industries. The government monopoly on foodstuffs was ended, resulting in higher prices for commodities. The high external debt was lowered by $2 billion.

Old problems—inflation and currency devaluation continued, however. Corruption within an overstaffed bureaucracy was notorious. As November 1996 elections drew near, it became apparent that Kenneth Kaunda ("KK") would attempt a come–back. President Chiluba averted this in a controversial constitutional amendment providing that any and all candidates would have to be native Zambians and further, could not in previous years have served as president. Kaunda was born of Malawian parents and, of course, had served as president. Furious, but helpless, his followers boycotted the election.

Nevertheless, the turnout was 40%; Chiluba and his *Movement for Multiparty Democracy (MMD)* won, gaining 131 seats in the legislature. Kaunda threatened continued civil disobedience and strikes, but was muted by a threat of criminal prosecution.

In many ways it is regrettable Kenneth Kaunda did not with greater grace depart the field of political combat. Gracious retirement is always becoming, especially in Africa where its appearance is so infrequent. The departure from power of Senegal's Leopold Senghor, Tanzania's Julius Nyerere and now Ketumile Masire of Botswana has given luster to their reputations. This will not be so with Kaunda. In the bitterness of rejection and defeat he became intemperate and hostile. In October he warned Zambians of an "explosion" soon to come if the *MMD* refused to dialogue with opposition parties, i.e., Kenneth Kaunda. "Something big will come, " he said, "and of course *MMD* will blame *UNIP* for that. But it won't be *UNIP*," he continued, "it will be the people of Zambia who are going to act."

The very next day an army captain, using the very improbable name of Capt. Solo, announced he had overthrown the government. Within a few hours the Gilbert and Sullivanesque interlude was over. Its greatest damage was probably done the studios of Zambian National Broadcasting from whence Solo had announced his takeover and rambled on for nearly four hours. Chiluba emerged stronger and more confident than after the disputed 1996 elections; most groups thoroughly condemned the coup. In its wake, Chiluba imposed a state of emergency giving the government broad powers.

The international donor community voiced concerns about the state of emergency, and Kaunda claimed his rival aimed at dictatorship. Lovers of irony noted that Kaunda had imposed a state of emergency throughout his 27-year rule. One of President Chiluba's first decisions as president was to remove the government's sweeping powers to search and detain without trial. By March the state of emergency had been lifted and awkward dialogue between the Zambian political parties seemed more genuine than before.

The war in the Congo has dominated Zambian politics, directly and indirectly, since 1998. President Chiluba was mandated by the Southern African Development Community (SDAC) to travel the region and help negotiate a cease-fire. His efforts culminated in the Lusaka Accord of July 1999, which set forth a framework for ending the conflict. He remains near the center of efforts to gain its acceptance and enforcement.

Angola, fixated on the complete elimination of Jonas Savimbi and his *UNITA* forces, continues to keep the pressure on Zambia. Its accusations that Zambia was helping *UNITA* replenish its armaments were given additional impact by a UN Security Council committee report on sanctions busting. Zambia was named among ten African states violating the UN sanctions against *UNITA*.

Local elections in late 1998 produced a massive victory for candidates of President Chiluba's *MMD*. Some 16 parties and over 400 independent candidates participated in the elections for 1,286 municipal seats. A potentially strong new party, the *United Party for National Development* (*UPND*) emerged in the election. Led by Anderson Mazoka, the outgoing head of the Anglo–American Corporation's East African operations, *UPND* stressed poverty alleviation as its goal. It committed itself to reduce Zambia's poverty from the current 50% level to below 20%. Kenneth Kaunda campaigned widely for *UNIP* candidates, but to little avail. When the final results came in, from abysmally low participation, *MMD* had won 880 seats and *UNIP* 234. The new kid on the block, *UPND*, won 28 seats.

Events in Zambia certainly seem to prove the adage that power is an aphro-

President Frederick Chiluba

disiac capable of generating passionate lust for itself. President Chiluba, elected to office as a reformer and committed to term limits, spent most of 2000 and 2001 seeking ways to secure himself a third term. Teams of lawyers and parliamentarians were sent to Namibia to see how it had been done there. *MMD* members were prohibited from announcing candidacy for the 2001 elections, and when one cabinet member, Ben Mwila, violated the edict, he was summarily dismissed.

President Chiluba coyly refrained from expressing any public desire for a third term, but everywhere his minions were busy pursuing the president's ambition. It was an aspiration that divided cabinet, party and country. Those who opposed a third terms were ruthlessly dispatched. After Mwila, four more cabinet members were sacked in early 2001, and six senior members of the Zambian security services were "retired" after indicating that the political environment in the country was not conducive for Chiluba's third-term quest.

Requiring a constitutional amendment, the quest for a third term involved several steps. The amendment had to be approved by the *MMD*'s national executive and recommended to a party convention. If approved, it would then go to the National Assembly where the *MMD* had more than a two-thirds majority—if the party whips were effective.

It never got that far. After the *MMD* expelled Vice-President Tembo and eight other cabinet members for opposing the project, and after more than half the *MMD* parliamentary delegation also objected, Chiluba loyalists still managed to ram a third-term resolution through the party convention. The president himself seems to have been given pause when violent protests erupted, and police had to intervene with tear gas. After Serbia and Côte d'Ivoire, Zambia witnessed the ventilation of political frustration in the streets. Finally, President Chiluba listened. In early May he announced that he would not seek a third term.

Culture: The territory of Zambia contains some of the most interesting ethnic groups of all Africa. The people are conservative and closely knit within their communities—the majority are Christian, particularly in the more densely populated South and West, but many in the rural section of the North retain their traditional beliefs.

In March 1999 the ministry of health reported that 70% of Zambia's estimated 9 million people were infected with tuberculosis. Thirty percent of Zambia's TB is related to the HIV/AIDS pandemic.

In Zambia HIV prevalence is at 20%. The northern town of Livingston has a 28% rate, making it the most afflicted town in Zambia. The cost of AIDS treatment has risen uncontrollably and continues to do so. Zambia's Central Health Board has said the budgetary costs of treating AIDS patients will rise from $1.7 million in 1990 to $21 million in 2005.

As Zambia enters the new century it is estimated that the number of AIDS orphans in the country will be surpass 600,000.

Economy: Zambia is one of sub-Saharan Africa's most urbanized countries. One-half the population is concentrated in a few urban zones, and rural areas are under-populated. While agriculture supports half the population, with corn the principal food crop and money earner, it is copper that dominates the Zambian economy.

Zambia has been historically copper-dependent. The metal produces 80% of national export revenues, and one mining company, Zambia Consolidated Copper Mines (ZCCM), contributes 25% of GDP. Socialist-style planning and administration during the Kaunda years did not help the industry develop. Two decades of under funding and a shortage of capital investment in new mines dragged copper production from its peak of 720,000 tons in 1969 to 320,000 in 1996.

The economy deteriorated rapidly as copper revenues sank. State enterprises, already bureaucratically inefficient, became heavily indebted. Deficit budgeting increased debt and inflation. Goods and services were in short supply. Business confidence disappeared and consumer frustration mounted. The pressures forced the authoritarian Kaunda to open the political system to competitive multiparty elections. Given a voice, electors tossed him out in 1991.

The Chiluba government introduced far-reaching, market-oriented reforms. Markets were liberalized so prices were determined in the market place, not the bureaucratic office. By 1997, a total of 204 state enterprises had been privatized. About 82% of the companies had been sold to Zambians, most of them well within the ambit of Zambia's governing party.

The state mining conglomerate, ZCCM, was broken up and its constituent parts sold off after much hesitancy and delay on the part of the government. This only diminished the value of what was being sold.

The sell-off of ZCCM continues to generate controversy. A recent audit speaks of "irregularities"—particularly in the sale of millions of dollars worth of cobalt well below market prices shortly before privatization. New management and capitalization have failed to halt production declines in copper. The industry produced 256,000 tons of copper in 2000, slightly down from the 260,300 tons produced in 1999.

There are signs of promising diversity, allowing Zambia to move away from its copper dependence. The country earned $660,000 in the sale of emeralds in 1997, and in the month January 1998 alone it earned $1 million from gemstone sales. Zambia now produces 20% of the world's emeralds. A flourishing export market in flowers is emerging, sending bright blooms to enliven the winter gloom of northern Europe.

The Future: President Chiluba's pursuit of a third term deeply divided party, parliament, and people. His withdrawal from this ill-conceived project throws the presidential race wide open. Any *MMD* candidate will have to overcome the burden of a divided party and the consequences of a fundamentally incoherent economic policy that has seen inflation skyrocket, unemployment rise, and per capita GDP fall from $390 in 1991 to $330 in 1999.

Early morning in Lusaka

The Republic of Zimbabwe

The ancient ruins which gave their name to the nation

Area: 391.090 sq. km. = 151,000 sq. mi. (slightly larger than Montana)
Population: 11,163,160 (July 1999 est.)
Capital City: Harare (Pop. 883,000, estimated).
Climate: Hot and humid in the southern Limpopo and Sabi River regions; temperate in the central and northern highlands. A rainy season normally lasts from October to April and there is a dry season from May to September. Drought conditions prevailed from 1981 to 1984.
Neighboring Countries: Zambia (North); Namibia (South–West Africa, West); Botswana (Southwest); Republic of South Africa (South); Mozambique (East).
Official Language: English.
Other Principal Languages: Shona, Sindebele (the language of the Ndebele, sometimes called Ndebele).
Ethnic groups: Shona 71%, Ndebele 16%, other African groups, 11%, white 1%, mixed and Asian 1%.
Principal Religions: Syncretic (part Christian, part indigenous beliefs) 50%, Christian 25%, indigenous beliefs 24%, Muslim and other 1%.
Chief Commercial Products: Tobacco, gold, ferroalloys, and cotton.
GNP per capita: 610 US$
Currency: Zimbabwean Dollar.
Former Colonial Status: Administered by the British South Africa Company (1889–1923); Autonomous state within the British Commonwealth (1923–1965); unilateral independence as *Rhodesia* (1965–1980), recognized independence (1980).
Chief of State: Robert Mugabe, President.
Independence Date: April 18, 1980.
National Flag: Seven horizontal stripes (top to bottom) of green, gold, red, black, red, gold, green. A white triangle at the staff contains a red star in which is centered the gold Zimbabwean bird.

Zimbabwe is hot and humid in the southern river basin areas. Cluttered forests of hardwood predominate in these lowlands, with both teak and mahogany towering above the scrub vegetation that is the breeding ground of the tsetse fly, carrier of dreaded sleeping sickness.

In the central areas the altitude rises in a series of fertile plateaus, with corresponding modification of the tropical climate. During the winter, the land sometimes gives off enough heat at night to allow the intrusion of a thin frost by dawn. The land that is not forested by tall trees, growing in a less densely vegetated woodland, is under cultivation.

Victoria Falls, located on the Zambezi River above the Kariba Lake is one of the greatest sights of Africa—they are more than twice as high as Niagara Falls and have a width of about one mile. The sparkling waters of the lake, the largest man–made body of water in the world, stretch narrowly to the northeast, held back by the 420–foot–high walls of the Kariba Dam that provides electric power to both Zimbabwe and Zambia.

History: There were successive waves of Bantu migration into Zimbabwe which may have started as early as about the 4th century A.D. The Zimbabwe ruins, the only pre–European remnant of architecture found below the Sahara in Africa, is attributed to people known as the Monoma, and are dated sometime between the 6th and 13th centuries, A.D. The Mashonas settled at an unknown time in the region; the Zulu and Barotse passed through during their migration to the south, and the Ndebele eventually came to dominate both the Shonas and the region. For details of earlier history, see Historical Background and *The British in Africa.*

By 1923 white settlers had gained self-rule. This was confirmed in 1923 when white electors rejected the possibility of joining South Africa. Instead Rhodesia became an autonomous member of the British Commonwealth. Although Britain reserved authority in the areas of foreign relations and military defense, that authority was never in fact exercised. A parliament of British settlers was chosen; Africans could not, with very few exceptions, pass the educational tests required to gain voting rights.

White control was further solidified in 1931 with the passage of the Land Apportionment Act. About 150,000 settlers were given exclusive rights to roughly one-half of the choicest land; 3 million Africans were relegated to the remainder. Land would always be central to Zimbabwean politics.

In 1953 Southern Rhodesia was joined with Northern Rhodesia and Nyasaland to make the Central African Federation. The federation was dissolved in 1963, and Northern Rhodesia and Nyasaland were given independence as Zambia and Malawi respectively. Fearing a similar development, white Southern Rhodesians rejected the governing United Federal Party and replaced it with the more conservative *Rhodesian Front (RF)*. By 1964 the *RF* was led by Ian Douglas Smith. Smith's *Rhodesian Front* swept the elections of 1965 and after several attempts to persuade Britain to grant independence, his government announced the Unilateral Declaration of Independence (UDI) on 11 November 1965.

After UDI

African nationalist organizations began to flourish after 1953, a development greeted with hostility by colonial officials. The first commanding nationalist figure was Joshua Nkomo. In 1961, Nkomo (an Ndebele) joined with Robert Mugabe (a Shona), and Reverend Ndabiningi Sithole (an Ndau) to form the *Zimbabwe People's Union (ZAPU)*. By 1963, however, Sithole, Mugabe and other Shona intellectuals, disiappointed with his leadership, split from Nkomo and formed the *Zimbabwe African National Union (ZANU)*. The split shattered what had been a multiethnic and multiregional anti-colonial movement. It shaped political rivalries well into the post-independence period. Two movements claiming nationalist goals would each become ethnically specific and regionally localized. At the declaration of UDI, African anticolonial forces were thus divided.

UN resolutions condemned White rule in Rhodesia and one forbade any member nation to trade with Rhodesia. Since Rhodesia was one of the very few sources outside the U.S.S.R. of chrome ore vital to the manufacture of hard steel, the U.S. Congress allowed the resumption of Rhodesian chrome purchases in 1971, infuriating Black African nations. Faced with international sanctions Rhodesia turned to the development of import-substitution industries, ironically providing the basis of one of Zimbabwe's greatest economic strengths today: a richly diversified economy.

Negotiations with the Smith regime came to naught. Within Rhodesia Smith allowed the creation of a third nationalist movement, the *United African National Council (UANC)* led by Abel Muzorewa, a bishop of the American United Methodist Church. Anxious to deal with moderate nationalist elements, Smith opened talks with Bishop Musorewa and two other black leaders, Chief Jeremiah Chirau and Reverend Sithole, who had lost out in a *ZANU* leadership struggle with Robert Mugabe. Both Britain and the U.S. urged that *ZAPU* and *ZANU* be included in the talks, but this plea was ignored. Both groups had already established themselves in neighboring Zambia and had launched minor guerrilla attacks against the regime since 1965.

All-out guerrilla war began in 1972 against isolated white farmers in northeastern Rhodesia. With the collapse of Portuguese authority in 1974, *ZANU* guerrilla forces found a permanent base of operations in Mozambique under Robert Mugabe. Joshua Nkomo and his *ZAPU* supporters raised their own guerrilla army, largely Ndebele speakers from southwestern Rhodesia, and opened a second front in the guerrilla war. *ZAPU* guerrilla activities continued to operate out of Zambia. Both Mozambique and Zambia would suffer terribly as targets of Rhodesian retaliation. By 1976 Mozambique and Zambia pressured the two guerrilla movements to fight the Smith regime jointly. This resulted in the creation of the *Patriotic Front of Zimbabwe*. When the guerrilla war took on serious economic consequences in 1978 and whites began to flee the country at the rate of 1,000 per month, Prime Minister Smith signed an "internal settlement" with Muzorewa, Sithole and Chirau. The agreement provided for qualified majority rule and elections with universal suffrage. Mugabe and Nkomo scoffed at this internal settlement, branding the other Black leaders as "Uncle Toms." Even when total amnesty was offered to *Patriotic Front* guerrillas, their leaders rejected it. In the Parliamentary elections of 1979, Muzorewa's *United African National Council* won 51 of the 72 seats allotted to African candidates, beating the *ZANU* splinter led by Reverend Sithole which won only 12 seats. Muzorewa became Rhodesia's first black prime minister, but Whites retained key positions within both the government and the army.

The guerrilla war continued and sanctions were not lifted. Britain decided to end the crisis by creating a government which would include all nationalist elements. The Lancaster House Conference began in London in September 1979 with Muzorewa, Nkomo and Mugabe. After endless weeks of fruitless discussions against a background of continuous fighting back home—an average of 100 lives were lost each day—the white minority finally consented to hold multiracial elections, supervised by the British, in 1980. These, it was agreed, would lead to independence for Zimbabwe.

The Lancaster House constitution would operate from 1980 to 1990, guaranteeing whites representation in parliament and protecting white economic interests. A bicameral legislature was established, with reserved seats for Whites in both houses. Compulsory land acquisition was prohibited to the government as was the establishment of a one-party state before 1990. The draft constitution was accepted by the three leaders and a total of nine political parties prepared for the upcoming elections. Both elements of the *Patriotic Front*, Nkomo's *PF-ZAPU*, Mugabe's *ZANU-PF*, ran separate candidates, as did the Muzorewa and Sithole organizations.

The election resulted in a stunning triumph for Mugabe. *ZANU* won 57 of 80 Black seats in the House of Assembly. Nkomo's *ZAPU* was successful in 20 contests, mostly in Matabeleland, while Bishop Muzorewa was sent to humiliating defeat with only three victories. The white minority was badly frightened at the prospect of having the Marxist Mugabe as Prime Minister, but acting with conciliation he assured them they would be treated as all other Zimbabweans. With representatives of 100 nations on hand, Zimbabwe achieved recognized independence on April 18, 1980.

Post-Independence Period

President Mugabe's politics of practical reconciliation was initially successful. Nkomo was appointed to a high ranking cabinet position. Two prominent white Zimbabweans were also included. The new government's tasks were enormous. It had to integrate what were essentially three armies—the guerrilla forces of *ZAPU* and *ZANU* and the Rhodesian Defense Forces. It had to re-establish social services and education in the rural areas and resettle a million refugees, displaced by nearly 15 years of civil conflict. Mugabe adopted a cautious approach to socializing the economy. Farmers were placated when prices for cash crops were raised. Despite populist pressures for land reform, he assured white farmers that their property would not be confiscated. These incentives produced surpluses which allowed Zimbabwe to weather the draught-caused crop failures of 1982–84 better than most of her neighbors.

Fissures soon developed. A cache of arms was allegedly found on Nkomo's farm and he, along with his closest aides, was accused of trying to overthrow the government. They were expelled from the cabinet in 1981. Nkomo's followers began a loosely organized campaign of dissidence against the government. Centered in Matabeleland, the dissidence involved attacks on both white farmers and government targets.

The government responded with the full force of emergency powers first granted the Smith regime and renewed annually ever since. Sweeping raids were conducted in Matabeleland after 1981. A strict curfew was imposed on the area and food shipments were withheld to starve the area into submission. In 1983 the notorious Fifth Brigade, trained by North Korea, was sent in to suppress the dissidence. The brigade, known as Gukurahundi, or "storm that destroys everything" accomplished its goal with ghastly violence. According to the Catholic Commission for Justice and Peace it was responsible for the death of an estimated 20,000 people between 1983 and 1987. The Matabele campaign demonstrated the regime's willingness to use violence and fear against its own people to consolidate its power.

In the 1985 general election, held at the height of the Matabeleland conflict, *ZANU* increased its parliamentary majority by eight seats and garnered 76% of the vote. Two years later Parliament eliminated seats reserved for Whites. In November, the constitution was again amended to create the post of executive president, combining the roles of head of state and head of government. Mugabe was then elected to the new presidency for a term of 6 years.

In the same month the two main political parties agreed to unify. Nkomo's *ZAPU* was absorbed into the ruling party, *ZANU-PF*. This marked the triumph of the Shona branch of Zimbabwean nationalism and that created a de facto single-party state. The constitution was later amended to provide a second vice-presidency to which Nkomo was appointed. Leaders of Zimbabwe's single party agreed it would "seek to establish a socialist society, on the guidance of Marxist-Leninist principles, and to establish a one-party state."

Despite state repression of political opposition, four opposition parties contested the March 1990 general election. Mugabe won 78% of the vote. The Catholic Commission for Justice and Peace claimed in its electoral report that pre-election violence and intimidation was so great that it was "calling into question the freedom and fairness of the general election." Voter turn out was low—54%.

President Mugabe proved out of touch with his own party when he proposed to institutionalize the one-party state later that year. The proposal was strongly opposed by churches, trade unions and students, and led to strains within the party. Ultimately a majority of the Politburo rejected the Mugabe plan. With the collapse of the Soviet Union and the decline of communist ideology in Eastern Europe, enthusiasm for Marxist-Leninist doctrine and rhetoric declined in Zimbabwe. In June, 1991 *ZANU-PF's* central committee decided to drop references to "Marxism-Leninism" and "scientific socialism" from the party's constitution.

Economic issues dominated Zimbabwean politics in the 1990s. With the expiration of the Lancaster House prohibition on forced land purchases, President Mugabe announced that the government would amend the constitution to speed up land redistribution. The Land Acquisition Act, finally passed in 1992, allowed for the compulsory purchase of 5,500,000 hectares of predominantly white-owned land. The commercial farming community fiercely opposed the plan and its implementation was delayed. A regional drought in 1992 brought great suffering, The Mugabe government, blamed for inadequate planning for the anticipated crop failure, became increasingly unpopular.

With popular discontent rising, fear of the regime seemed to diminish. Parliament became less passively acquiescent in 1992 and defeated government plans for a new ministry. As it seemed to weaken in popular support, the government returned to one of Zimbabwe's genuine hot-button issues: land redistribution. It published a list of farms to be purchased in May of 1993. Seventy farms, some of them the most productive in the country, amounting to 190,000 hectares, were scheduled for compulsory purchase. A year later it was revealed that the first farm seized under the Land Acquisition Act had been leased to a government minister. Many came to believe the government was more concerned about self-enrichment than the needs of its constituents.

The general parliamentary election in April 1995 did nothing to change the political landscape. *ZANU-PF* won its fourth successive electoral victory, winning 118 out of 120 seats.

Unexpectedly, one of Mugabe's most outspoken opponents, Margaret Dongo, won a by-election victory in November. Dongo had been expelled from *ZANU-PF* in 1994 for criticizing high-level corruption. She ran as an independent and was defeated in the April elections. Presenting evidence of massive electoral fraud to the High Court, she won annulment of election results and campaigned a second time. The second campaign took place amid widespread anger over huge salary increases the legislature granted government officials and members of Parliament. The salary announcement came only days after civil servants sued the government for canceling their year-end bonuses to reduce government spending. Needless to say, Dongo won her election.

Mugabe was overwhelmingly reelected for another 6-year term in March 1996, but less than one-third of the electorate bothered to vote. A seeming triumph, the figures suggest *ZANU's* diminishing legitimacy. Emboldened by the example of President Mandela's moral leadership to the South, legislators have reacted vigorously to a series of corruption scandals that tainted the government. Margaret Dongo exposed the looting of the veterans' compensation fund by high *ZANU* officials and won the support of 100 *ZANU-PF* legislators in calling for an official audit of the fund. Legislators also rejected a contract for a new terminal at the Harare International Airport when it was awarded to an inexperienced Cypriot company with close ties to President Mugabe's nephew.

1996 and 1997 also saw an unprecedented increase in the number of public demonstrations against the regime. Civil servants, railway workers, doctors and nurses, among others have all protested wages and work conditions. Veterans of the liberation struggle, mostly poorly educated peasant farmers living in poverty, disrupted the President's speech at the annual memorial day services in 1997 to demand payment and pensions for service. Food riots in January 1998 forced the government to send in the army when the police could no longer control the situation. The regime seemed to be unraveling.

Harare

Courtesy: CALTEX Petroleum Corporation

A Regime of Personal Rule

By 1998 Robert Mugabe's control over party and state in Zimbabwe had little credible and effective opposition. Authority had increasingly been concentrated in his hands by every constitutional amendment, and there were no checks, no balances to assure accountability. His basic authoritarian impulses had no restrictions. Zimbabwe was subjected to a regime of personal rule, and suffered the consequences.

Economic mismanagement resulted in a virtual economic meltdown. The value of the Zimbabwe dollar plummeted. In 1980 it traded at parity with the American dollar; in January 1999, one US dollar was worth Z$40. Inflation soared. Prices on basic commodities rose beyond the capacity of most people to afford them. Mass "stay-aways" organized by the unions almost paralyzed the nation. The government's response was concession to populist demand. Fuel price increases were rescinded; price controls were introduced on basic commodities. The consequent reaction to this was withdrawal of the International Monetary Fund's seal of approval.

Hanging over all this, and intensifying the domestic political crisis, was President Mugabe's personal decision to intervene on behalf of Laurent Kabila when the Congo was convulsed by a second rebellion in August 1998. Mugabe's claim to be supporting a "legitimate" leader was pure sophistry, but then, one of the victims in any war is language. It was the case of one authoritarian coming to the rescue of another. It also demonstrated just how unaccountable leadership in Zimbabwe had become. The government went on an arms-buying spree. China, Zimbabwe's main arms supplier, became the source of fighter aircraft; Swiss-designed cluster bombs were added to the arsenal. Defense costs skyrocketed.

Despite the obvious drain the government would hear nothing of withdrawal. The Minister of Defense told interviewers in early May that the troops would not leave the Congo until peace was obtained. And just to emphasize the point, he added, "I know our economy is not doing well, but that will not stop us from fighting." So speaketh a regime without accountability.

Polls indicated that 70% of the citizenry opposed Zimbabwe's presence in the Congo, and Zimbabwe's political forum heated up significantly. President Mugabe's heightened rhetoric abused his critics left, right and center. Where the government controls radio and television, the few independent newspapers were subjected to ferocious criticism and threats of much closer control. The unions, which had led demands for political reforms and articulated public anger over economic hardship, were subjected to a six-month ban on strikes as Mugabe pursued a crackdown on his critics.

In 1999 and 2000 Zimbabwe continued its downward spiral into economic collapse and political chaos, driven by the ambitions of one man: Robert Mugabe. Tempers frayed when critical fuel shortages developed. The National Oil Company of Zimbabwe (NOCZIM), a state oil procurement monopoly, was so riddled with corruption that it had run up $237 million in debt and exhausted its credit lines. As the crisis continued into a second month, transport and industrial operations were seriously affected. Agricultural activities were equally impacted and there were worries that the tobacco crop would go unharvested..

In what would become an ominous foreshadowing of things to come, President Mugabe accused white industrialists and farmers of hoarding fuel to create shortages in retaliation against his controversial plans to grab mostly white-owned farms to resettle blacks. In reality, the fuel crisis reflected all the ills of twenty years of authoritarian rule. Economic mismanagement was everywhere evident. Corruption and cronyism were rampant and unilateral decision-making disastrous.

President Mugabe's unilateral decision to send Zimbawean troops to assist Laurent Kabila was a major factor in the country's tale of economic woe. The daily tab for keeping the 11,000 troops in Congo was $1 million. Despite acute shortages and massive lines at the gas pumps, NOCZIM continued shipping available fuel to support the war cause. To pay for its costs, Zimbabwe signed a variety of deals that tended to treat the Congo as a neo-colony, rich in exploitable resources. The deals suggested less public policy to amortize war costs, than a means to engage the loyalty of the army and provide enrichment for officers, cronies, and supporters.

In one of the most remarkable of deals, Zimbabwe's army—technically the Zimbabwe Defense Forces (ZDF)—created a company called Osleg to operate parallel to Comiex, a private company owned by the Democratic Republic of the Congo (DRC) army. The two companies were granted licenses to buy and sell diamonds and gold. There was even discussion about moving into diamond mining. Among others, Osleg directors included the permanent secretary of the Ministry of Defense and the ZDF commander, General Vitalis Zvinavashe.

In 1999 Osleg and Comiex, which is run by Kabila's right-hand man Victor Mpoyo, entered into a joint venture to corner the diamond market in the Mbuji-Mayi area. Zimbabwe was reportedly pumping in an estimated $3.5 million a month to support the ventures, but few if any profits were reported. The problem was that Zimbabwean officers had no experience with diamonds and no hard currency to buy them from independent miners.

The ZDF was reportedly sending retired army officers to Johannesburg for training in diamond grading and valuing. There they underwent a crash course of two-weeks, hardly adequate for beginners.

President Mugabe (early photo).

Even an experienced Zimbabwean business man like Billy Rautenbach, seemingly President Mugabe's personal choice to take over the Congolese mining conglomerate Gecamines, ran into trouble with the Congolese. He was removed as head of this cash cow, which seemed to have been milked dry.

The DRC's agricultural sector also seemed worthy of exploitation. Zimbabwe's Agricultural and Rural Development Authority was allocated 500,000 hectares (1.2 million acres) of land for the production of maize, soybeans, potatoes and rice in addition to beef, poultry and pork programs. And just to make sure the goods got to Zimbabwe, the national railways established a weekly goods train run to the DRC. One of the first shipments was 15,000 tons of copper concentrate from Gecamines.

Ineptitude, loss, and mismanagement in the Congo mirrored the general deterioration at home. Foreign exchange nearly disappeared. Inflation ran above 60%, as did the unemployment rate. Interest rates rose to 70%. The Zimbabwe dollar declined even more, trading at 45 to one US dollar. Over 60% of the population lived below the poverty line. This was the Mugabe legacy. It gave rise to two major political movements in late 1999.

In September the Zimbabwe Confederation of Trade Unions (ZCTU) launched a new political party, the *Movement for Democratic Change* (*MDC*). The confederation's dynamic and effective secretary-general, Morgan Tsvangirai, was designated party leader. In the months to come the *MDC* would provide consistent and focused opposition to the Mugabe regime. Its capacity to mobilize opposition was facilitated by the pre-existent structure of grassroots union organizations.

The confederation's dynamic and effective secretary-general, Morgan Tsvangirai, was designated party leader. In the months to come the *MDC* would provide consistent and focused opposition to the Mugabe regime. Its capacity to mobilize opposition was facilitated by the preexistent structure of grassroots union organizations.

The second movement sparked by deteriorating conditions was one to amend Zimbabwe's constitution. President Mugabe appointed an official Constitutional Commission to recommend changes. It held hearings and learned that Zimbabweans overwhelmingly wanted Mugabe's power to be limited.

The whole process ended in farce. A draft, which actually strengthened and consolidated the president's powers and allowed the confiscation of white-owned farms without compensation, was swept through the final meeting of the 400-member constitutional commission. No vote was taken. To delegates' roars of "No", Judge Godfrey Chidyausiku, the chairman, declared, "the draft is adopted by acclamation."

The *MDC* and commercial farmers organized a "No" campaign in the February referendum. The government, which had never lost an election in twenty years of power, used its power to make life as miserable as possible for its opponents. The state print and broadcast media rejected all opposition advertising and virtually all statements critical of the draft constitution.

Despite governmental control and intimidation, the opposition handed President Mugabe his first defeat since independence. Fifty-five percent of those voting rejected the proposed amendments. Even the promise of white lands for Africans could not silence a populace suffering the consequences of twenty years of misrule.

Like the wounded and cornered lion he was, Mugabe lashed out with special ferocity, unleashing a storm of violence that reduced Zimbabwe to a state of governance by thuggery and fear. The country witnessed seemingly "spontaneous" invasions of white-owned farms by self-styled "war veterans," "disillusioned," they said, by rejection of the constitutional amendment allowing confiscation and distribution of the lands. The reality was somewhat different.

Many of the so-called "war veterans" were far too young to have ever served. They were in fact part of the mass of urban unemployed, carefully organized and dispersed throughout the country with logistical precision. The farm invasions began within a week of Mugabe's referendum defeat in February and ultimately were estimated to involve 50,000 squatters invading up to 1,400 farms. London's *Sunday Telegraph* reported the man coordinating the land seizures and organizing food and transport for squatters was none other than General Perence Shiri.

The recently discovered stone carving of the Zimbabwe Bird

Courtesy: CALTEX Petroleum Corp.

The head of Zimbabwe's air force, General Shiri had also commanded the Fifth Brigade massacres in Matabeleland in the Eighties—probably the most notorious example of the state employing coercion against its own citizens. General Shiri's name also appeared on a list of 28 senior government and military figures given farms seized from white farmers.

The campaign was, quite simply, a program of state-sponsored terrorism. Its victims were initially white farmers who had been active in the campaign against the referendum and their black employees. Whites were humiliated and killed. Black farm workers had their homes and property destroyed and were forced to participate in the depredations of the next farm to be invaded. A state of law ceased, replaced by fear, intimidation, and violence.

This was the political climate in which the government held the June 2000 parliamentary elections. They were less about "landless veterans" than about *ZANU-PF* maintaining power. Fearful of losing power and perquisites, Mugabe and his minions resorted to force and terror to brutalize and silence rural supporters of the *Movement for Democratic Change* (*MDC*).

Zimbabwe's electoral geography explained the rural strategy. Rural parliamentary seats outnumber those in urban districts where the economic consequences of Mugabe's legacy are felt most and where opposition is greatest. Every rural victim of the regime's terror campaign became a living reminder of *ZANU-PF's* ability to destroy those who did not support it—a crude but effective way to rally party supporters in party strongholds.

The government-sponsored campaign of violence resulted in the death of some 30 people. Thousands were beaten, raped and intimidated, but *MDC* voters courageously made their way to the polls and handed *ZANU-PF* the surprise of its life. Out of 120 seats available through the election, the *MDC* won a remarkable 57; *ZANU-PF* won 62 and the remaining seat went to Rev. Sithole's *ZANU-Ndonga*.

Despite electoral intimidation, it was the best showing by any opposition party in Zimbabwe's history. Several *ZANU-PF* bigwigs were defeated, including Mugabe's right-hand man, Emmerson Mnangagwa. Zimbabwe's constitution allows the president to appoint an additional 30 members to parliament. Using this option, Mugabe returned Mnangagwa to the House of Assembly, where he was elected speaker.

The EU characterized the election as neither fair nor free, and the *MDC* challenged nearly 40 results in court. In several cases the justices have annulled election results that had been compromised by violence and intimidation, adding fuel to President Mugabe's sustained attack on the judiciary. That first started when courts ordered black squatters to end their illegal occupations of white-owned farms. War veterans, who had become the regime's storm troopers, invaded judicial premises and threatened judges. The police did nothing, and the regime informed the justices that it was unable to protect them or their families.

The chief justice of Zimbabwe's supreme court was thus forced into early retirement, and Mugabe appointed one of his cronies, Judge Godfrey Chidyausiku, to fill the vacancy. Judge Chidyausiku, it should be recalled, had chaired the notorious constitutional commission which had proposed constitutional amendments to increase, once again, President Mugabe's authority and allow confiscation of white-owned farms without compensation.

Mugabe and the Media

The regime's intimidation of judges was condemned by an international panel of judges and lawyers for placing the rule of law "in the gravest peril." But its attack on the judiciary was only one part of a campaign to destroy its opponents, wherever they were. The media, especially the *Daily News*, Zimbabwe's only independent newspaper and an outspoken critic of the Mugabe regime, were specifically targeted for harassment and intimidation.

War veterans, now the regime's enforcers, assaulted *Daily News* journalists, fired steel bolts into its offices, and set up road blocks outside Harare to confiscate copies of the newspaper and prevent its distribution to outlying areas. In January 2001, Chenjerai Hunzvi, the veterans' leader, declared that he would "ban" the paper. Within days the paper's printing works were blown up with such force that the explosion rattled houses fives miles away. Five of The *Daily* News's six presses were shattered, and the roof of the warehouse was blown off.

Investigators later determined the destruction had been caused by five anti-tank land mines, manufactured in the former Soviet Union and favored for their ability to toss a ten-ton tank into the air. Those who set them off knew how to place them for maximum effect. In other words, this was not an affair of street-crazies with a few pipe bombs.

When the government disliked the coverage it got, reporters were expelled, as happened to the BBC correspondent and a colleague working for a South African paper. Local reporters could fare worse and at least two were badly tortured. The government also kept its own puppet press in turmoil. When the government-controlled *Herald* and *Sunday Mail* both dramatically lost circulation and money, their editors were fired. Their successors lasted but a few months before being fired.

When the Media Institute of Southern Africa (MISA) released its 2001 report on the state of media freedom in the region, Zimbabwe had the highest number of media freedom violations. And in May, the Committee to Protect Journalists (CPJ), an international media watch-dog group, placed President Mugabe on a list of ten "worst enemies of the press." The CPJ citation of dishonor said the president had "launched an all-out war against independent media, using weapons that range from lawsuits to physical violence."

Radio, far cheaper than newspapers and more effective in reaching a rural audience, has been a major concern of the regime ever since Zimbabwe's supreme court declared the Zimbabwe Broadcasting Company's monopoly unconstitutional in September 2000. Since independence in 1980, there has been no private broadcasting station in the country. Shortly after the court's decision, Capital Radio, financed by foreign charities, started operations, broadcasting music. It had a brief life. Within days armed police swept into the station's office, seized its equipment and accused it of being a "pirate" station.

Not wanting any alternative voices to be heard, especially when there was a presidential election coming up in 2002, President Mugabe has used *ZANU-PF* majorities in parliament to pass a range of legislation that aimed to destroy free expression. A broadcasting act was rushed through parliament in April 2001with little debate, even after it was criticized as unconstitutional by one parliamentary committee.

By the provisions of the bill, potential broadcasters would require a license. National broadcast licensees would be severely limited, and radio stations could not be owned if financed by foreign interests. Broadcast content was mandated: at least 75% of the programs broadcast must have Zimbabwean content and be produced within Zimbabwe. For commercial broadcasters, at least 50% of the music broadcast must be produced within Zimbabwe, and at least 10% of the non-Zimbabwean music must be African.

The government also retained the power to close down broadcasters. The act allows the minister of information to suspend a license if the broadcaster does anything which is, in the words of the legislation, "prejudicial to the defense, public safety, public order, public morality or public health of Zimbabwe." It's the minister's license to kill independent broadcasters, and there should be no doubt the license will be used. Commenting on Capital Radio, Zimbabwe's information minister, Jonathan Moyo, made the government's position clear: "If there is a court which allows (independent broadcasting) in Zimbabwe, we will not allow it. It compromises our national security."

One provision of the broadcast act prevents political parties from owning radio stations. It is a direct attack on the *MDC*'s ability to get out the word and mobilize its constituency. Equally draconian is the Political Parties Act passed at the same time. It prevents political parties or candidates from accepting foreign funding either directly from a donor or indirectly from a third party.

In the Spring of 2001 Hunzvi and his "war vets" brought their circus of chaos to the cities. Businesses and even charitable institutions were subject to veterans' raids, which amounted to little more than an excuse to steal, kidnap and extort. When they threatened to invade embassies, the outcry was so great the plug was pulled on their depredations, but the regime's point had been made: it could destroy the source of support for the *MDC* within the business community. For Hunzvi it was a last hurrah of sorts. He died in early June, reportedly of malaria of the brain.

Morgan Tsvangirai, the *MDC* leader, has been charged with "inciting terrorism" against President Mugabe. At one political rally, it is alleged, he said that if Mugabe did not step down peacefully "we will remove you violently." The trial has been delayed on several occasions as the government searches for a compliant judge to hear the case. If convicted, Tsvangirai could be disqualified from running against Mugabe in next year's presidential elections.

Morgan Tsvangirai, MDC Leader

Culture: The white and African populations lived apart for decades; independence has not changed this. Black workers provided labor on white plantations as well as in urban homes and stores. Harare, Umtali, Gweru and Bulawayo were all modern, thriving cities possessing almost all conveniences of European or American urban areas, but have been in decline since 1980. There is no legal discrimination in the cities—the races mix in public places, but somewhat uncomfortably.

The majority of people combine their traditional tribal beliefs with Christianity (Protestant). The remaining white people are primarily Anglican and Presbyterian, and there is an active Catholic Church in which the Bishops openly oppose terrorist measures of the current government. But the Pope blessed Mugabe's belated marriage to his secretary, Grace Marufu. They have two children, both conceived before the death of his first wife. The marriage rites and post–nuptial celebrations in 1996 were attended by 20,000 people—important, and unimportant hangers–on.

AIDS rages throughout Zimbabwe and takes its horrific toll. In less than 15 years AIDS has gone from isolated occurrence to pandemic. Official figures as of March 1999 indicate that 220 people a day are dying from the disease. An estimated 26 per cent of people between the ages of 55 and 49 are infected with HIV. A University of Zimbabwe medical school survey indicated that one in every three pregnant women in the capital were HIV positive. An estimated 3 million Zimbabweans may be living with HIV. This year 80,000 deaths from AIDS are predicted.

The social consequences are devastating. Zimbabwe is well on its way to losing an entire generation. Left behind are the orphans—an estimated one million since the 1980s—deprived of traditional family support and often abandoned to life on the streets of the country's larger cities. There they turn to the only life available: begging and crime.

Zimbabwe's social and political problems, like the spread of AIDS, have long been the subject of song by Zimbabwe's foremost musician, Thomas Mapfumo. Born in colonial Rhodesia in 1945, Mapfumo has a personal history that reads like a biography of Zimbabwe. Early recognizing how Africans were exploited in their own land, he sympathized with those fighting against white rule and wrote songs in his native Shona that uplifted the hearts and sustained the action of Zimbabwe's guerilla forces.

It was *chimurenga* music, or music of the struggle. It articulated the concerns of those who had no voice, or as Mapfumo says, it gave voice to the voiceless. Inclusion of the sounds of the *mbira,* a traditional Shona thumb piano, provided a deceptively innocent packaging for revolutionary songs of justice and freedom. Traditional Shona proverbs disguised much of the meaning from those unfamiliar with the language, but the colonial regime could sense popular reaction. After one of his songs of liberation, "Hoyoko" (Watch Out), became a popular hit, Mapfumo's music was banned from the airwaves.

Since the heady days of the liberation struggle, the musician has become increasingly disenchanted with Zimbabwe under Robert Mugabe. His music still gives voice to those who suffer most, but it now criticizes the regime that betrayed their hopes for a better life. "Too many of my people," he says, "are still poor, hungry and without jobs, homes or land. As long as that's the case I have no choice to speak out for them."

"Chaunorwa" criticized Zimbabwe's pervasive corruption under Mugabe, and was duly banned from state-controlled airwaves. Other songs have criticized the farm invasions and Zimbabwe's involvement in the Congo War. His latest album, *Chimurenga Explosion* (aNOym reCOrds, 2000)—released only a few months before the June parliamentary elections—had at least one of its cuts, "Disaster," denied airtime. "Disaster" is Thomas Mapfumo's description of Zimbabwe under Robert Mugabe. "I'm very disappointed," he says. "After all our struggle, I never expected our own black government was going to destroy our country." Mapfumo has moved his family to the United States and vows not to return to Zimbabwe while President Mugabe remains in office.

Economy: Traditionally, Zimbabwe has gained its chief income from agricultural exports. Tobacco is the principal commercial export, but mineral resources, like gold and various ferroalloys, make a significant contribution. The economy is in free fall as a consequence of both government action and inaction.

Social violence orchestrated by *ZANU-PF* has disrupted the agricultural sector and especially tobacco. The government's plan to confiscate commercial farms for distribution to the landless could very well destroy the most vibrant component of a desperate economy. The big farms not only keep Zimbabwe fed, but produce 30% of its total exports. Tobacco alone is the single biggest earner of foreign exchange—about 30%, and it contributes 15% to Zimbabwe's GDP.

The effects of social chaos have been manifested in tobacco production. In the 2000/2001 growing season, Zimbabwe produced about 180 million kg of tobacco. A year earlier, farmers produced a record crop of 237 million kg, worth some $400 million. Production is likely to diminish further. On farms confiscated by government or squatter action, food crops have begun to replace tobacco.

Farm production in general has been hard hit by fuel shortages, higher costs attributed to an over-valued Zimbabwe dollar and an inability to borrow from banks leery of loaning of land that might be seized. Widespread disruption of agriculture, combined with a severe shortage of foreign exchange, means Zimbabwe could face a major food deficit of 600,000 tons of maize, the country's staple crop, this year. The country needs at least 1.8 million tons of maize to feed its population, but maize production fell by 43% last season. Overall agricultural output is estimated to decline by 15% in 2001. There were food riots in October 2000, and these may only be a precursor of more to come in Fall 2001.

Tourism, another source of foreign exchange, has also been hard hit by the violence. Hotel occupancy levels have plummeted. Industrial output, starved of fuel and other inputs, will slow significantly. Over 400 businesses have already declared bankruptcy.

The government has consistently spent more than it takes in despite the efforts of the International Monetary Fund to effect structural change. Even with the economy's dire state, the presidential family lives well. While 60% of the population lives below the poverty line, Mugabe and his wife Grace await the completion of their fourth private mansion in Harare's plushest suburb. It's a gift from his party and built by the same Cyprus-based company that won the contract to construct the capital's new airport. Mugabe, an inveterate traveler keen on creature comforts, is also said to be planning to buy a $38 million private plane for presidential travels. The presidential couple travels abroad frequently.

The regime has long existed on patronage and pre-electoral payoff. Tough elections are usually preceded by unbudgeted spending sprees. The last time around it was veterans' pensions. For the June parliamentary elections the government doubled the pay and allowances of MPs, increased civil servants' salaries by 90%, and boosted payments to rural leaders. Ruling party leaders are already privileged by being exempted from paying the customs duty of 200% on the value of imported luxury cars. Budget deficits are expected to reach the equivalent of 15% of GDP. The only conceivable source for such extravagance would appear to the printing press, and inflation already hovers around 70%.

The World Bank cut off funding for Zimbabwe because of debt arrears amounting to tens of millions of dollars. By May 2001 Zimbabwe's external payments arrears had reached $629 million. Foreign exchange had virtually dried up, and Zimbabwe received what fuel and electricity it did through the kindness of neighbors. South Africa, unwilling to have a total economic implosion on its borders, continued to supply fuel, while Mozambique still waits for payments due the Cabora Bassa generating plants.

Given the general instability, Zimabwe does not inspire investor confidence. Between January and April 2001, foreign investment declined 61%. Without investment new jobs are not being created, and old ones are being lost as business shrinks. Overall, Zimbabwe's economy is expected to shrink by 7 to 8%, at least, in the coming year.

The Future: Zimbabwe is essentially bankrupt, but unfortunately there is no receivership in the international community. President Mugabe's rule has reached such heights of despotism and caprice that even Nelson Mandela has referred to him, in barely disguised terms, as a "tyrant." He went on to say, for good measure, that ordinary people should depose tyrants who enriched themselves at the expense of their countrymen by "picking up rifles and fighting for liberation." It suggests the degree to which forbearance for the regime has evaporated. A survey released in October 2000 by the Helen Suzman Foundation, a South African Research group, found that 79% of Zimbabweans wanted President Mugabe to resign.

There would appear to be little chance of this. He has indicated his intention to run in 2004, and the brutal assaults on press, courts and political opposition only emphasize the campaign to eliminate anyone or anything that stands in the way of his electoral success. No election with Mugabe and *ZANU-PF* will be free and fair, and if falsified results are returned, one could easily see a replay of events in Bucharest or Abidjan where democracy was asserted in the streets.

The cost of basic food products like bread, fruits, and vegetables has escalated dramatically in the first half of 2001. This, coupled with looming food shortages, could produce social unrest which even regime violence might not be able to control. London's *Guardian* newspaper ran a fundamentally unrealistic article in the late spring that said Zimbabwe's high military command had informed their South African counterparts they were preparing a coup for the fall. There would be, the argument ran, food riots and the army would be asked by Mugabe to put them down, but would be unwilling to fire on its own people. They would, instead, depose the president.

Times are crazy in Zimbabwe, but nothing in the article makes much sense. Senior generals have done quite well under Mugabe and have profited from the endless opportunities provide by Zimbabwe's intervention in the Congo. None appears to be interested in losing such benefits. If there is antipathy to Mugabe and his regime, it comes from the middle and lower ranks of the army. Mugabe has less to fear from his generals than from his privates and corporals and sergeants.

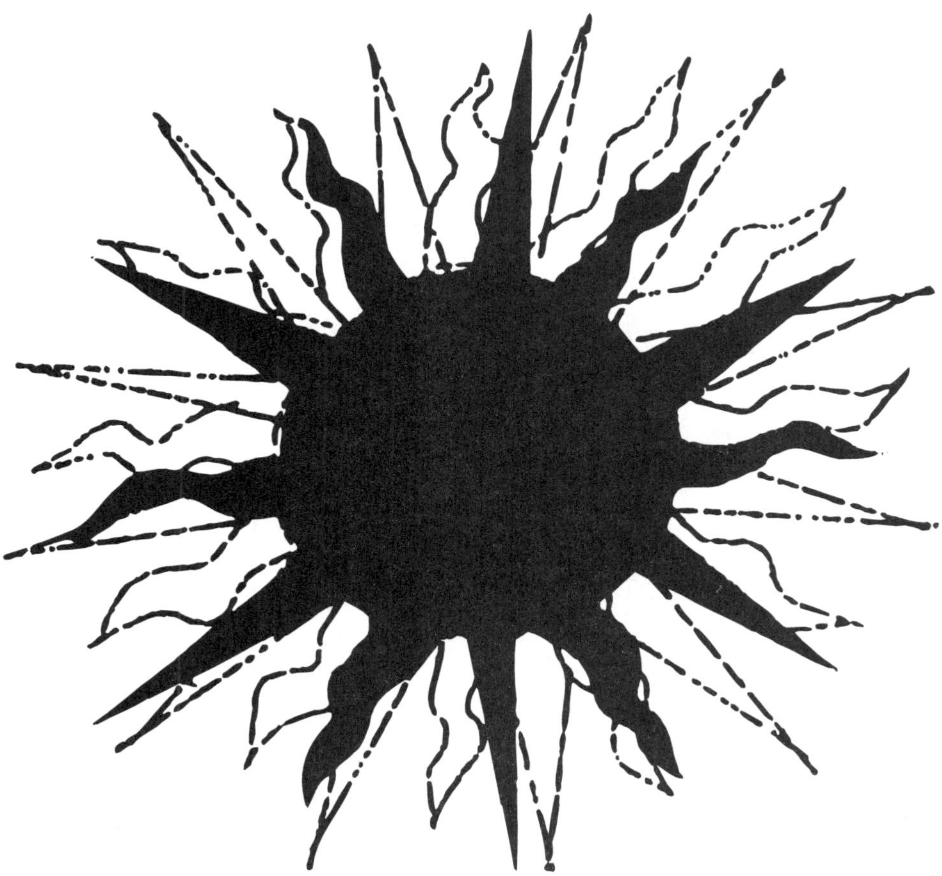

EAST AFRICAN ISLAND NATIONS

The Democratic Republic of Madagascar

Area: 595,000 sq. km. = 229,730 sq. mi. (somewhat smaller than Texas).
Population: 14,873,387 (July 1999 est.)
Capital City: Antananarivo (Pop. 1.5 million, est. 1996. Pronounced Tah-nah-nah-*reev.*)
Climate: Interior–warm and rainy (November–April); cool and dry (May–October); the southern portion of the island is semi–arid. The coastal areas are uniformly hotter than the inland altitudes. The east coast has a heavy, almost year–around rainfall brought by Indian Ocean trade winds and monsoons.
Neighboring Countries: The closest neighbor of this island republic is Mozambique, 300 miles west on the African mainland.
Official Language: Malagasy and French.
Other Principal Languages: Malagasy is universally understood and spoken by the people, although there are several dialects, particularly in the coastal areas.
Ethnic groups: Malayo-Indonesian (Merina and related Betsileo), Cotiers (mixed African, Malayo-Indonesian, and Arab ancestry—Betsimisaraka, Tsimihety, Antaisaka, Sakalava), French, Indian, Creole, Comoran.
Principal Religions: Indigenous beliefs 52%, Christian 41%, Muslim 7%.
Chief Commercial Products: Coffee 45%, vanilla 20%, cloves, shellfish, sugar, and petroleum products.
GNP per capita: 260 US$
Currency: Malagasy Franc (no longer tied to the French Franc).
Former Colonial Status: French Protectorate (1894–1960).
Independence Date: June 26, 1960.
Chief of State: Didier Ratsiraka, President (since Feb. 1997).
National Flag: A vertical stripe of white closest to the pole with two horizontal stripes of red and green.

The Democratic Republic of Madagascar, the fourth–largest island of the world situated in the Indian Ocean off the southeastern part of Africa is a land of contrast throughout its 990–mile length.

The west coast, facing the Mozambique Channel, is a low, tropically wet and dry region, particularly in the extreme South. A series of broad plateaus rise from the coast to increasing heights of 2,300 to 4,500 feet. More abundant rainfall occurs here, and the altitude tempers the otherwise hot climate. Almost daily rains fall during the summer; the weather from May to October is cooler when temperatures in the higher altitudes drop as low as the freezing point. Several mountain ranges rise above this plateauland—Mount Tsaratanana majestically looms to a height of 9,450 feet.

The eastern shore is a narrow strip between the sea and the steep sides of the mountains. Washed by the warm waters of the Indian Ocean, and visited by the trade winds and monsoons, this coastal strip is almost uniformly hot and humid, with an annual rainfall exceeding 110 inches.

History: The Indonesian, Arab and African heritage of the people of Madagascar gives some indication of its early history. From the time of the Christian era, there were successive waves of immigration to the island by people from what are now Indonesia and Malaysia. For early and colonial history, see Historical Background and *The French in Africa.*

Philibert Tsiranana (*Feel*–eh–bear Tsear–ah–*nah;* the last vowel in Malagasy names is not pronounced), a moderate, was the first president after independence. His health gradually failed, and he was unable to deal effectively with a Maoist uprising in the South in 1971. All power was given to the military in 1972, eventually headed by Lt. Commander Didier Ratsiraka (*Deed*–year Rot–see–rakh) as President of the Supreme Council of the Revolution.

Known as the Red Admiral, even issuing his only little red book of thoughts in emulation of Chairman Mao, Ratsiraka was the instigator of the Malgasy socialist revolution of 1975. The Malagasy Republic was replaced by the Democratic Republic of Madagascar. Government control of the economy under Ratisraka rose dramatically. Just as dramatically, the economy declined. Backed by the military, Ratsiraka was reelected to successive seven-year terms in 1982 and 1989, after advancing the election nine months. Violence marked the regime in early 1990's, when Ratsiraka used the military to resist a pro-democracy movement. The blackest day was 10 August 1991 when he ordered troops to fire on a huge crowd of protesters surging around the presidential palace. Fourteen people were killed and hundreds wounded. IMF economic support was suspended.

In 1991, a High Authority for the State for Transition, presided over by Albert Zafy, was instituted following large-scale protests. A new constitution creating a parliamentary democracy was adopted in 1992, and in 1993, Zafy won the presidential election after a long battle for multiparty democracy. It soon became apparent that constitutional democracy did not guarantee governmental stability. In a period of less than five years following its adoption, there would be six changes of government, three changes of Prime Ministers, two motions of censure and a presidential impeachment. Recognizing the weakness of executive authority confronted with a boisterously fragmented parliament, legislators revised the constitution to reinforce presidential powers. In 1996, after a long-running battle with parliament, President Zafy was impeached and ultimately deposed when the High Constitutional Court confirmed his impeachment by the National Assembly.

Presidential elections in December 1997

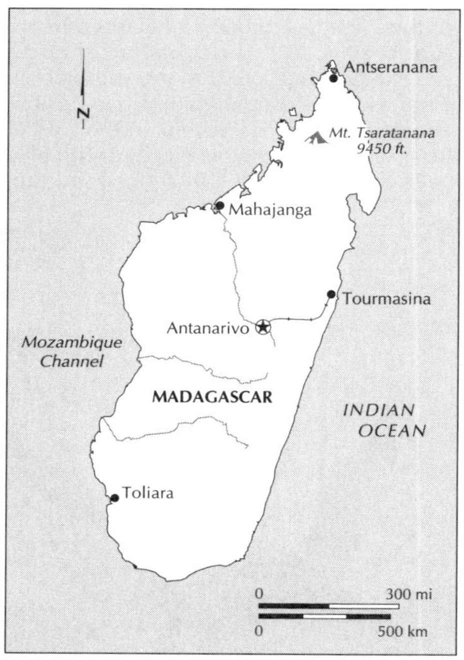

resulted in the return of the Red Admiral, Didier Ratsiraka, from political desert to Presidential palace. A reformed Marxist, like other chameleon presidents in Benin, Eritrea, Ethiopia or Uganda, Ratsiraka spoke of decentralization and economic liberalism. His first major political move was a referendum submitted to voters in March to decentralize governmental authority to six semi-autonomous provinces. These would be run by provincial councils elected by universal suffrage. In turn, provincial councils would elect a provincial governor and exercise control over economic and social programs. That provincial councils could be dissolved by the President of the Republic gave a clue to the real purposes of the constitutional referendum: the reinforcement of presidential power.

Obscured by public emphasis on provincial decentralization, new constituional provisions significantly enhanced presidential authority. The president would have the power to nominate the Prime Minister with no obligation to chose him from the political majority in parliament, and it would be the president, not the Prime Minister, who defined government policy. The president would have the power to dissolve parliament and even nominate the most important magistrates of an "independent judiciary." Conditions for impeaching the President would be considerably tightened. The goal of these provisions was to put an end to the permanent political instability created by the 1992 constitution. In effect, they ended the parliamentary regime of the Third Republic and returned the country to the pre-1991 situation.

Voters were confronted with a single, not particularly informative question: "Do you accept the project to amend the constitution to give greater dimension to the development of all regions and to reinforce national unity?" In a country where only 50% of the population is literate, only 50,000 copies of the revised constitutional text were distributed, and those in French, because translation into Malagasy ran into too many semantic problems. The opposition called for a boycott of the election, saying, not without some justification, it would be a return to a totalitarian regime. When final results were tabulated, only 34% of registered voters managed to bring themselves to the polls, and the referendum passed by the thinnest of margins: 50.62%.

The new regional assemblies mark a significant change for the island. Previous governments, both colonial and independent, had emphasized national unity by a concentration of authority at the center. Power and economic development focused on the capital Antananarivo to the detriment of distant regions. The new assemblies gain control of areas such as social services, development, education and health, with limited taxing abilities for funding regional programs. Money would still flow from the center for obvious reasons: Antananarivo currently accounts for three fifths of the state's tax collection.

Indeed, Antananarivo's dominance was one reason many opposed regional devolution, fearing the capital would no longer be willing to share the burden. Supporters argued that the regional assemblies would bring government closer to the citizenry and develop a sense of public responsibility on the part of politicians. They would, it was also argued, reduce what is seen as a generalized state of corruption.

Political skepticism dominates the Madagascan electorate. A poll by French Institute for Development Research found that 95% of the capital's residents felt that "politicians do not reflect people's needs and only defend their own personal interests." Sixty to seventy percent of that electorate responded to calls to boycott the December 2000 elections.

When the final results were in, President Ratisraka's *AREMA* (*L'Avant-Garde du Renouveau de Madagascar*) party or "independents" associated with it, captured most of the 336 regional assembly seats. Only in the capital did the conservative *AVI* party of former Prime Minister Norbert Ratsirahonana beat President Ratsiraka's supporters, winning 10 of the 18 contested council seats. After the election, the new councilors elected provincial governors who in turn formed administrations composed of a maximum of 12 commissioners.

The election of provincial councilors allowed the election of parliament's upper house. Members of the Senate are elected indirectly by an electoral college made up of what are known as "grand electors"—members of parliament, regional councilors, and mayors. Two-thirds of Senate members are appointed by the electoral college, and the remainder are nominated by the president. Senators serve a term of four years, and half of them will be elected or appointed every two years.

In the Senate elections of February 2001, the governing *AREMA* party, which already had a majority of supporters among the grand electors, easily grabbed a majority of senatorships—49 out of 60. The President will nominate 30 additional Senators. With *AREMA* dominating both center and periphery, President Ratisraka seemed well-positioned to call the shots in Madagascar's next presidential election in 2002.

A bridge to troubled waters.

The president himself became embroiled in a controversy which highlighted the electorate's skepticism and concern that corruption had become pervasive. In November 2000, the government stripped a deputy speaker of the National Assembly, Jean-Eugene Voninahitsy, of his parliamentary immunity and tried him for insulting the head of state and putting out false information. Voninahitsy's crime, in addition to allegedly passing bad checks, was to accuse the president of lying about an aging pontoon bridge secured from the Ukraine.

The bridge, to replace one washed out by the terrible storms of 2000, had cost, the president said, $400,000. It was installed and turned into a toll bridge. After a parliamentary visit to the Ukraine, Voninahitsy claimed to have been told the bridge had been a gift to Madagascar and accused the president of lying. He also challenged the right of a private company to impose a toll on a national highway in the absence of a toll-free alternative.

Voninahitsy, a member of the *Rally for Social-Democracy* (*RPSD*), which is part of

President Didier Ratsiraka

the presidential coalition, was imprisoned, tried and sentenced to 11 months in jail. Hundreds, including heads of political parties, coalitions and lobby groups, as well as members of parliament, took to the streets to protest daily in December 2000 and January 2001.

Ratsiraka, faced with a major challenge to his authority, gave only muddled explanations, including a statement that he was "talking to my children" – seeming to confirm more and more reports that members of the presidential family are involved in their own form of privatizing state resources. With a 15,000 Malagasy francs toll (about $2) for every crossing, the bridge brings in generous revenue for the operator, Decagon, whose board of directors includes Ratisraka children, nieces, and nephews.

Culture: The diversity in the heritage of the people of this great island is modified by the fact that all speak or understand the highly developed language called Malagasy and an estimated 53% are literate. It has some distinctively oriental features, derived from ancient Indonesia and Malaysia; there is a great deal of literature and poetry of a distinctive style.

Although about 41% of the people are Christian, most have joined traditional beliefs with ancestor worship of Hindu origin—a religious combination of east and west. The capital of Antananarivo is located on the site of the old capital city of the Merina Kingdom in the high plateau region. Its population of about one million consists largely of Merina people. The coastal ports of Toumasina, Mahajanga, Toliara and Antseranana are populated mainly by Malagasy Christians, with communities of Chinese and Indian merchants.

Economy: Agriculture dominates the Madagascan economy. It accounts for about a third of GNP and employs 75% of the working population. The sector is dominated by small-scale farms which produce both export and food crops. Vanilla used to be the number one export crop, but natural calamities, governmental inefficiencies in marketing, and high local taxes reduced production at the same time Mexico and Indonesia were increasing theirs.

Eyeing the huge Japanese market for prawns (Japan consumes some 300,000 tons of shrimps and prawns a year; imports make up 90 per cent of this) the government encouraged the development of crustacean fisheries. In 1996 prawns replaced vanilla as the number one export earner. More than 7,000 tons of prawns worth US$63 million were exported that year. Madagascar's main crops are now prawns, coffee, cotton, cloves, and vanilla. They provide about 60 percent of export earnings.

Rice is Madagascar's main food crop, while maize, bananas, sweet potatoes, groundnuts, pineapples, coconuts, and sugar are also grown for local consumption. The economy's dependence on agriculture makes it subject to the caprice of a frequently hostile Mother Nature.

Drought, locusts, and cyclones visit Madagascar nearly every year. The last couple of years have been particularly devastating. The locust swarms of 1998 were the largest for 50 years, causing in excess of US$300m worth of damage. The year 2000 cyclone season started off with two particularly malevolent ladies: Eline whipped across the island with winds of up to 75mph in early February, quickly followed by Gloria which brought two days of torrential rains. Rather than just passing through and leaving a trail of damage, both of these cyclones perversely returned, destroying what they had missed the first time. Trees were flattened, houses crushed, and rice paddies inundated with mud. More than half a million people were left homeless.

Rice production is predicted to decline sharply. Imports of rice, the principal element of the Madagascan diet, have averaged 80,000 tons per year over the past five years. That figure will be substantially higher in 2000-2001.

Under normal circumstances Madagascar produces nearly 75% of the world's vanilla supply. Annual export averages 1,000 tons, with a commercial value of $70 million. Depending on the variety, vanilla sells for $60 to $75 per kilo. Following the devastating 2000 cyclone season, however, it is estimated that about 25 to 30% of the vanilla inventory was destroyed while 25 to 30% of the beans ready for harvest were lost. Supplies in 2001 will be tight. Ice cream and sweets manufacturers, for whom vanilla is a base for practically every flavor, will be hard put to locate alternative sources.

In scenes worthy of Charlie Chaplin or Bertolt Brecht, southern Madagascar has seen the influx of thousands of miners, hot in pursuit of gem quality sapphires. What appeared an anomaly in 1995—the discovery of a huge 40-pound sapphire, nine times the size of the world's largest cut sapphire—had turned, by November 1998, into a treasure trove of easily accessible gemstones. The Ministry of Energy and Mines estimated that 200 new prospectors arrived daily. A small village at the edge of Isalo National Park mushroomed into a city of 100,000, devoid of any sanitary facilities, but ultimately serviced by bars, brothels, and traders. So rich was the strike that reports spoke of sapphires of a quality and color rarely seen on world jewelry markets being "crunched underfoot."

By mid-1999 an estimated US$ 100 million in gems had been excavated and sapphires were well on the way to replacing Madagascar's "pink gold"—shrimp and prawns—as the country's chief export earner. Despite the boom in the mining business, however, the government says it has earned only $2.2 million from the sapphire rush. As of April 1999 only 36 pounds of the gemstone had been declared and subject to government duties.

At musical performance in southern Madagascar

The chaotic development of the mining area only contributed to the ecological damage Madagascar already suffers. The tons of earth dug up by the mining (and the wastes of their producers) were washed into brooks downstream from the gem deposits and impacted on low-lying rice paddies. Environmental degradation in Madagascar is one of its saddest stories. Only an estimated 15 per cent of Madagascar's ancient forest remains, and most of that is in National Parks. Low technology slash and burn cultivation, employed by a desperately poor and expanding population, has contributed significantly.

Once one of the ecologically richest countries in the world, Madagascar now has its biological diversity at highest risk. Forest preservation and the creation of national parks are receiving large-scale international support, estimated to be worth US$4 billion. For many species, however, it might already be too late.

Lassitude continues to characterize government privatization plans. The state-owned petroleum products company, Solima, has only a partial and tenuous privatization of its refinery on record, while its distribution system remains in government hands. Monopoly positions in both cotton and sugar have yet to be privatized, and Air Madagascar, which continues to lose money and whose finances are perilous, remains a hard sell.

The Bretton Woods institutions, better known and the World Bank and IMF, have given the government some leeway, recognizing the extreme poverty of the country and at least a verbal commitment to privatization. In December 2000, Madagascar qualified for the Heavily Indebted Poor Countries (HIPC) Initiative and was granted about $1.5 billion in debt relief—nearly 40% of its total outstanding debt.

The Future: President Ratsiraka and his *AREMA* party dominate political life in Madagascar, but that dominance may well be unraveling. A recent poll of 1,550 people indicated that 41% did not believe they lived in a democracy. Sixty percent also believed that good governance did not exist in Madagascar, a sentiment which can only be further intensified as more and more revelations of how the president has facilitated the economic success of his children and relatives come to light. The affair of the pontoon toll bridge, where politicians united to condemn the president's government, may be an early warning of things to come.

The Republic of Mauritius

Area: 1,856 sq. km. = 717 sq. mi., excluding Rodrigues (40 sq. mi.) and other small islands (45 sq. mi.)—slightly larger than Kauai, one of the Hawaiian Islands).
Population: 1,180,915, 1999 est.
Capital City: Port Louis (pop. 146,000)
Climate: Tropically hot and humid, with slightly cooler temperatures in the highlands of Mauritius which rise as high as 2,500 feet.
Neighboring Countries: Mauritius is located 550 miles east of Madagascar; Rodrigues is 350 miles northeast of Mauritius.
Official Language: English.
Other Principal Languages: Creole, French, Hindi, Urdu, Hakka, and Bojpoori.
Ethnic Background: Hindu Indian (54%); Islamic Indian (14%); Creole, a group of African and African–European descent (25%); European descent, Chinese and other (7%). Figures are approximate.
Principal Religions: Hindu 52%, Christian 28.3% (Roman Catholic 26%, Protestant 2.3%), Muslim 16.6%, and other 3.1%.
Principal Commercial Products: Clothing and textiles 55%, sugar 24%.
GNP per capita: 3,700 US$
Currency: Mauritius Rupee.
Former Colonial Status: French possession (1715–1810); British possession (1810–1968).
Independence Date: March 12, 1968.
Chief of State: Cassam Uteem, President.
Head of Government: Aneerood Junauth, since September 2000 elections.
National Flag: Red, blue, gold and green horizontal stripes.

The land mass that is now the island of Mauritius is the result of volcanic activity that occurred thousands of years ago. The craggy, hardened lava, covered with fine ash and silt was in turn covered with a carpet of green vegetation, growing swiftly in the tropical sun. The island is a series of plateaus and interesting variations caused by small streams, waterfalls, crevices and coastal indentations. The island of Rodrigues is a dependency of Mauritius.

History: The Dutch arrived at this island, uninhabited by man prior to the time, in 1598, naming it after a prince of Holland. They remained for a century and started sugar production at the time the last clumsy dodo birds walked upon the island. Concluding that the island offered no profit, they withdrew, and the French arrived in 1715. The small group of settlers was augmented by African slaves, who worked the sugar plantations that came to dominate the island.

There was some intermarriage between the French and the Africans resulting in the evolution of a stable group of people now known as Creoles, the upper class of which remain pure White in ancestry. The British seized the island during the Napoleonic wars in 1810. Slavery had been abolished and a program of importing large numbers of people from India to perform the strenuous labor on the plantations commenced. When the Suez Canal opened in 1869, the island of Mauritius quickly became one of the earth's forgotten places; it formerly had been a port of call for ships going to and from the Middle and Far East.

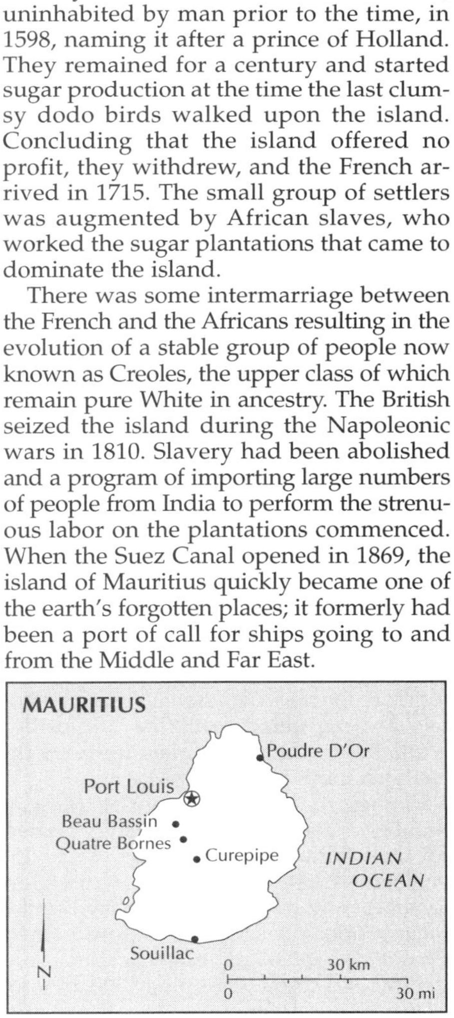

Following World War II, the world–wide surge of nationalism gradually entered Mauritius, particularly among those of Indian descent who had risen in numbers to be a majority of the population. When Great Britain announced the withdrawal "east of the Suez" in 1966, Mauritius was intended to be a part of this plan. Ethnic diversity was the biggest problem—the Indian majority favored independence, but the Creole people were opposed.

In order to placate the Creoles, a complicated plan was devised to apportion the seats of the legislature among the ethnic groups, and elections were held. The result was that the Hindu Indians were able to command a majority; the Creoles a minority and the Islamic Indians were unable to elect a single representative.

For about 41 years until 1982, Sir Seewoosagur Ramgoolam and his *Labor Party* dominated the political scene. The party was challenged in June 1982 elections by a French Maurician, Paul Berenger, and the vote was so split along party and ethnic lines that a coalition government emerged headed by Aneerood Jugnauth, which included Berenger as Finance Minister. A second collapse in the government in mid–1983 led to a second election. Jugnauth, realizing that he had to effectively compete with opponents, organized the *Mauritian Socialist Movement, (MSM)*, which won over Berenger's *Mauritian Militant Movement*. Jugnauth continued in power until late 1995 when he did something of dubious wisdom. A constitutional amendment was offered to incorporate oriental languages (Hindi, Urdu, Tamil, Marathi, Telegu, Mandarin and Arabic) into primary education. All of his principal associates in the coalition resigned and the amendment failed. He had to ask that the National Assembly be dissolved.

An opposition alliance won all 60 seats in the 20 island districts. Navin Ramgoolam, son of Sir Seewoosagur, became the new prime minister. No basic changes in government economic development policies resulted.

The language issue does highlight the multiracial, multilingual and multireligious nature of Mauritian society. Unlike many former British colonies, Mauritius retained the Westminster model, but without winner-take-all provisions. Each communal group constituting the Mauritian nation obtains representation in the National Assembly, but communal tensions can and do arise. In early 1998, Prime Minister Ramgoolam ordered a holiday to celebrate the Hindu festival, which drew the criticism of opposition leaders fearful of the economic consequences of too many sectarian holidays.

Communal, age and class tensions surfaced dramatically in February 1999 when

Mauritius experienced its worst riots in 30 years. They were sparked by the death, in police custody, of Joseph Topize, alias Kaya. A Creole singer and creator of "seggae"—a mixture of Jamaican reggae with the lilting Maurician dance rhythm known as "sega," Topize had been arrested for smoking marijuana at a rally to decriminalize the drug. His death, under mysterious circumstances, set off three days of rioting by mostly young Creoles.

Class differences are sharp on Mauritius. Seventeen white Franco-Maurician families own over half the island's cultivated land. They control not only agriculture but industry too. At the other end of the socioeconomic scale are the Creoles who often have no school certificates or vocational training. They often end up working as laborers, disaffected from a system in which they share so little—an urban poor, dangerous and volatile. Kaya was their idol.

For the Fall 2000 elections Berenger and Jugnauth formed an electoral alliance. In a pre-election pact the two agreed that if they won, *MSM* chief Sir Anerood Jugnauth, a Hindu, would serve as prime minister for the first three years; after that *MMM* leader Paul Berenger, a Franco-Maurician, would rule for the next three, becoming the nation's first non-Hindu leader since independence from Britain in 1968.

Discontent with the state of the economy and dissatisfaction with the handling of communal tensions lay at the heart of the campaign. The alliance appealed to that discontent with the slogan "We'll get the country back on track." Despite 43 parties fielding candidates, the election was a straightforward fight between the alliance and former Prime Minister Ramgoolam's *Labor Party*-led coalition. When the final tallies were in, the alliance won a smashing victory: 54 out of 62 seats in assembly.

Bitterness from Britain's 1968 removal of the Chagos archipelago from the administrative control of Mauritius still lingers. The archipelago, which includes the island of Diego Garcia, was cleared of nearly 5,000 inhabitants and leased to the United States for use as a military and nuclear base; in return the British reportedly were able to obtain Trident submarines on favorable terms. The military base, originally intended to counter the Soviet threat, proved its utility in the Gulf war when allied bombing missions took off from its 12,000 foot runway. The lease expires in 2016.

Culture: Its population is culturally diverse, reflecting the island's colonial history. Europeans brought in both Indians and Africans to work the sugar plantations. Today, about 63% of the population is Indian and overwhelmingly Hindu, 30% African–Creole, 5% Chinese and 2% European. The various ethnic groups tend to have limited interaction with each other. The government has managed to increase literacy from 60% to 100% in a mere three years, largely by making education free. University education remains élitist, restricted to a select few. Only 3% of Mauritians obtain university degrees—which could impact on the government's efforts to attract high–tech companies.

Economy: Mauritius has transformed its economy since independence when it was essentially dependent on the export of sugar to Great Britain. In the 1960s sugar accounted for nearly 80% of agricultural production and 86% of export earnings. Sugar is still king, but in the thirty years since independence, Mauritius has diversified its economy to create strong supports in light manufacturing, particularly textiles, and tourism.

In 1996 sugar accounted for 25.6% of export earnings, but only 7.7% of GDP. Severe drought conditions devastated Mauritius' sugar production in 1999. Production fell by 41 percent, to around 373,000 tons from 629,000 tons in 1998. It was the worst sugar harvest since 1960 when only 235,781 tons of sugar were produced. Sugar revenues for the 1999 season were at $208 million, nearly $160m less than 1998.

The sharp decline means Mauritius will not be able to meet its export obligations to the European Union. Under Lomé Convention protocols, Mauritius is committed to export around 507,000 tons a year to EU countries.

Light manufacturing, dominated by textiles, accounted for 23% GDP. There are 275 textile factories concentrated in Mauritius' Economic Processing Zone and they have made Mauritius the world's second largest exporter of woolen knits. Rising costs, however, are causing a drift of factory production to Madagascar. Recent tariff increases for drinking water costs, water freight services, and port dues, for example, have already increased textile production costs on Mauritius. Some companies found their costs had doubled, diminishing the island's allure to manufacturers.

Tourism constituted 5% GDP in 1996 and represents one of the greatest potential growth areas. In 1999 Mauritius received 578,100 visitors compared to 558,200 during the previous year, representing 3.5 percent increase in the country's tourism sector. Tourism in Mauritius is the third pillar of the economy with revenues accounting for more than $560 million. A hundred hotels are registered with the authorities while the travel and tourism industry directly employs 17,100 people.

Playing to developing tourist traffic, a number of theme parks are being planned for the island. The state-owned Sugar Investment Trust has entered a partnership to build an $8 million aquatic park, but the megaproposal is a Swiss venture named CirnePark. Installed on 40 hectares, the park would cost a whopping $300 million. With all due deference to Las Vegas and Disneyland, it would include the reconstruction of a 19th-century Port Louis shopping street, a cane sugar refinery, a naval battle between pirates, a fishing village, and even a volcanic eruption.

Touted to be the largest leisure park in the south-western Indian Ocean area (a title for which there is little competition) the park will not be profitable "in the short term" according to Robin Virahsawmy, adviser to the Maurician minister of tourism. One suspects this island fantasy is a proposal whose time will never come.

Mauritius is the region's leading center for international financial services—what tends to be called off-shore banking. Unfortunately, this may be associated with growing illicit drug trafficking which former Prime Minister Jugnauth blamed for two attempts on his life in 1988 and 1989.

Mauritius sees itself as an important economic link between Africa and Asia. Represented in ASEAN and the Asia Pacific Economic Cooperation (APEC) forum as well as being a member of the Southern African Development Community, Mauritius has recently taken a leading role in founding the 14-member Indian Ocean Rim-Association for Regional Cooperation (IOR-ARC) which would link the two economic areas.

Maurician businesses have already invested significantly in Mozambique. Sugar producers, for example, have committed themselves to rehabilitating Mozambican refineries and hope to produce 300,000 tons of sugar there by the year 2004.

Future: Both the sugar industry and garment manufacturing are threatened by the withdrawal of preferential access to international markets currently provided by international agreements. The basic thrust of the Maurician economy will be maintained: raw products from Africa exported to Mauritius for processing and then re-exported to Europe, America or neighboring countries. A major push will be made to upgrade the education of the country's workforce for new service industries.

Prime Minister Aneerood Jugnauth

EASTERN AFRICA

The Republic of Djibouti (Pronounced Gee-booty)

Area: 23,000 sq. km = 9,000 sq. mi. (slightly larger than Massachusetts).
Population: 447,439 (July 1999 est.)
Capital City: Djibouti (Pop. 300,000. 1997 est.; 400,000 including suburbs. Pronounced Gee-*boo*-tee.)
Neighboring Countries: Ethiopia (North, West, South); Somali Republic (Southeast).
Official Language: Arabic, French.
Other Principal Languages: Somali, Afar (Danakil), Arabic.
Ethnic groups: Somali 60%, Afar 35%, French, Arab, Ethiopian, and Italian 5%.
Principal Religions: Muslim 94%, Christian 6%.
Chief Commercial Products: Hides and skins, and coffee (in transit).
GNP per capita: N/A
Currency: Djibouti Franc.
Former Colonial Status: French Territory (1896–1977).
Independence Date: June 27, 1977.
Chief of State: Ismail Omar Guelleh, President (since April 1999).
National Flag: A white triangle upon which is centered a red star (at the staff) inserted into two broad horizontal stripes of dark blue and green.

The Republic of Djibouti is a tiny, sun-blistered pocket of land strategically located at the entrance to the Red Sea. The only reason for its separate existence as a colony was the deep, natural harbor at the city of Djibouti, through which Ethiopian exports and imports traveled overland since the beginning of the century. The desert country of the interior is parched and bleak, an irregular landscape seen infrequently by other than the nomadic herdsmen who pass through. It has been said that this area is even too hot for the devil.

History: The Republic of Djibouti was undoubtedly a focal point of African–Asian migration and travel for centuries. For details of early and colonial history, see Historical Background and *The French in Africa.*

France, after granting all of its remaining African colonies independence in 1960 did not concern itself with this remaining African territory until 1966. De Gaulle's August 1966 visit was marked by two days of public demonstrations by Somalis demanding independence. France conducted a referendum in March 1967 in which 60% chose to remain associated with France. In July of that year, the name French Somaliland formally changed to the French Territory of Afars and Issas to avoid any encouragement to expansionist ambitions in Somalia.

Hassan Gouled Aptidon, an Issa, easily won the ensuing presidential elections and an inter-ethnic government was formed with an Afar, Ahmed Dini, serving as Prime Minister. Successive elections in 1981 and 1986 returned the unopposed President with majorities of over 90% and affirmed Issa domination of Djibouti politics.

In November 1991 a devastating civil war erupted between the Issa-led government and a predominantly Afar rebel group which termed itself the *Front for the Restoration of Unity and Democracy (FRUD).* Responding to criticisms of its monopoly of political power, President Aptidon's government decided to permit multi-party politics and allowed the registration of four political parties in 1992. Only two, Aptidon's *People's Rally for Progress (RPP)*—the only legal party in Djibouti from 1981 to 1992—and the *Party for Democratic Renewal (PRD)* contested the national assembly election. Claiming there were too many opportunities for electoral fraud, the *PRD* withdrew its candidates. The *RPP* won all 65 assembly seats with a turnout of only 50%.

In 1994 a moderate faction of the *FRUD* signed a peace agreement with the government, ending three years of civil war. In this accord the government agreed to recognize *FRUD* as a legitimate political party and named two *FRUD* leaders, Afars, to cabinet positions in 1995. In December 1997 elections the ruling *RPP-FRUD* coalition won all 65 legislative seats.

At the age of 83, elderly and frail, President Aptidon announced that he would not stand for re–election in 1999. In April Djibouti conducted its second multiparty presidential elections and the overwhelming victory went to Aptidon's nephew, *Chef de Cabinet*, and long–time director of security services, Ismail Omar Guelleh. His campaign was slick and well–financed. Colored posters covered the walls of Djibouti; thousands of green T–shirts and hats bearing his name were distributed to Djibouti's numerous unemployed. His opponent was the seasoned politician Moussa Ahmed Idriss, a leader in the campaign for independence who served in the French parliament from 1962 until 1967. Much less well–financed, Idriss received about a quarter of the votes cast. It was an election in which both wings of FRUD participated rather than boycotted. Those who had reconciled themselves to the government supported Ismail Omar Guelleh; those who remained in armed opposition urged support of Idriss.

The usual severity of the regime to its critics continues under President Guelleh, who seems little tolerant of criticism. The government, which owns the principal newspaper, *La Nation*, has particularly little patience with the opposition press. Charges of "distributing false information" can land an editor in jail and earn the newspaper a lengthy banning. The government also owns the radio and television stations. Neither is a source of critical judgment against the government.

In February 2000 Ahmed Dini's unreconciled wing of *FRUD* signed an agreement on "reform and civil harmony" with the Djibouti government, seeming to bring closure to the Afar rebellion. The agreement called for rehabilitation of zones devastated by the civil war, compensation of victims of the conflict, and "real devolution, granting a wide degree of autonomy to the regions concerned."

A section of the agreement on democratization suggested *FRUD*'s sense of exclusion from Djibouti politics. It referred to the need for "equitable representation" and an administration within which "the various national communities are equally represented." The reality of political power in Djibouti is that the Issa, the dominant Somali clan, control the ruling party and are disproportionately represented in bureaucratic and military ranks. Among the Issa, the president's subclan, the Mamassan, predominates.

Negotiations between the government and representatives of FRUD's armed faction began in April 2000, but have dragged on with little of consequence to be seen. President Guelleh himself abstained from direct participation, claiming to be too busy with the on-going Somali reconciliation talks. Both negotiations were part of his general policy of seeking civil concord at both national and regional levels. The extended Somali talks were perhaps his greatest achievement. Lasting from May to August 2000, they concluded with agreements on a transitional government that might at last bring order to the chaos that has been Somalia.

Relations with Eritrea were severely strained during its two-year war with Ethiopia. Asmara constantly accused Djibouti of aiding Ethiopia, and President Guelleh went so far as to say the two countries were "almost in a state of war" after charging the country with aiding Djiboutian rebels. Diplomatic relations were restored in March 2000 with the help of Libyan mediation, and President Guelleh made an official visit to Eritrea in February 2001 to work out the details of future cooperation.

Relations with Ethiopia, by contrast, have tended to be a love fest. On a state visit during the war, President Guelleh was everywhere feted and honored. The Ethiopian President called Djibouti "a reliable asset for peace and stability in the Horn of Africa" and "a reliable partner for development." President Guelleh was honored by being invited to speak before the Ethiopian parliament, the first African president to do so in recent times.

In September 2000, Ethiopian Prime Minister Meles Zenawi raised the issue of integration between his country and Djibouti at the Washington National Press Club. Stressing the importance of regional economic consolidation, he went on to say that it "might require political integration."

Internally, tension has persisted in Djibouti, largely due to salary arrears to civil servants. Both teachers and postal workers have gone on strike, and there have been grumbles of discontent from equally unpaid security agents and soldiers.

In December 2000, President Guelleh faced the first serious challenge to his authority when approximately 150 police officers, led by Police Chief Yacin Yabeh Galab, attempted to overthrow the government. The attempt found little support in the mid-day sun and was quickly suppressed, but not before some nine persons had been killed during clashes between police and army.

Culture: The city of Djibouti is distinctly French in atmosphere; about 24,000 Europeans live in the capital, including the French military force and dependents. Djibouti is a very clean city, but it, like other African cities, is surrounded by squalid shanties on its fringes.

A widespread practice is the use of *khat*, a stimulant common throughout the Horn of Africa. Much of Djibouti's business activity grinds to a halt at midday, partly because of the heat and partly because this is when the daily plane from Ethiopia arrives bringing about 12 tons of the drug.

In late October 1999, the Djibouti police shut down about 40 "unauthorized bars" to preserve, in the words of the Interior Minister, "good morals in a Muslim country." The bars, which catered mainly to foreigners, notably to troops from France, were reportedly a focus of both male and female prostitution, drunkenness, drugs, fighting and pedophilia.

Economy: The 1991–94 civil war expanded the army from 3,000 men to 18,000, devastated infrastructure and bankrupted the state. The national debt is estimated to be around $250 million. To pay for the war, public utilities were raided and payments were delayed to creditors and state employees. When the government proposed reducing public salaries, which account for nearly 80% of the budget, a general strike was declared and the government had to suspend planned reforms. The IMF extended the reform timetable to March 1998, but provided only minimal fresh credit. With less than 1% of its soil arable and with virtually no industry, Djibouti is dependent on its strategic location on one of the busiest sea lanes of the world. Modernized to receive container cargoes, port facilities are the heart of the Djibouti economy.

The outbreak of hostilities between neighboring Ethiopia and Eritrea significantly increased activities at Djibouti port, for it became the principal means by which Ethiopia is supplied when cut off from the Eritrean ports of Assab and Massawa. Strenuous efforts were also made to improve rail and road connections between Ethiopia and Djibouti to speed the transfer of imports.

For the Djibouti to Addis railroad six locomotives were rehabilitated, for example, and four new ones purchased with the aid of the French Development Agency. In November 2000, the EU granted a $40 million loan to upgrade the line. With improvements the line will have the capacity to carry one million metric tons of freight annually.

President Guelleh's campaign poster

With the transfer of its maritime commerce to the port of Djibouti as of May 1999, Ethiopia became a major factor in the port's modernization and expansion. In the first half of 1999, over 272,000 tons of merchandise, including food aid, fertilizers and fuel, passed through the port en route to Ethiopia. The port is also the principal entrée for Ethiopian arms and military equipment.

More than 2,000 jobs have been created at Djibouti's port as roads and rail traffic surged to unprecedented levels during the Eritrean-Ethiopian conflict. These new jobs may only be temporary if Ethiopia and Eritrea resolve their differences amicably. They make only a small dent in estimated unemployment rates of 40%.

The Eritrean–Ethiopian war also effected a change in French deployments in Djibouti. As part of a turn to a professional army, France had begun to wind down its military commitments and presence in Africa. French troops withdrew completely from the Central African Republic and were reduced in Gabon and Chad. In this reorganization, French forces in Djibouti were scheduled to drop from 3,200 to 2,500 by 2002. The loss of income from taxes and expenditures by this French contingent would have been palpable, and the government sought to ease into the transition by a cash payment as compensation. The two governments worked out an agreement which entailed a payment of $11 million and an increase of taxes paid for services supplied by Djibouti. With war next door, however, re–deployment was slowed and France sent a hi-tech surveillance frigate to the Gulf of Aden to assure the security of Djibouti's harbor and airport.

Djibouti remains France's largest military post in Africa. It is estimated that the base generates about a quarter of Djibouti's GDP.

A major strain on government resources is the huge temporary population of individuals dislocated by drought and regional conflict. The country hosts nearly 100,000 of these refugees—nearly one-fifth of its population.

The Future: President Guelleh has few resources with which to confront Djibouti's crippling poverty. Unemployment stands at 40%. Promised funds to help demobilize and retrain soldiers have been slow to arrive. There hasn't been enough money to pay civil servants for months. The capital is deprived of electricity for several hours each day, and Ethiopia has offered to supply more. Djibouti's vegetables and beloved *khat* also come from Ethiopia. President Guellah will, of necessity, favor relations with Ethiopia. For a man born and raised in eastern Ethiopia himself, speaking fluent Amharic, federation may very well be a rational policy option.

The State of Eritrea

Downtown Asmara

Photo by Veronica Rentmeesters

Area: 93,679 sq. km. = 40,800 sq. mi. (larger than Maine).

Population: 3,984,723 (July 1999 est.)

Capital City: Asmara (Pop. 435,000, est.).

Climate: Generally dry, moderate to chilly in the central highlands; hot and dry in the desert regions, hot and humid along the coastline.

Neighboring Countries: Sudan (North and East); Ethiopia (South); Djibouti (Southeast).

Official Languages: None, though Arabic and English are often used on official letterheads.

Other Principal Languages: Afar, Amharic, Arabic, Tigre and Kunama, and Tigrinya.

Ethnic groups: Tigrinya 50%, Tigre and Kunama 40%, Afar 4%, and Saho (Red Sea coast dwellers) 3%.

Principal Religions: Muslim, Coptic Christian, Roman Catholic, Protestant

Chief Commercial Products: Livestock, sorghum, textiles, food, and small manufactures.

GNP per capita: 200 US$

Currency: Nakfa.

Former Colonial Status: Italian colony (1890–1941); British trusteeship (1941–1952); absorbed by Ethiopia 1962–1991, (defeat of Ethiopian forces), referendum in April 1993 resulted in total independence.

Independence Date: May 24, 1991.

Chief of State: Isaias Afwerki, President (April 1993).

National Flag: A red triangle at the pole divides a green field at the top, from a blue one at the bottom. A gold olive branch appears on the red triangle close to the pole.

Geological evidence indicates that Eritrea was a relatively flat plateau of green trees and grass prior to the arrival of modern mankind. At an known time, massive earthquakes caused the land to change into a terrain of sharp peaks accentuated by smoldering, active volcanoes which spewed their lava freely. Although the volcanoes are now dead, the peaks remain, often rising to more than 14,000 feet, with a craggy appearance caused by lava rock formations. If the land were lower in altitude, it would be arid and closely resemble that of Sudan to the west. Instead, except for the coastal areas, the climate is moderate, with frost appearing above 11,000 feet. Variation in temperature from noon to midnight may be as much as 60 degrees.

Eritrea is semi–arid at best, and rainfall is irregular. This, combined with the rugged terrain which dominates all but the coast along the Red Sea, makes the land

somewhat unhospitable and generally incapable of producing field crops. Rainfall amounts in a given year depend upon variations in the generally west to east prevailing winds. If the currents aloft are from southwest to northeast, moisture capable of generating rainfall arrives from central Africa's vast rain forest area. But if the prevailing pattern is from the northwest to the southeast, the hot winds of the Sahara and sub–Sahara, hot and dry, arrive and roast any crops that were planted.

Although almost 80% of the people are engaged in agriculture and animal husbandry, they provide Eritreans with only 70% of the calories necessary to reasonably survive. This borderline existence means starvation in years of drought; one out of every five children born does not live until its fifth birthday.

History: Nothing is known of the early Christian era history of this region. The Coptic Christian Church established outposts in Ethiopia and Eritrea in the 4th century, and Islam arrived most probably as a result of continued contact with Arabs by the first part of the 8th century. Today, the people are almost evenly divided between Christianity and Islam. Eritreans continued to live a life of unrecorded, localized independence until overtaken by the swirl of events in the late 19th century associated with Italian efforts at colonization and the efforts of Menelik II, King of Ethiopia, to assemble what became modern Ethiopia. For details of early history, see *Historical Background*, pp. 13, 33.

The Italian conquest of Eritrea and later of Ethiopia effectively created a separate identity for each. After the Italians were expelled in 1941, the British assumed control over the territory. Under pressure from the British and Ethiopia, the UN adopted a plan for federation of Eritrea and Ethiopia in 1950. This was intended to observe Eritrean autonomy, but almost immediately after the federation went into effect, Eritrean rights were abridged or violated. When Emperor Haile Selassie unilaterally dissolved the Eritrean parliament and annexed the country in 1962, the liberation struggle started. In the initial years the independence movement was led by a largely Islamic *Eritrean Liberation Front (ELF)*, but in the early 1970s, the Front divided. Breakaway members coalesced in the Christian-dominated *Eritrean Peoples Liberation Front (EPLF)* which soon became the dominant force fighting the Ethiopian government. Isaias Afwerki emerged as the Front leader.

In 1974 the monarchy collapsed and power was seized by the military. Lt. Col. Mengistu Haile Mariam assumed power as head of state and Chairman of the governing military council known as the Derg. The regime was totalitarian in style, financed by the Soviet Union and Eastern block and assisted by Cuba in a massive militarization of the country. War against the Eritrean rebels continued through the late 1980's, when the Soviet Union, otherwise occupied in Afghanistan, announced that it would not renew its defense and cooperation agreement with Ethiopia. Army morale plummeted and the *EPLF*, joining with internal opposition to the Derg, advanced on Ethiopian positions, ultimately driving Mengistu into exile in 1991.

The *EPLF* established a provisional government in May 1991 with its leader Isaias Afwerki as its head; the *EPLF* Central Committee served as the provisional legislature until a referendum on independence could be organized. Independence was overwhelmingly ratified in a UN-monitored referendum in April 1993. Freely-contested elections chose a National Assembly which in turn appointed Afwerki as President of the Provisional Government of Eritrea (PGE). The *EPLF* renamed itself the *People's Front for Democracy and Justice (PFDJ)* in early 1994 and became the country's only political party.

The new government faced enormous challenges. A constitution had to be written, a judiciary created, a school system reconstructed, refugees reintegrated and ex-guerrillas demobilized. Underlying all was the need to rehabilitate a badly damaged infrastructure and reform the collapsed institutions of a centrally planned economy. In March 1994 the National Assembly established a constitutional commission and members traveled throughout the country and to Eritrean communities abroad holding meetings to explain constitutional options and solicit input. The new constitution which resulted from this broad consultative process was ratified by the constituent assembly on May 24, 1997. Elections which would implement the constitution were postponed; they are planned for 1998.

A full judiciary system has yet to be installed. Given an absence of legally trained personnel, the Ministry of Justice has been unable to process a large volume of civilian corruption cases. These were handled by the Ministry of Defense and in 1997 some 2,314 civilians were tried by special military courts.

At its peak fighting strength the *EPLF* army grew to nearly 110,000 fighters—nearly 3% of the total population. Since a fragile peacetime economy could not support such numbers, the government began a phased program to demobilize 50% to 60% of the army in 1993. In the first phase, some 26,000 soldiers, most of whom had enlisted after 1990, were demobilized. They were given cash bonuses and a six-month supply of food. Government loans and grants of farmland in western Eritrea were available, as were vocational training courses. A second phase demobilized an additional 17,000, most of whom had joined the *EPLF* before 1990 and had had considerable combat experience. Indeed, many had virtually grown up in the army and lacked the skills to be competitive in the economy. These were given higher compensation, more intensive training and more psychological counseling. (Special attention has been given to women fighters who made up 30% of the *EPLF*'s combat forces.) By 1998 the army had shrunk to 47,000.

Eritrean law obliges every citizen between the ages of 18 and 40 to do national service, but national service in war has taken on a new meaning. In April 1999 the government conducted evening raids across the country, rounding up young people who might have skipped out on national service. Unless they could identify themselves as a mother, pregnant or a veteran, young Eritreans were put on buses and taken off to a police station for questioning.

President Isaias Afwerki

Eritrea faces periodic armed clashes along its border with Sudan, the neighborhood bully. As the only country on the Red Sea, aside from Israel, that is not majority Muslim, Eritrea has good reason to be obsessed with threats to its sovereignty. Ever pursuing Islamic expansionism, Sudan supports the extremist Eritrean group known as the *Eritrean Islamic Jihad (EIJ)*. Asmara itself has become a base of Sudanese political leaders in exile who have joined forces with the rebel *Sudanese People's Liberation Army (SPLA)*, which has been fighting since 1983 to free mainly animist and Christian southern Sudanese from domination by the Muslim, Arabised north. In fall 1997 posters went up on Asmara walls instructing veterans demobilized since 1995 to register for possible recall to the colors. The government has also evinced an interest in repatriating several thousand of its soldiers still serving in the armed forces of the *Ethiopian People's Revolutionary Democratic Front*. Prime Minister Meles Zenawi, faced with increasing Islamic activities in southeastern Ethiopia, insisted they were still needed there.

This, of course, all changed with the outbreak of hostilities between the two countries in May 1998. They quickly escalated to virtual war in early June. At issue was an obscure triangle of land, 155 square miles of rocky barrenness called the Badme Triangle. Unlocatable on most maps, the triangle became the focus of national pride on both sides of the border. Both Presidents Afwerki and Meles found themselves in a situation from which it was difficult to retreat. Pride and personality, on both sides, generated a cultivated knack for stubbornness. Negotiations had, by early May 2000, brought no resolution to the conflict. As soon as the last negotiators left, Ethiopia launched another massive attack. A surprise advance against a presumably impregnable pass brought crushing victory in nineteen days, after which Ethiopia announced its war aims achieved.

A ceasefire was announced in June and actually lasted through the conclusion of peace negotiations. The peace agreement, brokered by US envoy Anthony Lake and the Organization of African Unity, was signed by the leaders of the contending countries in December. It called for a pull back of troops and creation of a demilitarized zone manned by several thousand UN peacekeepers. A five-member border commission to demarcate the disputed border was established. The two parties agreed not to name their own nationals as commissioners. Appointed to the commission were officials from the Netherlands, Nigeria, the United Kingdom and the United States, who began meeting at the end of March.

By March 2001, both countries had basically fulfilled their commitments under the agreement, and UN troops had begun to settle in. Thousands of mines, set by both sides of the conflict, make movement hazardous and resettlement of inhabitants impossible. Bodies, mummified in the searing east African heat, still litter the battlefields, the victor often undistinguishable from the vanquished.

Culture: Asmara, Eritrea's capital, is a delightful Italian–style city, sometimes called a "second Milan." Its main street is lined with palm trees, and many of its 400,000 inhabitants can often be found sipping expresso at sidewalk cafes. Its best restaurant is Italian and service there is provided by courtly and elderly Italian– speaking waiters. Eritrea's favorite drink is cappuccino, and like Italians, Eritreans share a national passion for cycle racing. How striking then to think of this as a place at war.

Observers have admired the pluck and courage of Eritreans. Their war of liberation was fought without military assistance from either East or West. It cost them 250,000 lives, but in rehabilitating their land they turned to self–reliance. Unlimited foreign aid was rejected as corrupting. Recycling is encouraged. In Asmara a huge depot gathers scrap metal and refashions it into everyday objects: water tanks and spades from the weaponry of war.

Women are honored and possess an equality undreamed of elsewhere on the continent. During the war of liberation at least a third of the 100,000–strong rebel force was composed of women. After the war, new laws made women fully equal to men with rights to own land, to choose their own mates and even divorce them. Today, that same equality prevails in the trenches of the Ethiopian front. Men and women mount guard with their AK–47s to protect the homeland.

Much remains to do to change the status of women at home more completely. The National Union of Eritrean Women estimates that 90% of women are illiterate. They have thus far organized literacy classes for over 26,000 women.

There is still a stigma attached to HIV/AIDS in Eritrea. People do not talk about it openly, and figures on its penetration into the population are sketchy. The health ministry's AIDS control program estimates that there may be as many as 70,000 HIV-positive people in the country—about 2% of the population. More ominously, the ministry suggests the infection rate may be doubling every 18 months.

AIDS awareness programs have recently been taken to refugee camps. Between various entertainments, talks on the risks and dangers of the disease are given, the use of condoms demonstrated and prophylactics distributed. The World Bank has provided a $40 million credit to assist the government awareness programs.

Economy: In the 1930s Eritrea was an exporting nation, and when World War II disrupted East African imports from Europe, Eritrea supplied the markets. Postwar demand shrank in the 1950s, and in the 1960s, as a province of Ethiopia, the economy was starved of investment and began to deteriorate. With the installation of the Mengistu regime in 1974, Ethiopia adopted a command economy and economic decisions were made by *apparatchiks* working in the capital. Most private assets were nationalized, drying up foreign investment. Recurrent drought, famine and nearly three decades of armed struggle intensified the destructive effects of centrally directed policies.

At its liberation in 1991, Eritrea inherited an economy neglected, isolated and virtually destroyed by war. When independence was achieved in 1993, the government, turning its back on its own Marxist background, began a remarkable effort to rebuild infrastructure, liberalize the economy and aggressively seek foreign investment. Its goal is effective participation in a globalized economy.

That participation was effectively stopped by the 1998–99 war with neighboring Ethiopia. Plans for renovation of the seaport of Assab are in abeyance, its facilities languishing unused because Ethiopia has shifted imports to Djibouti. Treasure and manpower have been depleted in a war few can understand and even fewer can appreciate. In July 1998 before the outbreak of hostilities, the IMF had called Eritrea's economic progress "impressive," noting its gross domestic product growth rate of between 7 and 8 percent. In Spring 1999, Eritrea has virtually ceased to produce anything. It has had to accommodate and bear the costs of at least 40,000 refugees, driven out of Ethiopia. It has gone on an expensive shopping spree for armaments. Top of the line fighter planes, MiG–29s, too sophisticated for the experience of Eritrean pilots, have been purchased with scarce resources. Eastern European pilots fly them.

No longer is Eritrea a bright and shining model of development. The economy has slowed. Growth dropped to 4% in 1998, down from a previous 7%. It was expected to drop further for 1999. Cargo unloadings at the port of Massawa were off by 60%. Because of a needless war, the achievements of years have been lost in months, and reconstruction costs are estimated at $800 million.

Much of the costs of war were financed by the Eritrean diaspora. At the height of the war crisis in May 2000, when it was uncertain if Ethiopia would march on Asmara, 3,000 Eritreans living abroad bought land in the capital where they could ultimately build homes. These sales brought in a total of $29 million to the treasury. Throughout the war the government sold bonds and raised some $200 million in contributions from Eritreans who had emigrated abroad.

Elections for Eritrea's 150-seat legislature—which will select the next president—will be held in December 2001. Provisions will be made for Eritreans living abroad and holding dual citizenships to participate in these elections.

Eritrea faces critical shortages of well-educated and trained people, especially for its ministries. To meet this shortage, the government has begun to send hundreds of graduates of the University of Asmara to various South African universities for advanced work. On their return, students will be placed in a ministry and are expected to serve twice the time of their course work. Most are expected to undertake a two-year masters course related to the ministry of their placement.

The Future: Many contentious issues remain to be resolved between Eritrea and Ethiopia, such as repatriation of citizens and compensation for war damages. Rapid demobilization of troops to get them back cultivating their fields will be required. Drought and war together offer the sad prospect of diminished food supplies.

The Federal Democratic Republic of Ethiopia

Drought in an already parched land

Area: 1,178,450 sq. km = 455,000 sq. mi. (larger than Texas and New Mexico).
Population: 59,680,383 (July 1999 est.)
Capital City Addis Ababa (Pop. 2.3 million, est.)
Climate: Hot in the lowlands, cool and invigorating in the plateau highland. There are normally two wet seasons (June–September and February– April).
Neighboring Countries: Kenya (Southwest); The Sudan (West); Somali Republic, Djibouti (East, Southeast), Eritrea (Northwest).
Official Languages: Amharic, English.
Other Principal Languages: Tigrinya, Orominga, Guaraginga, Somali, and Arabic.
Ethnic groups: Amhara, Gurage, Oromo, Sidamo Shankella, Somali Afar, and Tigrean.
Principal Religions: Muslim 45%–50%, Ethiopian Orthodox 35%–40%, animist 12%, other 3%–8%.
Chief Commercial Products: Coffee, leather products, gold, oilseeds, beeswax and honey.
GNP per capita: 100 US$
Currency: Birr.
Former Colonial Status: Ethiopia has never been a colony in its history of almost 4,500 years. It was briefly occupied by the Italians (1936–1941).
National Holiday: National Revolution Day, September 12 (1974).
Chief of State: Negaso Gidada, President.
Head of Government: Meles Zenawi, Prime Minister.
National Flag: Three equal horizontal bands of green (top), yellow, and red with a yellow pentagram and single yellow rays emanating from the angles between the points on a light blue disk centered on the three bands. Ethiopia is the oldest independent country in Africa, and the colors of her flag were so often adopted by other African countries upon independence that they became known as the pan-African colors.

Many centuries before the advent of modern mankind, Ethiopia was a relatively flat land of green grass and trees. Severe earthquakes occurred, causing fiery volcanos to push skyward, spewing molten lava throughout the land.

Today, Ethiopia is a land of sharp mountains rising to more than 15,000 feet. Their rough appearance is produced by volcanic rock formations. The Rift depression enters the country in the Southeast, and the majestic peaks on either side of the gorge march in parallel formation towards the Red Sea. Slightly above Addis Ababa, the mountains separate and those on the left hand proceed north to the Red Sea at Asmara in Eritrea; the right hand peaks extend towards the Somali Republic.

The rugged terrain is one of the most isolated in the world. Surrounded by desert and arid land on all sides, the mountains rise so swiftly that they are almost impenetrable. The Blue Nile, originating from the cool waters of Lake Tana, flows through a gorge more magnificent that the Grand Canyon of Arizona. This river channel, more than a mile deep and 20 miles across, is surrounded by slopes of deep green vegetation.

There are three semi–arid regions in Ethiopia: in the southeast portion, enclosed by the Somali Republic; in the northwest bordering Eritrea and the Sudan. These areas have been hard hit by the drought which has continued since 1981.

The climate of the highland plateaus and mountains is temperate and invigorating. Frost occurs regularly above 11,000 feet, where the daily range in temperature may span as much as 80° from noon to midnight.

History: For details of earlier periods, see Historical Background and *The Italians in Africa.*

Haile Selassie became emperor in 1930 and within one year promulgated the first constitution which provided for a two–chamber legislature. In reality, he retained absolute power over the affairs of Ethiopia. A short time later, the Italians mounted their invasion of the country.

Following the return of the emperor in 1941 and during the postwar period, increasing emphasis was placed on modernization of what had been a very backward nation. The constitution was amended in 1955, providing for a Chamber of Deputies of 251 members elected by universal suffrage to four–year terms of office. The Senate was composed of 125 members selected by the emperor from among distinguished Ethiopians to serve for six years.

The Crown Council, a traditional institution, included Crown Prince Asfa Woosen and the Archbishop of the Coptic Church, which had separated from the Egyptian Coptics, as well as other dignitaries drawn from the ruling class; it assisted in forming basic policy and was convened at the call of the monarch.

Further constitutional reform in 1966 gave the Prime Minister the right to select his own cabinet, subject to the approval of the Emperor. Eritrea was joined with Ethiopia in 1962 after a popular referendum, but the *Eritrean Liberation Front,* a band of Islamic guerrillas, continued sporadic battles which escalated into an armed rebellion in 1970 and has continued since that time. The rebels, estimated to then number 1,500 to 2,000, were equipped with Soviet and Chinese weapons.

Ethiopia, financed by substantial periodic grants from the U.S. and considered in the post–World War II period to be trouble–free, was conservative and ruled by a clan of wealthy landowners. The beginning of the end of this was in the 1970's when a series of natural and man–made disasters occurred. Drought gripped the nation in 1972; rising prices and unemployment, accompanied by hordes of refugees in the cities from the parched countryside provoked a widespread strike. The military, reacting to high prices, *demanded* higher salaries and started a limited military rebellion. Emperor Haile Selassie, aged and shaken, granted a partial increase. Riots caused by lack of land reform occurred in the southern provinces; peasants demanded and seized productive plantation land owned by absentee landlords.

Civil unrest led to the deposition of the aging Haile Selassie on September 12, 1974. A provisional administrative council of soldiers known as the Derg ("committee") seized power from the Emperor and installed a socialist military dictatorship. Beginning what would become standard practice, the Derg summarily executed 50 members of the royal family, ministers, generals and dignitaries of the imperial government. The Emperor himself was strangled to death on August 22, 1975.

Lt. Col. Mengistu Haile Mariam assumed leadership of the Derg in February 1977, after having his two predecessors killed. Mengistu turned Ethiopia into a totalitarian state and a communist killing field. From 1977 through early 1978 thousands of suspected enemies of the Derg were tortured and killed in a purge known as the "red terror." Communism was officially adopted, a Soviet-style constitution promulgated, and the Workers Party of Ethiopia created, complete with a hammer and sickle flag. Resistance, equally inspired by Marxist-Leninist thinking and practice, developed in all the major regions of the country.

In connection with its efforts against the rebels the government embarked on vast programs of "resettlement" and "villagization." The first was intended to resettle people from the often arid north to the rainier southern regions. Illiterate and fearful, the people often fled, both before and after being moved, to Sudan and Somalia. Many were shot—in the back—while fleeing. They then lived in horrible squalor in refugee camps, where more arrivals occurred by the hundreds each week and disease was rampant, sapping what little strength the people had left. The second program was calculated to give the government more control over the people in rural, inaccessible areas so they couldn't support rebel movements. It also was intended to make the collectivization of agriculture easier. This was initially criticized by observers, who later correctly concluded this is the only lasting solution to frequent famine in this nation.

The government did not hesitate to use foreign aid to lure people into these programs who otherwise would have had nothing to do with them. As usual, with food shortages widespread, children were the first to starve, becoming living skeletons before drawing their last breath.

Sensing the weakened state of Ethiopia, the Somali Republic unleashed a band of rebels (and later regular army troops) to seize the Ogaden Desert region of its neighbor—most of the people of the Ogaden are ethnic Somalis. By mid-1977 they had penetrated as far as Diredawa. The Soviets stepped in and began to send massive quantities of arms and technical personnel to Ethiopia. This, however, placed the USSR in the embarrassing position of being patron and supporter of both sides of a war in which neither party had any interest in compromise. This was brief; the Somalis ejected the Soviets from their nation and turned to the United States for support.

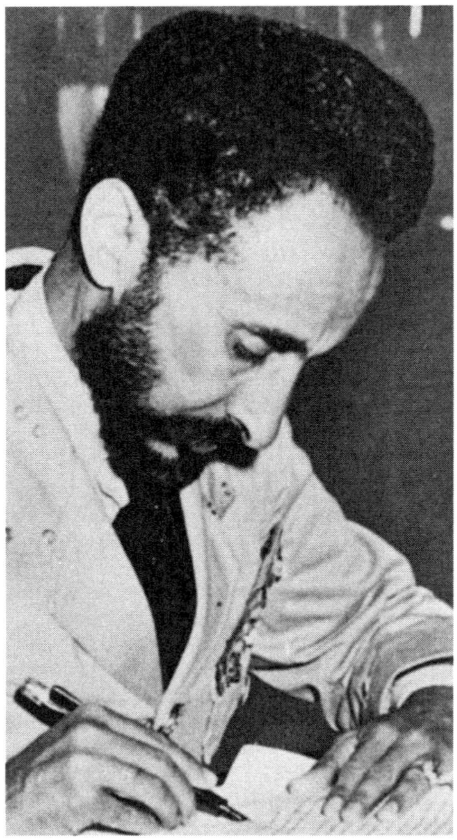

Former Emperor Haile Selassie

The war was short. Following massive arms shipments from the Soviets there came a wave of Cuban troops—flown from Angola—to support the fledgling communist regime. By early 1978 the Somalis had been routed, but the region would continue to be an area of instability to the present.

The Derg's military dictatorship was brought to an end by draughts, famine, and regional insurrections against its repression, particularly in the northern regions of Tigray and Eritrea. Officially set up in February 1975, the *Tigrayan Peoples Liberation Front (TPLF)* announced its first task was "the establishment of an Independent Democratic Republic of Tigray." Allied with the *Eritrean People's Liberation Front (EPLF*), the *TPLF* waged incessant guerrilla warfare against the Derg. In 1989, the *TPLF*, representing a minority of only 7% of the Ethiopian population, merged with other ethnically-based opposition groups to form the *Ethiopian People's Revolutionary Democratic Front (EPRDF).* By May 1991, *ERDPF* forces were advancing on Addis Ababa; Mengistu fled the country for Zimbabwe where he was granted asylum by President Mugabe. On May 27 *EPRDF* troops took control of the capital and a transitional government under the leadership of Meles Zenawi, head of the *TPLF*, was formed.

Meles Zenawi was born Legesse Zenawi, the third and youngest child of a member of the lower Tigrayan nobility. As such, he saw himself, as other Tigrayan students, as the victim of discrimination by the Amhara, who had dominated Ethiopian political life since the rule of Emperor Menelik. After two years as a pre-medical student, he dropped out of school to join the nationalist struggle in Tigray. It was at this point that he adopted his nom de guerre of Meles Zenawi, honoring Meles Tekle, a Tigrayan nationalist student killed in 1974. In 1985, Meles founded the *Marxist-Leninist League of Tigray* (*MLLT*) as a "vanguard party" within the *TPLF*. His intellectual model at the time was Envar Hodja, the repressive ruler of Albania. By 1989 the *MLLT* had became the vehicle by which Meles took over the leadership of the TPLF, linked with other opposition groups, and brought about the downfall of the military dictatorship of the Derg.

The transitional government of 1991 had originally included the *Oromo Liberation Front* (*OLF*) and members of the *Southern Ethiopia People's Democratic Coalition* (*SEPDC*), but by 1993, both had left the government and gone into opposition. (The *Eritrean People's Liberation Front* had already established a separate provincial government in the province in May 1991, and in April 1993, Eritreans voted for independence from Ethiopia.) The transitional government pledged itself to oversee the creation of a multiparty democracy and in June 1994 a 547-member constituent assembly was elected to draft a new constitution. Its work was completed in December 1994 with the adoption of the constitution of a Federal Democratic Republic of Ethiopia. The constitution established a federal state and emphasized decentralized administration based on 10 essentially ethnically defined regions. Regions are granted broad powers in economic and social development programs, the right to raise and spend their own revenues and most remarkably, the right, in theory, to secede from the Ethiopian state. For the Tigrayan leadership at the core the *EPRDF*, the constitution was a means of redressing the grievances of Ethiopia's various "nationalities" against the Amhara. At a superficially obvious level, the constitution represents a revolutionary break with the highly centralized structures of the Empire and its Marxist successor.

In reality, political power in Ethiopia continues to be relatively centralized around Meles Zenawi, the *TPLF*, and its allies within the *EPRDF*. Elections for Ethiopia's first popularly chosen parliament and regional legislatures were held in May and June 1995. Most opposition parties boycotted the elections, resulting in a landslide for the *EPRDF*. As head of the dominant force within the *EPRDF*, Meles was appointed to a five-year term as Prime Minister. In this parliamentary regime the office of President is largely honorary; its duties consist of signing legislation adopted by parliament, receiving the credentials of foreign ambassadors and awarding "medals, prizes and gifts in accordance with procedures established by law." Negaso Gidada, an Oromo, was elected by Parliament as Ethiopia's first Federal President.

With its ethnic and regional emphasis, the new system spawned a plethora of new political parties—65 in all are registered, but most were created by or are satellites of the *EPRDF*, itself dominated by the *Tigrayan Peoples Liberation Front (TPLF)*. The *EPRDF* links the *TPLF*, the *Amhara National Democratic Movement (ANDM)*, *Oromo People's Democratic Organization (OPDO)*, and the *Southern Ethiopian Peoples Democratic Front (SEPDF)*—which itself consists of members from some 20 ethnic parties. Meles Zenawi combines a variety of functions that emphasize his centrality: he is chairman of the *TPLF*, chairman of the *EPRDF* and Prime Minister.

Centrifugal forces tear at the heart of the new Ethiopia. Members of the *OLF* have resorted to urban terror tactics that have produced a repressive response by the government. Afar separatists shuttle back and forth across the border with Djibouti, and Islamist Somali separatists continue to convulse the Ogaden. For each the model is the province of Eritrea, now an independent state. Despite the constitution's commitment to regional and ethnic rights, the government seems more willing to repress than share power. People unwilling to join the *EPRDF* are castigated as "narrow nationalists," harassed and imprisoned. In the Oromia and Somali regions human rights groups have documented hundreds of "disappearances." Ethiopia held elections for a federal parliament, nine regional assemblies and council members for the capital, Addis Ababa, and the eastern city of Dire Dawa in May 2000. It was only the second time that nationwide elections had been held in the country. The opposition was given an unprecedented opportunity to air its grievances in a series of public debates. Largely attended, the debates were rebroadcast on state-run radio and television.

Lt. Col. Mengistu Haile Mariam

Candidates addressed issues ranging from Ethiopia's chronic unemployment to the war with Eritrea and some roundly criticized the government's human rights record. Land reform—the state owns all the land—and the constitutional provision allowing states to secede were also hot issues. Opposition groups unanimously voiced concern with what they saw as uneven regional economic development, with federal funds flowing more generously to the northern regions, which are the *EPRDF*'s political base.

Everywhere it was an uphill battle for the opposition. Not a single opposition candidate managed to secure the 500 signatures necessary for nomination in the northern Tigray region. Elsewhere the Front's satellite and creature parties completely dominated the electoral process. In the Amhara region, the opposition *All-Amhara People's Organization* could only sign up one candidate each for the federal parliament and the regional assembly.

In the Oromiya region, the *Oromo People's Democratic Organization*, another Front member, nominated 176 candidates for parliament and 531 for the regional assembly. The opposition *Oromo National Congress* could only offer 28 candidates for parliament and 38 for the regional assembly. An estimated 54% of Ethiopia's population are Oromo, 24% are Amhara and only 5% are from Tigray.

Prime Minister Meles' four-party coalition won overwhelmingly: 479 of the 547 parliamentary seats. When parliament convened in October, it reelected Meles to another five-year term. Local elections were held in February and March 2001 with a similar preponderance in favor of the *EPRDF*

War with Eritrea

Much to the surprise of the world community, hostilities between Ethiopia and Eritrea broke out in May 1998 and escalated to virtual war in early June. The issue focused on an obscure triangle of land, 155 square miles of rocky barrenness called the Badme Triangle. Unlocatable on most maps, the triangle became the focus of national pride on both sides of the border.

Both Presidents Afwerki and Meles found themselves in a situation from which it was difficult to retreat. The internal pressures on President Meles were particularly intense. Amhara imperialists had never accepted the loss of what they considered the Eritrean province, and the loss of the Red Sea ports rankled deeply, even among the Oromo majority. Galling too was the perception that the *TPLF* leadership had conceded too much by letting Eritrea secede and assume no share of the national debt.

If any war can be ranked as more absurd than others, this one should take pride of place near the top of any such list. Casualties probably exceeded 40,000 by the best estimates, and for far too long each party found reasons to pursue war rather than peace.

Pride and personality, on both sides, generated a cultivated knack for stubbornness. Negotiations had, by early May 2000, brought no resolution to the conflict. As soon as the last negotiators left, Ethiopia launched another massive attack. A surprise advance against a presumably impregnable pass brought crushing victory in nineteen days, after which Ethiopia announced its war aims achieved.

A ceasefire was announced in June and actually lasted through the conclusion of peace negotiations. The peace agreement, brokered by US envoy Anthony Lake and the Organization of African Unity, was signed by the leaders of the contending countries in December. It called for a pull back of troops and creation of a demilitarized zone manned by several thousand UN peacekeepers. A five-member border commission to demarcate the disputed border was established. The two parties agreed

The old town of Harar WORLD BANK Photo by Kay Muldoon

not to appoint their own nationals as commissioners. Named to the commission were officials from the Netherlands, Nigeria, the United Kingdom and the United States, who began meeting at the end of March.

The opposition protested in Addis Ababa, and Prime Minister Meles had to put down hard-line dissidents within his own party. But by March 2001, both countries had basically fulfilled their commitments under the agreement, and UN troops had begun to settle in. Bodies, mummified in the searing east African heat, still litter the battlefields, the victor often undistinguishable from the vanquished.

Culture: The Ethiopian Orthodox Church is one of the world's oldest, Christianity having become the state religion around the same time the Emperor Constantine converted to Christianity. Tradition has it that the first Christian to be baptized was an Ethiopian noble, a top treasury official to Queen Candace who was on his way home from a pilgrimage to Jerusalem when he met the Apostle Philip. Baptism scenes are a recurring motif in Ethiopian art.

An extraordinary feature of the Ethiopian Church is its historic connection to the Old Testament and Jerusalem. Ethiopians celebrated the Sabbath on Saturday for over a millennium. Most Ethiopian churches are consecrated with a symbolic Ark of the Covenant, and tradition has it that the original Ark was brought to Ethiopia by Menelik I, son of the Queen of Sheba, following a visit to his father, King Solomon. The story of Soloman and the Queen is a popular motif in Ethiopian religious art. The original Ark is claimed by some to be in the Church of St. Mary of Zion in Aksum.

Lalibela, in a mountainous region some 400 miles north of Addis Ababa, was a "New Jerusalem" for Ethiopian Christians in the 13th century. Eleven medieval churches were carved out of solid rock there. They have been declared World Heritage sites by UNESCO and are a principal tourist attraction for Ethiopian visitors.

Ethiopia's many churches, with their rich collection of manuscripts and artifacts, have been objects of plunder over the years. The government is making strenuous efforts to recover this cultural patrimony.

The government has made less strenuous efforts to deal with the AIDS pandemic. Years of half-hearted AIDS public awareness campaigns have proved ineffective. In April 2000 President Negaso Gidada publicly admitted that "The AIDS pandemic, which had been restricted to urban areas, has now spread to rural areas." Official figures are ominous. Nearly 300,000 people died in 1999 from AIDS-related diseases—a rate of more than 800 a day. Three million people are believed to be infected with the HIV virus.

The figures indicate that the AIDS crisis is of greater magnitude than the periodic famines which receive much greater international attention. The HIV infection rate has already reached the critical level of 10% of the sexually active population—those between the ages of 15 and 49. At that point economic growth begins to be impacted.

Economy: Despite its Marxist origins, or perhaps because of them (Hoxa's Albania was hardly an economic success story), the new government has embarked on a program of economic reform, including privatization of state enterprises. Liberalization of the economy is seen as essential for attracting foreign investment, and the project

President Negaso Gidada

Prime Minister Meles Zenawi

is not without its success: the economy grew a striking 12.4% in 1996.

Necessitously, industrial development will be agriculture-driven. Agriculture involves 85% of the population, generates 80% of Ethiopian exports and contributes 45% to the GNP. Only 10.9 per cent of Ethiopia's total land surface is under intense agricultural cultivation. The principal export crop is coffee, providing 65–75% of the country's foreign exchange earnings. In 1998 coffee earned well over $300 million, but lower market prices were expected to reduce that figure for 2000.

Ethiopia is a major producer of beeswax, surpassed only by Mexico and China. It is also the world's 10th biggest honey producer. The industry was hard hit by massive fires that destroyed large portions of the country's southern forests in March. More than 13,000 beehives were burnt. At least 50,000 hectares of forest were destroyed in Oromiya region.

"Khat," a shrub whose leaves have a psychotropic effect when chewed, is also a valuable traditional export to neighboring Djibouti and Somalia. Ethiopian producers are now a leading source of sesame seeds, with an 11% of world imports.

Ethiopia is estimated to have 75 million head of livestock, the largest concentration in Africa. Its pastoralists have recently had difficulty marketing their flocks because of the threat of Rift Valley fever. Traditional buyers, like Saudi Arabia and the Gulf states, prohibited import of East African livestock. In 2000 drought and fire impacted Ethiopian herds. Hides and skins remain important export items for Ethiopia.

Ethiopian economic development focuses on agricultural improvement. More than a million people died of starvation between 1984 and 1990, but 1999 is predicted to produce near record food crops. A good rainy season, increased use of fertilizers, improved seeds and fewer outbreaks of crop pests and disease have significantly improved food production. A joint report of the World Food Program and the Food and Agriculture Organization forecasts food production in 1999 at nearly 12 million tons, up 36 per cent from 1998. Record production was achieved in 1996—more than 13 million tons.

Since 1992 the government has established a series of grain storehouses to be better prepared when drought and famine occur. Without this advanced planning, the death toll from the spring 2000 drought would have been significantly greater. With all the humanitarian concern, often late, shown for Ethiopian drought and famine victims, it is useful to realize that these conditions are regionally specific: 86% of Ethiopians are supporting themselves.

The government has ambitious plans for the development of irrigation agriculture. Since water management is so essential for agricultural development and increased electricity is so essential for industrial development, the government plans to complete seven hydroelectric dams on the Blue Nile in the next five years. The dams would increase the present 340 megawatts electric-generating capacity of the country to 713 megawatts. Such proposals are viewed by Egypt, well down stream, but utterly dependent on the flow of Nile waters from the Ethiopian highlands, with the greatest concern.

Until it went to war with Eritrea, landlocked Ethiopia imported its fuel and oil products through the Eritrean seaports of Massawa and Assab. Now those supplies have been rerouted through Djibouti, which is connected to Addis Ababa by railroad, and the Somaliland port of Berbera, through which the EU has been sending food supplies. Deliveries increased so much at Djibouti that backlogs began to occur and alternative ports have had to be used. The Kenyan port of Mombasa has also handled cargo for Ethiopia during the conflict. There are plans to pave roads in Ethiopia and Sudan to provide access to Sudan's major Red Sea port.

The tensions between Eritrea and Ethiopia that led to war seem to have been largely economic, and came to a head when Eritrea issued a new currency. Both states had been using notes from the Mengistu regime, with Eritrea offering a slightly better exchange rate. In 1997, both issued new, more appropriate national notes. (As witness to poorly developed infrastructure and the absence of a national market, it should be noted that bank notes from the Haile Selassie era still circulate in rural areas.)

The economic impact of the war is significant. Before 1998, Ethiopia's government had sharply cut military spending. The 600,000-member army of the Marxist Derg had been reduced to less than 100,000. There was only a civil militia stationed at the border when the war began. Since then, the government has spent heavily on weaponry and increased its armed forces. Its army is now estimated at 350,000 and the country reportedly spends $1 million a day on the war effort.

Quite remarkably, tourists still come to Ethiopia. In March 2000, the government released figures showing $31.7 million brought in by tourism over the past two years. A total of 90,000 visitors arrived in 1999/2000, down from a high of 120,000 before the Ethio-Eritrean border conflict broke out in May 1998. The most popular destinations were the rock churches of Lalibela, the 17th century palaces at Gondar, the obelisks at Axum and Bahar Dar, and the source of the Blue Nile.

The Future: Many contentious issues remain to be resolved between Ethiopia and Eritrea, like repatriation of citizens and compensation for war damages. Recent drought conditions will put tremendous pressure on food supplies, and a debilitated economy will take a while to generate enough jobs to absorb demobilized soldiers.

Carrying a water jug

The Republic of Kenya

Among the world's greatest athletes

Area: 582,750 sq. km = 225,000 sq. mi. (larger than twice the size of Nevada).
Population: 29 million (estimated).
Capital City: Nairobi (Pop. 1.5 million, estimated).
Climate: Hot and dry in the area from the Tana River to the north and northeast; hot and dry, but with a short rainy season in the southeast area below the Tana River; temperate and usually moist in the central highlands and southwestern grassy plains, with two wet seasons.
Neighboring Countries: Tanzania (South, Southwest); Uganda (West); Sudan (Northwest); Ethiopia (North); Somali Republic (Northeast).
Official Languages: KiSwahili, English.
Other Principal Languages: More than 60 languages are spoken. Prominently: Borana, Digo, Duruma, Embu, Gikuyu, Giryama, Gusii, Kalenjin, Kamba, Logooli, Luo, Luyia, Maasai, Meru, Pökoot, Saamia, Taita, Teso, and Turkana.
Ethnic groups: Kikuyu 22%, Luhya 14%, Luo 13%, Kalenjin 12%, Kamba 11%, Kisii 6%, Meru 6%, and other African 15%. Non-African (Asian, European, .and Arab) 1%.
Principal Religions: Protestant 38%, Roman Catholic 28%, indigenous beliefs 26%, Muslim 7%, and other 1%.
Chief Commercial Products: Tea 18%, coffee 15%, and petroleum products.
GNP per capita: 330 US$
Currency: Kenya Shilling.
Former Colonial Status: British Protectorate (1895–1963).
Independence Date: December 12, 1963.
Chief of State: Daniel T. arap–Moi, President.
National Flag: Three horizontal stripes of black, red and green separated by narrow white stripes; a shield with two crossed spears is in the center.

Lying immediately below the heart of Africa on the east coast, Kenya extends from the Indian Ocean to the lake region of East Africa. North of the winding Tana River, there is an arid countryside which slowly rises to the southern mountains of Ethiopia. The lack of rainfall in this half of the country has produced a semi–desert type of land the same as is found in the Somali Republic.

South of the Tana River, the coastline is hot and oppressively humid—this is the only part of Kenya that is truly tropical. This gives way immediately to a thornbush country of gently rising land extending about 175 miles from the coast.

The south central portion of Kenya is a beautiful land of high plateaus stretching between the mountains. Mount Kenya, in this area, reaches a height of 17,040 feet 80 miles north of Nairobi. The Gregory Rift, extending in an almost straight line to the south from Lake Rudolf, is an immense trench almost 3,000 feet lower than the mountains which enclose it.

From the western side of this rift formations, the land slowly descends to the shores of Lake Victoria. The cool climate of the southeastern and south central areas is invigorating—though the Equator divides these regions from northern Kenya, the climate is temperate because of the altitude. These are normally fertile lands; it is frequently possible in many sections to harvest two crops each year. Intermittent drought since 1982 has sharply curtailed production of food stuffs.

History: Arab traders called on the coast of Kenya for an undetermined time, establishing a community in the 8th century which remains to this day. Portuguese mariners landed in Kenya as early as 1498, seeking a sea route to the Far East. Colonial activity in this area was by the British and Germans; for details of early and colonial history, see Historical Background, *The Germans in Africa* and *The British in Africa*.

Elections conducted in May 1963 resulted in an overwhelming victory for the *Kenya African National Union (KANU)* led by Jomo Kenyatta. Under pressure from this majority, Britain recognized the independence of Kenya; although initially a part of the British Commonwealth, Kenya adopted a republic form of government in 1964.

Elections in 1966 gave an overwhelming majority to *KANU;* the *Kenya People's Union* led by Oginga Odinga, who had been expelled from *KANU,* won only a handful of seats. Internal rivalry in *KANU* after the elections led to a reorganization of the government. Charging Odinga with communist sympathies, Kenyatta jailed him.

Under continuing pressure, particularly from the Luo people, Kenyatta (a Kikuyu) released Odinga (a Luo) and in an effort to placate the opposition, he appointed another Luo as Minister of Finance.

Elections were scheduled for 1969, to be contested by candidates from *KANU* and *KPU.* This plan was abandoned when the finance minister was assassinated in July 1969 by a Kikuyu tribesman; the Luo rioted before and after his funeral, causing severe unrest.

The murder of the cabinet officer was symbolic of increasing tensions between the Kikuyu and the Luo. Although denied and ignored by the government, administration of *Mau Mau* type oaths (see colonial history) had been resumed. Bands of Kikuyu gangs had been attacking Luo people and engaging in other acts of terrorism.

Faced with the threat of serious unrest, Kenyatta threw Odinga back into jail, where he remained for most of the time until Kenyatta's death in August 1978. Things continued rather evenly in Kenya, with Kenyatta exercising vise–like control. *KANU* was the only legal party. But even within it, there was criticism of the aging leader.

President Kenyatta died suddenly in August 1978 and was immediately succeeded by Vice President Daniel T. arap– Moi (pronounced *moy)* who was duly elected in his own right in November 1979 to a five–year term. In mid–1982 a group of Air Force officers attempted to overthrow the government, blaming worsening economic conditions on the Moi regime. But the base was cleverly infiltrated by loyal government troops claiming to be in sympathy with the *coup* leaders; once inside the base they simply shot the rebels. There was massive looting following the news of the attempted takeover; over 100 people were killed and many hundreds were wounded. Final executions of officers occurred in 1985.

President Moi disbanded the Air Force and closed the University in Nairobi where student supporters of the *coup* were numerous, opening it so the students could complete their year the following April. Odinga remained in prison, finally being released in 1983.

Premature elections were called by *KANU* and held in September 1983; Moi was the only candidate for president. There were multiple candidates for the seats in parliament which were hotly contested, and more than 40 deputies were replaced.

Moi governed an ethnically divided Kenya with authoritarian firmness. Urban Kikuyus of Nairobi charged him with cronyism as he appointed fellow Kalenjin tribesmen to lucrative government positions. The secret ballot was abolished in favor of a "queuing" system where people have to publicly line up according to their political preferences. This led to intimidation and widespread election fraud; in some districts there was only a 20% turnout in 1988, down from the former 90%.

The International Monetary Fund indicated that Kenyans own $2.62 billion in overseas bank accounts. Charges of corruption did not result in efforts toward reform, but rather a crackdown on dissent. Many government critics fled the country. A massive demonstration in Nairobi in late 1991, punctuated with cries of "peace" and "democracy" was met with tear gas and riot batons. The government dismissed the participants as agitators and anarchists.

Further protest came from international aid agencies—the International Monetary Fund, the World Bank and several creditor nations, all of which cut off money destined for Kenya. This was more than the Moi regime could stand; quietly, provisions for multi–party election in 1992 were made. In order to protect *KANU* and his own tenure, Moi immediately embarked on a course intended to divide (and conquer). Exploitation of every difference possible among the opposition had the desired effect. *KANU* would have been soundly defeated by a united opposition.

They not only refused to cooperate, they carefully split among themselves; this included a division with the *Forum for the Restoration of Democracy (FORD),* which initially had wide suppport that transcended traditional tribal rivalries, including that of the Kikuyu and Luo.

In spite of last minute resignations of several reputable cabinet members, *KANU* rallied and went on the victory in December 1992. Moi personally campaigned vigorously. For added insurance, his people in the legislature ramrodded through a constitutional amendment providing that in order to be elected, a presidential candidate would have to win at least 25% of the vote in five of the seven districts. Since he and his Kalenjin tribesmen controlled the western mountain district and other significant areas through political patronage, this virtually assured that none of his three principal opponents stood a chance.

The result was Moi, 36%, three principal opponents (25%, 19.5%, 17.5%—a total of 63%). The election was tainted by widespread violence and intimidation. Notwithstanding the fact that 63% voted against him, he reveled in the "victory."

In the legislature, things were more realistic. *KANU* elected 95 delegates to 88 for the opposition. However, riots broke out on the opening day in 1993; Moi simply dissolved the legislature rather than face such vocal opposition, the first in a decade. The International Monetary Fund, infuriated by the printing of special shillings to finance *KANU's* effort in the election, imposed more rigid conditions on future loans, a move that was dismissed by an enraged Moi.

Richard Leakey, a famous White conservationist, spoke out against the Moi regime in 1995, forming a political party *(Safina)* to oppose corruption. The president denounced him as a racist and colonialist and arranged his public beating by a mob as police simply looked on.

The December 1997 elections reproduced the whole dreary cycle of violence, conflict, repression and lost opportunities, this time, on a lower scale. Candidates and human rights workers were harassed and intimidated. Members of the *KANU* youth wing, in addition to security forces, blocked meetings and rallies. Fourteen deaths resulted from police actions against supporters of constitutional reform in May and June.

Opposition parties once again proved incapable of uniting behind a single candidate. Their appeals were tribal rather than national. Moi was elected by winning a mere 40% of the popular vote and the required 25% of the vote cast in five of the eight provinces. His majority in parliament was razor thin. *KANU* emerged with only 109 out of 222 seats.

The 1997 elections were held in an environment of uncertainty, for in July the International Monetary Fund (IMF) refused to lend any more money to Kenya, partly because corruption had become so

Carrying water home

A pride of lions in safari country, Kenya

blatant it was holding back the nation's economy. Confirming the IMF's concern, the Commissioner-General of Kenya's Revenue Authority stunned the nation by disclosing the country loses $1.68 billion annually through corruption.

President Moi responded by declaring war on corruption and creating the Kenya Anti-Corruption Authority (KACA), but it wasn't until fall 1999 that the authority completed its organization and training and could begin its investigations. KACA's director, Justice Aaron Ringera, bluntly summarized corruption's impact on Kenya: "Corruption has, contaminated our politics, eroded our social fiber and thwarted our efforts to alleviate poverty."

Corrupt bureaucrats were reportedly gripped by panic, but remained calm enough to bring legal action against KACA. In December 2000 a three-judge constitutional court ruled the Authority illegal, setting off alarm bells within the donor community.

Kenya's chief justice threatened to dismiss all prosecutions brought to court by KACA, and in April 2001, one judge dismissed fraud and abuse of office charges against Water Development Minister Kipng'eno Arap Ng'eny. He was immediately re-arrested and charged afresh. The new case will now be prosecuted by Kenya's attorney general instead of KACA. Ng'eny is charged with conspiring to defraud the Kenya Posts and Telecommunications Corporation of $2.4 million while he was its head.

As part of a calculated set of responses to impress the IMF, Moi also appointed Richard Leakey, a well known critic of the ways things are done in Kenya, to head its civil service. The appointment produced astonishment at home and delight abroad. Leakey, part of the world-famous paleontology family, was a long-time friend of World Bank President James Wolfensohn, and his appointment achieved its desired goal. The IMF resumed lending to Kenya in July 2000, but not without the strictest of conditions.

Enactment of anti-corruption and economic crimes bills was required, as well as ethics legislation which would require public officials to declare their wealth and liabilities. Another condition required a weekly inspection by IMF officials of the Central Bank of Kenya balance sheet. The conditions were humiliating, but given the pervasive depth of corruption in Kenya, essential.

In May 2000, the Parliamentary Anti-Corruption Select Committee issued a 937-page report listing a whole galaxy of politicians, civil servants and businessmen implicated in corruption and fraud scandals. What came to be known as the "List of Shame" included Kenya's Vice-President George Saitoti and the powerful trade minister Nicholas Biwott, both close associates of President Moi. The report fell short of including President Moi, but it indicated that his son Philip should be prosecuted for evading duties of about $600,000 on six vehicles.

Vice-President Saitoti was named in connection with Kenya's biggest financial scandal—the fraudulent diversion of $690 million to Goldenberg International as compensation for exports of gold and diamonds in the early 1990s. Kenya produces neither gold nor diamonds in commercial quantities, and the amount of money diverted exceeded the total combined value of tea, coffee and horticultural exports—Kenya's principal sources of foreign exchange.

Parliament itself became a hall of shame when KANU used its numerical strength in parliament to delete the names of the top government officials, including Saitoti and Biwott, from the list of shame.

Leakey's tenure as head of Kenya's civil service was brief, less than two years, but long enough to dust up the chicken house and ruffle lots of feathers. He resigned in March 2001, and almost simultaneously the IMF once again put the brakes on its lending to Kenya, citing "serious setbacks" to the fight against corruption.

Culture: The AIDS pandemic has begun its terrifying march through Kenyan society. Cultural patterns and behaviors have facilitated rather than hindered its progress, and in November 1999 President Moi declared the disease a "national disaster."

The death toll, already staggering, continues to mount. Over 700,000 Kenyans have died of AIDS, and current projections suggest the total will reach 2.5 million by 2005. The disease kills 500 Kenyans every day and is expected to carry off 740 per day by 2005. More than half of Kenya's hospital beds are taken up with AIDS sufferers. It costs the government an estimated $2.7 million each day to deal with the disease, money it can ill afford.

The rapid progress of AIDS in Kenya reflects fundamental economic and cultural realities. Rural poverty has driven young girls, children really, to the cities where the best job they can find is child care. Their salary is $10 to $15 a month. Since this is insufficient to provide for family needs at home, many turn to prostitution. In Kisumu, a tourist site on the shores of Lake Victoria, for example, girls can find customers day and night—receiving less than a dollar for each transaction. Statistics from Kenya's National AIDS STD Control Programme (NASCOP) indicate that a third of girls aged 15 to 19 years in Kisumu are HIV-positive.

Wife inheritance is a cultural practice that contributes to the spread of HIV/AIDS. Here, a widow becomes the property of her late husband's brother. There is often little choice for the woman. Alone, she is unable to provide adequate care, food, clothing and school fees for her children. If she does not agree to be "inherited" she is barred from entering her husband's family compound; her brothers-in-law are prohibited by custom from even digging her grave.

In a deeply patriarchal society it is inappropriate for a woman to take the lead and ask a man to wear a condom. Until recently the government refused to encourage the use of condoms, deferring to pressures from church leaders who fear talking about condom use will only encourage youths to have sex.

Economy: Having meager mineral resources, the economy of Kenya has traditionally rested on agriculture and tourism. The fertile highlands produce coffee and tea which traditionally have dominated exports of Kenya.

Prior to 1979, contrasted with neighboring countries, Kenya was relatively prosperous—at least for the clique of politicians and businessmen who control the nation's wealth. A world oil "shortage" with sharply increased prices followed by a world–wide recession shook the economy, followed by drought in 1982. After that year, the fertile central highlands received less than 30% of the usual rainfall and the crops simply dried up. The government issued a plea for 1 million tons of corn. Aid came from external sources, but did not reach the drought–plagued northwest where there was the most need. Government corruption siphoned off far too much of that which was received.

Things improved in 1985–86 when tumbling oil prices and steeply rising coffee prices gave Kenya hope of a brighter future. But soon afterwards a world surplus of coffee dashed that hope. Overall, Kenya's economic performance has declined since 1974. International donors pressured President Moi to introduce a multiparty system in 1991 and insisted on economic liberalization, an end to corruption, and a transparent government. Unfortunately there was no effective system of monitoring or enforcing these conditions.

In July 1997, when the government refused to meet reform commitments earlier made, the IMF refused to make any further loans. Kenya was singled out for rough treatment not only because of blatant corruption, but also because it is relatively well developed and has much to lose if its infrastructure deteriorates. One simple example: if corrupt officials allow truckers to double the weight they carry on Kenya's highways, those roads will inevitably be severely degraded.

President Daniel arap–Moi addresses a gathering

(Kenya's notoriously high highway death rate is attributable not only to bad roads, but also to corruption. Road carnage is abetted by police officers who take bribes and allow mini-buses and buses to flout traffic laws. In less than a month, Kenya registered two of its worst ever road accidents—two buses collided killing 76 people in western Kenya and a bus-truck smash-up on the Nairobi-Mombasa highway killed 73 passengers.)

The IMF suspension brought the country's economy and financial market to steep decline. Central Bank figures indicate that real GDP growth had dropped consistently: from 2.8 percent in 1997, to 1.8 percent in 1998 and to 1.3 percent for 1999. Only in May 2000 would the IMF reopen discussions with Kenya, after demonstrable progress had been made on the high-level corruption, shrinkage of a bloated civil service, and privatization of inefficient state corporations.

Officials and heads of government corporations, police and other departments were dismissed as a result of corruption investigations. President Moi announced a reduction of cabinet ministries from 27 to 15 in a bid to improve efficiency and reduce public expenditures. The government also accelerated the privatization process and invested more in the agricultural sector, which contributes 30% of the country's GDP and 70% of its foreign exchange income.

Tea was one focus of the government's attention. Kenya is one of the world's largest black tea suppliers. In 1999 it exported more than 241,000 tons of tea, accounting for about a quarter of the country's foreign exchange earnings. The tea sector employs over two million people across the country. To help reverse a drop in production, the government allocated $12 million to import fertilizers for tea growers.

In February 2000 Germany's biggest condom manufacturer, Condomi AG, announced it was joining Kenya's Olago Enterprises to build a condom factory on the outskirts of Nairobi. Given the spread of HIV/AIDS, there is a need and market demand. Condom use grew 250% in the past three years following AIDS awareness campaigns. The new factory will have an

A young Masai herdsman

Courtesy: Jon Markham Morrow

initial capacity of 100 million condoms per year. With intensified AIDS education programs annual demand is expected to reach 650 million by the end of 2003. Current demand, according to the National AIDS Control Council, stands at 120 million condoms.

The Future: Can a tiger lose its stripes? Can old dogs learn new tricks? Those are the relevant questions in contemplating Kenya's future. Moi and his cohorts have presided over a regime that has been brutal, repressive, dictatorial and corrupt. Political patronage has impeded economic development. Fellow Kalenjins have been appointed positions on the basis of ethnic affiliation rather than merit and have proceeded to convert public resources to private gain. Change, or at least the appearance of change, has come in response to lender pressures, but frankly it is difficult to imagine a system so deeply and pervasively corrupt changing much and remaining transformed.

Kenya's personality-oriented parties, based on ethnic loyalty, seem helpless to change the structure, and if they did, would only operate to get their day at the feeding tough of public resources. Rising poverty and tribal polarization will fuel continuing ethnic violence. Since President Moi has designated no successor, internal rivalries within *KANU* will dominate the political scene. Kenya still looks like a risky investment.

The Somali Democratic Republic

The National People's Assembly, Mogadishu Photo by Ali Abdi Addaue

Area: 637,140 sq. km. = 246,000 sq. mi. (slightly larger than Texas).
Population: 7,140,643 (July 1999 est.)
Capital City: Mogadishu (Pop. 500,000 +/−).
Climate: Hot, with scarce and irregular rainfall and frequent droughts.
Neighboring Countries: Djibouti (Northwest); Ethiopia (West); Kenya (Southwest).
Official Language: Somali, Arabic.
Other Principal Languages: Italian, English.
Ethnic Background: Darod (North–Northeast); Hawiya (central area); Rahanwein (South); Ishaak (North Central area); all of the foregoing are collectively referred to as Somali (85%); Bantu derivation (14%).
Principal Religion: Islam (Sunni sect).
Chief Commercial Products: Livestock, bananas, hides, and fish.
GNP per capita: N/A
Currency: 1 Somali Shilling (So. Sh.) = 100 cents.
Former Colonial Status: The North was a British Protectorate (1897–1960); the South was an Italian Colony (1892–1941); British administration (1941–1949); Italian Trust Territory (1949–1960).
Independence Date: July 1, 1960.
Chief of State: Transitional President Abdulkassim Salat Hassan, selected by the Transitional National Assembly created at the Arta (Djibouti) Conference August 2000.
National Flag: A five–pointed white star on an azure blue background.

The Somali Republic, the easternmost nation of Africa, covers an area often referred to as the *Horn of Africa;* it has a 1700–mile coastline on the tropical waters of the Gulf of Aden and the Indian Ocean. Although the northern part of the country is hilly, reaching altitudes of 4,000 feet, the larger portion to the south is a flat, semi–arid land which is uniformly hot. But for the presence of sporadic rainfall, this land would be as oppressive as the central part of the great Sahara Desert. The endless expanses are covered with large volcanic boulders and stones having a sponge–like appearance, lying on a soil that resembles red dust. During the "dry season" when there is utterly no vegetation, these rocks absorb the heat of midday, which brings their temperature often to more than 150°F. There is no activity to be seen on the land during the daytime of this semi–arid area—both man and beast wait for the cool of the evening to travel and hunt.

Acacia trees, with their roots reaching far into the land to obtain precious water, spread their umbrella–like foliage, shading portions of the otherwise shadeless, vacant countryside. Goats and antelope must stand on their hind legs to reach their precious food from these trees. There are periods of rain which produce a cover of green grass and vegetation punctuated by widely scattered termite mounds which reach heights of 15 feet.

The locusts which invaded Egypt at the time of Joseph and his brethren probably came from Somalia, since this is one of the major breeding grounds of the African locust. The frankincense and myrrh carried to the cradleside of Christ by the three Eastern Kings possibly came from Somalia, where these aromatic woods are found today.

History: Although tradition holds that the ancestors of the Somali people, of Cushitic origins, lived in this region of Africa more than 2,000 years ago, the earliest traces of people date to the 7th century A.D. The Koreishite Kingdom was established at that time by a group of people from nearby Yemen. For details of early and colonial history, see Historical Background, *The Italians in Africa* and *The British in Africa.*

Modern Somalia is the result of the merger of fish and fowl: former British Somaliland and *Somalia Italiana* in 1960. Each came with a different colonial history and experience and those differences are at the heart of modern Somalia's present situation. British Somaliland became independent on June 26, 1960; five days later, on July 1, it joined Italian Somalia to form the Somali Republic. At independence there was no common administrative language. English was spoken in the former British protectorate, Italian in the larger *Somalia Italiana.* Somali, though spoken by all, did not exist as a written language until the 1970s.

The British interest in Somaliland had been purely strategic: control of the entrance to the Red Sea and cheap provisions for Aden, its garrison at the tip of the Arabian peninsula. As a consequence, indirect rule was administratively appropriate. Northern Somalis were left to follow their own customs; traditional procedures for resolving conflicts among nomadic clan groups remained in place. Italy's treatment of Somalia was much different. Colonial swagger, bravado and domination provided cheap compensation for humiliation and defeat in Europe. Italian Somaliland was subordinated to colonial will. Southern Somalis were forced to adopt Italian law, and nomad customs, especially traditional mechanisms for conflict resolution between clans, were abolished. Resistance was intense and military confrontation continued to the late 1920s.

From British Somaliland emerged a well–educated élite, the very best of which had been trained in British universities. Italy introduced mass education in the south, but at a relatively low level, creating a mass of very nationalistic semi–intellectuals. At unification, then, there was little in common between the two partners save a vague sense of "Somali" identity. To preserve the union which gave expression to that identity, Northerners gave up much. The capital was located in the southern city of Mogadishu. Most of the technical positions in the new government were filled by better–trained Northerners, but the bulk of political appointments went to Southerners. Political parties proliferated, reflecting the fragmentary nature of Somali clan politics, and at one point Somalia had more parties per capita than any democratic state aside from Israel. (In the last multiparty elections held, March 1969, more than 60 parties competed.)

This multitude of parties also expressed substantial differences in political style and orientation. With a dominant position in parliament, Southern nationalists, pro-Arab and militantly pan–Somali, pushed the idea of a "greater Somalia"—a claim on Somali–inhabited areas of neighboring Kenya and Ethiopia. "Modernists," mostly Northerners, stressed economic and social development and urged improved relations with other African states. Out of this welter of conflicting tendencies, the Somali Youth League gradually assumed a dominant position, successfully cutting across regional and clan loyalties. And under the leadership of Prime Minister Mohamed Ibrahim Egal (1967–69), a Northerner educated at English public schools from Exeter to London, Somalia significantly improved its relations with Kenya and Ethiopia, but its fledgling constitutional democracy was brought to an end in October 1969, when the army and police, led by Maj. General Mohamed Siyad Barré, seized power in a bloodless coup. Prime Minister Egal was thrown in jail where he remained for 12 years.

Siyad Barré was born in the Ogaden area of Ethiopia, an area once part of Italian East Africa but returned by the British to Ethiopia in 1948. Nicknamed "Afweyne" or "Mighty Mouth" by his fellow herdboys, Siyad later travelled to Mogadishu for what formal education he had and ultimately became a member of the *Polizia Africana Italiana*. He rose within police ranks to become the first Somali commissioned as a full police officer, and by 1960, when Somalia became independent, Siyad had won accelerated promotion to the rank of Brigadier–General of Police. With the formation of the Somali National Army in April 1960, Siyad transferred from Police to Army as one of its deputy commanders. He was promoted Commander–in–Chief in 1965.

Siyad moved quickly to eliminate the institutions and personnel of Somalia's democracy. Important political figures like Prime Minster Egal were detained, the constitution suspended, national assembly closed, parties banned and Supreme Court abolished. Notwithstanding this destruction of institutions, the country was renamed the Somali Democratic Republic. The coup–makers designated themselves the Supreme Revolutionary Council (SRC) and assumed full executive and legislative power, concentrated in the hands of Siyad Barré himself. Major–General Mohamed Siyad Barré became head of state and chairman of the SRC, its politburo, the cabinet and the committees for defense, security and judicial matters. His models were Nasser and Kim Il Sung, and like them, a cult of personality soon emerged. "Afweyne" would ultimately be touted as "The Father of Wisdom."

Sweeping changes were introduced into Somali life. Clan and kinship ties were officially banned and the new regime promised to root out all references to clanship. To replace traditional Somali private justice—blood vengeance or blood money payments between groups—the government introduced the death sentence for those convicted of homicide. In what is probably its most enduring achievement, the regime introduced a Latin script to make Somali a written language and aggressively pursued literacy in the new script.

In 1974, Siyad signed a treaty of cooperation with the Soviet Union. The institutional trappings of a Marxist dictatorship were gradually set in place. The regime opted for "Scientific Socialism" and in a few years most sectors of the economy were brought under state control. Banks, insurance companies, electrical power production, petroleum distribution, sugar estates and refineries were all nationalized. One exception to this nationalization program were the large banana

Somali nomads, who let their hair grow until married (left) and have it cut when married.

Xiddigta Oktoobar

Tusaalooyinka Madaxweynaha

Barnaamijka Cusub ee Hawlgalka Xisbiga Hantiwadaagga Kacaanka Soomaaliyeed, ujeeddadiisu waxay tahay la dagaallanka asluubxumida, caddaalad-darrida, sinnaan la'aanta, eexda, laaluushka, iyo xatooyada xoolaha Qaranka, meelmarintiisuna ay tahay waajibaad saaran muwaadin kasta.

(Jaalle Siyaad)

Waa Wargeys maalin walba ka soo baxa Wasaaradda Warfaafinta iyo Hanuuninta Dadweynaha ee J.D.S.

Waxaana lagu daabacaa W.M.Q., Qilmihiisuna waa 10 Sh. So., Tel. 21057 - 21012 - 20865 - S.B. 1178 - Muqdisho

ISNIIN 18ka Jannaayo 1988

Xoghayaha Guud ee XHKS oo ka warramay sida dhibaatooyinka dhaqaale ee dunida ay u saameeyeen waddamada soo koraya oo aynu ka mid nahay

Muqdisho, 17 Jan. (SONNA) — Shirkii Hoggaannada Golaha Dhexe ee XHKS oo uu shir Guddoomiye ka ahaa, Xoghayaha Guud ee XHKS, Madaxweynaha JDS Jaalle Maxamed Siyaad Barre ayaa shalay lagu qabtay Xarunta Dhexe Xisbiga ee magaalada Muqdisho.

Xoghayaha Guud ee XHKS, Jaalle Maxamed Siyaad Barre oo shirkaasi ka hadlay waxa uu ka warramay dhibaatooyinka dhaqaale ee maanta ka jira dunida, gaar ahaan sida arrintaasi ay u saameysay dalalka dunida saddexaad oo JDS ay ka mid tahay, wuxuuna sheegay in wadiiqada keliya ee looga gudbi karo duruufaha dhaqaale ay tahay in dhab ahaan loogu jeesto wax soo saar iyo shaqo adag.

Jaalle Siyaad waxa uu caddeeyay in Ummad kasta

Madaxweynaha oo qaabilay Kaaliyaha Xoghayaha Arrimaha Dibedda ee Mareykanka uqaabilsan Arrimaha Afrika

Jaalle Siyaad oo helay dhambaal hambalyo ah

Muqdisho, 17 Jan. (SONNA) — Madaxweynaha JDS, Jaalle Maxamed Siyaad Barre waxa uu shalay ku saabsan sannadka cusub dhambaal hambalyo ah oo ka helay Madaxweynaha dalka Faransiiska Mudane Francois Metterand.

Madaxweyne Metterad waxa uu dhambaalkaa uu u soo diray Jaalle Siyaad ku yiri:— "Waxaa farxad weyn ii ah inaan kuu soo diro Madaxweynow, dhambaalkan hambalyada ah oo ku beegan sannadka cusub ee

A Somali newspaper

plantations which represented significant foreign investment. State corporations were created and given absolute monopolies as the foundation of a socialist economy. Private traders were prohibited from importing, storing, purchasing or distributing food items.

The usual apparatus of state repression also emerged: The National Security Service (NNS), answerable to Siyad Barré himself, began to create its own interrogation and detention centers. Courts for the trial of those caught within its web were created and, of course, more prisons to hold the guilty were built. A vast propaganda machine emerged (obviously helped by literacy in the new script) and countless posters, poems, songs and speeches were generated to praise the "father of the revolution."

Resources were lavished on an expansion of Somali military forces which rapidly increased in size, technical ability and political influence, much to the consternation of neighboring countries, especially those with significant Somali minorities. For years Somalia had secretly assisted Somali, Oromo, Eritrean and other nationalities opposed to the central governments of Kenya and Ethiopia, but in June 1977, when the Ethiopian regime seemed weakened by drought and politically vulnerable, the policy of clandestine support ended. The government and party authorized the army to intervene directly in Ethiopia to assist the *Western Somali Liberation Front* fighting for the return of the Ogaden to Greater Somalia. The Somali army entered the Ogaden in July and overran it.

Expansionist excess was severely punished, however. The Soviet Union, with alliances to both Ethiopia and Somalia, turned against the unorthodox Siyad Barré. War materiel was airlifted to Ethiopia, and a Russian–directed Ethiopian army, with Cuban regiments in support, defeated Somali forces and sent their remnants scurrying back across the border. The army was humiliated and lost its legitimacy as the guardian of pan-Somali nationalism. The country was stunned, and soon it was nearly overwhelmed by an influx of refugees fleeing the re–imposition of Ethiopian authority in the Ogaden. By 1979 there were officially 1.3 million refugees in the country, more than half of which were located in the North. One out of four people in the North was a refugee, and the regime's limited resources and even more limited capacity to deliver services increased tensions between it and the Northern clans.

Clan–based opposition grew, but was brutally repressed. Siyad Barré became increasingly dependent on his own clan and family, to whom went the majority of appointments and the greatest opportunities for corruption. Alliances shifted, with the regime signing on with the Americans after the debacle of the Ogaden war. "Scientific Socialism" was abandoned and U.S. forces gained access to Somali military facilities, many of which were up–graded. Somali officers were given training in U.S. military schools, and America came to the country's aid when invaded by Ethiopia in 1982.

Regime incapacity, economic mismanagement and human rights abuses moved Somalis from disillusionment to anger. Opposition increased. A few senior officers who escaped a bungled coup attempt in 1978 fled to Ethiopia and created the first opposition movement: the *Somali Salvation Democratic Front (SSDF)*. In 1981 a second opposition movement, the *Somali National Movement (SNM)* was created in London by disgruntled businessmen, religious leaders, intellectuals and army officers, mostly from the Northern Isaaq clan. *SNM* guerrilla operations out of Ethiopia began against the regime. Siyad Barré focused his wrath, and American–supported military might, against his Northern opposition in a bloody civil war.

The regime acted without restraint against the northwest. Hargeisa, Somalia's second city and the former capital of British Somaliland, was bombed, strafed and rocketed. Some 50,000 people are believed to have lost their lives there as a result of summary executions, aerial bombardments and ground attacks. The city itself was destroyed. Streams of refugees fleeing the devastation were not spared by government planes. The term "genocide" came to be used more and more frequently by human rights observers.

Market centers throughout the northwest were destroyed by the war and the mining of transport routes rendered them unusable. Wells, on which nomadic pastoralists are dependent, were poisoned. Trade closed down and the Northern economy collapsed with the closure of Berbera port to animal exports from 1989 to 1991. Economic stress resulted in traditional kinship obligations of support being strained to the maximum. Social stress was intensified when a major drought hit the area in 1991–92 at the height of the civil war. Famine killed between 300,000 to 500,000 and affected millions more.

Civil strife gradually expanded throughout Somalia, leading to the formation of other opposition movements. The *United Somali Congress (USC)* was formed in 1987 by largely Hawiye–clan exiles in Italy. Dominated by the central Hawiye clan, the *USC* quickly divided into two rival factions based on different sub–clans. One faction led by General Aideed allied with the Somali National Movement, which provided arms. An Ogadeni–led *Somali Patriotic Movement* (*SPM*) was formed in 1989 when the highest ranking Ogadeni in the government, the Minister of Defense, was arrested. Siyad Barré was increasingly isolated, defended by only his heavily armed presidential guard, drawn exclusively from his Marehan clan. As 1990 drew to a close, rebel forces had entered Mogadishu, and early the next year Siyad Barré and his loyalists fled the city. By then, little was left of Somalia.

The army fractured into slivers of dedication focused on rival clan leaders who became warlords intent on control of territory and whatever resources remained that would sustain their power. The war in the south had produced major population dislocations. A third of the population became internal refugees, and at least a quarter of a million migrated to Mogadishu. When fighting in the capital intensified, there was a similar outflow of people.

The humanitarian disaster brought about Operation Restore Hope, launched in 1992 under UN auspices. The Somalia project was well–intended, but vague and shifting in direction. It was started to protect the delivery of humanitarian aid. It then refocused on creating a secure environment, which logically entailed demobilization of warlord factions. These, of course, had little interest in losing the source of their power and resisted. When General Aideed was identified as the chief trouble–maker, the project again refocused on his capture. When the wily general's forces shot down an American helicopter and killed several American troops in a pitched gun battle, the U.S. withdrew. The project yet again refocused, now seeking negotiation with the very General Aideed it had sought to capture. TV images of a dead American soldier dragged triumphantly through the streets of Mogadishu soured the American public on such foreign adventures and left with policy makers a residual horror of committing American ground troops anywhere in the world.

The international humanitarian effort in Somalia was budgeted at 1.5 billion dollars a year. It was the most expensive humanitarian effort ever undertaken, and in virtually every way it was a failure. By early 2000, four warlords still contended over divided Mogadishu. General Aideed, who was killed in a gun battle with rivals in 1996, was replaced as faction leader by his son, a young man who somewhat ironically held American citizenship and once had served in the U.S. Marine Corps. Various negotiations between southern faction leaders conducted in Egypt, Kenya, Ethiopia or Libya achieved nothing.

The 13th Somali national reconciliation conference began its discussions in Djibouti in May 2000. Convened by Djibouti's president, Ismail Omar Guelleh, the conference brought together clan elders, religious leaders, academics, businessmen and, for the first time, a group of women. Over two thousand Somali met for over three months at Arta, Djibouti, to thrash out new institutions for the Somali state. The contending warlords were, for the most part, excluded—by intention and choice. Much of the cost of the conference was underwritten by the Djibouti tycoon, Ahmed Bore, a close friend of President Guelleh.

Front and back of the Somali Shilling

Transitional President Abdulkassim Salat Hassan

The largest and most broadly representative of any conference, Arta proved the most sensitive to the segmentary nature of Somali society and thus the most successful. A Transitional National Assembly was selected, which then proceeded to elect a transitional head of state. Abdulkassim Salat Hassan, a former interior minister of the Siad Barré regime, won out over some twenty rivals for the new office of Transitional President. His term of office was set at three years, during which time procedures would be implemented to create permanent institutions for the renovated state.

The leadership of Somaliland, and especially Puntland, vigorously rejected the Arta results, complaining particularly about the predominance of individuals prominent in the Siad Barré regime, a government which had done so much to destroy the north. The warlords treated Arta as simply another faction and suggested that the transitional president would have to negotiate with them to bring lasting peace to Somalia.

Encouraged by Ethiopia, the major warlords met in Addis Ababa in early 2001 in what was nothing more than an anti-Arta conference. In March, claiming to be "leaders and representatives of the overwhelming majority of the political forces in Somalia," they announced creation of a *Somali Reconciliation and Restoration Council (SRRC)*. The council's purpose, they said, was "to lead the nation towards an all inclusive reconciliation conference and the establishment of a legitimate transitional representative government of National Unity."

The transitional government has established itself in Mogadishu and uneasily cohabits the space claimed by the city's long-term armed factions. It has much going for it in terms of international recognition and promises of reconstruction aid. The claims of the warlords seem increasingly to fall on deaf ears, but much remains uncertain as Somalia hesitantly moves towards peace and stability that have eluded it for a decade.

Somaliland: In northwest Somalia where British indirect rule did not destroy traditional Somali–systems of conflict resolution, leaders have opted for reconciliation rather than rivalry. Somali-style peace conferences, large-scale regional gatherings lasting anywhere from two to six months, managed to stabilize clan relationships. At a grand shir, or council, which concluded in February 1991, Isaaq clans representing 80% of the population of former British Somaliland reached an amnesty with other clans. Independence was declared in the

Mohamed Ibrahim Egal

same year with the rallying cry "No More Mogadishu."

There have been at least three of these grand councils, called "national conferences," to work out the form and structure of the state. Two elected assemblies have been created. One is essentially a small lower parliamentary house. The other is a council of elders, larger than the first and consisting of clan representatives. This chamber of elders cannot be dissolved by the president, and those who replace members who have died, been recalled or incapacitated must come from the same clan or sub–clan. The system was ratified in a constitution approved by two–thirds of the representatives in February 1997. Muhammed Ibrahim Egal, the last prime minister of democratic Somalia, was re-elected to a five–year term as president in 1997.

Denied recognition as a sovereign state by an international community fixated on a unitary state for Somalia, Somaliland made remarkable progress on its own. Heavy weapons were surrendered voluntarily and often stored unguarded. State controls on the economy were virtually eliminated, and trade and commerce began to thrive.

The Somaliland government has an annual budget of around $25 million. Employing something like 26,000 people, it spends 70% of its revenues on salaries. Revenues are mostly derived from port duties at Berbera where activity has recently increased. UN agencies have used it for transporting food relief to Ethiopia, and the Ethiopian government has turned to it in a search for alternatives to the Eritrean port of Asab.

Ethiopian Airlines has recently begun twice-weekly flights to Hargeisa, Somaliland's capital. International flights from the Gulf states, East Africa and Europe already land at Hargeisa and Berbera airports, generating about $1.5 million in revenues for the government. As of 2001, Somaliland businessmen will pay income and profit taxes, which will add to government revenues.

Wealth and profits are largely based on livestock trade, meat and hide exports. Some 1.5 million head of sheep and livestock were exported in 2000, while in 1999 about 2 million head had been exported. A new skin and hide factory has recently opened in Burao to produce export-quality leather.

In 2000, Somaliland would normally have expected to export two to two and a half million head of sheep to Saudi Arabia as well as 100,000 head of cattle to Yemen, but the states imposed a livestock ban in October after an outbreak of Rift Valley Fever (RVF). In normal years the country expects to earn between $150 to $200 million in foreign exchange from the livestock trade. This earns the government some $8-9 million in taxes, over 30% of its total budget.

While the livestock ban is in effect, Somaliland is largely dependent on overseas remittances by diaspora Somali, estimated at $500 million a year. Given the absence of international assistance, contributions by the Somaliland diaspora have been crucial in the country's development. Somaliland now has two universities and several vocational colleges whose construction was greatly aided by diaspora remittances.

The entrepreneurial spirit abounds in Somaliland. Businessmen there have created one of the cheapest telephone systems in Africa: International calls are $1.50 a minute in the day and only 80 cents at night. Traders are working to export frankincense and myrrh, and exploration has begun for oil and gemstones. A recently discovered reef of high-quality emeralds—several miles long—holds much promise as an alternative source of income.

Somaliland's two million people today enjoy the peace and prosperity that elsewhere in Somalia seems yet distant.

Economy: Livestock and bananas were Somalia's most profitable sectors. As with Somaliland, however, the Gulf states stopped buying Somali meat after another outbreak of RVF, and that source of foreign exchange was curtailed. Banana exports have also suffered. The "banana

View of Mogadishu and the ocean

wars" between the European Union and the U.S. over America's share of the European banana market hit Somali banana growers hard.

Coastal waters off northern Somalia contain rich fishing grounds, but the absence of any governmental control of its waters encouraged illegal plundering by a variety of fishing fleets. Using the newest and most destructive of fishing techniques—drift nets and dynamiting to break up coral reefs where lobsters and other highly prized catch live—these mechanized fishermen destroy the habitats and livelihood of local fishermen.

Traditionally, Somali fishermen used nets only between September and April. In the hot season between May and August, indigenous fishermen use only hooks to catch their prey. To industrialized fishing operations which know no such limitations, the profits are enormous. Within 75 days of fishing, each ship gets up to 420 tons of fish out of Somali waters. The catch is worth 6.3 million US dollars.

To stop illegal fishing, locals have begun to arm themselves and their boats and to keep watch on the coast. When they capture a foreign fishing vessel, its occupants are forced to pay a cash fine for the illegal practice. Taiwanese and Ukrainian ships have recently been captured, but the pirates are heavily armed, and it is likely that violence will increase until the government develops a capacity to patrol its shores. Already several local fishermen and their boats are unaccounted for and presumed lost in the fishing wars.

In the south the most important commercial crop comes from banana plantations. The plantations, controlled by two major firms, one Italian and the other American (Dole), represent the only examples of modern agricultural techniques in the country—irrigation system and modern farm machinery. Export duties through the southern ports seem to represent the most important source of income for the Hawiye faction of Hussein Aideed. The south also has its example of resources plundered as a result of governmental incapacity. Around Kismayu, hundreds of hectares of trees are felled daily to make charcoal for export to the Middle East.

Culture: In many ways the supreme cultural achievement of Somalia can be found in its poetry. Oral verse is central to the Somali way of life. It is a means of mass communication, preserving history and shaping contemporary events, expressing personal and public sentiment and experience. Travelers invariably comment on the Somali love of harmonious sound, elaborate image and alliterative arabesque. A poem could be as precious as a jewel; a great poet was a sage, a wise man an elder, even if not old.

Distinguished poets were heard by huge audiences of national radio and showcased by the BBC's Africa Service. Their allusive and metaphoric language could confound the foreign censor and stimulate the nationalist cause. The Somali poetic tradition remains today, not entirely muted by the thunder of arms, not entirely destroyed by political repression. So embedded in Somali consciousness is poetry that it is part of the texture and discourse of clan reconciliation meetings, the bedrock of Somali politics.

For Westerners, access to the power of Somali oral verse is indirect. One intimation of that power is the voice and music of the country's most famous musician, its first female pop star, Maryam Mursal. Her story is the story of Somalia. Possessed of a huge voice, an alto husky with the sadness of experience, Mursal was a star in the 1970s singing what was called locally "Somali jazz." It combined traditional African song and Arabic sound with influences derived from Western performers like Ray Charles and Etta James. As the oppression of the Siyad Barré regime increased, so did Mursal's political engagement. Her songs became more political, more critical. "When we have a president that oppresses us," she sang, "what president or what person should we turn to in order to get help?" The regime reacted quickly. The song was banned and Mursal fired.

Having five children to support, she took her savings and purchased a truck and taxi. She made deliveries by night and taxied by day, becoming Mogadishu's first female cabdriver. As the violence of civil war exploded in the 1990s, Mursal fled Somalia, trekking for some seven months through Kenya and Ethiopia and finally to Djibouti where she sought asylum at the Danish Embassy. That finally granted, she wound up with her family in a Danish refugee camp singing for her fellow escapees. Heard by a record producer who recognized hers as a voice he had thrilled to and recorded in Africa, Mursal was contracted to Real World records and introduced to the world at large.

Two CDs showcase her musical range and diversity. *Waaberi* is a compendium of traditional–style Somali songs, recorded live before a small audience. Her backup is a group of Somali expatriates, once members of the Somalian National Theater troupe, playing percussion and traditional *oud* or lute. (The term "lute" ultimately derives from the Arabic *al 'ud.*) *The Journey* transports Mursal's Somali melodies into the eclecticism of World Music. *Oud* and percussion are replaced by keyboard bass, guitars and horns, muted trumpet, violins and accordion. The album's longest song, "Qax" (The Refugee) tells the story of her harrowing trek through the Horn of Africa to ultimate refuge, the journey of life replicated in ever–changing soundscapes of complex rhythm and instrumentation.

The Future: For the first time in a decade there is a sense of optimism in Somalia as a consequence of the establishment of the Transitional National Government (TNG). The country's future depends on the TNG's capacity to reconcile obdurate warlords and the recalcitrant mini-states of Somaliland and Puntland.

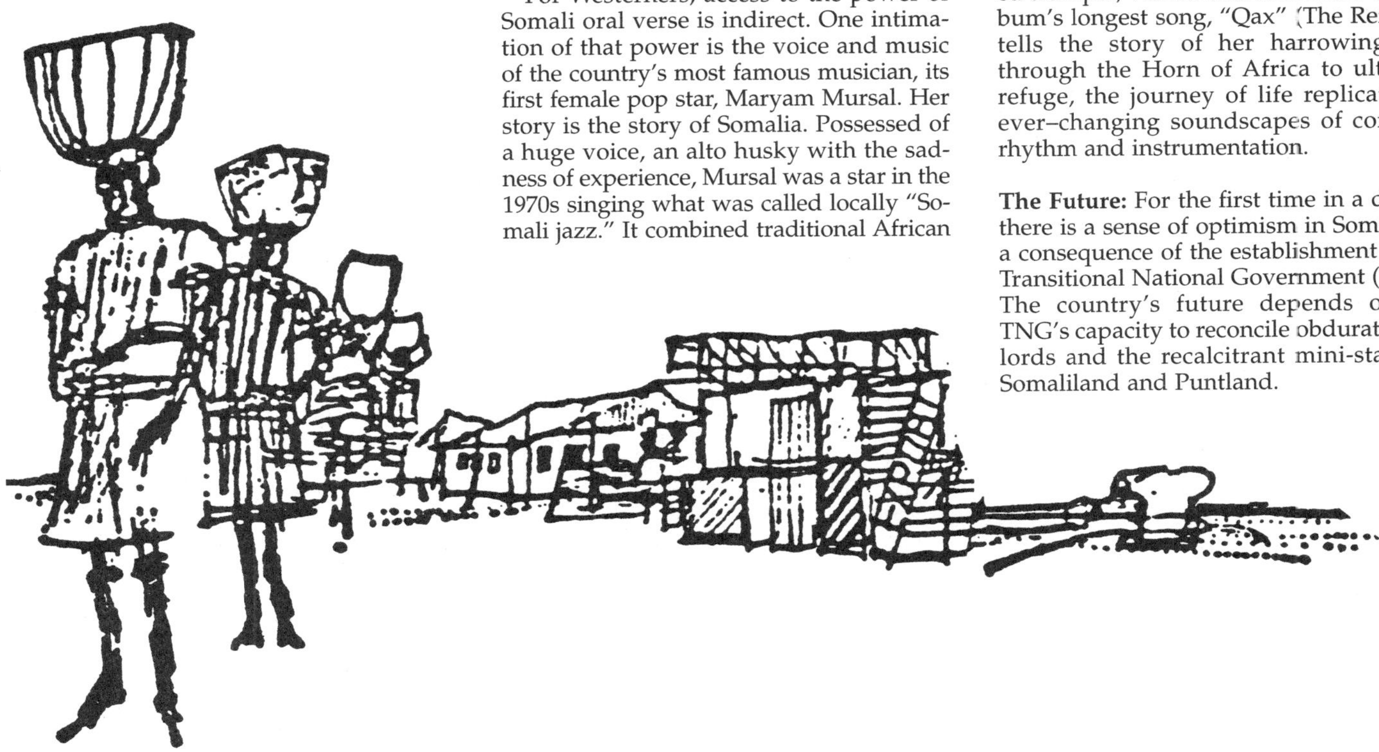

The United Republic of Tanzania

Mount Kilimanjaro

Area: 939,652 sq. km = 362,800 sq. mi. (includes the islands of Zanzibar and Pemba; as large as Texas and most of New Mexico.

Population: 31,270,820 (July 1999 est.)

Capital City: Dar es Salaam (Pop. 2.8 million, et). Some government offices have been moved to Dodoma which is to be the new capital at an undetermined time.

Climate: Tropically hot and humid in the coastal area, hot and dry in the central plateau and semi–temperate in the highlands where cooler weather prevails as the altitude increases.

Neighboring Countries: Mozambique (Southeast); Malawi, Zambia (Southwest); Congo (Kinshasa), Burundi, Rwanda (West); Uganda (Northwest); (Kenya (Northeast).

Official Languages: KiSwahili, English.

Other Principal Languages: Arabic (widely spoken in Zanzibar). Kiswahili (Swahili) is the mother tongue of the Bantu people living in Zanzibar and nearby coastal Tanzania; although Kiswahili is Bantu in structure and origin, its vocabulary draws on a variety of sources, including Arabic and English, and it has become the lingua franca of central and eastern Africa; the first language of most people is one of the local languages. Prominent among these are Bena, Chagga, Gogo, Ha , Haya, Maasai, Makonde, Nilamba, Nyakyusa, Nyamwezi, Nyaturu, Ruguru, Shambala, Sukuma, and Yao.

Ethnic groups: mainland—native African 99% (of which 95% are Bantu consisting of more than 130 tribes), other 1% (consisting of Asian, European, and Arab); Zanzibar—Arab, native African, mixed Arab and native African.

Principal Religions: mainland—Christian 45%, Muslim 35%, indigenous beliefs 20; Zanzibar—more than 99% Muslim.

Chief Commercial Products: Coffee, manufactured goods, cotton, cashew nuts, minerals, tobacco, and sisal.

GNP per capita: 210 US$

Currency: Tanzania Shilling.

Former Colonial Status: German Colony (1885–1917); British Mandate under the League of Nations and Trusteeship under the United Nations (1919–1961).

Independence Date: 26 April 1964. Tanganyika became independent 9 December 1961 (from UK-administered UN trusteeship); Zanzibar became independent 19 December 1963 (from UK); Tanganyika united with Zanzibar 26 April 1964 to form the United Republic of Tanganyika and Zanzibar; renamed United Republic of Tanzania 29 October 1964.

Chief of State: Benjamin Mkapa, President (since 1995).

National Flag: A triangle of green in the upper left corner; a triangle of blue in the lower right–hand corner with a broad band of black between the two. These three colors are separated by narrow yellow bands.

Tanzania is a large, picturesque country lying just south of the Equator, extending between the great lakes of Central Africa and the Indian Ocean, with a 500–mile coastline. A fertile plain of up to 40 miles in width stretches along the coastline; the land slowly rises in the interior to a large central plateau averaging 4,000 feet in altitude. A mountain range of moderate height in the middle of Tanzania extends from north to south.

At the north end of these peaks, Mount Kilimanjaro rises in majestic splendor to the height of 19,340 feet—the tallest peak in Africa, which, though only three degrees south of the Equator, is capped by snow and icy glaciers year around.

Farther to the northwest, immense, fresh water Lake Victoria spreads its sparkling breadth across the semi–arid plain.

A chain of towering mountains extends along the length of the entire western border, sharply descending to Lake Tanganyika which is 2,534 feet deep. This long, narrow body of water was created centuries ago when an immense fault of land descended sharply, creating an earthquake of immeasurable proportions, and forming what is now called the Great Western Rift Valley. The large East African lakes contribute an area of 20,000 square miles of inland water to the area of Tanzania. Abundant rainfall supports dense vegetation in the coastal area, but the central plateau, hot and dry, has an average of 25 inches of rainfall per year.

In the higher elevations, cooler weather prevails and there is more abundant rainfall, produced by the rush of warm air up the high slopes of the mountains. There are many game parks which protect large numbers of elephants, buffalos, lions, giraffes and other native species. A recent aerial survey of the Serengeti National Park revealed that more than one million animals live within its confines.

History: Countless centuries ago, Persian, Arabic, Indian and Portuguese traders called at the coast of Tanzania and engaged in lively trade with the various people. The country had been settled in unknown times by large numbers of Bantus and small groups of Nilotic and Nilo-Hamitic people. For details of early and colonial history, see Historical Background, *The Germans in Africa* and *The British in Africa*.

As a result of pre-independence elections in 1960, the *Tanganyika African National Union (TANU)*, energetically led by its founder, Julius Nyerere, was installed in power. Nyerere, the son of a minor chief of the small Zanaki tribe, had been sent to a Catholic mission school as a boy. He later trained as a teacher at Makerere University College in Uganda and with Catholic assistance, went on to Edinburgh University where he received a master's degree in 1949. When he returned home in 1953, he was one of only two Tanganyikans trained in foreign universities, and a year later he formed *TANU* to agitate against British rule. Under Nyerere's leadership, *TANU* developed into a successful vehicle for the mass mobilization of African sentiment. Tanganyika became fully independent of Great Britain on December 9, 1961, a *de facto* single party state. Within a year a republican form of government was adopted with Nyerere as the country's first president.

In 1964 Nyerere proceeded to institutionalize the one-party system. Following eastern European models, *TANU* would be the sole means of organizing political expression in the country. Meanwhile, the neighboring island nation of Zanzibar, independent in 1963, experienced a destabilizing revolution that would ultimately link it to Tanganyika.

Former President Nyerere

President Benjamin William Mkapa

Zanzibar

Before the 1964 revolution, Zanzibar—a collective noun which refers to both Zanzibar and Pemba islands and their volcanic neighbors—was a highly stratified society. A majority of the population, 76% were African; Arabs made up 16%, but monopolized political power and controlled the economy of clove plantations. Trade was dominated by a smaller Indian population. After World War II, the racial structure of Zanzibar society was increasingly challenged by the majority African population. They experienced economic and social discrimination and limited opportunities. Symptomatically, initial judicial hearings were conducted in Arabic rather than the more widely used KiSwahili. Political parties were first organized in the 1950s and reflected Zanzibar's racial divide. The *Zanzibar Nationalist Party (ZNP)* was largely Arab and Arabized Africans; the supporters of the *Afro-Shirazi Party (ASP)* were Africans, often descendants of a long mixture of Arab, Persian and African heritage. In June 1963 Zanzibar gained internal self-government and and *ZNP*-led coalition emerged victorious in July elections with Sultan Jamsid ibn Abdullah as head of state and Prime Minister Hamadi, an Arab, as government leader. Zanzibar was declared independent on December 10, 1963, but a month later on January 13, 1964, the Arab-dominated government was overthrown in a bloody revolution. Thousands of Arabs and Indians were massacred, the Sultan deposed and a Republic declared, under the control of a 32-man Zanzibar Revolutionary Council led by Abeid Karume of the *ASP*. Marxist-Leninist thinking was used to legitimize a tropical tyranny. The *ASP* monopolized political power as Zanzibar's sole legal party. All land was nationalized, political opponents thrown in jail and murdered, and a massive exodus of Arabs and Asians began amid continuing disorder. Karume appealed to neighboring Tanganyika for aid in maintaining law and order. Nyerere's government, fearing the consequences of continuing instability dispatched Tanganyikan police forces and in April 1964, Zanzibar and Tanganyika formed a union, later formally designated the United Republic of Tanzania. The governing parties of each partner shared similar outlook and had long cooperated with each other. Though Nyerere's socialism was more moderate than Karume's the union strengthened left-radical pressures on *TANU*.

Tanzania

In 1964 *TANU* was also facing instability on the mainland. Economic discontent had been fomented by trade unions and the army had mutinied in various parts of the country as soldiers protested low pay and the slow pace of Africanization of the lower officer grades. Nervous about a professional army, the government disbanded it and replaced it by a highly politicized Tanzanian People's Defense Force. The emulation of "popular democracies" was intensified following Nyerere's visit to China in 1965. The Chinese told him that farmers were the most conservative members of society and must be uprooted from the land if socialism were to be built. Nyerere had used the KiSwahili term "ujamaa," meaning familyhood, to describe the ideal of communal cooperation he sought to develop, but this was given a more conventional socialist definition in *TANU*'s Arusha Declaration of 1967. The government was asked to nationalize all means of production and to prepare development plans that relied in no way on foreign assistance. Planned villages, as in China, resulted. Peasants were forcibly transferred to new villages without consultation and without compensation for the loss of their houses and farms. Unremarkably, production declined.

In 1977 Tanzania adopted a new constitution which explicitly subordinated all organs of state to the party. At the same time, *TANU* and the *Afro-Shirazi Party* merged to form a single party known as the *Chama cha Mapinduzi*—the Revolutionary Party, or *CCM* for short. Within the union, Zanzibar has considerable autonomy—its own president, who serves as Tanzanian vice-president, and chief minister, responsible for most affairs aside from defense and international relations. Under the constitution, Tanzanian's lawmaking body, the National Assembly, consists of 228 members, of whom 118 are elected from mainland constituencies and 50 from Zanzibar. Others were appointed by government and various "mass organizations." Given the leading role of the *CCM* and its monopoly of power, however, the legislature was relatively meaningless. To reinvigorate a complacent party, an interesting variant on the one-party theme was introduced in the mid-1980s: *CCM* would approve two candidates for most constituencies, providing

Serengeti National Park

some illusion of democratic choice. Indeed, some government ministers were defeated in this manner.

President Nyerere was confirmed in office by plebiscites (it can hardly be called them an election when only one candidate is running) held in 1965, 1970, 1975 and 1985. In that year he retired from the presidency but retained the post of *CCM* chairman. His chosen successor was Ali Hassan Mwinyi, the former president of Zanzibar. It was during Mwinyi's two terms in office that the socialist chickens came home to roost. The economy was bankrupt and its intellectual model proved equally bankrupt with the collapse of the Soviet Union. Plans were made to privatize some state companies and open the economic door a crack. Courageously, the government introduced the notion of competitive democracy and the constitution was amended in 1992 to make Tanzania a multiparty state. In 1995, Ben Mkapa was elected President in Tanzania's first competitive election.

The elections, characterized by administrative ineptitude, were chaotic. The situation in the capital was so bad—election officials absent, ballots lost, polls opening late, if at all—that the whole thing had to be redone after being declared null and void. Opposition parties claimed it was all a CCM plot and withdrew, but when the dust settled, on the mainland at least, 30 years of single party rule had given way to actual party competition. *Chama cha Mapinduzi* continued to control parliament, winning 186 of 232 elective seats, and as *CCM* candidate, Mkapa beat three opponents winning a total of 61.8% of ballots cast.

The 2000 elections in many ways seemed a repeat of those held in 1995. President Mkapa overwhelmed his opposition with nearly 75% of the vote, and *CCM* continued its dominance in parliament, holding 244 of 274 seats.

Turmoil reigned in Zanzibar. The *CCM* organization there—always more authoritarian than its mainland counterpart—made life very much tougher for its *Civic United Front (CUF)* opponents. Government security forces and *CCM* toughs harassed and intimidated *CUF* candidates and supporters on both Pemba and Zanzibar; opposition officials were beaten by police. On election day, ballots and registration lists failed to arrive on time in opposition strongholds.

The situation on Pemba was such a disaster the Zanzibar Electoral Commission (ZEC) nullified the results and re-ran the elections in early November. *CUF* boycotted the re-runs, demanding that the entire election be conducted again, with the expected result: The ZEC announced that *CCM's* Amani Abeid Karume won the Zanzibar presidency with 67%, beating the *CUF's* Seif Shariff Hamad, who took 33%.

The European Union, the OAU and the United States all criticized the conduct of the election, but Amani Karume, the former minister of communication and transport and eldest son of Zanzibar's first president, Abeid Karume, seemed little inclined to make concessions to the opposition.

CUF protests continued, and members elected to parliament refused to attend its sessions. At the end of January 2001, an opposition meeting demanding nullification of the elections, new constitutional provisions granting greater autonomy for Zanzibar and a restructuring of the country's electoral commissions was violently broken up by Tanzanian security forces, resulting in the death of at least thirty-three people. Several thousand *CUF* supporters fled to Kenya in fear for their lives.

It took the death of over thirty people to force the two parties into negotiation. In March the *CCM* and *CUF* signed an accord to cool the political crisis, but in April Tanzania's parliament declared the fifteen Zanzibar seats vacant because the *CUF* deputies had missed three consecutive meetings. Under the Tanzanian constitution, by-elections to fill the vacancies should be held within ninety days. Instead, the ruling *Chama cha Mapinduzi* party used its huge parliamentary majority to pass a bill changing the ninety days to two years. It was hardly a move calculated to reduce tensions.

Pressure on the government continues to increase. In early April tens of thousands of demonstrators took to the streets of Dar-es-Salaam demanding electoral justice. "We declare the elections in Zanzibar null and void," they chanted, carefully watched by hundreds of policemen. More ominous for a government dependent on the goodwill of donors, one banner struck at the regime's vulnerability: "EU - USA - Don't support election thugs," it read.

With the death of its Founding Father, Julius Nyerere, in October 1999, Tanzania entered a new era. He had dominated the political scene from the beginning and continued to do so in retirement. With his passing it may be possible to open discussions on issues he suppressed. There are pressures from Zanzibar to re-examine the union between islands and mainland.

The April demonstrators also marched for a new constitution, but notions of greater autonomy for the islands probably won't get much of a hearing from President Mkapa. At Nyerere's funeral, he made his position clear: Anyone, he said, "dreaming about breaking the unity of Tanzania...will be dealt with ruthlessly and their activities curtailed."

Culture: The numerous tribes of proud Africans have a rich diversity of customs and traditions which contribute to the distinctiveness of Tanzania. The Kikuyus of the North extend into Kenya and are hunters and warriors. The fabled Masai, one of the best known tribes, actually are few in number—they are highly onamented cattle herdsmen with a singular custom of living on a diet principally of milk and blood from their cattle. Their main sport is killing lions with their spears in order to obtain material for their elaborate headdresses.

The larger group of Chaggas in the north–central plains around Mt. Kilimanjaro are an advanced, Christian people devoting their lives to business and coffee growing. Another Bantu group, similar to the Chaggas, the Sukuma, are well–educated, industrious people, constituting the largest tribal group in Tanzania.

Modern education is being extensively promoted by the government. Many students from Tanzania are pursuing advanced courses in universities located in Uganda and Europe. A program of adult education is now underway with a goal of eliminating illiteracy; literacy now stands at an admirable rate of about 85%.

KiSwahili is more and more becoming the national language and is credited with instilling a national pride within the country. Whereas most of the other former European colonies still use as their official tongue the language they inherited from them, Tanzania is an exception. The editor of an important newspaper in Dar es Salaam has been having a difficult time finding journalists qualified to *speak* and *write* in English. While KiSwahili has definitely been a major factor in unifying the Tanzanian people, English is still the "international" language, and many Tanzanians are concerned that the country will lose certain economic advantages by slowly "burying" the other official language.

The present capital, Dar–es–Salaam (Haven of Peace), is a majestic city of modern buildings with an incomparably beautiful beach on the warm waters of the Indian Ocean. It also is a crowded city. Merchants and traders from many other cultures have made this busy port city a "melting pot" of people. Two smaller cities, Moshi and Arusha, both lying within the shadow of Mt. Kilimanjaro, are centers of agriculture and commerce. In an effort to "open up" the interior regions of the country, centrally-located Dodoma, with a present population of about 90,000 has been selected as the new capital city. Actual transfer of the functions of government and completion of the building program to make this a reality will probably stretch over a period of ten years because of limited government funds.

The government–controlled *Daily News* is widely circulated on the mainland; publication on Zanzibar is sporadic.

Economy: Julius Nyerere knew little of economics, and his socialist program devastated an already poor country. Tanzanian policies emphasized government control over all aspects of the nation's economic life, with heavy spending on education and health services. In an agriculturally based economy, resettlement of peasant farmers into planned villages facilitated the distribution of those services but had disastrous effects on agricultural production, which plummeted. Government owned industries and businesses were costly failures and a drain on national resources. As agricultural production diminished and the expenses of nationalized companies rose, national income fell, foreign debt increased and Tanzania became increasingly dependent on the generosity of international donors.

President Mkapa has continued his predecessor's efforts to liberalize the economy. Agricultural policy allows for a play of market forces. Privatization of state-owned enterprises has been undertaken, exchange rates have been freed and red tape reduced. Corruption is pandemic in Tanzania ("In my country," said former Prime Minister Joseph Warioba, the chairman of Mkapa's anti-corruption commision, "you have to pay a bribe for everything.") The very public anti-corruption campaign which followed the Warioba Report resulted in hundreds of state bureaucrats being fired, though almost none have been prosecuted. All of this has created a better business climate and stimulated economic growth, but even so Tanzania remains desperately poor.

Economic growth has been sluggish for the past several years, barely enough to keep up with population growth. Agriculture accounts for 60% of GDP, employs 85% of the work force and contributes over 80% of export earnings. Like an unloved child of nature, however, Tanzania was subjected to meteorological extremes of drought and flooding with what seems cyclical regularity. Prices for its main agricultural products—coffee, sisal, cotton, tobacco, cashew nuts and tea—have declined. Tourism is one of its fastest growing sectors but most visitors reach the country from neighboring Kenya where roads and airport services are better developed. (Tourism has replaced cloves as Zanzibar's principal source of foreign exchange. The island expects to earn $72 million from a projected 100,000 tourists in 2000.)

Tanzania's mining sector is poised to make a major contribution to the economy. Gold mining companies invested $400 million in the country in 1998, and 4.3 tons of the metal were exported that year, bringing in revenues of $36 million. The mining sector recorded a growth rate of 17 percent in 1997 and grew by 27.4 percent in 1998. Total estimated gold deposits in Tanzania now stand at around 30 million ounces; its annual gold production is expected to reach at least 40 tons by 2001.

There are also considerable deposits of gemstones—green tourmaline, sapphire, garnet, diamonds, rubies and emeralds—in Tanzania. The country earned $8.1 million from gemstone exports in 1998, compared with only $200,000 11 years before when large quantities were smuggled out of the country. Smuggling remains a problem as the example of tanzanite indicates. Tanzanite is a precious blue stone produced only in Tanzania in the volcanic soils to the southwest of mount Kilimanjaro. Strangely enough, Kenya now stands as the world's largest exporter of this unique product.

For any type of mining venture in Tanzania, infrastructure is a problem. Roads are inadequate and in disrepair. Availability of water and electricity is often problematic.

The greatest drag on the Tanzanian economy remains its international debt. As of 1998 that debt was 8 billion dollars. The World Bank evaluates debt burden by a ratio of debt to exports. In severely indebtedcountries, the ratio of debt to exports is put at 220 percent or more. A debt burden in that range coupled with a debt service of 20-25 percent of annual exports can qualify a country for Heavily Indebted Poor Country (HIPC) relief. Tanzania qualified on both counts. Its debt/export ratio is 406 percent while its debt service 35 percent.

Debt payments consume 40% of state revenues. Another 40% goes to pay the salaries of government workers. Only 20% of state revenues is thus available for all other government services. Precious little remains for investment and development.

So restricted are Tanzania's revenues that it has delayed a customs union with Kenya and Uganda. It currently earns 30% of its tax revenue from Kenyan imports and stands to lose $80 million if tariffs are eliminated. The same fear of lost import tariff revenues motivates mainland opposition to Zanzibar's proposal to make Malindi a free port.

The International Monetary Fund and the World Bank announced a debt relief package worth two billion dollars for Tanzania in April 2000. It was testimony not only to Tanzania's poverty but the institutions' faith in the Mkapa government's economic policies.

The Future: Zanzibar remains in turmoil, and its parliament is paralyzed. Multilateral aid, business investment and tourism are all in jeopardy.

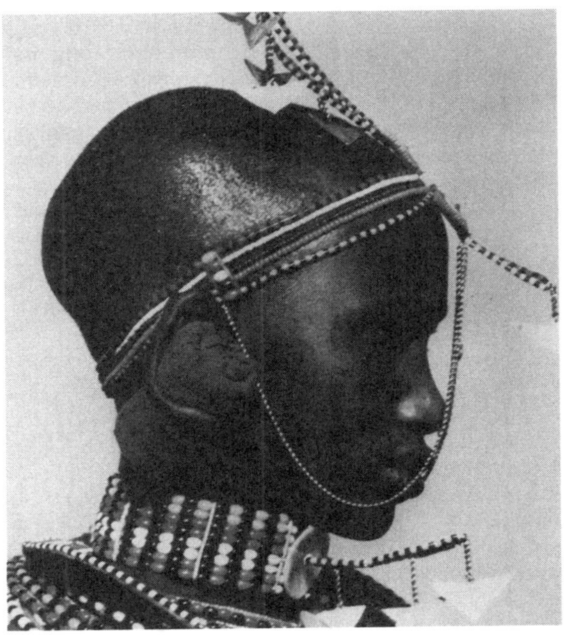

A young Masai woman

The Republic of Uganda

His Majesty Ronald Muwenda Mutebi II, King of Buganda, a traditional ruler of Uganda

Area: 235,690 sq. km. = 91,080 sq. mi.
Population: 22,804,973 (July 1999 est.).
Capital City: Kampala (Pop. 1.3 million, estimated).
Climate: Temperate, though equatorial, because of altitudes averaging 4,500 feet with ample rainfall in most years (except in the semi–arid northwest) interrupted by two short dry seasons.
Neighboring Countries: Rwanda, Tanzania (Southwest); Congo-Kinshasa (West); The Sudan (North); Kenya (Northeast).
Official Language: English is taught in grade schools, used in courts of law and by most newspapers and some radio broadcasts.
Other Principal Languages: Over forty. Prominently: Acholi, Alur, Chiga, Ganda, Karamojong, Kenyi, Lango, Masaba, Nyankore Nyoro, Rwanda, Sogo, Teso, Tooro.
Ethnic groups: Baganda 17%, Karamojong 12%, Basogo 8%, Iteso 8%, Langi 6%, Rwanda 6%, Bagisu 5%, Acholi 4%, Lugbara 4%, Bunyoro 3%, Batobo 3%, non-African (European, Asian, Arab) 1%, and other 23%.
Principal Religions: Roman Catholic 33%, Protestant 33%, Muslim 16%, indigenous beliefs 18%.
Chief Commercial Products: Coffee 54%, gold, fish and fish products, cotton, tea, and corn.
GNP per capita: 320 US$
Currency: Uganda Shilling.
Former Colonial Status: British Protectorate (1894–1962).
Independence Date: October 9, 1962.
Chief of State: Yoweri Museveni. (b. 1941), President.
National Flag: Six bands of black, yellow and red (repeated) with a silver circle in the center enclosing a crested crane.

This fertile expanse of highland lies astride the Equator in central East Africa between the Eastern and Western Rift formations. Uganda, dotted with lakes, and with immense Lake Victoria on the South, lies at an altitude of between 3,000 and 6,000 feet. If this country were at a lower altitude, its climate would be hot, moist and oppressive, but it is quite pleasantly temperate with ample rainfall to support intense cultivation. In the extreme Northeast, the climate is somewhat more dry.

Approximately 15% of the country is covered by fresh water. The Ruwenzori Mountains to the west divide Uganda from Zaïre, having altitudes of almost 17,000 feet. In the southwest, close to Rwanda, the Virunga range of active volcanos reaches skyward. In the East, Mount Elgon rises to a height of 14,000 feet, prominent among its neighbors of the Eastern Rift Mountains.

The Victoria Nile originates from the banks of Lake Victoria, heavily populated

with hippopotomi and crocodiles, and flows to Lake Kyoga, an irregularly shaped body of water with large swamps. From there the Nile flows north and west through immense mountains to empty into Lake Albert. The Albert Nile flows northward, leaving Uganda at the Sudanese border to continue its journey of more than 4,000 miles to the Mediterranean Sea.

The great expanse of plains traditionally has been dotted with many farms and plantations, and, as is true in Tanzania to the south, wildlife of many varieties is abundant.

History: It is difficult to trace the migrations of the Bantu people whose descendants live in Uganda today. The last Kabaka (King) of Buganda, claimed to be the 37th member of an uninterrupted line of monarchs. It is not possible to determine the exact time when the Nilotic groups came to northern Uganda. For details of early and colonial history, see Historical Background and *The British in Africa.*

The United Kingdom of Uganda was granted internal autonomy on March 1, 1962, becoming fully independent on October 9 of that year. The government initially consisted of a federation of the kingdoms of Buganda, Busoga, Butoro and Bunyoro, which retained local autonomy and the rest of the country was governed by the central government. Sir Edward Frederick Mutesa II, Kabaka of Buganda, became the first president and Sir William W. Nadiope, King of Bunyoro, was the first Vice–President. Prime Minister Milton Obote wielded considerable power within the central government. The cabinet was selected by a coalition of Obote's *People's Congress Party* and the *Buganda Kabaka Yekka Party;* the formerly dominant *Democratic Party* was in the minority.

The post independence era, more than 23 years long, was dominated by two figures which reduced Uganda to a grisly shambles, replete with starvation and widespread deaths. Milton Obote was the first (1963–1971, 1980–1985) and the second was a military figure, Idi Amin (1971–1979).

Milton Obote

Charging Mutesa with making personal profits from the supply of arms in connection with a rebellion in neighboring Zaïre, Obote dismissed him and seized the government. The hereditary king barely escaped when the army stormed the presidential palace; he lived in exiled poverty until his death in 1969. His remains were ceremoniously returned to Uganda in 1971.

Obote abolished the old constitution and the traditional kingdoms; his *PCP* became the sole party and he veered Uganda sharply toward marxism–socialism. As he appointed more and more of his fellow Lango (also Langi) tribesmen to public offices in what had become an overstuffed bureaucracy, army posts and the judiciary, tensions mounted. The country was proclaimed a republic in order to permanently end the old kingdoms. Finally the army revolted, uniting behind an initially curious leader, Idi Amin.

General Amin, a massive man who had been the Ugandan heavyweight boxing champion between 1951 amd 1960, was popular at the time of his takeover of Uganda. He had an overstuffed ego, however, and wasted no time alienating just about everybody. All Asians were ordered expelled from Uganda in 1972 without thought to the importance of the vital role they played as merchants and traders.

Amin's mental quirks became widely known and initial admiration quickly turned to fear. Educated Ugandans began to leave the country to escape his whims. He expelled African clergy and missionaries, claiming they were foreign agents, and completely outlawed some Christian denominations such as the Jehovah's Witnesses. Brutality became the order of the day by 1974. Secret executions, massacres and torture were among his favorite methods and he personally participated in some of these grisly acts.

Military efforts to oust him failed and the perpetrators were executed on the spot. His spies operated at every level and he became more mentally deranged. The economy all but disappeared by 1978 and the country seethed with unrest. In response to an army insurrection, Amin tried to distract attention from his shortcomings by claiming that Tanzania had invaded Uganda; he "responded" to this fabrication by having his troops invade Tanzania. They captured about 710 square miles before withdrawing.

But President Julius Nyerere of Tanzania used the invasion as an excuse to get rid of Amin. Nyerere had personally granted Obote asylum when he was driven from Uganda. The Tanzanian troops, augmented by Ugandan exiles, mounted a swift invasion. Amin's forces, demoralized by his behavior, crumbled after fierce fighting had claimed the lives of many.

Idi Amin

The conquering army entered Kampala in April 1979 and was greeted jubilantly. In the confusion, the dictator escaped and now is living comfortably in Saudi Arabia. In elections swiftly scheduled, it appeared that Obote's *UPC* would lose. But a military figure proclaimed himself sole judge of the elections. He announced Obote the winner and immediately became his vice president.

There ensued five years of strife, frequently inter–tribal, in which an estimated 1 million fled and 300,000 lost their lives. Although there was a general rebellion that resulted in the ouster of Obote, it was a revolt that involved traditional tribal and clan rivalries to the extent that general chaos prevailed in Uganda from 1985 until 1987. There was a vacuum of power which in 1986 was gradually filled by the *National Resistance Army,* armed by Libya and led by Yoweri Museveni.

In January Musevani's *National Resistance Army (NRA)* shot its way into Kampala and seized control of the country. Museveni became president of the country at the head of the *National Resistance Movement (NRM)* and began the difficult task of rebuilding Uganda. He was determined to break the cycle of violence which had destroyed Uganda, restore democracy and foster economic development. Those goals required an entire rethinking of the institutions and practices that had bedeviled and destroyed the country. Chief among the objects of his criticism were the traditional political parties, which he castigated as "sectarian and divisive," responsible for the country's political and economic ills. Political parties were prohibited and political participation organized within the framework of the broad-based *National Revolutionary Movement (NRM.)* This was the beginning of what would come to be known as the non-party movement system.

Since the regime had come to power by force of arms promising to restore democracy and individual liberties, one its first projects was a constitutional commission which could develop the framework which restored the rule of law. The commission was to seek the views of the ordinary citizen and was charged with holding public meetings, debates, seminars and workshops throughout the country. Once organized, the commission toured the entire country and consulted with elders, religious and other organizations, opinion leaders in a variety of sectors. From this followed the publication of *Guidelines on Constitutional Issues* which was intended to be the basis of continuing dialogue. It addressed such issues as the need for a new constitution, human rights, political parties, and the structure of any future government. The whole process demonstrated a remarkable shift from the traditions of constitutions created on high and presented to the people. Here, people would actually participate in the development of the document that would shape their lives and futures. The process was clearly designed to assure the document would receive the respect and legitimacy of the Ugandan people.

The transition from anarchy to constitutionalism was lengthy; the constitutional commission's draft was debated and ratified by a popularly elected constituent assembly on July 12, 1995, and promulgated by President Museveni on October 8. The product of deliberation was lengthier. In its final form, the constitution weighed in with 287 articles and seven addenda, making the Uganda Constitution ten times longer than that of the United States. Reflecting Uganda's turbulent past, it contains the hopeful piety that no person or group of persons shall "take or retain control of the Government of Uganda, except in accordance with the provisions of this constitution," but fundamentally, it incorporates President Musevani's ideological vision. This is particularly obvious on the issue of political parties.

The constitution outlaws political party activities, including opening and operating branch offices, holding delegates conferences, sponsoring candidates for election and staging political rallies. For Musevani, a society like Uganda, still divided on tribal and religious grounds, is not ready for political parties, though in reality they continue to operate. The constitution guarantees the right to form parties, but postpones their registration and organization to later parliamentary legislation. Parliament is constitutionally prohibited from establishing a single-party state. After five years experience with the movement system, voters were promised an opportunity to assess the system in a referendum.

Parliamentary elections were held July 1996. There are 214 directly elected members and a number of indirectly elected seats for representatives of women (39), youth (5), workers (3), the disabled (5) and the army (10).

President Museveni's personal rule was legitimized by May 1996 elections held in accordance with provisions of the new constitution. His election slogan was "No Change," and he campaigned on his record: He had ended Uganda's cycle of blood and dictatorship, boosted security through the army and built economic success that saw gross domestic product growth hit 10% in 1994. He won handily, beating two opposition candidates. It was the first free and open presidential vote in 30 years.

President Museveni

Economic rehabilitation was as important to Museveni as political reconstruction. He had inherited a wasteland of human devastation when he assumed power in 1986. Piles of skulls remained at crossroads, remainders of the grisly days since independence. The economy was stagnant. Transportation and communication systems had been destroyed by war, production disrupted. The state was bankrupt; revenue from taxation was virtually nonexistent. Agreements were made with the IMF, the economy was liberalized to include producer incentives, loans were secured to rehabilitate infrastructure and the economy, starting from virtually nothing, responded with eye-catching growth rates. Averaging 6.3% over a decade, Uganda's growth rate was ranked 15th in the world.

Although economic vibrancy has returned to Uganda, not all its citizens share in its changed conditions. In border areas to the west and north, the *Uganda Peoples Defense Force (UPDF)* faces on-going resistance and rebellion from those marginalized economically and politically. In the north, the *Lord's Resistance Army (LRA)* supported by Khartoum's meddlesome anti-Musevani regime, has waged war for years. Led by a former Roman Catholic altarboy, Joseph Kony, the LRA recruits its soldiers by kidnapping children, male and female, and sends them off to Sudanese camps for military training or sexual service. Those who flee or disobey—and disobedience includes riding a bicycle— have been maimed or murdered. His stated goal is to overthrow Museveni and rule Uganda in accordance with the Ten Commandments. Survivors describe him as a fanatic who claims visitations from the Holy Spirit which guide his actions. The rebels—Museveni calls them terrorists—have killed thousands, destroyed homes and property, prevented the distribution of social services or development projects in an already dirt-poor region. Some 300,000 displaced persons live in "protected villages" organized by the army to prevent the enemy from getting food and assistance from fellow Acholi tribesmen. War against the LRA ties down an entire Ugandan division, and the absence of any visible progress against the bandits prompted President Musevani to reshuffle the army's high command in early 1998. Sudan also supports two other rebel groups, the *Allied Democratic Forces*, and the *West Nile Bank Front*, active on Uganda's western border.

Sudanese support for these destabilizing elements is tit-for-tat response. President Musevani shares with his colleagues

A pineaple farm near Jinja

Courtesy: Dr. Robert J. Kowalczyk

in Eritrea and Ethiopia, fellow Marxists turned advocates of democracy and liberal economy, common hostility to Sudan's Islamist regime. Uganda is an important transshipment point for arms going to the southern Sudanese resistance under the leadership of John Garang. Uganda was the training ground for members of the Tutsi-led Rwandan Patriotic Front which invaded and defeated the genocidal regime installed in Kigali. Musevani was also central in organizing and supporting the forces responsible for the collapse of the Mobutu regime in Zaire. It all represented an enormously self-confident foreign policy, distinctly at odds with the OAU traditions of non-intervention and respect for borders.

Uganda's involvement in the Democratic Republic of the Congo dominated the events of 1998–99. First, the fight to overthrow Mobutu and install Laurent Kabila. Then the campaign to oust Kabila, who had become a second Mobutu and had failed to deal with the Uganda's concerns. The second intervention was justified on both security and human rights grounds. As with Rwanda, security issues were paramount: Kabila had done nothing to contain anti–Museveni rebels, members of the *Lords Resistance Army* (*LRA*) or the *Allied Democratic Forces* (*ADF*), comfortably nestled on his eastern borders.

Uganda's support of the anti-Kabila rebels raised fundamental questions about how a country as poor as Uganda could afford the increased defense expenditures necessary to conduct these operations. In part, the answer is simple: the war became self-financed through exploitation of Congo's rich resources. The war effort was early dominated by the question of resource extraction. Congo's wealth corrupted all who came near.

In September 1998 an airplane carrying Lt. Colonel Jet Mwebaze, brother of Uganda's army chief of staff, crashed in Rwanda. All those aboard died, as did the reputation of the Ugandan army. The plane carried, in addition to Mwebaze, a small group of shady international gold dealers and gold, undeclared, amounting in value to over a million dollars. Corruption permeated the entire army operation. Timber prices in Uganda fell sharply because Ugandan troops in the Congo had flooded the market with cheap wood smuggled from the war zone. The tentacles of corruption spread throughout the region as ports in Kenya and Tanzania served as points of transshipment for timber, coffee and minerals headed for Asian markets.

Corruption, already notable in Uganda, tended to become all-pervasive and inched closer to President Museveni himself. His half-brother, Major-General Salim Saleh, who seemed to shuttle back and forth between the private and public sectors, was everywhere touched by the taint of corruption. Businessmen talked about how difficult it was to work in Uganda without playing into the system of corruption, and lenders noted the high cost of corruption on development. It was estimated that perhaps no more than a third of a loan actually made it to a specific project.

In 1999 Uganda's partnership with Rwanda supporting the anti-Kabila coalition seemed to unravel. Clear policy differences began to emerge, and disputes over control of Congo resources drove a further wedge between the allies. The rebel *Congolese Rally for Democracy* (*RCD*) itself divided into factions.

After months of infighting, the rebels removed their original leader, Ernest Wamba-dia-Wamba, replacing him with Emile Ilunga. Rwanda and Uganda, themselves divided on the best way to fight the war, supported different rebel factions. Uganda supported Wamba, who moved to Kisangani where he was better protected by Ugandan troops; Rwanda backed Ilunga, whose *RCD* faction remained headquartered in Goma. Yet a third rebel faction emerged under the leadership of Jean-Pierre Bemba, the leader of the *Congolese Liberation Movement* (*MLC*). Backed by Uganda, Bemba took charge of the rebellion's northern front.

On at least two occasions the military forces of Uganda and Rwanda came to open conflict at the city of Kisangani. At heart, it appeared a conflict over control of the region's rich natural resources, but it compounded strains in the relationship. By mid-2000 each country had massed troops on its respective borders, and some feared a clash of former friends as unnecessary as the conflict between Ethiopia and Eritrea.

At home, the northern and western insurrections continue, though at reduced levels of intensity. Joseph Kony's *LRA* continues to "recruit" its fighters, porters or sex slaves by kidnapping children—despite behind the scenes negotiations mediated by the Carter Center in Atlanta. Before pulling out of the Democratic Republic of the Congo, the *UPDF* conducted a number of successful raids against *ADF* forces operating in the eastern regions. Several top commanders were reportedly killed, and one began to see a trickle of rebel surrenders by mid-2001.

In June 2000 Ugandans were called upon to reflect on their political system. Under transitional provisions of the new constitution, the "movement system" had been in place for five years. In late June a referendum was held on whether Uganda should adopt a multiparty system of democracy. The referendum campaign differed significantly from the intense educational drive to explain the constitution to inexperienced voters. One saw few workshops or other means of explaining and debating the nature and significance of the decision. The campaign became personalized—a referendum for or against Yoweri Museveni.

Sensing the mood of a country relatively satisfied with Museveni's tenure, the opposition decided to boycott the vote. More than 90% of those who voted chose to retain the Movement system; only 9.3% of referendum votes favored a return to multi-party democracy. Uganda remains, in effect, a single party state.

There was little interest in Uganda's presidential election scheduled for March 2001 until Kizza Besigye announced that he was entering the race. Suddenly there was the possibility of genuine competition. Dr Besigye was no ordinary challenger. He was one of the original NRA fighters and Musevani's personal physician during the long bush war. He went on to serve as a minister in Museveni's National Resistance Movement government. He knew, in other words, the regime from the inside. What he saw disillusioned him and formed the basis of his campaign against his old comrade in arms.

Corruption and nepotism were criticized, as was Uganda's involvement in the Congo war. He accused the president of becoming increasingly autocratic and of turning the ruling movement into a party intolerant of competition. For the president and his supporters there was, no doubt, a sense of betrayal. The campaign became unnecessarily violent and ramified regionally.

Tensions with Rwanda were magnified. Kigali was accused of contributing large sums to the Besigye campaign. Dr. Besigye's wife, a member of parliament, added to heightened suspicion between the two countries by accusing the Museveni government of aiding the Interahamwe, one of Rwanda's greatest *bête noirs*.

When all the votes were counted, President Museveni won by a huge margin, receiving 69.3% of the vote. Dr. Besigye, who ran second with 27.8% of the vote, refused to accept the results, charging fraud and intimidation. Bitterness remains, but many of the regime's problems have been laid bare. Whether President Museveni is willing or able to deal with them is another issue entirely.

Equally revealing and damaging was the April 2001 report of a panel of experts to the UN Security Council on "Illegal Exploitation of Natural Resources and Other Forms of Wealth in the Democratic Republic of the Congo." Names were named, and they came very near the President himself. The panel specifically singled out the president's half-brother, Major-General Salim Saleh and his wife Jovia Akandwanaho, as being "at the core of the illegal exploitation of natural resources in areas controlled by Uganda."

The panel's judgment on President Museveni was no less harsh. The president had "put himself in the position of accomplice," said the panel, by choosing not to act when information on corrupt practices was brought to his attention. Denials were, of course, issued. In high dudgeon, President Museveni announced withdrawal of Ugandan troops from the Congo and withdrawal from the whole Lusaka peace process.

Culture: Official figures indicate that Uganda is, by a large majority, a Christian nation. The two major immigrant religions, Islam and Christianity, far exceed indigenous religions, but these figures are misleading. Most Ugandans, even after converting to Islam or Christianity, do not abandon their traditional beliefs altogether but blend them with their adopted faiths.

Uganda is fertile ground for the foundation and growth of new sects and one, The Movement for the Restoration of the Ten Commandments of God, came forcefully to attention with widely publicized stories of mass murder. Over the last decade, East Africa has been a particular focus for cult groups led by charismatic figures. Students of such movements suggest they are the response of people overwhelmed by realities they neither understand nor control. Famines, ethnic genocide of unimaginable proportions, and a devastating AIDS epidemic have left people confused and traumatized. In these circumstances communities have turned to charismatic preachers whose doomsday scenarios provide a reasonable explanation of the irrational and hold out hope of a better world to come. Such, it seems, was what the Ten Commandments Movement offered its victims.

Uganda's HIV/AIDS program has come to be viewed as a model for states affected by the pandemic. A decade ago, more than 25 percent of Ugandan adults were living with HIV/AIDS. The death of a young and productive breadwinner left many families in poverty. AIDS orphans epitomized the problem. Innocent, they suffered. Most had no access to education, labor skills, and employment. They became street kids, an urban poor; alienated and unemployed, they became a potential threat to social stability. The problem was recognized early and a commitment was made to deal with it.

In many ways the program's success reflects the political culture of President Museveni's regime. Uganda's approach to the AIDS has stressed democratic flexibility. Museveni was as inclusive as possible, encouraging different actors to contribute in whatever way they could. He appointed a bishop for example, as one of the leaders of the Uganda AIDS Commission (UAC). To have a religious figure in UAC helped with the arduous task of moving AIDS from private to public spheres.

All the major sectarian communities participated. The Islamic Medical Association of Uganda (IMAU) created the Family AIDS Education & Prevention Through Imams project (FAEPTI). The project recognized Imams as trusted message bearers in the community and worked with them to incorporate HIV/AIDS prevention information into their spiritual teachings. It worked with leaders at 850 mosques and has trained 6,800 community volunteers who have visited 102,000 homes.

Openness of discussion and commitment to education, characteristics of Museveni's rebel insurgency from the beginning, have also characterized the country's approach to AIDS. In 1988 Uganda's most famous popular singer, Philly Lutaaya, returned from Sweden after four years of political exile. In April 1989 he shocked his fans and fellow Ugandans by announcing he had AIDS. For the next eight months he led a personal crusade against AIDS. Then, at the age of 38, he died. The admission and death of so public and esteemed a figure also elevated HIV/AIDS to public discussion from the dark recesses of shame. Once there, action was possible.

The Uganda AIDS program is reputed to be one of the most aggressive around. It features education and testing, counseling and condoms. Eighty percent of the nation's condoms are distributed by the health ministry. Usage has skyrocketed during the 1995-99 period: Forty percent of men reported condom use to guard against HIV/AIDS, up from seven percent.

The program is open to trials of new drugs, and indeed, nevirapine studies in Uganda showed the transmission of HIV from mother to child was reduced to about 13%.

In December 1999 President Museveni announced that the national HIV infection rate had declined from 30% in 1991 to 10%. Uganda is the only African country where AIDS prevalence rate is dropping. It aims to reduce the current infection rate from 10 percent to 7.5 percent by the year 2005. Despite the good news, the problem remains enormous. An estimated 1.9 million Ugandans carry the HIV virus that causes AIDS.

Economy: Uganda's economy is agriculture based. Coffee is the country's biggest export earner and the 1997 crop surpassed 1996's record production. Then, Uganda exported 4.15 million bags of coffee, which accounted for 65% of its export income. The productivity of Ugandan coffee farmers is due to President Musevani's deregulation of the coffee market in 1991. Uganda's Coffee Marketing Board, which had served as a convenient collection agency for dictators, was eliminated. Buyers became competitive, prices paid to farmers rose, providing higher savings and access to credit which permitted investment to improve both crops and harvesting. The price of coffee in 2001 dropped more than 40% from the previous year. A kilo of coffee brings only 64 cents. Earnings have fallen 50%, and the government is having a difficult time finding funds to pay its membership dues in both the Association of Coffee Producing Countries and the Inter-Africa Coffee Organization.

Significant efforts have been made to diversify the economy, once almost totally reliant on coffee exports. Fishing and fish processing rose steadily to provide 6% of export income, but the market faces an uncertain future. The European Union briefly halted sales of frozen fish—directed largely to Spain and the Netherlands—because of salmonella fears and pesticide poisoning. The government responded by quickly building better loading facilities to keep the fish clean.

Pesticide poisoning is related to a longer range but potentially even more damaging problem: the water hyacinth. Probably brought in by Belgians as an ornamental plant, the hyacinth has no known natural predators and, like a cancer, grows with amazing rapidity. The whole of Lake Victoria, the world's second largest fresh-water lake, is threatened, and the plant is making its way down the Nile river system. Already, 70,000 tons of hyacinth press against the outer walls of Uganda's Owen Falls hydroelectric dam, 80 km east of Kampala, which supplies electricity to Kenya and Tanzania. Engineers wonder how much weight it can take. Thus far spraying aquatic herbicides directly onto the plants has been the most effective method of reducing weed infestation quickly. The two chemicals used, rodeo and weedar, have been found safe to humans as well as fish.

In April 1998 Uganda's stellar economic performance was recognized by the World Bank and International Monetary Fund. As part of the Highly Indebted Poor Countries (HIPC) project, the lending institutions agreed to cut Uganda's $3.4 billion debt by about one fifth. By 2001, however, the proposed benefits of the HIPC debt cancellation had to be questioned.

A survey conducted by the Uganda National Bureau of Statistics between August 1999 and August 2000 indicated that the number of Ugandans living in absolute poverty had fallen 9%, from 44% of the population to 35%. Urban areas experienced a much larger drop than rural areas, and there were regional variations. In the North, poverty levels *increased* from 60% in 1997/98 to 65%.

Even more striking a challenge to proposed HIPC benefits was the growth of Uganda's debt stock. When included in the HIPC program, Uganda's debt was recorded at $3.4 billion. In 2001, after the program's debt cancellation, Uganda's debt stock had risen to $3.8 billion. Little wonder civil society was lobbying for greater input into how the program would operate.

The Future: It's clear the sheen of Museveni's star has begun to fade. Uganda's economic development is still dependent on external aid, and lender hesitancy, if not refusal, will certainly follow in the wake of the devastating Panel of Experts' report.

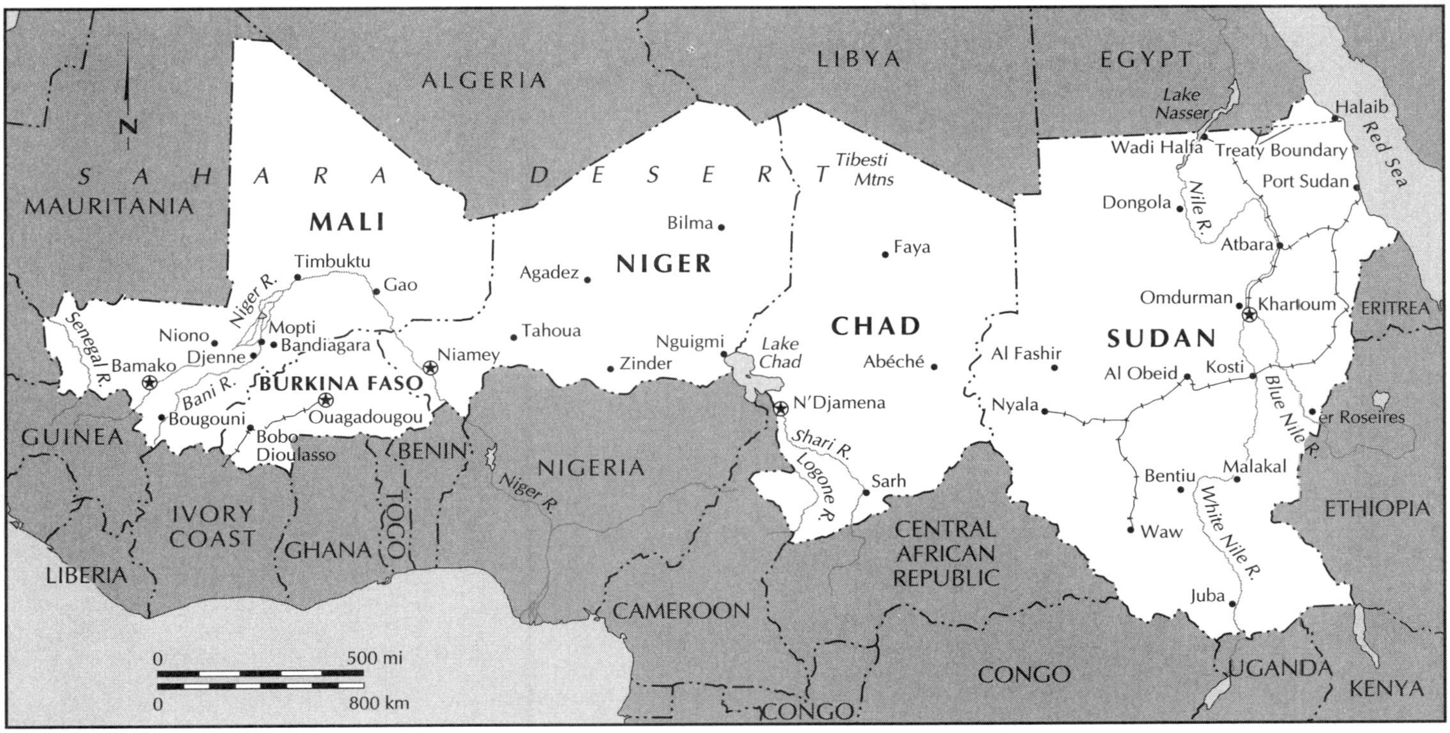

Burkina Faso

Area: 274,540 sq. km. = 106,000 sq. mi. (slightly larger than Colorado).
Population: 11,575,898 (July 1999 est.)
Capital City: Ouagadougou (Pop. 1 million, estimated. Pronounced Wah-gah-*doo*-goo).
Climate: Cooler and drier (November–March); warm and dry (March–May); warm with usually ample rainfall (June–October).
Neighboring Countries: Mali (West and North); Niger (East); Benin (Southeast); Togo, Ghana, Côte d'Ivoire (South).
Official Language: French.
Other Principal Languages: Bissa, Bobo, Fulfulde, Gourmanchéma, Jula, Lobi, Mòoré.
Ethnic groups: Mossi about 24%, Gurunsi, Senufo, Lobi, Bobo, Mande, Fulani.
Principal Religions: Indigenous beliefs 40%, Muslim 50%, Christian (mainly Roman Catholic) 10%.
Chief Commercial Products: cotton, animal products, gold.
GNP per capita: 240 US$
Currency: CFR Franc (no longer tied to the French franc).
Former Colonial Status: French Colony (1896–1932); part of Ivory Coast, Niger and French Soudan (1932–1957); French Overseas Territory (1958–1960).
Independence Date: August 5, 1960.
Chief of State: Col. Blaise Compaoré, President.
National Flag: Horizontal red and green stripes with a yellow five–pointed star in center.

This country of gently rolling hills, north of the hot, steamy equatorial zone, with an average altitude of 800 feet, has a comparatively pleasant climate. The tall grass of the plains and the green forest grow rapidly during the usual wet season from May to November in years of normal rainfall. Almost daily rains are usually short thunderstorms—the rest of the day during these months is warm and sunny.

Toward the end of November, the rains become less frequent and finally almost cease altogether. The grasses of the plains which have risen to heights of six feet turn brown, waiting to be consumed by localized brush fires.

A drier area is found in the North and Northwest, which is a transition zone between the plains and the hot Sahara further north. It is from this great desert that the *harmattan* (the hot wind of the dry season) comes, covering the whole country. The rivers of Burkina Faso, the Black, Red and White Voltas, and the tributaries of the Niger in the East—are not navigable. Travel to and from land–locked Burkina Faso is principally over the railway from Ouagadougou through Bobo–Dioulasso to Abidjan in Côte d'Ivoire.

History: More than 800 years ago, great numbers of conquering horsemen, the Mossi, penetrated a small region in the southeast of Burkina Faso, subduing the passive farmers of the plateau. They established a feudalistic system based on collective leadership.

The Mende and Bobo, related groups, have been in this country for countless centuries. Legend does not indicate the time of origin of the several other groups of Burkina Faso.

Although the Mossi became peaceful farmers through the centuries, they were able to forcefully defeat efforts of the Islamic people of the North to conquer them and convert them to Islam. The Arab Berbers, however, presented a continuing threat. For details of early and colonial history, see Historical Background and *The French in Africa*.

A treaty was signed in 1960 granting what was then Upper Volta independence from France. A new constitution was adopted, taking effect in that year. Upper Volta was governed by a president elected for a five–year term, and a 75–member National Assembly, both elected by universal suffrage. The constitution provided for a separate judiciary. Maurice Yameago's *Volta Democratic Union* captured all the seats of the Assembly and he became the first president. Although quite popular, a combination of corruption and adverse economic conditions, including high unemployment led to his downfall. Col. Sangoulé Lamizana assumed charge; Yameago was tried and imprisoned in 1969, but was released in 1971.

Col. Lamizana was a burly, imposing figure with tribal scars on his cheeks. A devout Muslim, he made a pilgrimage to the city of Mecca. He appeared to be making progress toward restoring civilian rule, but in 1970 a constitution was adopted providing that he serve for a transition period of four years; thereafter the president would be elected.

However, the National Assembly functioned until 1974, when Lamizana had it dissolved; he appointed himself to the additional positions of Prime Minister and Army Chief of Staff, declaring that Upper Volta would be a one–party nation. Upper Voltans voted in late 1977 overwhelmingly to return to civilian rule—and for political parties to be allowed to resume their activities. But by some strange quirk of Upper Voltan politics, a military man was elected to a seven–year term of office: General Lamizana.

During the next two years Upper Volta plunged to economic depths. Corruption was rampant in the government and little effort was made to relieve the suffering of the peasant majority or in overcoming the continuing effects of drought. Opposition parties were squeezed out of existence. But a powerful labor movement remained, and during late 1980, teachers, government workers and employees in private industry caused a series of paralyzing strikes. Lamizana tried to reassure the groups, but made no promises. The military looked on with increasing alarm as the government floundered and the nation seemed headed for civil war. In late 1980 the President was placed under house arrest.

The leader of the bloodless *coup* was Lamizana's former foreign minister, Colonel Saye Zerbo, who was immediately proclaimed President of the Military Committee for Reformation and National Progress—and, of course, chief of state.

The principal goal of the new government was to rout out corruption and to try to set the country back on its economic feet, but it made almost no headway; in late 1982 other officers staged a *coup* which toppled Zerbo's government. A Provisional People's Salvation Council was formed, which accused Zerbo of betraying the people and using his government as an instrument of terror. The new president, Col. Jean–Baptiste Ouedraogo had planned elections for November 1984, but in August 1983 Capt. Thomas Sankara led yet another *coup* and became President of the National Council for the Revolution.

After the coup Sankara formed the *National Council for the Revolution (CNR),* with himself as president. Committees for the Defense of the Revolution (CDRs) were organized to implement the *CNR*'s Marxist-Leninist programs. Sankara himself adopted a romantic self-denial. Virtually his only possessions were his guitar and his used car, a tiny Renault 5, which he chose as the official vehicle for his whole government. By word and deed the charismatic Sankara sought to lead and mobilize, but personal revolutionary idealism alone was insufficient. The CDRs, organized as popular mass organizations, deteriorated into gangs of armed thugs and clashed with several trade unions. Revolutionary People's Courts too often resembled a Robespierrean reign of terror. Fear and resistance grew, and on October 15, 1987, Sankara was assassinated in an action directed by his friend and colleague, Blaise Compaoré. The man who created modern Burkina Faso was unceremoniously buried in a common grave in Ouagadougou. Only later were his remains moved and the grave given a proper headstone. Ten years later followers regularly leave flowers, and Sankara has become an icon for youthful Africans who have dubbed him "Che Sankara." Like the famous Che poster, Sankara's thin, mustachioed features grace stickers that appear on motorcycles, taxis and trucks throughout West Africa.

Compaoré, along with two other members of the *CNR*, Jean-Baptiste Boukary Lengani and Henri Zongo, formed the *Popular Front (FP)* to continue the revolution.; its principal constituent was the leftist *Organization for Popular Democracy/Labor Movement (ODP/MT).*Recognizing the discontent aroused by the more extreme of Sankara's policies, he moderated them and opened the Front to non-Marxist organizations. In September 1989, while Compaoré was returning from an Asian trip, Lengani and Zongo were accused of plotting the overthrow of the *Popular Front*. Arrested, they were summarily executed the same night.

The *Popular Front* drafted a new constitution, that of Burkina Faso's Fourth Republic, in 1990; it was ratified by referendum in 1991. Compaoré resigned from the army to contest presidential elections held in December. Running unopposed, he was elected, but nearly 75% of the eligible electorate abstained from the polls. The following year legislative elections were held and the *ODP/MT* won a majority of the seats. In February 1996, the ruling party merged with several smaller opposition groups to form the *Congress of Democracy and Progress (CDP).*

Relations between government and populace were strained in 1996. A structural adjustment program adopted in 1991 had caused a number of austerity pinches. (The 1994 devaluation of the CFA franc had led to higher prices and diminished buying power.) In July the government agreed to increase civil servants' salaries by three to five percent, but warned the budget would not be able to stand a larger increase. On October 25 members of Burkina Faso's presidential guard were arrested in connection with an alleged coup plot. The arrests followed more than a month of rumors about divisions within the presidential guard, a crack group involved in the three military coups staged since 1982. It had been instrumental in placing Compaoré in power, and knew, shall we say, where the skeletons were buried.

Woman carrying a jar of water on her head WORLD BANK Photo

In early 1997 the *CDP* used its parliamentary majority to amend the constitution, eliminating the provision which limited Burkina Faso's president to no more than 2 terms. The opposition *Party for Democracy and Progress (PDP)* futilely protested the amendment would institute lifelong political power. "Should we speak of a republic, a monarchy or personal power," asked Joseph Ki Zerbo, the party's leader.

The same parliamentary session also changed the deposit required of presidential candidates, from two million CFA francs ($4,000) to five million CFA francs—about $10,000. Small parties need not apply. Suggesting the changes that had taken place in the world as well as in Burkina Faso, parliament also purged the constitution of such Sankara-era terminology as "the people," and "the toiling masses."

Legislative elections held in 1997 resulted in a large *CDP* majority—-101 out of 111 seats. Only 44% of voters managed to respond to the electoral call. It was a severe blow for the opposition which had won twice as many seats in 1992.

The October 1998 presidential elections posed few problems for President Compaoré who was easily returned to office against nominal opposition. Once again the opposition boycotted the elections and the only question was really about how many voters would even bother. President Compaoré needed a big enough turnout to retain his credibility, especially after the dis-

President Blaise Compaoré

mal participation rate seven years previously. Two other candidates entered the lists, but essentially this was a one–horse race. Ram Ouedraogo was Africa's first Green Party candidate, and his environmentalist campaign stressed ideas on sustainable development. The other candidate was a former Burkinabé diplomat, Frederic Guirma. Dubbed "grandfather," the 67-year-old Guirma unabashedly called for a return of Burkina Faso's old name, Upper Volta, and a return of its former red, white and black flag. The opposition charged both candidates were friends of President Compaoré, dragged in to provide a veneer of democratic legitimacy for the election. When the results came in Compaoré won nearly 88% of the vote. According to official figures, 56% of registered voters participated.

Two deaths that shook the nation

President Compaoré's inauguration in December was darkened by the mysterious death of Burkina Faso's most prominent journalist, Norbert Zongo, the managing editor of the weekly *Independent*. Celebrated for his hard–hitting critiques of the regime, Zongo (actually the pen name of Henri Segbo) was known as "the Incorruptible." His charred body was found, along with three others, in the burned out wreckage of an automobile. The exterior of the auto showed no signs of fire damage; the victims had been shot with 12 caliber bullets and given a *coup de grace* with a 357 Magnum. His death rocked the nation, prompting a wave of violent protests, demonstrations, tear gas, arrests, beatings, and deaths which continued through the spring. The president was forced to create an independent national commission of inquiry to examine the more than suspicious death. Places on the commission were reserved for representatives of the international press, human rights organizations, and members of the victims' families. Representatives of the ministries of Security, Defense and Justice joined them. Even before the work of the Commission was completed the details began to leak out.

A French ballistics expert and a pathologist had been brought in to conduct the scientific aspects of the investigation. Early findings from the probe confirmed the widespread belief that Zongo was the victim of a political assassination. Noting "contradictions and incoherence" in the testimony of members of the Presidential Guard, the commission pointed to them as "serious suspects" in the case. One commission member, the secretary–general of Reporters Without Borders, was hustled onto the first plane for Europe after giving an interview to a local radio station in which he referred to members of the Presidential Guard as "hoodlums." The security minister referred to the interview as holding forth ideas which were "inadmissible and dangerous to the public order" and which "incited people to take to the streets."

The commission's report linked Zongo's assassination to his relentless campaign to expose the earlier murder of a chauffeur of President Compaoré's younger brother, François. The evidence indicated that David Ouedraogo, the chauffeur, had been involved with three others in the theft of money from the younger Compaoré's wife. All four had been taken, on the order of François Compaoré, to a security prison and subjected to the most grotesque of tortures, both psychological and physical. They were taken out and forced to dig their own graves, lined up before a firing squad and subjected to the terror of mock execution. Ouedraogo himself reportedly died of the effects of torture, which included being roasted alive. Norbert Zongo's reporting and demand for justice made him a popular hero, and an enemy of the state. His assassination exposed the dark side of the Compaoré regime and generated vociferous demands that "impunity" for killers not be tolerated. Crowds chanted the names of nearly 50 people who died in suspicious circumstances. And striking at the very origins of the regime itself, an "International Committee for Justice for Thomas Sankara" was created.

Burkina Faso has been in a state of permanent crisis since the December 1998 killing of Norbert Zongo. For President Compaoré, it has been two and a half years of living nervously. Intense political, social and labor unrest in Burkina Faso has also proved a major embarrassment troubling the regional and perhaps continental ambitions of the president.

Two weeks after the commission of inquiry's report was issued, the president appointed a College of Sages, wise men to recommend policy and action to deliver the country from political crisis. The sixteen-member council was headed by the Bishop of Bobo-Dioulasso and consisted of three former heads of state, eight religious and traditional leaders and three "resource persons." Acting with dispatch, the group asked for the arrest of all those implicated in the death of David Ouedraogo. The next day, three members of the presidential guard close to President Compaoré were detained in Ouagadougou and charged for murder of François Compaoré's driver.

A market scene at Po WORLD BANK Photo

In August 2000, a military tribunal met to hear the case against five members of the *Régiment de la sécurité présidentielle* (Presidential Guard) charged with David Ouedraogo's murder. Three, including the Guard's former head, Marcel Kafando, were quickly found guilty and sentenced to long jail terms. In addition, the three were ordered to pay a staggering fine of 200 million CFA in damages to the Ouedraogo family. That works out to be nearly $270,000, and where three members of Presidential Guard would get such a sum was uncertain. Outside the courtroom, more than three thousand people gathered to denounce the trial as a miscarriage of justice, given the absence of the principal suspect, Francois Compaoré.

The Zongo murder has resulted in continuing social unrest. Demonstrations and strikes have taken place throughout the country on a nearly permanent basis. The protests are led by a loose group of activists known as the Collective Against Impunity which continues to agitate for a full investigation of the Zongo murder.

In early February 2001 the government acted to quell continuing unrest over the Zongo affair. Burkina Faso's attorney general announced the indictment of Marcel Kafando, the former head of the Presidential Guard, for murder and arson in journalist's death. Thirty-five francophone African newspapers collectively reacted by publishing an open letter demanding fuller action: "now that you hold the arm which killed, search a little higher and you will find the head."

Kafando's indictment was seen by many as a step towards resolving the political and judicial crises triggered by Zongo's assassination. Apparently hoping the populace was tired of protest and agitation and desirous of moving on, the government orchestrated a "national day of forgiveness" for late March. The event had been recommended by the College of Sages to assuage years of public anger. By any standard of evaluation, it was a remarkable event.

Standing before a crowd of 30,000 Burkinabé in a local stadium, President Compaoré delivered an unprecedented apology for crimes against the populace. "I ask for pardon," he said, "and express deep regret for tortures, crimes, injustices, bullying and other wrongs."

President Compaoré had much to apologize for, at home and abroad. The majority of his West African colleagues distrust the man intensely and see him as the patron of regional subversion. UN experts' panels have fingered him as a key figure in the lethal exchange of arms for diamonds that fuels destructive conflict in West Africa and Angola. The most notorious of his foreign adventures were the support of Charles Taylor in Liberia and Foday Sankoh's insurgency in Sierra Leone.

Culture: Beautiful handcrafted articles adorn the homes of Burkina Faso. The arts of spinning, dying and weaving and how to melt gold dust to create inimitable jewelry were learned centuries ago. Since 1969 Burkina Faso has taken the art of film to heart with gusto and enthusiasm. Indeed, it's probably the only country that's given film-makers their own public monument. Ouagadoudou, Burkina's capital and largest city, is the site of the important biennial Pan–African film festival known as Fespaco. The 17th festival was held in 2001 and featured some 108 films. Films by francophone directors predominated, but this year several came from countries such as Ghana, Zimbabwe, Ethiopia, Sudan and Nigeria.

Economy: When Compaoré and friends eliminated Thomas Sankara, they promised a "rectification" of his "deviancies." In effect, that has come to mean a slow liberalization of a socialist economy. A structural adjustment program launched in 1991 tries to eliminate cumbersome regulations, price controls and widespread government involvement in productive sectors, all of which were a brake on private investment. Government spending, especially on salaries and loss-making state enterprises, has been cut back. Some state companies have been privatized and the economy is more open to market forces. It remains, however, dependent on agricultural production; over 80% of the population is engaged in subsistence agriculture and at the mercy of often unfavorable weather conditions.

Cotton remains the most important money earner, while a number of international companies have begun to boost the country's gold production. Gold is now the country's second largest source of export revenue after cotton, though subject

to the fluctuations of the world market. Those hazards were seen in August 1999 when the government closed the Poura gold mine amid falling gold prices that made production increasingly uneconomical. Over 300 workers lost their jobs. A number of mining projects are still in the planning stages and could become operating mines within the next five years.

Burkina Faso's migrant workers, who annually fan out across West Africa in search of employment, traditionally send back remittances that contribute about 5% to GDP. Some 3 million Burkinabé live in neighboring Côte d'Ivoire, but in the past year, several thousand fell victim to rising anti-foreigner sentiment there. Ivoirian farmers in the southwest accused the Burkinabé farm workers of stealing their land in late 1999. Using rifles, machetes and clubs, they routed the laborers from their homes and plantations, where they had worked for years. Countless Burkinabé homes were destroyed and Ouagadougou estimated that some 12,000 Burkinabé had fled the country.

Future: Remarkable as it was, President Compaoré's apology will not reduce the claims of those who say he and his brother have been given immunity in the Zongo and Ouedraogo murders. Revelations of presidential profiteering from the sale of arms for diamonds can only erode support within the army and legitimacy within the general population.

The Republic of Chad

On the Chadian desert Courtesy: Embassy of Chad

Area: 1,284,640 sq. km. = 496,000 sq. mi. (the size of Texas, New Mexico and Arizona).
Population: 7,557,436 (July 1999 est.)
Capital City: N'Djamena (pop. 550,000. 1996 est.)
Climate: Dry desert in the North varies from 10° to 122°F.; the central and southern areas are warm with increasing rainfall and humidity in the South, where there is a six–month dry season; Chad has been gripped by drought and the advancing Sahara Desert.
Neighboring Countries: Cameroon (Southwest); Niger and Nigeria (West); Libya (North); The Sudan (East); Central African Republic (Southeast and South).
Official Languages: French and Arabic.
Other Principal Languages: Over 100, including Gulay, Kanuri, Karanda, Maba, Marba, Marfa, Masana, Mundang, Musey, Ngambay, Sango (a Creole trade language), and Sar.
Ethnic groups: Muslims: (Arabs, Toubou, Hadjerai, Fulbe, Kotoko, Kanembou, Baguirmi, Boulala, Zaghawa, and Maba). Non-Muslims: (Sara, Ngambaye, Mbaye, Goulaye, Moundang, Moussei, Massa). Nonindigenous: 150,000 (of whom an estimated 1,000 are French).
Principal Religions: Muslim 50%, Christian 25%, indigenous beliefs (mostly animism) 25%.
Chief Commercial Products: Cotton, cattle, and textiles.
GNP per capita: 230 US$
Currency: CFA franc (no longer tied to the French franc).
Former Colonial Status: French Colony (1910–1960).
Independence Date: August 11, 1960.
Chief of State: Idriss Déby, President.
National Flag: Three vertical stripes of blue, gold and red.

Landlocked Chad, more than 1,500 miles from any seaport, lies almost in the center of Africa and is one of the true transitional nations between the desert to the north and the fertile southern area of the continent. For centuries it has been the crossroads of traders going back and forth between the Sahara–Mediterranean Sea region and the tropical areas of West Africa.

Although Chad resembles a shallow basin in which Lake Chad, a former inland sea, occupies the "drain" position to the west, topographically it has three distinct regions. The Chadian Sahara in the North is a land of dry desert sand dunes gently rising to a height of 12,000 feet above sea level in the Tibesti Mountains. Only 1.2% of the population of Chad inhabits this area, mostly tribal nomads. The endless expanse of desert, scorching by day, sinks to below freezing levels at night.

The central portion is a semi–arid land of great treeless plains; this section traditionally has received just enough rainfall to support cattle raising, but is now in the throes of a devastating drought. The green southern area, with more ample rainfall, supports 45% of the country's population, who engage in cotton cultivation.

Lake Chad, fed by the Shari and Logone Rivers in the southwest corner of the nation, has been called a "crowned prairie" by some because of its tangles of grass and reeds that normally cover the surface and its surrounding marshlands. The area of this immense lake has been diminished by the drought which has gripped central Africa.

History: Not very much is known of the early history of the Chad area. Various Semitic tribes and kingdoms were successively established during the western Dark Ages, including the powerful Oueddai Empire. This was a hunting ground for the early slave traders who transported their human cargo to Egypt and the East. For details of early and colonial history, see Historical Background and *The French in Africa*.

At the time of independence, the constitution established a unicameral legislature composed of 75 delegates elected by direct, universal suffrage. There were from the beginning problems of mutual trust and cooperation between the essentially Arabic people of the North and the Sudanic–Bantu people of the South. The legislature was immediately dominated by the *Chadian Progressive Party* of President Tombalbaye, a southerner. There was a period of strife in 1963 which resulted in elimination of most opposition parties. Elections in 1969 further strengthened the position of the party and the president, who was reelected to a seven–year term.

Tombalbaye accused the French of trying to unseat him in July 1973, fuming about the presence of French troops in Chad which he had hitherto welcomed. The Chadian leader of a "dump Tombalbaye" movement was shot dead in Paris in 1973; Tombalbaye denied any involvement in the affair. The following day the President announced several changes. The party was renamed *National Movement for Cultural and Social Revolution,* the use of Christian forenames was abolished as was the use of French names for streets and places except for Avenue Charles de Gaulle in Fort Lamy (renamed N'Djamena).

Increasing dissatisfaction arising out of drought conditions, coupled with the jailing of a number of the military in 1973 led to changes in Chad in 1975. President Tombalbaye was killed and the army installed General Félix Malloum, its leader, who had been under house arrest since 1973. The country has been in turmoil ever since.

In 1976, the former leader of the northern–based rebellion of the Toubou tribesmen, Hissene Habré (pronounced Ah-*bray*), split with the group over Libya's claim to a large, uranium–rich portion of northern Chad. He was succeeded by the chief of this strict Islamic group, Goukouni Oueddei (Weh–*day*). Habré eventually joined forces with the central government, and in August 1978 General Malloum was proclaimed President and Habré became Prime Minister. The latter was given the task of seeking national unity after years of fighting between the Muslim north and non–Islamic south; sporadic fighting had occurred, occasionally accelerating into furious combat.

Rebellion and civil war broke out in N'Djamena in early 1979 and there was almost continuous fighting for five weeks. Tribal massacres occurred in the southern and central parts of Chad, with from five to eight thousand Muslims killed—in retaliation for similar human slaughter of non–Muslims in the central and northern areas.

Rumors flew that all non–Muslims would be forced to convert to Islam. During this period Habré and Oueddei somewhat reconciled their differences. In early 1979, both Malloum and Habré resigned their offices and handed over governmental authority to a provisional state council in an effort to finally end the bloodshed. Malloum was promptly replaced by Oueddei as *President* of the State Council.

Even though eleven rival groups signed an agreement in Lagos, Nigeria to form yet *another* provisional government, Oueddei was once again named president. The agreement called for an immediate ceasefire. But this was quickly forgotten. The situation eventually evolved into one where both Oueddei and Habré had their own private armies. Fighting ebbed and flowed in N'Djamena and throughout the country.

All French troops were asked to leave the country in May 1980; most Europeans went with them and the U.S. Embassy was closed. The streets of N'Djamena became a no–man's land. When Libya offered military help to Oueddei's beleagured forces in December, the President accepted, believing that his troops were no match for those of Habré's in the see–saw desert war. Habré's rebels, in turn, could not compete with well– equipped Libyans and faded into eastern Chad to await a better opportunity to seize power.

Oueddei at first welcomed the Libyans—even though that northern neighbor had in 1976 annexed a 60–mile–wide strip of Chad, renaming it "southern Libya." But when in January 1981 Libya announced a *merger* with Chad, the President knew things were out of control. Great pressure on Libya to withdraw was brought by other African governments and in late 1981, Oueddei asked them to leave. Seven thousand troops left for Libya and Habré saw his chance. Within a few days his forces had seized a large part of the country and he was on his way to an easy victory over Oueddei's 11–faction coalition, which actually had never coalesced. An OAU peace–keeping force moved quickly into Chad and easily checked the rebel advance, driving Habré back to eastern Chad.

Life in N'Djamena temporarily returned to a semblance of order; the U.S. Embassy reopened in early 1982. But in mid–1982 Habré's forces swept out of eastern Chad and, amid bitter fighting, seized N'Djamena. The OAU troops remained neutral, Oueddei escaped to Cameroon and Hissene Habré declared himself chief of state. The OAU troops withdrew by the end of June.

The Libyans returned to the assistance of Oueddei and, in response, French and Zaïrean troops came to the aid of Habré. Fighting was sporadic after early 1984. Diplomatic efforts all but totally failed because of the factionalism which gripped Chad. Southern Chadian rebels suspected of sympathizing with Oueddei were badly mistreated until they accepted an amnesty offered by Habré in early 1986.

When Libyan forces reentered Chad in substantial numbers, building an airfield at Ouadi (Wadi) Doum in the northern desert, the French returned, with aircraft. The airfield was hit, and N'Djamena was bombed by a Libyan plane the next day, February 17th. Then came the surprise: Oueddei announced his resignation as head of the rebels. Libya placed him under arrest in Tripoli, where he was wounded in violence during a clashbetween his bodyguard and Libyan soldiers. He declared his solidarity with Habré.

This left Libya's Qadhafi, the sponsor of a revolution, without a leader. Most of the Chadian rebels had simply deserted the cause. With French assistance, Chadian forces struck the Libyan force in northern Chad, devastating it. Libyans left about $1 billion in Soviet armaments, including tactical weapons. In November 1988 Habré regained control of N'Djaména, but he was unable to control divisive factionalism. In April 1989, Idriss Déby, one of Habré's leading generals, defected and fled to Sudan. From there Déby launched a series of attacks on the eastern region of Chad, fully invading the country in November 1990. On December 2, his troops entered war-exhausted N'Djaména without battle, President Habré and the forces loyal to him having fled. After three months of provisional government, a national charter was approved by the *Patriotic Salvation Movement (MPS)* in February 1991, with Déby as President. Since then President Déby has sought to maintain a fragile, always intermittent, peace. The political tools of amnesty, integration into the national armed forces and recognition as political parties have brought a number of armed opposition groups into the government fold, but as soon as one group reconciles with the government, a discontented faction hives off or another group springs up.

It is easy to analyze the absence of Chadian unity in terms of a north/south division. Northerners are Arabized pastoralists with a long warrior tradition. Southerners are sedentary and Christianized, long subject historically to slaving raids by their northern neighbors. In reality, the struggles have as much to do with a vision of power and the nature of the state. Once lodged in N'Djaména, the group in power imposes a centralized view of power and the state, snuffing out resistance and denying individuality. In a situation where there are over 200 different ethnic groups to be satisfied, a more reasonable course might involve greater decentralization and localized autonomy, but the central authority has usually rejected federalism, seeing it as a loss of power and control over the meager resources available.

In April 1993, opposition political and military groups attended a landmark National Conference which produced a time table for national elections. The country's first free, multiparty presidential elections were held in June 1996. Idriss Déby won nearly 70% of the vote in a run-off election in July, vigorously protested by the 14 other candidates who had run against him. (A government court had thrown out nearly 250,000 first round—mainly anti-Déby—ballots it declared fraudulent.) In the 1997 legislative polling, Déby's party fell short of an outright majority, winning only 55 of 125 seats. His southern presidential rival, General Wadal Abdelkader Kamougue, and his *Union for Renewal and Democracy (URD)* won 31. Bargaining among parties ultimately brought about a majority coalition for the government. Kamougue rallied to the government and was elected speaker of the National Assembly. Déby appointed a southerner, Nassour Guelengdoussia Ouaido , Prime Minister.

Chad's relative stability was interrupted in late 1997 by an upsurge of factional resistance. This occurred mainly in the south, where the development of a major oil field raises, once again, the question of who controls resources and how they will be used. To highlight demands for greater participation in making those decisions, groups have resorted to kidnapping Europeans.

No sooner had President Déby resolved things with Southerners, then one noted an upsurge of kidnappings in the North. By October 1998, it was apparent that there was another rebel movement to deal with here. Led by a former defense minister, Youssouf Togoïmi, the *Mouvement pour la démocratie et la justice au Tchad* (*MDJT*) was centered in the sparsely populated Tibesti region, a mountainous, semi-desert area ideal for guerrilla warfare. It is also one of the most heavily mined areas in the world, with thousands of anti-tank and anti-personnel mines left over from the days of Chad's war with Libya. The rebels seem to rely on support from local Toubou nomads, traditionally warriors and do not appear to be supported by neighboring Niger or Libya.

The war continues, though it often appears to be a war of dueling press releases with each side claiming victory and listing a body count. The *MDJT* has also linked up with two other armed rebel groups to form the *Political Committee for*

Action and Liaison. Its fundamental purpose seemed to be additional opposition to the government's Doba oil field project. Also included was the *Movement for Democracy and Development* (*MDD*), one of the oldest armed opposition groups engaged in fighting the government of President Idriss Déby and the *Revolutionary Democratic Council* (*CDR*).

Chad's political culture is highly fragmented. Its varied sectional and ethnic interests create a constantly changing set of oppositional organizations and alliances. The *Concertation des Partis Politiques (CPP)*, for example, is an umbrella organization representing most of the 50-odd opposition parties. *The Coordination of Opposition Armed Movements and Political Parties* (*CMAP*) involves 13 opposition groups, but is rejected by the *MDJT*, certainly the most active armed opposition at this time.

France, which stations troops at two sites in Chad, has seemed to follow a hands-off policy. Although it had favored President Déby's rise to power in 1990, tensions had built up between the two. French advisors were involved in training and supervising the Zakawa Guard as a personal security force for the president, but when France refused to help it stamp out unrest in the South, Déby reportedly sent 20 French security officials packing. The French armed forces Chief of Staff even traveled to N'Djamena to soothe ruffled feathers.

Franco-Chadian relations have been tense ever since the French oil giant, Elf-Aquitaine, withdrew from the Doba Oil field project. More than 10,000 Chadians took to the streets of N'Djamena to protest in a two-hour demonstration. The government declared the French ambassador *persona non grata* and forced his departure. Rumors persist that the ambassador had refused the use of French planes in the fight against *MDJT* forces in the north.

Chad has also protested a map of the country published by the French embassy. It shows the border between Chad and Libya—the northern desert strip of Aouzou claimed by both countries—drawn with a dotted line, indicating, for Chadians, France's neutrality in the touchy territorial dispute.

President Déby has oriented his foreign policy towards breaking Chad's natural land-locked isolation. He was the first to fly into Tripoli after the OAU rejected further implementation of the UN air embargo and spoke highly of how Libya could help Chad gain access to Mediterranean markets. Libya also provided gasoline to avert a fuel crisis in Chad and funded the participation of a small force of Chadian soldiers fighting in support of Laurent Kabila.

Chad was a founding member of Col. Qadhafi's latest regional grouping, the Community of Sahel-Saharan States (COMESSA) and hosted its second summit meeting. During the sessions, Col. Qadhafi was given a mandate to act as mediator between the Chad government and the rebels of *the Movement for Democracy and Justice in Chad*. By Spring 2001, Col. Qadhafi had brought President Déby and Youssouf Togoïmi together for face-to-face talks at least three times, but these remain inconclusive. Presidential elections took place May 2001.

Economy: Chad is one of the poorest countries in the world. It has always relied on agriculture as the basis of its economy. More than 80% of the population is engaged in farming, and most of that is subsistence. Cotton and livestock have traditionally been the country's principal moneymakers, but government budgets are highly dependent on foreign assistance. Chad's development is irregular and inconsistent, characterized by alternations of growth and decline brought on by drought, civil war and continuing political instability. Together they have crippled the economy.

Cotton is the main export crop and Chad's most lucrative source of income. It traditionally accounts for nearly 50% of export revenues. Cotton fields cover 10 per cent of Chad's cultivated land. Production stood at 134,000 tons in 1995, and increased to 262,000 tons in the 97/98 season. The Asian economic crisis affected sales and world cotton prices have dropped catastrophically. The 98/99 production figures showed a marked drop off: Only 161,000 tons were harvested.

Exports of livestock are the second largest source of income for the country. There are some 12 million head of livestock in Chad, including five million cattle, six million sheep and goats, and one million camels. Livestock generated about $35 million in officially declared revenues. Smugglers, it is estimated, deprive the Chadian economy of close to two thirds of its potential livestock taxes. Putting an end to smuggling and tax evasion in this industry has become a major priority for the government.

The most important element in Chad's plans for future improvement is the Doba oil field in the south. Reserves are estimated at 900 million barrels, and peak production is projected to be around 225,000 to 250,000 barrels per day. Crude oil from some 315 wells would be transported through a 650-mile pipeline to an offshore marine terminal near Kribi, Cameroon. Total investments in the project were estimated to be near $3.5 billion.

Despite stiff opposition from environmentalists, the project received backing from the World Bank, and a consortium of major oil companies has been put in place. ExxonMobil, Petronas (the Malaysian National Oil Company) and Chevron will undertake construction of the project.

President Idriss Déby

An aggressive construction schedule has been drawn up, involving rapid mobilization and commencement of critical infrastructure work by the end of 2001. The project is expected to create between 3,000 and 4,000 jobs, while roads will have to be resurfaced and bridges built.

Production is expected to begin in three or four years, and depending on the world price for oil, Chad could earn between $2.5 billion and $8.5 billion from royalties and taxes over 25 years. That translates into $80-100 million a year.

Fears persist that oil income will be siphoned off by corruption or diverted away from poverty alleviation projects. Desperately poor, more than half of Chad's population live on less than 50 cents a day. Responding to these concerns, Chad passed a law in January 1999 creating an oversight body to monitor the management of oil revenues.

The law mandates that 70% of the oil earnings be dedicated to health, education, agricultural and infrastructure projects, and another 10% deposited directly in an offshore account as savings for future generations. The World Bank has also established its own watchdog panel to determine whether the government sticks to those commitments.

Whole kennels of watchdogs will be needed. In May 2000, the government spent $4 million of a $25 million "bonus" paid by the oil companies on the purchase of arms.

The Future: Déby has proved to be the most politically skilled of Chad's military rulers. He will need all those skills to resolve the battles surrounding Doba production and construction of the pipeline.

The Republic of Mali

The Great Mosque of Niomo, Niomo, Mali

Area: 1,204,350 sq. km. = 545,190 sq. mi. (more than four times the size of Nevada).
Population: 10,429,124 (July 1999 est.)
Capital City: Bamako (Pop. 400,000, estimated).
Climate: Hot and dry in the northern two thirds of the country; increasing rainfall and more temperate in the southern third. Two short rainy seasons have watered the South, but high temperatures cause rapid evaporation.
Neighboring Countries: Senegal (Southwest); Mauritania (North, Northwest); Algeria (Northeast); Niger (East, Southeast); Burkina Faso, Côte d'Ivoire, Guinea (South).
Official Language: French.
Other Principal Languages: Bambara (spoken by 80% of the population). Bomu, Boso, Dogon, Fulfulde, Kassonke, Malinke, Senoufo, Songai, Soninke, Tamajeq, Tamasheq.
Ethnic groups: Mande 50% (Bambara, Malinke, Sarakole), Peul 17%, Voltaic 12%, Songhai 6%, Tuareg and Moor 10%, other 5%.
Principal Religions: Muslim 90%, indigenous beliefs 9%, Christian 1%.
Chief Commercial Products: Cotton 50%, gold, and livestock.
GNP per capita: 250 US$
Currency: CFA franc. (no longer tied to the French franc).
Former Colonial Status: Part of French West Africa (1890–1960).
Independence Date: September 22, 1960.
Chief of State: Alpha Oumar Konaré, President (elected April 1992).
National Flag: Three vertical stripes of green, yellow and red.

Northern Mali is a flat, dry stretch of land which is part of the Sahara Desert. This empty land, inhabited by descendants of the Berber tribes, who live a nomadic, pastoral life, has virtually no rain. The otherwise flat terrain is broken occasionally by rocky hills. The country becomes more hospitable to the south of fabled Timbuktu, which lies along an ancient caravan route of Arab merchants. The Niger River, lifeblood of Mali, flows in an irregular pattern through lakes from Timbuktu to Bamako, the capital city.

This is the farmland of Mali. In a manner similar to the Nile River, the Niger overflows its banks each year, flooding the surrounding crop lands, rendering them fertile. Most of the people of the country are gathered in this section surrounding the river, which is navigable from mid–June to mid–December. The river abounds in many varieties of fish.

The country becomes slightly more temperate south of the Niger, receiving greater

rainfall in average years. This section is part of the so–called Guinea Savanna, a brush and low tree belt stretching from the Atlantic coast 3,000 miles inland to the east. It is principally in this region that the wild life of Mali is abundant, including giraffes, elephants and other species.

History: The known history of the Republic of Mali dates back to the 11th century when a powerful Islamic king succeeded in establishing his authority over the area about the same time William the Conqueror invaded Saxon England. For details of early and colonial history, see Historical Background and *The French in Africa.*

Known as French Soudan, Mali became part of the *French Community* in 1958, with almost complete internal autonomy. With French permission, Soudan and Senegal joined in 1959 to form the Mali Federation, but this was dissolved in 1960 when Senegal withdrew. After achieving independence in 1960, the government headed by Modibo Keita withdrew from the *French Community* which had evolved into a post–independence economic union of former French colonies in association with France.

Keita, announcing that Mali was a socialist nation, sought assistance from the Soviet Union and later from communist China. Russian aircraft and weapons were received, and the Chinese sent technical assistance and limited financial aid. The result was a gradual decline in the limited economy of Mali during the ensuing years which was obscured by government propaganda and continuing small amounts of communist–bloc assistance. The government, ruled by the *Soudanese Union Party,* which also controlled the press, labor unions and state youth organizations, gradually splintered into two groups. One favored a total commitment to the economic power of the Soviets and Chinese, whereas the other saw advantages in moving toward economic cooperation with the former French colonies and with France itself.

By 1967 the economy was totally disorganized and the government bankrupt. It was clear the socialist model had failed. The pro-French faction prevailed and in 1967 it was decided to rejoin the Franc Zone and modify some economic excesses. This had the effect of halving the income of the small segment of Malians who were engaged in the wage economy. Unrest resulted, and Keita dissolved the Political Bureau of the state party because "it ceased to enjoy the confidence of the people."

In this unstable situation a group of young army officers seized control in a move unopposed even by the president's personal guard. Keita was shipped off to prison in distant desolate Kidal deep in the Sahara, and a *Military Committee for National Liberation (CMLN)* was established. Lt. Moussa Traoré became its president and dominant figure. The new military leaders renounced socialism and attempted economic reform, but were confronted with debilitating internal political struggles and a disastrous Sahelian drought. Ultimately corrupt and repressive, the Traoré regime sustained itself in power for years and had no interest in returning Mali to civilian rule. A new constitution created a single-party state in 1974, and in 1976 Traoré created a new party, the *Democratic Union of the Malian People (UDPM).* He led the party in what were basically sham elections in 1979, winning 99% of the vote. Challenges to his power, by students or from within the military, were brutally suppressed.

Desperate to improve the economy, the government approved plans for economic liberalization and signed an agreement with the IMF. By 1990, the austerity demanded of such plans had begun to pinch all but the ruling clique. Collapse of the Soviet Union encouraged demands for an end to one-party rule and the implementation of multiparty democracy, something Traoré was unwilling to concede. In early 1991, student-led anti-government rioting broke out. It gained the support of government workers and others and resulted in four days of bloody street rioting; an estimated 200 people were killed by government forces. On March 26 a military coup d'état overthrew the president, suspended the constitution and set in motion the process by which Mali would be returned to civilian rule.

The new *National Reconciliation Council* was headed by Lt. Col. Amadou Toumani Touré who promised democratic reforms, lived simply and kept his word, becoming the most popular military figure in Africa after Thomas Sankara. He governed for 14 months during which he established the processes for multiparty democracy and then stepped down. From January to April 1992 Malians enthusiastically participated in presidential, legislative and local elections. Twenty-one political parties participated, with eleven of them winning seats in parliament. Alpha Oumar Konaré, an archeologist, defeated 9 other candidates for the presidency, and his *Association for Democracy in Mali (ADEMA)* secured a parliamentary majority.

During his first five year term Konaré won plaudits for his devolution of more governing powers to local authorities, and when Secretary of State Warren Christopher visited Mali in fall 1996, he high-

Sheep sale in rural Mali

lighted the significant progress Mali had made under Konaré. Political expression flourished: some 40 independent newspapers and journals, in French, Arabic and local languages appeared, often criticizing the government. Fifteen radio stations, a more important source of news in a largely illiterate population, blossomed in Bamako alone; 40 others broadcast elsewhere in the country. Freedom of expression is everywhere apparent.

In 1995 he brought an end to the long-term Tuareg rebellion which had ravaged the north. There, Tuareg nomads, pastoralists whose flocks had been decimated, whose water holes had dried up, and whose people were on the brink of starvation, had been driven to revolt by a callous and corrupt regime. They took up arms against the military dictatorship of Moussa Traoré in 1990, after thousands of tons of food destined for starving nomads had been stolen by the army. When the army proved ineffective in limiting Tuareg raids on farmers along the Niger river, the farmers themselves organized a militia, which they called Ghanda Koy—Masters of the Land—to strike back at nomads. Both groups rallied to Konaré's peace and reconciliation program in 1995. The armies were disarmed, some 9,000 fighters were paid $210 and efforts were made to integrate some of them into the army—always a difficult task given the preference of Tuaregs to speak Arabic rather than French. In March 1996, President Konaré symbolically set fire to several thousand weapons to seal the peace.

A committed democrat and a man of the most humane instincts—he has commuted death sentences meted out to Moussa Traoré and several of his cronies to life imprisonment and closed the terrifying prison at Kidal—President Konaré had no trouble in his search for a second five-year term in 1997. Unfortunately, the 1997 presidential and legislative elections proved a disaster. Poorly administered and producing such dubious results that a court had to throw them out, they had to be repeated. The opposition—and there are some 62 parties in Mali, many organized around a single personality—screamed foul and took to the streets. Security forces had to use tear gas to control mobs and one policeman was lynched by a Bamako crowd. Ten opposition leaders were charged with inciting a riot leading to violence. The second round of elections were boycotted by the opposition, and. given the circumstances, thousands stayed away from the polls fearful for their personal safety. Konaré and *ADEMA* won handily, but their mandate was weakened by events.

The consequences of this fiasco produced a permanent political tension in Mali ever since. Municipal elections had to be postponed again and again. As a way out of this impasse, President Konaré proposed a National Political Forum that

President Alpha Oumar Konaré

would examine Mali's governing legislation. The suggestion, at once simple and radical, found support. For once, most politicians and the civil society agreed to take part in a common endeavor. Regional forums met in December 1998 and discussed constitutional revisions, the organization of future elections, party financing and the power of the Independent National Electoral Commission (CENI).

Once these regional consultations were concluded, official delegates met in Bamako in January 1999 to draw up conclusions and recommendations. The final document, 200 pages in length, was called *A Summary of the National Political Forum.* Included, at the suggestion of Konaré himself, was a constitutional provision that explicitly limits a president to no more than two terms. The state agreed to find the necessary funding for any political party playing a positive role in the civic education of the population, and it was recommended that journalists no longer be imprisoned for offending press laws.

Municipal elections were finally held in May and June 1999. Some 190 municipalities went to the polls to elect 2,840 members of municipal councils. *ADEMA* won about 60% of the seats, while the former government party, *US-RDA*, won less than 10% of the vote. Two additional parties, the *National Renaissance Party* and the *Party for Democracy and Progress* registered victories on a smaller scale. The elections were part of the government's general policy of decentralizing power to local communities.

Mali's hyperactive political climate has been warming considerably in anticipation of presidential elections in 2002. *ADEMA*, Mali's governing party, has been convulsed by internal struggles organized around personalities and party identity. Ibrahim Boubakar Keïta, the party president and prime minister, had been actively cultivating the notion that he was the natural successor to President Konaré, but in February 2000, Konaré dismissed him from the premiership. Next, a group of young technocrats and reformers around the president effected a take-over of the party's executive committee, ousting several of Keïta's supporters.

The party remains deeply divided between reformers and old guard backers of Keita, a man unlikely to shy away from a run at the presidency. Support committees for Amadou Toumani Toure, the former military ruler who brought about the peaceful transition to democracy in Mali, have sprung up across the country and seem to have the quiet backing of President Konaré.

During the past year President Konaré has served as chairman of the West African Economic Community, better known by its acronym, ECOWAS. It has been a particularly demanding year with crises

Market Scene in Bamako

in Sierra Leone, Liberia, Guinea-Bissau and the Ivory Coast calling for the application of his diplomatic skills.

In addition to a presidential election, Mali will also host the finals of the 23rd African Nations Cup in 2002.

Culture: Much of Lassiné Minta's lifetime career as a master stonemason has been devoted to the transformation of a small local mosque into a monument of Islam—the Great Mosque in Niomo. Commissioned by a Committee of Elders, and assisted by his sons with the support of the entire community, the structure is elegantly beautiful. He received the 1983 Aga Khan Award for Architecture at a ceremony in Turkey that year.

Mali's musical traditions are among the most distinguished in West Africa. Traditionally the preserve of craft specialists called *griots,* music has breached the boundaries of caste in the modern era. One of Mali's greatest musical stars is Salif Keita. Born in 1949, Salif was an albino in a culture where albinos are believed cursed. Ostracized by his father, Keita and his mother were only allowed to return to his village when the local Imam predicted great things for him. Limited by sensitive skin and poor eyesight, Keita was unable to become a teacher and when he decided to become a professional musician he was practically disowned. He made his way through the music scene in Bamako and became a central figure in the synthesis of traditional Malian music with other styles from near and far. Today he is one of the luminaries of World Music, capable of touching audiences throughout the world.

Mali's, and indeed Africa's, most distinguished scientist is the astrophysicist Cheikh Modibo Diarra. Dr. Diarra works for NASA and was the mastermind of the Pathfinder mission to Mars. He joined the Caltech/NASA Propulsion Laboratory in 1988 and was earlier involved in the Magellan mission to Venus, the Ulysses mission around the sun and a mission to Jupiter. In 1998 he was appointed as the UNESCO Goodwill Ambassador to Africa—the first African and the first scientist to hold that post. His principal assignment in that role is the promotion of science and mathematics in Africa.

Excision—the removal of the female clitoris—is currently practiced by all of Mali's ethnic groups, with the exception of some Tamashek, Songhay and Dogon groups. A national Demographic and Health Survey conducted in 1996 indicated that 94% of all Malian women had been excised. The same survey concluded that overall, 75% of Malian women were in favor of continuing the practice. Urban women were less supportive than rural, and the more educated the women, the less likely they were to support the practice.

The Bamako-based Association for the Progress and Defense of Women's Rights, led by Fatoumata Sire, leads the battle against female genital mutilation in Mali. Educational plays and musical performances that focus on female health issues have been taken to villages and have reported some success in convincing villager elders to end the practice. The association also works to retrain women who traditionally performed the circumcision so that they might have an alternative source of income.

Economy: As with other Sahel states, Mali's economy is agriculture based and subject to meteorological caprice. Despite its arid climate, Mali's cotton industry has flourished and it now ranks behind Egypt as Africa's second producer. Cotton accounts for half of Malian exports and has traditionally earned the country around $30 million annually. During the 1999-2000 seasons, 459,000 tons were produced, but low prices on the international market discouraged farmers. Production for the 2000-2001 season is estimated to be only 230,000 tons.

Mali's biggest boom may be in minerals, especially gold. The Sadiola Hill mine, near Kayes on Mali's western border, has brought Mali to the top ranks of West African gold producers. Run by Canadian and South African mining interests, Sadiola is one of the largest industrial projects ever undertaken in Mali. During construction the work force numbered some 2,400 and when fully operational, the mine will employ more than 600 people for at least 12 years. The mine, which poured its first ingot in January 1997, has reserves of 140 tons. Annual gold production is projected to be 10 tons a year over 13 years.

The opening of Morila Gold Mines in February 2001 in south-western Mali has consolidated the country's place as the third largest gold producer in Africa after South Africa and Ghana. Morila will increase the country's annual total gold production to 50 tons.

The Future: President Konaré seems to have brought about a solution to Mali's seemingly permanent crisis. Recognizing the need for term limits, he will leave office in the year 2002. His most likely successor is the enormously popular Amadou Toumani Touré.

Anti-excision Poster by Ruth Evans

The Republic of Niger (pronounced Nee–*zhair*)

Children at a primitive well Photo by Ken Brown

Area: 1,266,510 sq. km = 489,000 sq. mi. (three times the size of California).
Population: 9,962,242 (July 1999 est.)
Capital City: Niamey (Pop. 508,000, estimated).
Climate: Hot and dry desert in the North; semi–arid and warm in the South with a wet season from June to September producing 9 to 30 inches of rainfall in normal years.
Neighboring Countries: Burkina Faso (Southwest); Mali (West); Algeria (Northwest); Libya (North); Chad (East); Nigeria and Benin (South).
Official Language: French.
Other Principal Languages: Arabic, Fulfulde, Hausa, Kanuri, Songai, Tamajeq, and Zarma.
Ethnic groups: Hausa 56%, Djerma 22%, Fula 8.5%, Tuareg 8%, Beri Beri (Kanouri) 4.3%, Arab, Toubou, and Gourmantche 1.2%, about 1,200 French expatriates.
Principal Religions: Muslim 80%, remainder indigenous beliefs and Christians.
Chief Commercial Products: Uranium ore 50%, livestock products 20%, cowpeas, onions (1996 est.).
GNP per capita: 190 US$
Currency: CFA franc (no longer tied to the French franc).
Former Colonial Status: French Colony (1921–1960).
Independence Date: August 3, 1960.
Chief of State: Tandja Mamadou, President, elected 1999.
National Flag: Three horizontal stripes of orange, white and emerald green. There is an orange globe in the middle of the white stripe.

The Republic of Niger covers an immense area in north central Africa. It is one of the most thinly populated nations of the continent. A huge plateau, the country is desolate but diversified, sometimes rocky and sometimes sandy, furrowed in many places by fossilized beds of ancient Sahara rivers. Hot and dry, it is pockmarked with small basins in the southern area which briefly turn into ponds during the "winter."

A narrow belt of territory in the south stretches along the entire width of the country and is the only fertile region. This area of trees and shrubs, interspersed with cultivated land supported by irrigation or wells, gives way quickly to a transition zone where the trees become smaller, and the lack of moisture supports only sporadic grazing by nomads' animals. In the northern two–thirds of the territory, the shifting sands of the hot desert render human life impossible except in the region of uranium mines, and only sparse, rudimentary animal life is found.

Little more than 2% of the land area is under cultivation, most of which is gathered around the 185–mile–long portion of the Niger River within the country's boundaries. The river floods from June to September, helping to provide moisture for the surrounding vegetation. The climate is exceedingly hot and dry during eight months of the year.

History: An empire was established in Niger by the Songhai people in the 7th century. Not much is known of the life of the people in the centuries of the Dark Ages. The Toubous conquered the Songhais at an unknown time and they were succeeded by the Djermas in the 17th century, who migrated from the north in large numbers. At the same time, the Hausas were asserting their power in the West and the semi–arid section, while the Tuaregs were moving into their confederations in the lonely north. For details of early and colonial history, see Historical Background and *The French in Africa.*

Niger was a member of the *French Community* from 1958 to 1960, but with the proclamation of independence it withdrew from that organization.

Under the first post–independence constitution, the president held office for a term of five years and was elected by universal suffrage. The National Assembly of 60 members, elected in the same manner, sat for five years. The government could be ousted and the Assembly dissolved either by a motion of censure requiring a two–thirds majority or a vote of *no confidence* by a simple majority.

After independence, the largest political party, led by Diori Hamani, dominated the government of Niger; the *Niger Progressive Party* held all seats of the National Assembly. Its membership was composed chiefly of persons of moderate outlook.

Niger was especially hard–hit by the drought which began in late 1972 and has continued since then. This, together with the usual African pressures for change, led to a bloodless *coup* which ended the 14–year rule of Diori Hamani in 1974. The slender head of the army, Seyni Kountché seized the government and installed himself as president of a twelve–man military council in 1974. There were at least three attempted *coups.* Frequent cabinet changes followed by executions reflected the restive state of Niger politics. Opposition groups formed, merged, split and disappeared. When President Kountché died in Paris of AIDS in late 1987, his cousin, Col. Ali Saibou, became chief of state.

President Saibou grudgingly agreed to a new constitution; it was promulgated after he was elected president in 1989. It was approved in 1992, greatly curtailing the power of the military and mandating elections which were held in 1993 after being postponed three times. A 43-year-old economist, Mahamane Ousmane won a majority, but could not reign in the chaotic political climate of Niger.

He quickly alienated most of the National Assembly and government came to a virtual standstill. The military, led by Brig. Gen. Ibrahim Mainasssara staged a *coup* in January 1996, arresting the president and prime minister. A new constitution was adopted and elections were held in July. Mainassara, running as an independent, won. The opposition contested the results of the presidential election and the crisis deepened four months later when the eight main opposition parties boycotted legislative elections. Pro-government parties and sympathizers claimed all 80 seats in the National Assembly.

On a more positive note, the government seemed to effect an end to the northern rebellion of Tuareg and Toubou peoples. Two main rebel movements, the *Organization of Armed Resistance (ORA)* and the *Coordination of Armed Resistance (CRA)* had long fought for autonomy, and a peace pact had been signed in April 1995. The agreement called for reintegration of these former rebels into Nigerien society. Some would be integrated into the army or paramilitary ranks, but this process had been painfully slow. *ORA* and *CRA* fighters had been encamped at government sites for more than a year; only a third had been integrated. Finally a breakthrough was made. Parliament finally voted amnesty for all desert guerrilla groups in March 1998. Shortly afterwards, the two main rebel fronts handed over their arsenals to military authorities. They consisted of heavy machine guns, rocket-launchers, anti-tank mines and ammunition.

From the point of General Maïnassara's transformation into a civilian ruler Niger became increasingly ungovernable. The country was wracked by a continuing series of strikes, protests, mutinies, and rebellions. Salaries to soldiers and civil servants, and scholarships to students went unpaid for months. The political opposition found the streets a comfortable place for political theater.

Niger's long political instability reached a climax in early 1999. Local elections were held for the first time, and when early results showed the opposition winning handily, armed men appeared in those polling areas where it seemed most successful. Ballots and official tabulation reports were destroyed, the vote disrupted. The opposition was justifiably outraged. Supporters were called to the streets to protest and widespread unrest ensued; a day later they called upon the General to resign.

Ex–President Ibrahim Mainassara Barre

The next day, April 9, 1999, the President's own security command shot him to death as he was preparing to leave the Niamey airport. With Orwellian glibness the commander of the Presidential Guard, Major Daouda Mallam Wanke, emphasized to reporters that Maïnassara's death was totally unpremeditated, merely an "unfortunate accident." Eyewitnesses reported that Presidential Guard members repeatedly shot the President with a truck-mounted large-caliber machine gun, nearly severing his body in two.

Very quickly the National Assembly and Supreme Court were dissolved, the constitution and political parties suspended, and a *National Council for Reconciliation (CRN)* put in place. Major Wanke, was chosen as President and head of the CRN, which consisted of 14 junior officers. The CRN announced that it would govern the country for a period of nine months. Not surprisingly, it also announced there would be no inquiry into the death of President Maïnassara.

Expressions of outrage were heard from every part, and France, on whom the Niger economy is largely dependent, suspended all military aid and economic assistance. Most politicians, however, seemed ready to collaborate with the new regime. When the military junta announced its cabinet, the solidarity of Niger's political class, including the close ties between soldiers and civilians, became apparent. Thirteen of the nineteen new ministers were from parties that had fiercely opposed Maïnassara.

With the Japanese—major trading partners with Niger—announcing that they would re-examine their economic cooperation unless democracy were restored, the new regime had to respond quickly. Major Wanke went on radio and television to announce that the junta intended to return the country to civilian rule by the end of the year. Elections would be held in November and the new president would be sworn in on 31 December. Members of the military and security forces were specifically banned from standing for election, as were civilian members of the transitional government. The major also indicated that there would be a referendum on a new constitution in June. The junta's timetable was scrupulously followed.

A number of technical committees were established to elaborate the new constitution, and after turbulent debates a consensus emerged: a parliamentary regime with a relatively strong president. The final draft provided for a single house legislature with executive power shared between the president and the prime minister. The president must name the prime minister from a list of three candidates proposed by the parliamentary majority. Clearing the way for army support of the new Fifth Republic, Article 141 of the new constitution provided amnesty to those responsible for "the coups d'état of 27 January 1996 and 9 April 1999."

The referendum of July 18 approved the new constitution by a nearly 90% majority, a figure made less impressive by the fact that only a little over 30% of the electorate participated. The referendum was the first step in a transition back to civilian rule. As promised by Major Wanke, multiparty presidential and parliamentary elections followed in October and November.

Seven candidates competed for the presidency. In the runoffs, Tandja Mamadou the candidate of the *National Movement for the Society in Development* (*MNSD*), beat Mahamadou Issoufou, the candidate of the *Niger Party for Democracy and Socialism* (*PNDS*) by a margin of nearly 60% to 40%.

Tandja, a retired military officer, had first become prominent when he helped oust Niger's first president, Diori Hamani, in 1974. He served as interior minister for both presidents Kountché and Ali Saibou. Under the latter, he was responsible for the bloody repression of Tuaregs in 1990. An ethnic Kanouri, Tandja profited by a runoff alliance with Mahamane Ousmane, a member of Niger's influential Hausa majority, leader of the *Convention Démocratique et Sociale* (CDS) and the country's last democratically elected president. His younger Hausa opponent, Mamamdou Issoufou (who had served as Prime Minister under Mahamane Ousmane) spent lavishly (with money rumored to have come from Burkinabé and Libyan sources) and campaigned vigorously in what Nigerian commentators called "an American style."

In elections for the National Assembly, Tandja's *MNSD* and *CDS* alliance won an absolute majority of 55 out of 83 seats. Much to the relief of many, the electoral system eliminated minor parties. Only three other parties would be represented in the new parliament. Issoufou's *PNDS* won 16 seats, and the *Rally for Democracy and Progress* (*RDP*) of former president Maïnassara won eight. The remaining four seats were won by the *Alliance nigérienne pour la démocratie et le progrès* (*ANDP*).

Niger's democratic transition remains extremely fragile. Donors have only slowly restored funds, and agreements with the Bretton Woods institutions have not yet kicked in. Resources available to the government are desperately limited, and fundamental problems remain. Civil servants and teachers remain unpaid and regularly take to the streets to demand back wages.

The University of Niamey has become a troublesome center of dissidence. Instruction deteriorated as lecturers, always underpaid and usually unpaid, quit to find jobs elsewhere. When students protested conditions in February 2001, clashes between protesters and government forces resulted in several injuries and the death of one gendarme.The University was closed, and the opposition brought a motion of censure—its second in the new year.

President Mamadou Tandja has announced ambitious plans to improve living conditions. One thousand villages housing a minimum of 1,000 inhabitants would each receive a school, a well and a health center equipped to fight malaria, meningitis and AIDS.

Culture: *National Geographic* has financed an expedition into the Niger desert to make casts of the most extraordinary rock carvings ever discovered—huge giraffes carved into desert sandstone 9,000 years ago. The largest stands over 20 feet tall; its proportions are meticulously accurate and its reticulation beautifully created in low relief. Wavy lines come from the mouths of these giraffes and to them are attached small human figures. No one is sure what they mean, but their artistic achievement is undeniable. For preservation purposes the actual site of this Sistine Chapel of rock art remains hidden. Casts will allow worldwide audiences to appreciate the consummate skill of their unknown creators.

Tourism in Niger had virtually ceased as a consequence of five years of Tuareg rebellion in the north, but in late 1998, the Niger desert became the improbable site of an international fashion show. Africa's best fashion designers gathered with representatives of the great fashion houses of Europe, political dignitaries and assorted cultural glitterati for the first International Festival of African Fashion (FIMA). The brainchild of Alphadi, Niger's best-known fashion designer, FIMA served to showcase African creativity and proved to the world that peace had returned to the Agadès region, a necessary stimulant to tourism.

Local religious leaders were less encouraging in their assessments of FIMA. They handed out leaflets before and during the show to express disgust with clothes that revealed arms, legs and breasts. It was, they said, a ceremony of perversion opposed to the principles of the Koran. They were no more receptive of FIMA's second edition in 2000.

Police had to use tear gas and batons to disperse more than 800 Islamic clerics and students who gathered outside parliament demanding FIMA's cancellation. The fashion show, they shouted, would only incite people to fornication.

For the government, committed to defending Niger as a secular state, the fashion show was simply a harmless distraction which could bring much needed investment to Niger. And as the interior minister gently reminded people, "There was already debauchery and adultery in Niamey before the show."

Economy: President Tandja inherited a shattered economy. The UN Development Program (UNDP) ranks Niger as the second poorest country in the world. Its GNP grows at a rate of 0.9% annually, while its population grows at a rate of 3.3%—one of the highest rates in the world. Annual per capita income is estimated at $190, and over 60% of the population survives on less than $1 per day. Niger has huge debts, and thousands of government workers remain unpaid.

As a profoundly poor state, Niger represents all the social and medical consequences of devastating poverty. The country has been spending three times more on debt payments than on health and education. The consequence is seen in raw statistics: In Niger, more than a quarter of children will die before they are five years old. Their deaths result from long-term starvation diets that weaken the immune system and allow children to be killed by measles, malaria, meningitis and diarrhea. The most horrifying of the child killers is Noma. It starts as a small black spot on the face and progresses by devouring facial tissue, muscle and bone.

Barge of the Niger River

Niger has qualified for participation in the Highly Indebted Poor Countries (HIPC) program, and in December 2000 the World Bank and IMF signed debt reduction agreements with the government. These will free up about $40 million per year to help implement government health, education and rural infrastructure plans. Debt service as a percentage of government revenue will drop from nearly 44% in 1999 to 10.9% in 2003 and average 4.3% during 2010-2019.

For years Niger's main source of export revenues was uranium, accounting for 80% of the national budget in the 1980s. Proven reserves total 280,000 tons, but production peaked at 4,360 tons in 1981. Since then, diminished demand has reduced production and seriously affected government revenues. In 1998 only 3,731 tons were mined.

Gold seems the most promising alternative in a desperate effort to diversify away from an uncertain reliance on uranium. Two neighboring gold mines are schedule to go into production in 2001—Samira Hill and Libiri. Ore will be jointly milled at the Samira site, and first year production is targeted at 150,000 ounces.

Niger's 6.7 million-head national livestock herd is an important economic resource, and cattle are the second most profitable export after uranium. Around 95% of the national production of leather and hides is exported and accounts for around 20% of export earnings.

The Future: Economic problems are crushing, with little prospect for improvement. President Tandja will emphasize the development of Niger's agricultural sector, but even here, the problems are staggering. The flow of foreign aid, on which the Niger budget is dependent, is only slowly returning now that transparent democratic elections have successfully returned the army to its barracks. Realistically, it is unlikely that foreign aid can ever arrive in amounts sufficient to cope with Niger's multiple problems. The collapse of the state and its capacity to provide and distribute social services opens the way for Islamic fundamentalists, who have shown elsewhere that they can fill such needs. Violent protests in Niamey against a fashion show suggest the forceful presence of fundamentalist currents.

The Republic of the Sudan

The Nile River at Khartoum

Busy street in downtown Khartoum

Area: 2,504,530 sq. km = 967,000 sq. mi. (An area as large as the U.S. east of the Mississippi joined by Louisiana, Arkansas and Missouri).
Population: 34,475,690 (July 1999 est.)
Capital City: Khartoum (Pop. 7.7 million, estimated, including the city of Omdurman and surrounding areas filled with squatter camps).
Climate: The northern half is arid desert, the middle and southern areas are temperate and semi–arid; the southwest is hot with a six month rainy season.
Neighboring Countries: Congo-Kinshasa and Central African Republic (Southwest); Chad (West); Libya (Northwest); Kenya and Uganda (Southeast).
Official Language: Arabic.
Other Principal Languages: Acholi, Bari, Bedawi, Dinka, Fulfulde, Fur, Hausa, Kanuri, Kenuzi-Dongola, Masalit, Nobiin, Nuer, Otuho , Shilluk, Toposa.
Ethnic groups: Black 52% (prominently including Acholi, Dinka, Nuer, Shilluk), Arab 39%, Beja 6%, foreigners 2%, other 1%.
Principal Religions: Sunni Muslim 70% (in north), indigenous beliefs 25%, Christian 5% (mostly in south and Khartoum).
Chief Commercial Products: Cotton 23%, sesame 22%, livestock/meat 13%, and gum Arabic 5%. Oil production just beginning.
GNP per capita: 290 US$
Currency: 1 Sudanese Pound (£Sd) = 100 piastres.
Former Colonial Status: Egyptian (1821–1885); British–Egyptian (1899–1956).
Independence Date: January 1, 1956.
Chief of State: Brig. Gen. Omar Hassan Ahmed el–Bashir, Chairman of the Revolutionary Council (b. 1947).
National Flag: Three horizontal stripes of red, white and black with a green triangle at the pole.

Sudan is the largest nation of Africa, covering an area of almost one million square miles. The vast Sahara Desert lies in the northern sector and is succeeded by a semi–arid plains country in the region near Khartoum, the capital city. This gently rolling territory is succeeded in the south by tropical plains land with more abundant rainfall; in the extreme south, the land becomes choked by dense jungle growth. The historic Nile River, the longest in the world, virtually divides the country and is the main route of north–south communication and travel between the Mediterranean Sea and the lower part of the African continent. The river has two points of origin—the waters of Lake Victoria flow into a portion known as the Victoria Nile. After a short distance, the river becomes lost in the Sudd swamp region of southern Sudan, which covers an immense area of land. The stream emerges again to flow northward through central Sudan. The Blue Nile originates to the east near Lake Tana in the mountains of Ethiopia. The two rivers join at Khartoum to form the main Nile, which, as it proceeds through northern Sudan, has a slight downward slope, interrupted periodically by rough cataracts. As it nears Wadi Halfa on the Egyptian border, the Nile shapes itself into an almost perfect "S" curve. Were it not for the predominantly muddy waters of this river, much of Sudan and Egypt would be empty and desolate.

High mountains rise in the extreme east of Sudan, close to the Ethiopian border and along the Red Sea coast. Other mountains are found to the west on the Chad border, and in the South.

History: The ancient history of Sudan, one of the oldest civilizations in the world, re-

volves around the Pharaohs of Egypt and the Nubian people in central Sudan. Gigantic formations of stone in the Nile area to the north furnished the material from which many of the picturesque temples and burial grounds of ancient Egypt were craved and built. In the eighth century BC Kushite kings from Nubia, now northern Sudan, conquered Egypt and created the 25th Dynasty. At the beginning of the Christian era, Sudan split into a collection of small, independent states. There were some conversions of people to Christianity in the 6th century, but much of the country remained pagan until there was a widespread adoption of Islam, primarily in the North, at the end of the 13th century. For details of early and colonial history, see Historical Background and *The British in Africa.*

Col. Jaafar Mohammed al Nimeri

Sudan has been riven by internal conflict for most of its history. That conflict has usually been referred to a one between a Muslim North and a Christian South, but that description is highly misleading. Conflict in Sudan is neither exclusively regional nor exclusively religious given the country's enormous complexity. Indeed, Sudanese themselves refer to the country as *laham ras* (literally "headmeat"), a term which refers to the highly divergent taste, texture and appearance of parts of cooked sheep's head, a popular Sudanese dish.

In this culturally complex situation, a central problem facing the state is defining its identity. Contemporary conflict is fueled by vastly divergent historical identities. For Sudan there is no unifying identity; diversity is division. Northern Sudan was conquered and unified by the Egyptian viceroy of the Ottoman Sultan in 1821. Egyptian rulers claimed southern Sudan, but were unable to establish effective control over its fragmented animist populations. Access to the south was not possible until after 1839, and from that point both the Ottoman rulers and their Arab Sudanese subjects saw the south only as a source of manpower. Slavers from both groups aggressively raided southern peoples.

Not until the 1880s was a sense of Sudanese identity articulated in opposition to the Egyptian conquerors. In 1881 a religious leader proclaimed himself the Mahdi or "expected one" and began to unify peoples in western and central Sudan. Drawing upon discontent with Ottoman-Egyptian exploitation, the Mahdi led a nationalist revolt culminating in the fall of Khartoum in 1885. The Mahdi died shortly afterwards, but his state survived until destroyed by an Anglo-Egyptian army under Lord Kitchner in 1889. Sudan was proclaimed a condominium in 1899, and governed by a joint British-Egyptian administration until 1956. Northern Arab Muslims were privileged by the condominium administration and in turn, looked down on the black African animists of the south. For black Africans of southern Sudan, the memory of slave raids meant that any pale-skinned person was a potential slaver.

Though one speaks of northern Muslim populations and southern animists, neither of these populations is in any way monolithic. Sudanese Muslims are divided by affiliation with rival religious brotherhoods. The Mahdi's followers called themselves *ansars*, and the Ansar sect today is the largest of the Sudanese Muslim brotherhoods. During the period of Ottoman-Egyptian rule, Turkish-Egyp-

A truck meets a camel caravan on a bridge over the Blue Nile in the Sudan

tians developed close relations with another Muslin brotherhood, known as the Khatmiyya. The second most important brotherhood today, the Khatmiyya retains its original pro-Egyptian anti-Mahdist identity. Each of these two rival brotherhoods is associated with a separate political party. Mahdists are the core of the *Umma Party*, while the Khatmiyya forms the core of the *Democratic Unionist Party (DUP)*. The leader of the *Umma Party*, Dr. Sadiq al-Mahdi, is a descendent of the first Mahdi. Smaller than either the Ansar or Khatmiyya is the more militant and fundamentalist Muslim Brotherhood led by Hassan al-Turabi and very much the core of the *National Islamic Front* (*NIF*). These sectarian groupings also have their secular opponents in the North, Muslims and non-Muslims whose vision of Sudanese identity is not based on political Islam.

Southern black African animists (and today a small number of Christians) are even more divided. Symptomatically, over a hundred languages are spoken in Sudan, most of them in the south. The two major southern ethnic groups, the Dinka and Nuer, are segmentary societies with no traditions of overarching leadership and governance. Both are cattle raising people. Both were traditional rivals for pasturage and objects of mutual cattle raids. Khartoum governments, dominated by northerners, have traditionally exploited such rivalries. Within each group segments vie with each other for scarce resources and produce intra-ethnic rivalries that can be exploited by the Khartoum government. Similarly, historical antagonisms between cattle pastoralists like the Nuer or Dinka and settled farming peoples create fissures that work against southern political unity.

These cultural diversities help explain Sudan's continuing history of political instability and conflict. At independence in 1956, a civilian regime, deeply divided between its Muslim partners, was incapacitated by internal division and overthrown by a military coup in 1958. The military in turn, reneging on its promises to restore civilian government, was driven from office and succeeded by another coalition government. Power sharing between *Umma* and *Unionist* parties could not overcome problems of factionalism, economic stagnation and ethnic dissidence in the south. Espousing pan-Arab-Nationalism and professing pro-Soviet sentiments, General Jaafar Nimeri took advantage of dissatisfaction with this civilian regime and overthrew it in 1969. Soviet arms poured into Sudan. But only two years later disputes between Marxist and non-Marxist elements within the ruling military coalition resulted in an abortive communist coup. Anti-Marxist elements quickly restored Nimeri, who, seeing the light, did a political about face and sought aid from the United States. After Emperor Haile Selassie was overthrown in neighboring Ethiopia by a Marxist military coup in 1974, Sudan was seen as a bulwark against Communism in the region. American arms poured into the country, and Sudan became another pawn on the chessboard of cold war politics.

Secure with American arms and support, General Nimeri began an Islamization campaign in 1983. Traditional Islamic punishments drawn from the *Sharia* were incorporated into the penal code. Amputations for theft and public lashings for alcohol possession became common. When religious leaders like Sadiq al-Mahdi questioned the general's credentials for creating an Islamic state, they were thrown in jail. Civil liberties were suspended and a state of emergency declared. Rights granted southerners for a degree of autonomy were curtailed and two army battalions mutinied under the

Dr. Sadiq al–Mahdi

leadership of a southern Dinka, Colonel John Garang, in 1984. This began Sudan's on-going civil war. General Nimeri himself fell in a bloodless coup a year later and was ultimately replaced by a civilian coalition again headed by Sadiq al-Mahdi.

The *Southern People's Liberation Army* (*SPLA*), founded by Garang, found a ready supply of arms from Marxist Ethiopia and by 1987, Soviet tanks and artillery supplied to the *SPLA* allowed it to fight positional battles and capture population centers. Subject to government bombardment and raids by its militias, massive numbers of southerners were displaced from their homes or fled to neighboring countries. The civilian government in Khartoum remained faction ridden and indecisive, incapable of winning the war. At the very moment negotiations with the rebels seemed on the verge of success, the regime was overthrown by General Omar Hassan al-Bashir in 1989.

The new military regime came to power with the backing of the militant *National Islamic Front* (*NIF*) party headed by Hassan al-Turabi. It quickly abolished the constitution, all political parties (except the *NIF*), and trade unions. Press freedoms were curtailed, strict dress and behavior codes imposed on women. More than 78,000 people were purged from the army, police and civil administration to make way for those of more militant Muslim faith. Support for the new regime came from Iran, enabling the government to make massive purchases of arms from China and the former Soviet republics. These were used to step up the war against the south. In addition to an ideology of militant Islam, the discovery of huge southern oil reserves in the 1970s also fueled the desire of Khartoum to control its southern provinces, even at the price of massive destruction and loss of life. Indeed, emptying the oil producing regions of their black African animist populations seemed to be a deliberate government goal.

The overthrow in 1991 of Ethiopia's Marxist regime and questions about continued arms supply led to a factional breakup of the *SPLA*. Under the leadership of Riek Machar, a Nuer faction broke off and proclaimed its goal independence from Sudan. John Garang remained head of the, now, largely Dinka SPLA and claimed his goal a unified, secular Sudan. The clash of these three visions of Sudanese identity—an Arab-Muslim Sudan, a Sudan divided into two separate states, or a unified secular Sudan—continues to the present. Fluid loyalties and deliberately divisive strategies by the Khartoum regime have led to a bewildering complex set of shifting alliances and coalitions, few of which can be identified with much more than a desire to overthrow the present regime.

By 1995 northern and southern opponents of the regime had joined forces in the *National Democratic Alliance* (*NDA*), and January 1997 the NDA could mount an offensive on three fronts in Eastern Sudan. Troops involved came from all the members of the *Alliance*. The main spearhead came from the Sudan People's Liberation Army commanded by Colonel John Garang, but also included elements from the *Beja Congress* and northern groups such as Sadiq al-Mahdi's *Umma* and Mohamed Osman al-Mirghani's *Democratic Unionist Party* (*DUP*). The strategic objective was the capture of ed-Damazin, the provincial capital and site of the Roseires hydroelectric dam that supplies Khartoum with 80 percent of its electricity. Even more threatening for the government was the possibility that these forces, with bases in Ethiopia and Eritrea, would link up with SPLA forces in the south with bases in Uganda.

In response, Khartoum rallied Southern dissidents and signed a peace agreement with Riek Machar and other breakaway SPLA faction leaders in April 1997. Pro-government southerners were linked together under the name of the *United Democratic Salvation Front* (*UDSF*) headed by Machar. In the months to come he was rewarded an impressive series of titles—President of the Coordinating Council of the Southern States and Assistant of the President of the Republic—and made a member of President Bashir's cabinet.

NDA forces demonstrated their capacity to inflict damage by conducting raids against the Roseires hydroelectric dam and at least twice blowing up the pipeline that transports oil from the south to refineries on the Red Sea. Khartoum's infrastructure looked increasingly vulnerable.

In February and March 1999 a seemingly successful series of reconciliation meetings between Dinka and Nuer leaders were held, suggesting the enemies of the regime were more unified than ever before. Meeting under the auspices of the New Sudan Council of Churches (NSCC), several hundred Dinka and Nuer chiefs and community leaders met at Wunlit in the state of Bahr el Ghazal. The meeting culminated in a peace agreement called the "Wunlit Dinka-Nuer Covenant."

More than 300 Dinka and Nuer chiefs and community leaders, local administrators, church leaders, and representatives of women and youth signed the covenant. A permanent cease-fire promised an end to the seven- and-half-year conflict between the Dinka and Nuer of the West Bank of the Nile. Amnesty provisions forgave offenses committed prior to January 1 1999.

The Wunlit Covenant demonstrated the vitality of traditional conflict resolution procedures. Agreements were reached through consensus. Rituals surrounding the agreement stamped it with the mark of tradition. The slaughter of a large white bull by traditional spiritual leaders of both communities symbolized peace and an end to the conflict. The sacrifice was also a symbolic warning that anyone who violates the covenant would go the way of the white bull.

President Bashir had to face not only the growing unity of his Southern enemies, but also a growing threat to his authority from within the *National Congress Party* (*NCP*), the renamed *National Islamic Front*. His approach was twofold. A peace agreement was signed with Sadiq al-Mahdi, driving a wedge in the NDA and rallying a leading Muslim cleric to his side in preparation for his struggle with Hassan al-Turabi. Turabi, speaker of parliament and also al-Mahdi's brother-in-law, seemed to be on the verge of reducing the president's position in both party and state. Bashir's response amounted to an internal coup. In late 1999 he acted decisively to curtail al-Turabi, the regime's chief ideologue and advocate of exporting Islamist militancy. Parliament was dissolved and a state of emergency declared, allowing the President to rule by decree.

With the principal spokesman for political Islam sidetracked, President Bashir moved into a remarkable charm campaign, vaunting newly minted secularist credentials and signing agreements with formerly hostile neighbors. Algeria, Egypt, Libya, Eritrea and Ethiopia are now friends of Khartoum, though the fragility of such flirtations is suggested by the agreement signed with Uganda only last December. Each party agreed not to arm opponents, but by this March, President Bashir was charging President Museveni of Uganda with violating the accord, continuing to supply arms to the SPLA and desiring to create "an empire in central Africa."

President Bashir's foreign policy moves seemed froth to mislead the eye. Deeper, more troubling events were happening within Sudan. In February 2000 Riek Machar resigned his lordly titles and leadership of the *United Democratic Salvation Front* (*UDSF*). He accused the government of failing to implement the peace agreement of April 1997. He also accused it of having sent troops to fight his soldiers in southern Unity state, heart of the southern oil-producing areas.

Following Machar's defection the government launched an offensive of unprecedented brutality against civilians living around the disputed Bentiu oil fields. Fugitives from the offensive reported that troops backed by tanks, helicopter gunships and aerial bombardments were torturing, slaughtering and burning men, women and children in a drive to evict all non-Arabs from oil-producing areas—largely Machar's own Nuer people. Aerial

In the south, a dugout canoe glides silently by AP/Wide World Photo

President Omar Hassan al–Bashir

bombardment, with increased intensity and larger instruments of death, continues today as the government pursues a policy of depopulating the oil producing regions of the south.

President Bashir has continued his campaign to isolate Hassan al-Turabi. In May 2000, the Islamic leader was suspended as secretary-general of the *National Congress* ruling party and accused of plotting against the government. Suggesting the falling out between the two former partners was total, Turabi responded by likening the government to a dictatorship and warned that dictatorship did not have a history of enduring in Sudan. Formally expelled from the *National Congress* party in June, Al-Turabi announced creation of a new political party, the *Popular National Congress* (*PNC*).

To bolster support among Islamic faithful, President Bashir induced Sadiq al-Mahdi's *Umma* party to break with the *NDA* and begin reconciliation talks with the government. Al-Mahdi himself returned from exile in November 2000, but he rejected talk of power sharing with the current regime, saying he could not support a "totalitarian" government.

When al-Bashir called presidential and legislative elections for December 2000, few were interested and few participated. No elections could be held in the south for security reasons, and where they were held in the north, they were actively boycotted by the major opposition parties. So lackluster was the whole affair that Bashir even permitted ex-President Nimeiry to return from exile and run against him.

Official reports indicated 63% of eligible voters went to the polls, a figure that produced hoots of derision from the opposition who claimed not more than 7% had participated. Bashir and the *National Congress* party won, overwhelmingly. What they won is more in question, for the regime remains thinly supported and totally isolated, dependent for survival on repressive force against its northern opposition and murderous warfare against its southern foes.

In February, Hassan al-Turabi was arrested and jailed when it was announced that his *PNC* had signed a memorandum of understanding with the southern rebel group, the Sudan People's Liberation Army (SPLA). The linkage between Turabi and his arch foe, John Garang, was unexpected, unprecedented and to many of his followers, inexplicable, unless, that is, one accepts the infinite mutability of Sudanese politicians.

For some of his followers, the memorandum represented a crisis of belief, for it rejected all he had stood for and implemented while in power. For Turabi loyalists, it was a visionary statement on Sudan's future, calling for democracy, a just peace and a federal government.

Failing to get Turabi to recant, the government has moved ahead with plans to bring him and a number of his followers to trial. Clearly it senses a propaganda victory over the Sorbonne-educated Turabi, easily identifiable now as a man without principles. At a meeting called to inspire "mujahedeen martyrs," President Bashir told the gathered throng that "the will of Allah has exposed the hypocrites in our ranks, by their signing of the memorandum of disgrace."

At mid-year Hassan al-Turabi remains a prisoner of the state he helped to create. For his loyalists, convinced he will emerge triumphant, each day adds to his martyrdom.

Culture: The issue of slavery in the Sudan highlights the age-old rerlationship between expansive Arab nomads in the North and sedentary animist or Christian farmers in the South. In January 1999 Christian Solidarity Inernational (CSI), a Swiss-based human rights group, announced its redemption of 1,050 slaves in the Sudan, the largest number ever liberated at one time. The group accused Sudanese armed forces of capturing and using Christian and animist black Africans as slaves and war booty. It was, the group said, "one of the most potent instruments of its declared *jihad* (holy war) against communities that resist its totalitarian policies of forced Islamization and Arabization." A few months later it announced that during the five day period of April 12–17, it redeemed a further 1,783 slaves, mostly women and children captured as war booty by the Sudanese armed forces. CSI said the slaves were redeemed from four different networks of Arab slave retrivers, for a fee of $50 per slave. Interviews with the liberated confirmed beatings, rape, female genital excision, forced conversions to Islam and unpaid labor. CSI says it has redeeed 7,725 slaves from the Sudan since 1995.

The regime employs a network of government informants to provide surveillance in schools, universities, markets, workplaces, and neighborhoods. So-called "popular committees" monitor household activities in the neighborhoods, generating a climate of suspicion. Sharia law applied by the regime makes for rules of conduct that tightly circumscribe the individual. The 1991 Criminal Act makes apostasy, including conversion to another faith, punishable by death. In June 1998 a Sudanese teacher was accused of deserting the religion of Islam. The court gave him two months in which to repent and return to Islam or be executed.

The on-going civil war in Sudan has transformed traditions that once constrained conflict. Beliefs that mitigated violence have given way to a culture of unmitigated violence. Among both Nuer and Dinka, for example, it was believed that causing a death created "spiritual pollution." A bit of the blood of any man a Nuer speared to death was thought to be in the slayer, there to haunt the killer. It had to be bled out of the upper arm by an earth priest.

With modern warfare and new weaponry, beliefs have been modified. Rebel commanders argued that gun death was a different matter; spiritual pollution, they argued, did not apply in a "government war." This effectively removed moral consequences from killing. Killing became easier and a culture of violence was created. Researchers have found that arguments once settled by fighting with sticks are now decided with assault weapons.

Economy: War, continuous and with few prospects of ending soon, has sapped Sudan's capacity for growth, development or improved life for its citizens. It costs the government half of its budget annually, President Omar al-Bashir admitted in early 1999. Sudan's 1999 budget projected spending at a level of S1.09 billion, which would indicate the war is costing the country nearly $1.5 million a day.

Sudan's economy has been traditionally dependent on agriculture and pastoral activity. About 65% of the population makes its living through crop growing or animal grazing. Principal food crops consist of millet, sorghum, rice, cassava, wheat, peanuts, beans and bananas. Exports are primarily cotton, livestock and gum Arabic.

Sudanese cotton production began in the 18th century and became commercially important in 1925 following the development of Al-Jazirah (Gezira), one of the largest irrigation projects in the world. The Gezira project distributes the waters of the Blue Nile captured by the Sennar and Roseires dams through a 2,700-mile network of canals and ditches to irrigate fields growing cotton and other cash crops. Constructed by the British, Gezira was originally developed to supply cotton for the textile factories of Lancashire. The irrigation project made Al-Jazirah the most productive agricultural area of Sudan. It takes up about half the country's total irrigated area and is, in effect, a 2 million-acre cooperative farm.

Gum Arabic is a substance obtained by tapping the *Acacia Senegal* tree. It is produced commercially in areas on the southern periphery of the Sahara desert and is widely used by U.S. candy, cosmetics and medical industries. Indeed, when the possibility of economic sanctions against Sudan arose in 1997, many interest groups lobbied for a gum Arabic exception, considering the Sudanese gum unrivaled in quality. More than 80 per cent of the world gum Arabic supplies come from Sudan.

In the south, agricultural activity is mainly pastoral, with the main domestic livestock being cattle. Sheep, goats, camels and chickens are also reared. In 1994–95 Sudan was estimated to have over a million head of livestock. Sudan is an important supplier of sheep meat to the Arab world and is building new slaughterhouses in order to service this huge market. Its fresh meat production increased 53 per cent in 1997, reaching 1.3 million tons of meat against 686,000 tons the year before.

While fresh meat and live animal exports produce the most income from the livestock sector, the leather industry in Sudan is an important adjunct. It consists of two main branches—raw hide processing and footwear manufacturing. In 1996 some 300 million square feet of cattle hides were produced, with another 60 million square feet of sheep and goatskins and 13 million of camel hides. The domestic footwear industry has a capacity to produce 18 million pairs of leather shoes and 60 million pairs of other types of shoes.

For obvious reasons, tourism is not a factor in the Sudanese economy. Still, a five-star foreign-owned hotel officially opened in Khartoum in November 1999. The Grand Holiday Villa Hotel, owned by Malaysian interests, is the first hotel offering first class international standards to open there in almost 20 years. It was considered commercially viable because of the large number of Malaysian companies involved in the Sudan's oil and gas sector. (Presumably most Malaysians would not be affected by Sharia law prohibitions on alcohol that went into effect in 1983.)

It is of course Sudan's oil that drives the current civil hostilities. The government desperately wants the oil income to buy the weapons to crush its southern opponents and impose its vision of an Arab-Muslim nation on the country. Southerners want, with equal desperation, to share and control a significant portion of the revenues generated by a resource extracted from their territory to develop lands and populations marginalized by the central government in Khartoum.

Picking cotton in Butri — WORLD BANK photo

Sudan began to export crude oil in August from its 1,600-km (1,000-mile) 28-inch pipeline in southern Sudan to the Red Sea. By the end of 1999, Sudan had exported 15 million barrels of oil in just four months. The pipeline, with a capacity of 250,000 barrels per day (bpd), was built by the Greater Nile Petroleum Operating Company (GNPOC), a consortium including Canadian oil company Talisman and the state oil firms of China, Malaysia and Sudan.

Malaysia's national oil company, Petronas, not only owns a 30% share in the Greater Nile Petroleum Operating Company; its state-owned power company, Tenega National, was responsible for building a power station at Port Sudan The station would generate power and sell it to Sudan's National Electric Corporation. The Chinese National Petroleum Company owns a 40% share of GNPOC and China reportedly sent 2,000 "engineers" to Sudan to build GNPOC's pipeline. Work on the pipeline was remarkably fast, beginning only in May 1998. Human rights organizations have suggested that Chinese prisoners were used on the project, promised a reduction in their sentences. There are also persistent rumors that Malaysia and China exchange arms for oil in the Sudan, fueling, as they say, the government's war on its southern citizens. All parties deny it of course.

The inextricable linkage of oil and conflict has brought those companies operating in democratic countries under increasing pressure from human rights and humanitarian groups. In Canada, first Arakis and then Talisman, which took over Arakis interests, have been the objects of protests and stockholder requests for divestment. The government of Canada went so far as to investigate Talisman's activities, but chose not to act on what it found. British protesters have focused on Weir Pumps of Glasgow, which provided the pumping stations for the pipeline.

The Future: Friendship and alliance in Sudan remain fluid and fragile. Competing visions of Sudan's identity—secular or sectarian state, unified or divided state—remain mutually incompatible. Despite the exhaustion of resources on both sides of the conflict, the political will to end the war and agree on a common vision of what the Sudanese state should be seems absent. Sudan's oil wealth has only made civil conflict more vicious. The SPLA claims the oil producing regions as a historical part of the south. One should not expect peaceful extraction of oil without a solution in the south.

NORTH AFRICA

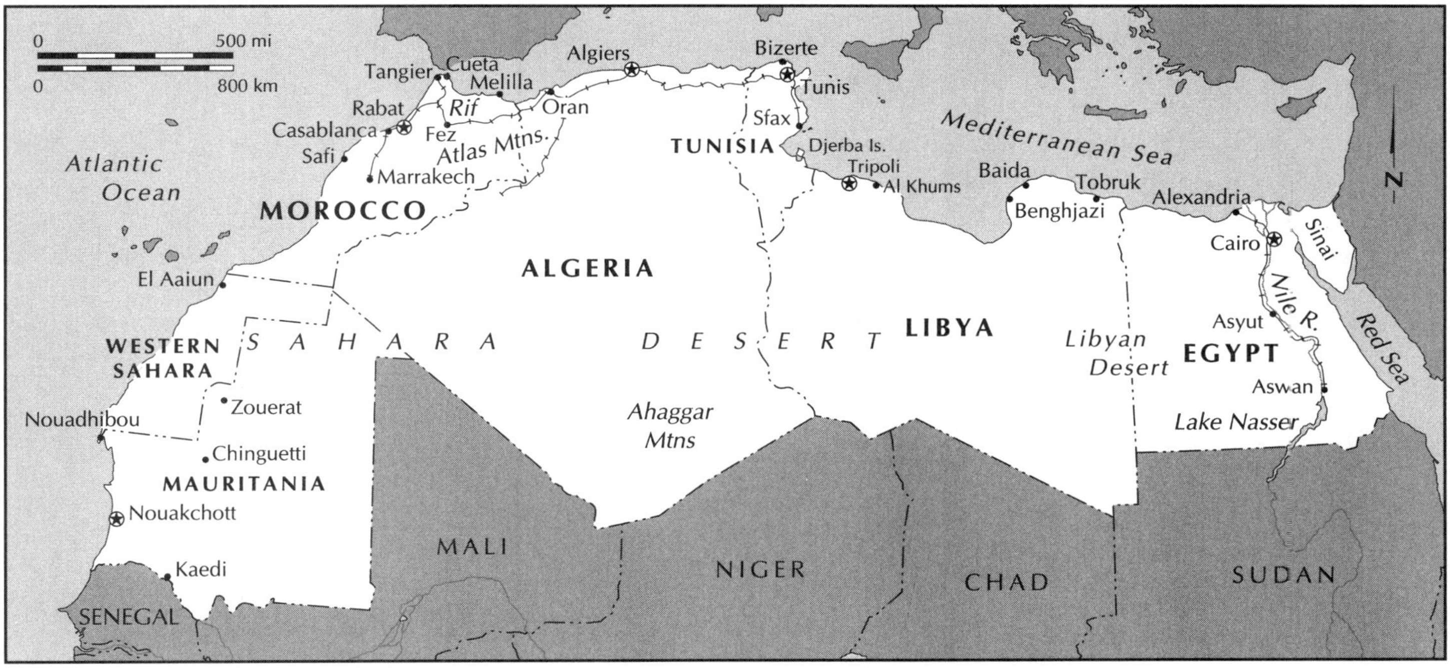

The Democratic and Popular Republic of Algeria

Area: 2,460,500 sq. km. = 950,000 sq. mi. (Almost as large as the U.S. east of the Mississippi River).

Population: 31,133,486 (July 1999 est.)

Capital City: Algiers (Pop. 4.2 million, estimated).

Climate: In the coastal region, temperate Mediterranean weather prevails. Inland, it is temperate and cooler in the high altitudes of the mountains. South, in the Sahara Desert, it is hot and dry—90 | SDF.–170 | SDF.

Neighboring Countries: Morocco (Northwest); Tunisia and Libya (East); Niger (Southeast); Mali, Mauritania (Southwest).

Official Language: Arabic.

Other Principal Languages: Berber langauges, including Kabyle, Tamazight, Taznatit, Tumzabt; Tamahaq, spoken by Tuaregs, and French.

Ethnic groups: Arab-Berber 99%, European less than 1%.

Principal Religions: Sunni Muslim (state religion) 99%, Christian and Jewish 1%.

Principal Commercial Products: Petroleum and natural gas 97%.

GNP per capita: 1500 US$

Currency: Algerian Dinar.

Former Colonial Status: French Colony (1831–1870); integral part of France (1870–1962).

National Day: Revolution Day, November 1st.

Chief of State: Abdelaziz Bouteflika, President (since March 1999).

National Flag: Two vertical stripes, green and white, with a red crescent enclosing a five–pointed star in the center.

Algeria existed as a seat of civilization long before recorded history. Its ports and commerce were the lifeblood of early times. The dazzling white city of Algiers, founded about 1,000 years ago, is a cosmopolitan crossroads of the East and West, climbing the Atlas Mountains from the blue Mediterranean. South of the fertile coastal regions and the mountainous areas stretches the vast Sahara Desert, where caravans similar to those of prehistoric days still cross the parched wastelands. Gleaming modern highways now lead to green oases and oil fields. Atomic science has invaded the silence of the desert.

Algeria has a 620–mile coastline on the Mediterranean. Two Atlas Mountain chains cross the country horizontally, dividing Algeria into three geographic zones: the northern Mediterranean zone, the high arid plateau between the ranges and the Sahara. The northern zone, known as the *Tell,* is a sun–bathed coastal area where vineyards, orange, fig and olive trees flourish in the valleys and hillsides. The high plateau is primarily the home of grazing herds of goats, sheep and camels. South of the Sahara, the immense Ahaggar Mountains are the territory of the Tuaregs, a Berber group with singular customs—the men, not the women, are veiled. Although this is a land of extremes, the most heavily populated areas have a pleasant climate.

History: Some of the first traces of human culture are to be found in the mountain range of the southern Sahara, including neolithic frescoes and carvings. The people who have lived the longest in Algeria are the Berbers, thought to be descendants of ancient Numidians who lived during Roman Empire times. For details of early and colonial history, see Historical Background and *The French in Africa.*

After a bitter eight–year struggle against Arab nationalists from 1954 to

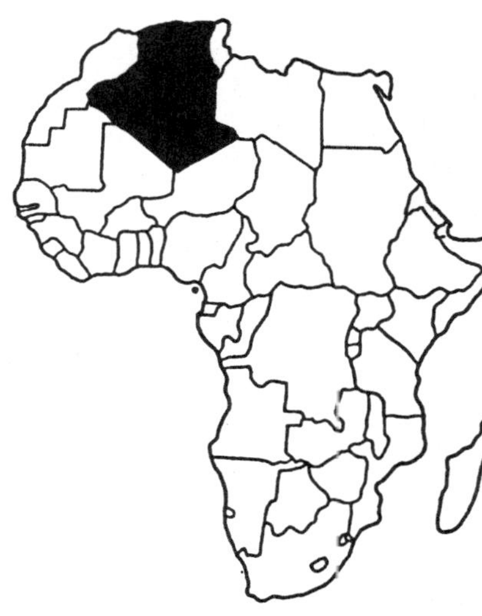

A workman with wire for new railway signal lines

1962, France granted independence to Algeria four months after a cease–fire had been negotiated. More than one million French citizens and other European residents left the country.

Ahmed Ben Bella, a prominent member of the *National Liberation Front (FLN)* which had led the fight for independence, headed the new government. Although leftist and socialist, he quickly outlawed the communist party and shortly thereafter was elected president. A wide range of reforms was undertaken, including the redistribution of land—drastic changes in a country which had only recently been shaken by the departure of skilled Europeans. Closer tieswere established with the European communist–bloc nations.

Constant bickering within the *FLN* led to the quiet removal of Ben Bella in 1965. He was placed under house arrest, but was never charged nor tried for any crime. In July 1979 he was placed under reduced restriction, provided with a villa, and was even allowed to receive visitors—but prohibited from making political statements or meeting with the press.

Colonel Houari Boumedienne was installed as chief of state with widespread support of the party leadership. The National Assembly was dissolved and the constitution suspended. Boumedienne, the former defense minister, established a 26–man Revolutionary Council to assist in governing the nation. He continued in power with the assistance of tight security measures which were able to successfully resist a 1967 attempt to oust him, and in 1968 a plot to assassinate him. Widespread changes in the army took place in 1969 and 182 political prisoners were tried by a hand–picked military court.

Starting in 1967, the Algerian government began the process of building new political institutions, beginning with communal assemblies and then provincial assemblies. A new constitution was finally adopted in late 1976 which was openly Marxist in tone; President Boumedienne was reelected with a 99% majority. A new National Assembly was elected in 1977. The 261 members were selected from a list of 783 candidates, all *FLN* members who had gained party approval. The new assembly includes several women and numerous young people. The farmers and lower class workers were not as successful in their campaigns as were teachers and government personnel.

One of the problems which created tension between Algeria and Morocco was the status of the former Spanish Sahara—see *Western Sahara.* in the section on Morocco. However, with increased successes of Morocco in dealing with the rebel movement (or "independence movement" if you prefer), Algerian enthusiasm for the insurgents waned.

President Boumedienne died in late December 1978, the victim of a rare blood disease from which he had been suffering for several months. In early 1979 elections were held in which there was but one candidate: Colonel Chadli Bendjedid, former commander of the military district in western Algeria and informal coordinater of defense during Boumedienne's illness. He also became Secretary General of the *FLN*, the two positions interwoven in the one–party governmental structure. The president appeared to be somewhat more moderate than his predecessor, yet he stated that he would continue to uphold the traditional goals of the Algerian revolution—the usual ones . . . improve the social and economic conditions of the nation.

In early 1980 Algeria was shaken by riots led by Muslim fundamentalists who sacked hotels, cafes and restaurants where alcohol—a violation of Islamic teachings—was served. Algeria has always been one of the most secular nations of the Arab world, keeping religion *strictly* out of government, but the successful Islamic revolution in Iran has sparked a wave of "back to the basic teachings of the holy Koran" atmosphere in the country. The rioters also attacked several "pleasure houses" provided for Algerian troops stationed near the border with Tunisia. Alcohol and sin *had* to go if Muslim standards were to be held high.

President Chadli felt the riots were inspired by outsiders—and he may well have been referring to Libyan President Gadhafi. Some blamed Marxist–inspired students at the University of Algiers. If true, it was a curious alliance—Marxists who *deny* religion banding together with Muslims who place religion before all.

A serious problem occurred when there was a strike by about a quarter of the 70,000 students at the University. The group spoke only Arabic. This presented a problem in a country where French had been the predominant language of government and commerce, especially in higher–paying positions. This remnant of colonialism remained in spite of efforts to "arabize" society, which included the appointment of 600 young Arabic–trained judges.

President Chadli was elected to a third five–year term in 1989. But in a decade, Algeria had changed drastically, and at last painfully reflected years of foolish spending by the *FLN*, and fluctuations of world oil prices. The external debt was impossibly high—$28 billion—and required 80% of export earning to pay principal and interest on it. Algeria's population had changed dramatically in a generation. Literacy had more than doubled from 25% to 57%, agricultural workers had declined from 57% to 14% and service employment had increased from 26% to more than 75%.

The leadership of the *FLN* had squandered oil royalties in "window–dressing" spending on visible projects that sustained its popularity (at least on the surface) but *failed to invest for the future.* Business loans to sound, job–producing enterprises should have been the first priority, but weren't. Widespread corruption in the government added insult to injury. By the 1990s the unemployment rate of skilled people exceeded 30%. Young people faced with this bleak picture had been raised with the expectation of creature comforts associated with western life, and had rejected Islamic laws that banned alcohol and bikini bathing suits. With their dreams shattered, they felt that they had one of two alternatives: emigrate, or adopt Islamic fundamentalism. The first choice was not available.

Islamic fundamentalism offered an alternative to the *FLN*, and *any* alternative would be better, they reasoned, without thinking. What they did not and do not realize is that they were being used by ruthless manipulators who cared not one whit for their future. The message of Islamic fundamentalists throughout North Africa and the Middle East is quite simple: anti–westernism. And the fundamentalist leaders seek not religious purity—they seek the treasury of Algeria, for themselves, not for Algerians.

The president, in response to external and internal pressures, legalized political parties in 1989 and the first to register was the *Islamic Salvation Front (FIS)*. It had already been at work, clandestinely exploiting discontent among young people. As the movement gathered steam, President Chadli declared very firmly, "all attempts to return Islam to the era of charlatism (sic) and myths, or to use it an an instrument of demagogy (sic) and political opportunism" would be rejected. But that is exactly what has been and is now happening in Algeria.

But it didn't work. *FIS* candidates won a plurality but not a majority in the first

President Abdelaziz Bouteflika

round of multi–party elections in late 1991. The military, supported by hundreds of thousands of marchers in Algiers, cancelled the second round of balloting. President Chadli resigned and a five–man National Consultative Council was proclaimed to advise during a 12–month state of emergency. It initially was led by Mohamed Boudiaf, but he lasted three weeks before being gunned down. Subsequently, Brig. Gen. Liamine Zeroual was chosen as interim president. Murders, massacres and destruction became common; modern weaponry was widely available and used, received by the terrorists from Iraq and Iran via Sudan.

Terror and subversion continued from 1992 onward and still is found widely in Algeria. The Islamists are hopelessly split into at least 100 factions, each claiming to be the "correct one." Violence was increasingly directed against innocent foreigners and Algerian females, who were raped and tortured for months and then put to death.

The military embarked on an anti-terrorist campaign in 1994–5 calculated to demoralize the Islamists. The violent rebels were interned in camps in the remote desert where they burned during the day and froze at night. Word of this spread. This, other anti–terrorist measures, the arming of informal militias in rural areas and a very active female electorate, produced 64.5% of the vote for Liamine Zeroual; turnout was 75%. The liberal press and Islamists protested that the military stole the election. But international observers pronounced the contest fair and within accepted standards. The biggest factor was enraged women, fed up with an interpretation of Allah's will that permitted endless rape, torture and murder.

The victorious military decided to ensure the victory with a new constitution. It presented a new constitution to the electorate in November 1996 to accomplish this. Even though it proclaimed Islam as the state religion, it provided that no party or candidate could have a religious affiliation as a basis for candidacy. It established a new chamber in the legislature *appointed by the government,* the approval of which was necessary to pass any legislation. Infuriated, the Islamists opposed it; the *Armed Islamic Group (GIA)* vowed to slit the throat of any person who left home to vote.

The government mustered about 300,000 military and police to safeguard the election and the vote was 80% for adoption. Some called the referendum a vote to confirm a military dictatorship; there is a degree of accuracy to that accusation. But it is also accurate to conclude that voters, particularly middle class ones, were sick and tired of all the killings since 1992, and wanted anything which would put an end to this. Unfortunately, their hope has not been rewarded.

The brutal, unspeakably horrible massacres of the innocents continued into 1998. Savagery was not murder alone. When *GIA* roving bands swept into villages on their killing rampages they would often carry off young women to their mountain hideaways. Estimates vary, but up to 1600 young women between the ages of 13 and 20 have been abducted. Many who escaped were pregnant and, given an absolute ban on abortion in the country, were forced to bear the consequences of political violence. In April 1998, the Islamic Supreme Council, the highest religious authority in the country, authorized abortion for rape victims. The decision came following pressure from women's groups and firmly rejects those who would use rape as a political weapon.

Parliamentary elections in 1997 resulted in Algeria's first multiparty legislature, despite intense criticism of electoral procedures. The National People's Assembly,

Algiers' *Casbah*, the native section of the capital AP/Wide World Photo

or lower house, has 380 members, elected for five year terms in multi–seat constituencies by proportional representation. President Zeroual's *Rassemblement national pour la démocratie* (*RND*) was the big winner, taking 156 seats with 38% of the vote. Despite comfortable majorities in parliament and in the government, President Zeroual surprised his countrymen by resigning his office in September 1998, effective with the selection of a successor in April 1999 elections.

In the shadowy world of Algerian politics, characterized more by opacity than transparency, Zeroual had lost the confidence of Algeria's real rulers, the army. With the president's resignation, hopes that new elections could help national reconciliation and move Algeria beyond its current impasse abounded. The army's top officier, Lieutenant-General Mohamed Lamari, announced that "access to power through free election will be an irreversible practice." Zeroual himself had promised free and fair elections, but they were not to be.

By January 1999 it was clear the army had rallied to a consensus candidate, the former Foreign Minister Abdelaziz Bouteflika. The secretary-general of the ruling *RND*, Tahar Benbaïbeche, charged that there had been "pressure amounting to threats" on party members to support Bouteflika. The very next day Benbaïbeche was roundly criticized as a failure by the retired former Defense Minister General Khaled Nezzar. The party's policy-making council met in special session and sacked Benbaïbeche as secretary-general, replacing him with the currently

Lounès Matoub

unemployed former prime minister, Ahmed Ouyahia.

In March, seven candidates were in the running, but when President Zeroual refused to meet with them shortly before actual balloting to discuss charges of electoral fraud, six withdrew, leaving Abdelaziz Bouteflika the sole candidate. The election was held; Bouteflika was "elected." Once again Algerian hopes were dashed.

Given the dubious nature of his election, President Bouteflika needed to show progress on ending Algeria's violence and assert his own identity—to prove, in other words, he was more than a creature of the generals. In July he launched a "civil concord" initiative, putting his credibility on the line almost immediately. To achieve stability he offered amnesty to all but the worst offenders in Algeria's 8-year civil war. They would have to lay down their arms by mid-January 2000; if not they would be wiped out.

The results of the amnesty are debatable at best. The government formalized a deal with the *Islamic Salvation Army* (*AIS*), the largest rebel group and military wing of the banned *Islamic Salvation Front* (*FIS*), but in fact, *AIS* had been observing a cease-fire since 1997. The two most notorious armed movements—the *Armed Islamic Group* (*GIA*) and the *Salafist Group for Preaching and Combat* (*GSPC*)—rejected the amnesty and stepped up their attacks. Nine thousand more Algerians were killed in 2000.

The army seemed incapable or unwilling to apply the second half of President Bouteflika's amnesty proposal—destruction of those who did not sign on. Only when he shifted from speaking of "civil concord" to talking of "national harmony," a concept which seemed to imply a broadening of the amnesty offer, did the army massively engage the armed Islamists. Organized into small cells, the militants have proved difficult to eradicate. Violence remains as intractable as ever.

President Bouteflika has failed to establish his authority as separate and independent of the army, and every attempt to do so puts a further chill in their relationship. Retired General Labri Belkheir, long a heavy-weight within the army and government, has been made head of the presidential office presumably to facilitate communication between the two realms.

Relations with the parties that form a governing coalition have also worsened. In early 2001 the coalition, which includes the *National Liberation Front* (*FLN*), *National Democratic Rally* (*RND*), *Rally for Culture and Democracy* (*RCD*), *Movement of Society for Peace* (*MSP*), *National Republican Alliance* (*ANR*) and the *Ennahda Movement*, attributed the country's declining security to the president's isolation and refusal to involve his political partners in a discussion of the country's vital issues. He had, it appears, not consulted with them in two years.

The coalition also criticized the president for failing to deal with the nation's on-going social and economic crises. Almost 40% of Algeria's 30 million people now live below the poverty line, and the gap between rich and poor steadily increases. Official figures put unemployment at 40%. Housing stock is inadequate, and there have been riots of the government's allocation of apartments.

Like the governing coalition of parties, the General Union of Algerian Workers has criticized the government's lack of consultation. In March 2001, it organized two days of demonstrations to protest a new law liberalizing the hydrocarbon sector. The disturbance signals the disillusionment and discontent felt by average Algerians and, coupled with army suspicion of the President, suggest how difficult it might be to finish out his term.

The army itself stands in the glare of international critical attention resulting from the publication of Habib Souaïdia's *The Dirty War* (*La Sale Guerre*, éditions La Découverte). Confirming what many had long suspected, the author describes his experiences as a junior officer in the Algerian army in horrific detail: "I saw colleagues burn alive a child of 15, soldiers disguised as terrorists massacre civilians, colonels kill mere suspects in cold blood, officers torture Islamists to death."

The Parisian daily newspaper *Le Monde* called for an international inquiry into the Algerian army, and a group of French intellectuals publicly attacked the French government for its uncritical support of the Algerian regime during the 1990s, including arms sales and military training. There were also calls for the EU to condition any further aid to Algeria on its cooperation with an international inquiry into the affair.

To calm things down the army chief of staff, General Mohamed Lamari, condemned the "mad media campaign from abroad" and claimed the book was an attempt to divide the army. Certainly the army does not take dissidence easily. In February, just as Souaïdia's book was making headlines, a group of army dissidents calling themselves the Algerian Free Officers' Movement (MOAL) reported that 47 officers had been massacred in a barracks prison.

The officers, who had completed their sentences and were supposed to be freed shortly, were killed in cold blood, said MOAL's communiqué, by a special commando group dispatched by General Lamari and the head of military intelligence, Gen Mohamed Mediene. At mid-Spring the atmosphere within the army was described as "tense."

Culture: The conflict between the army and Islamists in Algeria is a struggle to define the country's identity and future. The army, francophone and secular, is adamantly opposed to Arab-speaking Islamists who advocate an Arab and Muslim identity for Algeria.

Struggling to maintain its own language and identity is Algeria's Berber-speaking minority. Representing 20 to 30% of the population, Berbers are the original inhabitants of North Africa. They fled to the mountains to resist successive waves of invaders—Romans, Arabs, Turks and French—and preserved both language (*tamazight*) and customs despite conversion to Islam. Berber women, for example, go without the veil.

Algeria's Kabyle mountains, the Berber heartland, remain a focal point of opposition to the government. Kabylia is one of the country's poorest and most populous regions. Unemployment is rife, and Berber youth have few future expectations beyond present misery. People there complain of a lack of government assistance and claim they must survive on remittances from relatives who have emigrated to France.

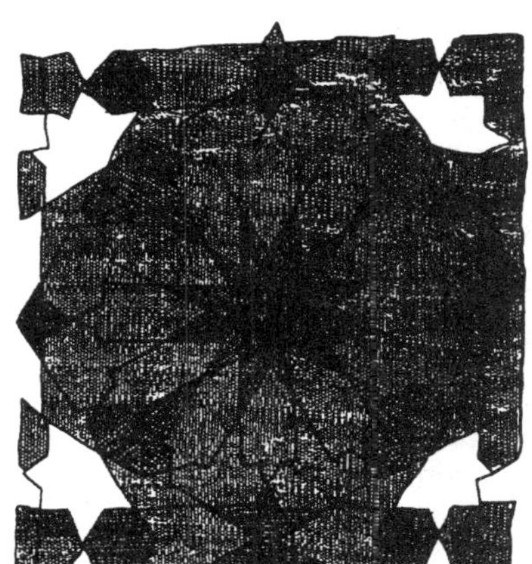

The Sahara's ever–shifting sand dunes hide a tiny fresh–water oasis

The singer Lounès Matoub, who was assassinated in an ambush in 1998, gave musical voice to Berber nationalism. But bloody Kabylia riots in the Spring of 2001 showed that the disaffection of Berber youth had moved beyond cultural claims. Their shouted slogans laid bare the social and economic crisis the regime faces. "You cannot kill us," they screamed at the national police, "we are already dead." "Give is work and housing and hope and there will be calm." The targets of their destructive rage were the symbols of government presence and occupation.

Economy: Oil production started in 1957 at Hassi Messouad and Ejelek; it was quickly expanded through pipelines, refineries and additional wells made possible by investment of foreign oil companies. Since that time oil has come to dominate Algeria's economy. Proven reserves remain at 9.2 billion barrels, but new discoveries and continuing exploration will add even greater depth to these reserves. The hydrocarbon industry accounts for 97% of Algeria's export earnings. With the rise of oil prices, the country has had windfall income. Some 802,000 barrels a day of crude oil are pumped from southern wells for export. In 2000 total export earnings were up 56%, producing a trade surplus of over ten billion dollars.

Although the state's coffers are full, there are few plans in the 2001 budget that would improve the condition of the bulk of Algeria's population. Fifty-eight percent of the population is younger than 25, and unemployment stands at 49% among those aged between 20 to 25. Economic growth in 2000 was about 3.5%, hardly enough to keep up with growing unemployment. Monthly wages average around $110.

Aside from the oil and gas sectors, there is little direct foreign investment given the prevailing violence. Algeria has 130 trillion cubic feet of proven natural gas reserves and is Europe's most important supplier of natural gas. Two important pipelines, with an export capacity of 1.15 trillion cubic feet per year, transport the gas to Europe. The 667-mile Trans-Mediterranean line carries 847.6 billion cubic feet to Italy and ultimately to Slovenia. The Maghreb-Europe Gas line, 1,013 miles long, carries 300.2 billion cubic feet of gas to Spain, Portugal and beyond. Algeria has had a longstanding policy of converting to gas for energy, freeing up petroleum for exportation. Currently, about 95% of the country's electricity is generated by gas.

In early 2001 the state-owned hydrocarbon monopoly, Sonatrach, signed an investment agreement with two French and Malyasian companies for oil and gas field exploration and development. Under the agreement, Gas de France and Petronas will invest about $22.5 million over the next three years to determine the potential of the gas field. If results prove satisfactory and the project goes ahead, investment will reach $2 billion. Petronas would put up 45% of the total, Sonatrach 30% and Gas de France the rest.

Agriculture makes up about 10 to 12% of the economy and consists mainly of grains, fruits, cattle, vegetables and poultry. Private industry is dominated by crony networks of former military chiefs and government leaders. Algeria's thriving black market is believed to account for around 20% of the country's economic activity

The country's external debt is well over $26 billion, and debt service payments absorb much of the government's windfall earnings from higher oil prices. Debt relief from France is dubious following the furor created by Souaïdia's *The Dirty War*. Further tension between the two was generated in April 2001 when a French court accepted a law suit against the former Algerian defense minister, General Khaled Nezzar, for systematic use of torture in the 1990s.

Heavy arms purchases from Russia may be part of Algeria's working off some $4 billion of outstanding debt to that country. For years Algeria was a leading customer for Russian jets, tanks, armored cars and other weapons, becoming one of Moscow's largest debtors. In late 2000, Russia and Algeria signed a contract on supplying Su-24 bombers costing $120 million. During a visit of President Bouteflika to Russia, there was much talk of cooperation in the energy and weapons sectors, and Russian firms are salivating at the prospects of upgrading and refurbishing the Algerian armed forces.

The Future: Key to any success for an Algerian president is the ability to assert the status and prestige of the presidency without threatening what Algerians call *"Le Pouvoir"*—the power of the generals. President Bouteflika has failed to do this. Neither the presidency nor army has the popular legitimacy to deal successfully with simmering discontent on the streets and in the factories. The Berber intifada revealed the enormous gulf between regime and populace. The criticism of young Berbers—that the regime is corrupt, nepotistic and repressive—has resonance throughout the land. The future looks rocky indeed.

In the Valley of the Kings . . . the Pharaohs gaze into Eternity Photo: Jon Markham Morrow

The Arab Republic of Egypt

Commuters at rush hour in Cairo

WORLD BANK Photo by Ray Witlin

Area: 1,000,258 sq. km. = 386,200 sq. mi. (The size of Texas and New Mexico).
Population: 67,273,906 (July 1999 est.)
Capital City: Cairo (Pop. 16 million, estimated, including numerous suburbs).
Climate: Dry, semi–tropical and hot. Temperatures are lower in the north during winter.
Neighboring Countries: Libya (West); Israel (Northeast); The Sudan (South).
Official Language: Arabic.
Other Principal Languages: Armenian, Domari, (spoken by Muslim Gypsies), Kenuzi-Dongola, and Nobiin. English and French are widely understood by educated classes.
Ethnic groups: Egyptians, Bedouins, and Berbers 99%, Greek, Nubian, Armenian, other European, primarily Italian and French 1%.
Principal Religions: Muslim (mostly Sunni) 94% (official estimate), Coptic Christian and other 6% (official estimate).
Chief Commercial Products: Crude oil and petroleum products, cotton yarn, raw cotton, textiles, metal products, and chemicals.
GNP per capita: 1200 US$
Currency: Egyptian Pound.
Former Colonial Status: British Protectorate (1914–1922); British exercised domination in various forms over Egypt from 1882 to 1952.
Independence Date: July 23, 1952.
Chief of State: Hosni Mubarak, President.
National Flag: Three horizontal stripes of red, white and black with the golden Eagle of Saladin centered on the white stripe.

Strategically occupying the northeast corner of Africa, the land route between Africa and Asia, and commanding the sea route between the Mediterranean and Indian Ocean via the Suez Canal, Egypt is a rainless expanse of desert. The habitable portion of this country has historically been only about 4% of its area. The remainder, within the great Sahara Desert, is a hot, endless landscape of sand dunes dotted with occasional green oases. It is not difficult for the inexperienced traveler to become lost in the sands of the desert since there are utterly no landmarks. The nomads have no trouble finding their way along the routes through the desert which have existed for centuries. Irrigation projects are slowly transforming the desert wasteland into fertile ground in areas close to the Nile River.

The people of Egypt are gathered on the banks of the Nile with a population density of more than 2,000 people per square mile. The Nile is the lifeblood of Egypt, providing water for irrigation and (in former years) fertile silt for the farmlands. With the exception of Mt. Sinai located on the peninsula named for it, there are few other mountains in Egypt.

History: Egypt is the oldest cohesive nation in the world, its history dating back to before 3,000 B.C. For details of early and colonial history, see Historical Background and *The British in Africa.*

By the end of World War II in which Egypt was neutral, restiveness of the lower classes rose to feverish heights. The people were governed and exploited by King Farouk and a number of wealthy landowners *(Pashas)* who controlled almost all the wealth and spent long periods of their time in Europe.

A huge mob revolted and seized Cairo in early 1952; in the succeeding months, a *junta* of military officers assumed control of the nation and in mid–1952 ousted King Farouk and his court of followers. The succeeding years were ones of strife and turmoil because of continuing friction with the newly–founded Israeli state in nearby Palestine. Egypt found itself in the difficult position of being the front offensive/defensive line against a group deeply hated by Arabs because of their seizure of land from Palestinians.

The United States refused in 1956 to finance a high dam at Aswan on the Nile

River. Egypt nationalized the Suez Canal with the intent of using income from that source to build the dam. British, French and Israeli forces invaded, withdrawing only under intense pressure from the U.S. and the Soviet Union. Ultimately, Egypt signed an agreement to compensate the shareholders of the Canal Company.

There was a brief period of union with Syria from 1958 to 1961 which created the name United Arab Republic; Syria withdrew and Egypt later reverted to its old name.

Gamal Abd–al Nasser (Nasir) completely dominated the Egyptian government after the ouster of the King; he dissolved two parliaments and ruled through a tightly–controlled *Arab Socialist Union* which was the only political organization permitted. Nasser's desire for power, not only within Egypt, but in the whole Middle East, caused him to make several mistakes. After nationalization of the Suez Canal, he announced as a gesture of support for Arabs displaced from Palestine by Israel that no shipping either to or from Israel would be permitted through the waterway. Israeli shipping to and from the Indian Ocean was then diverted through the Gulf of Aqaba and the port city of Eilat; Mediterranean ports served as terminals for vessels from Europe and the Western Hemisphere. This arrangement prevailed for a decade, but in 1967, pressured by other Arab nations, Nasser decided to change things.

Announcing sympathy for the Syrian government which was loudly protesting *possible* aggression on the part of Israel, in 1967 Nasser demanded withdrawal of UN forces located along armistice demarcation lines with Israel, supposedly to enable Egypt to assist Syria (if necessary).

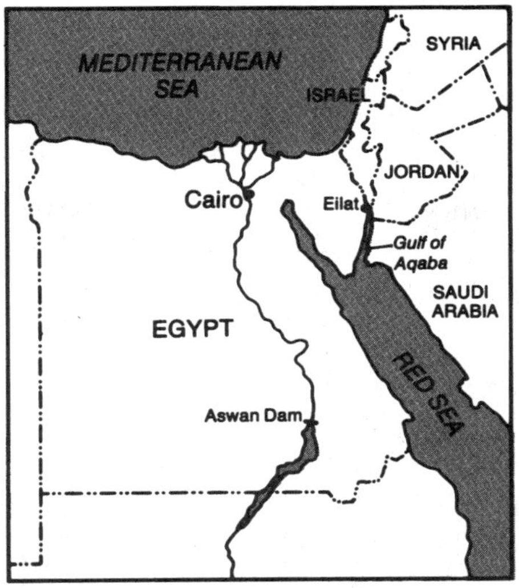

Mild–mannered Secretary General U Thant of the UN ordered the immediate withdrawal of the forces without consulting the Security Council or the General Assembly. Nasser's forces quickly occupied the heights of Sharm–al–Sheikh, a strategic overlook commanding the entrance to the Gulf of Aqaba. It was announced that all shipping to or from Israel was barred from the Gulf. *Al Ahram,* the semi–official newspaper of Cairo, published an editorial gleefully declaring that Israel had no choice but to fight if it wished to have access to the Red Sea.

Seizing the offensive, Israel made a three–pronged attack against Egypt, Syria and Jordan in mid–1967, bombing Iraqi airfields to eliminate air assistance from that country. The initial surprise assault on Egypt was by air from the *west,* catching almost all Egyptian aircraft (supplied by the Soviets) on the ground. In the ensuing five days of battle, the Arab forces were completely routed. A UN–imposed cease–fire established an uneasy peace, which continued in effect until the fighting gradually escalated in 1970–1971, requiring another informal cease–fire agreement. In order to replace $5 billion in lost arms, the USSR supplied almost $7 billion in equipment to Egypt after 1967.

Nasser continually threatened a war to regain occupied territory. Trial of the 1967 military leadership of Egypt for incompetence resulted in sentences of 10 to 15 years, which were protested as being too lenient. Most of those still in prison were quietly released in 1974. Unrest continued in 1968 and at one point Cairo was torn by riots.

Nasser died unexpectedly in 1970 from a reported heart attack; Egypt and the Arab world were plunged into mourning. There was a dramatic funeral for the fallen leader.

Anwar Sadat, installed as Vice–President in 1969 and elected president by a vote of 70% in 1970 was supposed to be a weak figurehead, but things turned out otherwise. He quickly ousted his rivals and made frequent and dramatic threats to "invade" and "crush" Israel, but until 1973 took no actual move in that direction. This delay was the basis of criticism, which was dealt with by cabinet changes, party expulsions and threats. When the Soviets leveled criticism at the quality of the Egyptian military prowess, Sadat decreed the ouster of all Soviet military advisors in 1972, charging that the fault lay with the Soviet failure to furnish enough modern weaponry to enable Egypt to conquer Israel. The reasons for the move were threefold—(1) to satisfy anti–Soviet feeling among conservative Egyptians and the leadership of Saudi Arabia with which a closer alliance was being promoted; (2) to move toward closer relations with the United States (which did not respond); and (3) to fight a war without the close observation and direction of the Soviets, who would take credit for any successes in battle.

Israeli control in the Sinai peninsula after the 1967 war tightened; there were Israeli settlements, and oil wells appeared. In an effort to wrest the occupied area from Israel, Egypt and Syria launched a two–front attack with the military and financial support of other Arab states and the USSR. The move, made during the Jewish religious festival of *Yom Kippur,* in October 1973, took Israel completely off guard and it appeared that Egypt might well be successful during the initial days of the conflict. Israel responded by first driving the Syrians back to within shell range of their capital city of Damascus, then turned to the Egyptian front. After the largest tank battle in history, the Israelis made daring crossings of the Suez Canal, launching a "pincer" attack which

View of Cairo from the Mohammed Ali Mosque Photo: Jon Markham Morrow

Dhows **catching the Nile's breezes** Photo: Susan L. Thompson

threatened to surround the Egyptians. Within hours the tide of battle had shifted and Cairo itself was threatened.

In such a situation, a cease–fire was arranged with U.S. mediation. The U.S. literally strong–armed the Israelis into giving up all territory west of the canal and enough territory in the Sinai Peninsula to salvage Sadat's reputation. Additional Sinai territory, including the Abu Rudeis oil field, was ceded to Egypt in late 1976. The Suez Canal, closed since the 1967 strife, was in operation by mid-1975 with U.S. assistance.

Although progress toward some basic settlement of the Egyptian–Israeli conflict was supposed to take place in 1974, because of Israeli stubbornness, the parties were as far apart in 1977 as they ever had been, particularly after election of a conservative, militant and expansionist government in Israel. Although the Soviets rearmed Egypt and Syria, in 1977 Soviet–Egyptian relations were at an all–time low, with Cairo newspapers and *Pravda* exchanging insults. Egypt shifted away from Soviet support to contributions from Arab oil states (principally Saudi Arabia) and from the United States. During the period 1957–1977 the Soviets had poured more than $20 billion into Egypt with nothing to show for their investment.

Elections in late 1976 resulted in an overwhelming victory for Sadat's *Arab Socialist Party* (280 out of 342 seats). The elections for the People's Assembly were genuinely free. By–elections and appointed members filled the remaining seats.

Following thirty years of strife, Sadat undertook the most controversial move of his career: he flew to Jerusalem to address a session of the Israeli Knesset. The Israelis were stunned and excited at this "breakthrough." Sadat delivered an impassioned plea for a just and lasting peace, but he held fast to the position that Israel must withdraw from occupied Arab territory and must grant Palestinians "their rights." Israeli Prime Minister Begin countered with the Israeli position: we are willing to negotiate, but your price is too high. He insisted that Israel must have "defensible borders."

After much "shuttle diplomacy," a peace treaty between Egypt and Israel was signed at The White House on March 26, 1979. When each nation was assured it would be protected from surprise attack, placement of their respective troops and a UN peace–keeping contingent, the treaty boiled down to these key points: (1) Israel agreed to withdraw all its armed forces and civilians from the Sinai Peninsula within a period of three years; (2) Egypt guaranteed passage of Israeli ships and cargoes through the Suez Canal; (3) both nations pledged full diplomatic, cultural and economic relations and (4) there would be a free movement of people and goods between the two countries. There was some extremely vague language about some sort of autonomy for the Gaza Strip and the West Bank of the Jordan River, both of which remain yet to be accomplished.

While reviewing a military parade in late 1981, Sadat was fatally gunned down by rebel soldiers who were members of *Al Jihad* ("Holy War!"). Eight days after the slaying and one day after a overwhelming nationwide referendum, Vice–President Hosni Mubarak took the oath as Egypt's fourth president, pledging to continue the policies of the fallen leader.

Egypt's president is a stocky former bomber pilot with a style totally different from that of Sadat. Hosni Mubarak is plain–spoken, quiet and practical. He has conferred with a wide range of advisors, experts and even opposition leaders before taking any important action. He immediately was faced with a boycott of Egypt by Arab nations other than the Sudan. But by 1985 he largely placated the would–be enemies of Egypt and relationships were informally resumed. In 1987 it became official—Egypt was again accepted as a member of the Arab League.

The president had tried to reconcile the many factions within Egypt—Muslims, Christians, the political elite, professionals, leftists, and even the *Muslim Brotherhood,* the arch foe of Sadat during his final years. Multitudes of political prisoners have been freed, but until 1990, many were retained without being charged. Muslim extremists, including those of *Al Jihad,* are not tolerated; more than 2,000 have been imprisoned and about 200 were convicted. President Mubarak visited Washington in 1982 and succeeded in obtaining a substantial aid package, both financial and military, over which Egypt has a large degree of control. He unsuccessfully tried to pressure Washington into derailing Israel's attempted colonization of the West Bank territory.

Mubarak decreed the legality of political parties and guaranteed them freedom of the press. Elections were held in 1984. Somewhat less than half of the 12.4 million registered voters cast ballots, but gave an overwhelming vote of confidence to Mubarak's *National Democratic Party,* which won 73% of the total seats in the People's Assembly—391 out of 448 which were contested. The *New Wafd Party* won 15.1% and a total of 57 seats.

The years 1984–86 were not kind to the president, however, No matter what was been done, one or more factions hotly opposed it. Food price increases led to widespread riots. The conservative Muslims continued to snipe at Mubarak. When he released the Coptic Pope from desert exile imposed by Sadat and within a few days attended a midnight mass at which the president urged peace between the two groups, the Muslim Brotherhood denounced Mubarak as an infidel.

With an external debt of about $25 billion, economic conditions in Egypt declined sharply in the mid–1980s. Foreign

Anwar Sadat

credit, principally from Arab nations, had been refused because of what was perceived to be Mubarak's conciliatory attitude toward the Israelis. In the latter part of the decade, foreign assistance again became available. U.S. aid and assistance has been steady, about $3 billion per year.

The basic problems of the late 1980s substantially remain: falling oil revenues, lowered receipts fram canal revenues and smaller remittances from Egyptians living outside of their country. Widespread subsidies for just about everything and everyone are costly, and have been steadily opposed by the International Monetary Fund which desires a structured, organized welfare system for the truly needy.

April 1987 elections resulted in an outstanding victory for the *National Democratic Party,* successor to the *Arab Socialist Party.* The Muslim Brotherhood, although officially banned in the 1950s by Nasser, reemerged by entering into an alliance with the *Liberal Party* and the *Socialist Labor Party.* This combination became the official opposition. The government had allowed the Brotherhood to resume operations to counter the rigidly fundamentalist *Islamic Jihad,* emanating from Iran and responsible for the assassination of Sadat.

Elections in late 1990 resulted in an equally impressive victory by President Mubarak and his party (348 out of 444 elected seats) in the National Assembly. The president's periodic attempts to mediate the lingering impasse between Israel and the Palestinians over the West Bank have met with little success because of (1) Israeli rigidity reflecting the desires of its citizens and (2) Mubarak's unwillingness to alienate Arab nations by seeming to be too conciliatory.

The intensity of Islamic fundamentalist action rose dramatically in 1992 and has been a matter of paramount importance since then. With support from Iran and Sudan, it has sought, in the name of Islam, to oust the Mubarak government from power because of Egypt's reputation as a secular rather than a religious state. Violence and terrorism, allegedly to enforce the will of Allah on earth, became more and more frequent, and has been directed particularly against tourists. Severe counter–measures taken by the government, including trial by military courts, gave rise to international criticism for human rights violations.

Although there are several fundamentalist groups, *Al–Jihad* is the principal organization behind fundamentalist violence. It has had a unit in New York City, under the guidance of fugitive Sheikh Abdul Rahman, which bombed the World Trade Center in 1992 and conspired to commit similar acts elsewhere. Several have been convicted and sentenced.

Terrorist attacks steadily escalated in 1993–5, including execution–style slayings of security force personnel. After brief trials by military courts, several dozen terrorists were publicly hanged without appeal. Attempts on the lives of prominent government officials have been made. An offer to negotiate was made by the terrorists in mid–1996. The government responded with the statement "There can be no dialogue with killers and criminals who betray their own country." The government attitude reflected a decision made by President Mubarak in 1996 to take all measures necessary to eradicate the Islamists.

President Sadat speaks before the Israeli *Knesset* AP/Wide World Photo

The military, 430,000 strong, is in sympathy with the efforts of the Mubarak government to control (and preferably eliminate) the fundamentalists.

With tourism income sagging, President Mubarak made a decision in 1995 to widen an anti-terrorist, anti-Islamist campaign. Widespread arrests occurred, followed by military tribunals and public, publicized death sentences for some and prison terms for a great many more. Enthusiasm for this accelerated greatly when there was an attempt on the president's life while he was visiting Addis Ababa, Ethiopia, in midyear. Some claim all of this was calculated to influence November 1995 elections.

Held in November, they resulted in an overwhelming victory for the ruling *National Democratic Party* (*NDP*). Political power in Egypt is concentrated in the *NDP* which occupies almost all the seats in the lower house of Egypt's parliament—the People's Assembly. Elections to Egypt's upper house, the Shura (Consultative) Council took place in mid–1998 amid general apathy among voters and a boycott by those parties capable of fielding candidates. Two–thirds of the largely powerless body is elected directly, and half of these must be workers and farmers. The President of the Republic appoints the other third.

There are no balloon-dropping political party nominating conventions in Egypt. Instead, the presidential candidate must be nominated by parliament—the People's Assembly and the Shura Council—and then approved in a countrywide referendum. Unsurprisingly Hosni Mubarak was nominated to a fourth presidential term in July 1999; his National Democratic Party controls 94 per cent of the seats in parliament. In September Egyptian voters marked their ballots—a green circle to approve, a black circle to disapprove—and 93.97% voted to approve Mubarak's nomination.

The People's Assembly election of October 2000, the first conducted with the supervision of judges to assure fairness, proved something of an embarrassment for President Mubarak's *National Democratic Party.* While the party nominally holds 85% of the seats in the Assembly, most of the new MPs representing the party originally ran as independents. As a consequence, the government's control of its parliamentary majority may not be as sure a thing as it has been in the past. The Assembly elections also marked the return of the *Muslim Brotherhood,* which managed to win 17 seats despite the usual harassment by the authorities.

Given the dominance of a single party in Egypt, one can understand how opposition sometimes is expressed in outrageous political violence. In November 1997 members of the *Gama'a al-Islamiyya,* Egypt's main Islamic militant group, perpetrated the deadliest attack since the Islamic insurgency started in 1992. Nearly 60 tourists were murdered at Luxor, some of their bodies maimed and mutilated before police killed the attackers. President Mubarak fired his Interior Minister, but the extremists achieved their goal: the impact on tourism was catastrophic. Hotelkeepers reported occupancy down 90% following the attack.

President Hosni Mubarak

In Egypt, stability has been privileged over expression. As a consequence the regime is authoritarian and political life is stifled. Dissent and criticism are seen, in varying degrees, as a threat to stability. Islamist organizations, which range from the moderate *Muslim Brotherhood* to the radical *Gama'a al-Islamiyya,* have been viewed as a collective threat. All have been banned. Their leaders have been harassed and arrested, their supporters silenced.

The search for stability through silence is itself destabilizing. Denied voice in the political arena, Islamist sentiment erupts elsewhere, as three days of student rioting in Cairo over an eighteen-year old Syrian novel indicate. Haider Haider's 1983 novel, *Seaweed*, refers to a despairing religious skeptic who commits suicide by drowning himself in the sea. Reprinted in November 1999, it ignited violent student protests in May 2000, suggesting a calculated search for alternative means of expression outside a severely circumscribed political arena. Some indeed saw it as an attempt to gain popular support for Islamist candidates in the upcoming fall 2000 parliamentary election campaign.

The most radical of Islamist organizations, *Gama'a al-Islamiyya* or *Islamic Group,* has been militarily defeated, crushed by force of arms. Militarily defeated the group splintered internally. Its military wing declared a unilateral cease-fire in 1999, but some cells refused the call.

Confident in its military victory over *Gama'a al-Islamiyya,* the government has begun to release some of its jailed supporters. Some 2,500 members of the *Gama'a* have been released since the cease-fire declaration. Reports indicate the remaining prisoners are no longer subjected to torture. Up to 30,000 prisoners are still believed to be behind bars.

The *Muslim Brotherhood* has long been outlawed, although in the past it has operated under other parties' labels. The government has frustrated younger Islamists in efforts to form a more modern-minded party. And recently the authorities arrested several members of the *Brotherhood* to prevent them from gaining influence in Egypt's labor unions.

The determination to control political life in the name of stability has had a corrosive effect on Egypt's political system. Power is dangerously concentrated in the hands of one man, the president. An aging generation of politicians has been ossified in place, with little intention of giving up the benefits of power. The system has become hermetically sealed off from social reality and desperately needs to be opened up. Its reinvigoration requires new blood and ideas.

Like Libya, Egypt has turned its attention to sub–Saharan Africa in the past years. The interest is both economic and political. Africa represents potential markets for Egyptians. African states also represent potential allies for Egypt on the issue at the center of Egyptian concern: the sharing and use of Nile waters. Egyptian Foreign Minister Amre Moussa criss-crossed the continent in April 1997 strengthening ties and opening markets. In Uganda, Egypt is involved in hydroelectricity. In Mali, agreements were made to set up joint ventures in cotton. In South Africa joint economic research teams have been created. Like their Libyan counterparts, though without so public an aspect, Egyptian diplomats have offered mediation services in a variety of African conflict situations. They have offered mediation in the Sudanese civil war. Egypt even got involved in trying to resolve the Somali conflict, though was politely told by IGAD (Intergovernmental Authority for development) mediators, Ethiopia in the lead, to mind its own business.

Confronted with Ethiopian opposition to present water-sharing agreements, Egypt has begun to normalize its relations with the *National Islamic Front (NIF)* government in Sudan. It was the NIF regime that had once sent a hit squad to assassinate President Mubarak in Addis Ababa, so observers were caught off guard when Egyptian authorities set about improving relations in late 1997. Since then, Egypt and Sudan have relaunched the joint Nile steamer service, moved to resolve disputes over confiscated properties (seized and nationalized by Sudan in 1993 and 1995) and begun discussions about ministerial exchanges. Hosni Mubarak also met with John Garang, leader of the southern rebellion against the NIF regime. He was assured that Garang's *Sudan People's Liberation Front* had no desire to break up the territorial unity of Sudan. The last thing Egypt wants on its Southern border is an imploding state.

Culture: The backbone of Egyptian society traditionally has been the peasant. Largely immovable, remaining in the area of their ancestors, they are energetic and fatalistic. An age–old class system is now virtually extinct, replaced by a large measure of individual pride among the people. Formerly termed *Fellahin* (plowmen), in recent years these peasants, densely packed along the Nile, are engaging in increasingly modern methods of farming, although beans and dark bread are still the staple food for millions.

Illiteracy, once widespread, has been substantially reduced; 44% are literate in Arabic or another language. In the upper Nile region there are a large number of Nubian–descended people with a culture derived from ancient traditions and customs. A small number of Bedouin nomads live in black tents in the desert. There are an estimated five million Christians in Egypt, members of the Coptic Church established in the days of the Apostles. Tens of thousands of college and university students periodically cause disturbances in the large cities for the usual reasons.

Cairo contains more than 16 million people—the largest city in Africa and the Middle East. Nearly two million automobiles clog its streets and pour asphyxiating exhausts into the atmosphere. To this cement, iron, chemical and metal factories and smelters offer their noxious contributions. Fumes from tons of daily garbage, uncollected, rise to join the smog. The city of a thousand minarets is almost always veiled in a cloak of yellow–gray haze. With too much of everything—noise, dust, heat, garbage and hawkers—Cairo ranks high among the world's urban stress zones. For the tourist, the city is a difficult stop. Noses run, eyes water. Many try to see the

Suez Canal

His Holiness Pope Shenuda III of the Egyptian Coptic Church, a prelate who also enjoys an occasional Coca-Cola
Photo: Wayne C. Thompson

major sights—the pyramids, the Museum, the grand market—in a day and then move to less polluted centers.

Cairo's new governor has plans for the chaotic city: extending water, sewage and telephone systems; reclaiming the banks of the Nile for public parks. There are also plans to restore crumbling Islamic architecture and remove squatter settlements. Contractors are being found to haul away the 8,000 tons of garbage generated daily. Taxis, minivans and city buses are switching to compressed natural gas—a fuel system in which Cairo is now a world leader.

Egyptian women are slowly gaining legal protection and rights in a male–dominated society. The tortured course of rules governing female circumcision finally concluded at the end of 1997. In December the country's highest judicial authority, the Council of State, banned the practice of excision, even when the consent of child or parent is given. The court ruled that excision—surgical removal of the clitoris—was physical mutilation as defined in the Penal Code and was therefore punishable by the law. Although there is no Koranic sanction for the practice, female circumcision has long been practiced in Egypt. Indeed the operation has traditionally been seen as a mark of virtue and guarantor of modesty. In 1997 a detailed demographic survey indicated that more than 97% of women and girls had been through the ordeal.

In early 1999 the government introduced a modification of law codes to give women greater divorce rights. Islamic law allows a man divorce by simple repetition of a ritual formula three times—and divorce is immediate. A woman, on the other hand, might have to go through years of litigation if her husband were unwilling to grant divorce. Every year some 20,000 women went before the courts requesting a divorce and if it is not given immediately, the woman remained under the legal tutelage of her husband who could, for example, prevent her from getting a passport.

The new code was finally approved in January 2000 after rousing heated controversy. (Hard-line Muslim clerics had described it as a threat to the stability of society.) The reforms of Egyptian family law are far-reaching. A woman will now be able to divorce her husband, with or without his assent. She is required to return any dowry or its equivalent in cash or property. And she will also be able to call on the Egyptian government to garnishee her husband's wages if he refuses to provide for her. If he disappears or cannot pay a court-ordered living allowance, she will be able to draw from a special state bank to keep her family afloat.

Lost in the politics of compromise was a provision that would have allowed Egyptian women to travel abroad without the permission of their husbands.

Egyptian moral standards are being severely tested by pornography that comes from the skies. Draconian Egyptian censorship finds itself impotent before satellite broadcasts coming from the Dutch "Erotica" channel, or the French "Eros TV." Originally encrypted, the channels required the purchase of a decoder which usually had to be arranged under the table. Decoders are now more and more openly sold and advertisements for them have even appeared in the official press. In early 1999, however, Eros TV began broadcasting its erotic films in the clear, from 1 am to 6 am. It's meant a boom business for all–night cafes, which have raised their prices during broadcast hours. The cafes became especially popular during Ramadan when Egyptians do not go to bed 'til dawn. Conservative editorial writers spoke of "traditional enemies" who wanted "to sap the foundations of an Arab and Islamic society by means of massive perversion."

Over the years three Egyptian citizens have been honored as Nobel laureates. The late President Anwar Sadat was the first to receive the Nobel prize for peace; he was followed by the celebrated novelist Naguib Mahfouz, who won the prize for literature. In 1999, the Egyptian scientist, Dr Ahmed Zewail won the Nobel prize in chemistry. Dr. Zewali received his award for studies on the transition states of chemical reactions using spectroscopy.

Economy: Prior to 1967, the government was having a moderate degree of success in diversifying the one–crop economy (cotton); oil production and light industry were started. To make up for lost revenues caused by the closing of the Suez Canal, Saudi Arabia and Libya contributed substantial sums and the Soviet Union provided tremendous loans to purchase military equipment.

The Aswan High Dam was dedicated in early 1971 and is capable of supplying water for the farming of an additional 30% of the land. Land reclamation is now a major project, but in the past has met with only partial success. Further, there is only a fraction of the former quantities of fertile silt below the dam, making it necessary to purchase fertilizer to grow crops. Water patterns close to the Mediterranean have changed, eroding the land and altering fishing activities. The High Dam was refurbished with U.S.–built generators which increased its generating capacity by 10%, about a third of Egypt's electricity. It was lower than normal due to falling river volume associated with the African drought of the 1980s. In spite of greater areas of land being available for cultivation as a result of the dam, Egypt still imports half of its food.

As a highly competitive arena in the cold war, Egypt was well–endowed with armaments from both East and West and it remains the object of generous bestowals by the United States. Part of the Camp David Accords involved weaning Egypt away from Soviet to Western arms, and since then, the flow of arms has been regular. In 1997 the Egyptian Air Force purchased Harpoon missiles for its F–16 aircraft; in 1998, 1,058 Stinger anti–aircraft missiles, to be installed on vehicle–mounted launchers, were sold.

Beginning in 1999 US economic aid to Egypt will be cut by 50% over 10 years, from $815 million annually to $407.5 million by the year 2009. Military aid will remain essentially static.

Egypt has a significant employment problem. Unemployment levels are high, while the wages of those employed are abysmally low. Civil servants frequently sell the services they should be dispensing or work more than one job to make ends meet.

The government hopes to create jobs by making Egypt an export-driven economy. Since a cabinet reshuffle in October 1999, the government has refocused its energies on achieving higher growth through export promotion. The goals are lofty. To attain a growth of seven percent, which has been targeted, exports must rise by 11 percent annually. Privatization, though sluggish, is envisioned as one means of increasing productivity, but perhaps there are even greater problems in finding markets for the goods produced.

Currently Egypt only exports 20% of its manufactured goods. Egyptian politicians remain wary of a trade agreement with the EU, fearing domestic manufacturers will be unable to compete with European companies in a free market. They also fear Egyptian agricultural products will find no advantage in such agreements.

High-value agricultural products offer one of the best opportunities for export expansion, but the country faces fundamental infrastructure problems. A well developed highway system to speed products to distant markets and cold storage facilities are two of the most obvious. Only recently has Cairo airport been equipped with cold storage facilities that allow perishable goods to be transported. Until now 40% were lost due to poor storage before export.

Egyptian tenant farmers have been in a state of uncertainty since 1997 when new rent control and security of tenure laws began to be implemented. The problem goes back to 1952, when one of President Nasser's first acts was to establish rent controls and give tenants an almost complete guarantee that they could pass leases on to their children in perpetuity. The policy's goal was twofold: to gain favor with peasantry and break the back of the landlord class.

By 1992 the distribution of political power had shifted. The People's Assembly was completely dominated by President Mubarak's *National Democratic Party* where landlords were well represented. The assembly passed new legislation that abolished rent controls and any presumptive security of tenure. Lagtime was built into the legislation to give both tenants and landlords time to adjust; it was not to be implemented for five years.

Since 1997 the process of implementation has had its difficulties. Rents tripled and tenants became dismissable at a year's notice. To break the connection between the land and its tenancy holder, some landlords forced farmers to move to another plot of land. When police were called in to enforce landlord rights, a number of regrettable incidents occurred. Skirmishes between the two parties have resulted in 87 deaths, 545 injuries and 798 arrests according to human rights groups.

Some 42,000 tenant farmers are landless and the government has insufficient lands to offer. In this situation one can easily understand the government's interest in two vast reclamation projects. In many ways they are Hosni Mubarak's pharaonic legacy to Egypt when he leaves office: two enormous water projects, both involving Nile waters, both designed to create hundreds of thousands of acres of arable soil for land-starved Egyptian farmers, both costing billions of dollars.

In the south, the Toshka project is designed to pump 5 billion cubic meters of water a year from Lake Nasser into the Western Desert to put some 420,000 hectares of land under cultivation. Construction work on the pumping stations continues nightly to avoid Toshka's inhospitable temperatures, which can reach 125F in the summer. Water will be pumped in what has been described as the world's longest canal and distributed along four tributaries.

The Kingdom Agricultural Development Company, owned by a billionaire Saudi prince, has agreed to invest around $300 million to set up agro-industries on around 100,000 acres of land. It might be tough to attract farmers here, no matter how land-hungry they may be. The nearest town is 100 km away and has little excess labor supply.

The 200-mile long canal is estimated to cost nearly $2 billion. President Mubarak has named it the Sheikh Zaid al-Nahayan Canal, to honor the Emir of Abu Dhabi and recognize the sheikh's aid to earlier irrigation projects. Ethiopia, which claims to contribute over 80% of the Nile water and to use a mere 1%, has raised diplomatic storm signals over the project. Internal criticism of the project is also mounting, especially since one investment bank has recently downgraded Egypt. The *Financial Times* of London reported the bank thought mega-projects like Toshka were "putting an unbearable strain on the government's finances, helping to create unacceptably high interest rates, a deteriorating balance of payments and putting pressure on the currency."

In the north a similar irrigation project has already started to bring water to the parched Sinai desert. The first phase of the project, which has been dubbed the "Peace Canal", was opened in late 1997. It consists of four 42-meter deep ducts that actually carry Nile waters under the Suez Canal. The project, which is designed to add 260,400 hectares of arable land, will cost an estimated $1.7 billion. Financing has come mainly from the Emir of Kuwait, Sheikh Jaber al-Ahmed Al-Sabah.

In recent years, oil revenues have represented about 40% of Egypt's export revenues, but oil production has been declining. The oil fields of the Gulf of Suez and Sinai are mature. Egypt's crude oil production peaked at just over 900,000 barrels a day in the early 1990s; it now hovers around 700,000 b/d. Egypt's last major discovery was 20 years ago in the Western Desert. The fields are not large—one American producer pumps 32,000 barrels a day—but production is relatively low cost and attracts further exploration.

Shell Egypt has sunk two wells in the North East Mediterranean Deepwater concession, and at least one has indicated the presence of oil. If exploration in the area proves successful, the Egyptian oil sector may yet have new life.

More immediately, declining oil production is being replaced by a host of natural gas discoveries. In May 1999, the tenth successful find off the Nile delta was announced. The Mediterranean fields are estimated to contain some 37 trillion cubic feet of gas. In early 2000, the petroleum minister spoke of reserves as great as 120 trillion cubic feet. At that level Egypt could easily become a significant exporter of natural gas to fast-growing Mediterranean markets. Export projects have the potential of bringing in $1.5 to 3 billion annually.

Tourism, which had reached a level of 4 million visitors in 1996–97, was dealt a terrific blow by the bloodletting at Luxor. Under normal circumstances, the industry is the second largest foreign exchange earner after petroleum, raking in about $5 billion. Official figures released by the government indicated that the number of tourists was down 13% in 1998, but most tour operators think it was much more; the economy lost over $1 billion.

To ensure greater safety for visiting tourists, the government has proceeded aggressively against militant Islamic movements. Some 16,000 suspect members of militant groups languish in Egyptian jails, many still awaiting trial. Armed soldiers and police maintain a heavy presence around tourist sites. At the Cairo Museum, where an attack on a tourist bus left 10 dead in September 1997, 30 guards control its access.

Tourism officials also seek to broaden the country's appeal beyond pharaonic monuments. Water sports on the Red Sea and the hot nightclubs of Cairo are part of the new emphases. And as part of its Millennium programs, Egypt has developed pilgrimage tours—visiting the various sites associated with Jesus Christ, Mary and other biblical saints.

The Future: Military and financial assistance from the U.S. will continue. But the illiteracy, poverty and alienation that helped fuel the Islamist movement remains as much a presence as the pyramids. The basic illiberal nature of the regime does nothing to alleviate these concerns.

Students stroll on the grounds of the American University, Cairo

Photo: Wayne C. Thompson

Socialist People's Libyan Arab Jamahiriya

Marketplace in Benghazi

Area: 1,758,610 sq. km = 680,000 sq. mi. (about the size of Alaska plus Arizona).

Population: 4,992,838 (July 1999 est.)

Capital Cities: Tripoli (Pop. 1.2 million, estimated) and Benghazi (Pop. 750,000, estimated), co–capitals; Baida is the administrative center; moves are now underway to transfer the administrative sector to Al Jofor.

Climate: Mediterranean, with summer and winter in a narrow 50–mile–wide band along the coast; semi–arid in the region adjoining the coastal belt, arid and hot in the remainder within the Sahara Desert.

Neighboring Countries: Algeria and Tunisia (West); Egypt (East); The Sudan (Southeast); Chad and Niger (South).

Official Language: Arabic

Other Principal Languages: Berber languages, including Jabal and Zuara; Tamahaq, spoken by Tuaregs; Italian, English, all widely understood in the major cities.

Ethnic groups: Berber and Arab 97%, Greeks, Maltese, Italians, Egyptians, Pakistanis, Turks, Indians, and Tunisians.

Principal Religion: Sunni Muslim 97%.

Chief Commercial Products: crude oil, refined petroleum products, and natural gas.

GNP per capita: 7,100 US$ est.

Currency: Libyan Dinar.

Former Colonial Status: Turkish Colony (1553–1911); Italian Colony (1911–1943) British–French jurisdiction (1943–1951).

Independence Date: December 24, 1951.

Chief of State: Col. Moamer al–Qadhafi, "Leader of the Revolution."

National Flag: A plain green field.

Libya covers a vast area of central North Africa, most of which lies within the blistering Sahara Desert. The coastal area is fertile and populous—in reality it is a series of oases in an otherwise dry countryside. Further inland, mountains rise in plateaus to heights of up to 3,000 feet. There is irregular rainfall in the region due to the perpetual struggle between the moist winds of the Mediterranean and the dry, hot air of the desert.

A short distance inland, rainfall becomes increasingly light. Sudden showers, when they occur, fill otherwise dry river beds to overflowing, sweeping valuable topsoil to the sea. Temperatures in the winter often go below freezing, but they may rise quickly to as high as 80°F. in January because of the *Ghibli,* a hot, arid wind from the desert.

The low mountains, with scattered scrub vegetation, provide forage for the Barbary sheep which need little water to survive. The sands of the Sahara take charge about 50 miles from the sea, where temperatures may soar as high as 137°F. in the shade. In the extreme South, the land rises abruptly to heights of 10,000 feet and more in the majestic and remote Tibesti Mountains.

History: Since unknown times Libya was subject to foreign rule. As early as 1000 B.C. Phoenician traders established themselves along the coastline, founding what later became the city of Cyrene. Three coastal cities to the west were given the name *Tripolitania,* or *three cities,* by the Romans—Sabratha, Leptis Magna and Oea. The first two are now ruins. Oea became Tripoli. Ruins of the empire structures are intermingled throughout Libya with those of earlier temples and buildings dating back to 1000 B.C. In Tripoli, Marcus Aurelius constructed a great arch as a monument to Roman power.

After the fall of the Roman Empire, Libya was successively invaded and ruled by Vandals, Byzantines and Greeks. A massive Arab invasion from the East subdued the people in the 8th century, bringing Islam to the native Berber people. For details of early and colonial history, see Historical Background and *The Italians in Africa.*

By the turn of the 20th century, Libya had been historically divided into three provinces—Cyrenaica, Tripolitania and Fezzan. At the close of World War II, the allied powers, the United States, France,

Great Britain and the Soviet Union could not agree on the future of Libya. Italy had renounced all rights to the colony under the terms of the peace treaty it signed in 1947. The provinces of Cyrenaica and Tripolitania were under British control and the French administered Fezzan.

At about the same time that the so–called "Big Four" submitted the question of Libya to the UN for a decision, the British recognized Emir El Sayyid Muhammad al–Mahdi el–Senussi as the head of state in Cyrenaica; he took the name King Idris. A grandson of the founder of the *Senussi* sect of Islam, he set up a government and proclaimed independence of all Libya. The UN debated for many months, and then in 1949 passed a resolution providing for Libyan independence by 1951. The National Constituent Assembly met and passed a resolution proclaiming Idris to be King of Libya; a constitution was prepared which came into effect with the formal declaration of independence in 1951.

Initially a loose federation under the monarch, a new constitution was adopted in 1963 which provided for a central government and merged the provinces. The Kingdom had a two–chamber legislature; the Senate was appointed by the King and the Chamber of Deputies was elected by the people. There were no political parties.

Because of the failure of Idris to ally Libya firmly enough with the Arab cause against Israel, a group of army officers, headed by 1st Lt. Moamer al–Qadhafi deposed the King in September 1969. Ironically, the King, because of illness, was prepared to announce his abdication the next day. He died in Cairo in 1983.

The government was placed in the hands of a revolutionary council and radical changes were undertaken—U.S. military bases were closed and 25,000 Italians either left or were expelled, many of them leaving their property, including $25 million in bank deposits, to be confiscated.

From that point Qadhafi became the darling of any hysterical revolutionary who came down the road. He yearned for Arab unity, and he has spent his years in power financing various revolutionary movements throughout the world, but especially in Africa and the Middle East, using Libya's immense oil–produced bankroll. He attempted to persuade the leaders and people of virtually every Arab nation to enter into a union with Libya—with Syria, Tunisia and even with tiny Malta. Failure to achieve a single union has led to frustration which he has expressed in statements denouncing the leadership of states unwilling to join the ranks of Arab unity.

Egypt's *El Ahram*, that nation's semi-official newspaper, reporting alleged Libyan involvement in a terrorist attack on Egypt's military college, accused Qadhafi of being a "maniac and mere highwayman, even though he may own the gold of Midas." His frequent visits at European mental institutions are a very poorly kept "secret."

The restless Qadhafi convened a General People's Congress in late 1976; it met again in 1977. The Revolutionary Council was dissolved and an organization took its place called the "Secretariat." There have been numerous attempts on Qadhafi's life, but he has been able to survive by keeping his movements and whereabouts secret. The latest have been in 1984–1985 by conservative army elements who see power slipping into the erratic hands of "People's Congresses" and the "General Secretariat."

In 1976 Qadhafi annexed a sixty–mile–wide strip of northern Chad based on an unratified 1935 agreement between Italy and France. It is reported to be rich in uranium ore. He did not waste the opportunity to become involved in what had been a sporadic civil war in Chad, supporting rebel troops against the central government, probably with the ambition of seizing even more of that nation. The battles subsided after Chadian troops, with French assistance, routed the Libyans, capturing about $1 billion of Soviet-manufactured military materiel. This occurred in 1987 while Qadhafi was moping in seclusion after American air raids on Libya.

King Idris I on his 75th birthday, 1965

Although during his years in power he frequently denounced the Soviet Union, actually he was not unfriendly with that nation, even though he did not always see eye to eye with it; he denied repeated requests for port facilities along Libya's 1100–mile coastline. The Soviets sold Libya billions of dollars in military equipment during the 1970s and 1980s—in fact more weaponry than it had troops to use and pilots to fly. The hard, western cash Libya used to pay for this materiel was badly needed by its supplier. Qadhahi made friendly visits to several of the former Soviet client states in Eastern Europe.

The relationship between Libya and the United States has been a strange one. Libya has needed food and technical experts from the U.S. and America has, until imports were halted, been a major importer of Libyan oil. In spite of this, in 1979 Libyan mobs swept down on the U.S. Embassy and sacked it; diplomatic personnel, forewarned, had left the building safely. Relations between the two countries came to a standstill while the U.S. insisted that Libya take full responsibility for the attack. The Libyans (Qadhafi), however, called it a "spontaneous demonstration by *students*".

The verbal offensive against the United States escalated in 1981 when two U.S. fighters shot down two Libyan jets over the Gulf of Sidra in what Libya regards as its territorial waters. The U.S. responded that the incident was caused by an unprovoked attack on U.S. jets, but Qadhafi raged that the U.S. was the aggressor.

Qadhafi instituted his own version of a "back to Islam" movement which is distorted and subject to change without notice. He does not use the title of president; he prefers "leader of the revolution." He decreed that Libya has no central government, just a series of "Basic People's Congresses" the decisions of which are carried out by layer upon layer of committees and a General Secretariat. He made military training under the congresses mandatory for girls as well as boys in secondary schools, in spite of the Islamic tradition which seeks to *shelter* women. This program, as well as the formation of a "People's Army" containing school and university students, made conservative elements of the military very apprehensive. There have been countless attempts on Qadhafi's life.

Perhaps the classic exposé of Qadhafi's terrorism occurred in Egypt in late 1984. A team of British and Maltese assassins were given the task of murdering Abdel Hamid Bakoush, an exiled Libyan opposition leader who had been Prime Minister under King Idris. Imprisoned, he escaped in 1977 and fled to Egypt. Egyptian security forces became aware of the plot and "joined" the assassins; the Egyptians faked a photograph of the Libyan lying in a pool of blood and issued a press release announcing the murder. The Libyan radio triumphantly announced that "the sentence of execution" on the target, who had "sold his conscience to the enemies of the Arab nations" had been accomplished by a "revolutionary force" thereby carrying out "the resolution of the Basic People's Congresses" which had formed internal and external committees to "liquidate the enemies of the revolution" (He is alive and well). Egypts's Mubarak announced his secret police had uncovered several other plots involving

Moamer al-Qadhafi

persons in Britain, France, West Germany and India.

In 1984–1986, terrorism, both within Libya and in foreign nations was primarily directed at Libyan dissidents living in exile and randomly selected foreign targets. By late 1985, President Reagan urged all Americans living illegally in the country to leave Libya and again forbade the issuance of travel visas to that country. About 1,500 had remained behind because of high pay associated with the oil industry; others were admitted without a visa to circumvent the President's order. In early March 1986, Qadhafi made an ominous pronouncement: threats of the U.S. against Libya "turned us into terrorists and [gave] us legitimacy to be so and to act as terrorists." The U.S. then sent a naval task force into the Gulf of Sidra past what Qadhafi had labeled "the line of death," sinking two Libyan patrol boats and conducting air raids against Libyan radar and missile installations on the mainland. Shortly thereafter a bomb ripped a discotheque in West Berlin, killing two U.S. servicemen; irrefutable evidence indicated Libya to be responsible.

With European nations perspiring nervously, President Reagan in April 1986 ordered an air strike against Libya, conducted from bases in England because France would not allow the U.S. aircraft to fly over its territory. A sea route via the Mediterranean was therefore necessary. Among the hits made was Qadhafi's residence. American spokesmen curtly stated "We didn't know he was home." He was, and the attack visibly shook him. When he finally appeared on television about five weeks later, he was at times incoherent—listeners could not understand his Arabic. He appeared to be heavily sedated.

For the next 18 months Qadhafi was continuously on the move, fearful of losing his power, his life or his mind. He alternately wept and uncontrollably raged against what he considered the unreasonable enmity of others, particularly former President Reagan. His popularity sank to an all-time low when basic commodities disappeared from markets because of lowered oil prices which prevailed during this period. But starting in 1988 he emerged and erratically embarked on a course to show that he was a reasonable and rational person. His popularity at home soared with the return of basic goods for the people as oil prices rose, ultimately to $20 per barrel.

Recognizing the toll UN economic sanctions took, Qadhafi organized a remarkable and ultimately successful campaign to eliminate them. The sanctions had resulted from alleged Libyan complicity in terrorism against two airliners—a Pan America flight which exploded over Lockerbie, Scotland in December 1988, and a Brazzaville-to-Paris UTA flight which exploded over Niger in March 1989. In the first, 270 people had been murdered, including a number of American citizens; in the second, 170 largely French citizens had died. Qadhafi's refusal to hand over the alleged perpetrators resulted in air and military embargoes ordered by the Security Council in 1992.

In 1993 the sanctions were tightened to include the freezing of Libyan funds and financial resources in other countries and a ban on the sale of equipment for oil and gas operations. Unlike sanctions applied against Iraq, however, Libyan sanctions never prohibited the sale of petroleum or froze petroleum investments. Unable to convince the UN on these matters, the United States imposed tougher unilateral sanctions in 1996 that applied to investments in Libya's oil or gas sectors. The lifting of the UN sanctions was conditioned on the two Libyan suspects in the Lockerbie case being turned over to the British and Americans.

By 1998 the sanctions were extracting a severe price from the Libyan economy, and at some point Colonel Qadhafi made the decision to eliminate these two obstacles to Libya's reinsertion into the world community. The two cases had different velocities and followed different trajectories, both equally improbable. In the UTA case, Qadhafi allowed a French investigating judge to question some 50 members of the Libyan intelligence services in Tripoli in 1996. During this visit, the judge "found" and seized a suitcase at the intelligence service offices. Not only was the suitcase identical to the one believed to have been stuffed with explosives that brought the plane down, but somewhat miraculously the judge also found timers and detonators similar to those used in the bombing. Those who believe in miracles are encouraged to maintain their faith. Others should see the clear political calculation: Qadhafi abandoned his officers so that the international community might abandon its isolation of Libya.

The French judge drew up charges accusing the second-in-command of the Libyan intelligence services, Abdallah Senussi, Qadhafi's own brother-in-law, of giving the order to bomb the UTA flight. Five others were also named in the indictment, and their trial *in absentia* took place in Paris in March 1999. All were found guilty and sentenced to life in prison. Libya later paid some $31 million as compensation to the victims' families.

Largely marginalized by other Arab states, Qadhafi turned increasingly to his African neighbors. Indeed, solidarity with them has become the "priority of priorities" for Libya. In June 1998 the OAU voted to ignore the UN air embargo on Libya, and several African presidents flew into Tripoli to visit the Colonel. Arab countries were assailed for their "silence and capitulation" to Western interests and for being "missing during the trying days." Libya downgraded its "permanent" status at the Arab League, scrapped its Arab Ministry and changed the name of its radio from the Voice of the Arab Nation to Voice of Africa. The ever-mercurial Qadhafi was quoted as telling an Arab delegation that "for good or worse, nothing will ever link me to Arabs," and that he wanted "Libya's interests to be in Africa and remain there."

Some of Libya's African friends, including Nelson Mandela, facilitated the final arrangement to resolve the Lockerbie case. The mechanism was unique, precedent-setting and diplomatically complex: The Lockerbie duo would be tried in the Netherlands, under Scottish law. The two suspects were transferred in April 2000, and UN sanctions were automatically suspended

The Lockerbie trial began in April 2000, and the panel of three Scottish judges hearing the case rendered their verdict in late January 2001. They found Abdel Basset al-Megrahi, a Libyan intelligence agent, guilty of murdering 270 people. Al-Megrahi's sentence was life imprisonment in a Scottish jail, but his lawyers plan to appeal the verdict. With a conclusion to the Lockerbie case, Libya has high hopes that all sanctions against it will be lifted.

The United States and the United Kingdom, however, still demand that Libya take responsibility for the bombing and agree to a compensation package for families of the victims. In March 2001, President Bush announced that American sanctions against Libya would be maintained. American oil companies desperately want access to potentially rich oil and gas fields in Libya and will lobby hard for their lifting.

Internationally, Col. Qadhafi presents himself as the new and revised edition, a rogue reformed. No longer the sponsor of terror and destabilization, the Colonel is now the sponsor and protector of stability among his African neighbors. Qadhafi and Libyan diplomats have been active in seeking resolution to conflicts in Chad, the Horn of Africa and the Democratic Republic of the Congo.

The high point of Libya's Africa-first policy came in March 2001, when an extraordinary OAU summit met in Sirte and agreed to the creation of an African Union. By midyear more than the requisite number of states had ratified the Act, and the union exists in legal fact. The practical results of the Union are uncertain, though certainly Libya gave financial expression of its thanks and pan-Africanist commitment by pledging $7 million to begin work on an African satellite. The pledge was a downpayment to France's Alcatel—a portion of the $18 million Alcatel requires to begin work on the project.

Internally, the government has faced continuing opposition which intensified as economic conditions deteriorated. Violent clashes with militant Islamist opposition groups occurred in 1997, particularly in the Eastern region. In response the government tightened security measures, made hundreds of arrests and conducted military operations in the affected areas. Members and sympatheizers of banned Islamic groups were closely monitored; activities at mosques were surveilled.

Colonel Qadhafi spent much of 1998 and early 1999 on crutches or in a wheel chair, the result, suggested a French news agency, of an attempted assassination in June. The Colonel, who travels somewhat flamboyantly, accompanied by stiletto-heeled female guards in military fatigues, a 200 motor caravan, and his desert tent rolled up in an army truck—the very model of a modern nomad officer—inexplicably called off a trip to Egypt. Rumors abounded. Amnesty International reported that over 100 intellectuals, including university lecturers, engineers, medical doctors and civil servants, had been arrested in June on suspicion of oppositional activities.

To deal with its opposition, the government has elaborated a new form of rule by terror. In March 1997 the Libyan General People's Congress approved a collective guilt and punishment law. By this law any group, large or small, including towns, villages, local assemblies, tribes or families can be punished *in their entirety* if accused by the People's Congress or a People's Committee of sympathizing, financing, or in any way helping, protecting or failing to identify perpetrators of crimes against the state. The crimes included in this package include "obstructing the people's power, instigating and practicing tribal fanaticism, possessing, trading in or smuggling unlicensed weapons, and damaging public and private institutions and property." The scope of the law is staggering.

Members of so-called "Popular Committees" have brought economic terror to the bazaars of Tripoli and other cities. Formed in 1996 and made up of volunteers, often students and army officers, the committees had been charged by Colonel Qadhafi with purifying cities of the "satanic filthiness of the West." "Our enemies will conquer us," said the Guide of the Revolution, "if we eat his products and renounce our customary foods." Ambulatory peddlers selling a few items on the streets in one of the few expressions of a free market were one object of the Committees' attention. Imported items are confiscated; sellers are fined; examples are made. One Palestinian merchant was accused of "inundating the Libyan market with Israeli aphrodisiac chewing gum," proving how ever–vigilant revolutionary Puritanism needs to be.

The Popular Committees, sometimes known as purification committees, are part of Colonel Qadhafi's efforts to curb "speculation and corruption." They also act as the administrative means by which price controls are enforced in the market place. In November 1998, Qadhafi warned merchants that "prices must be cut by whatever means, and if they are not cut, there will be violence." Shopkeepers who did not act quickly enough, warned the Colonel, might find that demonstrators would "set their shops ablaze." Half the shopkeepers in Tripoli closed down for fear their prices might be exposed as too high. As well they might. Under laws passed in 1996 any Libyan can be punished by death for speculations in food, currency, clothes or housing during a state of war or blockade—which includes the UN sanctions.

Clearly multilateral sanctions worked, and the social consequences of economic constriction were something the regime ultimately chose not to bear. Qadhafi's concession in the Lockerbie case was the clearest sign the regime had changed course. Pragmatism triumphed over ideology. The Colonel-Guide now speaks of free markets and investments, and the Revolutionary Committees have been marginalized.

In September 2000 he articulated his vision of the new Libya: "Now is the era of economy, consumption, markets, and investments. This is what unites people ir-

Tripoli in the shimmering heat of midday

respective of language, religion, and nationalities." Despite such globalist geniality, vestigial anti-Americanism remains, as does an implacable opposition to Israel. Libya's development of a missile program with Chinese assistance remains a principal US security concern.

September also saw a brief distortion in the Colonel-Guide's Pan-African vision. During that month African migrant workers became the target of ugly and violent incidents in several Libyan towns; scores died. Shortly before these incidents the General People's Congress (GPC) had ordered a crackdown on employing foreigners. The employment of foreign workers was restricted to the public sector, and unneeded migrants were to be deported. Apparently these measures allowed underlying tensions to be manifested in violence.

Libya's wealth had long attracted migrant workers, and the trend was accelerated in the 1990s when many African economies suffered major recessions. Most take menial jobs, often as day laborers. But their numbers had grown over the years, and there was a sense that immigration needed to be regulated. The GPC speaker was quoted as saying: "The great principle of our sharing our income and revenues with our Arab and African brothers is being betrayed."

The government put 331 people, both Libyans and immigrants, on trial in January 2001. They were charged (this is Libya) with political crimes: "carrying out actions aimed at harming the Libyan Jamahiriyah (popular rule) system, attempting to block the African unity project and plotting against Libya's leadership in Africa." Given the political nature of the charges, the defendants face harsh sentences, including life imprisonment, if found guilty.

Culture: The Islamic Libyans tend to be basically conservative in their outlook. The lodges of the Islamic Senussi brotherhood have been the traditional centers of art, religious philosophy and learning, but they are gradually giving way to a system of public education based on more modern concepts and "Qadhafi ideology." Compulsory, free education greatly reduced a pre–1951 illiteracy rate of 90% to less than 50%. High schools and technical colleges emphasize the development of practical skills calculated to contribute to the growth of the economy.

The cities of Tripoli and Benghazi are beautiful combinations of round, arched Arab architecture and modern skyscrapers, interspersed with the classic ruins of past civilizations and the towers of gleaming mosques. Several modern supermarkets have taken their place alongside the traditional open–air markets, and many of the comforts of European and American living are available—if you can afford them.

Libya contains a remarkable collection of sites that bear witness to the life that flourished their during prehistoric, Punic, Greek, Roman and Byzantine eras.

One rock art site alone--Tadrart Acacus on the southwest border, east of the city of Ghat—contains thousands of cave paintings in very different styles, dating from 12,000 BC to 100 AD. They catalogue the changing fauna, flora and life styles of the populations that succeeded one another in this Saharan region.

Three sites, Cyrene, Leptis Magna and Sabratha all hold enormous tourist potential.

Cyrene, founded in the seventh century BC, is one of the most complex archaeological sites in the Mediterranean region. Cyrenians built the biggest Greek Doric temple in Africa in the sixth century BC—the Sanctuary of Zeus, comparable to the Temple of Zeus at Olympia.

Leptis Magna was enlarged and embellished by Septimius Severus, who was born there and later became emperor. It was one of the most beautiful cities of the Roman Empire, with its imposing public monuments, market place, storehouses, shops and residential districts.

Sabratha, once a Phoenician trading-post that served as an outlet for the products of the African hinterland, was later Romanized and rebuilt in the 2nd and 3rd centuries AD. Its theater, victory arch and arena all bespeak the efforts of Roman city planners.

Economy: Libya's economy is dependent on its petroleum industry. Oil accounts for 95% of foreign earnings and 50% of government revenues, but over the years, as fields matured and prices declined, oil production and revenues have been sliding downwards. It is clear U.N. sanctions also hurt the economy. Libya reported estimated losses amounting to nearly $27 billion resulting from them. Economic growth has become pinched. Growth of 2% was reported in 1995, but this fell to .7% in 1996 and .6% in 1997.

Even when higher oil prices returned, Libya was unable to take full advantage of the situation. With sanctions curtailing investment, Libya's oil capacity has remained stagnant at 1.3 million-1.4 million b/d for a decade.

Sanctions hit hardest at petroleum facilities, which haven't been modernized in years, and air and ground infrastructure. With only internal flights, airport maintenance and upgrading had deteriorated, and road construction languished. The lifting of sanctions has opened enormous opportunities for Libya and foreign business investment.

The Libyan prize is huge. There are 30 billion barrels of proven oil reserves, and Libyan oil is extremely high-quality, low-sulfur content crude. Low production costs in Libya add incentives. Onshore costs can be as little as $1 a barrel, and given the shallowness of the Mediterranean, even offshore costs are low by world standards. Current oil production, estimated at 1.6 million b/d, is expected to rise to 2 million b/d in two years. In 2001 the National Oil Corporation will open more than 322,000 square miles to foreign companies for exploration in production-sharing agreements.

The Iran Libya Sanctions Act (ILSA) of 1996 restricted US oil companies' investment in Libya, but the act is up for review in August 2001. The major oil companies will lobby the Bush administration for exemptions that will allow participation in the Libyan developments lest they be shut out by their European competitors.

Natural gas production also has enormous potential and is a high priority for Libya. Proven reserves are estimated at 46.3 trillion cubic feet and believed by some industry experts to be even larger—in the 50-70 trillion cubic foot range. Libya would like to shift to the greater use of gas rather than oil domestically, freeing up more oil for export. It also has great expectations for gas exports to Europe. In June 1996, the Italian oil group ENI signed an agreement with Libya for a project envisioning importation of 280 billion cubic feet of gas per year. It would be transported through a pipeline under the Mediterranean to Sicily and then on to the Italian mainland. The cost of the project is estimated at $3.8 billion.

In their campaign against sanctions, Libyans have dangled the lure of huge investment prizes before the eyes of eager businessmen: $4.5 billion for petroleum industry improvements; another $4 billion for railroad construction. Two lines were proposed: one would connect with the Egyptian and Tunisian frontiers; the other would connect the Fezzan to the Mediterranean. In all, 3,000 kilometers of track, 96 stations, 244 locomotives, and 544 bridges were envisioned. For air transportation, $2.5 billion was offered for the purchase of 25 new and used airplanes, completely renewing the Libyan fleet, largely made up of Soviet-era Russian models. An unspecified sum was designated for the modernization of airports at Tripoli, Benghazi, and Sabha. All told, it was $11 billion to generate corporate pressure against sanctions.

After almost 10 years of isolation, the whole of Libya's weapons arsenal needs to be updated. The government looks to Russia, its principal arms supplier previously. The president of the Russian firm, Oboronitelnye Sytemy (Defense Systems), announced that Libya would be the next country to be outfitted with its ground-to-air missile defense system. Employing Russian S-300 missiles, the system is capable of destroying both ballistic and cruise missiles as well as combat aircraft. Its manufacturers consider the system better than the American Patriot missiles. In May 2000 the general director of the Promeksport [Industrial Export] said his company had started carrying out contracts with Libya worth about $100 million.

Virtually all of the government's spare investment funds have been channeled into the Great Man-made River project. The project involves a 620 mile-long canal to transport water from deep below the Sahara desert to the North. Better provision of drinking water to the Northern cities and the development of irrigation-based agriculture are the project's goals. Under construction since 1983 and estimated to cost $30 billion, the project may not produce water any more cheaply than desalinization. More importantly, it draws down a non-renewable source of water.

In Libya, investment is an adjunct to foreign policy. The government-owned Libyan Arab Foreign Investment Company (Lafico) operates in 40 countries. It owns shares of the Banco di Roma and Italy's ENI oil company. It participates in the modernization of the Minsk (Ukraine) Automobile Factory (MAZ). It has purchased a share of a cigarette factory in Mali and a hotel in The Gambia, for example, and has set aside over $450 million for investment in Algeria.

The Future: The tarmacs of Libyan airports will further deteriorate with the influx of businessmen and diplomats to post–sanctions Libya. The lifting of sanctions promises jobs for the unemployed—more than 30% of the population—and a chance at improved living standards. An end to the air embargo will facilitate a greater exchange of ideas and experiences for Libyans, neither of which will make Colonel Qadhafi's authoritarian regime any more comfortable.

Roman ruins near Tripoli

The Islamic Republic of Mauritania

Crane operator at a mining site near Nouadhibou

Area: 1,085,210 sq. km. = 419,000 sq. mi. (One and one–half times the size of Texas).
Population: 2.6 (July 1999 est.)
Capital City: Nouakchott (Pop. 735,000, estimated).
Climate: Hot and arid; drought conditions have existed for the last decade.
Neighboring Countries: Senegal (Southwest); Western Sahara (Northwest); Algeria (Northeast); Mali (East and Southeast).
Official Languages: Hasaniya Arabic, Wolof.
Other Principal Languages: Fulfulde, Soninke, Zenaga; French.
Ethnic groups: mixed Moor/black 40%, Moor 30%, black 30%.
Principal Religion: Islam.
Chief Commercial Products: Fish and fish products, iron ore, and gold.
GNP per capita: 410 US$
Currency: 1 Ouguiya (UM) = 5 khoums
Former Colonial Status: French Colony (1920–1960).
Independence Date: November 28, 1960.
Chief of State: Maouya Ould Sidi Ahmed Taya, President.
National Flag: Green with a yellow five-pointed star above a yellow, horizontal crescent; the closed side of the crescent is down; the crescent, star, and color green are traditional symbols of Islam.

Mauritania lies on the upper west coast of Africa, almost wholly within the immense Sahara Desert. The northern two–thirds of the country is totally flat and stony, with virtually no rain.

Thunderstorms occasionally intrude and brief but heavy rainfall collects into streams and rivers within a few minutes. Two hours after the end of the storm, there is no sign of moisture. In some places, the water descends to great depths, supporting a few green oases which stand out in the otherwise vacant countryside.

A narrow band of semi–arid land stretches from west to east in the southern region of the country. Its rainfall of about four inches per year supports low, sparse scrub vegetation. The most heavily populated area of the country lies along the Senegal River. The rich soil ia periodically flooded during normal years by the river which, when added to the rainfall of 10 to 25 inches, permits cultivation and cattle raising.

History: The first inhabitants of Mauritania were of West African Negro heritage. Thinly scattered throughout the immense country, these people who were not carried off into slavery were pushed to the south by a Berber invasion in the 11th century. The few Negroid people who remained adopted the Islam faith of their conquerors. For details of early and colonial history, see Historical Background and *The French in Africa.*

Mauritania achieved full independence in 1960; the government adopted the presidential system, replacing the original parliamentary form.

The president was elected for a five–year term by all citizens. The first presidential elections were held in 1961; those which took place in 1966 resulted in a second term for President Moktar Ould Daddah, who was also returned to office in 1971 and 1976. The unicameral National Assembly of forty members was also elected by universal suffrage.

The *People's Party* was dominant after 1959, holding all seats in the National Assembly. It was formally created by a union of all political groups in 1961.

Relations with Morocco and Algeria were quite close—the three nations desired

to jointly share the 10 billion tons of phosphate in former Spanish Sahara. However, in a flurry of diplomatic and guerrilla activity, Spain, weary of trying to appease internal and external opinion over its continued possession of a colony on the African continent, decided to surrender Spanish Sahara to literally anyone. Mauritania joined with Morocco to exclude Algeria from the desert wasteland. The end result was a *de facto* partition of the former Spanish colony, with Mauritania receiving a portion in the south and Morocco receiving a larger northern area. In proceedings before various international bodies, some parties insisted that the land was *terra nullius*—it belonged to no one, probably the most accurate analysis if there were not such immense phosphate deposits.

France pledged to help Mauritania against attacking *Polisario* guerrillas supported by Algeria in its effort to obtain some or all of the wealth. These guerrillas established the *Saharan Arab Democratic Republic* in the former colony of Spanish Sahara. Air strikes were frequently made from bases near Dakar, Senegal.

Without warning, a military *coup* toppled the Ould Daddah government in mid–1978. There had been growing dissatisfaction with the fragile state of the economy, badly drained by a staggering military budget which had increased army strength in two years from 1,500 to 15,000 men. *Polisario* attacks on the railroad which shipped iron ore to Nouadhibou caused up to two month delays in the export of iron ore which accounted for over 70% of the nation's exports.

In 1979 Mauritania officially ended its role in the desert war over the southern half of Western Sahara. Drained financially by its costly struggle with *Polisario* guerrillas, it renounced all claims to the territory. It recognized the Saharan Arab Democratic Republic in 1983.

Mauritanian politics has traditionally been dominated by the cultural and ethnic divide which separates the population. An artificial creation of the colonizer, Mauritania joins Moors, northern nomadic peoples of Arab-Berber culture, with southern, sedentary black Africans, agriculturalists concentrated in the Senegal River valley. The Moor segment of the population itself is divided into two groupings. So-called "White Moors," descended from the region's Arab-Berber conquerors, and "Black Moors," black Africans of Arab-Berber culture, traditional servants of the conquerors. Moors speak Arabic, while the Afro-Mauritanians of the south tend to speak French in addition to their indigenous languages. Virtually all are Muslim, but Moors tend to take a single wife, while Afro-Mauritanians take up to the legally-permitted four. This has resulted in a more rapid population increase among Afro-Mauritanians, now about one-third the population. It is these racial identities which have been the base of tensions historically.

At independence, White Moors held political power, while Afro-Mauritanians were more numerous within the civil administration. Founding president Mokhtar Ould Daddah was able to keep the tensions in check, but with the beginning of the Saharan conflict in 1978 power became increasingly concentrated, especially after Ould Daddah's overthrow in 1978, to the benefit of Moors. "Arabization" policies were pursued in schools and workplaces, to the protests of Afro-Mauritanians. Several military regimes followed until Colonel Maouya Ould Sidi Ahmed Taya took power in 1984. Afro-Mauritanians became fearful when Moors began to invest in southern agricultural lands as early as 1983. Municipal elections of 1986 seemed to increase the power of Moors even further, just as the economic consequences of the first phase of economic liberalization began to impact most heavily on Afro-Mauritanians. There was a failed coup d'état in 1987, the core of which was the clandestine *Front for the Liberation of Africans in Mauritania (FLAM)*. Racial incidents in the Senegal River valley in 1989 resulted in massacres of African farmers there and retaliatory racial onslaughts against Moors in Senegal. Approximately 95,000 Afro-Mauritanians were expelled or fled from 1989 to 1991. Both Mali and Senegal, which received the bulk of those fleeing, had massive refugee problems as a consequence.

The discovery of another plot against the regime in 1991, the details of which remain obscure to this day, resulted in hundreds of Afro-Mauritanian soldiers being arrested, tortured, maimed and executed. Parliament passed an amnesty bill in 1993 to preclude any legal pursuit of those involved and has not acknowledged responsibility or wrongdoing. It has, however, given pensions to the widows of some of those killed.

The appearance of what seemed to be racial purges, coupled with the regime's support of Iraq following the Gulf War, led to international isolation and diminished foreign aid in the early 1990s. Col. Taya effected a turnabout beginning in 1991. A new constitution was adopted by referendum in 1991which permitted multiparty elections. Presidential elections in 1992 allowed Col. Taya to remain in power, though the electoral process was severely criticized. His principal opponent was Ahmed Ould Daddah, brother of the first president, who took a respectable 33% of the vote.

President Taya demonstrated keen political pragmatism by reversing alliances. In October 1995 the Iraqi ambassador was thrown out and the government announced that secret missions were being set up in the country by Iraqi citizens loyal to the Arab nationalist *Ba'athist* movement of Saddem Hussein. The government in November recognized Israel, and the same month 52 alleged pro-Ba'ath militants were arrested and charged with holding illegal meetings. Found guilty in December, they were acquitted in January 1996 by an appeals court.

Multiparty legislative elections in 1996 did little to bring Mauritania into the democratic camp. October voting brought one opposition member and six independents into parliament. The remaining 72 seats were controlled by the President's *Republican Democratic Social Party (PRDS)*. Massive fraud on both sides was reported, with the opposition charging the government of running voters from polling station to polling station in minibuses.

President Taya was reelected to a second 6-year term in December 1997, winning more than 90% of the vote against four opposition candidates. His main challenger, economist Ch'Bih Ould Cheikh Malainine, did particularly well in Mauritania's two major urban centers. In Nouakchott, he reportedly won about 23% and in Nouadhibou, the economic capital, some 41% of the vote. The election was not without its usual protests from the opposition, major elements of which boycotted it. After his victory President Taya announced that he would "wage war without mercy" on poverty, but no mention was made of the growing concentration of wealth in the hands of an emerging, but extremely narrow, middle class. During the campaign Malainine revealed that 39 Mauritanians held 70% of the country's wealth and 27 of them were members of a single tribe.

Municipal elections in early 1999 were boycotted by both Ahmed Ould Daddah's *Union des Forces Démocratiques* (*UFD*) and *Action for Change* and resulted in an unsurprising electoral sweep by the *PRDS* —officially winning virtually 100% of all municipal council seats. This of course put

A handsomely decorated doorway in Oualata

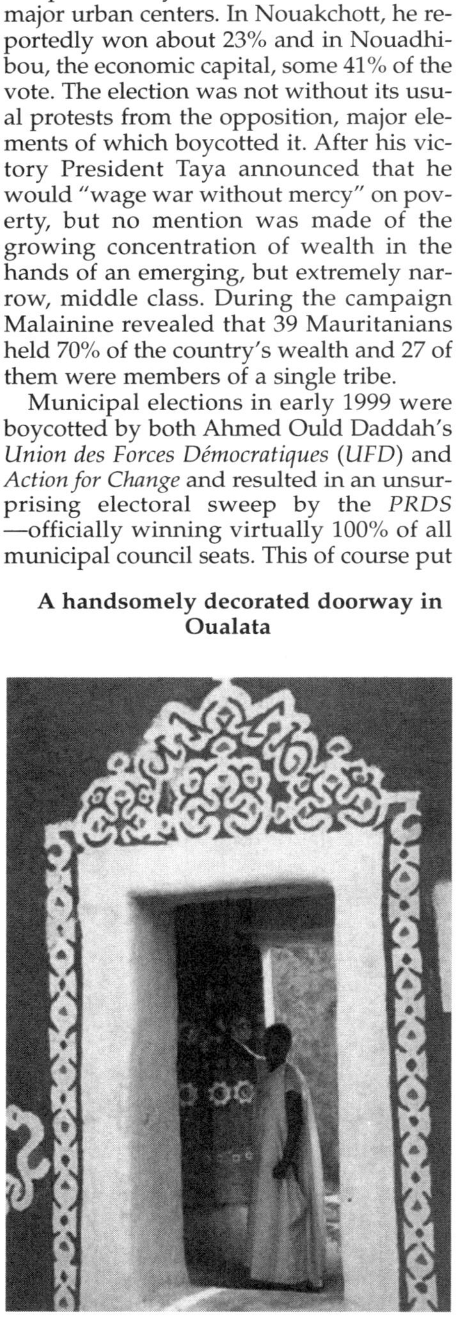

the party in a position to control the upper house of parliament, which is indirectly elected through an electoral college consisting of mostly municipal councilors. What was surprising about the election was the government's implicit admission of the fraudulence involved when it annulled elections in the capital because of the extensive use of forged identity papers. Less than a quarter of the eligible voters in the capital actually took the time to vote.

The clandestine Afro-Mauritanian political movement calling itself *FLAM* continues to call for the autonomy of southern Mauritania and a resolution of the issue of some 70,000 deported black Mauritanians who have been living in Senegal and Mali since 1989. *FLAM* accuses the regime of "Mauritanian apartheid," characterized by the exclusion of Afro-Mauritanians from public affairs, generalization of Arabizing policies and affirmation of the exclusively Arab character of the country.

Igniting a firestorm of controversy within and outside the country, Mauritania agreed in October 1999 to establish full diplomatic relations with Israel. With Jordan and Egypt, Mauritania became only the third Arab state to establish diplomatic relations with Israel. The al-Aqsa intifada that began in September 2000 has brought more pressure on the government, which has steadfastly refused to cut relations with Israel. The opposition has organized regular and ongoing protest demonstrations. In the port of Nouadhibou some 15,000 people took to the streets.

As always, the government's response was repression. Ahmed Ould Daddah's *Union des forces démocratiques - Ere Nouvelle* (*UFD-EN*) was banned in October 2000 because, said the government, it was waging a "smear campaign against the country" and calling for violence. The chairman of *the Front populaire Mauritanien* (*FPM*), Ch'Bih Ould Cheikh Malainine—who was the runner-up in the last presidential election—and two of his associates were arrested in April 2001 and charged with "criminal conspiracy."

In December 2000, President Ould Taya announced a series of political reforms that suggested an effort to give his image a more liberal sheen. A limited degree of proportional representation would enhance the chances of political parties to have more members elected to the senate and national assembly. Parties would be funded on the basis of their showing in forthcoming municipal elections and would be given access to state-controlled media.

Relations with France have deteriorated. Two Afro-Mauritanian exiles living in France discovered one of their Arab-Mauritanian torturers living there. Backed by the International Human Rights Federation, the two had Captain Ely Ould Dah arrested. The incidents went back to the late 1980s when the Mauritanian government was repressing the nationalist aspirations of Black Mauritanians. Members of *FLAM* were aggressively pursued after the group diffused its "Manifesto of Oppressed Afro-Mauritanians."

President Maouya Ould Sidi Ahmed Taya

Captain Oud Dah, then a lieutenant in the presidential guard, had allegedly had the victims tied hand and foot, suspended upside down and beaten mercilessly to reveal members of the group. Now he was in France as part of a military training program. When the officer was arrested, outraged Mauritanian authorities ordered the expulsion of 40 French military advisers. President Taya ended Mauritania's military training ties with France, its long-term military trainer and provider. Mauritanian officers will henceforth be trained by Spain. Visa requirements were imposed on all French citizens. The captain fled minimal confinement restrictions in April 2000, well before any judicial determination could be made in the case.

In December 2000, Mauritania's withdrawal from the Economic Community of West African States (ECOWAS) was officially confirmed. The government had linked the decision to community plans to promote greater regional integration with a single currency. The cross border mobility this entailed might easily result in a massive influx of Black Africans and threaten the dominance of Mauritania's Arab ruling class. Of this, it wanted no part.

Culture: At independence in 1960, some 83% of the population was nomadic. Today that figure is about 20%, the consequence of devastating droughts in the 1970s. Animal herds were decimated, and traditional family life and the rural economy were virtually destroyed. The result was a massive migration to the principal urban centers. Nouakchott and the port Nouadhibou are among the fastest-growing cities in the world. The capital's population of more than 700,000 is growing by nearly 6% annually.

Surrounding both Nouakchott and Nouadhibou today are encampments of the impoverished, mud-built shanty towns from which the poor can view the privileged position of the ruling class. Forty per cent of the country's entire population lives within the environs of the capital. Most live from odd jobs, and their home have neither electricity nor running water.

Urban agglomerations like Nouakchott and Nouadhibou both destroy and recreate social relationships. Clan solidarity and social control are breaking down in the new environment. Stealing, traditionally such a shame-filled crime that the thief might commit suicide, is on the increase as newcomers are exposed to material pressures and temptations. Divorce is also rising. On the more positive side, sociologists have noted that as rigid clan ties break down, people begin to think of themselves less in terms of clan and caste and more in terms of a nation.

Desert oases, once thriving commercial and cultural centers, are now prey to an advancing Sahara. Chinguetti, the legendary seventh holiest city in Islam, once boasted a population of 3,000; 30,000 camels annually drank its waters. Today it is almost a ghost town. UNESCO has named it part of the world's patrimony in recognition of its spiritual and cultural importance. In Chinguetti eight families guard its greatest treasures: thousands of manuscripts—verses of the *Koran*, treatises on religion, astronomy and traditional medicine, works of poetry. The oldest go back to the 12th century. None have been translated and almost all are in advanced stages of deterioration. In 1999 UNESCO launched a program to save some 3,500 volumes at Chinguetti and Ouadan.

Economy: Mauritania has emerged from the terrible draught conditions of the 70s and 80s with decent rainfall in the past few years. Animal flocks that had been devastated have been gradually reconstituted. Cattle, which had fallen to 7.6 million head in 1973, have risen to 11 million head. Agricultural production has benefited from more merciful weather. The sector employs 50% of the population and contributes 24% of the GDP. Sorghum and millet are the principal cereal grains grown, producing some 136,000 tons. An important rice-growing culture is located in the Senegal River valley, aided by irrigation dams at Diama, Senegal, and Manantali, Mali. The irrigation dams are part of the *Senegal River Development Organization (OMVS)* which brings together Mali, Mauritania and Senegal.

Mauritania earned around $400 million in foreign exchange in 1997, almost exclusively from iron ore and fishing. The iron ore industry is centered on the open–pit mines of Zouerat in the North. Ores are subjected to low intensity magnetic separation and then transported to the coastal port of Nouadhibou, some 400 miles away by train. Convoys of up to 250 ore–bearing cars, pulled by four engines and extending a mile and a half in length evacuate the desert's wealth. On their return trip, the trains bring food, water and supplies to Zouerat, a town of 40,000 built to sustain the mines.

Annual iron production amounts to nearly 12 million tons, generating about $200 million in earnings and employing some 4,000 workers. The industry is operated by *SNIM* (*Société Nationale Industrielle et Minière de Mauritanie*) which is 80% state–owned. Kuwaiti and Jordanian investors, along with the Islamic Bank hold the remaining shares. As part of its privatization efforts the government has discussed selling some 25% of *SNIM* stock. In 1998 iron exports produced about $200 million and contributed more than 10% of GDP.

Waters off the Mauritanian coast are rich fishing areas—perhaps too rich. From 200 ships harvesting the sea in 1996, more than 500 were working the waters in 1998. Contrary to normal expectations, increased fishing boats have resulted in reduced catch and income. The explanation lies in the devastation of fish stock by damaging industrial-scale fishing techniques. Species like dolphins, sharks and turtles have declined dangerously.

In 1998, the government decreed a two-month "biological rest" to help fishing stocks renew themselves, but even this has proved ineffective. It has recently banned all fishing, except traditional non-motorized fishing by local communities, in the Banc d'Arguin National Park, a 12,000 square km coastal wetland that is home to the world's most endangered marine mammal, the monk seal, and over two million migratory water birds.

The depletion of fishing stock resulted from the agreement signed between Mauritania and the European Union. In exchange for $600 million in cash over 6 years, EU ships were allowed unrestricted fishing rights. Giant Dutch factory trawlers, for example, can catch and freeze 300 tons of sardines a day.

The state-run *SMEP* (*Société mauritanienne d'exploitation du poisson*) reported revenues had dropped from $180 million to $130 million 1992 to 1997. Fishing currently accounts for about half of Mauritania's export income and contributes 10% of GDP. Japan is the biggest buyer of Mauritanian fish, and the country maintains a sizable trade surplus with the Asian country.

Despite the importance of the fishing industry, however, there are no port facilities for processing the catch nor, indeed, is there a Mauritanian fishing fleet. If there are no processing facilities aboard their ships, fishermen take their catch to the Canary Islands for processing. Since Europeans can't eat enough sardines to match the Mauritanian catch—their main goal is to keep expensively subsidized fleets employed—the canned sardines are shipped back to West Africa. In other words, the markets for canned sardines are the countries that would have normally eaten fresh sardines caught by local fishermen. The Mauritanian government and Dutch shipowners are currently studying the feasibility of constructing port and processing facilities in the country.

Despite the importance of the fishing industry, however, there are no port facilities for processing the catch nor indeed is there a Mauritanian fishing fleet. If there are no processing facilities aboard their ships, fishermen take their catch to the Canary Islands for processing. And since Europeans can't eat enough sardines to match the Mauritanian catch—their main goal is to keep expensively subsidized fleets employed—the canned sardines are shipped back to West Africa. In other words, the markets for canned sardines are the countries that would have normally eaten fresh sardines caught by local fishermen. The Mauritanian government and Dutch shipowners are currently studying the feasibility of constructing port and processing facilities in the country.

Given its dependence on iron and fish, Mauritania desperately needs to diversify its economy, but diversification requires investment and there is little money available for that. International financial aid accounts for 80 percent of the country's investment budget and international lenders have justifiable concerns. Mauritania has faithfully followed structural adjustment programs; the budget is balanced (with foreign assistance) and inflation is down. There has been reasonable growth but little distribution of its consequences. The staggering inequalities of Mauritanian life are suggested by a simple fact: 80% of Mauritania's value added tax is paid by a mere 12 individuals.

Mauritania is also faced with a huge foreign debt of $2.6 billion. In 1999, the country began repayment of the principal—about $150 million, which amounts to a debt service ratio of 50%. In December 2000, the country qualified for relief under provisions of the Highly Indebted Poor Countries (HIPC) initiative, which might reduced its debts by 40%. The opposition is less than enchanted, believing that much of the benefit will be siphoned off to the benefit of the government and its supporters.

The Future: Racial tensions are always under the surface, and with a continually frustrated opposition, subject to exacerbation. Any escalation of tension within the country will have its spill over effects on Senegal and Mali. The question of slavery will continue to embarrass the government. Severe restrictions on industrial fishing are absolutely essential for the industry's continued existence.

A train crosses the vast and lonely Mauritanian desert

The Kingdom of Morocco

The ancient city of Ait Benhaddou in the High Atlas Mountains, now abandoned, which the UN considers one of the world's cultural treasures.
Photo by Susan L. Thompson

Area: 458,730 sq. km. = 200,320 sq. mi. (larger than California; does not include Western Sahara, now actually a part of Morocco).

Population: 29,661,636 (July 1999 est.).

Capital City: Rabat (Pop. 955,000, estimated).

Climate: Semi–tropical and moist along the coastline and inland for 125 miles. Cool, with frost and snow in the high altitudes of the Atlas Mountains. A hot, semi–arid plateau on the south side of the Atlas Mountains quickly gives way to the Sahara Desert. The dry season of the coastal regions is from April to October.

Neighboring Countries: Algeria (East, Southeast); Mauritania (South); Morocco claims the entire territory of Western Sahara, formerly Spanish Sahara, most of which it occupies.

Official Language: Arabic.

Other Principal Languages: Berber languages, including Ghomara, Tachelhit, Tamazight, Tarifit; French, Spanish (largely in the enclaves of Melilla and Ceuta).

Ethnic groups: Arab-Berber 99.1%, other 0.7%, Jewish 0.2%.

Principal Religions: Muslim 98.7%, Christian 1.1%, and Jewish 0.2%.

Chief Commercial Products: Food and beverages 30%, semiprocessed goods 23%, consumer goods 21%, and phosphates 17%.

GNP per capita: 1260 US$.

Currency: Dirham.

Former Colonial Status: French Protectorate (1912–1956).

Independence Date: March 2, 1956.

Chief of State: King Mohamed VI (since July 1999).

National Flag: A five–pointed star in green outline on a red background.

Situated on the northwest corner of Africa, Morocco is the closest nation of Africa to the European continent, separated from Spain by the Strait of Gibraltar. The country has three distinct geographical areas: the coastal belt, the High Atlas Mountains and the semi–arid plateaus close to them and, finally the Sahara Desert. The coastal region is fertile, with a gentle climate and ample rainfall; intense cultivation of the land is possible. White beaches along the seacoast stretch for almost 1700 miles along the Atlantic Ocean and the Mediterranean Sea. The Rif Mountains are located close to the Mediterranean, forming a crescent of land 6,000 feet high. The view of these mountains from the sea, with the sandy beaches at their base, is one of the most beautiful in Africa.

One hundred miles inland, the Middle Atlas Mountains rise sharply, descend slightly and are succeeded by the High Atlas which reach a height of 13,000 feet. The Atlas, stretching almost the entire width of Morocco, form a natural barrier between the fertile coast and the dry Sahara Desert. Temperatures are cool in the highlands and bitterly cold in the winter. They are often snow–capped in the summer, permitting skiing at the same time bathers relax in the sun along the coast.

History: Many centuries before the birth of Christ, the Phoenicians had established trading posts in what is now Morocco and settled numerous people in the land. From the 1st century B.C. until the 5th century A.D. Morocco was a Roman province, providing foodstuffs for the people of the Empire.

After the fall of the Roman Empire, there was a quick succession of Vandals, Visigoths and Byzantine Greeks, who conquered Morocco. In the ninth century Arab forces arrived, bringing Islam to the people whom they subdued. The Berbers of inland Morocco were readily converted to this religion. The first rulers of the country claimed to be direct descendants of the Prophet Mohammed. The next centuries were a period of strife between the Muslim-Berbers and the Arab invaders.

After achieving some degree of unity in the 12th century, Morocco began to expand. Its borders ultimately reached from the Atlantic to Egypt and as far as Timbuktu to the south. After consolidating this immense territory, the Moors (the name given to the mixture of Arab and Berber people) conquered almost all of Spain, which became a Moroccan province. There was a slow decline of this vast empire, culminating in the first part of the 16th century.

In 1664, the Alaouite Dynasty succeeded to the throne of Morocco and has reigned ever since; King Hassan II, the present monarch, is a member of that dynasty.

One ruler of this family, Mulay Ishmael (1672–1727) was noted for widespread cruelty, particularly directed against Christian captives. He took thousands of lives, many with his own hand, to accomplish the construction of his new palace at Meknes, near Fez. Most of Morocco became united under this sovereign. Moroccan seamen joined with other mariners of North Africa in widespread piracy on the high seas which persisted for more than 100 years.

There was another period of decline in the 19th century, and at one point, Morocco requested the United States to protect it from European expansion. Because of the country's strategic position, France indicated an interest in Morocco. After the conquest of Algeria, France slowly subdued Morocco, and a joint French-Spanish administration was set up in 1906. This quickly gave way to a French Protectorate under the terms of the treaty of Fez in 1912.

When Sultan Moulay Yusuf died in 1927 the French chose his younger son, Sidi Muhammad, as sultan. Known for his retiring disposition, the prince turned into a skilled and forceful king as Muhammad V. Around him Moroccan nationalists of all stripes gathered and challenges to French rule mounted. French attempts to divide Berbers and Arabs backfired and nationalists initiated a new national day, the *Fête du Trône* or Throne Day in 1933. It accentuated the monarch's role as symbol of national unity.

Popular enthusiasm for the young king was often accompanied by anti-French demonstrations. Political parties soon emerged seeking greater Moroccan self-rule. The explicit demand for independence followed logically on the country's experiences in World War II. Muhammad V urged cooperation with France when war broke out in 1939 and Moroccan troops fought valiantly to defend the colonial ruler. A defeated France shone less brightly and Vichy's racial laws were offensive to a monarchy that had a large Jewish population. The Allies, meeting in Casablanca in 1943, expressed little enthusiasm for continued French presence in Morocco and by 1944 an *Independence Party, Hizb al-Istiqlal*, was formed.

The monarch's willingness to permit existence of the independence movement was more than annoying to French administrators. He roused further hostility by refusing to countersign decrees of the French resident general, denying them legal validity. Ever seeking to divide Arabs and Berbers, French administrators began to cultivate Berber leadership as a counter foil to a nationalist monarch. One of the most formidable, Thami al-Glaoui, the feudal overlord of Marrakesh, condemned Muhammad V as not being the sultan of Moroccans as much as he was the sultan of *Istiqlal*.

Together al-Glaoui and France worked to depose the Sultan, but when the French removed him from office in 1953, it only made Muhammad more a nationalist hero. The Algerian uprising in 1954 diverted French attentions from Morocco and under the overwhelming influence of a popular monarch and a strong nationalist party, Morocco became independent in 1956.

Power in independent Morocco was concentrated in the hands of the monarch. Sultan Muhammad V (who officially adopted the title of king in August 1957) chose his ministers personally and kept personal control of the all-important army and the police forces. He was assisted, if that be the word, by a Consultative Assembly of 60, which he himself named. His eldest son, Moulay Hassan, became chief of staff and learned the art of politics and power from a skilled practitioner. Royal absolutism was slightly modified by a royal charter issued in May 1958 creating a constitutional monarchy.

When *Istiqlal* split along generational and ideological lines in 1959, the King positioned himself as neutral arbiter, well above the political fray. *Istiqlal*'s main faction, containing older and more traditional elements, was headed by Muhammad 'Allal al-Fasi. A smaller section headed by Mehdi Ben Barka was formed of younger men, intellectuals who favored socialism and had republican leanings. To pursue these goals, they formed the *National Union of Popular Forces (UNFP)*.

Serving the traditional mint tea. Photo by Susan L. Thompson

Moulay Hassan was elevated to the throne as King Hassan II upon the unexpected death of his father in 1961. He promptly drafted a new constitution providing a parliamentary government. Elections were held in 1963 and the National Assembly began to function. Both *Istiqlal* factions were in opposition, while a miscellany of royal supporters coalesced in the *Front for the Defense of Constitutional Institutions*. Political bickering led to political paralysis. The king dissolved parliament after only a year and established a regime of personal rule. Over the years it was clearly Hassan II's preferred form of governance.

The king's most formidable opponent, Mehdi Ben Barka, was forced into exile. Once the king's mathematics instructor, Ben Barka later turned radical, touting a Nasserist "Arab revolution" against Morocco's "reactionary" monarch. His support of revolutionary Algeria led to subsequent charges of high treason, including allegations of plotting against the life of Hassan II. He was sentenced *in absentia* to death. From his home in Paris Ben Barka became leader of the opposition to Hassan—until, that is, he was kidnapped and disappeared in October 1965. Numerous observers have suggested the Ben Barka plot was managed by General Muhammad Oufkir, the king's minister of the interior.

There followed a period of constitutions and coups, none of which were successful. Army rebels attempted it in 1971, raking the king's birthday party with gunfire and killing 98 guests, one of which was the Belgian ambassador. A year later General Oufkir apparently led a second coup which almost downed the royal plane. Hassan survived, as he did some eight other attempts on his life. For the faithful, such luck meant he must be a good ruler, gifted with *baraka*—a kind of divine grace.

His opponents were less fortunate. General Oufkir died at the royal palace, supposedly by his own hand. Hundreds of suspects, including members of his family, were imprisoned. It was a tad more genteel than the fate of rebels against his father. While Crown Prince and army chief in 1958 Hassan had suppressed a rebellion in the Rif mountains. Rebellion ringleaders, so the story goes, were flown out to sea in helicopters and shoved overboard. True or not, it certainly contributed to the prince's image: fear not love was a more likely policy. Indeed, force seemed to be respected by Moroccans. Hassan's forceful policies to absorb Spanish Sahara increased his popularity in the mid-1970s.

Hassan turned Western Sahara into a fervent nationalist cause. Good relations with Israel and Washington provided the weaponry to defeat the Polisario Front, a guerrilla insurrection seeking independence for the area. Ultimately the war evolved to a stalemate, with Moroccans hunkering down behind massive walls of sand. Nationalist fervor over Sahara could not for long disguise the country's real social and economic and political problems.

Constitutional tinkering, and it was frequent, never threatened the king's personal rule. Royal decrees could not be debated, for that would be like challenging the will of God. It was also a crime to question the royal finances. Repressed political energy will always find a way out and the regime faced not only plots against its ruler, but periodic riots, strikes and other manifestations of discontent.

By the early 1980s bad harvests, a sluggish economy, and the continuing financial drain of the Sahara war increased domestic strains. Islamic fundamentalism

King Mohamed VI

was finessed by the king's claim of descent from the Prophet, but its growing influence among both the educated and the impoverished suggested fundamental weaknesses in the system. The need for reform was pressing and made more so by international lenders and human rights organizations looking more closely at Morocco's troubled state.

The king responded, as always, with a combination of symbol and reality. There seemed to be a greater liberalization. Amnesties were granted to some long imprisoned in remote places; curbs on the powers of security and police forces were announced. Another constitutional referendum was held in 1992, but its provisions were superseded by yet another constitutional change submitted to referendum in 1996. There would be a new bicameral parliament. It would consist of an indirectly–elected upper house and, for the first time since independence, a directly elected popular assembly. It was still change from above—royally-directed political reform.

The 1997 elections were Morocco's first direct elections for the lower house of parliament and were an attempt to spread democracy to rural areas. More than 3,000 candidates contested 325 seats under conditions of greater openness than ever before seen. Three main political groups took almost equal numbers of seats in the Chamber of Deputies. The *Koutla* left-wing opposition block took 102 seats. Its dominant partner, the *Socialist Union of Popular Forces* (*USFP*) won 57 seats to become the largest party in parliament. The right-wing *Wifak* block won 100 and the center-right grouping received 97. The relatively equal distribution of seats among the principal forces hinted at stalemate rather than action.

For the first time ever a fundamentalist religious party, the Islamist *Popular Constitutional Democractic Movement* (*MPCD*), would be represented in parliament, winning nine seats. The remaining seats in the 325-seat chamber went to a scattering of minor parties. The big loser in the elections was *Istiqlal*. It won only 32 seats, down from 43 in 1993 elections.

Though a parliamentary system, the government emerged less from parliament than from the king. Hassan II reserved the right to appoint and fire ministers. In February the king asked Aberrahmane Youssoufi, the 73-year old leader of the *USFP*, to form a government. The cabinet would ultimately include representatives of five opposition parties with *USFP* and *Istiqlal* taking the majority of posts. The King retained control over two of the most important ministries. The Interior assignment went to the current minister (and king's right-hand man) Driss Basri. Defense remained in the hands of the king as supreme commander of the general staff of the Royal Armed Forces. Hassan had learned much from his father: meaningful power still lay in the hands of the monarch.

To Moroccans Driss Basri was the most powerful and feared of Hassan's ministers. As minister of the interior for over 20 years, Basri controlled a web of security agents and spies who informed him of the slightest hint of dissent or opposition. He controlled appointments of governors and other regional and local officials. The police were under his control and his jails were places of detention and torture. Even critical foreign-policy questions have been under his purview. In many ways the interior ministry was a parallel government operating above the law and responding only to the king. Basri was Grand Vizir of the king's dark side.

After thirty-eight years of less than progressive rule King Hassan died in July 1999. He was succeeded by his unmarried elder son, Crown Prince Sidi Mohamed. Mohamed VI's first speech ignited a spark of optimism brighter than any generated by the half-hearted reforms of his father. He evoked the poverty of his people, the fate of women and the need for change. Action followed words. Corrupt gover-

The Hotel Rif in Tangier WORLD BANK photo

nors were fired and some 10,000 prisoners released from Moroccan prisons. Victims of human rights abuses and relatives of those who had simply "disappeared" were recognized and offered compensation by the state. Before a December 1999 deadline, the Moroccan human rights commission received 5,500 requests for compensation from victims of the former regime.

Mohamed also began the process of bringing his father's political opponents home from exile or freeing them from house arrest. The most notable of the exiles was the 73-year old Abraham Serfaty. Head of the Marxist-Leninist *Ila al-Amam* group, Serfaty had been sentenced to life in prison for making statements in favor of self-determination for the Western Sahara. International pressure brought release from jail and expulsion from Morocco after 17 years' imprisonment. He had been living in exile for 8 years when the young king allowed him to return, a free citizen once again. The family of Mehdi Ben Barka, who "disappeared" under mysterious circumstances in 1965 while living in France, had their passports restored and were allowed to return to Morocco.

The other notable political opponent restored was the Islamist leader Sheikh Abdessalam Yassine, the most radical of Hassan's challengers. The 72-year old Yassine was head of *al-Adl wal-Ihsane* (*Justice and Charity*). Active mainly on university campuses and in the poor districts of large cities, *Justice and Charity* is the country's biggest Muslim fundamentalist organization.

Sheikh Yassine had long been a thorn in the side of King Hassan. In the 1970s he had been detained without trial for more than three years for sending a 114-page letter to the royal palace criticizing the king for copying Western values—described as barbarous, materialistic and egoistic—and demanding the application of *sharia* law. Government ministers had long called for his release but palace officials argued he should first acknowledge the religious authority of King Mohamed VI, who bears the title *Amir al-Mu'minin* or "Commander of the Faithful." In May 2000 Yassine was finally released from 10 years of house arrest for challenging the monarchy.

The Sheikh, seemingly an inveterate letter writer, persisted in his ways even while under house arrest. In February 2000 he addressed a 35-page letter to the king raising one of the most taboo of subjects—the royal family's wealth. It called on the king to return billions of dollars that Islamists allege his father had stashed abroad.

In November 1999 King Mohamed confirmed his commitment to change by dismissing his much feared interior minister, Driss Basri. The process was gradual but obvious. Basri's image was badly damaged following violent September protests in Western Sahara, and in October both the secret service bureau and the Western Sahara portfolio were taken from his hands. His replacement was 51-year old Ahmed Midaoui, former head of the domestic intelligence service (*Sûreté Nationale*).

Despite fresh vigor and a new optimism generated by the new king, it is difficult to say that much progress has been made on Morocco's most pressing problems. Hesitancy rather than boldness characterizes the Youssoufi government. It is certainly cautious after Islamists effectively and easily mobilized as many as half a million people to protest proposed legislation that would have broadened women's rights. The government also seems uncertain as to its policy leadership versus that of the king. Following demonstrations against its proposed modifications of marriage statutes, the government appointed a special committee, including Muslim scholars, to examine the issue, but the committee never met. In April 2001 it was the king who then acted to appoint an advisory commission to study civil code revisions.

It was also the king who, drawing upon his religious authority as commander of the faithful, took practical action to deal with two of the country's abiding problems: illiteracy and unemployment. In August 2000 he announced that Morocco's mosques would be used to dispense literacy courses, as well as religious, civic and health education. Women—whose literacy in the rural areas is estimated to be as low as 10%—were a primary target of the program. The other targets were unemployed university graduates, and it would be from these, said the king, that instructors for the new literacy program—male and female—would be hired.

In a system long accustomed to turning to the monarch to solve problems and provide assistance, it would appear the government's capacity to assert its own policy leadership and autonomy will only slowly develop.

Western Sahara

Western Sahara, formerly known by the names of its two former subdivisions, Saguia el–Hamra and Rio de Oro, is totally within one of the most oppressive parts of the immense Sahara Desert. A narrow band along the coast receives torrential thunderstorms wafted inland by the steady trade winds. The only thing that remains after the rain is more erosion—the water either spills into the short rivers emptying silt into the Atlantic Ocean or is quickly swallowed up by the scorched land that has a thirst which cannot be quenched.

This thinly populated desert region became a Spanish colony because no other nation wanted it during the rush of European claims to African territory at the close of the 19th century. For details of earlier and colonial history, see Historical Background and *The Spanish in Africa*.

The territory, then known as Spanish Sahara, came under Moroccan–Mauritanian domination as a result of a series of diplomatic and military actions after the Spanish left in 1975. The Spanish had been principally occupied with administration of the colony and with the extraction of phosphate deposits which are located in the desert and transported to the sea by a conveyor belt.

Morocco, Algeria and Mauritania had joined together in the early 1970s to bring anti–colonial pressure upon Spain to relinquish the territory. Spain dragged its feet as long as possible, mining the phosphate resources. When guerrilla activity commenced in 1974 and resulted in sabotage of the conveyor belt in 1975, Spain, led by an aging Franco who died in late 1975, decided to surrender the territory. The question, of course, was to *who* or *what* it should be relinquished. Cooperation between Morocco and Mauritania continued, but Algeria, sensing that it would receive little or nothing, went its separate way.

The Algerians supported the *Polisario*, a name which was derived from *Popular Front for the Liberation of Saguia el–Hamra and Rio de Oro,* an organization which demanded "independence" for the whole territory.

Morocco, then backed by Mauritania, insisted that Spain should "return" the western Sahara to its "homeland" rather than setting up an independent nation under *Polisario,* which it claimed was a gang of mercenaries that didn't represent the nomadic people who wandered in and through the region. The UN had decided earlier that Spain should determine the wishes of "the people."

Seizing the initiative, King Hassan announced a "green march" of Moroccans into Spanish Sahara. Spain nominally resisted the move and Algeria, needless to say, was furious. Some 200,000 civilians crossed the border from Morocco and penetrated six miles into the territory. A visit by soon–to–be King Juan Carlos of Spain convinced the Spanish that action could no longer be postponed. A tripartite agreement was reached in Madrid whereby Spain would withdraw from Spanish Sahara and transfer administration to Morocco and Mauritania. The matter came before the Organization of African Unity after the *Polisario* proclaimed the existence of the *Saharan Democratic Arab Republic,* which was immediately recognized by Algeria and later by other African nations as the only legitimate government.

Moroccan and Mauritanian troops quickly solidified their position in Western Sahara, while Algeria supported *Polisario* sabotage and violence.

It initially appeared that Morocco and Mauritania were in firm control, but guerrilla activities of *Polisario* posed substantial problems for both nations. Incursions into Mauritania itself posed a threat to the capital city. Spanish Sahara, divided in a manner which gave Morocco two–thirds of the land and all of the phosphate deposits, was a battlefield with no clear lines of control.

Mauritania, a poor nation with an all but non–existent military capability, folded in August 1978. The guerrillas, supported by Algerian oil money were just too much to overcome. When it recognized the *Polisario* as the legitimate government of Western Sahara, King Hassan branded it a "traitor" and proclaimed southern Western Sahara to be the 37th province *of Morocco.*

Morocco now controls all but the easternmost small portion, which is walled by a ten–foot–high "berm" intended to keep the native *Sahrawi* "rebels" out. They are accused of being mercenaries, which until recently, was correct.

Since that time the rebel activity has been irregular. Most are sheltered in camps near Tindouf, Algeria. As Algeria was threatened by Islamic fundamentalists, widespread unrest, violence, and fell on hard economic times, its support for the cause waned sharply in 1992. In order to solidify his position in Western Sahara, King Hassan ordered that the territory be included in the Moroccan national referendum of September 1992. This meant that the multitude of Moroccan settlers in the territory were treated as resident Moroccan citizens.

Former Secretary of State James Baker, Kofi Annan's personal representative for Western Sahara, launched another drive to resolve the dispute in mid-May 2000. The Polisario's 30-year frustration threatens to turn into armed conflict once again. Driss Basri's dismissal removed one stumbling block to real negotiations. There may be an opportunity for a settlement at long last. A UN-sponsored referendum was postponed from 1992 to 1993, then to 1994, 1995, 1996, and yet again to 1998 because of constant haggling over *who* is a voter. By early 1998 the UN mission had identified over 120,000 Sahrawi refugees eligible to vote in the December elections, but the parties refused to accept this determination and the elections were once more postponed to March 2000, a deadline now come and gone.

In a November 2000 speech commemorating the 25th anniversary of the Green March, King Mohammed VI excluded any notion of independence for Western Sahara. "No solution is feasible," he said, "outside national unanimity and sovereignty..." What Morocco offers instead is the promise of greater autonomy within a program of increased decentralization. The two sides agree on so little that UN Secretary General Kofi Annan told the Security Council in February 2001 "a climate of increased mistrust and bitterness has set in between the parties and this is undermining the agreed cease-fire regime."

Culture: The historic city of Meknes, founded in the 11th century by Almoravid rulers as a military town, is a major tourist attraction. Meknes became a capital under Sultan Moulay Ismaïl (1672–1727), the founder of the Alawite dynasty. The sultan transformed the city into a impressive center of Spanish-Moorish style surrounded by high walls. Monumental entrance doors show the harmonious blending of Islamic and European styles of the 17th-century Maghreb.

A note on royal names and titles. Moroccan princes are referred to with the title Moulay (master), unless their name is Mohamed. Since the only "Master Mohamed" is the Prophet, princes named Mohamed are addressed as Sidi (my lord). Princesses are given the title Lalla.

The Alawite dynasty has provided the country's sultans since the mid-17th century. Like his predecessors, King Mohamed bears several titles—Commander of the Faithful, Savior, and Shadow of the Prophet on Earth—that reflect the dynasty's claim to be directly descended from the Prophet Mohammed. The claim has been the traditional means by which Moroccan kings have legitimized their rule and more recently checked the claims of Islamists.

Boosting the social and economic status of women has been a major policy focus of the Youssifou government. In a traditional, male-dominated society women are disadvantaged. More than 50 percent of Moroccan women are illiterate, for example, with the rate rising to 90 percent in poor rural areas. This limits their ability to contribute significantly to the country's economic development.

In March 1999 the government introduced a series of proposals that would alter the country's traditional Islamic marriage statutes. The plan would ban polygamy and raise the minimum age for marriage from 15 to 18. A system of legal divorce would replace the current norm of simple verbal dissolution through repudiation by the husband. Under the new proposals divorce would be in the hands of a judge. The new statutes also stipulated that a couple's assets must be shared after divorce.

After the government announced its reforms in March 1999, most political and religious groups expressed passionate reactions. A year later fundamentalists and modernists staged dueling marches in Casablanca and Rabat. An estimated 500,000 traditionalists demonstrated in Casablanca against the project, dwarfing a demonstration by supporters of the plan, who rallied about 40,000 people in Rabat.

More and more restrictions against women are being lifted. The mail, for example, may soon be delivered by female hands. The government has authorized the post office to recruit women for the position of postwomen. In March 98, for the first time, road traffic was regulated by policewomen.

Economy: Agriculture contributes about 16% of Morocco's economy and accounts for 40% of the labor force, but it is highly dependent on rainfall patterns. As a consequence, economic growth tends to be erratic. According to government statistics, GDP grew in 1998 by 6.7%, but only 1.5 percent growth occurred in 1999, when it was hurt by a serious drought. The drought of 2000 was, perhaps, even more serious. With agricultural production down considerably, economic growth is not expected to exceed 0.8% for the year.

After two years of drought and recession, Morocco appears to be the beneficiary of plentiful winter rains, which have made growth prospects for 2001 much rosier. Economists are predicting growth may range from 8% to 10% for the year.

There are no government statistics on Morocco's cannabis crop (known locally as *kif*), the amount of which, no doubt, also fluctuates with rainfall conditions. Morocco is among the world's largest producers of cannabis. Its cultivation and sale are the economic basis for much of northern Morocco, where up to 85,000 hectares are devoted to its production. Over 2,000 metric tons are estimated to be exported yearly to Europe and may account for as much as a quarter of Morocco's hard currency earnings. Most Moroccan cannabis is processed into hashish, resin, or oil and exported to Algeria, Tunisia, and Europe—smuggled to Spain, Portugal, and France by sea, then by road to other countries in Europe.

Attempts to diversify have produced a modestly mixed economy. The mining sector remains crucially important. Morocco has the largest phosphate reserves in the world and produces significant amounts of fertilizers and phosphoric acid. Raw phosphate exports formed about 30% of total international exports, up from 2% in 1996. Phosphate revenues are expected to reach $2 billion in 2000 through expansion of Asian markets. The Royal Family, which is said to own about a fifth of the country's land, also controls the country's rich phosphate mines.

Morocco's manufacturing base is expanding and currently contributes around 17% to the country's GDP. While the country has virtually no energy reserves, having to import 90% of its energy needs, it does act as an important transit center for natural gas exports from Algeria to Spain and Portugal. A fishing industry is developing, perhaps even a bit too quickly. Morocco has had to declare an occasional "biological repose" in response to overly zealous Atlantic fishing. Morocco has become a major exporter of snails, earning approximately $3 million annually. Tourism is thriving, registering 2 million visitors in 1999, an increase of 18% over the previous year. (A short way across the Mediterranean, however, tiny Gibraltar attracted 6 million visitors.)

Not endowed with the fabulous wealth of some of its neighbors, Morocco's economic growth has been modest, but opportunity has often been frittered away. In 1974 Morocco's GDP per person was the same as South Korea's. Today South Korea's is about eight times as high and Morocco is the regional sluggard. A major reason, argues the World Bank, is the country's bloated and heavily unionized administration. It employs some 750,000 people, including security forces and para-military forces under the direct control of the interior ministry. The wages of this army of civil servant devour a full 12% of Morocco's $35 billion GDP and the share is growing. The effects are immediate and real: Morocco budgets more for education than its neighbors but achieves less because of excessive administrative costs. One out of two children of school age do not go to school in Morocco. One in two Moroccans can neither read nor write, a literacy rate worse than India's.

In a situation of scandalous disparities of wealth and poverty (in Morocco the richest 10% consume 14 times what the poorest 10% consume) it does not help that government ministers are paid $95,000 a year, plus perks for life. There are currently 41 ministers. Elsewhere, at least 4 million Moroccans live on less than $1 a day and the number of poor has steadily increased between 1991 and 1999—from 3,5 million to nearly 5 million. Unemployment has also increased. In 1982 10 percent of the active population was unemployed. Presently it's 16 percent and more in the urban centers—up to 25%. Among young people, unemployment figures rise to 30%.

Social statistics paint an equally gloomy picture of King Mohamed's inheritance. Less than one household in five has access to potable water. For electricity the ratio is higher. More mothers die in childbirth than anywhere else in the Arab world.

Over all Morocco's economic development hangs the debt guillotine. The country has an external debt of $19 billion and debt servicing weighs heavily on the national budget. Once debt servicing and civil service salaries are paid, there is precious little left to invest.

There are some potentialities. Morocco has stayed the course of the economic liberalization it launched in 1991 and this has brought significant foreign investment. Its privatization program has been described by the *Financial Times* as "North Africa's most advanced...." In July 1999 a consortium led by Spain's *Telefónica* paid $1.1 billion for a second mobile telephone network license, which could turn Morocco into a regional telecommunications hub. The investment helped produce a record $1.8 billion in foreign investment in 1999.

In early 2001 Vivendi Universal paid the government a little over $2 billion for a 35% interest in Maroc Telecom, the national telephone company. The check helps balance the excess the government has had to pay out in increased oil prices.

Perhaps the most important potential for the Moroccan economy lies with the discovery of oil in the Talsint region of southeast Morocco. For years Morocco has had to import virtually all of its oil and gas. To encourage exploration and development, it drastically overhauled its investment code: required participation by the state in such endeavors was reduced from 50% to 25%, and companies were offered a full ten years tax abatement once production begins.

The American independent oil company, Skidmore, through its Moroccan subsidiary, made the Talsint discovery. Reserves are estimated at 100 million barrels—enough to encourage others to explore. Offshore exploration permits brought bids from several majors in Spring 2001.

In announcing the discovery to the nation, Mohammed VI demonstrated a keen ear for Islamic critics. These riches, he told his audience, would never be allowed "to engulf us in fatalism, indolence and consumerism, paralyzing our energy and our human and natural potentialities." Perhaps more importantly in terms of Morocco's economic development, he seemed to look to neighboring Algeria as a negative model: "The wealth discovered," he affirmed, "will never constitute an alternative to our agricultural heritage, but rather a tool for its enrichment."

The Future: Morocco's political system remains fragile. The dynamic for change has shifted from a government headed by an unwell septuagenarian to the monarch. Proclaimed "King of the Poor," the young monarch owes his adulation as much to reaction against the dark days of his father as to his own personality. Despite having a parliament, all major decisions still reside in the hands of the king, and the whole system seems unable to function without direction from that source.

The challenges Mohamed faces are formidable. Relations with Algeria remain tense. Western Sahara cries its urgency. An estimated 167,000 people remain encamped around geographically inhospitable Tindouf in southwest Algeria awaiting some resolution of their fate. More than 60 per cent of the population remains illiterate. Mass migration to the cities by the rural poor has created an enormous urban underclass, potentially vulnerable to those preaching radical change.

Political Islam still threatens the monarchy's political and religious dominance. The huge march organized in Casablanca against proposed changes in the status of Moroccan women gives some hint as to the potential of Sheikh Yassine and his followers.

The king has said he would prefer to be a constitutional monarch and has spoken favorably of the Spanish model. It remains to be seen if the political forces unleashed by his accession to the throne can be contained enough to move in an orderly fashion to such a reasonable goal.

The Republic of Tunisia

A group of men discuss the day's events at the harbor of Sousse

Area: 164,206 sq. km. = 63,431 sq. mi. (slightly larger than Florida).
Population: 9,513,603 (July 1999 est.)
Capital City: Tunis (Pop. 2 million estimated).
Climate: Warm, Mediterranean in the northern and central parts; hot and dry in the semi–Sahara south–southwest.
Neighboring Countries: Algeria (West); Libya (East, southeast).
Official Language: Arabic.
Other Principal Languages: French; possibly some Berber languages.
Ethnic groups: Arab 98%, European 1%, Jewish and other 1%.
Principal Religions: Muslim 98%, Christian 1%, Jewish and other 1%.
Chief Commercial Products: Hydrocarbons, textiles, agricultural products, phosphates and chemicals.
GNP per capita: 2,110 US$
Currency: Dinar.
Former Colonial Status: French Protectorate (1881–1956).
Independence Date: July 20, 1956.
Chief of State: Zine Abidine Ben Ali, President.
National Flag: A white disk bearing a red crescent and a five–pointed star centered on a red background.

Tunisia, the smallest country of North Africa, lies almost in the center of the Mediterranean Sea coastline, with a seashore almost 1,000 miles long. The coastal belt, with an average of 50 miles in width, is the site of farmland. The coastline extends horizontally for 140 miles in the North and then proceeds irregularly southward for a lineal distance of 300 miles. There are three large gulf areas of gentle warm waters which carve semi–circles. The coastal strip is succeeded by a gently rolling tableland with an average altitude of 1,600 feet—an area of grass and forestland. This, in turn, is followed by the semi–desert to the south–southwest where there is little rainfall, and shallow salt lakes. Though this sparsely settled territory is within the desert, it is not quite as bleak and hot as the central Sahara.

History: The early history of Tunisia includes the presence of almost every powerful empire of old. An early settlement of Phoenicians developed in the 6th century B.C. Ruins of the city of Carthage as it existed in the days of Hannibal lie today a short distance north of Tunis. Elephants undoubtedly were present in this northern area at the time Hannibal used them in his famed offensive against the Roman Empire. For details of early and colonial

history, see Historical Background and *The French in Africa.*

France recognized Tunisian independence on July 20, 1956. The old monarchy was abolished in 1957 when the Constituent Assembly established a republic, naming Habib Bourguiba president. Following adoption of a Constitution, the first elections were held in 1959 in which there was only small opposition to the *New Constitution Party* of President Bourguiba.

The single–chamber Assembly is elected for terms of five years. There is a separate judiciary patterned on that of France. Elections since independence have uniformly resulted in overwhelming victories for the *New Constitution Party* and Bourguiba. Although aging, the President was elected to a third term in October 1969 and in late 1974 he was proclaimed president for life.

Close ties have been maintained with France after some tension caused by a delay in the withdrawal of French forces. The lands of French farmers were nationalized in 1965 and an attempt was made to organize them into collectives. This, coupled with a 1969 drought, had a highly damaging effect on the economy.

During 1970–71, when Bourguiba was suffering from a liver ailment, there were increasing pressures for constitutional reform. The basic issue was whether the National Assembly should have the power to vote a censure of an administration when dissatisfied on a particular issue. Bourguiba, somewhat recovered, wisely resisted the move, arguing that such a system was bound to result in a new government several times a year. Fully recovered in 1974, he presided over a party congress which "erased" the memory of the 1971 reform movement.

Libya's Qadhafi made energetic and sometimes hysterical moves to persuade Tunisia to unite with Libya in 1973. It was approved "in principle" by Bourguiba, who undoubtedly thought such a move would take years and years. Qadhafi did not understand what "in principle" meant and demanded immediate action; the whole idea died a quick death—Bourguiba was the undertaker. There remains nominal cooperation between the two nations, which have roller–coaster relations.

An open split between the government and trade unions occurred in 1977; they had been consistent supporters of the president. The government held a hard line, putting down strikes and refusing to negotiate with the strikers. Tunisia has been plagued since independence by widespread unemployment (20%–30%), low wages and an uneven distribution of income; these conditions have sparked many clashes. The *Destour Socialist Party (DSP)* of which President Bourguiba was chairman, continued a tough policy by making many arrests and removing from the cabinet ministers who felt the government should assume a more moderate position.

A general strike in 1978 lasted 24 hours; a state of emergency was declared and there was rioting in Tunis and some of the larger cities. Other strikes and riots occurred since that time, usually after announcement of increases in food costs; the latest was in early 1984.

As in other North African nations, there is a rising tide of Muslim fundamentalism. Zealots want to oust the "old men" governments and replace them with "Islamic" administrations patterned after that of the late Khomeini of Iran. The Tunisian constitution recognizes Islam as the state religion, but this has always been a tolerant and open society. Bourguiba, however, did many things to make the Muslim fanatics angry. He permitted wives to institute divorce proceedings against their husbands and encouraged women to enter all trades and professions. He also westernized the court system by abolishing most of the powers of the Muslim religious courts and rabbinical tribunals by turning their functions over to the civil courts. All distinctions between religious and public schools were abolished. He even went further in 1984, and included two women in his cabinet after a reorganization. The fundamentalists see these moves as cutting the tap roots of the Islamic traditions.

Some 3,000–4,000 Islamic fundamentalists were arrested by the government from 1981 until the departure of Bourguiba, who refused to allow them to function as a political party; stiff prison sentences were substituted for death penalties. The straw that broke the camel's back came in June 1981 when the "brotherhood," as they call themselves, made a raid on a summer vacation beach resort where Europeans in sometimes scanty attire lived "the good life;" the resort was all but destroyed. This was a terrible blow to Tunisia's profitable tourist industry and marked the beginning of the crackdown on the zealots.

Former President Bourguiba remained quite popular in spite of advancing years. When a dispute erupted over succession to the presidency in 1984 he quickly settled it. The Prime Minister (who wielded considerable power) would immediately become president and name a successor prime minister.

After thirty years in power, Habib Bourguiba, suffering from Parkinson's Disease, became visibly senile—he could not remember things he had done the previous day and started taking irrational actions. His persecution of Islamic fundamentalists, whose number had been swollen by migration to the cities from rural areas, reached an intolerable level. Acting swiftly, former Prime Minister Zine Abidine Ben Ali declared Bourguiba incapable of

Relief from the desert heat in a cool oasis

Habib Bourguiba

carrying out his office and removed him on November 7, 1987, thus becoming president of Tunisia. The move had widespread support from all elements and factions within Tunisian society. Among his first moves, the new president commuted the sentences of several hundred Islamic fundamentalists and suggested he would dissolve the parliament and hold elections earlier than the scheduled date in 1991. He had scheduled them for November 1989.

When it appeared that he and his party were well ahead of any competitor, President Ben Ali advanced the contest to April 1989. His judgment was correct—the *Democratic Constitutional Rally (RCD)*, the new name of Bourguiba's party, won more than 80% of the vote and all 141 seats in the National Assembly.

By late 1991 the Islamic fundamentalists had again bloomed and seriously threatened a tourist industry which was reaching new heights of prosperity. The government, acting through the military in 1992, brought 171 members and leaders of the outlawed *Nahda* group before the Tunis military court. Thirty–five received life sentences, 142 received sentences of 3 to 20 years and four were acquitted.

The firmness with which the Islamists were handled sent a clear message to other political groups in Tunisia. It has become increasingly clear that President Ben Ali is a man who is not comfortable with opposition. Repression in one form or another has been extended out from the fundamentalists. Amnesty International claims that some 2,000 political prisoners are held behind bars in Tunisia. The consequence is clear: Tunisia's opposition parties are some of the most restrained in Africa. The press more often than not appears more as lap dog than watch dog.

In the 1994 presidential elections no opposition party was able to put forth a candidate. The Tunisian constitution requires potential presidential candidates to secure the nominating signatures of 30 members of parliament, but with the president's *RCD* in a monopoly position there, it's hard for any candidate to get his papers signed. Unopposed, Zine Abidine Ben Ali won 99.9% of the vote. In the legislative balloting of the same year, four opposition parties were only able to win 19 seats in parliament, but it was the first time the opposition would be represented there; Ben Ali's *RCD* won 144 seats. Tunisia remained firmly within the President's iron grip.

In the 13 years since President Ben Ali first came to power the apparatus of surveillance and control has come to dominate Tunisian life. The number of police is four times larger than it was in 1987, and it is aided by a host of additional agencies of surveillance that have been created by authorities. The secretary-general of Amnesty International has spoken of a strategy of "interiorizing fear" within the citizenry and the International Federation for the Rights of Man has called Tunisia a "police state." Membership in the *RCD* is a political necessity. One's membership card is often a survival tool, the first thing shown police when stopped for questioning. Perhaps apocryphally, but suggestively, the story goes about that Tunisian children, asked to design a new symbol for their country, drew a police van.

Presidential elections were held in October 1999 with new election laws permitting the possibility of multiparty elections for the first time in Tunisian history. No longer would the signature of 30 political grandees be required. Leaders of political parties who had been in that role for five years and whose parties were represented in parliament, were eligible to run for the office of president. Only two candidates besides the president met these requirements: Mohamed Belhaj Amor, secretary general of the *Parti de l'unité populaire* (*PUP*), and Abderrahmane Tlili of the *Union démocratique unioniste* (*UDU*).

President Ben Ali

Election results were scarcely credible: President Zine el Abidine Ben Ali was reelected by 99.4% of the voters. It was enough to assure Tunisia a place in the Jurassic museum of retrograde political forms.

Despite a network of 132,000 policemen and 5,000 wiretaps on the telephone lines of its citizens, the regime did not anticipate the social unrest that rocked both Tunis and several southern cities in early 2000. Taxi drivers disabled the capital for three days in February, protesting a new driving code with increased fines. In the same month several Tunisian cities witnessed protests against stiff increases in

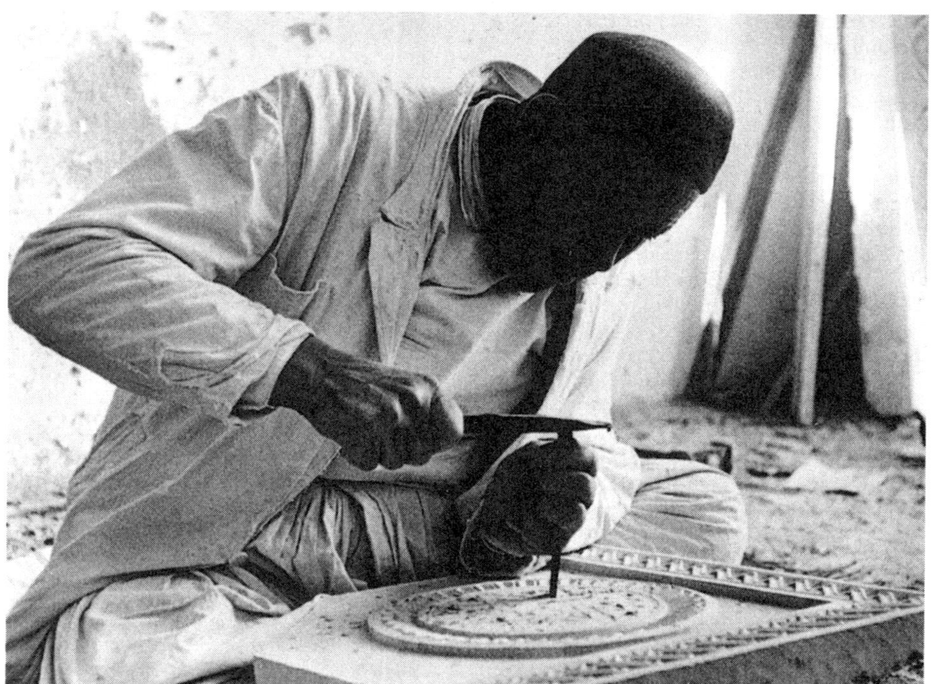

A stone carver

the price of gasoline, transport, and food products, especially bread.

In some places the protest began in secondary schools and colleges. When students went out to protest in the streets, they clashed with police, but were supported by locals, mainly youth and mostly unemployed.

None of these events was, of course, reported in the local press. Censorship is a basic element of a security state, and the Tunisian Press Code allows the government to pre-censor and ban publications. Any information that might be used to criticize the government is eliminated. Politically sensitive articles are sent to the interior ministry for review, and each edition must be registered with the ministry before publication.

The regime's efforts to muzzle reporters were highlighted by the hunger strike of Taoufik Ben Brick, who had written articles critical of President Ben Ali for French newspapers. In one he called the president "a second-rate dictator." His reward: banned from writing for any Tunisian newspaper, telephones cut off, arrested, interrogated and beaten, prevented from leaving the country. He began his hunger strike when Tunisian authorities lifted his passport, and the case received international attention. Much embarrassed, the authorities relented. Ben Brick went into asylum in France, where he reflected on the death of journalism in Tunisia.

On the occasion of the thirteenth anniversary of his accession to power in November 2000, President Ben Ali spoke soothing words to his critics. Stressing his "unshakeable faith in the principles of human rights," he announced the state would pay compensation to any individual unlawfully arrested and detained. This, of course, was merely days after a Paris news conference where four Tunisian students had given graphic accounts of beatings, rape and torture they endured at the hands of Tunisian security agents. The press conference also announced publication of a 200-page report entitled "Torture in Tunisia," issued by the Committee for the Respect of Freedom and Human Rights in Tunisia (CRLDHT).

In the same November address he announced future amendments to the Press Code to eliminate physical punishment of journalists. He specifically noted punishments for "libel of public order," a crime of infinite breadth and ambiguity the president called "rather murky" and open to "various interpretations."

One would be right to remain skeptical. In Tunisia the problem is not legislation, but its non-respect. In a security state behavioral patterns long established are difficult to change.

In late January 2001, police surrounded the home of Taoufik Ben Brik (returned from exile in September 2000) where his brother, Zoghlami, was to launch a new newspaper, *Kaws el Karama* or *The Arch of Dignity*. Officers stopped people from entering the house and confiscated copies of the paper taken by those leaving the conference. Some attendees were followed and beaten. Perhaps it was the headline of the first issue they found offensive: "Ben Ali, Thirteen Years, Enough!" A few days later Zoghlami himself was assaulted by plainclothes police officers armed with iron bars.

The medina in Kairouan

Culture: A variety of well-maintained museums offer testimony to the diverse cultural heritage of Tunisia. The National Museum of the Bardo, located in the old palace of the Bey in a Tunis suburb, is the finest archeological museum in the Mahgreb. Its stellar attractions are the mosaic floors from the Roman cities of northern Tunisia, rich evidence of the extraordinary wealth and luxury of Rome's breadbasket province. Further evidence of Tunisia's importance to Rome is the grand amphitheater of El Jem. After the coliseums of Rome and Capua, the one at El Jem was the third largest ever built by the Romans; it accommodated some 30,000 spectators.

Near Kairouan, the sacred city of Islamic Tunisia, one can visit the national Museum of Islamic Art with its stunning collection of ceramics and calligraphy. In Mahdia, in the heart of the East Coast tourist areas and still an important weaving center, one can visit the Textile Museum of the Dar el-Himma. The museum features a fine collection of traditional Tunisian costumes, one of the principal manifestations of women's artistic creativity.

A secular state, Tunisia allows greater freedom to its women than many other Muslim countries. The 1956 personal status code declared polygamy illegal and granted the right of judicial divorce to men and women equally. President Bourguiba, who did so much to create modern secular Tunisia and liberate its women, died in April 2000.

One rarely sees a woman dress in the body-covering *chador.* In the cities younger women are usually dressed in Western attire. Women have played an important role in traditional Berber culture and two of Tunisia's most heroic figures are women: Dido, or Alyssa, the Phoenician princess who founded Carthage and dallied with Aeneas, and Kahina, a warrior-queen who led the Berber resistance to the Arab invasion of the eighth century.

The government pursues a policy of Arabization, the speed and fervor of which often depends on relations with France. Bilingualism is still tolerated, for it is not the intention of the government to eliminate French, but merely to readjust its place in an Arab nation. Shopkeepers have already been forced to remove signs employing the Latin alphabet and the administration is under orders to use the country's official language in all its documents by the end of 2000.

In education the problems are greater. First, it is a question of which Arabic to use. A Tunisian's mother tongue is a dialectical Arabic, spoken on a daily basis but nonwritten. At school, the student is introduced to written classical Arabic, the language of instruction. In the larger society an Intermediate Arabic, halfway between the two, has been developing, and for the past three years a fourth alternative has been offered by the daily presence of Arabic-language television broadcasts emanating from the Persian Gulf state of Qatar.

The new private television network, Al Jazirah, is based in Qatar and is frequently referred to as the CNN of the Arab world. Tunisians watch to learn something about their own country, but at the same time the broadcasts may be leading to a homogenization of Arabic, or at least an elevation of the standards of spoken Tunisian Arabic.

Dialectical differences in Arabic suggest the second problem facing the government's Arabization program—the availability of textbooks. Given the absence of standardized terminology in some of the sciences, for example, there are no university textbooks available.

Economy: Historically a granary of the Mediterranean, Tunisia's agricultural sector has been eclipsed by its petroleum production. For years its biggest money-maker has been oil, but production, from aging wells, is in decline. According to the US Department of Energy, oil production in 1999 was around 82,000 barrels per day, down nearly 25% from the year before.

A booming economy has meant increased energy demand, only partially compensated by increased production of natural gas. To meet these demands, the government has sought to encourage new exploration with a more liberal hydrocarbon code, but success rates have been low.

Tourism replaced oil as Tunisia's biggest foreign exchange earner in 1999. It accounts for around 10% of GDP. Some 5.06 million tourists visited the country in 2000. Despite impressive growth, the sector may actually have expanded too rapidly. An excess of bed capacity has meant remarkable bargains for the traveler—$20 a night for a five-star hotel room—and less than full occupancy in many hotels.

Agriculture employs about 30% of the workforce and accounts for around 13% of GDP. Relatively rich and productive, around 30% of the land is arable. Some 55 million olive trees occupy a third of that, and olive oil is Tunisia's most important agricultural export. In the 1999-2000 farming season, 225,000 tons of oil were produced. Estimates for the 2000-2001 season are slightly lower because of reduced rainfall.

The government always points to its economic success when pressed on its restraint of political life. The figures are impressive. Per capita income has increased sevenfold under its management, from $300 in 1956 to over $2,800 in 2000. The country has experienced an average growth rate over 5.7% between 1996 and 2000. Tourism and trade are growing as is the pace of privatization. Job creation has been significant, but the unemployment rate remains stuck at about 15%.

The IMF has forecast economic growth in 2001 at more than 6%, and foreign investors, undeterred by human rights issues, have responded to the economy's stability and success. Foreign direct investment in Tunisia exceeded $1 billion for the first time in 2000.

All in all, Tunisia is an economic success story, and its citizens, 60% of whom are middle-class, seem willing to accept economic benefit at the cost of political freedom. Political control may be the price Tunisians are willing to pay for a stable and growing economy.

For the Ben Ali regime, security and stability are contingent on control. But control in Tunisia has weakened potential checks on the government. An effective secular opposition has not been allowed to develop, and Islamic fundamentalists have thrived most where no meaningful secular opposition has existed. Without a free press, corruption can flourish and the rule of law vanish. These are the kinds of concerns that face potential investors. For the Ben Ali government the tension between political control and economic liberalization will dominate the next few years.

The Future: Constitutionally, President Ben Ali is serving his final term. However, attempts to suppress all form of criticism, be they from opposition politicians, human rights advocates or journalists, seem only a prelude to efforts to secure a fourth term of office in 2004. Tensions between the state and civil society will continue to mount, and the regime faces a crisis of identity. It is a system based on control, and a genuine pluralist political system almost inevitably means loss of control. The years to come will test its capacity to change.

Modern interpretations of traditional architecture on the island of Djerba

The Republic of Cape Verde (*Vair*–day)

Mindelo, São Vicente. Cultural and intellectual capital of Cape Verde. *Photo by Carlos da Sousa*

Area: 4,030 sq. km = 1559 sq. mi. (slightly larger than Rhode Island). Ten rather mountainous islands and eight additional islets about 400 miles off the coast of Senegal.
Population: 405,748 (July 1999 est.).
Capital City: Praia (on São Tiago island. Pop. 78,675).
Climate: Temperate; warm, dry summer; precipitation meager and very erratic, producing prolonged droughts; harmattan winds from the Sahara can obscure visibility.
Official Language: Portuguese
Other Languages: Crioulo (a blend of creole Portuguese and West African words).
Ethnic groups: Creole (mulatto) 71%, African 28%, European 1%.
Religions: Roman Catholic (infused with indigenous beliefs); Protestant (mostly Church of the Nazarene).
Principal Commercial Products: Shoes, garments, fish, bananas, hides.
GNP per capita: 1,060 US$
Currency: Cape Verdean escudo
Former Colonial Status: Portuguese colony
Independence Date: 5 July 1975 (from Portugal).

President Pedro Pires

Chief of State: President Pedro Pires (since March 2001).
National Flag: Three horizontal bands of light blue (top, double width), white (with a horizontal red stripe in the middle third), and light blue; a circle of 10 yellow five-pointed stars is centered on the hoist end of the red stripe and extends into the upper and lower blue bands.

History: Cape Verde had no indigenous people. It was settled by Portuguese, Jews, and Africans in the fifteenth century; they mingled, creating a Creole culture. Only 405,000 Cape Verdeans live on the islands of the archipelago. Another 500,000 live in the eastern United States, primarily in Rhode Island and Massachusetts.

Under the leadership of Amilcar Cabral, the struggle to free Cape Verde from Portuguese colonial rule began in the early 1960s. Cabral's mother was from Guinea-Bissau and the nationalist party he created, the *African Party for the Independence of Guinea-Bissau and Cape Verde (PAIGC)*, fought to liberate and unite both colonies. Cabral saw neither. He was assassinated in early 1973 and the colonies were granted independence in 1975 under the leadership of Aristides Pereira.

Efforts continued to unite Cape Verde and Guinea-Bissau, but following the 1980 *coup d'état* in Guinea-Bissau, which resulted in the overthrow of Luis Cabral by Nino Vieira, union was no longer possible. In Cape Verde, the governing party renamed itself the *Partido Africano da Independencia de Cabo Verde*, or *PAICV*.

Pereira's authoritarian rule lasted until multiparty elections in 1991. These were

Former Prime Minister Carlos Veiga

won by the *Movimento para a Democracia* (*MPD*) led by Antonio Mascarenhas. President Mascarenhas was reelected in 1996 without much opposition or participation. Only about 40% of the electorate managed to turn out.

The electoral rivalries of the *PAICV* and *MPD* continue to divide the community of Cape Verdean immigrants in America. As expected in color-conscious America, the community is also divided over conceptions of race and color. Lighter-skinned, longer-established Cape Verdeans frequently refer to themselves as Portuguese. Others live in the black community and identify themselves as black.

This division of the community has worked against a collective response to elevated levels of youth unemployment, crime, and urban violence. At least 300 Cape Verdeans, children of immigrant families and mostly in their early 20s, have been deported to Cape Verde in the 1990s. They were convicted of certain felonies and fell under provisions of a 1996 law that required the US Immigration and Natural Service to deport convicted felons. In impoverished Cape Verde they have few prospects and often resort to a life a crime.

Cape Verde grants voting rights to anyone born in the islands, so many Cape Verdean emigrants participated in the parliamentary and presidential elections of 2001. Absentee ballots are not employed in the process. Instead, polling places are set up in community centers wherever a concentration of islanders lives. There were nine official polling places in Massachusetts, Rhode Island, and Connecticut for this cycle of elections.

Based largely on diaspora support, the *PAICV*, which had governed the islands for the first fifteen years after independence, re-captured political power by winning 39 out of 72 parliamentary seats in January elections. The *MPD* won 31 seats, and an alliance of three opposition parties captured the remaining two seats.

The two parties faced each other again in the February presidential elections. Former Prime Minister Carlos Veiga represented the *MPD*, while Cape Verde's first head of government, Pedro Pires, led the *PAICV*. Three other candidates, David Hopffer Almada, a former minister of justice, Jorge Carlos Fonseca, a former minister of foreign affairs, and Onesimo Silveira, a former mayor of San Vicente, also entered the electoral competition.

The run-off pitted the two former prime ministers against each other: Veiga, a Lisbon-educated lawyer against the ex-guerrilla fighter Pedro Pires. The balloting was so close that results were not official until March. Once the Supreme Court had heard a number of electoral challenges, the National Electoral Commission announced a winner: Pedro Pires by a mere twelve votes.

Culture: Cape Verde has always been a cultural crossroads. Its rich musical heritage reflects its isolation and poverty, and its synthesis of intersecting cultures. For generations the islands sent their men abroad to work, manning, in the nineteenth century, the ships of the American whaling fleet. Longing and loneliness characterize the most famous Cape Verdean musical form, the *morna*. It combines the sadness and longing of the Portuguese *fado* melodic line with a quickness of rhythm that is distinctly African.

The singers of *morna* sing of *"saudade,"* a Portuguese word meaning longing and yearning, homesickness and nostalgia. It is the haunting sadness of an island people driven to leave by poverty, but always looking back to home and loved ones. One of the greatest Cape Verdean singers is Cesaria Evora. Her recordings are perennially near the top of World Music charts and her live performances have captivated an international audience.

Economy: Cape Verde has extremely limited natural resources. An archipelago of ten larger islands, only nine of which are habitable, and eight smaller islets, Cape Verde has little land to cultivate. Only 20 percent of the land can be used for agriculture. A rugged volcanic terrain, Cape Verde is subject to persistent periods of drought, interrupted by torrential rains and floods that erode what useful land is available.

Beans and maize are the most important foodstuffs grown, but production fluctuates with climatic conditions. Other crops include bananas, sweet potatoes, yams, manioc, pumpkins, sugar-cane, coffee, and groundnuts, but the country must import nearly 90 percent of its food. This results in a large trade deficit.

According to official figures, unemployment affects about 26% of the labor force. Annual growth in GDP has averaged a modest 3.8 percent from 1987 to 1997, but the IMF has recorded growth of 5 percent in 1998. This was largely fueled by growth in tourism. With an abundance of good quality beaches, coupled with a sunny climate, tourism has strong growth potential. The government recognizes this and has encouraged foreign investment in the industry.

Since attaining power in 1991, the *MPD* government has reversed the socialist policies of its predecessor and liberalized the economy. The state is now less an agent of intervention. Prices and exchange rates have been freed from government control and a privatization program is selling off state corporations. These policies have encouraged foreign investors, donors, and lenders.

The Future: The country's future is very limited by climate and geography. The government's privatization program should bring badly needed revenue to the treasury. Tourism and fishing look like the most promising areas of development.

Given the closeness of the presidential elections, there will inevitably be some tension between the parties in parliament. It is unlikely that the *PAICV*, despite its socialist orientations, will reverse the economic liberalism of the past ten years.

The Democratic Republic of Sao Tome and Principe (Sow Toe–*may* and *Preen*–see–pay)

São Tomé city

Land: 1001sq. km.=385 sq. mi. São Tomé is 275 miles off the coast of The Gabon; Príncipe is 125 miles off mainland Equatorial Guinea. Both lie just north of the Equator.
Population: 154,878 (July 1999 est.)
Capital City: São Tomé
Climate: Tropical; hot, humid; one rainy season (October to May).
Official Language: Portuguese
Other Principal Languages: Crioulo
Ethnic groups: Mestico, Angolares (descendants of Angolan slaves), Forros (descendants of freed slaves), *Servicais* (contract laborers from Angola, Mozambique, and Cape Verde), Tongas (children of *servicais* born on the islands), and Europeans (primarily Portuguese).
Principal Religions: Roman Catholic, Evangelical Protestant, and Seventh-day Adventist.
Chief Commercial Products: Cocoa 90%, copra, coffee, palm and oil (1997).
GNP per capita: 280 US$
Currency: Dobra (Db)
Independence Date: 12 July 1975 (from Portugal).
Chief of State: President Miguel Trovoada (since 4 April 1991).
National Flag: Three horizontal bands of green (top), yellow (double width), and green with two black five-pointed stars placed side by side in the center of the yellow band and a red isosceles triangle based on the hoist side; uses the popular pan-African colors of Ethiopia.

São Tomé and Príncipe form an archipelago of two main islands and several associated islets lying just north of the Equator. Of volcanic origins, the islands have fertile central highlands from which numerous fast flowing streams carry soil to the ocean. Tropical rainforests cover 75% of the land area and shelter flora and fauna similar to that found on mainland Equatorial Guinea.

History: Portuguese navigators discovered the uninhabited islands in the late 15th century. By the mid-16th century slaves had been imported, and the islands had become a major exporter of sugar. A slave-based plantation economy characterized the islands well into the 20th century based, after the decline of sugar exports, on coffee and finally cocoa.

The rich volcanic soils proved well-suited to cocoa trees, and by 1908 São Tomé had become the world's largest producer of coco. The crop was grown on extensive plantations called *rocas*—owned by Portuguese companies or absentee landlords—that occupied all productive farmland. The *rocas* system inevitably led to abusive treatment of African farm workers, and the history of the islands is filled with slave revolts and resistance to labor demands.

Local dissatisfaction with working conditions on the plantations led to an outbreak of riots in 1953. In what became known as the "Batepa Massacre," over 1,000 *forros* (the descendants of freed slaves) were shot by Portuguese troops for refusing to work the *rocas*. The massacre is seen as the beginning of the nationalist movement in the islands.

A Committee for the Liberation of São Tomé and Príncipe was created in exile in 1960. It changed its name to the *Movement for the Liberation of São Tomé and Príncipe* (*MLSTP*) in 1972. Unlike its counterpart in Guinea-Bissau, the *MLSTP* never mounted a guerrilla campaign against the Portuguese.

Following the overthrow of the Salazar dictatorship in 1974, African troops in São Tomé mutinied, and the new government agreed to hand over power to the *MLSTP* in 1975. Independence was granted on July 12, 1975. Most Portuguese had already departed, taking skills and capital with them. At independence, the Portuguese legacy was a 90% illiteracy rate, few skilled workers, and abandoned plantations.

At independence the *MLSTP* became the nation's sole political party and ruled with little tolerance for opposition for 15 years. Its leader, Manuel Pinto da Costa, assumed the new nation's presidency, and Miguel Trovoada, another founder of the *MLSTP*, was elected prime minister.

To cope with the country's disastrous economic inheritance, President Pinto da Costa turned to Marxist-Leninist models of political and economic organization. Most plantations were nationalized, and no one was allowed to own more than 247 acres. The single ruling party largely absorbed the country's organizational life. Social control and surveillance were organized through a series of people's militias set up in workplaces and villages.

When cocoa prices collapsed in the mid-1980s, the economy was severely damaged. Popular dissatisfaction led to a process of liberalization which culminated in the establishment of multiparty democracy in 1990. Constitutional reforms included the direct election of the president, and Miguel Trovoada, whom Pinto da Costa had accused of complicity in a coup plot and had jailed from 1979 to 1981, returned from exile to battle his old comrade-in-arms for the presidency. Running as an independent, Trovoada won. He survived a coup attempt in 1995 and went on to win re-election to a second five-year term in 1996 against his old foe, Manuel Pinto da Costa. Since then São Tomé has been characterized by continuing political and economic crisis.

In November 1998 legislative elections the *MLSTP*, in alliance with the *Social Democratic Party* (*PSD*), won an absolute majority 31 of 55 seats in the National Assembly. President Trovoada's *Independent Democratic Alliance* (*ADI*) became the official opposition. São Tomé's politics remain bitter, personal and contentious.

The government continues to face serious social agitation. Workers see their own conditions deteriorating while rumors of a huge oil bonanza are rife. Oil companies have publicly paid the government nearly $8 million in "bonuses," but the mass of the population has little to show for it.

President Trovoada of São Tomé and Príncipe

Civil servants, including doctors and teachers, regularly strike to protest their salaries and working conditions. In July 1999, president Trovoada recognized the validity of the protests. "Salaries and pensions are clearly not enough to cover people's basic needs," he said.

More darkly, he sent a warning to the government: "São Tomé's oil cannot be a matter for political colleagues, friends and relatives. Its revenue should benefit citizens and the population as a whole." The president's speech was a high point of political candor, but it only highlighted what seemed normal in a country suddenly exposed to the possibility of immense oil riches: the politically well-placed jockey to control sources of wealth. Trovoada unveiled the process in São Tomé, accusing "a number of citizens and political leaders of eagerly getting themselves into positions to reap fabulous personal benefits."

São Tomé's next presidential elections are scheduled for Fall 2001. President Trovoada, having served two terms, is constitutionally ineligible to run again. His traditional foe, Pinto da Costa, has indicated he is not interested in running again. Given the political stalemate produced by divided government, there is some talk of amending the constitution to strengthen the hand of the president.

Culture: Wilder than Cape Verde and closer to Europe than the Caribbean, São Tomé and Príncipe represent a relatively unspoiled paradise for tourists. Clean beaches, a stunning Blue Lagoon, rain forest and mountains with the Obo Natural Park are all available to the intrepid. These would appear to be few: in 1998 there were only some 2,000 tourist visitors to the islands.

The climate is equatorial, and to avoid oppressive humidity it's best to arrive during the driest and coolest months—from June to September. Roads are few, and any serious tourism requires four-wheel drive vehicles.

São Tomé, the capital, has a wealth of somewhat down-at-the-heel colonial architecture. The city's atmosphere is unrushed and unhurried. Blackouts are frequent, adding to the somnambulant mood. For many the best cup of coffee in the world comes from local beans.

Economy: The country has been traditionally dependent on the export of cocoa. In 1975 Portuguese plantation farmers held 90% of all cultivated land on the islands. After independence, with a regime in the thrall of Stalinist economic thinking, the cocoa plantations were collectivized. Production collapsed and the plantations deteriorated. From exports of 11,400 tons of cocoa in 1900, production plummeted to 4,000 in 1996, despite efforts to re–privatize the plantations in 1990. São Tomé's dependence on cocoa is virtually total. Foreign exchange earnings in 1998 totaled $4.7 million, with $4.6 million derived from cocoa sales. Such dependence is subject to the hazards of price fluctuations, and cocoa prices have recently tumbled. In 1999 cocoa was valued at $1,400 per ton, but by March 2000 the price had dropped to $700. The fall in prices was especially disastrous for small producers, some of whom went into debt.

São Tomé has faced vertiginous inflation and high unemployment. Its currency, the *dobra*, traded at the rate of 200 per dollar in 1991, sank to a low of 7,000 per dollar, and by 1999 was traded at 2,366 per dollar. Government action has begun to control inflation. In 2000 the inflation rate was 10%, down from the preceding year's 12.6%. Unemployment has reached 75%, and those who do work average $10-15 dollars per month. The economy is periodically paralyzed by employee strikes.

Worker salary agitation can be understood in a situation where virtually all consumer goods have to be imported. A pair of shoes costs about $95, more than the new monthly minimum salary of a government worker. Most workers live in abject poverty.

Diversification is essential, and the government is exploring a variety of options. Sweet peppers and flowers, which have a high value on the international market, are seen as viable alternatives. Fishing agreements bring in some revenue to the national treasury. Commercial timber operations are mostly geared to local usage, though the bark of cinchona trees is commercially harvested for quinine production.

São Tomé's Volcanic Shoreline *Photo by Fabien Violas*

The most important potential for São Tomé lies in its oil prospects. Nigeria and São Tomé have settled their maritime boundary dispute and agreed to jointly explore for oil and other resources in a disputed area. Seismic tests conducted by Mobil have already discovered petroleum blocks in the São Tomean economic zone bordering Nigeria. It is estimated the archipelago has a production capacity of 500,000 barrels a day, with reserves expected to last 200 years. Extraction has not yet started.

The relationship between Environmental Holdings Corporation (ERHC) and the São Tomé government remains, apparently, at issue in the courts. ERHC mapped out the country's maritime economic zone and established a grid for oil exploration, but by October 1999 the bloom appeared to have faded from its relationship with the government.

The company announced it was dissolving the partnership with the São Tomé and Príncipe National Petroleum Company (STPETRO) for breach of contract. The government, said the company, seemed to have "much personal interest rather than collective" in negotiating oil exploration accords. The government announced that it would begin legal action, alleging defamation.

The Future: Covetous eyes are being cast on these volcanic islands by imaginative entrepreneurs. Plans for a duty free zone on the island of Principe have roused the ire of environmentalists who have managed to slow down its development. The forced cohabitation between the president and his opponents in the national assembly has not been not a recipe for progress. But all things change, and if petroleum reserves are proved, oil will greatly lubricate the possibilities for change.

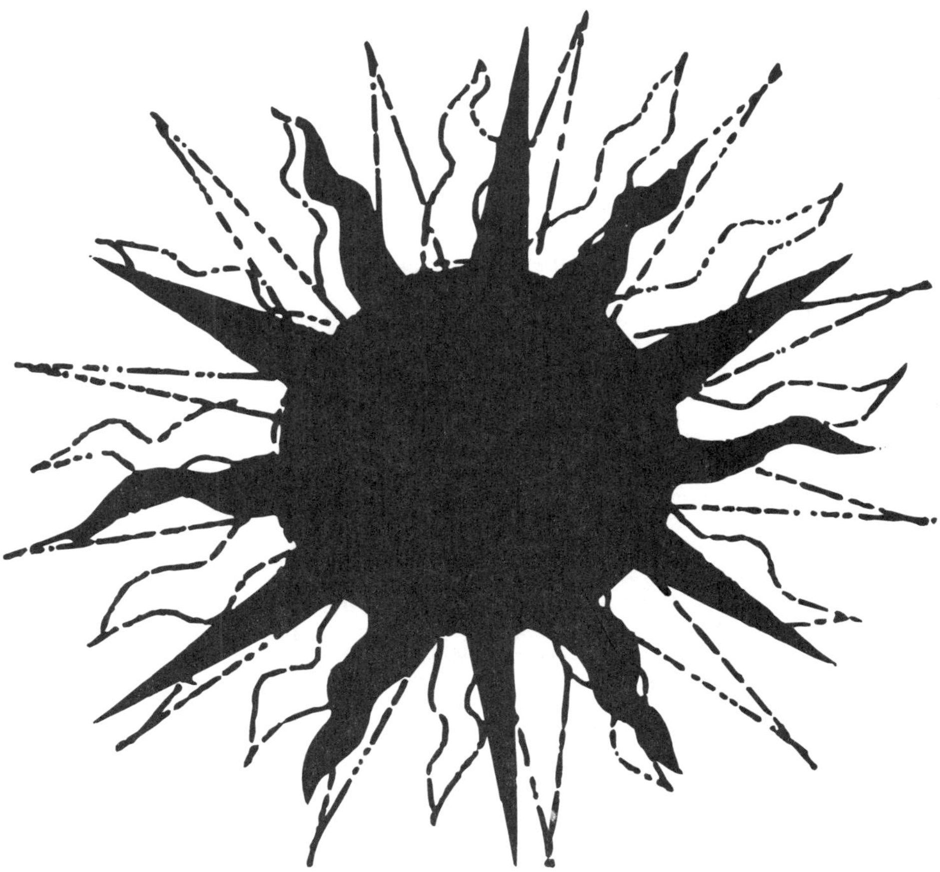

The Republic of the Seychelles *(Say–shells)*

Intendance Beach, Mahe

Photo by Angelo Cavalli, STMA (Seychelles Tourism Marketing Authority)

Land area and terrain: 100 sq. mi., about 1,000 miles off the east coast of Kenya in the Indian Ocean, consisting of some 92 islands, half of which are mountainous and very scenic. The others are little more than coral atolls.
Population: 79,164 (July 1999 est.)
Capital City: Victoria (on Mahe, pronounced Mah-*hay*, pop. 21,000 estimated.)
Climate: Tropical marine; humid; cooler season during southeast monsoon (late May to September); warmer season during northwest monsoon (March to May).
Official Languages: English, French
Other Principal Languages: Creole
Ethnic groups: Seychellois (mixture of Asians, Africans, and Europeans).
Religions: Roman Catholic 90%, Anglican 8%, and other 2%.
Chief Commercial Products: fish, cinnamon bark, copra, tea and vanilla.
GNP per capita: 6,450 US$
Independence Date: 29 June 1976 (from UK).
Chief of State: France Albert René, President.
National Flag: Five oblique bands of blue (hoist side), yellow, red, white, and green (bottom) radiating from the bottom of the hoist side.

Located in the western Indian Ocean, 1,000 miles off the coast of East Africa, the Seychelles comprises nearly 100 islands, spread over 154,000 square miles of the Indian Ocean. Lying just below the Equator, the islands have been dubbed a "Garden of Eden" because of the lushness and diversity of their scenery: some are volcanic, some are coral, all are different. Mahé is the largest and most populated of the islands, with almost 90% of the nation's total population of 80,000.

History: The first recorded landfall on the islands was made by an expedition of the British East India company in 1609. France colonized the islands in the 18th century, but lost them to Britain as a consequence of the Napoleonic wars. French colonists established plantations worked by African slaves, but the abolition of slavery in the 1830s forced a shift away from cotton to smaller-scale agricultural cultivation. The nineteenth century saw an influx of Asians—Chinese, Indians, and Malays. Over the years the populations intermarried, producing the islands' present mixed population. The descendants of former slaves have tended to remain an underclass.

The British colony was granted self government in 1975 and independence in 1976. James R. Mancham, the islands' first president, was overthrown in 1977 by a leftist coup d'etat led by his prime minister, France Albert René. In 1979 René revised the constitution and created a one-party socialist state controlled by his *Seychelles People's Progressive Front* (*SPPF*). President René has been in power ever since.

A multiparty political system was not permitted until 1991, and Seychelles' first democratic multiparty elections were held in 1993. René triumphed over former president James Mancham, and the SPPF retained control of the National Assembly.

President René of The Seychelles

In March 1997 elections, President René was once again returned to power with 66.65% of the votes cast. James Mancham, leader of the opposition *Democratic Party (DP)*, was the big loser, receiving only 14% of the vote, down from the 35% he had won in 1993. The *DP* also saw its legislative representation reduced from 5 to 1. Wavel Ramkalawan, leader of the *United Opposition (UO)*, drew 20% of presidential ballots, and his party replaced the DP as official opposition by winning 26% of votes cast in legislative elections. President René's *Seychelles People's Progressive Front (SPPF)* holds 30 legislative seats. Its nearest rival, the*UO*, has only 3.

In July 1998 the UO changed its name to the *Seychelles National Party* (*SNP*). The party's leader, Reverend Ramkalawan, has proved to be much less conciliatory as leader of the opposition than his predecessor. Fifteen minutes after the first sessions of parliament began, he was expelled for protesting rulings by the speaker. Despite its overwhelming majority, the *SSPF* makes few concessions to its opposition.

Seychelles'one daily newspaper and single radio and television service are government controlled, and opposition spokesmen are not, shall we say, given extensive coverage. In February 2001, President René filed several lawsuits against *Regar*, an opposition weekly, and *Vizyon*, an information bulletin of the *SNP* claiming defamation. The two publications represent the only alternative to state controlled media and could be bankrupted if found guilty by the courts. President Rene appoints all Seychelles judges.

Culture: The population of the Seychelles is relatively homogenous, the result of frequent intermarriage between the island's original French settlers and Africans who settled after the islands were ceded to Britain in the early 1800s. Small Indian and Chinese minorities also exist. Most of the population is Roman Catholic, and almost everyone speaks Creole.

Fish and rice are the basic staples of Seychelles cuisine. Islanders eat some 165 pounds of fish annually and face reduced catches from the sea. The 1998 catch was down some 60%, attributable to increased temperatures of the Indian Ocean waters. Fish are migrating to cooler waters.

Economy: Isolated in the vast Indian Ocean, the Seychelles promote themselves as an idyllic tourist location. More than 130,000 people visited the islands in 1999 and accounted for 70% of their hard currency. It's up-scale tourism only—charter flights are not permitted. With the weakening of Asian economies in the late 1990s, however, tourism weakened. The flow of hard currency slowed, but government spending did not.

In December 2000, the International Monetary Fund reported that the Seychelles' net international reserves were depleted and that government debt had grown alarmingly. Twenty-three years of comprehensive welfare state spending had brought the socialist Garden of Eden to the brink of bankruptcy.

Seychelles has one of the highest living standards in Africa with a remarkable per capita GDP of more than $6,000. But the economy has been stagnant, and in 1999 it posted a negative growth of 3%. Foreign exchange reserves are exhausted.

The Seychelles Chamber of Commerce and Industry estimates there are around 650 million Seychelles rupees (over $111 million) awaiting conversion into foreign exchange within the national banking system. The foreign exchange crisis almost led to British Airways and Kenya Airways stopping flights to Seychelles because they were unable to convert rupees. The effect on tourism would have been devastating, and after prolonged negotiations the government permitted the airlines to slowly exchange their rupee earnings for hard currency.

Seychelles is taking advantage of its greatest natural resource, fish. Its exclusive economic zone gives it control of more than 386 thousand sq. miles of Indian Ocean, abundant in rich fishing grounds.

Since 1979 foreign vessels fishing in the zone have had to secure a license. A fleet of patrol boats enforces the exclusion zone, and all fishing vessels must stop in Victoria port, register their catch, and pay the appropriate fees. Registered hauls have increased from 60,000 tons of tuna in 1983 to 250,000 tons in 1998. The European Union sends the most vessels to the zone, with more than 40 ships working its waters.

Global warming has had a double impact on the Seychelles. Several species of fish have moved on to cooler waters, and many of the islands' coral reefs are dying. The reefs cannot tolerate a rise in sea temperature of over 1-2 ° C for more than a few weeks. In 1998 temperatures rose 3° for several weeks, killing the once-colorful reefs and turning them into crumbling gray rubble.

Fishing licenses and fees bring in about $ 7million annually, but the government decided added value could be better achieved by processing the catch locally. In 1995, it joined with Heinz to build the new cannery on reclaimed land in Victoria harbor. The factory currently cans 250 tons of tuna daily, but has a capacity of 400 tons a day. By the year 2000 the Indian Ocean Tuna factory was expected to can around 100,000 tons a year—about 50% of the annual the tuna catch.

With 2000 workers, scheduled to increase to 2500 in the early months of 2000, Indian Ocean Tuna has nearly replaced tourism as Seychelles' largest foreign currency earner. Given the country's high employment rates, the factory brings in nearly 40% of the workforce from overseas—mainly women from the Philippines. The factory generated about $100 million in 1999, almost as much as Seychelles tourism.

When a new prawn farm was inaugurated on the island of Coetivy, 155 miles south of Mahé in 1992, President France Albert René predicted that aquaculture would overtake tourism revenues. After seven years of operation those expectations have failed to materialize. The state-owned Seychelles Marketing Board (SMB) has built a new $22 million prawn processing plant, but the endeavor increasingly looks like a costly failure.

Failed investments and mismanagement result from excessive government involvement in the economy. According to a recent EU study, government expenditures account for 62% of GDPover the last six years. The economy is dominated by the Seychelles Marketing Board (SMB), the islands' largest employer. Headed by president René, SMB possesses a variety of import and export monopolies and has a share of almost every enterprise.

A good socialist at heart, René claims SMB saved the islands from dishonest merchants who imported low-quality products to make maximum profits and could not assure regular supplies to a population largely dependent on imported foodstuffs. Critics note that SMB's monopolies have not prevented shortages in a wide variety of products.

The IMF and EU offer a simple prescription for Seychelles' welfare-state woes: privatize government monopolies, eliminate price controls, devalue the rupee, permit foreign investment and scrub controls on foreign exchange. It may be a hard sell, but the government, desperate for revenue, has begun to sell off its housing stock, encouraging, in very un-socialist terms, private home ownership.

The Future: Economic realities will force the government, kicking and screaming, to loosen the state's grip on Seychelles' economy. The free lunch enjoyed for so long by the Seychellois will become a bit more like lean cuisine.

The Federal Islamic Republic of the Comoros

The south shore of Nzwani, between Sima and Moya.

Photo courtesy Martin Ottenheimer

Land area and terrain: 2,170 sq. km. = 838 sq. mi. The Comoro *group* consists of four mountainous islands lying between Tanzania and the northern coast of Madagascar: Grand Comore (also known as Njazidja), Anjouan (Nzawi), Mohéli (Mwali) and Mayotte. The latter, with a substantial Christian minority, opposed joining the other three and, although claimed by the Republic, remains a dependency of France.

Climate: Tropical marine; rainy season (November to May); cyclones possible during rainy season.

Population: 562,723 (July 1999 est.)

Capital City: Moroni (on Grande Comore, pop. 32, 000, estimated).

Ethnic groups: Antalote, Cafre, Makoa, Oimatsaha, Sakalava.

Principal Religions: Sunni Muslim 86%, Roman Catholic 14%.

Official Languages: Arabic, French

Other Principal Languages: Comoran (a blend of Swahili and Arabic).

Chief Commercial Products: Vanilla, ylang-ylang, cloves, perfume oil, and copra.

GNP per capita: 370 US$

Currency: Comoran franc

Independence Date: 6 July 1975 (from France).

Chief of State: Colonel Azali Assoumani.

National Flag: Green with a white crescent in the center of the field, its points facing downward; there are four white five-pointed stars placed in a line between the points of the crescent; the crescent, stars, and color green are traditional symbols of Islam; the four stars represent the four main islands of the archipelago—Mwali, Njazidja, Nzwani, and Mayotte (a territorial collectivity of France, but claimed by Comoros); the design, the most recent of several, is described in the constitution approved by referendum on 7 June 1992.

Political History: After WWII the islands became Overseas French Territories and were represented in the French National Assembly. Agreement was reached in 1973 to grant independence in 1978, but on July 6, 1975, the Comoran parliament declared unilateral independence. Deputies from Mayotte abstained from this vote, and as a result the Comoran government had effective control over only Grand Comore, Anjouan, and Mohéli. Mayotte remains under French jurisdiction to this day.

The government of President Mohamed Taki Abdoulkarim, a deeply religious Sunni Muslim, was elected in 1996 following a mercenary-led coup which deposed then-president Djohar Said Mohamed. He went on to reintroduce the death penalty, announce restrictions on the consumption of alcohol and censure women who wore mini-skirts. In October 1996, Taki amended the constitution, strengthening the powers of the presidency and sharply eroding the powers of individual islands—the source of much future disturbance.

Taki's government directed little development money to Anjouan and Mohéli; unemployment there rose to 90%. Islanders also thought of themselves as unfairly taxed in indirect ways by Grand Comore. They had, for example, to make an expensive trip across the 50-mile straits to the capital to obtain any official documents. And always there was the nearby example of Mayotte. By remaining with

Colonel Azali Assoumani

France, the citizens of Mayotte enjoyed free education, health benefits and a minimum wage. Rebuffed by France when reunion with the former colonial power was proposed, Anjouan and Mohéli declared unilateral independence in August 1997.

In September a misguided and misdirected government invasion was repulsed and only hardened the resolve of secessionists. A February 1998 referendum adopted a new independence constitution, but economic reality argued against the case for independence. Both Anjouan and Mohéli are volcanic islands with few exports, poor economies and a population problem; there is little likelihood they could go it alone. To make matters worse, bloody factional disputes broke out among the secessionists. Armed militias of unemployed youths supporting Anjouan "president" Foundi Abdallah Ibrahim fought pitched battles with those supporting the man he had sacked as "prime minister," Chamassi Said Omar. The two had been bitterly divided over the island's future. Omar preferred a return to rule by France while Ibrahim argued for full independence. After a failed assassination attempt against Ibrahim in late November, numerous deaths resulted from machine gun and artillery battles between militias and the Anjouan capital, Mutsamudu, was left in ruins. In August 1999 Ibrahim signed a declaration indicating that he no longer claimed to be president, and delegated most of his powers to the separatist Lieutenant-Colonel Said Abeid Abdelemane.

On Grand Comore, President Taki died suddenly of natural causes in November. His death left the Islamic federation leaderless, with no designated successor and facing the political impasse of secession. Tadjiddine Ben Said Massounde, the elderly president of the Comoros high court, was persuaded to accept an interim presidency. More technician than politician, the acting president appointed the opposition leader Abbas Djoussouf as prime minister in an effort to create a government of national unity. France, the OAU, South Africa and other island states stepped up diplomatic pressures to resolve the crisis and ultimately representatives of the three islands agreed to attend a reconciliation conference on the island of Madagascar in April 1999.

The Madagascar conference produced agreement on the tentative outlines of a new Comoran state. Anjouan was represented by a unified delegation and seemed to agree on a number of fundamental points. The Federal Islamic Republic would become the Union of Comoran Islands. The new federation would grant greater autonomy to the constituent islands, each of which would have its local executive and parliament after a one-year transition. To the central government would be reserved defense, foreign affairs, the issuance of currency, higher education and research. The federal presidency, elected by the National Assembly, would be rotated between the three islands every three years.

Nothing was said about disarming Anjouan militias. Delegates from Mohéli and Grand Comore initialed the agreement, while the Anjouan delegation held back, claiming that it had not been given a mandate to cede the island's independence. Consultations back home were necessary.

There were economic pressures in abundance on all parties to accept the agreement. France promised millions if political accord could be reached. A follow-up meeting was similarly scheduled on Mauritius by international lenders—if political agreement could be found.

On Grand Comore, anti-Anjouan riots broke out when the details of the agreement were announced. Youth gangs attacked and threatened residents from Anjouan, ordering them to leave the island, and confiscated the cars of Anjouan taxi drivers. Around 1,000 Anjouanais, despoiled of all they had, fled back to their island by sea and air, no doubt adding to sentiments for full independence. The government accused oppositon politicians of fomenting the troubles and sent in heavily armed troops to restore order. Since the best order to a military mind is martial order, the Comoran army effected the nation's 18th *coup d'état*, avoiding what seemed to be a slide into chaos and anarchy.

The army commander, Colonel Azali Assoumani, told his countrymen that the army had assumed "its role as the last bastion in the survival of our nation and state." Constitution, government, parliament and parties were dissolved. A majority of the 800-man army was reportedly Anjouanais and had brought pressure from within the ranks to end the attacks on that island's citizens. Col. Azali, from Grand Comore himself, said there would be heavy punishment for anyone harassing people of Anjouanese origin. He also announced commitment to the recent Madagascar accord. The army, he said, would remain in power for a year.

That year came and went in April 2000, and little had changed. There was no return to civilian government, and no one had been able to put Comoros together again. Anjouan continued its separatist ways under Lt. Col. Said Abeid, who organized a series of farcical "elections." A "National Assembly" was elected in August; a referendum held, and the Madagascar agreement "massively" rejected and independence affirmed. Municipal elections were called in March, and Lt.Col. Abeid was reported to be clearing the streets and villages of his opponents.

The two colonels met and agreed on a looser relationship among the constituent elements of the Federal Republic in August 2000, but the arrangement was roundly condemned by the political class as too concessionary to secessionists and destructive of national unity. Finally, after months of torturous negotiations facilitated by both the OAU and La Francophonie, a Comoran national reconciliation forum brought together delegates of the federal government and Anjouan authorities with members of civil society and opposition in February 2001.

In the agreement which emerged, Anjouan would return to the federal fold, but with recognition of the need of constituent communities to administer and freely manage their own affairs. A National Reconciliation Commission (NRC) would later work out the specifics, including a constitution; its decisions would be "binding for the institutions in the country."

It was also agreed that Col. Azali would head a transitional administration charged with establishing the constitutional and electoral commissions and overseeing the collection of small arms from various militia. When all parties showed commitment to the process, said the OAU representative, aid to the impoverished nation would once again begin to flow.

In March, Col. Azali announced he would not be a candidate in elections scheduled for December, freeing himself to implement the procedures established by the NRC. This being the Comoros, several groups still had reservations and quibbles as the June deadline for a constitution neared, and the whole process remains dicey at best.

Economy: The Comoros islands are one of the poorest countries in the world. Some 80% of the population is involved in the agricultural sector, but still the islands must import a significant portion of their foodstuffs. Rice is the country's main staple and accounts for 90% of Comoran imports.

In many ways, the islands are caught in a poverty spiral. GDP growth was negative in four out of five years between 1995 and 1999. It fell by 2.3% during the period 1995-1998 while the population was growing rapidly—between 2.5 and 3% annually. (For comparative purposes there are slightly over 40 births per 1000 population in Comoros; in the United States the figure is 14.2 birth per 1000.) Transfers from Cormorans living abroad and foreign assistance from European Union and Arab countries are critical economic props. External debt remains high—estimated at $218 millon—roughly equal to the country's total GDP.

Endemic political stability is exacerbated by the government's regular revenue shortfall. Civil servants weren't paid at least four months' salaries in 2000, and the government faces regular strikes by workers agitating for payment of wages due and salary increases to keep up with rising prices.

The export economy is based on vanilla (65% of the total), cloves (18.5%) and ylang ylang (12.5%), an essence popular in perfume making. Traditionally, Comoros generates about 200 tons of processed vanilla per year, but the 2000 harvest is not expected to rise too much above 140 tons. The decline has been attributed to aging vines, bad weather and farmers discouraged by previous poor sales. Prices paid the farmers, on the other hand, have risen following the cyclones which devastated Madagascar's vanilla plantations.

A similar increase in demand for cloves may have had longer-term negative consequences. Last year planters harvested 2,500 tons of cloves to take advantage of high sale prices, but the rapid picking damaged many trees; harvests for the next two years have been compromised, and this year's is not expected to surpass 1,000 tons.

The Comoros have long been the world's leading producer of the essence of ylang-ylang, an oil widely used in the perfume industry. Production is localized on Anjouan Island

Less exotic are the islands' undeniable fish resources, a sector which is still largely underdeveloped. The government signed a three-year agreement with the EU that begins in February 2001. A sizeable amount of money will be spent on developing the fisheries sector, while 65 EU ships are allowed to catch tuna. Annual compensation will be about $311,000.

The stunning natural landscapes of the islands are an obvious area for future touristic development. But for the moment political instability remains dissuasive.

Future: Whatever *is* there to say about a country whose history is dominated by coups, assassinations, and attempted secession? Stability, not to mention agreement or consensus, seems little likely.

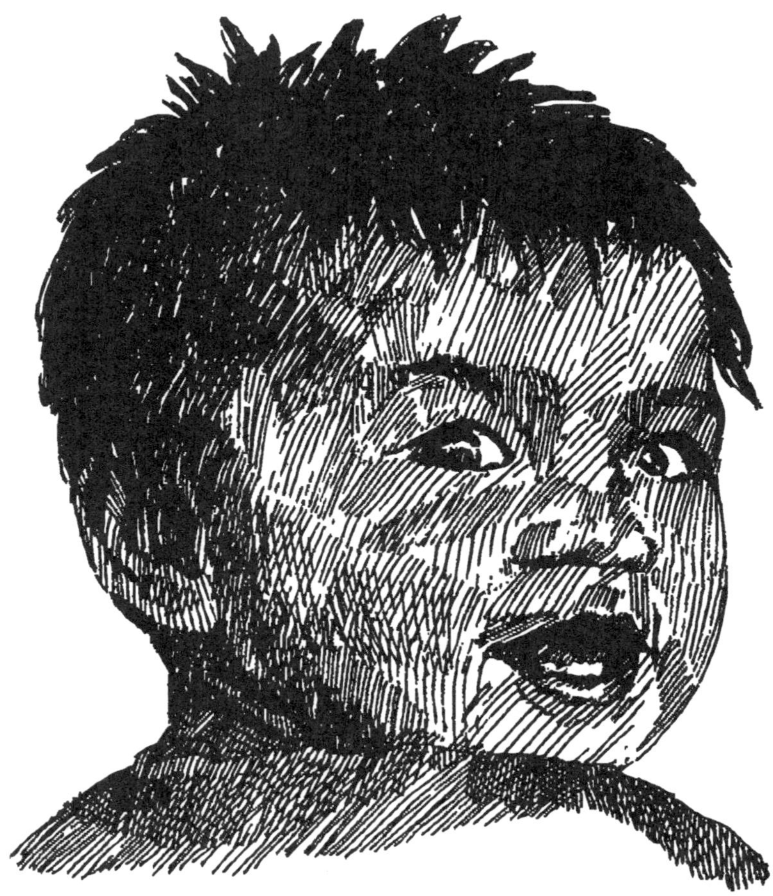

Selected Bibliography of Key English Language Sources

General

Adams, William and Andrew Goudie, eds. *Physical Geography of Africa.* New York: Oxford University Press, 1999.

Adjustment in Africa: Reform, Results, and the Road Ahead. Washington, DC: The World Bank, 1994.

Africa South of the Sahara 1996. London: Europa Publications Ltd., 25th ed. 1996.

Alemayu, Makonnen. *Industrialization in Africa.* Lawrenceville, NJ: Africa World Press, 1998.

Ali, Taisier M. and Robert O. Matthews, eds. *Civil Wars in Africa: Roots and Resolution.* Montreal: McGill-Queen's University Press, 1999.

Amadiume, Ifi. *Reinventing Africa: Matriarchy, Religion, and Culture.* Northampton, MA: Interlink Publishing, Group, 1998.

Ambrose, Brendalyn P. *Democratization and the Protection of Human Rights in Africa: Problems and Prospects.* Westport, CT: Greenwood Publishing Group, 1995.

Asante, S.K. *Regionalism and Africa's Development: Expectations, Reality, and Challenges.* New York: Saint Martin's Press, 1997.

Ayittey, George B. *Africa in Chaos.* New York: Saint Martin's Press, 1998.

Bever, Edward. *Africa.* Phoenix, AZ: Oryx Press, 1996.

Beyene, Asmelash and Gelase Mutahaba, eds. *The Quest for Constitutionalism in Africa: Selected Essays on Constitutionalism, the Nationality Problem, Military Rule, and Party Politics.* New York: Peter Lang Publishing, Inc., 1994.

Binns, Tony, ed. *People and Environment in Africa.* New York: John Wiley & Sons, 1995.

Callaghy, Thomas M. and John Ravenhill, eds. *Hemmed in: Responses to Africa's Economic Decline.* New York: Columbia University Press, 1993.

Cohen, Ronald, et al., eds. *Human Rights and Governance in Africa.* Gainesville, FL: University Press of Florida, 1993.

Conyers, James L., Jr. and Alva Bennett. *Africana History, Culture and Social Policy: a Collection of Critical Essays.* Bethesda, MD: International Scholars Publications, 1998.

Cooper, Brenda and Andrew Steyn, eds. *Transgressing Boundaries: New Directions in the Study of Culture in Africa.* Athens, OH: Ohio University Press, 1997.

Copson, Raymond W. *Africa's Wars and Prospects for Peace.* Armonk, NY: M.E. Sharpe, Inc., 1994.

Cordell, Dennis D. and Joel W. Gregory, eds. *African Population and Capitalism: Historical Perspectives.* Madison, WI: University of Wisconsin Press, 2nd ed. 1994.

Decalo, Samuel. *Civil-Military Relations in Africa.* Gainesville, FL: Florida Academic Press, 1998.

Decalo, Samuel. *The Stable Minority: Civilian Rule in Africa, 1960-1990.* Gainesville, FL: Florida Academic Press, 1998.

Delancey, Mark W., et al., *African International Relations: an Annotated Bibliography.* Boulder, CO: Westview Press, 2nd ed. 1997.

Deng, Francis M. and Terrence Lyons, eds. *Africa Reckoning: a Quest for Good Governance.* Washington, DC: Brookings Institution Press, 1998.

Ellis, Stephen, ed. *Africa Now: People, Policies, and Institutions.* Portsmouth, NH: Heinemann, 1996.

Fage, J.D. *A History of Africa.* New York: Routledge, 3rd ed. 1995.

Furley, Oliver and Roy May, eds. *Peacekeeping in Africa.* Brookfield, VT: Ashgate Publishing Company, 1998.

Gates, Henry Louis, Jr. and Kwame Anthony Appiah, eds. *Africana: the Encyclopedia of the African and African-American Experience.* New York: Basic Books, 1999.

Graybill, Lyn and Kenneth W. Thompson, eds. *Africa's Second Wave of Freedom: Development, Democracy, and Rights.* Lanham, MD: University Press of America, 1998.

Greenfield, Sidney M. and André Droogers, eds. *Syncretism in Africa and the Americas: the Reinterpretation of Cultural Patterns.* Lanham, MD: Rowman & Littlefield Publishers, 2000.

Griffiths, Ieuan Ll. *The African Inheritance.* New York: Routledge, 1995.

Grovogui, Siba N'Zatioula. *Sovereigns, Quasi Sovereigns, and Africans: Race and Self- determination in International Law.* Minneapolis, MN: University of Minnesota Press, 1996.

Hove, Chenjerai. *Shebeen Tales: Messages from Harare.* Chicago: LPC InBook, 1997.

Howe, Herbert M. *Ambiguous Order: Military Forces in African States.* Boulder, CO: Lynne Rienner Publishers, 2000.

Hughes, Arnold, ed. *Marxism's Retreat from Africa.* Portland, OR: Frank Cass & Co., Ltd., 1992.

Iheduru, Obioma M. *The Politics of Economic Restructuring and Democracy in Africa.* Westport, CT: Greenwood Publishing Group, 1999.

Ihonvbere, Julius O. *Africa and the New World Order.* New York: Peter Lang Publishing, 2000.

Iliffe, John. *Africans: the History of a Continent.* New York: Cambridge University Press, 1995.

Ishikawa, Kaoru. *Nation Building and Development Assistance in Africa: Different but Equal.* New York: Saint Martin's Press, 1999.

Isichei, Elizabeth. *A History of Christianity in Africa: from Antiquity to the Present.* Grand Rapids, MI: Eerdsmans, 1995.

Jalilian, Hossein, et al. *Industrial Development and Policy in Africa: Issues of De- Industrialisation and Development Strategy.* Northampton, MA: Edward Elgar Publishing, 2000.

Joseph, Richard, ed. *State, Conflict, and Democracy in Africa.* Boulder, CO: Lynne Rienner Publishers, 1999.

Khapoya, Vincent. *The African Experience.* Upper Saddle River, NJ: Prentice-Hall, Inc., 1994.

Lancaster, Carol. *Aid to Africa: So Much to Do, So Little Done.* Chicago: University of Chicago Press, 1999.

Lumumba-Kasongo, Tukumbi. *The Dynamics of Economic and Political Relations between Africa and Foreign Powers: a Study in International Relations.* Westport, CT: Greenwood Publishing Group, 1999.

Maddox, Gregory, ed. *African Nationalism and Revolution.* New York: Garland, 1993.

Mahadevan, Vijitha, et al., eds. *Contemporary African Politics and Development: a Comprehensive Bibliography.* Boulder, CO: Lynne Rienner Publishers, 1994.

Maier, Karl. *Into the House of the Ancestors: Inside the New Africa.* New York: John Wiley & Sons, 1997.

Mazrui, Ali A. and Alamin M. Mazrui. *The Power of Babel: Language in the African Experience.* Chicago: University of Chicago Press, 1998.

Mbaku, John M. *Institutions and Reform in Africa: the Public Choice Perspective.* Westport, CT: Greenwood Publishing Group, 1997.

McCann, James C. *Green Land, Brown Land, Black Land: an Environmental History of Africa, 1800-1990.* Westport, CT: Greenwood Publishing Group, 1999.

McIlwaine, John. *Africa: a Guide to Reference Material.* New Providence, NJ: Bowker-Saur, 1993.

McIntosh, Susan K., ed. *Beyond Chiefdoms: Pathways to Political Complexity in Africa.* New York: Cambridge University Press, 1999.

McLynn, Frank. *Hearts of Darkness: the European Exploration of Africa.* New York: Carroll & Graf, 1993.

Miers, Suzanne and Martin A. Klein. *Slavery and Colonial Rule in Africa.* Portland, OR: Frank Cass Publishers, 1999.

Mohan, P.C., ed. *Bibliography of Publications: Africa Region, 1990-97.* Washington, DC: The World Bank, 1998.

Mungazi, Dickson A. *The Mind of Africa.* Westport, CT: Greenwood Publishing Group, 1996.

Nzongola-Ntalaja, Georges and Margaret C. Lee. *The State and Democracy in Africa.* Lawrenceville, NJ: Africa World Press, 1998.

Oyebade, Adebayo. *Africa after the Cold War: the Changing Perspectives on Securi-*

ty. Lawrenceville, NJ: Africa World Press, 1998.
Paulson, Joann. *African Economies in Transition.* New York: Saint Martin's Press, 1999.
Rasmussen, R. Kent. *Modern African Political Leaders.* New York: Facts on File, 1998.
Reader, John. *Africa: a Biography of the Continent.* New York: Alfred A. Knopf, 1998.
Reno, William. *Warlord Politics and African States.* Boulder, CO: Lynne Rienner Publishers, 1998.
Royle, Trevor. *Winds of Change: the End of Empire in Africa.* North Pomfret, VT: Trafalgar Square, 1998.
Rwomire, Apollo. *Social Problems in Africa: New Visions.* Westport, CT: Greenwood Publishing Group, 2001.
Schraeder, Peter J. *African Politics and Society: a Continental Mosaic in Transformation.* New York: Saint Martin's Press, 1999.
Shams, Feraidoon, ed. *State and Society in Africa: Perspectives on Continuity and Change.* Lanham, MD: University Press of America, 1995.
Stewart, John. *African States and Rulers.* Jefferson, NC: McFarland & Company, 1999.
Sundkler, Bengt and Christopher Steed. *A History of the Christian Church in Africa.* New York: Cambridge University Press, 1999.
Thomas, Caroline and Peter Wilkin, eds. *Globalization, Human Security, and the African Experience.* Boulder, CO: Lynne Rienner Publishers, 1999.
Vogel, Joseph O., ed. *The Encyclopedia of Precolonial Africa: Archaeology, History, Languages, Cultures, and Environment.* Walnut Creek, CA: AltaMira Press, 1997.
Wesseling, H.L., trans. by Arnold J. Pomerans. *Divide and Rule: the Partition of Africa 1880- 1914.* Westport, CT: Greenwood Publishing Group, 1996.
Wiseman, John A., ed. *Democracy and Change in Sub-Saharan Africa.* New York: Routledge, 1995.
Wohlgemuth, Lennart, et al., eds. *Institution Building and Leadership in Africa.* Piscataway, NJ: Transaction Publishers, 1998.
Wright, Stephen. *African Foreign Policies.* Boulder, CO: Westview Press, 1998.
Yansane, Aguibou Y. *Prospects for Recovery and Sustainable Development in Africa.* Westport, CT: Greenwood Press, 1996.
Young, Crawford. *The African Colonial State in Comparative Perspective.* New Haven, CT: Yale University Press, 1994.

Coastal West Africa

Alie, Joe A. *A New History of Sierra Leone.* New York: Saint Martin's Press, 1990.
Berry, LaVerle, ed. *Ghana: a Country Study.* Washington, DC: U.S. GPO, 3rd ed. 1995.
Cann, Joseph P. *Counterinsurgency in Africa: the Portuguese Way of War, 1961-1974.* Westport, CT: Greenwood Publishing Group, 1997.
Clapham, Christopher S. *African Guerrillas.* Bloomington, IN: Indiana University Press, 1998.
Clark, Andrew Francis and Lucie Colvin Phillips. *Historical Dictionary of Senegal.* Lanham, MD: Scarecrow Press, 1994.
Daniels, Morna. *Côte d'Ivoire.* Santa Barbara, CA: ABC-CLIO, 1996.
Decalo, Samuel. *Historical Dictionary of Benin.* Lanham, MD: Scarecrow Press, 1995.
Decalo, Samuel. *Historical Dictionary of Togo.* Lanham, MD: Scarecrow Press, 3rd ed. 1996.
Dzorgbo, Dan-Bright S. *Ghana in Search of Development: the Challenge of Governance, Economic Management and Institution Building.* Brookfield, VT: Ashgate Publishing, 2000.
Eades, J.S. and Christopher Allen. *Benin.* Santa Barbara, CA: ABC-CLIO, 1997
Forrest, Joshua B. *Guinea-Bissau: Power, Conflict, and Renewal.* Boulder, CO: Westview Press, 1992.
Gellar, Sheldon. *Senegal: an African Nation between Islam and the West.* Boulder, CO: Westview Press, 1995.
Handloff, Robert E., ed. *Côte d'Ivoire: a Country Study.* Washington, DC: U.S. GPO, 3rd ed. 1991.
Huband, Mark. *The Liberian Civil War.* Portland, OR: International Specialized Book Services, 1998.
Hutchful, Eboe. *Ghana's Adjustment Experience: the Paradox of Reform.* Lawrenceville, NJ: Africa World Press, 2000.
Kludze, A. Kodzo. *Chieftaincy in Ghana.* Bethesda, MD: Austin & Winfield, 1998.
Kulah, Arthur F. *Liberia Will Rise Again: Reflections on the Liberian Civil Crisis.* Nashville, TN: Abingdon Press, 1999.
Lobban, Richard. *Cape Verde: Crioulo Colony to Independent Nation.* Boulder CO: Westview Press, 1995.
Lobban, Richard. *Historical Dictionary of Cape Verde.* Lanham MD: Scarecrow Press, 3rd ed. 1995.
Marah, John K. *African People in the Global Village: an Introduction to Pan African Studies.* Lanham, MD: University Press of America, 1998.
McDaniel, Antonio. *Swing Low, Sweet Chariot: the Mortality Cost of Colonizing Liberia in the Nineteenth Century.* Chicago: University of Chicago Press, 1995.
Mundt, Robert J. *Historical Dictionary of Côte d'Ivoire (the Ivory Coast).* Lanham, MD: Scarecrow Press, 1995.
Pinkney, Robert. *Democracy and Dictatorship in Ghana and Tanzania.* New York: Saint Martin's Press, 1997.

Central West Africa

Aborisade, Oladimeji. *Politics in Nigeria.* Reading, MA: Addison-Wesley Educational Publishers, 1999.
Akiba, Okon. *Nigerian Foreign Policy towards Africa: Continuity and Change.* New York: Peter Lang Publishing, 1998.
Amadi, L.O. *Dictionary of Nigerian History: from Aba to Zazzau.* Bethesda, MD: International Scholars Publications, 1998.
Apena, Adeline. *Colonization, Commerce and Entrepreneurship in Nigeria: the Western Delta, 1914-1960.* New York: Peter Lang Publishing, 1997.
Chiabi, Emmanuel. *The Making of Modern Cameroon: a History of Substate Nationalism and Disparate Union, 1914-1961.* Lanham, MD: University Press of America, 1997.
DeLancey, Mark W. *Historical Dictionary of the Republic of Cameroon.* Lanham, MD: Scarecrow Press, 3rd. ed. 2000.
Dibie, Robert A. *The Military-Bureaucracy Relationship in Nigeria: Public Policy Making and Implementation.* Westport, CT: Greenwood Publishing Group, 2000.
Falola, Toyin. *The History of Nigeria.* Westport, CT: Greenwood Publishing Group, 1999.
Fegley, Randall. *Equatorial Guinea.* Santa Barbara, CA: ABC-CLIO, 1992.
Human Rights Watch. *The Prince of Oil: Corporate Responsibility and Human Rights Violations in Nigeria's Oil Producing Communities.* New York: Human Rights Watch, 1999.
Kalck, Pierre and Thomas O'Toole. *Historical Dictionary of the Central African Republic.* Lanham, MD: Scarecrow Press, 2nd ed. 1992.
Kalu, Kelechi Amihe. *Economic Development and Nigerian Foreign Policy.* Lewiston, NY: The Edwin Mellen Press, 2000.
Kastfelt, Niels. *Religion and Politics in Nigeria: a Study in Middle Belt Christianity.* New York: Saint Martin's Press, 1994.
Krieger, Milton H. *An African State and Society in the 1990s: Cameroon's Political Crossroads.* Boulder, CO: Westview Press, 1998.
Liniger-Goumaz, Max. *Historical Dictionary of Equatorial Guinea.* Lanham, MD: Scarecrow Press, 1998.
Maier, Karl. *This House Has Fallen: a Journey through Nigeria's Heart of Darkness.* New York: PublicAffairs, 2000.
Metz, Helen Chapin, ed. *Nigeria: a Country Study.* Washington, DC: U.S. GPO, 5th ed. 1992.
Oke, Tayo. *Radicalism, Political Power, and Foreign Policy in Nigeria.* Lewiston, NY: Edwin Mellen Press, 1999.
Osaghae, Eghosa E. *The Crippled Giant: Nigeria since Independence.* Bloomington, IN: Indiana University Press, 1998.
Oyewole, Anthony. *Historical Dictionary of Nigeria.* Lanham, MD: Scarecrow Press, 1998.
Titley, Brian. *Dark Age: the Political Odyssey of Emperor Bokassa.* Toronto: University of Toronto Press, 1997.
Wright, Stephen. *Nigeria: Struggle for Stability and Status.* Boulder, CO: Westview Press, 1998.

Equatorial West Africa

Adelman, Howard and Astri Suhrke, eds. *The Path of a Genocide: the Rwanda Crisis from Uganda to Zaire.* Piscataway, NJ: Transaction Publishers, 1998.

Barnes, James F. *Gabon: Beyond the Colonial Legacy.* Boulder, CO: Westview Press, 1992.

Black, Richard. *Angola.* Santa Barbara, CA: ABC-CLIO, 1992.

Brittain, Victoria. *Death of Dignity: Angola's Civil War.* Chicago: LPC InBook, 1998.

Broadhead, Susan H. *Historical Dictionary of Angola.* Lanham, MD: Scarecrow Press, 1992.

Ciment, James. *Angola and Mozambique: Post-Colonial Wars in Southern Africa.* New York: Facts on File, 1997.

Colello, Thomas, ed. *Angola: a Country Study.* Washington, DC: U.S. GPO, 3rd ed. 1991.

Decalo, Samuel. *Historical Dictionary of Congo.* Lanham, MD: Scarecrow Press, 1996.

Destexhe, Alain. *Rwanda and Genocide in the Twentieth Century.* New York: New York University Press, 1995.

Eggers, Ellen K. *Historical Dictionary of Burundi.* Lanham, MD: Scarecrow Press, 1997.

Human Rights Africa Staff. *Genocide in Rwanda: the Planning and Execution of Mass Murder.* New Haven, CT: Yale University Press, 1997.

James, W. Martin. *A Political History of the Civil War in Angola, 1974-1990.* New Brunswick, NJ: Transaction, 1992.

Keane, Fergal. *Season of Blood: a Rwandan Journey.* New York: Viking Penguin, 1996.

Lemarchand, René. *Burundi: Ethnocide as Discourse and Practice.* New York: Cambridge University Press, 1994.

Meditz, Sandra W. and Tim Merrill, eds. *Zaïre: a Country Study.* Washington, DC: U.S. GPO, 4th ed. 1994.

Peterson, Scott. *Me against My Brother: at War in Somalia, Sudan and Rwanda.* New York: Routledge, 2000.

Shaw, Caroline S. *São Tomé and Principe.* Santa Barbara, CA: ABC-CLIO, 1994.

Tvedten, Inge. *Angola: Struggle for Peace and Reconstruction.* Boulder, CO: Westview Press, 1997.

United Nations and Rwanda, 1993-1996. New York: United Nations Publications, 1996.

Williams, Dawn Bastian, et al., *Zaïre.* Santa Barbara, CA: ABC-CLIO, 1995.

Southern Africa

Adler, Glenn and Jonny Steinberg. *From Comrades to Citizens: the South African Civics Movement and the Transition to Democracy.* New York: Saint Martin's Press, 2000.

Andersson, Hilary. *Mozambique: a War Against the People.* New York: Saint Martin's Press, 1992.

Azevedo, Mario Joaquim. *Historical Dictionary of Mozambique.* Lanham, MD: Scarecrow Press, 1991.

Bauer, Gretchen. *Labor and Democracy in Namibia, 1971-1996.* Athens, OH: Ohio University Press, 1998.

Beck, Roger B. *The History of South Africa.* Westport, CT: Greenwood Publishing Group, 2000.

Beinart, William and Saul Dubow, eds. *Segregation and Apartheid in Twentieth Century South Africa.* New York: Routledge, 1995.

Booth, Alan R. *Historical Dictionary of Swaziland.* Lanham, MD: Scarecrow Press, 2000.

Brink, Andre. *Reinventing a Continent: Writing and Politics in South Africa, 1982-1998.* Cambridge, MA: Zoland Books, 1998.

Byrnes, Rita M., ed. *South Africa: a Country Study.* Washington, DC: U.S. GPO, 3rd ed., 1997.Chanock, Martin. *Law, Custom and Social Order: the Colonial Experience in Malawi and Zambia.* Westport, CT: Heinemann, 1998.

Ciment, James. *Angola and Mozambique: Post-Colonial Wars in Southern Africa.* New York: Facts on File, 1997.

Crosby, Cynthia A. *Historical Dictionary of Malawi.* Lanham, MD: Scarecrow Press, 1993.

Dale, Richard. *Botswana's Search for Autonomy in Southern Africa.* Westport, CT: Greenwood Press, 1995.

Davis, Geoffrey V. *South Africa.* Santa Barbara, CA: ABC-CLIO, rev. ed. 1994.

Decalo, Samuel. *Malawi.* Santa Barbara, CA: ABC-CLIO, 2nd ed. 1995.

Dzimba, John. *South Africa's Destabilization of Zimbabwe, 1980-89.* New York: Saint Martin's Press, 1998.

Eades, Lindsay Michie. *The End of Apartheid in South Africa.* Westport, CT: Greenwood Publishing Group, 1999.

Elbadawi, Ibrahim and Trudi Hartzenberg. *Development Issues in South Africa.* New York: Saint Martin's Press, 2000.

Fine, Ben and Zavareh Rustomjee. *The Political Economy of South Africa: from Minerals-Energy Complex to Industrialization?* Boulder, CO: Westview Press, 1996.

Finnegan, William. *A Complicated War: the Harrowing of Mozambique.* Berkeley, CA: University of California Press, 1992.

Gillis, D. Hugh. *The Kingdom of Swaziland: Studies in Political History.* Westport, CT: Greenwood Publishing Group, 1999.

Ginsberg, Anthony. *South Africa's Future: the Struggle Ahead.* New York: Saint Martin's Press, 1999.

Goodman, David. *Fault Lines: Journeys into the New South Africa.* Berkeley, CA: University of California Press, 1999.

Grotpeter, John J. *Historical Dictionary of Zambia.* Lanham, MD: Scarecrow Press, 1998.

Hall, Margaret and Tom Young. *Confronting Leviathan: Mozambique since Independence.* Athens, OH: Ohio University Press, 1997.

Hayes, Patricia, et al., eds. *Namibia under South African Rule: Mobility and Containment, 1915-1946.* Athens, OH: Ohio University Press, 1998.

Jackson, Ashley. *Botswana 1939-1945: an African Country at War.* New York: Oxford University Press, 1999.

Johnston, Deborah. *Lesotho.* Santa Barbara, CA: ABC-CLIO, rev. ed., 1997.

Keegan, Timothy J. *Colonial South Africa and the Origins of the Racial Order.* Charlottesville, VA: University Press of Virginia, 1997.

Khadiagala, Gilbert M. *Allies in Adversity: the Frontline States in Southern Africa Security, 1975-1993.* Athens, OH: Ohio University Press, 1994.

Koelble, Thomas A. *The Global Economy and Democracy in South Africa.* Piscataway, NJ: Rutgers University Press, 1999.

Meer, Fatima. *Higher than Hope: the Authorized Biography of Nelson Mandela.* New York: Harper & Row, 1990.

Munro, William A. *The Moral Economy of the State: Conservation, Community Development, and State-Making in Zimbabwe.* Athens, OH: Ohio University Press, 1998.

Nelson, Harold D., ed. *Zimbabwe: a Country Study.* Washington, DC: U.S. GPO, 2nd ed. 1983.

Newitt, Malyn. *A History of Mozambique.* Bloomington, IN: Indiana University Press, 1995.

Nyeko, Balam. *Swaziland.* Santa Barbara, CA: ABC-CLIO, 1994.

Ohlson, Thomas and Stephen John Stedman. *The New Is Not Yet Born: Conflict Resolution in Southern Africa.* Washington, DC: Brookings Institution Press, 1994.

Potts, Deborah. *Zimbabwe.* Santa Barbara, CA: ABC-CLIO, rev. and expanded ed. 1993.

Rich, Paul B., ed. *The Dynamics of Change in Southern Africa.* New York: Saint Martin's Press, 1994.

Ross, Robert. *A Concise History of South Africa.* New York: Cambridge University Press, 1999.

Saunders, Christopher C. and Nicholas Southey. *Historical Dictionary of South Africa.* Lanham, MD: Scarecrow Press, 1999.

Schoeman, Stanley and Elna Schoeman. *Namibia.* Santa Barbara, CA: ABC-CLIO, rev. ed. 1997.

Schrire, Robert, ed. *Malan to De Klerk: Leadership in the Apartheid State.* New York: Saint Martin's Press, 1994.

Simon, David E., ed. *South Africa in Southern Africa: Reconfiguring the Region.* Athens, OH: Ohio University Press, 1999.

Spanger, Hans-Joachim and Peter Vale, eds. *Bridges to the Future: Prospects for Peace and Security in Southern Africa.* Boulder, CO: Westview Press, 1995.

Sparks, Donald L. and December Green.

Namibia: the Nation after Independence. Boulder, CO: Westview Press, 1992.
Swatuk, Larry A. and David R. Black, eds. *Bridging the Rift: the New South Africa in Africa.* Boulder, CO: Westview Press, 1997.
Switzer, Les and Mohamed Adhikari, eds. *South Africa's Resistance Press: Alternative Voices in the Last Generation under Apartheid.* Athens, OH: Ohio University Press, 2000.
Thede, Nancy and Pierre Beaudet, eds. *A Post-Apartheid Southern Africa?* New York: Saint Martin's Press, 1993.
Tutu, Desmond M. *No Future without Forgiveness.* New York: Doubleday, 1999.
Waldmeir, Patti. *Anatomy of a Miracle: the End of Apartheid and the Birth of the New South Africa.* New York: W.W. Norton & Company, 1997.
Welsh, Frank. *South Africa: a Narrative History.* New York: Kodansha America, 1999.
Woods, Anthony. *The Creation of Modern Malawi.* Boulder, CO: Westview Press, 1998.

East Africa Island Nations

Allen, Philip M. Madagascar: *Conflicts of Authority in the Great Island.* Boulder, CO: Westview Press, 1995.
Bennett, George and Pramila Ramgulan Bennett. *Seychelles.* Santa Barbara, CA: ABC-CLIO, 1993.
Bowman, Larry W. *Mauritius: Democracy and Development in the Indian Ocean.* Boulder, CO: Westview Press, 1991.
Bradt, Hilary. *Madagascar.* Santa Barbara, CA: ABC-CLIO, 1994.
Metz, Helen Chapin, ed. *Indian Ocean: Five Island Countries.* Washington, DC: U.S. GPO, 3rd ed. 1995.
Ottenheimer, Martin and Harriet Ottenheimer. *Historical Dictionary of the Comoro Islands.* Lanham, MD: Scarecrow Press, 1994.
Scarr, Deryck. *Seychelles since 1770: History of a Slave and Post-Slave Society.* Lawrenceville, NJ: Africa World Press, 1999.
Storey, William K. *Science and Power in Colonial Mauritius.* Rochester, NY: University of Rochester Press, 1997.

Eastern Africa

Adelman, Howard and Astri Suhrke, eds. *The Path of a Genocide: the Rwanda Crisis from Uganda to Zaire.* Piscataway, NJ: Transaction Publishers, 1998.
Bigsten, Arne and Steve Kayizzi-Mugerwa. *Crisis, Adjustment, and Growth in Uganda: a Study of Adaptation in an African Economy.* New York: Saint Martin's Press, 1999.
Byrnes, Rita M., ed. *Uganda: a Country Study.* Washington, DC: U.S. GPO, 2nd ed. 1992.
Crummey, Donald. *Land and Society in the Christian Kingdom of Ethiopia: from the Thirteenth to the Twentieth Century.* Champaign, IL: University of Illinois Press, 1999.
Darch, Colin. *Tanzania.* Santa Barbara, CA: ABC-CLIO, rev. ed. 1996.
Donham, Donald L. *Marxist Modern: an Ethnographic History of the Ethiopian Revolution* Berkeley, CA: University of California Press, 1999.
Fegley, Randall. *Eritrea.* Santa Barbara, CA: ABC-CLIO, 1995.
Forster, Peter G. and Sam Maghimbi, eds. *Agrarian Economy, State, and Society in Contemporary Tanzania.* Brookfield, VT: Ashgate Publishing Company, 1999.
Fozzard, Adrian. *Djibouti.* Boulder, CO: Westview Press, 1999.
Ghebre-Ab, Habtu. *Ethiopia and Eritrea: a Documentary Study.* Trenton, NJ: Red Sea Press, 1993.
Gregory, Robert G. *South Asians in East Africa: an Economic and Social History, 1890-1980.* Boulder, CO: Westview Press, 1993.
Hansen, Holger Bernt and Michael Twaddle, eds. *Developing Uganda.* Athens, OH: Ohio University Press, 1998.
Hansen, Holger Bernt and Michael Twaddle, eds. *Religion and Politics in East Africa: the Period since Independence.* Athens, OH: Ohio University Press, 1995.
Haugerud, Angelique. *The Culture of Politics in Modern Kenya.* New York: Cambridge University Press, 1995.
Henze, Paul B. *Layers of Time: a History of Ethiopia.* New York: Saint Martin's Press, 1999.
Killion, Tom. *Historical Dictionary of Eritrea.* Lanham, MD: Scarecrow Press, 1997.
Levine, Donald N. *Greater Ethiopia: the Evolution of a Multiethnic Society.* Chicago: University of Chicago Press, 2000.
Maloba, Wunyabara O. *Mau Mau and Kenya: an Analysis of a Peasant Revolt.* Bloomington, IN: Indianan University Press, 1998.
Marcus, Harold G. *A History of Ethiopia.* Berkeley, CA: University of California Press, 1994.
Metz, Helen Chapin, ed. *Somalia: a Country Study.* Washington, DC: U.S. GPO, 4th ed. 1993.
Munro-Hay, Stuart and Richard Pankhurst. *Ethiopia.* Santa Barbara, CA: ABC-CLIO, 1995.
Negash, Tekeste. *Eritrea and Ethiopia: the Federal Experience.* New Brunswick, NJ: Transaction Publishers, 1997.
Neyko, Balam. *Uganda.* Santa Barbara, CA: ABC-CLIO, rev. ed. 1996.
Ocitti, Jim. *Political Evolution and Democratic Practice in Uganda, 1952-1996.* Lewiston, NY: The Edwin Mellen Press, 2000.
Oded, Arye. *Islam and Politics in Kenya.* Boulder, CO: Lynne Rienner Publishers, 2000.
Ofcansky, Thomas P. and LaVerle Berry, eds. *Ethiopia: a Country Study.* Washington, DC: U.S. GPO, 4th ed. 1993.
Ofcansky, Thomas P. and Robert M. Maxon. *Historical Dictionary of Kenya.* Lanham, MD: Scarecrow Press, 1999.
Ofcansky, Thomas P. and Rodger Yeager. *Historical Dictionary of Tanzania.* Lanham, MD: Scarecrow Press, 2nd ed. 1999.
Ofcansky, Thomas P. *Uganda: Tarnished Pearl of Africa.* Boulder, CO: Westview Press, 1996.
Pankhurst, Barbara. *The Ethiopians.* Malden, MA: Blackwell Publishers, 1998.
Peterson, Scott. *Me against My Brother: at War in Somalia, Sudan and Rwanda.* New York: Routledge, 2000.
Pinkney, Robert. *Democracy and Dictatorship in Ghana and Tanzania.* New York: Saint Martin's Press, 1997.
Prouty, Chris and Eugene Rosenfeld. *Historical Dictionary of Ethiopia and Eritrea.* Lanham, MD: Scarecrow Press, 2nd ed. 1994.
Ricciuti, Edward R. *Somalia: a Crisis of Famine and War.* Brookfield, CT: Millbrook Press, 1993.
Schraeder, Peter J. *Djibouti.* Santa Barbara, CA: ABC-CLIO, 1991.
Tesfai, Alemseged. *Post-Conflict Eritrea: Prospects for Reconstruction and Development.* Lawrenceville, NJ: Red Sea Press, 1999.
Tripodi, Paolo. *Colonial Legacy in Somalia.* New York: Saint Martin's Press, 1999.
Tripp, Aili M. *Changing the Rules: the Politics of Liberalization and the Urban Informal Economy in Tanzania.* Berkeley, CA: University of California Press, 1997.
Watson, Mary Ann, ed. *Modern Kenya: Social Issues and Perspectives.* Lanham, MD: University Press of America, 2000.
Widner, Jennifer A. *The Rise of a Party-State in Kenya: from "Harambee!" to "Nyayo!".* Berkeley, CA: University of California Press, 1992.

South Sahara Africa

Amnesty International. *Sudan: the Human Price of Oil.* London: Amnesty International, 2000.
Azevedo, Mario. *Chad: a Nation in Search of Its Future.* Boulder, CO: Westview Press, 1997.
Burr, J. Millard and Robert O. Collins. *Africa's Thirty Years' War: Chad, Libya, and the Sudan, 1963-1993.* Boulder, CO: Westview Press, 1999.
Burr, J. Millard and Robert O. Collins. *Requiem for the Sudan: War, Drought, and Disaster Relief on the Nile.* Boulder, CO: Westview Press, 1994.
Collelo, Thomas, ed. *Chad: a Country Study.* Washington, DC: U.S., GPO 2nd ed. 1990.
Decalo, Samuel. *Historical Dictionary of Chad.* Lanham, MD: Scarecrow Press, 1997.
Decalo, Samuel. *Historical Dictionary of Niger.* Lanham, MD: Scarecrow Press, 1996.

Deng, Francis Mading. *War of Visions: Conflict of Identities in the Sudan.* Washington, DC: Brookings Institution Press, 1995.

Englebert, Pierre. *Burkina Faso: Unsteady Statehood in West Africa.* Boulder, CO: Westview Press, 1996.

Keen, David. *The Benefits of Famine: a Political Economy of Famine and Relief in Southwestern Sudan, 1983-1989.* Princeton, NJ: Princeton University Press, 1994.

McFarland, Daniel M. *Historical Dictionary of Burkina Faso.* Lanham, MD: Scarecrow Press, 1998.

Metz, Helen Chapin, ed. *Sudan: a Country Study.* Washington, DC: U.S. GPO, 4th ed. 1992.

Mosely Lesch, Ann. *The Sudan: Contested National Identities.* Bloomington, IN: Indiana University Press, 1998.

Peterson, Scott. *Me against My Brother: at War in Somalia, Sudan, and Rwanda.* New York: Routledge, 2000.

Petterson, Donald. *Inside Sudan: Political Islam, Conflict, and Catastrophe.* Boulder, CO: Westview Press, 1999.

Zamponi, Lynda F. *Niger.* Santa Barbara: ABC-CLIO, 1994.

North Africa

Abdo, Geneive. *No God but God: Egypt and the Triumph of Islam.* New York: Oxford University Press, 2000.

Adamson, Kay. *Algeria: a Study in Competing Ideologies.* Herndon, VA: Cassell Academic, 1998.

Ahmida, Ali Abdullatif. *The Making of Modern Libya: State Formation, Colonialization, and Resistance, 1830-1932.* Albany, NY: State University of New York, 1994.

Arnold, Guy. *The Maverick State: Gaddafi and the New World Order.* Herndon, VA: Cassell Academic, 1996.

Beattie, Kirk J. *Egyptian Politics during Sadat's Presidency.* New York: Saint Martin's Press, 2000.

Borowiec, Andrew. *Tunisia: a Democratic Apprenticeship.* Westport, CT: Greenwood Publishing Group, 1998.

Boutros-Ghali, Boutros. *Egypt's Road to Jerusalem: a Diplomat's Story of the Struggle for Peace in the Middle East.* New York: Random House, 1997.

Burr, J. Millard and Robert O. Collins. *Africa's Thirty Years' War: Chad, Libya, and the Sudan, 1963-1993.* Boulder, CO: Wesview Press, 1999.

Calderini, Simonetta, et al., *Mauritania.* Santa Barbara, CA: ABC-CLIO, 1992.

Ciment, James. *Algeria: the Fundamentalist Challenge.* New York: Facts on File, 1997.

Daly, Martin W., ed. *Modern Egypt from 1517 to the End of the Twentieth Century.* New York: Cambridge University Press, 1999.

El-Kikhia, Mansour O. *Libya's Qaddafi: the Politics of Contradiction.* Gainesville, FL: University Press of Florida, 1997.

Findlay, Anne M., et al., *Morocco.* Santa Barbara, CA: ABC-CLIO, 1995.

Handloff, Robert E., ed. *Mauritania: a Country Study.* Washington, DC: U.S. GPO, 2nd ed. 1990.

Harik, Iliya F. *Economic Policy Reform in Egypt.* Gainesville, FL: University Press of Florida, 1997.

Lawless, Richard I. *Algeria.* Santa Barbara, CA: ABC-CLIO, 1995.

Malek, Jaromir, ed. *Egypt: Ancient Culture, Modern Land.* Norman, OK: University of Oklahoma Press, 1993.

Metz, Helen Chapin, ed. *Algeria: a Country Study.* Washington, DC: U.S. GPO, 5th ed. 1994.

Metz, Helen Chapin, ed. *Egypt: a Country Study.* Washington, DC: U.S. GPO, 5th ed. 1991.

Metz, Helen Chapin, ed. *Libya: a Country Study.* Washington, DC: U.S. GPO, 4th ed. 1989.

Murphy, Emma C. *Economic and Political Change in Tunisia: from Bourguiba to Ben Ali.* New York: Saint Martin's Press, 1999.

Naylor, Phillip Chiviges and Alf Andrew Heggoy. *Historical Dictionary of Algeria.* Lanham, MD: Scarecrow Press, 2nd ed. 1994.

Nelson, Harold D., ed. *Morocco: a Country Study.* Washington, DC: U.S. GPO, 5th ed. 1985.

Nelson, Harold D., ed. *Tunisia, a Country Study.* Washington, DC: U.S. GPO, 3rd ed. 1988.

Park, Thomas K. *Historical Dictionary of Morocco.* Lanham, MD: Scarecrow Press, 1996.

Pazzanita, Anthony G. *Historical Dictionary of Mauritania.* Lanham, MD: Scarecrow Press, 1996.

Perkins, Kenneth J. *Historical Dictionary of Tunisia.* Lanham, MD: Scarecrow Press, 1997.

Quandt, William B. *Between Ballots and Bullets: Algeria's Transition from Authoritarianism.* Washington, DC: Brookings Institution Press, 1998.

Ruedy, John. *Modern Algeria: the Origins and Development of a Nation.* Bloomington, IN: Indiana University Press, 1992.

Simons, Geoff. *Libya: the Struggle for Survival.* New York: Saint Martin's Press, 1993.

St. John, Ronald Bruce. *Historical Dictionary of Libya.* Lanham, MD: Scarecrow Press, 3rd ed. 1998.

Stone, Martin. *Agony of Algeria.* New York: Columbia University Press, 1997.

Sullivan, Denis J. *Islam in Contemporary Egypt: Civil Society vs. the State.* Boulder, CO: Lynne Rienner Publishers, 1999.

Swearingen, Will D. and Abdellatif Bencherifa, eds. *The North African Environment at Risk.* Boulder, CO: Westview Press, 1996.

Takeyh, Ray. *The Origins of the Eisenhower Doctrine: the U.S., Britain and Nasser's Egypt, 1953-57.* New York: Saint Martin's Press, 2000.

Vandewalle, Dirk. *Libya since Independence: Oil and State-Building.* Ithaca, NY: Cornell University Press, 1998.

Vandewalle, Dirk, ed. *North Africa: Development and Reform in a Changing Economy.* New York: Saint Martin's Press, 1996.

Willis, Michael. *The Islamist Challenge in Algeria: a Political History.* New York: New York University Press, 1997.

Zartman, William, ed. *Tunisia: the Political Economy of Reform.* Boulder, CO: Lynne Rienner Publishers, 1991.